M

Georgia

D1409988

Explore
2013

Georgia

Carol Thalimer and Dan Thalimer
with photographs by the authors

The Countryman Press ✳ Woodstock, Vermont

Interior photographs by the author unless otherwise specified

Maps by Erin Greb Cartography, © The Countryman Press
Book design by Bodenweber Design
Composition by PerfecType, Nashville, TN

Published by The Countryman Press, P.O. Box 748, Woodstock, VT 05091

Distributed by W. W. Norton & Company, Inc., 500 Fifth Avenue, New York, NY 10110

Printed in the United States of America

Explorer's Guide Georgia

Second Edition

10 9 8 7 6 5 4 3 2 1

DEDICATION.

To David Torrisi, son-in-law, husband, father, son, brother, uncle, nephew, and friend extraordinaire.

May a strong breeze fill your sails to ensure a safe journey to the other shore.

EXPLORE WITH US!

We've lived in Georgia since 1979 and have been writing about it for newspapers, magazines, and guidebooks since 1987. In the course of living here, enjoying our state for our own pleasure, and researching Georgia for our readers, we've traveled the state countless times—constantly seeking out the new and checking up on the tried and true. More and more communities are recognizing the value of tourism, so the number of attractions, lodgings, dining opportunities, and fairs and festivals continues to grow. We make our recommendations selectively based on years of research and personal experience.

WHAT'S WHERE

This section is an alphabetical listing of special highlights and other important information. Here you'll find recommendations on everything from where to buy fresh seafood to where to write, call, or go online to find information about parks and camping.

LODGING

We selected hotels, bed & breakfasts, resorts, and other lodgings based on their merit. Although we may not have stayed in every accommodation, we've tried to visit each or, in some rare cases, have relied on the advice of locals in the know. Accommodations cannot pay to be included in this guide.

RESTAURANTS

We've made a distinction between *Dining Out* and *Eating Out*. In the *Dining Out* category, we've generally listed more formal restaurants with entrée prices higher than $20. The *Eating Out* restaurants are generally more casual and more inexpensive. Note that we list entrée prices—you can easily double a meal price by adding appetizers, soups and salads, desserts, and alcoholic beverages. No restaurant can pay to be included in this guide.

PRICES

Changes are inevitable—especially with information in a book, which is hopefully in use for many years. We give prices only to give you a ballpark figure for whether a lodging is inexpensive, moderate, or expensive. In almost all cases, there will be some kind of local tax added to the basic rate. When you make your reservation, you might want to check about taxes or gratuities that are added on to the basic rate.

SMOKING

Georgia has a law banning smoking in buildings open to the public. There's still a lot of leeway, however. Large hotels, for example, may still have smoking and nonsmoking rooms available. B&Bs, which are often in someone's home, are usually smoke-free for various reasons, including insurance requirements. Restaurants are generally smoke-free unless they do not admit anyone younger than 18, but they may allow smoking in the bar or in outside eating areas. If smoking is an issue because of allergies or personal preference, be sure to ask.

KEY TO SYMBOLS

☜ **Special value.** This symbol appears next to lodgings, restaurants, and attractions that are inexpensive.

✂ **Family friendly.** This symbol appears next to attractions, eateries, and lodgings that are of particular value or appeal for families.

♿ **Handicapped access.** This symbol appears next to attractions, lodgings, and restaurants that are partially or completely handicapped accessible. Note that in the case of lodgings such as bed & breakfasts, in particular, there may be a ramp to get into the building, but bathrooms may not be completely outfitted for the handicapped.

🐾 **Pets.** This symbol appears next to lodgings, campgrounds, and attractions that accept pets. Please note that many of these have restrictions, may require advance notice, and may have additional fees associated with your pet.

We would appreciate any comments (good or bad) or corrections so that our next edition will be as complete as possible. Please write to Explorer's Guide Editor, The Countryman Press, P.O. Box 748, Woodstock, VT 05091, or e-mail countrymanpress@wwnorton.com.

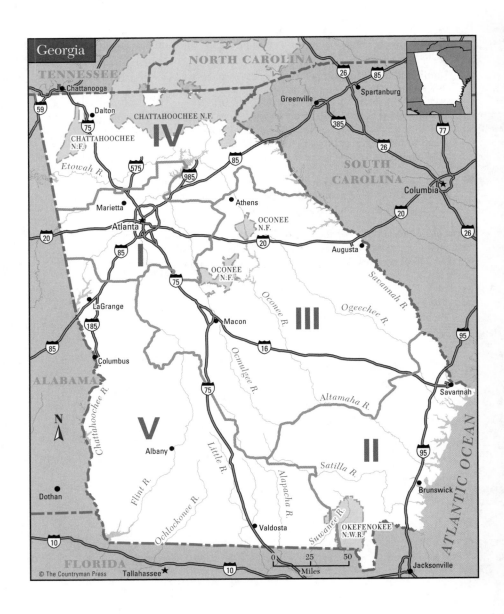

CONTENTS

5   Southern Rivers / 427

MAPS

ACKNOWLEDGMENTS

Although we've written 15 other books about Georgia and the South, the gargantuan size and complexities of this book resulted in a process we'd liken to birthing an elephant: It was quite often painful, but we're proud of the result. We'd especially like to thank our editors at the Countryman Press—Kermit Hummel, Lisa Sacks, Doug Yeager, and Justine Rathbun for this edition, and Kermit, Jennifer Thompson, and Kathryn Flynn for the first edition—for their guidance, suggestions, and infinite patience.

Our daughter Elaine Pyle was an invaluable researcher and fact checker on the first edition, and we also thank her husband, Eric, for lending her to us for prolonged periods.

No matter how much traveling we do throughout the state, we could never keep up-to-date with the latest activities, attractions, lodgings, restaurants, shopping, and events in Georgia without the assistance of the state regional representatives at the Georgia Department of Economic Development, Tourism Division: Fay Tripp, director; Atlanta Metro, Brittney Warnock Gray; Colonial Coast, Carey Ferrara; Classic South, Jeannie Buttrum; Historic Heartland, Mandy McCullough Barnhart; Magnolia Midlands, Lori Hennesy; Northwest Georgia Historic High Country, Janet Cochran; Northeast Georgia Mountains, Cheryl Smith; Plantation Trace, Jeff Stubbs; and Presidential Pathways, Maggie Potter. We've worked with many of these representatives for 20 years, and they are amazing founts of information.

To the countless others at specific activities, attractions, lodgings, restaurants, shopping, and events—thank you.

WHAT'S WHERE IN GEORGIA

This section offers some general information that is helpful to travelers but would be too repetitive to include in each individual chapter—information about airports and airlines, car rentals, mass transit, bus and train travel, and the like. In addition, in this section we offer information about some of the state's most outstanding attractions, fairs and festivals, activities, and lodgings to spur your curiosity. These brief mentions are more fully described in the pertinent chapters. In this chapter, we merely reference these without contact information; in the separate chapters, for each entry we give you the telephone number(s), website if there is one, address, hours of operation, and admission, lodging, or meal price. We also give you some information about associations and councils that might be helpful, references to other books or websites, and regulations such as those regarding fishing, hunting, smoking, building fires, and littering.

AFRICAN AMERICAN SITES In a state where a major part of the economy was once based on slave labor, where the Civil War often intruded, and where there were numerous events connected with the civil rights movement of the 1960s, it's not surprising that there are many significant historical sites related to the lives and history of African Americans. The most significant of these sites and one of the most-visited attractions in the state is the **Martin Luther King Jr. National Historic Site** on Auburn Avenue in Atlanta. The site contains Dr. King's birthplace and

Ebenezer Baptist Church. Adjacent to the historic site is the **King Center for Nonviolent Social Change,** which includes the tombs of Dr. King and his wife, Coretta Scott King. Also in Atlanta is a collection of six prestigious black colleges, known collectively as **Atlanta University.**

Throughout the state some other significant African American sites or tours include the **Black Heritage Trail Tour** in Columbus, the **Coweta County African American Heritage Museum and Research Center** in Newnan, **Hog Hammock** community on Sapelo Island, the **King-Tisdell**

Cottage in Savannah, **Lucy Craft Laney Museum of Black History** in Augusta, **Morgan County African American Museum** in Madison, the **Mount Zion Albany Civil Rights Movement Museum** in Albany, **Ralph Mark Gilbert Civil Rights Museum** in Savannah, **Seabrook Village** in Midway, and the **Tubman African American Museum** in Macon. Numerous festivals celebrate African American heritage.

AGRICULTURAL FAIRS Outside of Atlanta and a few other large municipalities, Georgia is largely rural, with an economy based on agriculture and forestry. These industries are often celebrated at annual agricultural fairs, the largest of which is the **Georgia National Fair** in Perry. Some other agricultural fairs include the **Georgia State Fair** in Macon, **Georgia Mountain Fair** in Hiawassee, **North Georgia State Fair** in Marietta, **Sunbelt Agricultural Exposition** in Moultrie, and the **South Georgia Jaycee Fair** in Swainsboro. Some of these are described in the pertinent chapter. For more information about fairs, contact the **Georgia Association of Agricultural Fairs** (706-746-3081; www.georgiafairs.org).

AIRPORTS AND AIRLINES Many travelers to Georgia will fly into Atlanta. Others may fly into Albany, Athens, Augusta, Brunswick, Columbus, Macon, Savannah, or Valdosta, although they may have to connect in Atlanta. In fact, there used to be a T-shirt on sale at the airport that read I DIED AND WENT TO HEAVEN, BUT I HAD TO CHANGE PLANES IN ATLANTA. No matter which airport travelers choose, they will then often need to rent a car to complete their journey, and the major airports have car rental firms on-site. Because travelers to the destinations described in so many additional chapters will fly into one of those airports, we do not give specific contact information about these airports, the airlines that fly into them, and on-site car rental firms in each individual chapter but simply reference "What's Where in Georgia." In some parts of Georgia, the most

convenient airport may actually be in another state: Asheville, North Carolina; Dothan, Alabama; Chattanooga, Tennessee; Greeneville/Spartanburg, South Carolina; or Jacksonville or Tallahassee, Florida. If those airports occur in more than one chapter, the specifics are in the text that follows. If an out-of-state airport occurs in only one chapter, we give the specifics about it in the appropriate chapter.

The following are the major airlines that serve Georgia (there are dozens of others): **Aeromexico** (1-800-237-6639; www.aeromexico.com), **Air Canada** (1-888-247-2262; www.aircanada.com), **Air France** (1-800-237-2747; www.airfrance.com), **Air Jamaica** (1-800-523-5585; www.airjamaica.com), **AirTran** (1-800-247-8726; www.airtran.com), **Alaska Airlines** (1-800-252-7522; www.alaskaair.com), **American** (1-800-433-7300; www.aa.com), **America West** (1-800-327-7810; www.americawest.com), **British Airways** (1-800-247-9297; www.britishairways.com), **Continental** (1-800-513-3273; www.continental.com), **Delta** (1-800-221-1212; www.delta.com), **ExpressJet** (formerly Atlantic Southeast Airlines) (404-856-1000; www.expressjet.com), **Frontier** (1-800-432-1359; www.frontierairlines.com), **Georgia Skies** (1-877-849-4997; www.pacificwings.com), **KLM Royal Dutch Airlines** (1-800-447-4747; www.klm.com), **Korean Air** (1-800-438-5000; www.koreanair.com), **Lufthansa** (1-800-645-3880; www.lufthansa.com), **South African Airways** (1-800-722-9675; www.flyssa.com), **Southwest Airlines** (1-800-435-4792; www.southwest.com), **United** (1-800-864-8331; www.united.com), and **US Airways** (1-800-428-4322; www.usair.com).

Following are the major airports and the airlines that serve each of them. The car rental companies available at each airport are listed under *Car Rentals*.

The primary airport, which serves much of Georgia, is **Hartsfield-Jackson Atlanta International Airport** (1-800-897-1910; www.atlanta-airport.com). One of the busiest airports in the world, it is served by 21 airlines. The primary airlines are Delta and AirTran (which will be transitioning into Southwest during 2012), but the entire list includes **Aeromexico, Air Canada, Air France, Air Jamaica, AirTran, American, America West, British Airways, Continental, Delta, ExpressJet, Frontier, KLM Royal Dutch Airlines, Korean Air, Lufthansa, United,** and **US Airways.** Transportation into the city is available from the airport by taxi (see the "Taxis" sidebar), MARTA rail (see *Bus/Rail Service*), limousine, and rental car.

Visitors to Albany may fly into **Southwest Georgia Regional Airport** (229-430-5175; www.ifly/southwest-georgia-regional-airport), 3905 Newton Road, which is served by **ExpressJet.**

Travelers to Athens and surrounding destinations will use the **Athens–Ben Epps Airport** (706-613-3420; www.athensairport.net), which is served by **Georgia Skies Airline** and **US Airways Express.**

Visitors to Augusta and nearby destinations arrive at **Augusta Regional Airport** (706-798-3236 or 1-866-860-9809; www.AugustaRegionalAirport.com), which is served by **American Eagle, ExpressJet,** and **US Airways Express.**

Travelers to Columbus and nearby destinations will use the **Columbus Metropolitan Airport** (706-324-2449; www.flycolumbusga.com), which is served by **American Eagle** and **Delta.** Visitors to the southern Georgia coast and resort islands may fly into the **Brunswick Golden Isles Airport** (912-265-2070; www.glynncountyairports.com), which is served by **Delta/Atlantic Southeast Airlines.**

The most convenient airport for some destinations is **Middle Georgia Regional Airport Macon** (478-788-3760; www.macon-airport.com), which is serviced by **Georgia Skies.**

Travelers to several destinations on or near the Georgia coast will fly into **Savannah/Hilton Head International Airport** (912-964-0514; www.savannahairport.com), which is served by **American Eagle, Continental Express, Delta** and **Delta Connection, United Express,** and **US Airways.** Numerous car rental companies,

public transportation, hotel shuttles, and taxis offer transportation from the airport to Savannah and Tybee Island.

Passengers to the northernmost part of Georgia may fly into **Asheville Regional Airport** (828-684-2226; www.flyavl.com), 61 Terminal Drive, Fletcher, North Carolina, which is served by **Allegiant, Continental, Delta, United,** and **US Airways.**

Those visiting the northwestern part of the sate may choose to fly into **Chattanooga Metropolitan Airport** (423-855-2200; www.chattairport.com), 1001 Airport Road, Chattanooga, Tennessee, which is served by **Allegiant, American Eagle, Delta, US Airways,** and **Vision Airlines.**

Travelers to the northeastern corner of the state may wish to use **Greenville-Spartanburg International Airport** (864-877-7426; www.gspairport.com), 2000 GSP Drive, Greer, South Carolina, which is served by **Allegiant, American Eagle, Continental, Delta, Southwest,** and **United Express.**

Those visiting the extreme southwestern part of the state may chose to fly into **Dothan Regional Airport** (334-983-8100), 800 Airport Drive, Dothan, Alabama, which is serviced by **ExpressJet.**

It may be most convenient for travelers to the extreme southeastern part of the state to fly into **Jacksonville International Airport** (904-741-4902; www.jia.aero), 2400 Yankee Clipper Drive, Jacksonville, Florida, which is served by **AirTran, American, Continental, Delta, Jet Blue, Southwest, United,** and **US Airways.**

Other travelers to the south-central part of the state may fly into **Tallahassee Regional Airport** (850-891-7802; www.talgov.com/airport), 3300 Capital Circle SW, Suite 1, Tallahassee, Florida, which is served by **American, Continental Express, Delta,** and **US Airways.**

AMTRAK AMTRAK (1-800-USA-RAIL; www.amtrak.com) makes only five stops in Georgia. The Crescent route, which runs from New York to New Orleans, stops in

TAXIS

Sometimes getting around Atlanta is best via taxi. Atlanta's professional taxicab drivers know the city's streets like the back of their hands and are used to the massive traffic jams. What's more, Atlanta has more than 1,500 taxis available to take you between accommodations and attractions. With preset rates for trips to and from the airport, downtown, and Buckhead, taxis provide an economical mode of transportation in Atlanta. Ask the concierge at your hotel for a list of taxi services in the area or simply flag down an on-duty cab. All cab companies are regulated under the same rate schedule, so it seldom makes any difference which taxi you take. From the airport the following flat rates apply:

Flat Rate for One Person*
Zone from Hartsfield

To Downtown	$30
To Midtown	$32
To Buckhead	$40

*There is an additional charge per each added person.

Rates to areas outside the central business district are computed by a meter. These are the standard charges:
$2.50 for the first ⅛ mile
$0.25 for each additional ⅛ mile
$21 per hour wait time
$1.50 flag drop fee

Toccoa and Gainesville in northeast Georgia and Atlanta in northwest Georgia. The Silver Service/Palmetto route, which runs along the Atlantic seacoast from the Northeast to Florida, stops in Savannah and Jesup. Because the **Atlanta station** (404-881-3067), 1688 Peachtree Street NW, is the closest station to so many towns described in this book, we give that information only here and do not list it in each chapter—simply referencing "What's Where in Georgia." There is bus service between the Atlanta station and Hartsfield-Jackson Atlanta International Airport. We give the Toccoa, Gainesville, Savannah, and Jesup information in the appropriate chapters and simply reference those in chapters about towns close to them. Several extreme-south Georgia towns are closer to AMTRAK stops in Florida; the specifics are noted in those chapters. On the whole, arrival in Georgia by train and sight-seeing throughout the state is not very practical unless your sole destination is one of the towns in which the trains stop (or very nearby) or you plan on renting a car.

AMUSEMENT PARKS No matter what your age, you can indulge the kid in you at Georgia's amusement parks, which can be found all over the state—some large, others small. All have rides; some have entertainment and even small zoos. The granddaddy of theme parks is **Six Flags over Georgia** in Austell, just outside Atlanta. Six Flags also operates a sibling park in Georgia: **Six Flags White Water** water park in Marietta, just outside Atlanta. Hot on their heels in size and number and variety of rides, entertainment, and other attractions is **Wild Adventures Theme Park** in Valdosta. Other amusement parks include the **All-American Fun Park** in Albany, **Dixieland Fun Park** in Fayetteville, **Fun Bowl of Henry County** in McDonough, **Lanierworld Beach and Water Park** in Buford, **Lake Winnepesaukah** in Rossville, **Splash in the Boro** in

Statesboro, **Summer Waves Water Park** on Jekyll Island, and **WaterWiz** in LaGrange.

ANTIQUES Georgia has a plethora of antiques shops in all regions. **Georgia's Antiques Trail** (www.georgiaantiquetrail .com) stretches 200 miles, from Conyers to McDonough, and lists 200 shops and dealers. There's also a **Tri-County Antique Trail,** which includes Elbert, Franklin, and Hart counties in northeast Georgia.

APPALACHIAN TRAIL The beginning and first 80 miles of the 2,144-mile Georgia-to-Maine trail is at Springer Mountain in north Georgia. The **Georgia Appalachian Trail Club** (www.georgia -atclub.org) was founded in 1930 in Dahlonega. In cooperation with the Appalachian Trail Conservancy and the U.S. Forest Service, the club maintains and manages the Georgia portion of the trail, much of which passes through the Chattahoochee National Forest. For information about the entire trail, contact the **Appalachian Trail Conference** (304-535-6331), P.O. Box 807, Harpers Ferry, WV 25425-0807.

APPLES A combination of favorable climate and soil conditions makes north Georgia ideal for apple production. The apple is so important to the economy of north Georgia that the fruit is honored with the **Apple Monument** in Cornelia. A particularly good place to find apples is **Apple Orchard Alley** along GA 52 in Gilmer County. In the autumn some farms offer visitors the opportunity to pick their own (www.pickyourown.org/GA.htm). Others offer apples and innumerable apple products for sale. Some of these farms include **Appletree Farms** and **Jaemor Farm Market,** both in Alto, **Hillcrest Orchards** in Ellijay, and **Mercier Orchards** in Blue Ridge. A popular annual fair is the **Georgia Apple Festival** (www.georgiaapplefestival .org). To learn more about apple-related activities or to find apple orchards, consult the website www.allaboutapples.com /orchard/ga01.htm.

AQUARIUMS The **Georgia Aquarium,** opened in November 2005, is the largest aquarium in the world. Visitors are particularly entranced with the beluga whales and the whale sharks. Tickets are for specified days and times, so be sure to make your reservations well in advance to avoid disappointment. In southwest Georgia, the **Flint RiverQuarium** in Albany is on a much smaller scale but is educational and enjoyable nonetheless and is not to be missed if you're in the area. The **University of Georgia Marine Science Complex and Aquarium** on Skidaway Island near Savannah is the state's only public saltwater marine aquarium.

AREA CODES Georgia has several area codes. The Atlanta metropolitan area alone has four, making it necessary to dial all 10 digits whenever you make a call. It is not unheard of for a business with more than one phone line to have two different area codes. In general, the area of the metropolitan region inside the I-285 perimeter highway that circles Atlanta uses the 404 area code, while the areas outside the perimeter highway use the others. There are exceptions, however, so be sure to check the number. Other area codes include 470, 706, and 762 in the northern areas of the state outside the Atlanta metro area; 478 in the central part of the state; 912 along the coast and in southeastern Georgia; and 229 in southwestern Georgia. With the proliferation of cell phones, all bets are off when it

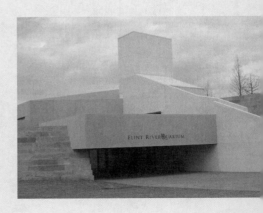

FLINT RIVERQUARIUM

comes to how many area codes will be in use when you travel to Georgia and whether you may have to dial all 10 digits in areas other than metro Atlanta.

ART ASSOCIATIONS AND COUNCILS
Georgia has 200 arts associations and 30 local arts groups as well as 11 symphony orchestras, 8 major art museums, and 30 community theaters. Some of the groups in the state include the **Albany Area Arts Council, Atlanta Fine Arts League, Blue Ridge Mountain Arts Association, Ohoopee Regional Council for the Arts** in Vidalia, **Rome Area Council for the Arts,** and the **Thomasville Entertainment Foundation,** all of which are described in the pertinent chapters, as are smaller organizations.

ART MUSEUMS
The **High Museum of Art** in Atlanta is the state's premier art museum. Not only are the collections impressive, but the structure is an outstanding work of art itself. The striking primary building was designed by Richard Meier, and an addition was designed by Renzo Piano. The second-biggest art museum in the state is the **Columbus Museum** in Columbus. The official Georgia art museum is the **Georgia Museum of Art** in Athens. Other significant art museums, which are described in separate chapters, include the **Albany Museum of Art** in Albany, **Madison Museum of Art** in Madison, **Marietta/Cobb Museum of Art** in Marietta, **Michael C. Carlos Museum of Emory University** in Decatur, **Morris Museum of Art** in Augusta, the **Museum of Arts and Sciences** in Macon, and the **Telfair Museum of Arts and Science/Jepson Center for the Arts** in Savannah. There are also entries in several chapters describing smaller and university art museums. For more information, consult the **Georgia Association of Museums and Galleries** (www.gamg.org) or the website www.georgia.worldweb.com/Sights Attractions/Museums.

ATTRACTION/RESTAURANT/ SHOP HOURS
We list the days of the week and the hours that attractions, restaurants, and shops are open as of publication time. Obviously many of these will change in the future. In general, museums, some other attractions, and many restaurants are closed on Monday, and almost all attractions and many restaurants are closed on Christmas and some other holidays. It would make the individual entries about these sites too unwieldy to list all the days they are closed. To avoid disappointment, please check ahead if you're traveling on major holidays such as New Year's Day, Martin Luther King Day, St. Patrick's Day (in Savannah), Easter, Memorial Day, Labor Day, and Thanksgiving. With the state forced to make drastic budget cuts, many of Georgia's state parks and historic sites are closed Sunday through Wednesday, except when a major holiday falls on a Monday. Always check the appropriate websites or call before you travel to get the most up-to-date times of operation for attractions, restaurants, and shops.

AUTO RACING
Auto racing in the state was supposedly spawned in mountainous north Georgia in the days of fast cars and moonshine—a combination that resulted in whirlwind races between whiskey runners and revenuers. Georgia is dotted with racetracks—everything from the **Atlanta Motor Speedway** and **Road Atlanta,** which rival the tracks in Daytona, Indianapolis, and Talladega, to quarter-mile dirt tracks in small towns. Space prohibits us from describing more than a few of these tracks.

BALLOONING
There's an exciting and romantic way to get a bird's-eye view of parts of Georgia: a ride in a hot-air balloon (www.balloonrideus.com). In the mountains of north Georgia, rides are available from **Balloons over Georgia** in Helen. Near the coast, rides are available from **Feather Air Hot-Air Balloons** in Ellabelle, near Savannah. In general, rides are offered in the early morning or just before dusk and are highly dependent on the weather, so check ahead. Two major balloon events include the **Sky High Hot Air Balloon**

Festival at Callaway Gardens Resort in Pine Mountain and the **Helen to the Atlantic Hot Air Balloon Race,** which starts in the mountains of northeast Georgia and ends at the coast.

BEACHES Georgia may have a small coastline compared to states such as Florida, but the state offers many wonderful, wide, hard-packed beaches perfect for sunning, swimming, bike riding, fishing, and other activities. The most pristine beaches are found at the **Cumberland Island National Seashore** on Cumberland Island and the beaches of privately owned **Little St. Simons Island,** both of which accept a limited number of overnight guests and day-trippers. Some of Georgia's barrier islands are national wildlife refuges and are also in a pristine state. **Tybee Island** and the Golden Isles of **Jekyll Island, St. Simons Island,** and **Sea Island** are developed resort areas with hotels, condominiums, rental cottages, restaurants, and shops. Parks at many of Georgia's lakes have man-made beaches, as do several state parks. Other beaches include the **Beach at Clayton County International Park** in Jonesboro, **Lanierworld Beach and Water Park** in Buford, **Lake Tobesofkee Recreation Area** in Macon, and **Robin Lake Beach** at Callaway Gardens in Pine Mountain.

BED & BREAKFASTS Many travelers prefer accommodations in small historic properties with breakfast included. Georgia has many such properties in cities and rural areas. These range from grand plantation homes in the deep southern part of the state to painted ladies in Atlanta to rustic homes in the mountains. A smaller portion of B&Bs are contemporary, and some were built specifically to be bed & breakfasts. Savannah has the largest concentration of B&Bs in the state. Prices vary from $50 to $650 but average $150–200 per night.

Not all that long ago Carol was the only person who had ever seen every single B&B in Georgia. With new ones opening all the time, however, it's hard to keep up, and there are a few listed here that we haven't visited but depended on the recommendation of tourism officials in the area.

The upside of a stay in a bed & breakfast is personal attention, recommendations about attractions and restaurants from your host, and the greater likelihood that guests will interact with each other than if you stayed in impersonal hotels. If you think you'd like to try a B&B, keep in mind that bed & breakfasts are usually in someone's home and that there are often strict rules about pets, children, and smoking, as well as deposit and cancellation policies that are more stringent than at other types of accommodations. B&Bs may not be wheelchair accessible and certainly don't have all the amenities of a large hotel. A stay in a B&B is usually by reservation only, with no walk-ins.

The prices we quote are for one night for one or two people; there is almost always an additional charge for more than two guests. See also *Farm Bed & Breakfasts.*

BICYCLING Every biker, from the occasional weekend recreational rider to the serious mountain biker, can find what he or she is looking for in Georgia. The entire southern part of the state is relatively flat, making recreational biking easy even for young family members. Biking is particularly popular at and around the beaches, which are usually hard-packed and easy to ride on, and rentals are plentiful. The mountains in north Georgia offer enough challenges for mountain bikers. Fees are charged for using the mountain bike trails at several of Georgia's state parks. Daily use is $2 at Fort Yargo, Hard Labor Creek, and Unicoi state parks and $3 at Fort Mountain State Park. An annual pass can be purchased for $25.

For information on biking in Georgia, consult the state's travel website, www.exploregeorgia.org, and choose the "Adventure" link.

Readers might like to contact the following organizations about bicycling in the state: **Atlanta Bicycle Campaign** (404-881-1112; www.atlanta.bike.org), a bicycle advocacy group in the Atlanta metro area;

Georgia Bicycle Federation (www
.bicyclegeorgia.com), which is dedicated to
making Georgia a friendlier place to ride;
and Georgia Bikes (706-372-9529; www
.georgiabikes.org), a nonprofit organization
dedicated to improving bicycling conditions
and promote bicycling.

Several excellent books describe bicy-
cling in Georgia: *Cycling through Georgia:
Tracing Sherman's March* by Susan C. Bai-
ley and *Road Bike North Georgia: 25 Great
Rides in the Mountains and Valleys of
North Georgia* by Jim Parham.

See also *Mountain Biking.*

BIRDING The Audubon Society (www
.audubon.org/states) has several chapters in
Georgia. The society has designated 29
regions of Georgia as important bird areas,
including Jekyll Island and the entire
mountainous area of north Georgia. Several
birding trails attract casual and serious birdwatchers. The Colonial Coast Birding
Trail stretches 112 miles from St. Marys to
Savannah along Georgia's coast and has 18
stops. More than 300 species of birds have
been spotted along the trail that includes
shoreline, salt marshes, old rice fields,
woodlands, tidal rivers, and freshwater wetlands. These are trails described in the
Savannah, Brunswick, and Darien chapters.
Another important birding trail is the Georgia Department of Natural Resources's
Southern Rivers Birding Trail, which
stretches from the piedmont area through
the coastal plain, ending at the Okefenokee
Swamp. It is described in the Bainbridge
chapter.

Some excellent book resources include
Birding Georgia by Giff Beaton, *Birds of
Georgia Field Guide* by Stan Tekiela, *Geor-
gia Birds* by James Kavanagh, and *Georgia
Bird Watching: A Year-Round Guide* by Bill
Thompson III.

BOOKS Georgians traveling within their
own state and visitors from elsewhere can
get the flavor of different eras in the state's
past by reading fictional and nonfictional
accounts set in Georgia—most written by
Georgians. Still the second-best-selling
book in the world after the Bible, *Gone
with the Wind* by Margaret Mitchell paints
the stereotypical portrait of the Old South.
Tobacco Road by Erskine Caldwell is a
searing portrayal of the life of a tenant
farmer during the Great Depression. Lillian
Smith's 1944 novel *Strange Fruit* is a grip-
ping story of miscegenation and murder. In
more recent years, *Peachtree Road* by Anne
Rivers Siddons and *A Man in Full* by Tom
Wolfe put the old and new moneyed classes
of Atlanta at the end of the 20th century
under the microscope.

Some other books set in the state or by
Georgia authors include *Ugly Ways* by Tina
McElroy Ansa; *Cold Sassy Tree* by Olive
Ann Burns; *The Lonely Hunter* by Virginia
Spencer Carr; *The Gospel Singer* and *Feast
of Snakes* by Harry Crews; *Deliverance* by
James Dickey; *A Circuit Rider's Wife* by
Corra Harris; *Told by Uncle Remus: New
Stories of the Old Plantation* by Joel Chan-
dler Harris; *Lamb in His Bosom* by Caro-
line Miller; *Wise Blood* and short stories by
Flannery O'Connor; *The Beloved Invader*
and *New Moon Rising,* books set on St.
Simons by Eugenia Price; *Run with the
Horsemen* by Ferrol Sams Jr.; *The Color
Purple* by Alice Walker; and *The Foxes of
Harrow* by Frank Yerby.

In the humor genre, two authors imme-
diately come to mind: Lewis Grizzard and
Bailey White. Some of Grizzard's books
include *If I Ever Get Back to Georgia, I'm
Gonna Nail My Feet to the Ground; Chili
Dawgs Always Bark at Night;* and *When
My Love Returns from the Ladies Room,
Will I Be Too Old to Care?* Some of White's
books include *Mama Makes Up Her Mind
and Other Dangers of Southern Living,
Sleeping at the Starlite Motel,* and *Quite a
Year for Plums.*

In the nonfiction category, *Midnight in
the Garden of Good and Evil* by John
Berendt examines a real-life murder mystery at the same time it skewers Savannah's
eccentricities. "The Book," as it is known in
Savannah and elsewhere, has earned a
worldwide cultlike following that brings
scores of visitors to Savannah. Going back
to the early 19th century, the recounting of
the horrifying conditions endured by slaves
in *Journal of a Residence on a Georgia

Plantation in 1838–1839 by English actress Frances Anne "Fanny" Kemble was instrumental in keeping England out of the Civil War. In the mid-20th century, *The Year the Lights Came On* by Terry Kay recounts the electrification of rural Georgia. Some other factual accounts about Georgia include *A Childhood: The Biography of a Place* by Harry Crews; *The Souls of Black Folk* by W. E. B. Du Bois; *Praying for Sheetrock* by Melissa Fay Greene, a sociological study of coastal Georgia; *In My Place* by Charlayne Hunter-Gault, who broke the color barrier at the University of Georgia; and *And the Dead Shall Rise: The Murder of Mary Phagan and the Lynching of Leo Frank* by Steve Oney, a shocking case of anti-Semitism in Atlanta at the turn of the 20th century. As a matter of fact, Georgia seems to have spawned a large number of books about infamous murders—not only *And the Dead Shall Rise* and *Midnight in the Garden of Good and Evil*, but others such as *Murder in Coweta County* by Margaret Ann Barnes. Several of these have been made into movies.

In the children's book category, Joel Chandler Harris is, of course, famous for the tales he incorporated into the Uncle Remus stories in the late 19th century. He also wrote *Little Mr. Thimblefinger and His Queer Country: What the Children Saw and Heard There,* a collection of Negro tales outside the Uncle Remus genre, as well as middle Georgia folklore tales and pure inventions. *Turn Homeward, Hannalee* by Patricia Beatty is a fictionalized version—told from a child's point of view—of the true story of the women and children taken from Roswell during the Civil War, charged with treason, and sent north to be imprisoned or placed in servitude. Youngsters will enjoy *A Tree That Owns Itself and Other Adventure Tales from Georgia's Past* by Gail Langer Karwoski. Some of these oddities, such as the tree in question, are described in our various chapters.

Some other travel guides you might want to consult include one of our other guides: *Fun with the Family: Georgia,* a collection of activities, attractions, festivals, lodgings, and restaurants specifically of interest to families with young children. Both *Georgia Off the Beaten Track* and *Georgia Curiosities* by William Schemmel examine some of Georgia's most eccentric or hard-to-find attractions.

BUS/RAIL SERVICE The **Greyhound Lines** (404-584-1738 or 1-800-231-2222; www.greyhound.com) station at 232 Forsyth Street in Atlanta is open 24 hours a day and is the eighth-busiest station in the country. There is another station at the Atlanta airport, 6000 North Terminal Parkway; call 404-765-9598. Because the Atlanta station is the closest one to towns described in many other chapters, we simply reference "What's Where in Georgia" rather than repeat the information. In addition, Greyhound stops at 26 other locations throughout Georgia. Those stops are noted in the appropriate chapters with the address of the station and the local telephone number if there is one. In our opinion, bus travel is not a viable way to see the state. Although it is possible to map out a route that includes only towns with Greyhound service, once in each town, a traveler would have to use a taxi service if one was available or get a rental car. To see any of the state outside the towns where Greyhound stops, a visitor would need a rental car.

Only the largest cities, such as Atlanta, Macon, Savannah, and a few others, have mass transit, so a visit to any town other than these would require using a taxi or a rental car. Because the areas described in several chapters include the Atlanta metro area, to avoid repetitive material, we describe the various mass transit systems that serve the metro area here and simply reference "What's Where in Georgia" in the individual chapters. We describe mass transit systems in Macon, Savannah, and a few other cities within the pertinent chapters.

The Atlanta metro area is served by the **Metropolitan Atlanta Rapid Transit Authority,** known locally as **MARTA; BUC (Buckhead's Uptown Connection); Georgia Tech Technology Square Trolley; Cobb Community Transit; Gwinnett County Transit;** and **Xpress,** which serves several outlying counties.

MARTA (404-848-5000; www.itsmarta .com), the city's bus/rail system, is the most cost-effective and convenient way to get around the metro Atlanta area (specifically Fulton County), with a variety of routes and pass options available. A station at the airport makes access to the city and suburbs easy. The regular fare is $2.50 one-way, and transfers are available between buses or buses and trains. Exact change, tokens, or Breeze fare cards (available at all station entrances) can be used. Visitor passes are available beginning at $8 for one-day unlimited use up to $17 for a seven-day pass. Buses generally run between 5 AM and 1:30 AM weekdays and between 5 AM and midnight on weekends and holidays. Trains run 5 AM–1 AM daily. MARTA allows bicycles on all its trains, and there are bike racks on the front of most buses (the racks handle only two bikes at a time). Many MARTA stations have bike racks for commuters who wish to bike to the train. Transfers are free between MARTA and Cobb Community Transit (CCT), Gwinnett County Transit (GCT), and Xpress.

In Marietta and Cobb County, mass transit is provided by **Cobb Community Transit** (770-427-4444; www.cobbdot.org /cct.htm). The transit authority provides bus service throughout the county and connecting service to MARTA at the Arts Center Station. Fare is $2 one-way.

For mass transit transportation in Gwinnett County, **Gwinnett County Transit** (770-822-5010; www.gwinnettcounty.com) provides express, local, and paratransit services. Express buses to and from Atlanta operate weekdays and include six routes using the HOV lanes on I-85. Free park-and-ride lots are located at I-985, Discover Mills shopping mall, and Indian Trail. Local bus service within Gwinnett County operates five routes Monday through Saturday, connecting neighborhoods and businesses to cultural, shopping, and educational opportunities. Fares $3–4 express service, $2 local.

Xpress (404-463-4782; www.xpressga .com) is metro Atlanta's newest public transit service. Fares are $3–4 one-way depending on zone, $5–7 round-trip. Routes operate 5:30 AM–9:30 PM weekdays. Operated in partnership with the Georgia Regional Transportation Authority and 12 counties, the service provides an easy-to-use connection to downtown Atlanta and MARTA rail stations from Conyers, Cumming, Fairburn, Jonesboro, Morrow, and Woodstock.

CAMPING Georgia is dotted with campgrounds on the shores of lakes and rivers, in forests or near the beach, in developed tourist areas or in the wilderness. Some of them are in state or national parks, while others are privately operated. Because of the mild climate, most of these campgrounds are open year-round, but it's always wise to check ahead—especially in the north Georgia mountains. An excellent resource is *Camping Georgia* by Alex Nutt. There are also dozens of camping websites, of which avid campers are probably already aware.

Most state parks have a campground, and we note that in each state park description along with the nightly camping fee. A two-night minimum stay is required for most reservations, except a three-night minimum is required for Memorial Day, Labor Day, and Independence Day weekends. RV and most other campsites offer electric and water hookups, grills or fire rings, and picnic tables. Comfort stations with hot showers, flush toilets, and electrical hookups are conveniently located. All campgrounds have a dump station, and some offer cable TV hookups. Campers younger than 18 must be accompanied by an adult, and pets are welcome if kept on a 6-foot leash and attended at all times. A deposit is required, and there are cancellation penalties. To find out about camping at specific state parks, consult the website at www.gastateparks.org.

CANOEING, KAYAKING, TUBING, AND WHITE-WATER RAFTING Because Georgia is crisscrossed with rivers, dotted with lakes, and edged by the Atlantic Ocean, the state offers all kinds of water conditions for any paddler's experience and interest level:

smooth-as-glass lakes, slow-moving rivers, tumultuous white-water rivers, calm estuaries, and the ocean, which may be calm or rough depending on the weather. Canoeing, kayaking, and tubing can be good ways to see Georgia's wildlife. Families with small children might enjoy floating down a placid river in an inner tube or gliding across a tranquil lake in a canoe or kayak. Tubing is popular in the Helen area of the northeast Georgia mountains as well as in the Chattahoochee River National Recreation Area, which runs from Lake Lanier through the metro Atlanta area. Those who want a little more adventure might like hurtling down a white-water river in a raft or challenging themselves to an ocean tour in a sea kayak. Two rivers in north Georgia—the Chattooga and the Toccoa/Ocoee, site of the 1996 Centennial Summer Olympic Games white-water events—provide plenty of thrills for white-water rafters. Some sections of the Flint River in western Georgia have rapids as well.

Sea kayaking is very popular around Tybee Island and the Golden Isles, while canoeing is a popular way to see the Okefenokee Swamp. Except for white-water rafting, which is usually offered only spring through fall, most of these paddling sports are available year-round. There is no shortage of outfitters who provide rentals, lessons, and guided tours, some of which may include overnight trips. Just a few outfitters include the **Chattahoochee Outfitters** in Roswell, **Flint River Outdoor Center** near Thomaston, **Nantahala Outdoor Center** near Clayton, **Sea Kayak Georgia** on Tybee Island, and **Up the Creek Xpeditions and Outfitters** near St. Marys. Some guided excursions are led by **Altamaha Coastal Tours** near Darien, **Appalachian Outfitters River Trips** in Helen, and **Three Rivers Expeditions** in Hazelhurst. In most chapters we describe various outfitters in the area and describe canoe trails such as the **Altamaha River Canoe Trail** near Baxley.

CAR RENTALS All the major car rental companies have numerous locations throughout Georgia, although all of them are not found everywhere. Rather than give car rental contact information in every chapter, we list that information here and simply reference "What's Where in Georgia" in most cases. These car rental firms include **Alamo** (1-877-222-9075; www.alamo.com), **Avis** (1-800-230-4898; www.avis.com), **Budget** (1-800-527-0700; www.budget.com), **Dollar** (1-800-800-3665; www.dollar.com), **Enterprise** (1-800-261-7331; www.enterprise.com), **Hertz** (1-800-654-3131; www.hertz.com), **National** (1-877-222-9058; www.nationalcar.com), and **Thrifty** (1-800-847-4389; www.thrifty.com).

Car rentals are available on-site at Hartsfield-Jackson Atlanta International Airport from **Avis, Budget, Dollar, Enterprise, Hertz, National/Alamo,** and **Thrifty.** At Southwest Georgia Regional Airport in Albany, car rentals are available from **Avis, Budget, Enterprise,** and **Hertz.**

Car rentals are available at Athens–Ben Epps Airport in Athens from **Hertz.**

Passengers arriving at Columbus Metropolitan Airport can rent cars from **Alamo, Avis, Budget, Enterprise, Hertz, National,** and **Thrifty.**

Car rentals are available from **Avis, Budget, Enterprise,** and **Hertz** at the Brunswick–Golden Isles Airport in Brunswick.

At Middle Georgia Regional Airport, rentals are available from **Alamo/National, Avis,** and **Budget.**

At Savannah's airport, car rentals are available from **Alamo, Avis, Budget, Dollar, Enterprise, Hertz, National,** and **Thrifty.**

At Asheville Regional Airport, car rentals are available from **Alamo/National, Avis, Budget, Enterprise,** and **Hertz.**

Car rentals are available at the Chattanooga airport from **Avis, Budget, Enterprise, Hertz, National,** and **Thrifty/Dollar.**

Car rentals are available at Dothan Regional airport from **Avis, Hertz,** and **National.**

At Greenville-Spartanburg International Airport, car rentals are available from

Alamo/National, Avis, Budget, Enterprise, and Hertz.

Jacksonville International Airport offers car rentals from Alamo/National, Avis, Budget, Dollar, Enterprise, Hertz, and Thrifty.

In Tallahassee on-site car rentals are offered by Alamo, Avis, Dollar, Enterprise, Hertz, and National. Off-site car rentals are also available at several locations around town from Enterprise and U-Sav (850-575-7368).

CHAPTER HEADINGS Chapters are divided among the five principal regions of the state: Atlanta Metro, a vast area including the city as well its suburbs and some towns that have been swallowed up by urbanization; the Coast, which includes many of Georgia's barrier islands as well as towns that line the mainland; Historical South, the central heartland of Georgia; the Mountains, which covers the northern part of the state; and Southern Rivers, towns and areas in the southern part of the state. Whether the chapter title lists only one city or several, the text of the chapter will cover a broader area then just that identified in the title. Descriptions will also be included for attractions, activities, special events, restaurants, and/or lodgings in small towns in the immediate vicinity of the featured town(s).

CHILDREN, ESPECIALLY FOR Throughout this book, attractions, restaurants, and lodgings that are of special interest to families with children or that are particularly child friendly are indicated with the ✣ icon.

CHILDREN'S MUSEUMS Youngsters aren't neglected when it comes to Georgia's museums. There are several museums geared specifically to the wee ones, including the Georgia Children's Museum in Macon, Imagine It! The Children's Museum of Atlanta, the Interactive Neighborhood for Kids in Gainesville, and the Museum of Arts and Sciences in Macon. Several important museums aren't just for adults but offer

interactive children's rooms in their facilities, including the Columbus Museum in Columbus, the High Museum of Art in Atlanta, and the Jepson Center for the Arts in Savannah. The Center for Puppetry Arts in Atlanta is of special interest to both adults and children.

CHILDREN'S PROGRAMS A real vacation for parents often includes special activities and programs geared to children so that the youngsters are occupied while the parents are enjoying other pursuits. One program that has been attracting families for several generations is Camp Cloister at the Cloister at Sea Island. Another extremely popular program is the Callaway Summer Family Adventure Program in Pine Mountain, which includes the Flying High Circus.

CHRISTMAS TREES AND WREATHS Many folks prefer to choose and cut their own Christmas tree both for the fun of doing so and to ensure freshness. A couple places where you can cut your own Christmas tree are Bradley's Pumpkin Patch and Christmas Trees near Dawsonville and Southern Tree Plantation near Blairsville. To find more about Christmas tree farms and to find other locations, consult the Georgia Christmas Tree Association website (www.gacta .com) and click on the "Find a Farm" link. Or call the organization, which is located in Hawkinsville (478-919-8733).

CIVIL WAR SITES Georgia has significant Civil War history. As Union troops pushed into the state from Chattanooga, the Confederacy had an important victory at Chickamauga (now a national battlefield park) but later couldn't stop the relentless advance toward Atlanta, which was targeted by the Union because it was the Confederacy's primary rail center and supply distribution point. After taking Atlanta, Union general William Tecumseh Sherman's March to the Sea headed across central Georgia to Savannah, destroying just about everything in his path. One of the most infamous Civil War prisons was Camp

Sumter in Andersonville (now the **Andersonville National Historic Site**).

When in Georgia, don't be surprised to hear the Civil War described as The War, as if there were no other. You'll also hear it referred to as the War of Northern Aggression and, our personal favorite, the Recent Unpleasantness. General Sherman is snidely referred to as That Pyromaniac from the North. Hardly a chapter in this book doesn't feature something about the Civil War and William Tecumseh Sherman.

Just a few of the Civil War sites in Georgia are **Allatoona Pass Battlefield Trail** in Cartersville, **Andersonville Civil War Village** and **Andersonville National Historic Site,** both in Andersonville, **Chickamauga and Chattanooga National Military Park** at Fort Oglethorpe, **Kennesaw Mountain National Battlefield Park** in Kennesaw, **Gordon-Lee Mansion** and **Lee and Gordon's Mills,** both in Chickamauga, and the **Tunnel Hill Heritage Center/ Western and Atlantic Railroad Tunnel** in Tunnel Hill. All these sites and many more are described more fully in the appropriate chapters. Numerous battle reenactments, living-history camps, and other Civil War–related activities occur throughout the year and are described in the *Special Events* section of individual chapters. See also *Reenactments.*

COTTAGE RENTALS Cottage rentals are a popular and usually reasonably priced lodging alternative for stays of a week or more at the beach, a lake, the mountains, or a state park. We list rentals of individual cottages as well as rental agencies in many chapters. Another source of information about cottage rentals is a local chamber of commerce; many of these are listed in the *Guidance* section of each chapter.

Most of Georgia's state parks offer fully equipped cottages with a fireplace and a screened-in porch, and we note those that do in state park descriptions with the nightly rental rate. In general, state parks require a two-night minimum stay (three nights on Memorial Day, Independence Day, and Labor Day weekends), although

some require a five- or seven-night minimum in the summer. Shorter stays may be available at the last minute. There is a maximum 14-night stay, although if you have vacated the cottage for four nights, you may return. Young people under the age of 18 must be accompanied by an adult. After a successful experiment with allowing pets in selected cottages at three state parks in 2005, all state parks with cottages now welcome pets in selected cottages. In general the charge is $40 per dog, and there is a maximum of two. Prior arrangements are required, so don't just show up with your pet. Deposits are required, and there are cancellation penalties. To learn more about state parks with cottages, consult the website www.gastateparks.org.

COUNTIES Georgia has 159 counties; most of them are very small, and many have only one municipality. Georgia has the second most counties of any state in the country behind Texas, which is a bigger state. In fact, Georgia has the smallest average county size of any state. Why so many and why so small? Years ago the thinking was that a county shouldn't be any larger than the distance a person could travel by horseback from his farm or plantation to the courthouse in the county seat, transact his business, and return home in the same day. Today the small sizes mean individual boards of education and many other county services that might be better consolidated, but most visitors are totally unaware of crossing so many counties as they travel. The only impact on a traveler would be if a medical emergency arose in a county without a hospital. All counties are now covered by 911, however, and a patient would be transported to a medical facility in a surrounding county. On the positive side, the large number of counties has created a collection of Georgia treasures: impressive county courthouses. Most of these were constructed after the Civil War but before the turn of the 20th century and are magnificent examples of a variety of styles of architecture. Most are still in use and may contain small museums; others have been converted to other uses, including museums. Unfortunately a few have burned and been replaced by much more forgettable structures. Some folks have made it their mission to see and photograph every historic courthouse in Georgia. A piece of trivia: Clarke County is the smallest county in Georgia and consists primarily of the City of Athens.

COVERED BRIDGES Georgia once had more than 200 covered bridges. Today there are only 16, and not all of them are historic. The following historic covered bridges are described in separate chapters: **Auchumpkee Creek** near Thomaston, **Big Red Oak** near Woodbury, **Coheelee Creek** near Blakely, **Concord** near Smyrna, **Cromer's Mill** near Carnesville, **Elders Mill** near Watkinsville, **Euharlee Creek Covered Bridge and Historic Museum** near Cartersville, **Parrish Mill** in George L. Smith State Park near Twin City, **Stovall Mill** near Sautee-Nacoochee, and **Watson Mill Bridge** in Watson Mill Bridge State Outdoor Recreation Area near Comer. For more information about these and other Georgia covered bridges, consult the **Georgia Department of Transportation**'s website (www.dot.state.ga.us and navigate through the prompts to "Covered Bridges") or check out the website www .n-georgia.com/coveredbridges.htm.

CRAFTS Locally made crafts can be found all over Georgia. Appalachian crafts are most often found in the mountainous areas of north Georgia. Pennsylvania Dutch crafts are created and sold by the Mennonite community in Montezuma in southwest Georgia. Amish furniture, artwork, quilts, and crafts from Pennsylvania and Ohio can be purchased from the **Amish Red Barn** in Clarkesville. Many crafts created along the coast reflect the African American Gullah culture.

Just a few excellent places to find a variety of quality crafts created by numerous Georgia artisans and craftspeople include **Genuine Georgia, an Artist Marketplace** in Greensboro and **Mark of the Potter** near Clarksville. In the individual chapters, we often describe shops that sell

Georgia arts and crafts. See also *Georgia Made.*

If you have an interest in a particular craft and want to find the best locations to purchase examples, there are dozens of craft guilds, such as the **Chattahoochee Handweavers Guild** (www.chgweb.com) and the **Georgia Basketry Association** (www.georgiabasketry.org). Search the Web for any other specific crafts in which you might be interested.

CRUISES The term *cruise* can cover a lot of territory, but in the context of this guide it generally means a boat ride or excursion of fairly short duration and might be focused on sight-seeing, wildlife observation, fishing, or even gambling. These cruises may be on the ocean or an inland lake or river. *Emerald Princess II* **Casino Cruises** (www.emeraldprincesscasino.com) out of Brunswick offers gambling cruises in international waters. **River Street Riverboat Company** (www.savannahriverboat .com) offers sight-seeing cruises on the Savannah River aboard nostalgic paddlewheelers. **Romantic Lake Cruises** (www .romanticlakecruises.com) offers sightseeing cruises on Lake Chatuge near Hiawassee. Check various chapters for dolphin watching and nature cruises (see also *Dolphin Watching*).

CULTURAL ORGANIZATIONS
The world-renowned **Atlanta Symphony Orchestra** offers classical and pops series. There are also symphonies based in Albany,

Athens, Augusta, Cobb, Columbus, Decatur, Gainesville, Gwinnett, LaGrange, Macon, Rome, Savannah, Statesboro, Toccoa, and Valdosta, as well as at all the major colleges and universities. Atlanta also offers the **Atlanta Ballet,** the **Atlanta Opera,** and the **Capitol City Opera Company.** (See *Theaters/Summer* and *Theaters/ Year-Round*).

CURIOSITIES Part of the fun of traveling around any state is finding the offbeat attraction. Georgia is no exception. The state's oddities include the **Big Chicken** in Marietta, an unusual Kentucky Fried Chicken restaurant; the *Cyclorama,* the world's largest oil painting; the **Double-Barreled Cannon** in Athens, an innovative but unsuccessful weapon developed during the Civil War; the **Georgia Guidestones** in Elberton, a gargantuan Stonehenge-like structure erected in a field by an anonymous group; **Paradise Gardens,** the compound of visionary artist Howard Finster; **Pasaquan** in Buena Vista, the flamboyantly decorated home and compound of the late visionary artist Eddie Owens Martin; **Rock Eagle Effigy** in Eatonton and **Rock Hawk Effigy** nearby, gigantic figures of birds created thousands of years ago by Native Americans; the **Smallest Church**

in America in Eulonia, which seats only 12; and the **Tree That Owns Itself** in Athens. You'll find many more in the individual chapters, and on your travels you may come across some we haven't listed. We'd love to hear about any others you discover.

DINING AND EATING OUT The prices we list for your guidance are for entrées only, unless otherwise noted. You could easily more than double the price of a meal by adding appetizers, soup, salad, side dishes, dessert, and cold beverages, tea, or coffee. Certainly the meal price would be greatly increased by adding alcoholic beverages. The *Dining Out* category is considered to be fine dining in a more formal setting. This category is usually more expensive, too; in general, we list restaurants here when entrées are $20 or higher. The *Eating Out* category is much more casual and also more affordable, with entrées less than $20. Some restaurants are hard to categorize. Perhaps a restaurant's entrées are less than $20, but the ambience is formal, with linen tablecloths and napkins, mood lighting, candlelight, soft music, and flowers. In that case, we've listed it with fine dining. Although we try to put each restaurant in the category in which we

THE BIG CHICKEN

When relating Marietta's rich historical background, one can go from the sublime to the ridiculous. Around Marietta, all things point to or away from the much beloved Big Chicken, so directions anywhere in the vicinity generally include references to the giant fowl: "Turn right at the Big Chicken," "Go 4 miles past the Big Chicken"—you get the idea. The 56-foot-tall, red and white sheet-metal chicken with its opening and closing beak and rolling eyes presides over the intersection of US 41/Cobb Parkway and GA 20/Roswell Road east of Marietta proper, where it has been since 1963, when it was erected as the landmark identifying a local fast-food joint. Scores of Northerners saw the big bird on their way to and from Florida when US 41 was the main route. The eatery was bought by Kentucky Fried Chicken in 1980, and as the end of the century approached, company executives began making noises about tearing the chicken down to make this KFC conform to others. But the citizenry grumbled. In 1993 a tornado severely damaged the big fella, and KFC decided once and for all to tear it down, but the company was soon flooded with protests from locals and folks around the world. The company even had to install a special toll-free number to handle the volume of calls that were coming from as far away as Japan. Bowing to the inevitable, executives spent $700,000 to restore the big guy to his former glory. Thank goodness the icon remains at his post. How else would we be able to find our way?

think it fits best, it might also fit into the other category, so we hope our description makes it possible for you to make a decision about whether this is what you're looking for or not. Also be aware that prices will almost inevitably have changed by the time you travel.

DOLPHIN WATCHING The official state marine mammal of Georgia is the right whale, which bears its young off the coasts of Georgia, South Carolina, and northeastern Florida. Extremely endangered, it is rarely seen within sight of land. Visitors are entranced, however, with cavorting dolphins, which are often seen. Just a few companies that offer dolphin-watching tours are **Capt. Mike's Dolphin Tours** out of Tybee Island, **Dolphin Magic** out of Savannah, and **St. Simons Transit Company** out of St. Simons Island. Anglers on deep-sea fishing charters often sight dolphins. Better yet, do as our multigenerational extended family does and stay several weeks each year in a cottage on the Back River on Tybee Island, where schools of dolphins cruising up and down the river keep us entertained all day long. Sometimes they come in almost to the shore. When various family members have been sailing or kayaking in the calm waters of the Back River, they've actually been sprayed by dolphins that were that close to them. Our grandson said, "That dolphin sneezed on me!" So plentiful and frequent are the sightings that we always say, "A day without dolphins is a day without sunshine."

DRIVING TOURS Throughout the book we describe many state-designated trails, just a few of which include the **Andersonville Trail** from Perry to Cordele, the **Blue and Gray Trail** from Chattanooga to Dallas, **Chattahoochee–Flint River Heritage Highway** from Roscoe to St. Marks, **Chieftains Trail** from Carrollton to Dalton, **Colonial Coast Birding Trail** from St. Marys to Savannah, **Georgia's Antebellum Trail** from Athens to Macon, **Heartland of the Confederacy Civil War Trail** from Athens to Madison, the **Liberty Trail** from Hinesville to

Riceboro, and the **Russell-Brasstown Scenic Byway** from Helen to Blairsville.

Many cities and towns have devised driving tours of historic neighborhoods. Just a few of these include the **Azalea Trail, Camellia Trail,** and **Valdosta Historic Driving Tour** in Valdosta; **Gone with the Wind Driving Tour of Homes** in Jonesboro; the **Thomasville Black History Heritage Trail Tour;** and driving tours in Historic Grantville, Moreland, and Senoia.

EMERGENCIES/MEDICAL Georgia's 159 counties are universally covered by 911 services.

EVENTS We list outstanding and often highly unusual annual events within each chapter. In addition to large festivals such as the **Atlanta Dogwood Festival,** the **Renaissance Festival** in Fairburn, and the **Savannah Irish Festival** and **St. Patrick's Day Parade** in Savannah, there are dozens of festivals dedicated to buggies, fire ants, honeybees, mayhaws (a type of berry), mules, peanuts, rattlesnakes, swine, Vidalia onions, watermelon, wild chickens, and wild hogs. We give a brief description, contact information, and an admission price if there is one. More events can be found by checking the websites of convention and visitors bureaus and chambers of commerce, which are listed in the *Guidance* section of each chapter. Other listings can be found at the state's travel website (www.exploregeorgia .org). Even more information can be obtained from the **Southeast Festivals and Events Association** (www.southeast festivals.com).

FACTORY OUTLETS Georgia has clusters of outlet stores scattered throughout the state, primarily along I-75, I-85, and I-95, but other places as well. These are described in the pertinent chapters. If you're in the market for carpet, Dalton, which is located 90 miles north of Atlanta and 25 miles south of Chattanooga on I-75, boasts more than 100 carpet outlets. Other outlet centers include **Commerce Factory Stores** in Commerce, **Georgia Islands Factory Shoppes** in Darien, **Lake Park**

Outlets in Lake Park, **North Georgia Premium Outlets** in Calhoun and Dawsonville, **Peach Festival Outlet Shops** in Byron, **Tanger Outlet Center** in Locust Grove, and **Tanger Outlets of Commerce.** Many individual off-price shops can be found throughout the state.

FALL FOLIAGE Autumn colors are usually at their most flamboyant in north Georgia the last week in October through the first week in November. The air is usually clear and crisp, making travel especially appealing. The downside is that the winding, two-lane, mountainous country roads are clogged with sight-seers. Restaurants and shops are crowded, and it's essential to have made overnight reservations far in advance. Unlike some other states where leaf season is considered off-season with reduced prices, in Georgia fall is still high season. In fact, hostelries may require three-night minimum stays and full nonrefundable payment in advance. A website to consult about fall foliage is www.forestry.about.com.

FARM BED & BREAKFASTS Farm B&Bs offer a complete change of pace for city dwellers: lots of wide-open spaces, farm animals, hearty breakfasts, and a casual atmosphere. Some are on working farms, some are not. One of the most outstanding is **The Inn at Serenbe,** located in Palmetto just south of Atlanta. Accommodations exude casual elegance; meals are gourmet delights. In addition to farm animals to feed or pet, guests enjoy a collection of folk art, the swimming pool, hiking trails, and a waterfall. Others are described in appropriate chapters.

FARMER'S MARKETS The state's numerous farmer's markets are the best source of fresh fruit, produce, and many other food and plant items. The largest is the **Atlanta State Farmer's Market** in Forest Park just south of the city, which even offers a trolley tour of the huge site. State farmer's markets also can be found in Albany, Augusta, Cairo, Cordele, Fitzgerald, Moultrie, Pelham, Savannah, and Thomasville. Other popular farmer's markets include **Buford Highway Farmer's Market** in Atlanta, **Harry's Farmer's Market** in Roswell, **International Farmer's Market** in Chamblee, the **Sweet Auburn Curb Market** in downtown Atlanta, and **Your DeKalb Farmer's Market** in Doraville. For more information about farmer's markets, consult the website at www.n-georgia.com and click on "Farmers Markets."

FARM TOURS Agriculture is an important part of Georgia's economy. Many farms throughout the state have branched out from merely growing crops to also offering tours, fruit and berry picking, shopping for food and other items, and recreational activities such as hayrides, petting zoos, and Halloween activities. Some of these farms include **Bradley's Pumpkin Patch and Christmas Trees** near Dawsonville, **Burt's Farm** near Dawsonville, **Cagle's Dairy** near Canton and Ringgold, **Enota Mountain Retreat** near Hiawassee, **Pumpkin Patch Farm** near Adairsville, **Southern Tree Plantation** near Blairsville, and **Sweet Grass Dairy** near Thomasville. The number of pick-your-own farms is so large that we could not include very many of them.

FERRIES Georgia does not need regular ferry service for use as public transportation as some other states do. There are, however, several places that you can get to only by ferry: **Cumberland Island National Seashore, Little St. Simons Island,** and **Sapelo Island.** Details about ferries to these locations are found in the appropriate chapters. **Belles Ferry** (912-447-4000; www.savtcc.com) provides water taxi service from the City Hall dock in Savannah's historic district across the Savannah River to the hotel, convention center, golf course, and attractions on Hutchinson Island. The cost is free, and the taxis operate every 10 to 15 minutes between 7 AM and 11 PM daily.

FILM Since the inception of the **Georgia, Film, Video, and Music Office** (404-962-4052; www.filmgeorgia.org) in 1973, 700 major motion pictures and television programs have been filmed in Georgia, including *Midnight in the Garden of Good and Evil, Forrest Gump, The Legend of Bagger Vance, Driving Miss Daisy, Glory, Sweet Home Alabama, Fried Green Tomatoes, The Fighting Temptations, In the Heat of the Night,* and the Emmy-winning HBO film *Warm Springs.* Savannah also has a film commission, which can be contacted at 912-651-3696 or through its website, www .savannahfilm.org. Several film festivals occur annually, chief among them the **Summer Film Festival** at the Fox Theatre in Atlanta, a series of films shown in the magnificent theater.

FIRE PERMITS Permits are not required for campfires, but campers are responsible for any damage caused by their fire, which may include the cost of fighting the fire and the cost of timber destroyed, so exercise extreme caution. Only dead or downed wood can be used. Better yet, use a portable stove fueled by propane gas or Sterno. Permits are required for all other outdoor burning. You must contact the local **Georgia Forestry Commission** office (1-800-GA-TREES; www.gfc.state.ga.us) to obtain a permit before you proceed with any other outdoor burning.

FISHING Georgia boasts 4,000 miles of trout streams, 12,000 miles of warm-water streams, and a half million acres of impoundments. More than 1 million anglers try their luck each year, spending $1 billion and having a $2 billion total impact on the state's economy. Licenses are required for both fresh- and saltwater fishing. Call 1-800-ASK-FISH for detailed information about fishing in Georgia. In addition to fishing regulations and license information, the recording gives a weekly update on fishing conditions, as well as locations of boat ramps and the answers to commonly asked questions. Alabama, Florida, and South Carolina have reciprocal freshwater fishing agreements with Georgia, so residents of those states don't have to get a Georgia license if they already have a valid one. There may be differences

between the states, however, in the number or size of fish caught, so be sure to check local regulations. Licenses can be purchased at most sporting goods stores, bait and tackle stores, and large stores such as Wal-Mart that have a sporting goods department. You also can get a license by going to www.permit.com. A complete list of fishing regulations is available in the Georgia Department of Natural Resources, Wildlife Resources Division, brochure "Georgia Sport Fishing Regulations." A downloadable version of the brochure can be found on the website at www.gofish georgia.com. Whether you're a fishing enthusiast or not, plan a visit to the **Go Fish Education Center** in Perry (see the Macon chapter.)

FOLK PLAYS To keep Georgia's unique rural heritage alive, several communities produce folk plays, including *Swamp Gravy* in Colquitt and *Tales from the Altamaha* in Lyons.

FORTS Georgia boasts forts that span the history of the area from the time of early settlers through the Revolutionary and Civil wars to World War II and the present. Currently active bases that have one or more attractions interesting to travelers include **Fort Benning** near Columbus, home of the National Infantry Museum; **Fort Gordon** near Augusta, which has a museum

and recreational opportunities for visitors; and **Fort Stewart** near Hinesville, which has an interesting museum. Historical forts open to the public include **Fort Frederica National Monument,** St. Simons; **Fort Jackson,** Savannah; **Fort King George Historic Site,** Darien; **Fort McAllister Historic Park,** Richmond Hill; **Fort Morris Historic Site,** Midway; **Fort Oglethorpe,** home of the Chickamauga and Chattanooga National Military Battle-field; **Fort Pulaski National Monument,** Tybee Island; and **Fort Yargo,** which is located in a state park near Winder. These forts offer living-history programs and numerous annual special events.

FRUIT AND BERRY PICKING If you want the freshest and most succulent fruits and berries, you might like to pick your own. The activity also can provide a pleasant couple of hours' entertainment for the whole family. Georgia has a seemingly endless supply of opportunities to pick your own farms throughout the state. We describe a few of them in various chapters. For more information about pick-your-own facilities, consult the website at www.pick yourown.org/GA/htm.

GARDENS Georgia's ideal climate makes gardens possible year-round in all but the most mountainous areas of north Georgia. The largest and most famous garden in Georgia and the Southeast is **Callaway Gardens** in Pine Mountain, which features numerous types of gardens but is most famous for its azaleas. Destined to become famous is the **Gibbs Gardens** in Ball Ground, opened in 2012. It is the largest residential estate garden in the country, with exceptional Japanese, waterlily, and daffodil gardens. Some other outstanding gardens include **American Camellia Society/Massee Lane Gardens** in Fort Valley, the **Atlanta Botanical Garden,** gardens at the **Atlanta History Center, Dunaway Gardens** near Newnan, **Ferrell Gardens at Hills and Dales** in LaGrange, **Founders Memorial Garden** in Athens, **Fred Hamilton Rhododendron Gardens** near Hiawassee, **Georgia Botanical**

Gardens at the **Historic Bamboo Farm** near Savannah, **Georgia Southern University Botanical Gardens** in Statesboro, **Japanese Garden** at the **Jimmy Carter Presidential Library and Museum** in Atlanta, **Robert L. Stanton Rose Garden** at Fernbank in Atlanta, **Rock City Gardens** in Lookout Mountain, the **State Botanical Garden of Georgia** near Athens, and the **Thomasville Rose Garden** in Thomasville. Some of these gardens offer classes, talks, and demonstrations as well as special events and festivals.

GEORGIA FACTS Georgia is the largest state east of the Mississippi River, stretching 322 miles from Dalton near the Tennessee border in northwest Georgia to Valdosta near Florida in the southern part of the state, and 255 miles from Savannah on the coast to Columbus on the Alabama border. Its geographic regions are the Coastal Plain, the Piedmont Plateau in the center of the state, the Ridge and Valley area in the northwest, and the Appalachian Mountains in the northeast. It is the ninth-largest state in population, with a citizenry of 9.69 million. Sixty million tourists visit Georgia each year. Some famous Georgians include former president Jimmy Carter; CNN founder Ted Turner; civil rights figures Martin Luther King Jr., John Lewis, and Andrew Young; writers Margaret Mitchell, Joel Chandler Harris, and Alice Walker; sports figures Bobby Jones, Ty Cobb, and Bill Elliott; entertainers James Brown, Ray Charles, Julia Roberts, and Travis Tritt.

GEORGIA GROWN Georgia boasts 11.1 million acres devoted to farms. The state leads all others in the production of cotton, corn, peanuts, poultry, tobacco, and watermelons, and is among the leaders in pecans, eggs, and rye. Georgia, which ironically is known as the Peach State, actually lags behind California and South Carolina in peach production, although production is still significant. Other important food crops include tomatoes and sweet Vidalia onions—grown in only a 20-county area. Georgia is becoming increasingly well-known for the number and variety of its wineries throughout the state, but primarily clustered in north Georgia. While you're traveling through the state you might want to sample the Georgia-grown products of **Ellis Bros. Pecans** in Vienna, **Farm Fresh Tattnall** in Reidsville, **Gooseneck Farms** in Hawkinsville, **Jolly Nut Company** in Fort Valley, **Lane Packing Company** in Fort Valley, and **Merritt Pecan Company** in Weston. Be on the lookout for farms and orchards that offer pick-your-own fruits, nuts, or vegetables. See also *Apples.*

GEORGIA MADE Although Georgia is not known as a manufacturing state (it has lost almost all its textile and American car manufactories), some products such as carpets are made here (see *Factory Outlets*). In fact, Georgia is the world leader in the manufacture of carpets. It is also the world leader in mining, production, processing, and application of kaolin—a white clay used in paper coating, plastics, rubber, pigments, and pharmaceuticals. It is found roughly along the fall line between the Piedmont Plateau and the Coastal Plain from Augusta to Macon to Columbus. On a smaller scale, Georgia craftspeople and companies create some other famous products, including rocking chairs produced by the **Brumby Chair Company** in Marietta.

GEORGIA PUBLIC BROADCASTING There's almost nowhere you can go in Georgia that you'd be out of range of a Georgia Public Broadcasting radio or television station. GPB television stations are found in Albany (WABW, channel 14), Atlanta (WGTV, channel 8), Augusta (WCES, channel 20), Chatsworth (WCLP, channel 18), Columbus (WJSP, channel 28), Dawson (WACS, channel 25), Macon (WDCO, channel 29), Savannah (WVAN, channel 9), and Waycross (WXGA, channel 8). Keep in mind that depending on the cable company that represents the area, these channel numbers may be different. Radio stations are found in Albany (WUNV, 91.7 FM), Athens (WUGA, 91.7/97.9), Augusta (WACG, 90.7), Brunswick (WWIO, 88.9), Carrollton

(WUWG, 90.7), Columbus (WJSP, 88.1), Dahlonega (WNGU, 89.5), Demorest (WPPR, 88.3), Fort Gaines (WJWV, 90.9), Macon (WDCO, 89.7), St. Marys (WWIO, 1190 AM), Savannah (WSVH, 91.1), Tifton (WABR, 91.1), Valdosta (WWET, 91.7), and Waycross (WXVS, 90.1). For information in Atlanta, call 404-685-4788; outside Atlanta call 1-800-222-4788; or consult the website at www.gpb.org. Atlanta also has public television (WABE, channel 30) and radio (WPBA, 90.1) stations operated by the Atlanta Board of Education. Call 678-363-7425 for the television station or 404-892-2962 for the radio station.

GHOST TOURS A state with so much history is bound to have more than a few ghosts. Savannah is called the "Most-Haunted City in America" by many. When visiting Savannah, be sure to take one of the spine-tingling walking or driving ghost tours—always scheduled after dark for the best effect (see the Savannah chapter for details). Several other options for ghost tours include **City Segway Tours Legends and Lore** in Atlanta, **Dalton Ghost Tours, Roswell Ghost Tours,** and **St. Simons Ghost Tours.**

GOLD MINING Most travelers don't know that the first gold rush in the country was not in California, but in Dahlonega in the north Georgia mountains. In fact, the phrase "There's gold in them thar hills" was coined in Georgia. It was the discovery of gold in Georgia that precipitated the removal of Native Americans from the area along the Trail of Tears to the west. The dome of Georgia's capitol in Atlanta is covered with gold mined in Dahlonega. Enough remnants of gold remain in the mountains to provide entertainment for tourists. Several locations around Dahlonega offer gold panning and/or mine tours: **Consolidated Gold Mine, Crisson Gold Mine, Dukes Creek Gem and Mining Company,** and **Gold 'n Gem Grubbin' Mine.**

GOLF Although Augusta is famous for the Masters golf tournament, very few members of the general public are ever lucky enough to attend and certainly can't play at Augusta National, but there are 523 golf courses across Georgia where they can play. We describe the state park golf courses and some resort courses in the appropriate chapters.

Eight state parks offer golf courses. Three are in north Georgia: the **Creek** at Hard Labor Creek State Park near Rutledge, **Highland Walk** at Victoria Bryant near Royston, and **Arrowhead Pointe** at Lake Richard B. Russell near Elberton. Five are in the southern part of the state: **Meadow Links** at George T. Bagby near Fort Gaines, **Georgia Vets** at Georgia Veterans near Cordele, **Wallace Adams** at Little Ocmulgee near McRae, **Brazell's Creek** at Gordonia-Alatamaha near Reidsville, and **The Lakes** at Laura S. Walker near Waycross. For more information about the state park golf courses, consult the website at www.georgiagolf.com.

The major resorts that cater to golfers are: **Barnsley Gardens Resort** in Adairsville, **Lake Blackshear Resort and Golf Club** in Cordele; **The Cloister at Sea Island** (restricted to guests only); **King and Prince Beach and Golf Resort** on St. Simons Island; **Sea Palms Golf and Tennis Resort** on St. Simons; **Kingwood Golf Club and Resort** in Clayton; **Innsbruck Resort and Golf Club** in Helen; **Chateau Elan Winery and Resort** in Braselton; **Legacy on Lanier Resort** at Lake Lanier Islands; **Brasstown Valley Resort** in Young Harris; **Westin Savannah Harbor Golf Resort and Spa; Cuscowilla Resort on Lake Oconee** and **The Ritz-Carlton Lodge at Reynolds Plantation,** both near Greensboro.

For information about all the golf courses in Georgia, consult the website www.golflink.com/golf-courses/state.asp?state=GA. More information can be obtained from the **Georgia State Golf Association** (770-955-4272 or 1-800-949-4742; www.gsga.org).

GORGES North Georgia is the mountainous area of the state, but for the most part travelers won't find spectacular gorges such as those in the western part of America. These ancient mountains have been worn down for millions of years. There are a few gorges, however. **Cloudland Canyon** is found in Cloudland Canyon State Park in Rising Fawn near the Tennessee border, and **Tallulah Gorge,** one of the deepest in the East, is found in the town of Tallulah Falls in northeast Georgia. The canyon that comes as a complete surprise is **Providence Canyon** near Lumpkin. Located in a relatively flat area near the Alabama state line, the canyon is the result not of millions of years of upheaval, but of erosion caused by a mere 100 years of poor agricultural practices. The gorge, contained in the Providence Canyon State Conservation Area, is the home of the biggest concentration of wildflowers in the state.

GUIDE SERVICES See *Canoeing, Kayaking, Tubing, and White-Water Rafting; Fishing;* and *Hunting/Shooting Sports.* Numerous guide services also are described in individual chapters.

GUIDED TOURS When we travel to a new place, we like to take a guided tour first to get the flavor of the area so we'll know which attractions we'd like to see in more detail. Many companies in the larger cities and towns offer guided tours—some walking, some by bus, trolley, or horse-drawn carriage. In Atlanta tours are offered by **American Sightseeing Atlanta, Atlanta Preservation Center Tours,** and **City Segway Tours.** In Athens tours are provided by **Classic City Tours** and **UGA Visitor Center Tours.** In Augusta **Augusta Canal Tours** offers tours. Savannah has dozens of tour companies. Some other guided tours throughout the state include **Milledgeville Historic Trolley Tour, St. Simons Trolley Tours, Saturday Guided History Tours** in Augusta, and **Spirit of Sapelo Tours** on Sapelo Island.

HANDICAPPED ACCESS Attractions, lodgings, and restaurants that are at least partially handicapped accessible are identified with the & icon. Keep in mind, however, that just because an entry is listed as wheelchair accessible doesn't mean it is fully wheelchair friendly. A multistory attraction such as a historic home may have a ramp to allow access to the first floor, but other floors may not be accessible at all. A hotel or other lodging may have wheelchair access to guest rooms on the first floor or access to rooms on other floors via an elevator, but bathrooms don't necessarily have full accessibility with roll-in showers, handrails, or other modifications. Likewise, restaurants may have access to rooms on the first floor only, and restrooms may have limited wheelchair accessibility. New or remodeled structures must conform to federal regulations; older sites may still have accessibility problems. We try to indicate the true conditions in each entry if we think the distinction needs to be made, but it's probably best to call ahead.

HIKING Georgia's vast areas of undeveloped land are conducive to both easy and challenging hiking. The most famous trails in the state are the 80-mile section of the **Appalachian Trail** in north Georgia (see entry above) and the 75-mile portion of the **Bartram Trail** from Augusta to Crawfordville, as well as the Georgia portion of the 300-mile **Benton MacKaye Trail** (www.bmta.org) and the **Pine Mountain Trail** between Warm Springs and Pine Mountain. The Bartram Trail actually runs from the North Carolina border in northeast Georgia 220 miles to Augusta, the Savannah River, and Savannah. The 55-mile Georgia Loop of the Benton MacKaye Trail is called "the toughest hike in Georgia." There are hundreds of miles of trails in the **Chattahoochee-Oconee National Forests.** State parks (www.gastateparks .org and www.fs.usda.gov) and other nature preserves are good places to hike. Some other trails include the **Aska Adventure Trails** in Blue Ridge, and the **Disney Trail** on Rocky Face Mountain and the **Pinhoti Trail,** both near Dalton in northwest Georgia.

Even the big-city areas have parks and other areas that provide hiking opportunities. The **PATH Foundation** (404-875-

7284; www.pathfoundation.org) is a non-profit organization working to build and maintain greenway trails throughout metro Atlanta and Georgia.

Some books particularly helpful to hikers are *Atlanta Walks* by Ren and Helen Davis, 45 self-guided tours in the metro area, including walking, running, and bicycling information; *Georgia Walks* by Ren and Helen Davis; *60 Hikes Within 60 Miles of Atlanta* by Randy and Pam Golden; *The Hiking Trails of North Georgia* by Tim Homan; *A Walk in the Woods: Rediscovering America on the Appalachian Trail* by Bill Bryson; *Hiking Georgia* by Donald Pfitzer; *Touring the Backroads of North and South Georgia* by Frank and Victoria Logue; and *Touring the Coastal Georgia Backroads* by Nancy Rhyne.

HISTORIC HOMES AND SITES

It's no surprise that, as one of America's original 13 colonies and a major player in the Civil War, the state has many historic treasures—some of them open for public tours. **Pebble Hill Plantation** in Thomasville is an example of a grand sporting plantation retreat of the early 20th century. **Callaway Plantation** in Washington, **Jarrell Plantation Historic Site** in Juliette, and **Hofwyl-Broadfield Plantation State Historic Site** are examples of working farms.

Three presidents called Georgia home, either full- or part-time: Jimmy Carter, Franklin D. Roosevelt, and Woodrow Wilson. The **Jimmy Carter National Historic Site** in Plains, the **Boyhood Home of President Woodrow Wilson** in Augusta, and the **Little White House State Historic Site** in Warm Springs give glimpses into their lives.

Savannah has one of the largest historic districts in the country, and many entire small Georgia towns are on the National Register of Historic Places—some of them in their entirety. The **Jekyll Island National Historic Landmark District** is a large and impressive restoration area.

In every chapter you'll find historic homes that are open for tours either because of the importance of the people who lived there or because of the architectural significance of the structure itself, or both. See also *African American Sites, Bed & Breakfasts, Civil War Sites, Covered Bridges, Forts, Lighthouses, Maritime Museums, Museum Villages, Native American Sites, Railroad Excursions and Museums, Theaters/Summer,* and *Theaters/Year-Round.*

HISTORY The history of Georgia can be traced through visits to the state's many historical sites. Thousands of years ago Native Americans inhabited the area. A strange remnant of their occupation is the **Rock Eagle Effigy** and the **Rock Hawk Effigy,** stone tumuli near Eatonton in central Georgia that represent gargantuan birds with outstretched wings. Mound Builders left evidence of their occupation along the western part of Georgia at what are now **Kolomoki Mounds Historic Park** near Baxley and **Etowah Indian Mounds Historic Site** near Cartersville, as well as in central Georgia at what is now the **Ocmulgee National Monument** near Macon. Some shell middens offer evidence that Native Americans of the Guale (pronounced WAHL-ee) Mocama tribe inhabited the coast and barrier islands. Numerous other sites depict the lives of Native Americans until they were driven out of the state in 1838 after the first gold rush in the country. This forced migration was known as the Trail of Tears. The Cherokee capital at New Echota, now the **New Echota Cherokee Capital Historic Site** near Calhoun, is a must-see stop in northwest Georgia, as are the homes of three Cherokee chiefs. See also *Native American Sites.*

Explorer Hernando de Soto and his men passed through Georgia in 1540. The Spanish later made more permanent incursions into what would become Georgia to build a chain of missions and establish a large Jesuit mission-presidio that later became a Franciscan mission on St. Catherine's Island. Although there is enough evidence of this occupation to interest archaeologists, little evidence remains that would attract tourists.

Fort King George, built in 1721 near present-day Darien, was the first English settlement in the area that would become Georgia. It was garrisoned by British soldiers for seven years. Now the **Fort King George State Historic Site,** the site contains a replica of the blockhouse and a museum that interprets the Native American, colonial, Scottish, and sawmilling periods of the immediate area.

Contrary to popular myth, Georgia was not founded as a penal colony nor settled by convicts but instead by yeoman farmers and small businessmen. Because the area lies roughly at the same latitude as China, Persia, and the Madeira Islands, Georgia's founders envisioned a robust economy based on silk and wine production. The state's charter banned slavery, Catholics, hard liquor, and lawyers.

Georgia was chartered and became the 13th colony in 1732. Savannah was settled in 1733 under the leadership of Gen. James Oglethorpe and was the first planned city in North America. Most of the city's original squares survive, although much of the historic architecture is from the postbellum years at the end of the 19th century. Oglethorpe and his Scottish Highlanders also moved down the coast to protect the colony from the Spanish in northern Florida. Sunbury became an important port, and Fort Morris, now the **Fort Morris Historic Site,** was built to protect it. The fort fell to the British in 1779, but it was used in the War of 1812. The town of Sunbury completely disappeared with the exception of its cemetery.

Fort Frederica on St. Simons Island was established in 1736 and, at its peak in the early 1740s, was the most elaborate British fortification in North America. After the British victory over the Spanish in the Battle of Bloody Marsh in 1742, the regiment disbanded and the fort was abandoned. The significance of this battle was that it cemented Britain's control of the southernmost colony and ended the threat of incursions by the Spanish. The site, now the **Fort Frederica National Monument,** has an interpretive center and ruins.

Because the initial crops and industries the founders envisioned never flourished, farmers turned to the planting of rice, indigo, and cotton, all of which were labor intensive. The ban against slavery was overturned in 1750. By 1760 one-third of the population was slaves, and by the Revolutionary War that figure had increased to almost half. A small affluent planter class developed.

Georgia played a relatively minor role in the American Revolution. It was the only colony to comply with the Stamp Act, and although there were three Georgia signers of the Declaration of Independence, Georgia didn't send a representative to the First Continental Congress. An important Revolutionary War battle was fought in Savannah in 1779 when occupying British forces repulsed an American and French assault. Confiscation of Tory property after the Revolution resulted in a vast reapportionment of land, which was particularly helpful to the average man away from the large plantations of the lowcountry. Heads of household could claim 200 acres of land, and few white men failed to qualify. More than 100,000 families claimed three-fourths of Georgia. Stripping the Native Americans of their lands in 1838 put even more property in the hands of individuals.

The invention of the cotton gin at the end of the 18th century made it possible for cotton production to increase twentyfold, which also increased the number of slaves. On the eve of the Civil War, Georgia had more slaves and slave owners than any other state.

Savannah's strategic importance continued after the Revolutionary War. It became a primary port, shipping cotton and other commodities from all over the state. Two brick forts were constructed near the city: **Fort Jackson** in 1808 and **Fort Pulaski** in 1829. Fort Jackson was manned during the War of 1812 and enlarged in 1845 and 1860. It didn't, however, prevent the Union from taking Savannah in 1864. The construction of Fort Pulaski, now **Fort Pulaski National Monument,** was overseen by Robert E. Lee. It was thought to be impregnable, but 30 hours of bombardment with rifled cannon by Federal troops resulted in its fall.

Georgia's dependency on slavery and its belief in the primacy of states' rights drove the state to secede from the Union on January 2, 1861, although only 51 percent of the legislature meeting at the capital in Milledgeville favored secession.

Fort McAllister, now **Fort McAllister State Historic Site,** was built by the Confederacy in 1862 to defend the Ogeechee River, the river plantations in the area, and Savannah's southern flank. It withstood Federal assaults in 1862 and 1863 but fell to Union troops in December 1864.

The war touched every area of the state—from Chickamauga in the northwest corner of the state to Atlanta and across the heartland to Savannah—whether any battles were fought in a particular area or not (see *Civil War Sites*). Margaret Mitchell's opus *Gone with the Wind* memorialized the war and its aftermath for people all over the world.

During the war and afterward under Reconstruction, the citizens of Georgia suffered terrible deprivation. The cotton economy never recovered after the war, which resulted in the tenant farmer system that continued to plague both blacks and whites until World War II. It was during this period that the Jim Crow and "separate but equal" laws were passed. Segregation became an urban way of life because so many African Americans were moving to the cities. Poll taxes, white-only primaries, literacy tests, and the county-unit systems disenfranchised blacks.

Georgia was in desperate straits in 1935 because of the Great Depression, the devastation wrought by the boll weevil, and a governor who fought all the New Deal programs designed to help the citizenry. The author of the New Deal, Franklin D. Roosevelt, got many of his ideas while visiting his home in Warm Springs, now the **Little White House State Historic Site.**

At the same time that much of the state was suffering, wealthy Northerners were enjoying an idyllic lifestyle in Georgia. From the late 1800s through the beginning of World War II, 100 Northern millionaires and their families spent winters at their exclusive retreat on Jekyll Island. Much of the area is preserved as the **Jekyll Island National Historic Landmark District.** Meanwhile, Northern industrialists maintained opulent plantations in the area of south Georgia between Thomasville and Tallahassee. Travelers can visit **Pebble Hill Plantation,** one of those retreats.

World War II was the pivotal event in turning around Georgia's economy because massive federal spending was infused into the state. Georgia was second only to Texas in military training facilities. Airplanes were built at Bell Aircraft (now Lockheed) in Marietta, and Liberty Ships were constructed in Savannah and Brunswick. After the war, automobile manufacturing came to Atlanta, and for the first time income earned by Atlanta workers surpassed the national average.

In the early 1960s, the civil rights movement was in full force in the South. The first sit-in in Atlanta was in 1960. The Albany civil rights movement, although not terribly successful, served as a training ground for Martin Luther King Jr., John Lewis, Julian Bond, Andrew Young, and many other familiar names. Atlanta, the "city too busy to hate," peacefully integrated its schools, and when King was assassinated, his funeral and mourning were also peaceful. Today one of the most visited sites in the state is the **Martin Luther King Jr. National Historic Site.**

Over the past 50 years Georgia has lost its textile manufacturing plants and is now losing its American automobile manufacturing plants—although it has attracted several foreign car companies—as well as several of its military bases. The state's economy suffered more than the national average during the recession that started in 2008. Still, the economy is multibased, and the population is multihued and multiethnic. CNN, the Cable News Network, makes its home in Atlanta, as does Coca-Cola. Tourists can take the **Inside CNN Tour** and visit the **World of Coca-Cola.** The 1996 Centennial Olympic Summer Games were a coup for Atlanta and the entire state. A lasting

legacy in downtown Atlanta is **Centennial Olympic Park.**

Indigenous folk arts, from the African American Gullah-Geechee culture on the coast to the Appalachian culture of the mountains, persist in pottery, folk plays, festivals, and the like. Travelers can visit **Hog Hammock** on Sapelo Island, the **Foxfire Museum** in Mountain City, and dozens of places in between. In addition to culture from the past, there have been striking changes in the fine arts, particularly the establishment of symphonies, operas, art museums, and ballets—not just in Atlanta but throughout the state.

Rapacious urbanization and suburbanization in the metro Atlanta area and some of the state's other cities have resulted in what we call "Anywhere USA," which can even be found in smaller towns. This is the strip or area of fast-food joints, big-box stores, shopping and strip malls, and gas station/convenience stores so familiar you could close your eyes and be anywhere in the country. Despite this intrusion of modern life, the state's natural beauty endures in many, many places. Georgia has well-maintained state highways and secondary roads, so get off the interstates and enjoy the nonhomogenized character of the state.

See also *African American Sites, Forts, Historic Homes and Sites,* and *Native American Sites.*

HORSEBACK RIDING Horseback riding is a popular activity here, whether along the beaches of southeastern Georgia, in the pastures of the heartland, or in the northern forests or mountains. For several years, companies offering horseback riding declined precipitously because of liability issues. The Georgia Legislature, however, passed a law that requires participants to sign a waiver releasing the company from liability. Since then, many companies are offering horseback riding once again. Several even offer overnight rides with meals, camping, and entertainment—à la *City Slickers.* Options for horseback riding can be found in almost every chapter. Some of the most outstanding are **Barnsley Gardens Resort** in Adairsville, **Brasstown**

Valley Resort in Young Harris, **Forrest Hills Resort** near Dahlonega, **Fort Mountain Stables** at Fort Mountain State Park near Chatsworth, **Lake Lanier Islands Equestrian Center** near Buford, **Roosevelt Riding Stables** at F. D. Roosevelt State Park near Pine Mountain, and **Victoria's Carriages and Beach Trail Rides** on Jekyll Island. These and many other options are described in the appropriate chapters. Many state parks and other nature preserves have riding trails open to visitors who BYOH (bring your own horse). Some of them even provide equestrian campsites and stalls for housing horses overnight. Those are described in the pertinent chapters. For those who bring their own horses, a current negative Coggins test for each horse must be in the rider's possession.

HORSE RACING Horse racing is not a widely available activity in Georgia, which makes the racing here that much more special. Two highly anticipated and well-attended annual events are the **Atlanta Steeplechase** in Kingston and the **Steeplechase at Callaway** in Pine Mountain. These events include the races themselves along with tailgating, special food tents, terrier races, other events, and, of course, fancy hats for the ladies.

Many Northern harness-racing horses winter and train in Hawkinsville at the **Lawrence Bennett Harness Training Facility.** Visitors can watch them daily during the season. Before the horses depart for

the North at the beginning of April, the **Hawkinsville Harness Horse Festival and Spring Celebration** fills two days with racing and other festivities.

There are few other horse races and events. Contact the **Georgia Thoroughbred Owners and Breeders Association** (1-866-66-GTOBA; www.gtoba.com) for information. Contact the **National Barrel Horse Association** (706-823-3728; www.nbha.com) for information about shows and events.

HOURS OF OPERATION The hours listed here for attractions, restaurants, shops, and so on are the most up-to-date we could get at publication time. Hours will undoubtedly change, however, so call ahead or consult an attraction or restaurant's website before traveling to avoid disappointment. Although we don't mention it when listing the hours for each entry, it should be understood that most attractions and many restaurants are closed on major holidays such as Thanksgiving, Christmas, Easter, and New Year's Day, and some other holidays. Assume attractions are closed on holidays or check ahead when in doubt.

HUNTING/SHOOTING SPORTS Georgia is famed for its game bird hunting—particularly in the plantation country of southern Georgia. Other types of hunting—including deer, wild boar, and turkey—are permitted in the national forests and most wildlife management areas throughout the state. Hunting regulations for all types of birds and animals can be found on the website for the **Georgia Department of Natural Resources** (www.georgiawildlife.com/hunting/regulations), as well as www.gunnersden.com, www.huntfind.com, and www.huntingsociety.org/Georgia.html.

Georgia is also filled with facilities that offer trap, skeet, and sporting clays, including the facility that was used for the 1996 Centennial Summer Olympic Games.

(OFFICIAL) INFORMATION ABOUT GEORGIA After reading this book, the place to go for more information about traveling in Georgia is the **Georgia Department of Economic Development, Tourism Division** (1-800-847-4842; www.exploregeorgia.org). You can request a free Georgia road map and a free "Georgia Travel Guide." The state also publishes a guide to African American–related attractions, a calendar of events, and a golf guide.

The state operates 11 welcome centers, most of which are at primary interstate highway access points into Georgia from other states: on I-20 westbound in Augusta from South Carolina, US 185 in Columbus, I-95 northbound in Kingsland from Florida, I-85 southbound in Lavonia from South Carolina, US 280 in Plains, I-75 southbound in Ringgold from Tennessee, I-95 southbound in Savannah from South Carolina, US 301 in Sylvania, I-20 eastbound in Tallapoosa from Alabama, I-75 northbound in Valdosta from Florida, and I-85 northbound in West Point from Alabama. These staffed centers can provide you with maps, the state travel guide, brochures on attractions and lodgings, and advice. There are numerous unstaffed rest areas on I-16, I-20, I-75, I-95, and I-475.

INNS Since 1979 we have personally stayed in and inspected hundreds of accommodations throughout the state. It's hard to keep up, however, so occasionally we've also relied on recommendations from travel professionals and others. No lodging has paid to be in this book.

ISLANDS Georgia is blessed with a small coastline and a series of coastal and barrier islands, most of which are accessible to travelers by road, ferry, or private boat. From north to south these are Tybee, Little Tybee, Skidaway, Wilmington, Wassaw, St. Catherine's, Blackbeard, Sapelo, Wolf, Little St. Simons, Sea, St. Simons, Jekyll, and Cumberland. Georgia's islands provide opportunities for numerous water sports, hiking, biking, and other outdoor pursuits. Lodging (when available) may be in hotels, cottages, and campgrounds.

LAKES When you look at a map and see how many significant lakes Georgia has, it's amazing to learn that the state has no large natural lakes. The major lakes were created for power generation and flood control, with recreation as a pleasant by-product. Some of the lakes are so large they are featured in several chapters. In addition, the state is filled with many small natural lakes, so access to a lake is available almost everywhere. Some lakes boast state parks, resorts, golf, and rental cottages.

Some of the most significant lakes in Georgia are **Clarks Hill Lake, Lake Hartwell,** and **Lake Richard B. Russell** in northeast Georgia; **Lake Allatoona** and **Lake Lanier** in north Georgia; **Lake Oconee** and **Lake Sinclair** in central Georgia; and **Lake Seminole, Lake Walter F. George,** and **West Point Lake** and in western and southwestern Georgia. These lakes and the lands surrounding them provide innumerable opportunities for water sports, hiking, camping, and other outdoor pursuits. These lakes and dozens of lesser lakes are described more fully in the appropriate chapters.

LIGHTHOUSES They once used their lights and day marks to warn sailors of danger or to guide them safely to harbor. Today several of these sentinels are open for visitors, and a climb to the top is rewarded with a spectacular view of the ocean and surrounding mainland: **Sapelo Island Lighthouse, St. Simons Lighthouse and Museum of Coastal History,** and **Tybee Island Lightstation and Tybee Museum. Cockspur Lighthouse** and **Little Cumberland Island Lighthouse** can be viewed only from afar.

LITTER There are 11 litter control laws in Georgia. Fines for littering may range from $200 to $1,000. Contact local law enforcement agencies to report violations. For more information, contact **Keep Georgia Beautiful** (404-679-4910; www .keepgeorgiabeautiful.org).

LODGES AT STATE PARKS Several state parks boast lodges with handicapped-accessible rooms, restaurants, and meeting facilities: **Amicalola Falls, George T.**

Bagby, Little Ocmulgee, and **Unicoi.** Occupancy is limited to four in regular hotel rooms and six in loft rooms. A deposit is required, and cancellation penalties are imposed within 72 hours of the anticipated arrival date. Visitors younger than 18 must be accompanied by an adult. Pets are not allowed in or around the lodges. Smoking is prohibited. For more information, consult the website at www.gastateparks.org.

MARITIME MUSEUMS Several museums along the coast are dedicated to Georgia's longtime relationship with the sea: **Maritime Center at the Historic Coast Guard Station** and **St. Simons Lighthouse and Museum of Coastal History** on St. Simons, **Ships of the Sea Museum** in Savannah, and **Tybee Island Lightstation and Tybee Museum** on Tybee Island.

MAPS Sources for Georgia maps include the *Georgia Atlas and Gazetteer*— available from Amazon, REI, and other sources—which provides DeLorme topographic maps that show highways and back roads as well as information on campgrounds, scenic routes, and natural features. The **Georgia Department of Economic Development, Tourism Division** (www.exploregeorgia.org) can provide a state road map. **Georgia Department of Transportation** (www.dot.state.ga.us) maps include the *Georgia Bicycle Map, State Highway Transportation Map,* city and county maps, and online maps. Click on "Maps." The **Chattahoochee-Oconee National Forests** (www.fs.usda.gov) can provide maps of the forests. Click on "Maps and Publications."

MOUNTAIN BIKING The best source of information about mountain biking in north Georgia is the **U.S. Forest Service** (770-297-3000; www.fs.usda.gov), which maintains many of the trails and can give you maps and advice. Places to ride are described in many chapters.

A good place to rent bikes is **Woody's Mountain Bikes** in Helen. Woody's also sponsors some guided rides. Some books

that are helpful to mountain bikers include *Backroad Bicycling in the Blue Ridge and Smoky Mountains: 27 Rides for Touring and Mountain Bikes from North Georgia to Southwest Virginia* by Hiram Rogers, *Mountain Biking Georgia: A Guide to Atlanta and Northern Georgia's Greatest Off-Road Bicycle Rides* by Alex Nutt, and *Off the Beaten Track: Guide to Mountain Biking in Georgia* by Jim Parham. See also *Bicycling* for information about bicycling organizations and other references.

MOUNTAINS Georgia's Appalachian and Blue Ridge mountains are ancient and worn down—and sometimes ridiculed by travelers from the western United States to whom Georgia's "mountains" are little more than bumps or hills. Not to be laughed at, however, is **Brasstown Bald**—one of the tallest mountains in the East. At almost 5,000 feet in elevation, it has weather comparable to that in Vermont. Visitors can drive almost to the top, and then a short, but steep, hike offers them breathtaking views of four states. **Kennesaw Mountain** north of Atlanta was the scene of fierce fighting during the Civil War. A climb to the top rewards hikers with an excellent view of Atlanta on a clear day. **Stone Mountain** is the world's largest exposed granite monadnock and the centerpiece of a recreational park. A carving of Confederate generals on its side was begun by the same sculptor who created Mount Rushmore. Visitors can hike to the top or take a cable car. Once at the top, they have excellent views of Atlanta. The entire northern part of Georgia is mountainous.

MUSEUMS We mention many different types of museums under the headings *Art Museums, Children's Museums, Maritime Museums, Museum Villages,* and *Railroad Excursions and Museums.* Some of Georgia's museums are special and difficult to categorize. Some unusual museums include **The Big House Museum** in Macon (the Allman Brothers Band Museum), **Booth Western Art Museum** in Cartersville, **Georgia Rural Telephone Museum** in Leslie, **Georgia Sports Hall of Fame** in

Macon, and, perhaps the most unusual of all, the **Loudermilk Boarding House Museum** in Cornelia, which houses the *Everything Elvis* exhibit. For an extensive list of museums, consult the website at www.answers.com/museumsingeorgia.

MUSEUM VILLAGES Museum villages provide a window into the past, and several of these villages exist in Georgia. Some were actual villages or townships; others have been created by moving historic buildings from around the state. The **Jekyll Island National Historic Landmark District** was the home of 100 millionaire families from the late 1800s to World War II. **Seabrook Village** near Midway was home to poor African Americans. These museum villages were created: **Frontier Village** in Fort Gaines, **Museum of Agriculture and Historic Village** in Tifton, and **Westville** in Lumpkin. Both the museum and Westville are staffed by costumed interpreters.

MUSIC CONCERT SERIES Georgia boasts not only the acclaimed **Atlanta Symphony Orchestra,** but a dozen other symphonies, not counting several college and university symphonies. The ASO offers a classical series, a pops series, family concerts, and free summer concerts in metro area parks. All the other symphonies have some kind of concert series, which are described in the appropriate chapters. Just a few of the state's concert series include **Arts and Entertainment Series/First Tuesday Series** in Tifton; **Fine Arts on the River** concerts in Savannah; and **Brown Bag Concerts** and **River Music Concert Series** in Bainbridge.

A pleasant spring-through-fall diversion in Atlanta is to attend an outdoor concert. One of the most famous venues is **Chastain Park Amphitheater** in Atlanta, which hosts two different series of musical acts, including one series with the Atlanta Symphony Orchestra. Other towns and cities that offer concert series, which may occur on the town square or in a park, include Blue Ridge, Dahlonega, Decatur, Kennesaw, Marietta, McDonough, Roswell, and

Stockbridge (see *Outdoor Venues* in this chapter and *Entertainment* and *Special Events* in the appropriate chapters). Numerous music festivals may vary in length from a day to a week or more. Some of the best-known festivals include the **Atlanta Jazz Festival** and the **Midtown Music Festival,** both in Atlanta, and the **Savannah Jazz Festival,** but there are many more described in individual chapters.

NATIVE AMERICAN SITES Before European explorers and settlers came to Georgia, Native Americans inhabited the region—primarily Cherokees in the north and Creeks and Seminoles in the south, but also Guale Indians on the coast. Even before these tribes, however, the state was inhabited by Mound Builders. Close to a dozen significant Native American sites, including a national monument and several state historic sites, are open to the public: **Chieftains Museum/Major Ridge Home** in Rome, **Chief Vann House Historic Site** in Chatsworth, **Etowah Indian Mounds Historic Site** in Cartersville, **Funk Heritage Center** in Waleska, **John Ross House** in Rossville, **Kolomoki Mounds Historic Park** in Blakely, **New Echota Cherokee Capital Historic Site** in Calhoun, and **Ocmulgee National Monument** in Macon. **Fort Mountain State Park** surrounds an ancient wall built by Native Americans. Many of these sites are on the 150-mile **Chieftains Trail** from Carrollton to Dalton.

NATURE PRESERVES/COASTAL Most of Cumberland Island—Georgia's largest barrier island, accessed by ferry from St. Marys—has been preserved as the **Cumberland Island National Seashore.** The national seashore offers 17 miles of pristine beaches, maritime forest, wild horses, and other wildlife, as well as campgrounds, mansion ruins, and a small museum. Some of the other coastal preserves include **Blackbeard Island National Wildlife Refuge,** which is accessed through several outfitters based in Brunswick, Darien, Savannah, St. Simons, and Tybee Island; **Melon Bluff Nature and Heritage Reserve** near Midway; and the **Sapelo Island National Estuarine Research Reserve** accessed from Meridian.

NATURE PRESERVES/INLAND

The **Chattahoochee-Oconee National Forests** cover a vast area of north and central Georgia, providing endless opportunities for hiking, bird-watching, camping, and other outdoor pursuits. Some other important nature preserves in the state include the **Bartram Forest** near Milledgeville; **Chattahoochee River National Recreation Area** in metro Atlanta; **Marshall Forest** in Rome; **Moody Forest Natural Area** near Baxley; **Okefenokee National Wildlife Refuge,** which can be accessed from Fargo, Folkston, and Waycross; **Panola Mountain State Conservation Park** near Stockbridge; **Phinizy Swamp National Park** near Augusta; **Piedmont National Wildlife Refuge** near Juliette; **Providence Canyon State Conservation Park** near Lumpkin; and **Scull Shoals Archaeological Site** near Greensboro.

OUTDOOR VENUES

Chastain Park Amphitheater, a horseshoe-shaped venue developed as a government works project in the 1930s, remains beloved by Atlantans, who bring gourmet dinners, fancy table settings, candles, and floral arrangements to enhance their concert experience. More casual are **Aaron's Amphitheatre at Lakewood** south of Atlanta, the **Frederick Brown Jr. Amphitheater** in Peachtree City, the **Verizon Wireless Amphitheater at Encore Park** in Alpharetta, and the **Villages Amphitheater** in Fayetteville. Many individual chapters list outdoor concerts or series that may take place in small towns across the state in a park or on the courthouse square (see *Entertainment* or *Special Events*). See also *Music Concert Series.*

PARKING

Nearly all the small towns and villages in Georgia have plentiful free on-street parking. Unless otherwise noted, assume that such parking is available. The larger cities, on the other hand, rarely have free on-street parking. In those cases, we give details about the parking situation, including metered parking, parking lots and garages, and special event parking. In Atlanta, for example, you may pay up to $15 for special event parking.

PARKING/STATE PARKS

The day-use parking fee (called the Daily ParkPass) in state parks is $5. The Daily ParkPass is valid for all state parks visited on the same day. Overnight guests in lodges, cabins, or campgrounds pay only one fee for the duration of their stay. Diners in lodge restaurants and conference attendees are exempt. Parking for golfers is included in the greens fee. Frequent visitors can purchase an Annual ParkPass for $50 (call 770-389-7401). There are discounted Annual ParkPass fees for seniors and disabled veterans. The Historic Site Annual Pass can be purchased for $35. Join the Friends of Georgia State Parks and Historic Sites and get both parking passes free. For more information, see the website at www.gastateparks.org.

PARKS/NATIONAL

Georgia boasts the following national parks and national scenic areas: **Andersonville National Historic Site** in Andersonville, the **Appalachian Trail** in north Georgia, **Augusta Canal National Heritage Area** in Augusta, **Chattahoochee River National Recreation Area** in the metro Atlanta area, **Chickamauga and Chattanooga National Military Park** in Fort Oglethorpe, **Cumberland Island National Seashore** off the south Georgia coast near St. Marys, **Fort Frederica National Monument** on St. Simons Island, **Fort Pulaski National Monument** on Tybee Island, the **Gullah/Geechee Cultural Heritage Corridor** on the coast, **Jimmy Carter National Historic Site** in Plains, **Kennesaw Mountain National Battlefield Park** in Kennesaw, **Martin Luther King Jr. National Historic Site** in Atlanta, and **Ocmulgee National Monument** in Macon. Each is described with its contact information in the appropriate chapter. For more information, consult the website at www.nps.gov.

PARKS/STATE Georgia State Parks celebrated its 81st anniversary in 2012. The system includes 48 state parks and 18 historic sites. **Chattahoochee Bend** is the newest state park. Although every park doesn't have every feature, combined the state parks offer accommodations in cabins, campgrounds, lodges, and even yurts; beaches; covered bridges; disc golf; flying model airplanes; forts; golf; hiking; historic homes and other structures; horseback riding; miniature golf; museums; Native American sites; waterfalls; water sports; and wildlife observation. Consult the website at www.gastateparks.org. In order to avoid giving repetitive information, the full street address, telephone number(s), and website address for each state park are given in full only once per chapter. The most natural place to give the full contact information is when the full description of the park is given under *Green Space—Nature Preserves and Parks.* If the park is going to appear under several headings that occur earlier in the chapter, however, we give the full contact information the first time the park appears. In subsequent entries, such as *Camping* or *Cottages,* for example, we give only the reservation telephone number.

PEACHES Peaches were introduced into what is now St. Simons Island and Cumberland Island in the 1570s by Franciscan monks who had come from St. Augustine, Florida. The Cherokees were growing them by the mid-1700s, and the first commercial production began in the mid-1800s. The first peaches were shipped to the New York market between 1858 and 1860. Georgia rapidly became associated with peach production and earned the nickname the Peach State. Today, however, the state is third in peach production behind California and South Carolina. The primary peach-growing area is in Crawford, Macon, Peach, and Taylor counties in middle Georgia along the fall line between the Piedmont and the Coastal Plain. The area is far enough north for the necessary winter chilling but far enough south to avoid late frosts. At **Lane Packing Company** in Fort Valley you can watch peaches being sorted and packed. You can buy peaches and peach products at **Dickey Farms** in Musella, the oldest packinghouse in Georgia. Consult the website at www.pickyour own.org to find other places to get fresh peaches. A much-anticipated annual event to celebrate the peach is the **Georgia Peach Festival,** held in June in Fort Valley and Byron.

PETS Unless you're traveling in the winter; visiting the relatively cooler mountains, lakes, or forested areas; or driving directly to and from your destination, traveling with your dog can be problematic. We tried touring the state with one of our dogs in an RV, and we ran into problems we didn't anticipate. Although Nero was perfectly comfortable while on the road with the air-conditioning running (in fact, he was often sitting regally in the passenger seat while one of us was working at the computer at the kitchen table), what to do when we stopped at a restaurant or attraction? In 99 percent of cases, with the exception of hiking trails, we couldn't take him with us. We couldn't leave him in the RV unless we left the air conditioner running, and with today's gasoline prices, that wasn't a very attractive option. We couldn't leave him tied outside the RV because it was too hot and we were concerned about his safety or the risk of him being stolen. We ended up running the RV so the air conditioner would be on. Although pets are welcome in state park campgrounds and selected cottages, they must be leashed at all times. And uncivilized though it may be, dogs are not welcome on Georgia's beaches. A few more hotels and even bed & breakfasts are realizing that many travelers won't be happy leaving their best friend at home. We've indicated with the 🐾 icon those lodgings, parks, and the like that are pet friendly. For more information about travel with pets, consult the **Pet Friendly Travel** websites (www.petfriendlytravel.com, www.dogfriendly .com, and www.pethospitality.com), which primarily list cabins and cottages.

POPULATION The 2010 census reports Georgia's population as 9,687,653 and the

Atlanta metro area's population as 5,268,860.

PUBLIC RESTROOMS In general, visitors can find public restrooms at welcome/visitors centers, government buildings such as city halls and courthouses, office buildings, public buildings such as libraries, restaurants, rest stops along major highways, large shopping centers, major attractions, city and state parks, and convenience stores/gasoline stations.

RAILROAD EXCURSIONS AND MUSEUMS Atlanta's existence was based on it being a railroad terminus and later a major rail hub, and rail traffic continues to play a significant role in the city's economy. Savannah was also a major rail center. Many, many small towns in Georgia were created as stops along the state's many railroad routes, and their fortunes waned as the railroads declined. Fortunately, many quaint, once-abandoned railroad depots enjoy new lives as museums, offices, restaurants, art galleries, and other uses. Several railbeds have been converted to Rails-to-Trails paths used by walkers, joggers, cyclists, and skaters. A few nostalgic rail excursions bring back pleasant memories to adults and create new ones for youngsters.

Among the excursions are the **Blue Ridge Scenic Railway,** which runs from Blue Ridge to McCaysville; the **Swamp Park Train** at the Okefenokee Swamp in Waycross; and the **SAM Shortline/Southwest Georgia Excursion Train,** which runs excursions from Cordele to Archery.

Museums range from large facilities with rolling stock, such as the **Roundhouse Railroad Museum** in Savannah and the **Southeastern Railway Museum** in Duluth, to smaller facilities with model trains, such as **Charlemagne's Kingdom** in Helen, the **Misty Mountain Train Museum** in Blairsville, and the **Walker County Regional Heritage Train Museum** in Chickamauga. The **Southern Museum of Civil War and Locomotive History** in Kennesaw contains The General, the famous locomotive that was stolen during the Civil War and resulted in the Great Locomotive Chase, and which has been immortalized in two movies.

RAIL SERVICE See *AMTRAK* for interstate rail transportation and see MARTA under *Bus/Rail Service* for a description of Atlanta's rapid rail service.

RATES The prices listed in all categories were the most up-to-date we could find at press time, but undoubtedly rates will change, so check ahead before you travel. The prices listed are merely a guideline so you can tell whether something is economical, moderate, or expensive. We've marked some entries with a 🦐 icon to indicate that it's an especially good value. In order to categorize an attraction, restaurant, or lodging as economical, we've decided that an attraction should have an admission fee of $10 or less, a restaurant should offer entrées at $20 or less, and lodgings should have room rates of $100 or less. This system isn't foolproof, however. An attraction such as a theme park, for example, may have an admission fee of considerably more than $10 but have so much to offer that it's actually economical.

REENACTMENTS Many Georgians have not forgotten the Civil War. The Sons of the Confederacy and other organizations reenact some of the battles that occurred in the state, including the **Battle of Resaca** and the **Battle of Tunnel Hill,** both of which occurred north of Atlanta. Reenactments consist of costumed soldiers, horses, the firing of weapons, and camps set up to reflect the life of a soldier. Sutlers often sell replica period clothing, weapons, and other wares. More detailed descriptions are given in the *Special Events* section of the pertinent chapters. See also *Civil War Sites.*

RESORTS We define resorts as properties with lodging, restaurants, and activities such as boating, children's programs, golf, horseback riding, tennis, spas, and the like. From the beaches to the mountains, Georgia boasts numerous properties that fit this definition. Among them are **Barnsley**

Gardens Resort in Adairsville, **Brasstown Valley Resort** in Young Harris, **Callaway Gardens** in Pine Mountain, **Chateau Elan Winery and Resort** in Braselton, the **Cloister at Sea Island, Cuscowilla Resort on Lake Oconee** near Eatonton, **Forrest Hills Mountain Hideaway Resort** near Dahlonega, **Innsbruck Resort and Golf Club** in Helen, **King and Prince Beach and Golf Resort** on St. Simons Island, **Kingwood Golf and Tennis Resort** near Clayton, **Lake Blackshear Resort and Golf Club** in Cordele, **Legacy on Lanier Resort** at Lake Lanier Islands near Buford, **Lodge on Little St. Simons Island, The Ridges Resort** in Hiawassee, the **Ritz-Carlton Lodge at Reynolds Plantation** on Lake Oconee near Greensboro, **Sea Palms Golf and Tennis Resort** on St. Simons Island, and the **Westin Savannah Harbor Golf Resort and Spa** in Savannah.

RESTAURANTS A few restaurants enjoy a multidecade life, while unfortunately most others turn over quickly. Even though they may not be the trendiest restaurants in town, we've tried to suggest eateries that have shown some staying power, but of course even some of those may be closed when you visit a particular locale, so it's best to call ahead to avoid disappointment. In the event that a restaurant you particularly want to visit has closed, consult our other suggestions, ask your concierge for help, or check with the welcome/visitors center.

Cuisine ranges from the sublime to the ridiculous, from gourmet to take-out. As you read the individual chapters, you'll find that BBQ and down-home-cookin' restaurants are prominently featured throughout the state—partly because these two cuisines are so popular and partly because in many small towns those are the only choices other than fast food. Fresh seafood is the top choice on the coast and islands, but good seafood can be found almost anywhere.

Some casual eateries that have enjoyed longtime renown in Georgia include the **H&H Restaurant** in Macon, where the

Allman Brothers band members used to eat; **Nu Way Weiners** in Macon; the **Varsity,** a hot doggery in Atlanta and Athens; **Mrs. Wilkes Dining Room** in Savannah; and the **Whistle Stop Café** in Juliette, which achieved fame in the movie *Fried Green Tomatoes.* A not-to-be-missed all-you-can-eat restaurant is the **Blue Willow Inn** in Social Circle.

RIVERS Georgia is laced with rivers and streams—some of them dammed into lakes. You'll notice that practically all of them still bear their Indian names. The major rivers in the state include the **Chattahoochee,** which flows all the way from Lake Lanier north of Atlanta to the Florida border and creates the border between Georgia and Alabama, and the **Flint,** which flows from the Atlanta metro area along the western border of the state and provides some white-water rapids. The best white-water river is the **Chattooga Wild and Scenic River** in northeast Georgia near Clayton. White-water conditions are also found on the **Ocoee River** in northwest Georgia, where the 1996 Centennial Olympic Games white-water events were held. Other rivers provide excellent conditions for canoeing: **Alapaha** (Lakeland), **Altamaha** (ends near Darien), **Ochlocknee** (Cairo), **Ocmulgee** (Macon), **Ogeechee** (Piedmont region to the sea at Ossabaw Island), and **Toccoa.** The **Conasauga, Coosawattee,** and **Oostanaula rivers** meet in Rome.

ROCKHOUNDING See *Gold Mining.* Those particularly interested in rocks and minerals will want to be sure to include a visit to the **Tellus Science Museum** in White in northwest Georgia.

SAILING The waters off Georgia's coast, which were the site of the 1996 Centennial Olympic Games sailing competitions, provide exhilarating sailing adventures for those who have their own boats as well as those who rent a boat or take a guided cruise. Georgia's many lakes are also meccas for sailors, although some lakes reputedly have "dead air" zones. **Lanier Sailing Academy** and **Windsong Sailing Acad-**

emy on Lake Lanier north of Atlanta offer sailing classes and rentals.

SHOPS Shops have the same problem as eateries in regard to staying power or lack thereof (see *Restaurants*). We tried to pick not the hottest flash-in-the-pan shops but those that have been around for a while. As with restaurants, in the event that a store you want to visit has closed, consider our other suggestions, ask your concierge, or check with the welcome/visitors center. These travel professionals also will be the best source of advice about the newest up-and-coming shops.

SKYDIVING Few are brave enough to jump out of an airplane or soar off a cliff in a hang glider, but if you're among those who thrive on an adrenaline rush, there are several adventures awaiting you in Georgia. Among these are **Atlanta Skydiving Center** in Cedartown, **Sky Dive The Farm** in Rockmart, **Skydive Atlanta** in Thomaston, and the **Lookout Mountain Flight Park and Training Center** in Rising Fawn for hang gliding.

SMOKING Beginning July 1, 2005, Georgia enacted a ban on smoking in any buildings open to the public, much to the joy of nonsmokers. That should have meant that we could simply list all hotels, lodgings, and so forth as nonsmoking. Nothing's ever that simple, though. As with most laws, there are still many loopholes and exceptions. Establishments such as bars and nightclubs that don't admit anyone younger than 18 can still allow smoking. Some restaurants still permit smoking in their bars and on patios and decks, so these areas may be even more packed with smokers than before. Few bed & breakfasts, which are often housed in historic homes, allow smoking indoors but may allow it on porches or decks. Insurance companies, however, may decree that bed & breakfasts not allow smoking even on the porches because of the possibility of fire. We have, therefore, still tried to indicate whether an establishment allows smoking or not, and if they do, where. Despite the loopholes in

the state law, more and more municipalities are enacting even more stringent laws prohibiting smoking in buildings open to the public.

SPECIAL LODGINGS Several historic homes and hotels offer exquisite accommodations. Among these are the **Greyfield Inn** on Cumberland Island, which was once a Carnegie family mansion; **Henderson Village** in Perry, which offers accommodations in historic homes and updated sharecroppers cottages; the **Jekyll Island Club Hotel** on Jekyll Island, which was once the private playground of 100 millionaires and their families; the **Mansion at Forsyth Park** in Savannah, a small luxury hostelry; the **Partridge Inn** in Augusta, a historic hotel dating from Augusta's grand hotel days in the late 1800s; and the **Windsor Hotel** in Americus, a fanciful concoction of styles. The Greyfield Inn on Cumberland Island, Jekyll Island Club Hotel on Jekyll Island, **King and Prince** on St. Simons Island, the **River Street Inn** in Savannah, and the **Smith House** in Dahlonega are Georgia's only five members of the National Trust for Historic Preservation's prestigious Historic Hotels of America. At the other

end of the spectrum is the **Len Foote Hike Inn** in Dawsonville, which actually requires overnight guests to make a 5-mile hike to the inn. See also *Resorts*.

SPORTS TEAMS This is the South, and college sports are still king, but there are numerous professional major- and minor-league teams. Atlanta has "America's Team"—the last-to-first **Braves** baseball team—as well as the **Falcons** football team, **Hawks** basketball team, and **Georgia Force** arena football team.

Not to be outdone, several other small cities have sports teams as well, and they are described in the appropriate chapters. Augusta has the **Greenjackets** minor-league baseball team and the **Riverhawks** hockey team. Columbus has the **Cottonmouths** hockey team. Rome has the **Braves** minor-league baseball team and the **Gladiators** basketball team; Savannah has the **Sand Gnats** baseball team. Another team is the **Gwinnett Gladiators** hockey team in Duluth. There are numerous other teams we didn't have the space to describe, so be on the lookout for them

THEATERS/SUMMER Most theater in Georgia is offered during a September-to-May season, but theater lovers don't have to be bereft during the summer season. Six Broadway musicals are brought to Atlanta each summer by **7 Stages Theatre** and **Theatrical Outfit** and performed at the Fox Theatre. The **Atlanta Shakespeare Festival** performs the Bard's plays and those of other playwrights on the campus of Oglethorpe University in the Buckhead section of Atlanta. In the southern part of the state, the **Peach State Summer Theater** performs three musicals in the Sawyer Theater in the Valdosta State University Fine Arts Building in Valdosta.

THEATERS/YEAR-ROUND Professional and amateur theater is alive and well in Georgia. The Atlanta metro area alone has dozens of theater groups ranging from the renowned **Alliance Theatre** at the Woodruff Arts Center to the **Theatre in the Square** in Marietta. Large-cast travel-

ing Broadway shows often perform at Atlanta's **Fox Theatre,** the **Cobb Energy Center,** or the **Boisfeuillet Jones Atlanta Civic Center.** Towns from Albany to Warner Robins have active community theater groups, and towns with colleges or universities offer theater as well. We try to include some choices for theatrical entertainment in every chapter.

Some historic theater structures, worth seeing in their own right in addition to attending a performance there, include the **Fox Theatre** in Atlanta, **Cotton Hall Theater** in Colquitt, **Rylander Theater** in Americus, **Madison-Morgan Cultural Arts Center** in Madison, and **Springer Opera House** (the official state theater) in Columbus.

TRAFFIC AND HIGHWAY TIPS One of the things the Atlanta metro area is most infamously known for is horrendous traffic. With I-75, I-85, and I-20 meeting in downtown Atlanta (one of only five American cities where that happens), it's no wonder that traffic is a problem—especially in the morning and evening. The I-285 perimeter freeway around Atlanta does little to speed you on your way. GA 400, a toll road that stretches north from Atlanta to near Dahlonega, is one of the most congested roads in the state. In the Atlanta metro area, getting off the major highways and using surface roads and streets gains you little except perhaps being easier on the nerves. And to make matters worse, the Atlanta metro area now stretches practically from Macon to the Tennessee border and from the Alabama line past Covington. Friday nights and Sunday nights are particularly heavily traveled as folks try to leave for and return from a getaway weekend.

Not that any of our readers would ever run a red light, but be forewarned that some municipalities are using photo enforcement at traffic lights. And be aware in driving around the Savannah Historic District that, as you approach a square, cars already in a square have the right of way over cars entering from a side street.

Happily, traffic is rarely a problem throughout the rest of the state. I-16 from

Macon to Savannah, for example, is lightly traveled. I-95, which skirts the coast, is heavily traveled but not often snarled. There are hundreds of two-lane country roads where you'll rarely see another car.

TROLLEYS Seeing the sights via a nostalgic trolley is a popular choice for travelers. Savannah has a plethora of choices, including **Gray Line Trolley Tours** (912-234-8687; www.graylineofsavannah.com), **Old Savannah Tours** (912-234-8128 or 1-800-517-9007; www.oldsavannahtours.com), and **Old Town Trolley** (1-888-910-8687; www.trolleytours.com). The **Express Trolley Tour** at the Atlanta State Farmer's Market in Forest Park is an interesting way to see the giant fresh market. See *Guided Tours* for a list of trolley tours in Milledgeville and St. Simons. More details are given in the appropriate chapters.

VACATION RENTALS In addition to campgrounds and cottages, condominiums are another lodging option for stays of a week or more (shorter stays may be available at the last minute) and are most often found at the beach resorts. On St. Simons Island condominium accommodations are offered by the **Beach Club and North Breakers Condominiums.** On Jekyll Island, various types of rentals are represented by **Jekyll Realty Vacation Rentals** and **Parker-Kaufman Realtors.** On Tybee Island, accommodations including condominiums are available through **Tybee Cottages and Tybee Vacation Rentals.** In the north Georgia mountains, condo accommodations are offered by **The Ridges Resort Condominiums** on Lake Chatuge in Hiawassee. See also *Cottage Rentals.*

WALKING TOURS Both guided (see *Guided Tours*) and self-guided walking tours are available throughout Georgia. One interesting tour is **Lights on Macon.** Various homes in one of Macon's historic districts participate in a special lighting project so that visitors can walk by and enjoy their outstanding architecture at night.

Athens is well-known as the cradle of many rock bands, such as REM and the B-52s. The **Athens Music History Walking Tour** points out many clubs and other sites where these bands got their start. While in Athens, a totally whimsical tour is **Who Let the Dawgs Out,** a tour of amusing public art represented by bulldogs (that's Dawgs to the uninitiated), the mascot of the University of Georgia.

At the other end of the spectrum are nature walks, such as **Sea Turtle Walks** on Jekyll Island. Many small towns and historic neighborhoods with structures from the turn of the 20th century are particularly conducive to walking tours. Some of these are **City of Decatur Walking Tours, Fort Gaines Walking Tour, Historic Darien Walking Tours,** six **Historic Downtown LaGrange Walking Tours, Historic Walking and Driving Tours of Thomasville, Walking Tour of Madison,** and **Walking and Driving Tour of Moultrie.**

WALKING TRAILS While hiking trails in the mountains and national forests can be strenuous, many other trails are more conducive to walking, jogging, bicycling, and in-line skating. Some of them are also stroller and wheelchair accessible. Some of these include the **Augusta Canal Trail** in Augusta; **Earth Day Nature Trail** in Brunswick; **Ocmulgee Heritage Trail** in Macon; **Savannah-Tybee Railroad Historic and Scenic Trail** on Tybee Island; the **Silver Comet Trail,** which stretches from northwest Georgia to the Alabama line; and the **Wild Horse Creek Trail** in Powder Springs, which connects with the Silver Comet Trail.

WATERFALLS North Georgia's mountains are conducive to sudden changes in elevation, creating many waterfalls along rivers and streams. The most accessible is **Amicalola Falls** in Amicalola Falls State Park near Dawsonville and Dahlonega. You can drive almost to the base of the falls or to an overlook near the top. Some other easily accessible waterfalls are **Anna Ruby Falls,** which is actually two falls near

Helen, and **Toccoa Falls,** on the campus of Toccoa Falls College in Toccoa.

From north to south in Georgia, the topography changes from mountains to the rolling Piedmont region and then to the flat Coastal Plain. The fall line where the Piedmont changes to the Coastal Plain is the site of **High Falls,** one of the farthest south waterfalls.

Many other waterfalls are listed and described in individual chapters. For information on other waterfalls in Georgia, good websites to consult are www.n-georgia.com /waterfal.htm and www.georgiatrails.com /waterfalls.html.

WEBSITES The intent of our descriptions of individual attractions, activities, lodgings, restaurants, special events, and the like is simply to whet your appetite. With the entries that particularly strike your fancy, we assume you'll want to know much more. Whenever they are available, therefore, we include websites with the contact information for each entry. Accessing the website enables you to learn more about an entry we describe, see numerous color pictures—perhaps even a live webcam— and check for the latest hours and prices before you travel. Be aware, however, that a website is only as good as the last time it was updated; we've found many that haven't been updated for years. We've listed many websites under specific entries and appropriate categories, but in order to reduce repetition, we list a couple here that would be found under several categories.

You can access lists of Georgia's ATV trails, bike trails, hiking clubs, hiking trails, horse trails, and waterfalls at the website www.georgiatrails.com. Or go to www .mountaintravelguide.com and click on "Georgia Mountains."

WHEN TO GO Georgia is blessed with a moderate climate year-round and doesn't really have a high season and low season as some states do. Spring and fall are long, pleasant, and colorful with flamboyant flowers or leaves. Winters are mild except in the mountainous areas in the northern part of the state, where freezing temperatures and snow and ice are rare but not unheard of. In the northern part of the state, some bed & breakfasts, campgrounds, and attractions close for the winter months, so it's best to call ahead if you're traveling there during this period to avoid disappointment. Occasional cold snaps, snowstorms, or ice storms in the rest of the state are rare and short-lived. In the majority of the state, winter daytime temperatures average 55 degrees, so a blazer or lightweight coat is usually sufficient for being outdoors. Nights can drop down to the 40s or even 30s, so a warmer coat, gloves, and hat may be necessary then.

Summers, on the other hand, can be quite hot, with daytime temperatures around 95 degrees for prolonged periods and sometimes even breaking 100 degrees for several days. Humidity can be high all over the state, but more so in south Georgia and the coastal areas. Temperatures and humidity on the barrier islands and in the immediate coastal areas are usually ameliorated by sea breezes, but as soon as you get inland, temperatures and humidity can be unpleasant. It is more comfortable, therefore, to travel to those areas in the fall through spring. Autumn is a good time to visit the coastal and barrier islands region, for example, because air temperatures have abated while the water temperature remains at its highest and the area is less crowded once children go back to school. (In Georgia, most schools start very early in August, so you don't even have to wait for Labor Day to reap the benefits of fewer crowds, although it is still quite hot.) Very warm temperatures can extend well into October.

Because weather in most parts of the state is so similar, we do not describe it in each separate chapter unless the weather in the area being described is unusual. We also give some information in the *When to Go* section about times when it might be better not to visit an area because of special events or other reasons that make the area crowded and lodging hard to get. The very things that make folks want to visit an area—fall foliage, for example—also make it the most crowded.

WILDLIFE MANAGEMENT AREAS The expense for the maintenance of Georgia's many wildlife management areas (WMAs) has long been borne by the license fees of hunters and fishermen. It has become obvious over the years that these areas were also being heavily used by hikers, mountain bikers, birdwatchers, nature photographers, and others. As of January 2012, a **Georgia Outdoor Recreation Pass (GORP)** is required for users ages 16–64 who do not otherwise have a valid fishing or hunting license at 32 specified WMAs. The pass is $3.50 for three days or $19 annually. Whenever we list a WMA, we try to indicate whether the GORP is required. To be sure, consult the website www.georgiawildlife.com /recreational-licenses or call 1-800-366-2661.

WINERIES Climate, topography, elevation, and soil conditions make wine production in Georgia viable, although the industry is still in its infancy. Most of the wineries and the widest variety of grapes are found in the northern part of the state. The **Georgia Wine Highway** stretches from Clayton to Braselton and includes 10 wineries. Wineries in the southern part of the state primarily grow muscadine grapes, which are sweet and often used in dessert wines.

We describe the primary wineries in the state, which include **Chateau Elan Winery and Resort** in Braselton, **Crane Creek Vineyards** in Young Harris, **Fox Vineyards and Winery** in Social Circle, **Frogtown Cellars** in Dahlonega, **Habersham Winery** in Helen, **Meinhardt Vineyards and Winery** in Statesboro, **Persimmon Creek Vineyards** in Clayton, **Still Pond Vineyard and Winery** in Arlington, **Three Sisters Vineyards and Winery** in Dahlonega, **Tiger Mountain Vineyards** in Tiger, and **Wolf Mountain Vineyards and Winery** in Dahlonega.

Some of the wineries have free tours and tastings; others charge a small fee. Several also offer a restaurant and/or shop.

There are also several tasting rooms around the state where you can sample a variety of Georgia wines rather than just those produced by an individual winery: **Dahlonega Tasting Room** in Sautee and **Georgia Winery Taste Centers** in Pine Mountain and in Ringgold.

For more information, contact the **Wine Growers Association of Georgia** (706-878-9463; www.georgiawine.com). Other sources of information are **Georgia Wine Country** (www.georgiawinecountry.com) and the **Georgia Wine Council** (www .georgiawinecouncil.org).

ZOOS/ANIMAL PRESERVES You don't have to travel to exotic foreign countries to see wild animals that aren't native to America or Georgia. Several zoos throughout the state showcase a variety of these wild animals. Other zoos may have more docile farm animals just right for petting.

Zoo Atlanta is the most prestigious of Georgia's zoos. It is one of only a few zoos in America to have an adorable pair of pandas on loan from China. The zoo also boasts an exceptional primate collection, as well as other wild and tame animals. Some other organizations with wild and tame animals are the **Center for Wildlife Education and Lamar Q. Ball Jr. Raptor Center** at Georgia Southern University in Statesboro, **Chestatee Wildlife Preserve** in Dahlonega, **Noah's Ark Animal Rehabilitation Center** in Locust Grove, **Wild Adventures Theme Park** in Valdosta, the **Wild Animal Park at the Parks at Chehaw** in Albany, **Wild Animal Safari** in Pine Mountain, and the **Yellow River Game Ranch** in Lilburn, which showcases animals indigenous to Georgia. Look for other small zoos and preserves listed in individual chapters.

Atlanta Metro 1

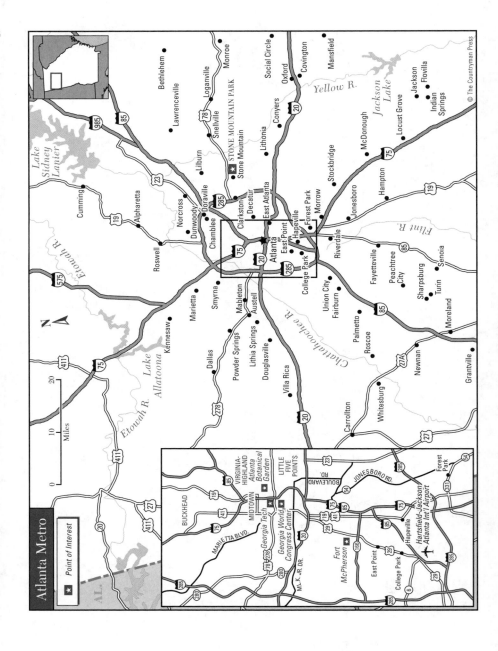

© The Countryman Press

ATLANTA

In 1782 a thriving Creek Indian village and trading post called Standing Peach Tree (some say it was actually Pitch Tree) existed along what is now called Peachtree Creek where it empties into the Chattahoochee River. Historians theorize that there was either a single peach tree or a pine (pitch) tree on the spot. From these humble beginnings grew what is now the capital of the South and a plethora of things named Peachtree.

Atlanta began taking shape in 1837, when the Western and Atlantic Railroad decided to make the area the southern end of its operations. (The honor had been offered to nearby Decatur, which turned it down; otherwise there might never have been an Atlanta at all.) The town was originally called Terminus since that's what it was—the end of the line. In 1843, it was renamed Marthasville for the daughter of Governor Wilson Lumpkin. In 1847, the town was renamed once again; this time it was called Atlanta—probably a feminine form of Atlantic (as in Western and Atlantic), and the name finally stuck.

By the beginning of the Civil War in 1861, Atlanta was a major rail hub, a manufacturing center, and a supply depot, so it's no wonder that the city was a target of destruction by Union forces under Gen. William Tecumseh Sherman. When the Union forces finally took Atlanta in 1864, all the railroad facilities, almost every business, and more than two-thirds of the city's homes were destroyed—making Atlanta the only major American city ever destroyed by war.

But the city wasn't held down for long—giving rise to the city's association with the Egyptian legend of the phoenix rising from the ashes. In 1868, the Georgia capital was moved from Milledgeville to Atlanta—making the city the fifth and last state capital. Newspaperman Henry Grady almost single-handedly created the image of the reconciled "New South," where business opportunities were rife. Colleges and universities opened, telephones and trolleys were introduced, and the 1895 Cotton States Exposition introduced 800,000 visitors to the vibrant city, all of which began a long upward economic surge that lasts to this day.

"The city too busy to hate" took the lead in peacefully strengthening minority rights in the Southeast during the 1950s and 1960s. In 1963, Mayor Ivan Allen Jr. was the only white Southern mayor to testify before Congress in support of the pending Civil Rights Bill. When native son Martin Luther King Jr. was assassinated in 1968, Mayor Allen pleaded for calm and was rewarded with peaceful mourning.

Ever optimistic, the city decided to build a stadium when it didn't even have a professional team to play there. That optimism paid off when major-league baseball's Braves moved from Milwaukee to Atlanta and the city was awarded the Falcons expansion football team. Today the city boasts not only baseball and football franchises but also basketball, soccer, and arena football teams.

Now a world-class city, Atlanta has one of the nation's busiest airports, an efficient public transportation system, convention facilities that have made it second in the nation in convention business, the Underground Atlanta shopping and entertainment complex, a new stadium, a sports dome, and a sports and entertainment arena. The city has hosted the 1988 Democratic National Convention, Super Bowls in 1994 and 2000, the NCAA Men's and Women's Basketball Final Four, and the NBA All-Star Game.

Another jewel in the city's crown was added when the 1996 Centennial Olympic Summer Games were awarded to Atlanta and 2 million people visited the city during the two-week event. The Olympics served as an impetus for a resurgence of downtown, with more than $2 billion in construction projects and other changes, the major legacy of which is Centennial Olympic Park.

Depending on whose statistics you're using, the metropolitan Atlanta area consists of 28 counties, up to 100 municipalities, and a population of more than 5 million people, but this chapter focuses on the area inside the city limits, which is generally also the area inside the I-285 perimeter highway. The population within the city limits is just 420,000, making Atlanta the 40th in size in the country.

GUIDANCE To plan a trip to Atlanta, contact the **Atlanta Convention and Visitors Bureau** (404-521-6600 or 1-800-ATLANTA; www.acvb.com), 233 Peachtree Street NE, Suite 100, Atlanta 30303. Open 8:30–5 weekdays. Also consult the website at www.atlanta .net for up-to-date information on hotel and restaurant reservations, directions, guidebooks, maps, and help in creating an itinerary. There are several Atlanta CVB Visitor Centers at various locations around the city to aid visitors. The **visitors center at Hartsfield-Jackson Atlanta International Airport** (see "What's Where in Georgia"), in the North Terminal near baggage claim, is open 9–9 weekdays, 9–6 Saturday, and noon–6 Sunday. Downtown, the **visitors center at the Georgia World Congress Center,** 285 International Boulevard, is open only during Georgia World Congress Center events, but the **visitors center at Underground Atlanta,** 65 Upper Alabama Street, is open 10–6 Monday–Saturday, noon–6 Sunday. To plan a trip specifically to Buckhead, contact the **Buckhead Coalition** (404-216-1662; www.buckhead.net/buckheadcoalition) or the **Buckhead Business Association** (404-467-7607; www.buckheadbusiness.org).

Also check out **AtlanTIX** (404-588-9890) at the Atlanta Convention and Visitors Bureau Underground Atlanta Visitor Center. Atlanta's same-day, half-price outlet offers tickets to a wide variety of theater, dance, and musical performances. AtlanTIX is open 11–6 Tuesday–Saturday, noon–4 Sunday.

GETTING THERE *By air:* Visitors to Atlanta fly into **Hartsfield-Jackson Atlanta International Airport.** Car rentals are available both on- and off-site. There are also numerous shuttle companies (some to distant cities), and several hotels have free shuttles to

ATLANTA AMBASSADOR FORCE

Begun during the 1996 Centennial Olympic Summer Games to aid the vast number of visitors from around the world, the 60-person Atlanta Ambassador Force was such a success it's still around to help present-day visitors. The AAF keeps an eye out for anyone who looks lost and can give directions, suggest attractions and restaurants, and relate history. For other information about the ambassadors, contact the Central Atlanta Progress (404-658-1877). The Ambassadors will be walking or riding a Segway or an all-terrain bike. Look for their pith helmets and turquoise windbreakers.

their properties (check ahead when you make your hotel reservation). See "What's Where in Georgia" for airline, car rental, and shuttle details.

By bus: **Greyhound Lines** (404-584-1738; www.greyhound.com), 232 Forsyth Street, is open 24 hours a day.

By car: Access to Atlanta is easy with I-75 and I-85 running north–south and I-20 running east–west. All of them meet in downtown Atlanta.

By train: **AMTRAK** (see "What's Where in Georgia"). The station is not located downtown but in Buckhead. Transportation from the station to downtown is available by taxi or MARTA bus (see Getting Around).

GETTING AROUND For car rentals, see "What's Where in Georgia."

Mass transit is another easy and economical alternative. The city's bus/rail system, **Metropolitan Atlanta Rapid Transit Authority,** known locally as **MARTA** (404-848-4711; www .itsmarta.com), is the most cost-effective and convenient way to get around Atlanta, with a variety of routes and pass options available (see "What's Where in Georgia"). MARTA also operates a shuttle to Six Flags Over Georgia and the Braves Stadium Shuttle. On days when the Atlanta Braves are playing at Turner Field (known locally as "the Ted"), MARTA offers easy service to the stadium from the Five Points rail station. Proceed from the station through Underground Atlanta to the shuttle buses waiting at the plaza. (Golf cart transportation from the rail station to the bus is available for elderly or disabled gamegoers.) The shuttle begins service 90 minutes before game time and continues until the stadium is empty. Each passenger needs a rail-to-bus or bus-to-bus transfer or a regular fare to ride the shuttle.

While in Buckhead, take advantage of the free ❧ **BUC (Buckhead's Uptown Connection)** shuttle (404-233-2228; www.bucride.com), which connects the Lenox Square and Buckhead MARTA rail stations with major hotels, dining locations, retail centers, and key office buildings. Operates 7 AM–7 PM Sunday–Friday, until 9 PM on Saturday.

In Midtown, another option for getting around town is the free ❧ **Georgia Tech Technology Square Trolley** (404-894-9645; www.pts.gatech.edu/ride/routes_schedules/pages /TechTrolley.aspx). These rubber-tired, alternative-fuel vehicles, designed to look like old-fashioned trolleys, provide service from the Campus Recreation Center in the center of the campus to Technology Square to the Midtown MARTA station. This means out-of-town visitors can take MARTA rail from the airport to the Midtown station, and then transfer to the trolley to reach the campus and the Georgia Tech Hotel and Conference Center. The Tech Trolley runs every 20–25 minutes weekdays, 36 minutes on weekends and is available to students, faculty, staff, and visitors.

PARKING There is little free parking downtown, in Buckhead, or in Midtown. What little on-street parking exists is metered, but it's free after 6 PM and on Sunday. Credit cards can be used at Park & Display kiosks. There are plentiful for-fee parking lots and parking decks. Consult the website www.atlantadowntown.com and search for "Parking."

WHEN TO GO Some times to avoid might include the Chick-fil-A Bowl, Big Peach Drop on New Year's Eve, or other major events that draw big crowds. It might be best to call the CVB before planning a trip to find out which events might be happening during your visit.

MEDICAL EMERGENCY Call 911.

NEIGHBORHOODS Atlanta was almost completely destroyed during the Civil War and also has been accused of tearing down everything more than a few decades old to build something new, so there are not as many historic buildings as might be found in a city of

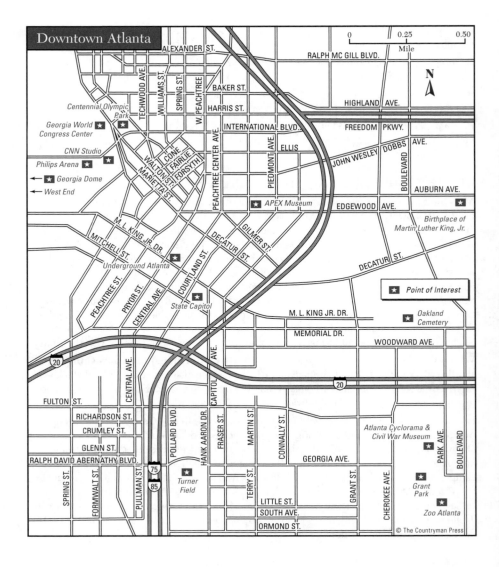

Downtown Atlanta

comparable age or size. There are, however, several historic neighborhoods dating from the late 1800s and early 1900s.

Ansley Park was built more than a century ago to attract Atlanta's wealthiest and most prestigious families. While downtown's Inman Park was the city's first trolley suburb, Midtown's Ansley Park was its first driving suburb. Today Ansley Park contains gracious residences and grand estates, tree-lined streets, broad lawns, and bucolic parks. The entire neighborhood is a National Register of Historic Places. Ansley Park is convenient to the arts district in Midtown.

Atlantic Station, Midtown Atlanta's newest, from-the-ground-up neighborhood, is being built on the site of the old Atlantic Steel Mill manufacturing complex, a long-abandoned eyesore along the I-75/I-85 corridor. The site is rapidly becoming an upscale mixed-use neighborhood.

Glitzy **Buckhead,** Atlanta's Beverly Hills, is a 28-square-mile district 4 miles north of downtown and immediately north of Midtown. Buckhead has been called "Where old money lives and new money parties" by the *Atlanta Journal-Constitution.* The area has the most beautiful and expensive neighborhoods, the finest restaurants, the most luxurious hotels, the best shopping, and the most nightlife. It's *the* place to see and be seen.

The historic neighborhood of **Candler Park,** which is listed on the National Register of Historic Places, was a large residential neighborhood near Chamblee dating from the late 19th and early 20th centuries. Candler Park is characterized by late-Victorian and bungalow/Craftsman architecture.

Downtown is primarily commercial, but in recent years many buildings have been converted to residential use and new neighborhoods have been built, resulting in a resurgence of in-town living. Downtown offers hotels, restaurants, and a wide range of attractions for visitors.

The vibrant **Fairlie-Poplar Historic District,** a short walk from major downtown attractions and hotels, is characterized by classic examples of commercial architecture largely developed in the early 20th century. Restaurants and boutiques occupy the street level of many of these buildings, and the district, on the National Register of Historic Places, is the site of several popular events.

Grant Park Historic District, bounded by Glenwood and Atlanta avenues and Kelly and Eloise streets, is one of Atlanta's oldest neighborhoods. Centered on Grant Park (see *Green Space—Nature Preserves and Parks*), the majority of the district's structures are residences built between the late 1800s and early 1900s. Grant Park is also home to the Atlanta Cyclorama and Civil War Museum (see *To See—Historic Homes and Sites*) and Zoo Atlanta (see *To Do—For Families*).

Once trolley transportation was available, Atlanta's well-to-do moved away from downtown. Begun in 1889, **Inman Park** was Atlanta's first suburb. Elegant Victorian-era homes were built northeast of downtown by wealthy magnates such as Coca-Cola's Asa Candler and Ernest Woodruff. The neighborhood is nationally renowned for its preservation efforts.

Little Five Points, located northeast of the residential Inman Park neighborhood, is a dining, entertainment, and shopping mecca for Atlanta's youthful consumers. Little Five Points (affectionately known as L5P) is the "in" place to go, with numerous offbeat restaurants, clubs, shops, and theaters—each with its own peculiar twist.

Midtown is the 9-square-mile district situated between downtown and Buckhead. Once known as Uptown, Midtown was developed in the 1870s as a streetcar suburb. It grew and prospered until the 1960s, when suburban growth moved even farther from the city. During the next decades, Midtown became much more commercial and much less residential. In the 1980s, however, the Midtown Alliance and renewed interest in in-town living sparked a renaissance in Midtown that continues to this day. The area's principal claim to fame is that it is Atlanta's arts district and the home of the city's most revered cultural institutions—the **Atlanta Symphony Orchestra,** the **Alliance Theatre,** the **High Museum of Art,** and the **Atlanta Botanical Garden**—as well as several other museums, swanky hotels, trendy restaurants, and the city's largest park. Midtown is known for its residential diversity and its energetic business district where bungalows coexist with skyscrapers, restaurants, and churches.

Poncey-Highland centers on the intersection of Ponce de Leon and Highland avenues and blends almost imperceptibly into Virginia-Highland. Businesses, shops, restaurants, and music venues make this a great place to walk and hang out.

Sweet Auburn is centered on Auburn Avenue, which was the epicenter of African American enterprise from the 1890s to the 1940s, when it was hailed as the richest black street in America. But once civil rights laws were passed and blacks were free to shop anywhere,

Auburn Avenue began to decline and, in fact, became quite seedy. Today, with sites to see including the **Martin Luther King Jr. National Historic Site** and the **African American Panoramic Experience Museum (APEX),** the district is undergoing a renaissance.

The trendy **Virginia-Highland** neighborhood is one of Atlanta's most popular for shopping, dining, and nightlife. The name derives from the intersection of Virginia and Highland avenues, and its history is traced to its initial settlement by farmers in the early 1800s. When the Atlanta Street Railway Company opened the area to development in the 1890s, the farms were subdivided into building lots for residential and commercial use. One of the earliest neighborhoods was Atkins Park at Highland and Ponce de Leon avenues, and the bungalow was the predominant style of architecture here through the 1920s. **Atkins Park** restaurant opened in 1927 and is said to have the oldest liquor license in the city of Atlanta. Virginia-Highland thrived into the 1960s but, like many other in-town neighborhoods, suffered deterioration and a loss of population soon thereafter. In the '70s, however, a few families moved into the neighborhood, and the rehabilitation of homes and businesses began. Today, Virginia-Highland is one of Atlanta's most desirable neighborhoods.

Around the turn of the 20th century, Atlanta's most affluent African Americans began to build or buy impressive homes in **West End.** But by the 1960s, West End's star had waned, and it was threatened with the loss of most of its historic architectural treasures to commercial development. In the 1970s, however, preservationists began restoring the remaining homes, and today the neighborhood is socially diverse and culturally rich. Sights to see in West End include the **Wren's Nest,** home of Joel Chandler Harris, creator of the Uncle Remus tales; the opulent Victorian-era **Westview Cemetery; the Herndon Home; Hammonds House Galleries and Resource Center;** and the **Atlanta University Center** complex of six historic black colleges and universities.

✳ To See

CULTURAL SITES ❧ ✍ ♿ **Robert W. Woodruff Arts Center** (404-733-4200; www.woodruffcenter.org), 1280 Peachtree Street. Open daily. The Woodruff, the fourth-largest arts center in the country, offers the finest in visual and performing arts in the Southeast. The center encompasses the **Alliance Theatre** and the **Atlanta Symphony Orchestra** under one roof, the **High Museum of Art** on the same campus (see separate entries under *Museums* and *Entertainment*), and the **14th Street Playhouse** nearby. Free access to the center, gift shop, and galleries; admission fee for plays, concerts, parking, and events.

FOR FAMILIES ✍ ♿ **Georgia Aquarium** (404-581-4000; www.georgiaaquarium.org), 225 Baker Street. Open 10–5 Sunday–Friday, 9–6 Saturday. Tickets are by reservation for a specific day and time, so make reservations before you travel to avoid disappointment. The aquarium, which resembles a huge ship (some have called it a modern-day Noah's Ark), is the largest aquarium in the world, with 8 million gallons of water containing more than 55,000 animals from 500 species. It's divided into five galleries and a 4-D theater. *Cold Water Quest* features the most popular residents: beluga whales and penguins; *Georgia Explorer* is an interactive experience with native species; *Ocean Voyager* showcases manta rays and whale sharks in the 6.3-million-gallon tank; *River Scout* is where you can see otters and alligators; *Tropical Diver* is inhabited with jellies, seahorses, and more. The newest exhibit is *AT&T Dolphin Tales,* a gallery with an underwater viewing window, theater, and show. Conveniently located near Centennial Olympic Park and the Georgia World Congress Center, the aquarium uses innovative technologies and interactive and interdisciplinary techniques to entertain visitors. Reptiles, amphibians, and invertebrates are also represented. But the sea life exhibited here isn't just to look at; it's meant to educate the public and impress upon them the need for protection and preservation. Guided tours are available. Adults

THE LARGEST AQUARIUM IN THE WORLD, THE GEORGIA AQUARIUM BUILDING RESEMBLES A HUGE SHIP.

$24.95, seniors $20.95, children $18.95. There are many specials, combos, and discounts.

🦽 ✍ ♿ **Imagine It! The Children's Museum of Atlanta** (404-659-KIDS; www.imagineit-cma.org), 275 Centennial Olympic Park Drive NW. Open 10–4 weekdays, 10–5 weekends. This is one place youngsters will never hear "Don't touch!" Instead, everything is designed to be touched. Geared for ages three to eight, the museum's high-energy, hands-on, larger-than-life, out-of-the-ordinary interactive displays encourage young ones to explore and discover. Anyone age two or older $12.75.

GUIDED TOURS 🦽 **Atlanta Preservation Center Tours** (404-688-3353; www.preserveatlanta.com), 327 St. Paul Avenue SE. Office open 9–5 weekdays. The organization, which is housed in the historic 1856 Lemuel Grant Mansion, offers separate guided walking tours showcasing the Fox Theatre, historic downtown, Sweet Auburn/MLK Jr. Historic District, Historic Midtown, SoNo Midtown, Inman Park, Druid Hills, Grant Park, and Ansley Park. Call or consult the website for tour schedules, which, with the exception of the Fox Theatre, are offered April through November. Fox Theatre tours are offered year-round. Reservations are not required. Tours last one to two hours and are canceled in the event of rain, except for the Fox Theatre tour. Adults $10, seniors and students $5; cash or check only.

City Segway Tours-Atlanta (404-588-2274 or 1-877-734-8687; www.citysegwaytours.com /atlanta), 250 Park Avenue NW. Check the website or call for times. The two city tours are offered twice each day; the two evening tours are offered only mid-March–August); reservations required. The two-wheeled Segway Human Transporter, a self-balancing personal transportation device, is perfect for a guided tour of downtown Atlanta because you can cover more territory than you could on foot. Imagine the looks you'll get from passersby as you cruise past. After a brief training session, you'll be off on your tour. Each is of varying lengths, and the choices include the Atlanta Segway Tour, the Segway Experience, an Evening Glide, and Legends and Lore (a ghost tour). Different tours include different sites, but some of the important attractions include Centennial Olympic Park, the Georgia Aquarium, CNN, World of Coca-Cola, Georgia Tech, the Fox Theatre, and the Shakespeare Tavern. Tours depart rain or shine (ponchos are provided for inclement weather). City tours $50–70, evening tours $60. Everyone must sign a liability waiver, and each party must sign a damage waiver that includes a deposit of $500 on a credit card. All riders must be at least 12 years old.

🦽 ✍ ♿ **Georgia Dome** (404-223-4636; www.gadome.com), One Georgia Dome Drive NW. Tours are offered on the hour 10–2 Monday, Wednesday, and Friday. Tours of the world's largest cable-supported dome are truly awe-inspiring. The 70,000-seat facility is not only the home of the Atlanta Falcons football team and the Chick-fil-A Bowl, but the complex also hosts many national and international championships and other events. Guests visit the observation level, press box, exclusive Dome suites, Verizon Wireless Club Lounges, the lower level, and the locker room before ending on the field, where they can toss a football. To commemorate annual college rivalries, a section of the Georgia Dome's floor level is dedicated to mini museums highlighting Southeastern Conference football and basketball championships, the Chick-fil-A Bowl, and the Bank of America Atlanta Football Classic. Adults $6; seniors, students, and active military $5; children 12 and younger $4. Special activities are offered at Falcons Landing, in the International Plaza between the Dome and Phillips Arena, on the days of Falcons games only. These include a free NFL Theme Park with interactive games, autograph sessions, live music, food, and drink. The festivities begin three hours before game time and continue until kickoff.

♦ ⌀ ♿ **Inside CNN Studio Tour** (404-827-2300; www.cnn.com/studiotour), One CNN Center (Marietta Street at Centennial Olympic Park Drive). Open 8:30–5 daily; tours begin every 20 minutes. Reservations for a specific time are required a day in advance, but visitors can take a chance to purchase same-day tickets. Tours of the high-tech, fast-paced, 24/7 news network show visitors behind-the-scenes action of the actual on-the-air newsrooms via glass-enclosed overhead walkways. A special, longer VIP tour is also available for an additional fee. Adults $15; seniors, college students, and children 13–18 $14; children 6–12 $10. (Children younger than 6 are not admitted.)

♦ ⌀ ♿ **Turner Field Tours** (404-614-2311; www.atlanta.braves.mlb.com/atl/ballpark/tours /index.jsp), 755 Hank Aaron Drive. Tours operate year-round and leave on the hour 10–2 Monday–Saturday. On game days, the last tour leaves at noon. No tours are offered on the day of any Sunday or afternoon home game. Tours begin at the Braves Museum and Hall of Fame and include Coca-Cola Sky Field, a luxury suite, the press box, broadcast booth, dugout, Scouts Alley, The Plaza, and the Braves Museum and Store. On game days when there are no tours, fans can see the museum alone. It opens two and a half hours before the game and closes in the middle of the seventh inning. Eating out at the stadium is easy thanks to several fast-food outlets. Adults $12, children $7; admission to museum only during games is $5. Free parking in the Green Lot on nongame days.

HISTORIC HOMES AND SITES ♦ ⌀ ♿ **Atlanta Cyclorama and Civil War Museum** (404-658-7625; www.atlantacyclorama.org), Grant Park, 800-A Cherokee Avenue SE. Open 9:15–4:30 Tuesday–Saturday. Before there were movies and television, there were cycloramas—huge, larger-than-life-size, wraparound paintings that could keep viewers occupied for hours. A major attraction in Grant Park since 1893, this cyclorama is the longest running show in the country as well as being the world's largest oil painting. Depicting the July 22, 1864, Battle of Atlanta, it measures 358 feet long (that's longer than a football field) by 42 feet high, covering 15,000 square feet. A diorama of 3-D life-size figures was added in the foreground in 1936, making the painting seem to come to life. Revolving stadium seating has been introduced into the circle created by the painting, and the addition of narration, dramatic lighting, and sound effects puts viewers right into the action. Before viewing the painting, watch the introductory film, *The Atlanta Campaign.* Also displayed at the Civil War museum are period photos, weapons, and uniforms, but another star shares the spotlight with the cyclorama painting: the locomotive Texas, which figured prominently in the Civil War episode known as the Great Locomotive Chase, which has been immortalized in two films (see the Northern Suburbs chapter to learn about the engine the General, which was the train that was chased). Right next door is Zoo Atlanta (see *To Do—For Families*), so visitors can make a day of seeing the two attractions. Adults $10, seniors and children 4–12 $8.

♦ ⌀ ♿ **Georgia State Capitol** (404-463-4536; www.sos.ga.gov/archives/state_capitol), Capitol Avenue and Martin Luther King Jr. Drive. Open 8–5 weekdays. Tours at 11:30 September–December; there's a Capitol Orientation at 1 PM January–April when the legislature is in session. The imposing Atlanta capitol was completed in 1889 in the Renaissance

Revival style with strong Victorian influences. Its gleaming dome rising 37 feet from the floor is plated in 23-karat gold mined in the north Georgia mountains and brought to the city by wagon train (even a few years ago, when the dome was replated, the gold was still brought by wagon train). The capitol has recently undergone extensive interior renovations. The tour includes a short film and showcases paintings and sculptures of prominent Georgians. Stop to visit the Georgia Capitol Museum (see *Museums*). Outside, stroll the grounds and admire the statues and monuments dedicated to well-known Georgians. Guided and self-guided tours. Free.

🏛 ♂ ♿ **Governor's Mansion** (404-261-1776; www.mansion.georgia.gov), 391 West Paces Ferry Road NW. Tours 10–11:30 AM Tuesday–Thursday; additional days and hours when it is decorated at Christmastime. Tour and learn about the traditionally Southern, 30-columned Greek Revival mansion, which was built in 1967. The three-story, 24,000-square-foot home boasts 30 rooms; the ceremonial rooms on the first floor are those open for tours. Set among 18 acres of sweeping wooded lawns, the mansion contains what is considered to be one of the country's finest collections of 19th-century neoclassical furnishings from the Federal period as well as fine paintings and porcelain. Free.

🏛 ♿ **Margaret Mitchell House and Museum** (404-249-7015; www.margaretmitchellhouse .com), 990 Peachtree Street NE. Open 10–5:30 Monday–Saturday, tours every half hour from 10:30; Sunday noon–5:30, tours every half hour from 12:30. Museum shop open 11:30–5:30 Monday–Saturday, noon–5:30 Sunday. Within this turn-of-the-20th-century Tudor Revival residence called the Crescent Apartments was the small, cramped flat of Margaret Mitchell. She lived there from 1925 to 1932, and it's where she wrote most of *Gone with the Wind,* a copy of which still sells every two and a half minutes. Mitchell and her husband, John Marsh, lived in No. 1, which she dubbed "the Dump." The tour of the Midtown site starts in the visitors center with exhibits such as *Margaret Mitchell: A Passion for Character* and *The Making of a Film Legend: Gone With the Wind.* In the apartment, visitors can see original Mitchell pieces such as her typewriter and her 1937 Pulitzer Prize, appropriate period furnishings, and other treasures such as the famous leaded-glass window out of which Mitchell looked while writing the book. After touring the apartment, guests proceed to the Gone with the Wind Movie Museum to see memorabilia from the Atlanta premiere, the original entryway to the Hollywood set of Tara, and the famous portrait of Scarlett from the Butler mansion. Adults $13, seniors and students $10, youth 4–12 $8.50 (check for an online discount). A combo ticket also allows admission to the Atlanta History Center: adults $22, seniors and students $17.50, children $12. Free parking is available adjacent to the property, and the Midtown MARTA station is only one block away.

🏛 ♂ ♿ **Martin Luther King Jr. National Historic Site** (404-331-5190 for the visitors center; 404-331-6922 for recorded information; www.nps.gov/malu), 450 Auburn Avenue NE. Open 9–5 daily; hours extended to 6 between June 15 and August 15. A memorial to the revered civil rights

THE ATLANTA CAPITOL'S DOME IS PLATED IN 23-KARAT GOLD.

THE STORY BEHIND *GONE WITH THE WIND*

Although Margaret Mitchell was something of a tomboy, she was unfortunately also fragile. A series of accidents and arthritis caused high-spirited "Miss Peggy" to resign her job as a reporter at *The Atlanta Journal* in 1926 to convalesce at "the Dump." At first she devoured every book her husband could bring her from the library, and when she exhausted that resource he suggested that she write a book herself. He counseled her to write about what she knew, so she began her opus by fictionalizing the stories told by her family and Civil War veterans. Mitchell took the manuscript (all 60 manila envelopes of it packed into a suitcase) to Harold Latham of Macmillan Publishing at the Georgian Terrace Hotel, where she told him, "Take it before I change my mind." The book won a Pulitzer Prize, has been translated into many languages, and is the second-best-selling book of all time, surpassed only by the Bible.

FAMOUS PAINTING OF SCARLETT O'HARA

leader, the site consists of King's birthplace and home, historic Ebenezer Baptist Church, his gravesite in the midst of a reflecting pool, an interpretive center, and the crypt of Coretta Scott King. The Gothic Revival–style Ebenezer Baptist Church is now used as a museum and a place for special services. Free, but tickets for the birthplace tour are required for scheduling purposes. They can be picked up at the visitors center. Adjacent to the historic site is the **Martin Luther King Jr. Center for Nonviolent Social Change** (404-526-8900; www.thekingcenter.org), 449 Auburn Avenue NE. Also open 9–5 daily, until 6 in the summer. The center serves as the international clearinghouse of official King programs, public information, and educational materials. Free.

🕯 **Rhodes Hall** (404-885-7800; www.rhodeshall.org), 1516 Peachtree Street NW. Open 11–3 Tuesday, 10–2 Saturday, tours every hour until one hour before closing. Along with the Margaret Mitchell House, this is one of the few grand homes left along what was once a fashionable residential street in Midtown. In 1904 furniture magnate Amos Rhodes had the Romanesque Revival, castlelike house built of Stone Mountain granite to resemble several Rhine Valley castles he'd seen in Europe. Among the interior highlights is the series of magnificent stained-glass windows representing the rise and fall of the Confederacy and including 15 Confederate heroes. Adults $7; seniors, students, and children $4.

🕯 ✎ ♿ **Underground Atlanta** (404-523-2311; www.underground-atlanta.com), 50 Upper Alabama Street SW. Shops are generally open 10–8 Monday–Thursday, 10–9 Friday and Saturday, noon–6 Sunday; restaurants and nightspots are open later. When Atlanta was a youngster in the mid-1880s, trains and horse-drawn buggies created the first traffic jams where streets crossed railroad tracks. At that time, the solution was to build viaducts over the tracks, but that left adjacent business owners with their entrances below street level. They responded by opening new entrances on the second floor at the new street level. Long forgotten, the lower level got a new lease on life as a shopping and entertainment mecca. Six blocks encompassing 12 acres are crammed with 75 shops, 19 restaurants and eateries, 5 nightspots, street vendors' carts, and sculptures that line both levels and create an urban playground for all ages. Street performers often keep visitors entertained. Numerous special events occur as well. Free.

🦐 ✿ ♿ **Wren's Nest House Museum** (404-753-7735; www.wrensnestonline.com), 1050 Ralph David Abernathy Boulevard SW. Open 10–2:30 Tuesday–Saturday; storytelling Saturday at 1 PM. This turn-of-the-20th-century building, Atlanta's oldest house museum, was the home of Joel Chandler Harris, a newspaperman, folklorist, novelist, and poet who preserved in print the folksy Uncle Remus tales he had heard as a child from slaves. (For more information about him and the Uncle Remus yarns, see the Madison chapter in part 3, Historic South.) The "briar patch" is furnished with original family pieces and Uncle Remus memorabilia such as a diorama built by the Disney Studios when it produced the movie *Song of the South,* which is based on the Uncle Remus tales. The museum hosts quarterly storytelling events. Adults $8, seniors and teens $7, children 4–12 $5.

MUSEUMS 🦐 ✿ ♿ **African American Panoramic Experience Museum** (404-523-2739; www.apexmuseum.org), 135 Auburn Avenue. Open 10–5 Tuesday–Saturday. Known as APEX for short, the museum is dedicated to presenting and preserving the culture, history, and traditions of people of African descent by tracing the details of that history and documenting the stories of Atlanta's African American pioneers, inventors, and storekeepers. The museum features a large exhibit, *Africa: The Untold Story,* as well as an exhibit dedicated to W. E. B. DuBois. A visual journey through the historic Sweet Auburn district includes a re-creation of the Yates & Milton Drugstore, one of the first black-owned businesses. Changing exhibits keep visitors coming back. Adults $4, seniors and children $3.

🦐 ✿ ♿ **Atlanta History Center** (404-814-4000; www.atlantahistorycenter.com), 130 West Paces Ferry Road NW. Open 10–5:30 Monday–Saturday, noon–5:30 Sunday; last ticket sold at 4:30; Swan House and Tullie Smith Farm Tours 11–4 Tuesday–Saturday, 1–4 Sunday. Four permanent and two changing exhibits in the architecturally striking main museum give historical perspectives about Atlanta and regional history, black history, the Civil War, and folk art, among other subjects. *Turning Point: The Civil War* includes the DuBose Civil War Collection, the largest collection of Civil War artifacts in America, with 5,000 Confederate and Union pieces. Other exhibits include *Metropolitan Frontiers,* the birth and growth of Atlanta; *Down the Fairway with Bobby Jones; Shaping Traditions: Folk Arts in a Changing Society;* Centennial Olympic Games Museum; and *Phillip Trammell Shutze: Atlanta Classicist, Connoisseur, and Collector.* Changing exhibits ensure return visits. But that's not all—there's so much more. In addition to the main museum, the complex includes two historic homes. The elegant **Swan House,** built for the wealthy Inman family in 1928, takes its name from the swan motif used discreetly throughout the mansion. In complete contrast to the Swan House, the house and outbuildings of the 1840s **Tullie Smith Farm,** which was moved to the site, show life on a simple farm. The modest Plantation Plain–style house is furnished with simple antiques. The grounds surrounding all three of the main buildings comprise 33 acres of formal and natural gardens with nature trails (see *Green Space—Gardens*). The **Chick-fil-A Café** serves lunch and snacks daily, while the elegant **Swan Coach House Restaurant,** located in the estate's former carriage house–garage, serves lunch 11–2:30 Monday–Saturday (see *Eating Out—In Buckhead*). Some attractions have limited wheelchair access. Adults $14.50, seniors and students 13–18 $11, children 4–12 $9. A combo ticket allows admission to the Margaret Mitchell House: adults $22, seniors and students $17.50, children $12.

🦐 ✿ ♿ **The Breman Jewish Heritage and Holocaust Museum** (678-222-3700; www .thebreman.org), 1440 Spring Street NW. Open 10–5 Monday–Thursday, 10–3 Friday, 1–5

64

Sunday; closed Saturdays and most Jewish and Federal holidays. The largest museum of its kind in the Southeast, this repository explores Atlanta's Jewish history from 1845 to the present through exhibits of everyday items. There is also an exhibit on the Holocaust and survivors who live in Georgia, a hands-on Discovery Center for children, educational programs, and genealogical archives. Adults $12, seniors $8, students $6, and children 3–6 $4.

🍴 ✂ ♿ **Center for Puppetry Arts** (404-873-3391; www.puppet.org), 1404 Spring Street NW. Museum open 9–3 Tuesday–Friday, 9–5 Saturday, 11–5 Sunday. Call for a schedule of performances. The center, dedicated to exploring the dazzling art of puppetry as an ancient, international, and popular art form, was opened in 1978 by Kermit the Frog and his creator, Jim Henson. Today the family of Jim Henson has lent a massive portion of his collection to the museum on a long-term basis. The first puppetry center in the country and still the largest American organization solely dedicated to the art of puppet theater, the center boasts an astounding collection of 350 one-of-a-kind puppets from different time periods and different countries—the largest permanent collection in the country. The center also produces daytime shows for children and families as well as cutting-edge evening shows for adults (see *Entertainment—Theater*). Museum admission: $8.25; shows $16.50; combo ticket with a guided tour $18.50. Free on Thursday 1–3.

✂ ♿ **Fernbank Museum of Natural History** (404-929-6300; tickets: 404-929-6400; www.fernbankmuseum.org), 767 Clifton Road NE. Open 10–5 Monday–Saturday, noon–5 Sunday. "Martinis and IMAX" 5:30–11 Friday evenings except December. Visitors can introduce themselves to some of the earth's earliest inhabitants at the largest museum of its type in the Southeast. The thrill begins with the Dinosaur Entrance Plaza. Then the *Giants of the Mesozoic* gallery features the largest dinosaurs ever discovered, including *Argentinosaurus;* at 123 feet long and weighing 100 tons, it was not only the most massive plant eater but also the largest known dinosaur ever to walk the earth. The much smaller, 47-foot-long, 8-ton *Giganotosaurus* was the largest meat eater. Visitors also see a flock of 21 *Pterodaustro*, small pterosaurs, and three *Anhanguera*, larger pterosaurs. In complete contrast, when looking down at the limestone floors, visitors see fossil remains of tiny sea creatures that lived during the Jurassic Period more than 150 million years ago. There's so much to see at this exemplary museum near Decatur, it's almost impossible to describe here. Other galleries include *World of Shells*, with its 900-gallon living-reef aquarium; *A Walk Through Time in Georgia; Sensing Nature; Reflections of Culture; Nature Quest;* as well as changing exhibits. The **Rankin M. Smith Sr. IMAX Theatre** offers spectacular movies on its five-story-high, 72-foot-wide screen with surround sound. Fernbank also offers special programs and family days. Plan to make a day out of a visit here; there is even a café for meals or snacks (see *Eating Out—In Atlanta*). Adults can enjoy a touch of class on Friday nights at "Martinis and IMAX," which includes a movie on the giant screen, live music, specialty martinis, a wine bar, and food (separate purchase). Also on the grounds is the **Robert L. Stanton Rose Garden** (see *Green Space—Gardens*). Adults $17.50, seniors and students $16.50, children 3–12 $15.50; IMAX $11–13; museum and movie $19–23.

🍴 ✂ ♿ **Fernbank Science Center** (678-874-7102; www.fernbank.edu), 156 Heaton Park Drive NE. Open noon–5 Monday and Wednesday, noon–9 Tuesday and Friday, 10–5 Saturday. Forest open 2–5 Monday–Friday, 10–5 Sunday; observatory open 9–10:30 PM Thursday and Friday. At this, one of the country's largest planetariums, visitors can explore the vastness of the universe with one of the center's specially choreographed shows. The center boasts an observatory, two electron microscopes, a NASA aeronautics education lab, a greenhouse, a botanical garden, and a 65-acre old-growth forest with paved walking trails, some adapted for heart patients and the visually impaired. The forest is the largest urban woodland forest in the Piedmont region. Seasonal guide sheets identify the flora and fauna. Check for numerous special events. Free except for planetarium; admission to planetarium: adults $4, seniors and students $3.

🍃 ✏ ♿ **Georgia Capitol Museum** (404-463-4536; www.sos.georgia.gov/archives/museum), 214 State Capitol. Open 8–5 weekdays. Located inside the state capitol, this modest museum preserves and interprets the history of the building and the state through memorabilia, artwork, Native American artifacts, fossils and minerals, scenes from Georgia's five diverse geographic regions, and 1939 World's Fair dioramas depicting Georgia industry, state symbols, and a replica of *Miss Freedom,* the statue that adorns the top of the Georgia Capitol. See also Historic Homes and Sites. Free.

🍃 ♿ **Hammonds House Museum** (404-612-0500; www.hammondshouse.org), 503 Peeples Street SW. Open 10–6 Tuesday–Friday, 1–5 Saturday and Sunday. The 1870 Eastlake-style residence in the West End was owned by several families until it was purchased by African American physician and art patron Otis Thrash Hammonds in 1979. He lived there, amassing his art collection, until his death in 1988. Today Hammonds House is Georgia's only exclusively African American fine art museum. The collection features 250 works from the mid-19th century to the present, including Haitian paintings and African sculpture. A piece of trivia: The Bingham family lived in this house from 1910 to 1979. Author Madge Bingham wrote *Sunny Elephant* and other children's books in her treehouse in the backyard. Adults $2, seniors and students $1.

🍃 ♿ **High Museum of Art** (404-733-HIGH or 404-733-4400; www.high.org), 1280 Peachtree Street NE. Open 10–5 Tuesday–Saturday, 10–8 Thursday, noon–5 Sunday; extended hours until 9 on first Thursday of each month, until 10 on third Friday. Guided tours at 1 Sunday and Wednesday. Located in the heart of Midtown as an integral part of the Woodruff Arts Center complex, the Richard Meier–designed High Museum of Art was already Atlanta's largest museum before it added another 177,000 square feet designed by Renzo Piano. The makeover includes new gallery space, special exhibition halls, and a pedestrian-friendly "village of the arts." Among the museum's collections are 19th- and 20th-century European and American paintings, art, and furniture; English ceramics; prints by French and German impressionists; sub-Saharan African pieces; decorative and folk art; modern and contemporary works; and photography. Important traveling exhibits always make a stop at the High. Interactive exhibits in the Children's Room keep the small ones from getting bored. Linger for a snack at the **High Café.** Adults $18, seniors and students with ID $15, children 6–17 $11.

🍃 ✏ ♿ **Jimmy Carter Presidential Library and Museum** (404-865-7100; www.jimmycarterlibrary.org), 441 Freedom Parkway. Open 9–4:45 Monday–Saturday, noon–4:45 Sunday. See a life-size re-creation of part of the Oval Office as it looked during the Carter administration and view state gifts from heads of foreign governments received during Carter's tenure, reproductions of first lady Rosalynn Carter's inaugural gowns, a formal White House dinner setting, and memorabilia from the 1976 campaign. Take time to stroll the rose garden and the beautiful and serene Japanese garden, where visitors can admire an unobstructed view of the Atlanta skyline (see *Green Space—Gardens*). Adults $8, seniors and students $6, children younger than 16 free.

ATLANTA'S LARGEST MUSEUM, THE HIGH MUSEUM OF ART INCLUDES A DIVERSE COLLECTION FOR ADULTS AND KIDS.

🍴 🖉 ♿ **World of Coca-Cola Museum**
(404-676-5151 or 1-800-676-COKE;
www.woccatlanta.com), 121 Baker Street
NW. Open 10–6:30 daily, but always check
ahead. Last admission one hour prior to
closing. Reservations strongly recommended. The story of Coca-Cola—from its
humble beginning as an 1886 drugstore
drink to its current position as a worldwide
phenomenon—is told through exhibits of
1,000 items of memorabilia, classic ads, and
a representation of the bottling process.
The attraction's proximity to the Georgia
Aquarium, Centennial Olympic Park, and
Imagine It! The Children's Museum of
Atlanta makes for a very convenient all-day
outing. Adults $16, seniors $14, youth and
children 3–12 $12.

THE WORLD OF COCA-COLA TELLS THE
STORY OF THE SOFT DRINK.

NATURAL BEAUTY SPOTS The 🍴 🖉 ♿ **Chattahoochee River** skirts the western
side of Buckhead in the metro region as it stretches from Lake Lanier north of Atlanta,
through the city and its suburbs on its 542-mile course to Apalachicola Bay, Florida. The
river corridor is one of America's premier urban greenways—a wild oasis within the metrop-
olis. Because the river is not navigable this far north and doesn't flow through downtown, the
waterway and the land surrounding it create one of metro Atlanta's best-kept secrets. It was
due to former president Jimmy Carter, a Democrat, and former speaker of the house Newt
Gingrich, a Republican—two Georgians whose outlook about many issues could hardly be
more dissimilar—that this section of the river was designated the **Chattahoochee River
National Recreation Area** (see *Green Space—Recreation Areas*). The 6,500-acre, 14-unit
recreation area is the most popular of Georgia's 10 National Park Service units, welcoming
more than 3 million visitors annually. Its parks contain more than 900 species of plants, old-
and new-growth hardwood forests, 20 species of fish, and numerous other animal species.
The park is a popular escape from the city for those who enjoy hiking, fishing, boating, and
other outdoor pursuits. One of the most popular activities is "shooting the 'Hooch"—floating
down the river on a raft on a hot summer day.

✳ To Do

BICYCLING You can rent bikes from Skate Escape in Midtown (see entry that follows),
but there are no rentals downtown or in Buckhead. **MARTA** (see *Getting Around*) allows
bicycles on all its trains, and there are bike racks on the front of some buses (the racks handle only two bikes at a time). Many MARTA stations have bike racks for commuters who
wish to cycle to the bus or train.

🍴 🖉 **PATH Foundation** (404-875-7284; www.pathfoundation.org), mailing address: P.O.
Box 14327, Atlanta 30324. The foundation has been instrumental in developing bike paths
throughout the metro area. The Atlanta-DeKalb Greenway Trail System includes the **Freedom Parkway Trail.** The east–west section, with its switchbacks and straightaways, was an
immediate hit with cyclists, joggers, in-line skaters, and strollers. The 3.3-mile **Chastain
Park Trail** is one of PATH's most popular trails. Visitors can download trail maps from the
website.

🍴 🖉 **Skate Escape** (404-892-1292; www.skateescape.com), 1086 Piedmont Avenue NE at
12th Street. Open daily 11–7. Located across the street from Piedmont Park, the company

rents bikes and regular and in-line skates that can be enjoyed in the park. Conventional or in-line skates $6 per hour or $15 per day. Bikes $6–12 per hour, $25–60 per day.

BOATING The **Chattahoochee River** provides numerous opportunities year-round for canoeing and kayaking, as well as motorboating and other small-boat use. Boating is allowed from sunrise to sunset; night boating is not permitted, nor are Jet Skis. No boat rentals are available in the park. Consult the website at www.nps.gov/chat for information about nearby outfitters who rent equipment.

CARRIAGE RIDES ✿ **Carriage For Hire** (404-622-0526; www.carriageforhire.com /atlanta.html). Carriage stands are located at Peachtree Street and International Boulevard, Centennial Olympic Park and International Boulevard, Underground Atlanta, and West Park Place and Baker. Available 7–10 PM weekdays, 4–10 PM weekends, except during exceptionally hot weather when it is dangerous for the horses to be out. These romantic carriage rides cover most of historical downtown and Centennial Olympic Park. $50 for 15 minutes, $100 for a half hour, $175 for an hour for up to six people in the carriage.

FISHING The **Chattahoochee River** is the southernmost habitat in the United States for trout. The state stocks the river with rainbow, brook, and brown trout, so fishing along the river's banks or from small boats is a popular activity. Several fishing outfitters, instructors, and guides are available for hire. A Georgia fishing license and trout stamp are required. There are special regulations along three sections of the river, so it's best to check ahead before planning to fish (consult the website at www.nps.gov/chat). Night fishing is not allowed.

FOR FAMILIES ✿ ✿ ♿ **Turner Field–Ivan Allen Jr. Braves Museum and Hall of Fame** (404-614-2311; www.atlanta.braves.mlb.com), 755 Hank Aaron Drive. Open 9–3 Monday–Saturday, 1–3 Sunday; open 9–noon on game days; off season open 10–2 Monday–Saturday. Located on the northwest side of Turner Field at Aisle 134 and named for a former mayor rather than a baseball player, the museum contains 600 Braves artifacts, which trace the team's 140-plus-year history, from its beginning in Boston (1871–1952) to Milwaukee (1953–1965) to Atlanta (1966–present). The Hall of Fame honors the careers of 21 Braves legends and includes memorabilia such as Hank Aaron's 715th home run ball and bat, and the team's 1995 World Series trophy. (See also **Turner Field Tours** under *To See— Guided Tours.*) Museum $2 on game days, $5 on nongame days. Free parking in the Green Lot on nongame days.

✿ ♿ **Zoo Atlanta** (404-624-5600; www.zoo atlanta.org), 800 Cherokee Avenue SE. Open 9:30–5:30 weekdays, until 6:30 weekends. Gates close one hour prior to closing. Zoo Atlanta, one of the 10 oldest, continuously operating zoos in the nation, is located in the historic Grant Park neighborhood. The original collection began with the animals of a traveling circus that was going out of business. In the 1980s, the conditions at the zoo had deteriorated to the point that it was named one of the worst in the country. A massive turnaround has made it one of the best. More than 700 animals representing 200 species from all

LUN LUN AND YANG YANG, GIANT PANDAS ON LOAN FROM CHINA, FROLIC AT ZOO ATLANTA.

over the world roam freely in habitats such as an Asian rain forest and an African savanna. The most popular stars right now are Lun Lun and Yang Yang, adorable giant pandas on loan from China and their offspring. They've had two babies here—one of which has now been returned to China but the other of which continues to charm visitors. He was named Po by Jack Black from the animated movie *Kung Fu Panda.* Not to be upstaged, however, is the outstanding primate collection, the largest collection in the country of gorillas and orangutans, but of many other primates as well. Keeper talks, training demonstrations, wildlife shows, and animal feedings are other popular activities. Adults $20.99, seniors $16.99, children 3–11 $15.99.

GOLF ✿ ✐ **Bobby Jones Golf Course at Atlanta Memorial Park** (404-355-1009), 384 Woodward Way. Open sunrise to sunset daily. The 18-hole, par-71 course is well suited to any level of play. The course meanders through beautiful neighborhoods and along Peachtree Creek, and boasts two clubhouses. $18.25–44.

✿ ✐ **Candler Park Golf Course** (404-371-1260), 585 Candler Park Drive NE. Open sunrise to sunset daily. The nine-hole, 2,064-yard, par-31 course provides a rare opportunity for in-town golfing. Built in 1928, it was once the private course of Coca-Cola founder Asa Candler. A forest of pines and oaks bisects the course, and the terrain varies from flat to hilly, which creates challenges for all levels of players. $10–22.

✿ **North Fulton Golf Course at Chastain Memorial Park** (404-255-0723), 216 West Wieuca Road. Open sunrise to sunset daily. Opened in 1937, the 18-hole, par-71 course features 6,570 yards of challenging play. The facility features a putting green, chipping area, pro shop, snack bar, club and cart rentals, and pro instruction. $24–27.25.

TENNIS ✿ ✐ **Bitsy Grant Tennis Center at Atlanta Memorial Park** (404-609-7193), 2125 Northside Drive. Open 9 AM–10 PM Monday–Thursday, 9–9 Friday, 9–6 Saturday and Sunday. Named for tennis star Bryan M. "Bitsy" Grant, who was a dynamo on the court despite his 5-foot-4-inch frame, the complex offers 13 clay courts and 10 hard courts. The center is also home to the **Georgia Tennis Hall of Fame.** $3–7 an hour.

✿ ✐ **Chastain Memorial Park Tennis Center** (404-255-3210; www.chastainpark.org), 110 West Wieuca Road. Open 9–9 weekdays, 9–6 Saturday, 10–6 Sunday. The park features nine tennis courts. $3–5 per hour. (see *Green Space—Nature Preserves and Parks.*)

✳ Green Space

GARDENS ✐ ♿ **Atlanta Botanical Garden** (404-876-5859; www.atlantabotanical garden.org), 1345 Piedmont Avenue NE. Open 9–7 Tuesday–Sunday, April–October; 9–6 Tuesday–Sunday, November–March. This tranquil 30-acre oasis bordering Piedmont Park (see *Nature Preserves and Parks*) has something blooming year-round in annual, dwarf conifer, fragrance, herb, ornamental grass, perennial, rose, spring and summer bulb, vegetable, and vine arbor gardens. The **Dorothy Chapman Fuqua Conservatory and Fuqua Orchid Center** overflows with exotic tropical plants, including lowland orchids, while Desert House showcases endangered succulents. Throughout the year, the garden sponsors festivals, flower and plant shows, demonstrations, plant sales, and social events such as "Cocktails in the Garden" and concerts on the lawn. Adults $18.75, children $12.95; additional fee for parking.

✿ ✐ ♿ **Atlanta History Center** (404-814-4000; www.atlantahistorycenter.com), 130 West Paces Ferry Road NW. Open 10–5:30 Monday–Saturday, noon–5:30 Sunday; last ticket sold at 4:30; gardens and grounds close at 5:15. See the Japanese maples and U.S. and Asian species in the Cherry-Sims Asian-American Garden; azaleas and rhododendrons in the Frank A. Smith Rhododendron Garden; native plants and wildflowers in the Mary Howard

Gilbert Memorial Quarry Garden; formal boxwoods, fountains, and statuary in the Swan House Gardens; the sculpture *The Peach Tree* in the Garden of Peace on the Swan Woods Trail; and the gardens and cotton patch at the **Tullie Smith Farm.** Children enjoy the seven interactive stations on the Connor Brown Discovery Trail. For the serious gardener, the center's Cherokee Garden Library houses more than 3,000 books and periodicals about gardening. Adults $16.50, seniors and students older than 13 $13, children 4–12 $11.

🌹 ✂ ♿ **Jimmy Carter Presidential Library** (404-865-7100; www.jimmycarterlibrary.org), 441 Freedom Parkway. Open 9–4:45 Monday–Saturday, noon–4:45 Sunday. Outside the facility (see *To See—Museums*) there is a 2,500-square-foot rose garden with 80 varieties, a wildflower meadow, and a tranquil Japanese garden with two waterfalls. Cherry trees blossom in the spring. Adults $8, seniors and students $6, children younger than 16 free.

🌹 ✂ ♿ **Robert L. Stanton Rose Garden** (678-874-7102; www.fernbank.edu/rosegarden .htm), 767 Clifton Road NE. Open daylight hours daily. This beautiful garden is located on the grounds of the Fernbank Museum of Natural History but maintained by the Fernbank Science Center (see *To See—Museums*). The garden is named in honor of Robert L. Stanton, who first established a rose garden at the museum in 1983. A trained horticulturist and employee of the science center, Stanton had a lifelong interest in roses and was a consulting Rosarian. His interest in educating the public about roses and his realization that there was no test site in Atlanta led to the establishment of this garden. Today the garden contains more than 1,300 rosebushes (the rose garden in Thomasville, "the Rose City," has only 500). The Stanton garden tests regular roses and devotes another garden to testing miniature roses. Free.

NATURE PRESERVES AND PARKS 🌹 ✂ ♿ **Centennial Olympic Park** (404-223-4412; 404-222-PARK for recorded message; www.centennialpark.com), 265 Park Avenue NW. Open 7 AM–11 PM daily (later during events). This 21-acre park is the living legacy of the 1996 Centennial Olympic Summer Games. Features of the park include gigantic lighted columns, Quilt Plaza, Centennial Plaza, the visitors center, water gardens, sculptures, and playgrounds—all connected by walkways laid with 500,000 bricks donated by local citizens to help pay for the park. As the park has matured, the 330,000 square feet of grass, 30,000 shrubs, and 575 trees have softened the appearance. The highlight of the park is the gigantic Fountain of Rings, the largest interactive depiction of the Olympic logo in the world. During the warm-weather months, different heights of water spurt out of 250 jets in the ground and invite the young and young at heart to jump in and get wet. An hourly dancing water show is set to music. Even in balmy Atlanta, modern technology makes it possible to have an outdoor ice-skating rink at Christmastime, when the park is aglitter with a holiday lights display. Numerous festivals and special events keep the park hopping year-round. Free.

A SAMPLING OF THE ROSES AT THE ROBERT L. STANTON ROSE GARDEN

🌹 ✂ ♿ **Chastain Memorial Park** (www .chastainpark.org), 135 West Wieuca Road. Open daily. The Buckhead park boasts nine tennis courts (see *To Do—Tennis*), seven ball fields, a swimming pool, 18-hole golf course (see *To Do—Golf*), gymnasium with basketball court, weight facility, the Chastain Arts and Crafts Center, stables, a

CENTENNIAL OLYMPIC PARK TRIVIA

- Some 800,000 bricks were used in the park. Laid end to end, they would stretch 100 miles, from Turner Field to Columbus, Georgia.
- The person-hours required to complete the park are equivalent to one person working full time for 100 years.
- Granite from each of the five continents represented by the Olympic Games was used in the park.
- Each of the five Olympic rings in the fountain is 25 feet in diameter—large enough to park two cars side by side.

state-of-the-art children's playground, an amphitheater (see *Entertainment—Music*), and a 3.3-mile circuit for jogging, bicycling, and walking (see *To Do—Bicycling*). Access to the 158-acre city park is free; some activities have a fee.

🦆 🐾 ♿ **Grant Park** (www.grantpark.org, click on "Attractions"). The 131-acre green space and recreational area in the center of the Grant Park Historic District was a gift to the city from Col. Lemuel P. Grant, the district's earliest settler. Today the park boasts a beautiful lake, numerous springs, swimming pool, playgrounds and picnicking facilities, the **Atlanta Cyclorama and Civil War Museum** (see *To See—Historic Homes and Sites*), and **Zoo Atlanta** (see *To Do—For Families*). The Grant Mansion is the home of the **Atlanta Preservation Center** (see *To See—Guided Tours*). Park free; admission to attractions.

🦆 🐾 ♿ 🐕 **Piedmont Park** (404-875-7275; www.piedmontpark.org), Piedmont Road. Open 6 AM–11 PM daily. Entrances: Prado, Westminster Gate, Worcester Gate, Park Drive Bridge, Charles Allen Drive Gate, 12th Street Gate, and 14th Street Gate in Midtown. Known and utilized as Atlanta's backyard for more than 100 years, Piedmont Park was created for the 1895 Cotton States and International Exposition. Today the 180-acre park with tiny Lake Clara Meer attracts cyclists, joggers, picnickers, in-line skaters, and walkers. In addition, the park features a visitors center, tennis courts, softball fields, boccie courts, basketball courts,

A CHILD COOLS OFF IN THE FOUNTAIN OF RINGS IN ATLANTA'S CENTENNIAL OLYMPIC PARK.

picnic shelters, fishing, a swim center, playgrounds, 0.7- to 1.7-mile walking loops, separate dog parks for large and small pooches, and a community garden. In summer, a Green Market purveys fresh vegetables. The city's most popular park also hosts festivals and special events. During the year the park is the scene of the **Atlanta Dogwood Festival** (see *Special Events*), **Screen on the Green** film festival, **Atlanta Jazz Festival** (see *Special Events*), **Atlanta Pride Festival,** and **Peachtree Road Race.** The **Park Tavern Restaurant** (404-249-0001; www.parktavern.com; 500 10th Street) and **Willy's Mexicana Grill** (404-249-9054; www.willys.com; 1071 Piedmont Avenue) anchor the two ends of the park. Adjacent to the park is the **Atlanta Botanical Garden** (see *Gardens*). All entrances and most areas are wheelchair accessible. With all these attractions, there is one drawback: The park has very little parking—almost none of it free. Visitors can use the parking facility at the Atlanta Botanical Garden; fee charged.

RECREATION AREAS 🐾 ✿ **Chattahoochee River National Recreation Area, East and West Palisades Unit.** The headquarters for the park is in Dunwoody at the **Island Ford Unit** (678-538-1200; www.nps.gov/chat), 1978 Island Ford Parkway. The Palisades Unit, accessible from Northside Parkway at the Chattahoochee River, is the only unit physically within Buckhead. Other units in this area include Cochran Shoals, Columns, Johnson Ferry, and Sope Creek. Open daily. The 50-acre unit features hiking, fishing, boating, tubing, picnicking, bird-watching, wildlife observation, and swimming. $3 parking fee.

LAKE CLARA MEER AT PIEDMONT PARK IS AN OASIS WITHIN THE CITY.

✳ Lodging
BED & BREAKFASTS

In Ansley Park
Shellmont Inn (404-872-9290; www .shellmont.com), 821 Piedmont Avenue NE. On the National Register of Historic Places, the Shellmont is an exquisitely restored mansion in Midtown. Outstanding architectural features include stained, beveled, and leaded glass; curved and bow windows; intricately carved woodwork; coved ceilings; and hand-painted stenciling. Public areas and guest rooms, which are in the main house and in a carriage house/ cottage, are furnished with antiques, Oriental carpets, and period wall treatments and embellished with luxurious amenities. Wicker-filled verandas overlook lawns, gardens, and a Victorian fish pond. A sumptuous breakfast is included. Smoking outdoors only. Not wheelchair accessible. $125–360.

In Buckhead
♿ **Beverly Hills Inn** (404-233-8520 or 1-800-331-8520; www.beverlyhillsinn.com), 65 Sheridan Drive. This simple, unassuming but cozy European-style inn, which was built in 1929, attracts a clientele that's 35 percent international. Each of the 18 guest rooms and suites features a private bath, antique furnishings, a balcony, hardwood floors, and a kitchen, which makes the inn particularly appealing for a long-term stay. Breakfast included and served in the Garden Room. No smoking. $99–165.

In Inman Park
1890 King-Keith House Bed and Breakfast (404-688-7330 or 1-800-728-3879; www.kingkeith.com), 889 Edgewood Avenue NE. The opulent Queen Anne–style King-Keith House, one of the most photographed houses in Atlanta, is characterized by 12-foot ceilings, carved fireplaces, spacious rooms, stained-glass windows, and period antiques. Accommodations include rooms, suites, and a private cottage with a Jacuzzi tub for two. Guests enjoy elegant public spaces, private gardens, complimentary snacks and beverages, and a full gourmet breakfast. No smoking. Not wheelchair accessible. Two-night minimum. $130–225.

🌸 **Heartfield Manor** (404-523-8633; www.heartfieldmanor.com), 1882 Elizabeth Street NE. This 1903 Craftsman cottage features a two-story entrance with a grand balcony, stained-glass windows, and wainscoting. All rooms and suites are furnished with period pieces. Some guest accommodations offer a full kitchen; some have a small refrigerator and microwave. No smoking. Not wheelchair accessible. $70–105.

Sugar Magnolia Bed and Breakfast (404-222-0226; www.sugarmagnoliabb .com), 804 Edgewood Avenue NE. Guest rooms and suites are offered in a magnificent, well-preserved Queen Anne–Victorian mansion and in a cottage. Built in 1892, the house is embellished with gables, ornate chimneys, whimsical turrets, and an inviting wraparound porch. The inside is characterized by 12-foot ceilings, a grand staircase, six fireplaces, beveled glass, and hand-painted plasterwork. The cottage boasts a whirlpool tub for two and a full kitchen. A generous continental breakfast is included. Smoking outdoors only. Not wheelchair accessible. $120–160.

In Virginia-Highland

St. Charles Inn Bed & Breakfast (404-875-1001; www.thesaintcharlesinn.com), 1001 St. Charles Avenue NE. Built in 1913, this Craftsman home actually has some flickering gaslight fixtures. A variety of accommodations—located in the Primary Residence, the Carriage House, and the Victorian Cottage—range from affordable guest rooms to luxurious suites. Some rooms and suites feature a fireplace, double whirlpool tub, private garden, or kitchen. Continental breakfast included. Another plus to staying at this B&B is that it's within easy walking distance of the shops and restaurants of Virginia-Highland. Smoking is permitted only outdoors. Not wheelchair accessible. $115–215; ask about numerous packages. Two-night minimum required on weekends.

Virginia-Highland Bed and Breakfast (404-892-2735; www.virginiahighlandbb .com), 630 Orme Circle NE. This restored 1920s Craftsman bungalow is nestled within a cottage garden, creating a true urban retreat. In fact the grounds are a designated Audubon Wildlife Sanctuary, and the classic labyrinth is included in the World-Wide Labyrinth Project. Guest rooms in the main house are furnished with antiques and feature a queen- or king-size bed and private bath. Some boast a whirlpool tub or a pri-

vate entrance. The family-friendly, self-catering Getaway Cottage is furnished in 1950s blond birch furniture. Full breakfast included for guests in the main house. The B&B is within walking distance of Highland Avenue shopping, dining, and entertainment. No smoking on the property. Not wheelchair accessible. $119–169; Getaway Cottage $219.

INNS AND HOTELS

In Buckhead

🐾 ♿ 🐾 **Grand Hyatt Atlanta** (404-237-1234; www.grandatlanta.hyatt.com), 3300 Peachtree Road NE. Recognized by AAA as a four-star hostelry, the 438-room Grand Hyatt is known for sumptuous accommodations, superior restaurants, exciting nightlife, and a solicitous staff. Other amenities include a heated outdoor pool open seasonally, a sauna, steam rooms, massage, **Cassis** restaurant, and the **Onyx** lobby lounge. Smoking and non-smoking rooms available. Pet friendly. $197–397.

🐾 ♿ 🐾 **InterContinental Buckhead** (404-946-9000; www.ichotelsgroup.com), 3315 Peachtree Road NE. This swanky, five-star hotel features such amenities as in-room libraries, Bose Wave sound systems, marble baths, an outdoor pool, a whirlpool, fitness center, and a spa. The hotel is adjacent to the Atlanta Financial Center and within easy walking distance of two upscale shopping malls, numerous restaurants, and the Buckhead MARTA station. Pets allowed. No smoking. $199–259.

🐾 ♿ **JW Marriott Buckhead Atlanta** (404-262-3344 or 1-800-623-2051; www .marriotthotels.com), 3300 Lenox Road. This AAA four-diamond hotel is physically connected to Lenox Square mall, which certainly makes it a favorite with shoppers. It's also within easy walking distance of the Lenox MARTA station. The sophisticated hotel features 367 elegantly appointed rooms and four luxury suites, as well as the **Lenox Grill** and the **Lobby Bar.** Smoking is permitted on the seventh floor, otherwise nonsmoking. No pets. $159–189; ask about special packages.

♪ & **The Ritz-Carlton Buckhead** (404-237-2700 or 1-800-241-3333; www.ritz carlton.com), 3434 Peachtree Road. Ritz-Carlton is synonymous with unparalleled luxury and service, and this 510-room AAA five-diamond hotel, one of only seven in Georgia, is always voted Atlanta's best. Accommodations are enhanced with ultra-luxurious linens, rich upholstery, and marble baths. The swanky hotel features a swim and fitness center with an indoor heated lap pool, whirlpool, sauna, steam room, and weight machines. The hotel's **Lobby Lounge** is the "in" place in Atlanta to spy visiting celebrities, and the four-star **Café** serves three meals daily and a fabulous Sunday brunch. The Ritz's afternoon tea, light tea, or royal tea are high-class affairs, and the hotel is known for imaginative room packages and fabulous holiday feasts. There's live piano music and a vocalist in the Lobby Lounge several nights. No smoking. $389 and up.

♪ & ❀ **St. Regis Hotel Atlanta** (404-563-7900; www.starwoodhotels.com/stregis), 88 West Paces Ferry Road. The latest of Atlanta's five AAA five-diamond hotels, the St. Regis provides unparalleled accommodations, dining, and service. Luxurious accommodations are provided in 120 rooms and 31 suites, each featuring maccasar ebony furnishings, handcrafted chandeliers, original artwork, marble baths, and amenities such as robes, turndown service, and the latest in entertainment technologies. Dining options include **Astor Court** for breakfast and afternoon tea, the **Wine Room** for personalized tastings and wine flights, the **Poolside Bar** in season, **Paces 88 American Bistro** for fine dining, and the **St. Regis Bar** for cocktails and light fare. A spa, pool, whirlpool, and an outdoor fireplace by a waterfall round out the amenities. Pet friendly. No smoking. $267–550.

♪ & ❀ **The Westin Buckhead Atlanta** (404-365-0065 or 1-800-253-1397; www .starwoodhotels.com/westin), 3391 Peach-tree Road NE. Those who have been to Atlanta before will recognize this outstanding hotel as the former Swissotel. The 365-room AAA four-diamond property features breathtaking architecture and an outstanding expressionist art collection. The hotel is also the home of the famed the **Palm Restaurant** (see *Dining Out—In Buck-head*). Other amenities include a fitness center and an indoor pool. The Westin is adjacent to Lenox Square mall and within easy walking distance of Phipps Plaza mall, two MARTA stations, and many highly rated restaurants. No smoking. Wheelchair accessible—-reserve in advance one of 17 rooms with adapted bathrooms. Pet friendly (small dogs only). $250–375.

Downtown

♪ & **Omni Hotel at CNN Center** (404-659-0000 or 1-800-843-6664; www.omni cnn.com), 100 CNN Center. The 1,070-room AAA four-diamond hotel's downtown location and easy accessibility to the MARTA rail system make it a popular base of operations when visiting the city. Attached to the CNN Center, the hotel has the advantage of its restaurants, bars, shops, and movie theaters. The hotel is adjacent to Philips Arena, where scores of sporting events and concerts occur, and across from the Georgia World Congress Center, Georgia Dome, and Centennial Olympic Park. Dining options include fine dining at **Prime Meridian,** casual dining at **Morsel's** and **Latitudes Bistro and Lounge.** No smoking. $139 and up.

♪ & **The Ritz-Carlton Atlanta** (404-659-0400; www.ritz-carlton.com), 181 Peachtree Street NE. Ritz-Carltons are world renowned for their not-to-be-topped personal service, flawless facilities, and superior dining. This AAA five-diamond downtown Atlanta property is no exception. The 25-story, 444-room hotel is situated in the heart of Downtown's business, finance, and government district within walking distance of many attractions, bars, restaurants, shops, and a MARTA station. Gracious guest rooms and suites have bay-window views of the downtown skyline. Exquisite dining is available at the **Atlanta Grill** (see *Dining Out—Downtown*) and the **Lumen Lobby Bar.** A fitness center is available. No smoking. $197 and up.

✦ ♿ **Westin Peachtree Plaza** (404-659-1400; www.starwoodhotels.com/westin), 210 Peachtree Street NW. The cylindrical-shaped hotel still reigns as the best publicly accessible place to get a view of Atlanta, not only from guest rooms but also from its revolving 73rd-floor **Sun Dial Restaurant, Bar, and View** (see *Dining Out—Downtown*). The hotel's 1,068 rooms are furnished with Westin's signature Heavenly Beds and Heavenly Baths. Amenities include an indoor/outdoor year-round swimming pool, shops, a fitness center, 24-hour room service, and high-speed Internet access in all rooms. Other dining options include the **Café** and the **Lobby Bar.** No smoking. $295–500.

In Midtown

♿ **Artmore Hotel and Suites** (404-876-6100; www.artmorehotel.com), 1302 West Peachtree Street. This boutique hotel in the heart of the cultural district occupies a historic property that began life in 1924 as an apartment building. Today it offers guest rooms, suites, and a penthouse suite. In keeping with the Spanish architecture, the intimate inn wraps around a courtyard with a bubbling fountain. The lobby contains the contemporary **Studio Bar and Lounge.** No smoking. From $159.

✦ ♿ **Four Seasons Hotel Atlanta** (404-881-9898; www.fourseasons.com/atlanta), 75 14th Street NE. All Four Seasons Hotels are renowned for incomparable personal service, outstanding amenities, elegant rooms and suites, and wonderful restaurants. The swanky AAA five-diamond, five-star (the only one in Atlanta) Four Seasons Hotel Atlanta meets each of these standards. The 244-room hotel occupies the first 19 floors of a 50-story building—the remaining floors are residential. For a room with a view of both Downtown and Midtown, ask for an upper-level corner Premier Room. The hotel's palatial Romanesque indoor pool is Atlanta's only saltwater pool, and its **Park 75 Restaurant** (see *Dining Out—In Midtown*) offers gourmet meals. The hotel is located in the heart of Midtown's arts district and offers special packages in conjunction with the High Museum of Art, the Atlanta Symphony Orchestra, and other cultural institutions. Smoking and nonsmoking rooms available. Weekend packages start at $186 with advanced purchase, $249 without.

✦ ♿ **Georgian Terrace Hotel** (404-897-1991 or 1-800-651-2316; www.thegeorgian terrace.com), 659 Peachtree Street NE. Known as the Grande Dame of Peachtree Street, this stately 1911 hotel has numerous connections with *Gone with the Wind.* Margaret Mitchell met Harold Latham of Macmillan Publishing in the dining room to deliver her manuscript. In 1939, when the movie premiered in Atlanta, the stars of the film stayed here and attended gala parties. Today the hotel consists of the original 10-story building, with marble floors, Palladian and French windows, spiral staircases, stained-glass skylights, intricate plaster moldings, crystal chandeliers, elegant latticework, and large murals. A stunning atrium connects a modern 19-story wing to the original building. Accommodations, which are offered in 326 standard rooms and junior to three-bedroom suites, feature antique-style furnishings, "dream" beds, and large bathrooms. Suites boast a living-dining area, a fully appointed kitchen, and even a washer and dryer. Other amenities include the elegant **Livingston Restaurant and Bar** and a fitness center. On the roof is a junior Olympic-size pool with a sweeping view of downtown Atlanta. The hotel is located directly across the street from the Fox Theatre and a block from the North Avenue MARTA rail station. No smoking. Getaway packages start at $151.

♿ **Georgia Tech Hotel and Conference Center** (reservations: 404-838-2100 or 404-347-9440; www.gatechhotel.com), 800 Spring Street NW. Located in the university's new Technology Square complex, this high-tech, upscale hotel offers 252 comfortable guest rooms, each with a flat-screen television, marble bath with upgraded amenities, and cutting-edge technology. The hotel also offers a full-service Club Room lounge with limited menu service from 3 PM to midnight, the Lobby Bar, advanced fitness center, indoor swimming pool, and concierge service. Technology Square features retail stores, restaurants, a day spa, and restaurants. Transportation and a connection to the Midtown MARTA station are available on the free **Tech Trolley** (see *Getting Around*). No smoking. $159–209.

✎ ♿ ❀ **Hotel Indigo-Atlanta Midtown** (404-874-9200; www.ichotelsgroup.com), 683 Peachtree Street NE. This trendy boutique hotel is located in a historic building across the street from the Fox Theatre. Plush bedding, area rugs on hardwood floors, spa-inspired baths, and a seashore theme make it a standout. The hotel also features a bar and restaurant, self-service laundry facilities, and a health and fitness center. Pets are allowed. In fact, from 5 to 8 PM on Tuesday, guests and locals can have cocktails with their dogs (Poochy gets a bowl of ice water). A dollar from each cocktail goes to the **Piedmont Park** dog park (see *Green Space—Nature Preserves and Parks*). Smoking and nonsmoking rooms available. $119–200.

✎ ♿ ❀ **W Hotel Midtown** (404-892-6000; www.starwoodhotels.com/whotels), 188 14th Street NE. Location, location, location—this 466-room hotel is across from the High Museum of Art and the Woodruff Arts Center. It's also within very easy walking distance of Piedmont Park, the Atlanta Botanical Garden, and the Arts Center MARTA rail station. Guest rooms feature the plush W Bed (the hotel even has comparable cribs for babies and beds for dogs), rain-forest showerheads, and state-of-the-art entertainment center. Hotel amenities include the **Jean-Georges Spice Market Restaurant, Whiskey Park Bar, W Cafe, Living Room Lounge, Bliss Spa,** an outdoor pool (open seasonally), and **SWEAT** fitness center. No smoking. From $149.

In Poncey-Highland
✎ ♿ **Emory Conference Center Hotel** (404-712-6000 or 1-800-933-6629; www.emoryconferencecenter.com), 1615 Clifton Road NE. The hotel, inspired by the architectural designs of Frank Lloyd Wright, provides a tranquil setting, contemporary elegance, spectacular landscapes, and

exceptional service. Nestled on 28 acres of forest preserve on the Emory University campus, it offers 197 beautifully appointed rooms, two full-service restaurants serving three meals daily, a lounge, an indoor and an outdoor pool, whirlpool, fitness center, bowling alley, pool tables, and spa. Free shuttle service within 1 mile. No smoking. Many rooms wheelchair accessible. $169–260.

🍴 ✎ ♿ **Emory Inn Atlanta Bed and Breakfast** (404-712-6000 or 1-800-230-4134), 1641 Clifton Road. Located adjacent to the Emory Conference Center Hotel and connected to it by a covered walkway, this more intimate inn offers 107 guest rooms, complimentary continental breakfast, a restaurant open for lunch and dinner, and an outdoor pool and hydrotherapy pool available seasonally. No smoking. Many rooms wheelchair accessible. $99–109.

🍴 ✎ ❀ **The Highland Inn** (404-874-5756; www.thehighlandinn.com), 644 North Highland Avenue. This quaint hotel was built in the 1920s as the Wynne Hotel and Tea Room. Today it offers simple, affordable rooms and suites with old-world charm. In addition to being pet friendly, the hotel has laundry facilities and offers continental breakfast. More than 60 restaurants are within walking distance. No smoking. Not wheelchair accessible. $86.85–110.95.

✳ Where to Eat
DINING OUT

In Buckhead
♿ **Aria** (404-233-7673; www.aria-atl.com), 490 East Paces Ferry Road. Open 6–10 PM Monday–Saturday. This upscale gourmet bistro, located in a historic house, specializes in slow-cooked food and organic produce. The sophisticated decor features unusual lighting and other flashy details. The lounge is sexy, and the wine cellar table is one of the most romantic in town. No smoking. Reservations recommended. $25–35.

♿ **Atlanta Fish Market** (404-262-3165; www.atlanta-fish-market.com), 265 Pharr Road NE. Open 11:30–11:30 Monday–

OPEN ALL NIGHT

Buckhead never sleeps, so visitors can find a quick bite, an alcoholic libation, coffee, or dessert at any time. These restaurants are always open: **International House of Pancakes** (404-264-0647), 3122 Peachtree Road NE; **Landmark Diner** (404-816-9090), 3652 Roswell Road NW, a 1950s-style diner; **OK Cafe** (404-233-2888), 1284 West Paces Ferry Road, a campy, folk-artsy place where you can always get breakfast (the jalapeño cheese grits are a favorite; brunch is served weekends until 2 PM); **R. Thomas Deluxe Grill** (404-872-2942; www.rthomasdeluxe grill.com), 1812 Peachtree Road NW, which serves breakfast, burgers, macrobiotic delights, and vegan and vegetarian cuisine prepared with the most natural and healthful ingredients; **Star-bucks** (404-261-8447), 2333 Peachtree Road NE and (404-240-5596) 3330 Piedmont Road NE; **Steak N Shake** (404-262-7051), 3380 Northside Parkway; and three **Waffle House** restaurants: (404-869-9215), 2581 Piedmont Road; (404-231-0023), 3016 Piedmont Road; and (404-816-2378), 3735 Roswell Road.

Thursday, 11:30–midnight Friday and Saturday, 4–10 Sunday. Look for the gigantic 65-foot steel and copper spawning salmon outside this seafood restaurant. So fresh are the fish and seafood here that the menu is updated twice a day. In terms of sheer variety of seafood, including everything from oysters to stone crab to halibut, no other Atlanta restaurant can compare. No smoking. $25–35.

& **Bone's** (404-237-2663; www.bones restaurant.com), 3130 Piedmont Road NE. Open 11:30–2:30 weekdays, 5:30–10:30 nightly. This private-club-like steakhouse has been a meeting place for the powerful for many years. The old-boys-network ambience is characterized by huge steaks and stiff drinks. Bone's has been designated the highest-ranking steakhouse in the country by Zagat's, and as of 2012, Bone's has received the Best Atlanta Steakhouse award for 16 years. The wine list is extensive. No smoking at dinner; smoking only in the lounge at lunch. Limited wheelchair access from a side entrance. Lunch $14–50, dinner $24–75.

& **Buckhead Diner** (404-262-3336; www.buckheadrestaurants.com), 3073 Piedmont Road NE. Open 11 AM–midnight Monday–Saturday, 10–2 for brunch and 5–10 for dinner Sunday. Pairing nostalgia and retro style, the glitzy, chrome, 1950s-style diner is no fast-food joint. Rather, it is a high-energy, upscale eatery where celebrities and other notables go to see and be

seen. The American menu features chic comfort food such as sweet and sour calamari or veal meat loaf with wild mushrooms. No smoking. Lunch $11–13, dinner under $30.

& **The Café at the Ritz-Carlton Buckhead** (404-237-2700; www.ritzcarlton.com), 3434 Peachtree Road. Open for three meals daily as well as Sunday; afternoon tea at 2:30 and 3:30 Monday–Saturday. The Café has earned four stars for its regional cuisine. It is renowned for its 50-item Sunday brunch. Breakfast is a substantial buffet; à la carte items are available for lunch and dinner. No smoking. Breakfast $16–27; lunch $16–24; dinner $24–37; brunch adults $59, children $29; afternoon tea adults $58, children $39.

& **Canoe** (770-432-2663; www.canoeatl .com), 4199 Paces Ferry Road. Open from 5:30 for dinner daily; 10:30–2:30 Sunday for brunch. Reservations required for dinner. This is one of the prettiest places in the metro area to dine. The Chattahoochee River just barely skirts the metro area, and this is one of the only restaurants located along its banks. In good weather the posh patio is the place to dine. Large windows overlooking the river and lush gardens are an acceptable substitute when the weather's less than ideal. The eclectic American menu features regional cuisine such as Vidalia spring onion soup, slow-roasted Carolina rabbit, and other delicacies. Try to visit Canoe for Sunday brunch, too. No smoking. Lunch $11–20, dinner $14–32, brunch $11–18.

& **NAVA** (404-240-1984; www.buckhead restaurants.com), 3060 Peachtree Road. Open 11:30–2:30 and 5:30–10 Sunday–Thursday, 5:30–11 Saturday. The cuisine is Southwestern with Native American and Latin influences. In addition to such dishes as enchiladas and tacos, the restaurant specializes in entrées such as pistachio-crusted mahimahi, lamb, and porterhouse steaks. Unusual desserts include banana enchilada, Southwest *tres leches* slice, or apple-piñon empanada. The eatery also offers a gluten-free menu. No smoking. $20–27.

& **New York Prime** (404-846-0644; www .centraarchy.com/newyorkprime-atl.php), Monarch Tower, 3424 Peachtree Road NE, Suite 100. Open 5–11 Monday–Saturday, 5–10 Sunday. The posh eatery serves classic New York strip, bone-in rib steak, barrel-cut filet, and other favorites such as lamb, veal, and lobster with delicious sides and salads. Diners also enjoy the martini bar and live entertainment. No smoking. $28–52.

& **The Palm Restaurant** (404-814-1955; www.thepalm.com/atlanta), Westin Buckhead Atlanta, 3391 Peachtree Road NE. Open for three meals daily. The famous full-service restaurant specializes in beef, lobster, and surf-and-turf combinations, as well as chops, veal, and other seafood. No smoking. $35–50.

& **Pricci** (404-237-2941; www.buckhead restaurants.com), 500 Pharr Road. Open 11:30–2:30 weekdays, 5–10 Sunday–Thursday, 5–11 Friday and Saturday. A dramatic interior and a creative menu of classic Italian cuisine with a modern flair guarantee an unforgettable dining experience. Selections include sliced Italian meats and cheeses, antipasti, salads, pizza, pasta, risotto, fish, and meat. No smoking. $19–30.

& **Prime** (404-812-0555; www.heretoserve restaurants.com), 3393 Peachtree Road, Lenox Square Mall. Open 11:30–10 Monday–Thursday, 11:30–11 Friday and Saturday, 4–9 Sunday. Many celebrities frequent this upscale surf-and-turf steakhouse, which offers steaks, seafood (including

sushi), and even vegetarian options. No smoking. $17–39.

& **Twist** (404-869-1191; www.heretoserve restaurants.com), Phipps Plaza, 3500 Peachtree Road. Open 11:30–10 Monday, 11:30–11 Tuesday–Thursday, 11:30–midnight Friday and Saturday, noon–10 Sunday. Peter Kaiser, a legendary chef in Atlanta, describes his gastronomy as "creative cuisine with an attitude." His hand-picked team of professionals creates innovative tapas, wraps, snacks, sushi, satays, seafood, and other finger food, as well as a few entrées and delicious desserts. Smoking allowed. $11–29.

Downtown

& **Atlanta Grill** (404-659-0400; www.ritz -carlton.com), 181 Peachtree Street NE. Open 6:30–2:30 and 5:30–10 daily; Sunday brunch 6:30–12:30. Located in the Ritz-Carlton, this upscale AAA four-diamond restaurant offers Southern-inspired cuisine featuring steaks and seafood in a clublike atmosphere. Jazz entertainment Thursday–Saturday. Smoking in the lounge only. $15–35.

& **Nikolai's Roof** (404-221-6362; www .nikolaisroof.com), 255 Courtland Street NE. Open 5:30–10:30 Tuesday–Saturday. Located on the 30th floor atop the Atlanta Hilton, this restaurant is the Fabergé jewel among the city's restaurants, being the first eatery downtown to earn a four-star rating. Russian influences are seen in the depictions of Fabergé eggs that adorn the gold-rimmed service plates, the waiters dressed in red Imperial Russian uniforms, the ambience, and twists to the French-Continental menu. Entrées include beef, seafood, duck, and even wild boar. The extensive wine list features more than 400 wine labels. Service is especially attentive. Smoking is permitted in the adjacent Point of View Lounge, but not in the restaurant. Restaurant is wheelchair accessible; restrooms are not. Reservations are required, as are a jacket and tie for gentlemen. À la carte $37–43, fixed price for four-course meal $78 (doesn't include wine).

& **Prime Meridian** (404-818-4450; www .omnihotels.com), 100 CNN Center. Open

6:30–11, 11:30–2:30, and 5:30–11:30 daily. The restaurant's location in the Omni Hotel at CNN Center provides views of Centennial Olympic Park and the downtown skyline. Fine Continental cuisine is blended with local and regional specialties. No smoking. $4–10.50 for breakfast, $12–23 for lunch, $10–44 for dinner.

& **Ruth's Chris Steak House** (404-223-6500 or 1-800-544-0808; www.ruthschris .com/locations/atlantasteakhouse.html), 267 Marietta Street, Centennial Olympic Park. Open 11–11 daily. Located in the Embassy Suites Hotel overlooking Centennial Olympic Park, the Atlanta incarnation of the world-famous restaurant chain serves aged USDA prime steaks as well as seafood, vegetarian choices, and other favorites accompanied by an exceptional wine list and classic desserts. No smoking. $24–44 (vegetarian $19).

& **Sun Dial Restaurant, Bar, and View** (404-589-7506; www.sundialrestaurant .com), 210 Peachtree Street NE. Open 11:30–2:30 daily, 6–10 Sunday–Thursday, 6–11 Friday, 5:30–11 Saturday. This trilevel revolving complex atop the Westin Peachtree Plaza hotel offers superb views of downtown as well as exquisite seasonally influenced contemporary American cuisine in the restaurant and wonderful jazz by the Mose Davis Trio in the bar. Visitors who are not customers of the restaurant or lounge may ride the glass elevators to the View level for $5, $3 for children 6–12. No smoking. Lunch $13–20, dinner $29–87, brunch $15–45.

In Midtown

& **Bacchanalia** (404-365-0410; www.star provisions.com/bacc), 1198 Howell Mill Road NW. Open 6–9:30 Monday–Saturday. One of the top restaurants in the city and certainly one of the most romantic, Bacchanalia serves lunch and an impeccable five-course, prix fixe dinner. Suave glamour is achieved in an old warehouse space where chef-spouses Clifford Harrison and Anne Quatrano blend cultural traditions as diverse as Californian nouvelle cuisine and Continental European dishes. No smoking. Dinner $85.

& **Einstein's** (404-876-7925; www.einsteins atlanta.com), 1077 Juniper Street NE. Open 11–11 Monday–Thursday, 11–midnight Friday, 9 AM–midnight Saturday, 9 AM–11 PM Sunday; bar open one hour past closing. Einstein's occupies a couple of bungalows just blocks from the arts district. Lunch and dinner choices range from salads and special sandwiches such as the jerk chicken or portobello and Brie melt to salads and hearty fare such as steaks and chops. Brunch, which is renowned for its famous martinis and Bloody Mary Bar, runs the gamut from French toast to steak and eggs. In good weather, dine outside on the tree-shaded patio, which has earned the restaurant the Best Outdoor Dining Experience in Atlanta from Creative Loafing. No smoking. Lunch $5–12, dinner $5–32, brunch $5–36.

& **Nan Thai Fine Dining** (404-870-9933; www.nanfinedining.com), 1350 Spring Street. Open 11–2:30 weekdays, 5:30–10 Monday–Thursday, 5:30–11 Friday, 5–11 Saturday, 5–10 Sunday. The decor in the soaring dining room follows the Thai zodiac. Cream banquettes, silk pillows in cream and mocha, and neutral carpet serve as a background for soaring red columns—and all of it combines to create a bold yet still understated look. Fancy ingredients such as duck, seafood, or lamb come in intricate presentations. The curries are especially noteworthy, and a chef's table at the exhibition kitchen provides a glimpse of culinary artistry. No smoking. $19–45.

& **Park 75 Restaurant** (404-253-3840; www.fourseasons.com/atlanta), 75 14th Street NE. Open for breakfast 6:30–11 Monday–Saturday, 7–10 Sunday; for lunch 11:30–2 Monday–Saturday; for tea 2–4 Saturday, 3–4 Sunday; for brunch 10–2 Sunday; and for dinner 6–10 Tuesday–Saturday. Afternoon tea reservations required 24 hours in advance. Located in the luxurious Four Seasons Hotel, the restaurant's ambience is a rich combination of styles and textures. What's more, it is described as "an opulent oasis and the best place in the world for Sunday brunch" by the Zagat restaurant survey. The New American cuisine is considered culinary art, from the sea scallops Rockefeller to the rack of spring meadow lamb. Tasting menus are available at a chef's table. No smoking. Reservations suggested for all meals. Breakfast $14–15, lunch $22, dinner $48, brunch $48, afternoon tea $32.

& **South City Kitchen** (404-873-7358; www.southcitykitchen.com), 1144 Crescent Avenue NE. Open 11–3:30 daily, 5–10 Monday–Thursday and Sunday, 5–10:30 Friday and Saturday. The Midtown restaurant is located in a renovated historic home near the Woodruff Arts Center and High Museum of Art. Not a faithful restoration, this remodeling involved gutting and opening up the interior to result in a sleek, steel-and-glass look with an open kitchen and a long, snazzy bar. Billed as "where the low country meets the high-rises," the South City Kitchen serves imaginative, nouvelle Southern cuisine with lowcountry and Southwestern influences. Some specialties include Charleston she-crab soup, buttermilk fried chicken, and grilled Georgia mountain trout. When the weather's warm and breezy, outdoor dining is popular. No smoking. Wheelchair accessible on the patio and ground floor; restrooms not wheelchair accessible. Lunch $14–21, brunch $8–19, dinner $15–36.

& **Veni Vidi Vici** (404-875-8424; www .buckheadrestaurants.com), 41 14th Street. Open for lunch 11:30–3 weekdays; dinner 3–10 Monday–Saturday, 5–10 Sunday. Reservations recommended. This northern Italian restaurant is the only fine-dining establishment we know of that's located in a parking garage. The restaurant, situated on the ground floor with a small outdoor area, is convenient to many of Midtown's soaring skyscrapers as well as to the Robert W. Woodruff Arts Center, making it perfect for preperformance dining. Sleek and sophisticated inside, Veni Vidi Vici serves entrées such as, salmon, beef, and veal, and rotisserie specialties such as suckling pig. Outdoor seating is available in good weather. No smoking. Entrées $19–34.

In Virginia-Highland

& **Babette's** (404-523-9121; www.babettes cafe.com), 573 North Highland Avenue. Open 5:30–10 Tuesday–Saturday, 5–9 Sunday; 10:30–2 Sunday for brunch. Babette's is a combination farmhouse and bistro located between Inman Park and Poncey-Highlands. Chef-owner Marla Adams creates dishes according to the seasons. The cuisine is a little French, Italian, Spanish, and Mediterranean. No smoking. Wheelchair accessible from a ramp on the side. Dinner entrées $15.50–27.50, brunch $8.50–12.

& **Sotto Sotto** (404-523-6678; www.sotto sottorestaurant.com), 313 North Highland Avenue. Open 5:30–11 Monday–Thursday, 5:30–midnight Friday and Saturday, 5:30–10 Sunday. This smashing Italian restaurant attracts a high-profile crowd to dine on a wide variety of antipasti and pasta. Check to see if one of the monthly "Tour of Italy" dinners is scheduled during your visit. Valet and street parking available. Nonsmoking area. Limited wheelchair accessibility. À la carte entrées $11–34; Chef's Choice three-, four-, or five-course dinners $40, $50, and $60.

EATING OUT

In Buckhead

& & & **Café Intermezzo** (404-355-0411; www.cafeintermezzo.com), 1845 Peachtree Road NE. Open 11 AM–2 AM Sunday–Thursday, 11 AM–3 AM Saturday. The Viennese-style café has a full menu of small plates, large plates, soups, salads, and sandwiches. But after a night out on the town attending the symphony or a play, it's a great place to stop in for a nightcap or coffee and dessert accompanied by live entertainment. Choose from 100 pastries, tarts, cakes, pies, and cheesecakes, as well as scores of coffee drinks, teas, beers, wines, and other alcoholic beverages. Lunch available until 5 PM; dinner until late night. No smoking. Breakfast $7–14.50, lunch and dinner $8–15, weekend brunch $6–8.

& & & **Eclipse di Luna** (404-846-0449; www.eclipsedeluna.com), 764 Miami Circle. Open 5–10 Monday, 11:30–10 Tuesday and

Wednesday, 11 AM–11:30 PM Thursday, 11:30–midnight Friday and Saturday, 5–10 Sunday. Latin American–, Spanish-, and Brazilian-influenced cuisine is presented in small, tapas-size portions. The artsy setting in an old warehouse creates a high-energy experience, as does the Sunday bottomless glass of sangria for $10. Live entertainment and a wine tasting on the first Tuesday of each month add to the ambience. No smoking. $2.25–6.95.

🍴 ♿ **Swan Coach House Restaurant, Gift Shop and Gallery** (404-261-0636; www.swancoachhouse.com), 3130 Sloan Drive. Open 11–2:30 Monday–Saturday. Just to the rear of the Atlanta History Center and reached by a separate entrance is the grand coach house–garage of the sumptuous Swan House mansion (see **Atlanta History Center** under *To See—Museums*). Magnificently restored and exquisitely decorated, the carriage house is a favorite place for ladies who lunch as well as for couples and families. Dine on brunch items, soups, salads, sandwiches, and desserts. By far, the most popular luncheon selection is the Swan's Favorite Chicken Salad accompanied by Frozen Fruit Salad and topped off with the French Silk Swans Dessert in the shape of a swan. Specialty drinks are served by the glass, pitcher, or punch bowl. The carriage house also has an upscale gift shop and art gallery open 10–4 Monday–Saturday. No smoking. $9–15.

In Candler Park

🍴 ✐ ♿ **Flying Biscuit Café** (404-687-8888; www.flyingbiscuit.com), 1655 McLendon Avenue. Open 7 AM–10 PM daily. Located in a cheerful and eclectically decorated Craftsman bungalow in the historic Candler Park neighborhood, the Flying Biscuit Café is the home of nonstop breakfast served all day, but the eatery also serves lunch and dinner. Breakfast includes everything from eggs to smoked salmon, and dishes are always accompanied by the famous biscuits. Lunch items include salads, sandwiches, burgers, and more. Dinner choices include salmon, chicken, and more. At the bakery next door, diners can purchase biscuits to take out. No smoking. Breakfast $7–12, lunch and dinner $8–15.

Downtown

🍴 ✐ **Busy Bee Cafe** (404-525-9212; www.thebusybeecafe.com), 810 Martin Luther King Jr. Drive SW. Open 11–7 Monday–Friday and Sunday; closed Saturday. For more than 50 years, locals have flocked to this soul-food café for the "beelicious" fried chicken, beef stew, and even chitlins, giblets, ham hocks, and neck bones. No smoking. Not wheelchair accessible. $10–15.

🍴 ✐ ♿ **Mary Mac's Tea Room** (404-876-1800; www.marymacs.com), 224 Ponce de Leon Avenue NE. Open 11–9 daily. A local favorite for more than 60 years, Mary Mac's is big on Southern hospitality and heaping helpings of comfort food. Diners pig out on fried chicken, chicken and dumplings, country-fried steak and gravy, fried catfish, meat loaf, turnip and other greens, fried green tomatoes, sweet potato soufflé, home-baked breads, banana pudding, bread pudding with wine sauce, and peach cobbler served with the table wine of the South: sweet tea. No smoking. Lunch $2–5.50, dinner $7.50–16.50.

In Little Five Points

🍴 ✐ ♿ **Front Page News** (404-475-7777; www.fpnnews.com), 351 Moreland Avenue NE. Open 11–11 Sunday–Tuesday, 11–midnight Wednesday, 11 AM–1 AM Thursday, 11 AM–2 AM Friday and Saturday. If you're looking for Cajun flavor and drinks galore, this is the place to come. Walls are covered with front-page newspaper clippings, but the ambience is more New Orleans–like. No smoking. See following entry for the location in Midtown. Entrées $8–15.

🍴 ♿ **The Vortex Bar and Grill** (404-688-1828; www.thevortexbarandgrill.com), 438 Moreland Avenue NE. Open 11 AM–midnight Sunday–Wednesday, 11 AM–3 AM Thursday–Saturday. For ages 18 and older only. The first hint a visitor has that this might not be a traditional restaurant is the giant skull with bulging eyes that creates the front of the building. Diners actually enter through the mouth of the skull. Once inside, they discover that this Atlanta institution serves high-quality pub food and a wide variety of alcoholic beverages. In fact, with 20 varieties of burgers, the eatery has earned the distinction of Atlanta's Best Burgers every year since 1992. There's another location in Midtown. Smoking and nonsmoking sections. $7–27.

In Midtown

♿ **Atmosphere** (678-702-1620; www .atmospherebistro.com), 1620 Piedmont Avenue. Open for brunch 11:30–2:30 Saturday and Sunday; for lunch 11:30–2:30 Tuesday–Friday; for dinner 6–10 Tuesday–Thursday, 6–10:30 Friday and Saturday, 6–9:30 Sunday. Reservations recommended on weekends. Located in a cottage near Ansley Mall, the French restaurant does bistro classics such as duck confit, escargot with white wine, rack of lamb, and salmon tartar, but don't decide what to order until you check out the specials. No smoking. Lunch $12–22, dinner $19–28, brunch $10–18.

♿ **Baraonda Café Italiano** (404-879-9962; www.baraondaatlanta.com), 710 Peachtree Street. Open 11–10:30 Monday–Thursday, noon–midnight Friday, 5–midnight Saturday, noon–10 Sunday. The house specialty at this friendly Italian eatery is thin Euro-style pizzas baked in an authentic wood-brick oven. In addition to pizzas, the eatery serves antipasti, *insalate,* calzone, pasta, and *secondi;* substantial entrées include lamb chops, veal scaloppine, and fish of the day. A plus to dining here is that the restaurant is within walking distance of the Fox Theatre. No smoking. Lunch $6–13, dinner $8–48, brunch $8–14.

♿ **Front Page News** (404-897-3500; www.fpnnews.com), 1104 Crescent Avenue. The presses start rolling at 11 AM for lunch or weekend brunch; the dinner edition goes until 11 PM, even later Wednesday–Saturday. With its brick courtyard, 12-foot-tall cast-iron fountains, flickering gaslights, and lush foliage, it's very reminiscent of New Orleans French Quarter eateries. FPN serves newsworthy Cajun- and Creole-influenced food as well as burgers, po'boys, sandwiches, salads, and fish

accompanied by microbrews, martinis, New Orleans–style Hurricanes, and other libations. No smoking. $8–15.

♿ **Joe's on Juniper** (404-875-6634; www.joesatlanta.com), 1049 Juniper Street NE. Open 11 AM–2 AM Monday–Saturday, 11–midnight Sunday; brunch until 3 PM Saturday and Sunday. A renovated historic cottage provides a home for Joe's, which purveys burgers, hot dogs, chili, soup, wings, munchies, salads, sandwiches, and desserts. The restaurant also serves brunch on weekends—here it is known as "blunch"—consisting of eggs Benedict, omelets, French toast, and other goodies. No smoking. $8–19, brunch $8–14.

♿ **ONE.midtown kitchen** (404-892-4111; www.onemidtownkitchen.com), 559 Dutch Valley Road. Open 5:30–10 PM daily, later Tuesday–Saturday. This hip eatery overlooking Piedmont Park attracts beautiful people, while the innovative and no-hype food focuses on the freshest ingredients and local products. No smoking. Less than $21.

♿ **The Varsity** (404-881-1706; www .thevarsity.com), 61 North Avenue NW. Open 10 AM–11:30 PM Sunday–Thursday, 10 AM–12:30 AM Friday and Saturday. This Varsity, the original, started out back in 1928 as a hangout for Georgia Tech students, but it grew to become the world's largest drive-in restaurant. Its parking lots and decks hold 600 cars, and there's room for 800 people inside at any one time. The menu is topped with chili dogs, onion rings, fried pies, and the eatery's famous Frosted Orange drink but also includes burgers, BBQ, chicken salad, ham salad, fries, and coleslaw. Diners can enjoy the luxury of curb service or go inside, but know what you want—carhops and counter workers don't brook any lollygagging. After all, they have to keep things moving to dispense 2 miles of franks, 300 gallons of chili, 2,000 pounds of onions, and 5,000 fried pies to 12,000 to 15,000 customers each day—30,000 on game days. So when they say "What'll ya have, what'll ya have, what'll ya have?" make sure to have your answer ready. Be sure to peruse the memorabilia and photos of all the famous people who've eaten here. No smoking. Wheelchair accessible downstairs. Under $5.

In Virginia-Highland

❦ ♿ **Atkins Park** (404-876-7249; www .atkinspark.com), 794 North Highland Avenue. Open 11 AM–3 AM Monday–Saturday, 11 AM–midnight Sunday. Atlanta's oldest continuously licensed restaurant and bar, Atkins Park has been serving food and drink since 1922. The Creole-influenced menu features gumbo, jambalaya, and po'boys. Although bar grub—including ample appetizers and bulging sandwiches—is served until the wee hours, full dinner service ends at 11 on weeknights and midnight on weekends. Smoking in the bar area only. Lunch $7–12, dinner $9–22, brunch $8–12.

❦ **George's Bar and Restaurant** (404-892-3648; www.georgesbarandrestaurant .com), 1041 North Highland Avenue NE. Open for lunch and dinner daily and until late night Wednesday–Saturday. Located here since 1961, the down-home neighborhood pub serves burgers, hot dogs, and finger foods such as chicken fingers. The decor features 1960s-era booths, sports memorabilia, and video games. Smoking at the bar only. Not wheelchair accessible. $7–11.

❦ ♿ **Manuel's Tavern** (404-525-3447; www.manuelstavern.com), 602 North Highland Avenue. Open 11 AM–2 AM Tuesday–Saturday, 11 AM–midnight Sunday and Monday; brunch until 3 PM Saturday and Sunday. This venerable Atlanta institution founded in 1956 by the late Manuel Maloof is now run by his family. Above-average bar fare includes wings, hot dogs, burgers, and other simple grub. Wide-screen televisions allow diners to watch the Atlanta Braves, other favorite sports teams, and CNN. Manuel's also hosts Atlanta's longest-running improvisational group, Laughing Matters, on the first Saturday each month. Designated smoking areas for over 18 only; the rest is nonsmoking. $7–16.

❦ ♿ **Murphy's** (404-872-0904; www .murphys-atlanta-restaurant.com), 997 Virginia Avenue. Open 11–10 Monday–Thursday, 11–11 Friday, 8 AM–midnight Saturday, 8 AM–10 PM Sunday; brunch until 4 PM Saturday and Sunday. Limited reservations accepted; call-ahead seating available for dinner only. Complimentary valet parking offered every evening after 5. A perennial favorite in the epicenter of the Virginia-Highland shopping and nightlife district, Murphy's has a jazzy new design and an ambitious menu. The community bistro is the ideal amalgamation of upscale comfort food, unassuming service, an inviting high-energy ambience, and good prices. The cuisine is described as contemporary American. The recent renovation made room for a sophisticated martini and wine bar, a bakery, and a retail wine shop where weekly wine tastings and seminars are held. No smoking. Limited wheelchair accessibility. Lunch $10–15, dinner $16–23, brunch $4.50–15.

✳ Entertainment

DANCE **Atlanta Ballet, Atlanta Ballet Centre for Dance Education** (404-873-5811 or 404-892-3303; www.atlantaballet .com), office: 1695 Marietta Boulevard NW. Office open 10–5 weekdays. Founded in 1929, the Atlanta Ballet is the oldest continuously running dance company in the nation. The company performs classic works and children's stories at various venues including the Cobb Energy Center, and the annual *Nutcracker* at the Fox Theatre. Check the website or call for a schedule of performances and ticket prices.

MUSIC **Atlanta Opera** (tickets: 404-881-8801; 404-881-8801; www.atlantaopera.org), office: 1575 Northside Drive, Suite 350. Box office open 9–5 weekdays. The group produces four fully staged grand operas annually at the Cobb Energy Center. Check the website or call for a schedule of performances and ticket prices.

Atlanta Symphony Orchestra (404-733-5000 or 404-733-4900; www.atlanta symphony.org), office: 1280 Peachtree Street NE. Started in 1945, the symphony is relatively young to have achieved such international prominence under the batons of maestros Robert Shaw, Yoel Levi, and Robert Spano. The symphony performs a classical season, a pops series, several family and holiday concerts, and performances by the Atlanta Youth Orchestra, all in the Woodruff Arts Center's Symphony Hall. The symphony also performs an outdoor summer series at Chastain Park Amphitheater and the Verizon Wireless Amphitheatre at Encore Park in Alpharetta, as well as several other free community concerts around Atlanta. Check the website or call for a schedule of performances and ticket prices.

Capitol City Opera Company (678-301-8013; www.ccityopera.com), office: 1266 West Paces Ferry Road NW, Suite 451. The opera company produces two or three main operas each year, as well as children's programs and monthly "Dinner and a Diva" shows at local restaurants. Check the website or call for a schedule of performances and ticket prices.

Center Stage and The Loft (404-885-1365; www.centerstage-atlanta), 1374 West Peachtree Street. This venue with stadium-style seating presents the very latest in musical acts. Check the website or call for a schedule of performances and ticket prices. Parking available free–$10 per car depending on the show.

& **Chastain Park Amphitheater** (information: 404-733-4900; tickets: 404-733-5000; www.classicchastain.com), 4469 Stella Drive NW. Atlanta's favorite outdoor venue is the site of summer concerts with big-name entertainers almost every night of the week. The section right in front of the stage has tables for six; in the rest of the facility folks bring their own TV tables. In either case, concertgoers bring colorful table linens, dinnerware, wine goblets, floral arrangements, candles, and, of course, an elegant picnic dinner. Instead of bringing their own picnic, visitors can reserve an elegant repast from Affairs to Remember (404-872-7859) or Proof of the Pudding (404-892-2359), and their order will be delivered to the park. In addition, light fare and even flowers and candles can be purchased at the park. Limited smoking.

Check the website or call for a schedule of events and ticket prices.

Tabernacle (404-659-9022; www.tabernacle atl.com), 152 Luckie Street NW. This historical landmark is a must-see entertainment complex. The decor alone is worth seeing. The former sanctuary is the main performance room where acts such as Lenny Kravitz, Smashing Pumpkins, Kid Rock, Lynyrd Skynyrd, Elvis Costello, and Willie Nelson have performed. Check the website or call for a schedule of performances and ticket prices (usually $25–45). Tickets available through Ticketmaster (404-249-6400) and at all Ticketmaster locations. The box office sells tickets only on the night of a performance, which might lead to disappointment in the event of a sold-out show.

NIGHTLIFE & **Andrews Upstairs** (404-869-1132; www.andrewsupstairs.com), 56 East Andrews Drive NW, Suite 10. Open 5 PM–2 AM Thursday, 5 PM–2:30 AM Friday and Saturday; Sunday through Wednesday only if there are special events. The upscale Buckhead music and entertainment venue (formerly the Celebrity Rock Café) features live regional and national music acts, late-night dancing with Atlanta's hottest DJs, and comedy acts. Smoking in designated areas. Also on the premises: cocktails at the main bar, tapas at **Cellar 56,** the **Stout Irish Sports Pub,** nightcaps at **Prohibition,** late snacks at **Sal's Pizzeria.** Dance to the tunes of a DJ in the domed courtyard. Check the website or call for a schedule and ticket prices.

& **Beluga** (404-869-1090), 3115 Piedmont Road NE. Open 4 PM–3 AM weekdays, 8 PM–3 AM Saturday. Buckhead's Beluga has been rated the Best Piano Bar by *Atlanta Magazine.* Billed as "drinks, dancing and debauchery," the club features 17 types of martinis and live music six nights a week. Smoking permitted; cigar friendly. No cover charge.

& **Blind Willie's** (404-873-2583; www.blindwilliesblues.com), 828 North Highland Avenue. Open Monday–Saturday beginning at 7 PM; music starts at 9:30.

Named for Thomson, Georgia, native "Blind Willie" McTell, whose "Statesboro Blues" was made popular by the Allman Brothers Band, this world-renowned bar showcases New Orleans– and Chicago-style blues. Cajun and zydeco are sometimes featured, and Cajun-style bar food is served. Smoking permitted. Cover charge $3–15.

🍴 ♿ **Churchill Grounds** (404-876-3030; www.churchillgrounds.com), 660 Peachtree Street NE. Tuesday through Sunday, the doors to the club's Whisper Room open at 9 PM for shows at 9:30 and 11:30. This intimate and sophisticated coffee shop offers much more than just java. In fact, it's considered one of Atlanta's premier jazz clubs. Those with a hunger for more than music can satisfy those cravings with light fare, espresso, cappuccino, and desserts. Smoking allowed only in a very small area in the back of the performance room. Check the website or call for a schedule of performances. Cover charge $7–15, plus $5–10 minimum.

🍴 **Dante's Down the Hatch** (404-266-1600; www.dantesdownthehatch.com), 3380 Peachtree Road NE. Open at 4 daily, except 5 Sunday; live music 6–11 Monday, 7–11 Tuesday–Thursday, 6–midnight Friday and Saturday, 7–11 Sunday. Ahoy, mateys! For a unique experience, descend into an 18th-century sailing ship anchored in a mythical Mediterranean village surrounded by a moat where live crocodiles lurk. Feast on fondue while listening to some of Atlanta's best live jazz, acoustic guitar, or vocalists. *Atlanta Magazine* has rated Dante's the place for the best live jazz in town. For a special treat, make reservations two nights in advance for the chocolate fondue. No smoking. Wheelchair accessible on the wharf but not on the ship. Cover charge $7 to sit on the ship weekdays, $8 weekends; no cover on the wharf.

🍴 ♿ **Euclid Avenue Yacht Club** (404-688-2582; www.theeayc.com), 1136 Euclid Avenue NE. Open 3 PM–2 AM Monday–Thursday, from noon Friday and Saturday. This Little Five Points neighborhood bar is always packed to the rafters with students,

regulars, bikers, and visitors. Activities include trivia nights, poker nights, and Pajamarama Fridays October–March. This is a smoking bar. No cover charge.

♿ **Fadó Irish Pub** (404-841-0066; www.fadoirishpub.com), 273 Buckhead Avenue. Open 11:30 AM–2 AM Monday–Thursday, 11 AM–3 AM Friday and Saturday, 10:30 AM–midnight Sunday. Fadó is the No. 2 seller of Guinness in America, and the eatery's warm, welcoming ambience is a rarity in frenetic Buckhead. Irish pub grub such as corned beef and cabbage, traditional Irish music, international soccer on television, and other fun complete the package. No smoking allowed. No cover charge.

♿ **Johnny's Hideaway** (404-233-8026; www.johnnyshideaway.com), 3771 Roswell Road. Open from 11 AM until the wee hours of the morning Monday–Saturday, from noon Sunday. The club is definitely popular with the older crowd, as is evidenced by the Sinatra Room and the King's Corner (Elvis, of course). It's all about the drinking and the dancing to live and recorded music, but light fare such as salads, entrées, and desserts are served. Smoking allowed. No cover charge, but there's a two-drink minimum.

♿ **Kenny's Alley at Underground Atlanta** (404-523-2311; www.underground-atlanta.com), 50 Upper Alabama Street SW. Occupying a wing at Underground Atlanta, Kenny's Alley features four nightclubs and restaurants that offer high-energy dance music, rock and roll, and reggae. This is the only place in Atlanta where patrons can carry a drink from bar to bar until 4 AM.

🍴 ♿ **Limerick Junction Irish Pub** (404-874-7147; www.limerickjunction.com), 822 North Highland Avenue. Entertainment 5 PM–1 AM Monday–Wednesday, until 2 AM Thursday–Saturday, until midnight Sunday. Atlanta's oldest Irish pub features traditional Irish music nightly. Tuesday is comedy night. Guinness and Harp are on tap, and hearty pub food is served. Parking is a big problem, so you might want to take a taxi. Smoking permitted. Cover charge $3 Friday and Saturday only.

♿ **The Masquerade** (404-577-8178; www.masq.com), 695 North Avenue. Open Wednesday–Saturday nights until 3:30 or 4 AM. The trilevel club (the levels are Heaven, Hell, and Purgatory) is located in an old warehouse in Little Five Points. Entertainment runs to heavy metal and punk bands. Smoking allowed. Wheelchair accessible, but crowding could make it very difficult to navigate. Show charges $8–35. For multiday events, special two- and three-day passes available.

♿ **Tongue and Groove** (404-261-2325; www.tongueandgrooveonline.com), 565 Main Street in Lindbergh City Center in Buckhead. Open 10 PM–2:30 AM Monday, 9 PM–2:30 AM Wednesday–Saturday. Weekend nights feature a DJ playing top 40 hits, hip-hop and R&B are played on Monday, and Latin music is played on Wednesday nights with free salsa lessons. The high-energy crowd is 21 to 40-plus. Smoking permitted. Wheelchair accessible on the Peachtree Road side. Cover charge $10 and up.

♿ **Variety Playhouse** (404-524-7354; www.variety-playhouse.com), 1099 Euclid Avenue. Located in Little Five Points, Variety Playhouse is a combination theater and nightclub with a mixture of theater seating, tables and chairs, and dancing and standing areas. It therefore presents a wide variety of entertainment—primarily live concerts. No smoking. Check the website or call for a schedule of events and ticket prices. All shows are general admission.

PROFESSIONAL SPORTS

♿ **Atlanta Braves** (tickets: 1-800-745-5000; www.atlanta.braves.mlb.com; Braves tickets www.braves.com/tickets), 755 Hank Aaron Drive. The major-league Atlanta Braves baseball team plays at **Turner Field** (see *To See—Guided Tours*). For transportation to the stadium, see the MARTA **Braves Stadium Shuttle** described in *Getting Around.* There are 200 "skyline" (we translate this as "nosebleed") seats along the far ends of the upper deck. Those adventurous enough to take a chance on waiting until two hours before game time

might snare one of them for $1. Check the website or call for a schedule of games and ticket prices.

♿ **Atlanta Dream** (1-877-977-7729; www.wnba.com/dream/frontoffice), office: 225 Peachtree Street NE, Peachtree Center, Suite 2400. The Women's NBA team plays at Phillips Arena. Check the website or call for a schedule and ticket prices. Single game tickets $7–105.

♿ **Atlanta Falcons** (770-965-3115; tickets: 404-223-8444 or 1-855-222-FANA; www.atlantafalcons.com), One Georgia Dome Drive. The National Football League's Atlanta Falcons play at the **Georgia Dome** (see *To See—Guided Tours*). Check the website or call for a schedule of games and ticket prices. Single game tickets $55–180.

♿ **Atlanta Hawks** (1-866-715-1500; www.nba.com/hawks), One Philips Drive. The National Basketball Association's Atlanta Hawks play at Philips Arena. Check the website or call for a schedule of games and ticket prices. Single game tickets $19–174.

SUMMER THEATER ♿ **Georgia Shakespeare Festival** (404-504-1473; www.gashakespeare.org), 4484 Peachtree Road. When driving up Peachtree Road in Buckhead, castle- and battlement-like structures, fluttering flags, and a cheery, circular, yellow and white tentlike building come as a complete surprise. These out-of-place and out-of-time buildings make up Oglethorpe University. Located on the grounds of the university, the flags and tentlike building announce the **Conant Performing Arts Center,** home of the Georgia Shakespeare Festival. In midsummer and in October, the Bard's classics, comedies, and opuses come to life along with works by other playwrights. Eat, drink, and be merry by picnicking before the show with catered meals or your own from home. No smoking. Check the website or call for a schedule of performances and ticket prices.

THEATER ♿ **Actor's Express Theatre Company/King Plow Arts Center**

(404-607-7469; box office: 404-875-1606; www.actorsexpress.com), 887 West Marietta Street NW, Suite J-107. Office open 10–6 weekdays. Located in a renovated plow factory, the troupe produces six main-stage shows each year, often reflecting original works and perspectives particular to Atlanta. No smoking. Check the website or call for a schedule of performances and ticket prices.

♿ **Agatha's—A Taste of Mystery** (information: 404-584-2211; reservations: 404-584-2255; www.agathas.com), 161 Peachtree Center Avenue. Shows at 8 Friday, 7:30 Saturday, 6 Sunday. Participants are asked to arrive 15–30 minutes early. Reservations must be made by phone. Named for—who else?—Agatha Christie, the queen of mystery writers, this campy interactive dinner theater unfolds a mystery during a five-course dinner. Always a farce with humor ranging from lowbrow to literate, the performance is presented by several actors with help from audience members. Shows run for 13 weeks, so you could go back numerous times throughout the year and see different shows. No smoking. $62 Sunday and Friday, $64.50 Saturday. Parking $5 with a ticket stub.

♿ **Alliance Theatre Company** (box office: 404-658-7159; www.alliancetheatre.org), Woodruff Arts Center, 1280 Peachtree Street. Check the website or call for a schedule of performances and ticket prices. The Southeast's premier professional theater and one of the nation's largest regional theater companies presents 10 productions yearly, including classic dramas, comedies, contemporary plays, musicals, and regional and world premieres. All are performed in its main theater, the more intimate Hertz Stage in the same building, or in the nearby 14th Street Playhouse. No smoking.

♿ **Boisfeuillet Jones Atlanta Civic Center** (404-523-6275; www.atlantaciviccenter.com), 395 Piedmont Avenue NE. Named for a prominent Atlanta philanthropist, the civic center hosts many diverse productions, including concerts, comedy, and gospel. As the largest stage in the Southeast, the center attracts big productions

such as *Miss Saigon.* The center also provides space for large traveling exhibitions such as *King Tut: The Exhibition, Titanic: The Artifact Exhibition,* and *Diana: A Celebration.* Check the website or call for a schedule of events and ticket prices. No smoking.

♿ **Buckhead Theatre** (404-843-2825; www.thebucktheatre.com), 3110 Roswell Road. This fine old restored building in Buckhead was built as a movie theater in 1931 in the Spanish Baroque style. After several incarnations and names, it serves today as an intimate venue for plays, national touring musical acts and comedians, as well as regional and local bands. Check the website or call for a schedule of performances and ticket prices. No smoking.

♿ **Center for Puppetry Arts** (office: 404-873-3089; tickets: 404-873-3391; www.puppet.org), 1404 Spring Street NW. Day and evening performances. The center (see *To See—Museums*) produces numerous children's and adult shows throughout the year. Check the website or call for a schedule of performances. $16.50.

♿ **Ferst Center for the Arts at Georgia Tech** (404-894-9600; www.ferstcenter.org), 349 Ferst Drive NW. Box office open 9–7 weekdays, 10–5 Saturday. This venue features an outstanding selection of concerts, recitals, dance, film, opera, music, and theater from September through May. The center is also the performance venue for **Atlantic Lyric Theatre, Ballethnic Dance Company,** the **Atlanta Gay Men's Chorus,** and numerous one-time events. Check the website or call for a schedule of performances and ticket prices. In addition, the facility houses the **Richards and Westbrook Galleries,** which display visual arts by a wide spectrum of artists. No smoking.

♿ **Fox Theatre** (404-881-2000; www.foxtheatre.org), 660 Peachtree Street NE. Box office open 10–6 weekdays, 10–3 Saturday, only on performance Sundays. Originally planned to be the Yaarab Temple Shrine Mosque in 1929, the theater was lavishly designed with Moorish, Egyptian, and art deco influences to reflect the then-recent discovery of King Tut's tomb in 1922. It then became a movie palace for 40 years. The threat of demolition in the 1970s to make room for a parking deck galvanized the local citizenry to form Landmarks, Inc., which saved and restored the theater, now known affectionately as the Fabulous Fox. To date $37 million has been spent on the restoration. Today the magnificent 4,500-seat performance venue, which is designated a National Historic Landmark and a Georgia Museum Building, hosts a wide variety of events, from movies to traveling Broadway shows to ballet to rock concerts. Among the premier series are the Delta International Series, Broadway Across Atlanta, and Theater of the Stars. A tribute to the Fox's movie-palace heritage is the

THE RESTORED FOX THEATRE IN DOWNTOWN ATLANTA, AFFECTIONATELY KNOWN AS THE FABULOUS FOX, HOSTS A VARIETY OF EVENTS THROUGHOUT THE YEAR.

Summer Film Festival, a popular series of classic and contemporary films. For a more in-depth tour, the Atlanta Preservation Society offers tours of the theater on Monday and Thursday mornings and twice on Saturday (see *To See—Guided Tours*). No smoking. Check the website or call for a schedule of performances and ticket prices.

&. The New American Shakespeare Tavern (404-874-5299; www.shakespeare tavern.com), 499 Peachtree Street NE. Box office open 1–6 Tuesday–Saturday, 3–5 Sunday. Performances at 7:30 Thursday–Saturday, 6:30 Sunday. Dinner is available from one hour and 15 minutes before the show until five minutes before the show. After dining on British pub food such as Cornish pasty, gobble, the King's Supper, or shepherd's pie accompanied by Irish ales and premium wines, enjoy the Elizabethan scenery, Renaissance and medieval costumes, and live acoustic music, all of which enhance the boisterous action of one of the Bard's plays. The tavern also performs original works, variety shows, and classics by other playwrights. No smoking. Wheelchair accessible from the entrance behind the building, but balcony not wheelchair accessible. Tickets $15–36. Check the website or call for a schedule and specific ticket prices. Ask about discounts and special programs. Dinner prices ($5.25–10.25) are in addition to tickets for the play, so it's possible to purchase tickets to the play only. Seating is on a first-come, first-served basis. Table seating is limited, but all seats can accommodate food and beverages.

Rialto Center for the Arts at Georgia State University (404-413-9TIX; www .rialtocenter.org), 80 Forsyth Street. Box office open 10–4:30 weekdays. This lovely historic movie theater in the Fairlie-Poplar Historic District has been fully restored and hosts international musical artists as well as theatrical and dance performances. Check the website or call for a schedule of events and ticket prices.

Seven Stages Theater (404-522-0911; box office: 404-523-7647; www.7stages.org), 1105 Euclid Avenue NE. This avant-garde, cutting-edge theater in Little Five Points presents plays that delve into the social, political, and spiritual values of contemporary issues. Call for a schedule of performances and ticket prices.

Theatrical Outfit (678-528-1500; www .TheatricalOutfit.org), 84 Luckie Street. The longtime Atlanta theatrical organization got a new home in 2004, the intimate 200-seat Balzer Theater located in the old Herren's restaurant space next door to the Rialto. Productions run the gamut from comedy to drama to musicals to one-person shows. Check the website or call for a schedule of performances and ticket prices.

✷ Selective Shopping

A shopper's mecca, Buckhead boasts 1,400 upscale retail shops. In addition, two of Atlanta's premier shopping malls are located in the heart of Buckhead. Between the two malls, shoppers can visit 350 trendy stores and numerous restaurants. A shuttle service whisks shoppers from one mall to another.

First there's upscale **Lenox Square** (404-233-6767; www.lenoxsquare.com), 3393 Peachtree Road NE. Open 10–9 Monday–Saturday, noon–6 Sunday (restaurants, bars, and cinemas are open longer). The largest mall in the Southeast features a Neiman Marcus, Bloomingdale's, Louis Vuitton, and Brooks Brothers, among many others. Then there's posh **Phipps Plaza** (404-261-7910; www.phippsplaza.com), 3500 Peachtree Road NE. Open 10–9 Monday–Saturday, noon–5:30 Sunday (restaurants, bars, and cinemas open longer). This swanky mall features a Sak's Fifth Avenue, Gucci, Giorgio Armani, Jimmy Choo, Barneys New York CO-OP, Nordstrom, and Tiffany & Co., among others

Visitors looking for the perfect antiques, works of art, or home accessories need look no further than Buckhead, which has several major interior decorator districts.

Atlanta Decorative Arts Center (404-231-1720 or 1-888-568-ADAC; www.adac atlanta.com), 349 and 351 Peachtree Hills Avenue, is primarily wholesale (a business license and a tax ID number are required

for entrance), but the facility is open to members of the public who are accompanied by a designer and for occasional sales and seminars.

BOOKS A Cappella Books (404-681-5128 or 1-866-681-5128; www.acappella books.com), 484-C Moreland Avenue NE. Open 11–8 Monday–Saturday, noon–7 Sunday. Shop in this Little Five Points store for new, used, and out-of-print books, including Beat literature, progressive and counterculture subjects, and books about music. Check the website or call for a schedule of appearances by national authors.

FOOD Star Provisions (404-365-0410; www.starprovisions.com), 1198 Howell Mill Road. Open 10–8 Monday–Saturday. This Midtown cook's market is owned by the masterminds behind Bacchanalia (see *Dining Out—In Midtown*) and Floataway Café. You'll find everything here, from restaurant-quality cookware and gadgets to seasonal tableware and linens to gourmet food products such as A-grade foie gras, $100 bottles of vinegar, ahi tuna, and 200 varieties of cheese (most of which are available to taste).

Sweet Auburn Curb Market (404-659-1665; www.sweetauburncurbmarket.com), 209 Edgewood Avenue SE. Open 8–6 Monday–Saturday. Built as an outdoor marketplace in 1918, the market moved indoors in 1924. Today you can buy not only fresh meat, fish, and produce from local and organic farms, but also African and Caribbean foods, African clothing, cell phones, flowers, hair-care products, and prescription drugs.

SPECIAL SHOPS Junkman's Daughter Alternative Superstore (404-577-3188; www.thejunkmansdaughter.com), 464 Moreland Avenue. Open 11–8 Monday–Friday, 11–9 Saturday, noon–7 Sunday. Located in the heart of Little Five Points, this fun, funky alternative shop, which has been named among the 25 Best Independent Stores in America, carries inexpensive club clothing—often leather and often embellished with chains and studs—and other off-the-wall and utterly tacky items. Climb the stairway encased in a 20-foot-tall red high heel to check out the shoe department on the mezzanine.

✳ Special Events

January: **King Week** (404-526-8961; www .thekingcenter.org). Check the website or call for a schedule of events and prices. The weeklong event, sponsored by the **Martin Luther King Jr. Center for Nonviolent Social Change** (see *To See—Historic Homes and Sites*), produces live performances, religious and inspirational concerts, international speakers, and educational seminars at various venues around the city to honor Nobel Laureate Martin Luther King Jr.

March: **St. Patrick's Day Family Festival** (404-523-2311; www.stpatsatlanta.com). The event, which takes place over three days at **Underground Atlanta** (see *To See—Historic Homes and Sites*), features live traditional Irish music and performances by Celtic rock bands, Irish dance contests, children's activities, Irish food and beverages, and unique Irish vendors. The festival ends with the **St. Patrick's Day Parade**. Free.

April: **Atlanta Dogwood Festival** (404-817-6642; www.dogwood.org). Spring in Atlanta is heralded with a three-day art and music festival in Midtown's **Piedmont Park** (see *Green Space—Nature Preserves and Parks*). The fun includes kids' village activities, entertainment, and an artist's market. The ever-popular **U.S. Disc Dog Southern Nationals,** hosted by the Greater Atlanta Dog and Disc Club, features demonstrations and competitions Friday and Saturday. Free admission; fee for some activities.

Late April: **Inman Park Festival and Tour of Homes** (770-242-4895; www .inmanparkfestival.org). This festival, held anually since 1971, consists of the city's largest street market, a juried arts-and-crafts show, a tour of historic Victorian homes, live entertainment, children's activi-

ties, a funky parade, and a wide variety of food and beverages. Free for festival; fee for tour of homes.

May: **Atlanta Jazz Festival** (404-546-6820; www.atlantafestivals.com). An international roster of artists performs throughout May in numerous venues around the city. The celebration culminates with a three-day festival at **Piedmont Park** (see *Green Space—Nature Preserves and Parks*). The majority of events are free and open to the public. Check the website or call for a schedule of events.

National Black Arts Festival (404-730-7315; www.nbaf.org). The 10-day festival celebrates the creative contributions of people of African descent through visual arts, music, theater, and dance in venues all over the city. Associated events occur throughout the year. Check the website or call for a schedule of events and ticket prices.

Sweet Auburn SpringFest (www. sweet auburn.com/springfest2005). Held 5–9 Friday, 11–9 Saturday, 2–8 Sunday. Activities include live performances on 10 stages, the Fantastic Fun Zone for kids, Technology Expo, International Craft Market, the Sweet Auburn Film Festival, and more. Check the website for a schedule of events. Free; some activities have a fee.

December: **Chick-fil-A Bowl and Parade** (404-586-8496; www.chick-fil-abowl.com). Prior to the Chick-fil-A Bowl, more than 30 bands; classic cars; giant helium balloons; floats; participating team presidents, bands, cheerleaders, and mascots; and the Chick-fil-A cows parade down Peachtree Street. After the parade, the NCAA football bowl game begins at the **Georgia Dome** (see *To See—Guided Tours*). Thirty activities connected with the game occur the week prior. The annual event sells out before the teams are even selected, so book early to avoid disappointment.

Children's Health Care of Atlanta Christmas Parade (404-785-NOEL for recorded information; www.choa.org /support-childrens/events/ChristmasParade -Main). Parade 10–noon (televised live on WSB-TV Channel 2—ABC). The parade consists of marching bands, costumed dogs, antique cars, dance groups, holiday-themed floats, giant helium-balloon characters, specialty groups, clowns, and the grand finale: the arrival of Santa and Mrs. Claus (who coincidentally are portrayed by your authors). Free; bleacher seats $12.

Holiday in Lights (404-223-4412; www .centennialpark.com). Open 7–11 daily. Mid-November through December, **Centennial Olympic Park** (see *Green Space—Nature Preserves and Parks*) is decked out with millions of lights that create lighted scenes. As an extra-special treat, an outdoor ice skating rink provides hours of entertainment for Southerners not used to this activity. Skating hours 4:30–10 weekdays, 10 AM–11 PM Saturday, 10–10 Sunday. Free for park and lights display; $7 for skating, $2 for rentals.

New Year's Eve Peach Drop (404-523-2311; www.underground-atlanta.com). Held at **Underground Atlanta** (see *To See— Historic Homes and Sites*), the annual midnight drop of the 800-pound peach is preceded by entertainment and activities, and followed by a fireworks display and more live performances. Family-oriented activities begin at noon. Free.

MCDONOUGH, HAMPTON, JACKSON, AND LOCUST GROVE

McDonough, now known as "the Geranium City," was incorporated in 1823, two years after Chief William McIntosh of the Creek Indian Nation stood on a large rock at Indian Springs and signed a treaty giving the state of Georgia all rights to the Creek territory between the Ocmulgee and Flint rivers. Henry County was created from these lands and was named for statesman and orator Patrick Henry. Eventually, five counties were carved out of Henry County, earning it the sobriquet "Mother of Counties."

Because this was a highly productive area of Georgia, it was important to the Confederacy. That significance put it high on William Tecumseh Sherman's list to be destroyed by Union troops on the March to the Sea. During Reconstruction, cotton came into importance and prosperity returned.

McDonough grew and thrived until 1843, when it was bypassed by the railroad. In recent years, Pennsylvanian Bob Oglevee was instrumental in getting Oglevee Products to set up a nursery in McDonough to test their hot-weather geraniums. The company offered to plant hundreds of geraniums in the town square, and the town agreed. The City Council then had McDonough recognized as "the Geranium City," and it now hosts a Geranium Festival on the courthouse square, one of metro Atlanta's most popular events. The landscaped square around the 1897 Romanesque-style courthouse boasts ancient oaks and a Confederate monument. Surrounding the square are bustling specialty shops, antiques stores, and boutiques.

McDonough makes a good base of operations for exploring the surrounding area and small towns that are rich in attractions, historical sites, sporting venues, outdoor pursuits, and special events. Easy access to I-75 gives visitors the convenience of going into Atlanta or Macon as well. Venture onto the back roads to see rolling green pastures, quiet leafy woodlands, serene lakes, and quaint towns.

GUIDANCE When planning a trip to the McDonough area, contact the **McDonough Hospitality and Tourism Bureau–McDonough Welcome Center** (770-898-3196 or 1-866-380-6154; www.tourmcdonough.com), 5 Griffin Street, McDonough 30253. Open 8–4 weekdays, 10–4 Saturday. Stop at the 1920s prototype Standard Oil gas station for local tourism information and admire the black 1920 Model T Ford waiting for a fill-up at the hand-cranked gas pumps. Pick up the brochure *Historic Sites of McDonough, Georgia* for a walking-driving tour. For more information about the area, including Hampton and Locust Grove, consult the **Henry County Chamber of Commerce, Convention and Visitors Bureau and Welcome Center** (770-957-5786 or 1-800-HENRYCO; www.henrycounty .com), 1709 GA 20 West, McDonough 30253. Open 8–4 weekdays.

GETTING THERE *By air:* The area is served by **Hartsfield-Jackson Atlanta International Airport.** For airport, airline, and car rental information, see "What's Where in Georgia."

By bus: The nearest station is in Atlanta (see "What's Where in Georgia").

By car: Most of the towns described in this chapter are easily accessed from I-75 south of Atlanta.

By train: **AMTRAK** (see "What's Where in Georgia"). The nearest station is in Atlanta.

GETTING AROUND In addition to car rentals at the airport, car rentals are available from **Enterprise** (678-432-0130), 444 Industrial Boulevard, McDonough. Public transportation is available from **Xpress** (see "What's Where in Georgia"). The service provides an easy-to-use connection to downtown Atlanta, where passengers can transfer to the MARTA bus/rail system, from Hampton and McDonough.

MEDICAL EMERGENCY Call 911.

VILLAGES When the railroad bypassed McDonough, **Hampton,** then known as Bear Creek because two surveyors had seen two bears in a tree there, profited from being on the Central of Georgia route. The center of all business activity in the area, the town shipped all the cotton for the surrounding counties. It wasn't unusual to see hundreds of wagons lining the roads, waiting to be unloaded. The town changed its name in 1873 to honor Civil War hero Gen. Wade Hampton of South Carolina. Hampton's historic railroad depot, circa 1881, was constructed with fireproof brick—both an innovation and an extravagance in the 1880s—and is graced with ornate brick detailing in several patterns. Today, Hampton is best known as the home of races at the **Atlanta Motor Speedway,** which draw more visitors than any other sporting event in Georgia. Beautiful historic homes and ancient oaks line the streets. In the spring, dazzling daylilies line the streets, too.

Indian Springs–Flovilla is noted as the site where an infamous Indian treaty was signed. The Indian Springs Hotel, which was built around 1822, even before the community was founded, was owned by Chief William McIntosh. Tours are offered during special events. **Indian Springs State Park** is the oldest state park in the nation.

Jackson, the county seat of Butts County, was incorporated in 1826. The courthouse, which was built in 1898 (Union troops had burned its predecessor in 1864), has Victorian architectural elements, marble floors, and an intact courtroom. The courthouse is open to the public when court is not in session. The most imposing home in Jackson, indeed in most of Georgia, is the Queen Anne–style Carmichael House on Second Street, which was built by a buggy builder in 1897 for the then-astronomical price of $16,000. It remained in the Carmichael family until the 1990s. Although it is a private home, art festivals and other events are often held on the lawns. Jackson's new brick sidewalks, light fixtures, planters, and refurbished storefronts combine to create an inviting atmosphere. Butts County's oldest restaurant, Fresh Air Barbecue, has been run by members of the same family since 1929. Jackson also hosts several annual events: the **Scot-**

COTTON WAS IMPORTANT IN THE EARLY DAYS OF MCDONOUGH AND SURROUNDING AREAS.

tish Festival in April, the **Native American Festival** in September, the **Civil War Days** in November.

Locust Grove was named for a grove of flowering locust trees that could be seen throughout the town. It was a major rail distribution center for cotton, peaches, and other farm products and had three cotton gins and several warehouses. Beginning in 1894, the prosperous town was the home of the Locust Grove Institute, a top-notch college-preparatory school founded by the Locust Grove Baptist Church and Mercer University. It was one of the first schools in Georgia to be accredited by the Association of Schools and Colleges of the Southern States. The Great Depression and the introduction of public schools led to the demise of the school in 1930, but its beautiful main building now houses city government offices. Today, Locust Grove is the home of **Noah's Ark,** a facility for animal rehabilitation, and the **Tanger Outlet Center.**

✸ To See

FOR FAMILIES 🐾 ✐ ♿ **Noah's Ark Animal Rehabilitation Center** (770-957-0888; www.noahs-ark.org), 712 Locust Grove–Griffin Road, Locust Grove. Office open 9–4 Tuesday–Saturday, animal habitats open for tours noon–3 Tuesday–Saturday. (*Note:* All tours are subject to cancellation because of rain, extreme heat or cold, or lack of volunteers.) Noah's Ark, which is located on 250 acres, was created to provide a home for abused, unwanted, and orphaned wild, domestic, and exotic animals and birds. Rehabilitated animals are returned to the wild or their place of origin; animals that can't be released live out their days here in as natural a habitat as possible, as do unwanted exotic animals such as lions, monkeys, and tigers that have no natural habitat in North America. Visitors can walk the nature trails through 40 acres and view the animal habitats. Free; donations accepted.

HISTORIC HOMES AND SITES 🐾 ✐ ♿ **Heritage Park** (www.hcprd.org), 101 Lake Dow Road, McDonough. Park open daylight hours daily; tours of the buildings by appointment. The 129-acre park straddles two centuries. The **historic village**, which represents what Henry County was like at the turn of the 20th century, was created by moving historic structures from around the county to one location. It includes a 100-year-old corn crib, an 1827 settler's log cabin, an original two-room country schoolhouse, a typical detached cookhouse, the first library building in the county, a 1934 steam locomotive and tender, and Lane's Store, which was built in 1921 and served as a general store for

A RESIDENT OF NOAH'S ARK

NOAH'S ARK FACTS
- The center rehabilitates more than 1,300 animals each year.
- Around 800 to 900 animals are usually in residence at any one time.
- It costs $600 per day to feed all the animals or $18,000 per month.
- The yearly budget at Noah's Ark is $997,000.
- There are only 27 full-time and part-time employees.
- It takes 300 volunteers to help with animal care and feeding, tours, group projects, and annual events.
- Noah's Ark had to turn away 2,500 animals last year for lack of funds.

quarry workers as well as a service station and local gathering place. The **Barn Museum** houses county artifacts. A unit in the county's parks and recreation system, the park also features a community garden, the 0.9-mile paved Brian Williams Trail, two playgrounds, a senior center, and a softball complex. Free.

🐾 ♂ ♿ **Nash Farm Battlefield** (770-288-7300; www.henrycountybattlefield.com), 4361 Jonesboro Road, Hampton. Grounds open daylight hours daily; museum open 9–3 Monday–Saturday. This 204-acre site was the scene of the largest Cavalry raid in Georgia history and a huge Confederate campsite during the waning days of the Civil War Atlanta Campaign. It is one of the few intact battlegrounds in the country. Contained in the **Veteran's History Museum** are archaeological finds from the property, uniforms and military paraphernalia from World War I to the present, as well as a room devoted to vintage ladies' fashions. Guided tours of the battlefield can be arranged by appointment.

✳ To Do

AUTO RACING ♂ ♿ **Atlanta Motor Speedway** (770-946-4211; tickets: 770-707-7970; www.atlantamotorspeedway.com; www.gospeedway.com), 1500 Tara Place/US 41 North, Hampton. Office open 8:30–5 weekdays. Check the website or call for a schedule of events and ticket prices. Track tours operate daily from the gift shop. The 1.54-mile track is one of the premier motor-sports facilities in America. Its NASCAR Sprint Cup Series races held in March and on Labor Day are the two largest single-day sporting events in Georgia. In fact, the track is the biggest revenue-producing venue in the state. Approximately 160,000 fans converge there to watch their favorite drivers race around the track at heart-stopping speeds. The track sponsors the AdvoCare 500, NASCAR Nationwide Series and NASCAR World Truck Series, Legends and Bandolero racing, and Friday Night Drags and Show-N-Shine. In use more than 300 days a year, the track also hosts driving schools, concerts, air shows, dog shows, circuses, weddings, and car shows, bringing in more than $455 million annually. The facility also offers tours and behind-the-scenes looks at the entertainment complex. Official track tours are offered depending on use of the track and include track history, a visit to Petty Garden, a tour of a luxury suite, a peek at the garages and Victory Lane, and two laps in the speedway van. Adults $5, children $2. Camping is also available.

FOR FAMILIES ♂ ♿ **Fun Bowl of Henry County** (770-898-4272), 370 GA 155, McDonough. Open 9 AM–midnight Monday–Thursday, 9 AM–3 AM Friday and Saturday, noon–midnight Sunday. The 8-acre indoor-outdoor family entertainment complex offers two video arcades, billiards, 32 lanes of bowling, go-carts, 18 holes of mini golf, an eight-station batting cage, and a snack bar. Limited wheelchair accessibility on some rides. $4 per activity.

✳ Green Space

GARDENS 🐾 ♂ ♿ **Dauset Trails Nature Center** (770-775-6798; www.dausettrails.com), 360 Mount Vernon Road, Jackson. Open 9–5 Monday–Saturday, noon–5 Sunday. In the Woodland Garden, visitors can see native azaleas, fairy wands, pink lady's slippers, ferns, merry bells, asters, jack-in-the-pulpits, shooting stars, bird's-foot violets, lilies, bloodroot, mayapple, columbine, galax, phlox, trillium, Solomon's seal, and others. Children can get a list at the visitors center for the Pleasure Hunt, a quest to find fun garden ornaments. The Woodland Garden path ends at the Bog Garden, which features two ponds connected by a waterfall, a covered bridge, and a bog filled with irises, lily pads, ferns, turtles, frogs, and the occasional water snake. The Children's Garden features plants that inspire the senses of smell and touch. There is a formal knot garden in the middle. Free; donations accepted.

LAKES 🐾 ♂ **Lake Jackson** (770-775-4839; www.georgiapower.com/lakes), Jackson. Open 7 AM–10 PM daily. The 4,700-acre, power-generating lake was created when a dam was built in 1910. Recreation is a secondary benefit. Lake Jackson has several marinas, parks, recreation areas, and campgrounds and offers innumerable opportunities for boating, fishing, swimming, and other water sports. One of the best fishing lakes in the state, it yields trophy-size bream, crappie, largemouth bass, hybrid bass, catfish, and carp. Waterskiing can be enjoyed on the lake and up three major river tributaries.

NATURE PRESERVES AND PARKS ☙ ✿ **Cubihatcha Outdoor Education Center, Towaliga River Preserve** (678-583-3930; www.hcwsa.com/cubihatcha-reservoir -management), 100 Collins Road, Locust Grove. Loop Trail open 8–5 year-round; River Trail open 8–5 weekdays, April–October. The center is a wetland enhancement and protection corridor created to improve and protect existing wildlife habitats, as well as for public education and enjoyment. Almost 1,000 acres of bottomland, hardwood forest, wetlands, and uplands typical of the Piedmont region provide diverse habitats for mammals, birds, fish, reptiles, amphibians, and insects. The 8-mile River Trail runs along the Towaliga River, while the Loop Trail is 2 miles around. Visitors can take a self-guided tour or arrange in advance for a walk led by a staff naturalist. (*Note:* The trails may be closed due to inclement weather or management discretion.) Free.

☙ ✿ ♿ **Dauset Trails Nature Center.** See *Gardens.* Open 9–5 Monday–Saturday, noon–5 Sunday; trails open sunrise–10 PM, provided users sign the release form located at the trailhead parking kiosk. (*Note:* The main entrance gate closes at 5 PM; after that, park at the trailhead outside the fence. Also note that trails are closed when wet.) The nature center offers 1,200 acres of creeks, lakes, ponds, and wildflower fields, while 17 miles of scenic wooded trails attract bikers, hikers, and observers of birds and other wildlife. The trails, marked for beginner, intermediate, and advanced hikers, include rocky terraces, bottomlands, and creeks. Ten miles of trails (separate from the hiking and biking trails) are open for horseback riding (BYOH—bring your own horse). The Wonder Room in the environmental nature education center interprets the area and exhibits live rehabilitated animals, such as alligators, turtles, and snakes, that are not releasable into the wild. Farm animals—chickens, guinea hens, goats, horses, mules, burros, cows, and pigs—are on view, too. The center also includes several gardens. Allow yourself at least two to three hours to see the main exhibits, more if you are hiking or biking. A piece of trivia: *Dauset* was created from the last names of the two people who started the nature center in 1977—Hampton DAUghtry and David SETtle. Free; donations accepted.

☙ ✿ ♿ **High Falls State Park** (478-993-3053; lodging reservations: 1-800-864-7275; www .gastateparks.org/info/HighFalls), 76 High Falls Park Drive, Jackson. Open daily 7 AM–10 PM. Two hundred years ago, this site was a booming industrial village with a blacksmith shop, cotton gin, gristmill, shoe factory, several stores, and a hotel. In the late 1880s, it became a ghost town when the railroad bypassed it and all the buildings virtually disappeared. All that remains is the foundation of the gristmill. The scenic area and a waterfall on the Towaliga River led to the creation of a state park where visitors now come for many recreational opportunities. The 1,050-acre park features 4.5 miles of hiking trails and a 650-acre lake for boating and fishing. Seasonally, visitors can play miniature golf and swim in the park's pool (additional fees). For boaters, the park offers two ramps, along with canoe, kayak, and pedal boat rentals in season. Private boats are allowed, but there is a 10-horsepower limit. Accommodations are available at the campground (see *Lodging—Campgrounds*). Parking $5.

☙ ✿ ♿ **Indian Springs State Park** (770-504-2277; lodging reservations: 1-800-864-7275; www.gastateparks.org/IndianSprings), 678 Lake Clark Road, Flovilla. Open 7 AM–10 PM daily. The springs at this park, considered to be one of the oldest state parks in the country, were used by Creek Indians for centuries. The Native Americans believed the spring waters healed the sick and bestowed additional vitality to the well. During the 1800s, the area became a bustling resort town when settlers came to partake of the springs themselves. During the Great Depression, the Civilian Conservation Corps (CCC) built many of the structures within the park, including the springhouse. A museum, which is open seasonally, focuses on the Creek Indians, the resort era, and the CCC. Today the 528-acre park offers water sports on the 105-acre lake, a playground, miniature golf (additional fee), and a short 0.75-mile nature trail. Boating facilities include a boat ramp and seasonal pedal-boat rentals. Private boats are permitted, but there is a 10-horsepower limit. The park also offers camping and cottages (see *Lodging—Cottages and Cabins*). Parking $5.

🐾 𝄞 ♿ **Newman Wetlands Center** (770-603-5603; www.ccwa.us/newman-wetlands-center), 2755 Freeman Road, Hampton. Visitors center open 8:30–5 weekdays, September–May; 8:30–5 Tuesday–Saturday, June–August. Trail open 7–7 daily, March–October; 7–5 daily, November–February. A

VISITORS TO INDIAN SPRINGS STATE PARK CAN TAKE TO THE WATER IN PEDAL BOATS.

project of the Clayton County Water Authority, the area was created to demonstrate the importance of preserving wetland environments and to provide public education about natural resource conservation. The 32-acre facility consists of a trail and a visitors/interpretive center. The easy 0.5-mile trail alternates between crushed stone through forested areas and a boardwalk over the swamp. Wheelchairs and strollers can be accommodated on the trail. The visitors center contains a central exhibit and learning lab area, an auditorium where a wetlands video is presented, and restrooms. During the summer, weekday guided walks are often scheduled. In addition to 130 species of birds, other wildlife such as beaver, river otter, fox, raccoon, muskrat, deer, wild turkey, opossum, and mink have been sighted. Some species stop here during their migrations; others are permanent residents. The Atlanta Audubon Society holds Saturday-morning bird walks here all year. Birding classes and workshops are offered, too. Special programs on topics such as waterfowl, bats, reptiles, and gardening are scheduled annually. The **Wetlands and Watershed Festival,** held on the first Saturday of October, features environmental exhibits and activities, guided trail hikes, live animal exhibits, nature crafts, and a scavenger hunt. Free.

✳ Lodging
CAMPGROUNDS

In Flovilla
🐾 𝄞 ♿ 🐾 **Indian Springs State Park** (camping reservations: 1-800-864-7275). The park offers 88 tent, trailer, and RV sites. See *Green Space—Nature Preserves and Parks.* $25–28.

In Jackson
🐾 𝄞 ♿ 🐾 **High Falls State Park** (camping reservations: 1-800-864-7275). The park offers 103 tent, trailer, and RV sites, as well as six yurts. See also *Green Space—Nature Preserves and Parks. Campsites* $25–28, yurts $65.

In McDonough
🐾 𝄞 **Atlanta South RV Resort** (770-957-2610 or 1-800-778-0668; www.atlantasouth rvresort.com), 281 Mount Olive Road. The campground provides 140 sites with water, sewer, and electric hookups, 80 of them pull-through, as well as tent sites. Other amenities include restrooms, showers, laundry facilities, a dump station, a pool, fishing, and a playground. The new clubhouse recreation room features a TV viewing area and Internet access. Five cabins offer a bed and a roof over your head. They each have a queen bed and a bunk bed, but no bathroom or sink. Tent sites $23, RV sites $36, cabins $32.

COTTAGES AND CABINS

In Flovilla

🦫 ♿ 🐾 **Indian Springs State Park** (lodging reservations: 1-800-864-7275). The park features 10 fully equipped cottages. Two are dog friendly ($40 per dog; two maximum). See *Green Space—Nature Preserves and Parks.* $115–125.

✳ Where to Eat

DINING OUT

In McDonough

♿ **Pilgreen's Steakhouse** (770-957-4490; www.the-t-boneking.com), 1720 Lake Dow Road. Open 5–9 Monday–Thursday, 5–10 Friday and Saturday. A favorite with locals and well-known for steaks and seafood for more than a half century, Pilgreen's offers white-table service with a view of the lake. No smoking. $14–25.

EATING OUT

In McDonough

🦫 🐾 ♿ **Gritz Family Restaurant** (770-914-0448), 14 Macon Street. Open 7–3 Monday–Saturday, 8:30–3 Sunday. Down-home Southern cooking is served for breakfast and lunch in a casual atmosphere. Start the day with a hearty breakfast of pancakes, omelets, or eggs fixed any way. Breakfast meats include bacon, sausage, ham, steak, chicken, pork, or corned beef hash. Of course, grits and biscuits make an appearance. Lunch entrées such as chicken and dumplings, salmon patties, fried chicken livers, and country-fried steak include two sides and bread. No smoking. $7–10.

♿ 🐾 **PJ's Café** (770-898-5373; www.pjs cafemcdonough.com), 30 Macon Street. Open 11–9 Tuesday–Thursday, 11–10 Friday and Saturday, 11–3 Sunday; early-bird specials 4:30–6:30. Steaks, seafood, and pasta are served in a casual atmosphere. The restaurant features a wine bar, international beers, and outdoor dining. Enjoy the cozy bar and the beautiful mural in the dining room. Live music Friday and Saturday evenings. No smoking. You can even bring your dog if you're eating outside. Lunch $7–13, dinner $8–20; early-bird specials $8–14; Tail Wagging menu for your pooch $1–3.

✳ Entertainment

DANCE Atlanta Festival Ballet (770-507-2775; www.atlantafestivalballet.com), mailing address: 416 Eagles Landing Parkway, Stockbridge 30281. The only professional dance company on the south side of metro Atlanta, the organization has 12 full-time professional dancers as well as numerous student apprentices in the Festival Ballet School. The company presents two full-length productions each year, including *The Nutcracker* at holiday time and a spring production, as well as a summer repertory program. Although the company is based in nearby Stockbridge (see the Southern Suburbs chapter), performances are held at the **Henry County Schools Performing Arts Center** and the **Clayton County Schools Performing Arts Center.**

MUSIC Henry Singers (770-957-0987; www.henrysingers.com). The vocal group performs several concerts annually, including a holiday concert in December. Concerts include a variety of musical styles from formal to lighthearted themes. Performances are at various venues. Check the website or call for a schedule. Free, but donations appreciated.

Southern Crescent Symphony Orchestra (404-981-SCSO; www.scsymphony.net), mailing address: 950 Eagles Landing Parkway, Suite 241, Stockbridge 30281. Check the website or call for a schedule of events and ticket prices; some concerts are free. The volunteer community orchestra composed of professional musicians, music educators, amateur musicians, and students presents four to six concerts annually ranging from Christmas sing-alongs to movie music, children's favorites to classical concertos. Although the symphony is based in Stockbridge (see the Southern Suburbs chapter), it performs at the **Henry County Schools Performing Arts Center** in McDonough, as well as other venues.

THEATER Henry Players (www.henry players.com), mailing address: P.O. Box 3083, McDonough 30253. Check the website for a schedule of performances. Tickets are available at several businesses (listed on the website) and online. The theatrical company, which consists entirely of volunteers, presents four productions annually, including drama, classics, comedy, and musicals. Productions are held at the **Henry County Schools Performing Arts Center** in McDonough. Adults $12, seniors and children younger than 12 $10.

✳ Selective Shopping

Jackson's historic turn-of-the-20th-century downtown features antiques stores, quaint shops, and restaurants. **McDonough**'s historic town square abounds with antiques shops and also features an old-fashioned hardware store and an art design studio. Many of the merchants in McDonough have banded together to offer a booklet of shopping discounts at many of the town's shops, restaurants, and activities. The booklet can be obtained from the **McDonough Hospitality and Tourism Bureau** (see *Guidance*).

FLEA MARKETS Peachtree Peddlers Flea Market (770-914-2269 or 1-888-661-3532; www.peachtreepeddlers.com), 155 Mill Road, McDonough. Open 9–6 Saturday, 10–6 Sunday. The 80,000-square-foot, all-weather flea market features antiques and craft booths as well as booths for just about every item imaginable. Find books, floral arrangements, Georgia produce, gifts, and much, much more. In addition, the facility has a restaurant and hosts craft shows and other special entertainment events. Free.

Sweetie's Flea Market (770-946-4721), 2316 US 19/US 441, Hampton. Open 6–4 Saturday and Sunday year-round. Georgia's oldest flea market has a fun country-fair atmosphere and bargains galore. Since 1947 the old-fashioned outdoor market has featured more than 100 dealers who sell antiques, collectibles, farm and country items, primitives, and more. There is a snack bar on the premises, too. Free.

OTHER GOODS Atlanta Motor Speedway Gift Store (770-707-7970; see *To Do—Auto Racing*). Open 9–5 daily.

Shop here for Atlanta Motor Speedway and NASCAR apparel, flags, pins, jewelry, pens, postcards, electronics, and kitchen supplies. The gift shop is in the same building as the ticket office, and tours leave from here as well.

OUTLET STORES Tanger Outlet Center (770-957-5310 or 1-800-406-0833; www.tangeroutlet.com/locustgrove), 1000 Tanger Drive, Locust Grove. Open 9–9 Monday–Saturday, 11–7 Sunday. One of the largest outlet centers in the country, this one features more than 60 of the nation's leading brand-name stores, from Aeropostale to Ultra Diamonds, with quality merchandise at discount prices. It attracts more than 3.5 million shoppers annually.

✳ Special Events

May: **Geranium Festival** (www.geranium festival.com). A more-than-third-century tradition on the square in McDonough, the festival features an arts and crafts exhibition and sale with vendors from all over the country, as well as music, other entertainment, and great food. Held the third Saturday. Free.

Summer: **Music on the Square concert series** (770-898-9868). Music on the Square concerts 7–11 PM on specific dates in May, July, and August at the McDonough town square. Talented bands and soloists perform jazz, rock and roll, classical, and pop music. Concertgoers are invited to bring blankets or chairs, snacks or a picnic meal, and beverages to enjoy while listening to music outdoors. Free.

October: **Fall Festival and Chili Cook-Off** (770-898-9868). Held on the McDonough town square, the event features a different kind of chili cooking contest. Instead of being judged according to certain criteria, participants are judged by the public. Participants (applications required) prepare their secret chili recipes ahead of time and bring them to the festival, where they're sold in sample-size cups. The person who sells the most cups wins. Other festival activities include entertainment, arts and crafts, and face painting and other children's activities. $5; nominal fees for some activities.

NEWNAN, MORELAND, AND SENOIA

Coweta County was named for the Coweta Indians, a Creek tribe, and its name means "water falls." The county was formed in 1825, when Chief William McIntosh—who was part Scot, part Indian—signed the Treaty of Indian Springs, for which he was killed by his fellow tribesmen.

Coweta County has produced loads of famous folks, from literary giants to entertainers. In addition to authors Erskine Caldwell and Lewis Grizzard (see *To See—Museums*), other celebrities include David Boyd, who illustrates the *You Might Be a Redneck If . . .* books; Margaret Anne Barnes, who wrote *Murder in Coweta County*; country music stars Alan Jackson and Doug Stone; classical music personality Charles Wadsworth, who serves as the musical director of Charleston's Spoleto festival; and football great Drew Hill. Minnie Pearl began her career as a drama coach here as well.

The area should be familiar to moviegoers who have seen *Fried Green Tomatoes, Driving Miss Daisy, Pet Sematary II,* and *The War.* Numerous TV series and productions have been filmed here as well: *I'll Fly Away, Passing Glory, A Christmas Memory,* and *Andersonville,* to name just a few. Raleigh Studios, located on 105 acres in Senoia, is a complete production facility with several sound stages.

Two of the state's designated Scenic Trails travel through this area: the Chattahoochee-Flint Heritage Highway and the Georgia Antiques Trail.

GUIDANCE When planning a trip to the Newnan area, including Grantville, Moreland, Roscoe, Senoia, Sharpsburg, and Turin, contact the **Coweta County Convention and Visitors Bureau and Welcome Center** (770-254-2627 or 1-800-826-9382; www.coweta.ga.us), 200 Court Square, Newnan 30263. Open 9–5 Monday–Saturday. Pick up a brochure for the Newnan antebellum and Victorian driving tour as well as brochures for Moreland, Senoia, and Grantville tours (see *To See—Scenic Drives*).

Visitors can also consult the **Newnan–Coweta County Chamber of Commerce** (770-253-2270; www.newnancowetachamber.org), 23 Bullsboro Drive, Newnan 30263. Open 9–5 weekdays.

To learn more about Whitesburg, contact the **Carrollton Area Convention and Visitors Bureau** (770-214-9746 or 1-800-292-0871; www.visitcarrollton.com), 102 North Lakeshore Drive, Carrollton 30117. Open 8:30–5 weekdays.

GETTING THERE *By air:* The nearest airport is in Atlanta. For airport, airline, and car rental information, see "What's Where in Georgia."

By bus: The nearest **Greyhound Lines** station is in Atlanta at 232 Forsyth Street; call 404-584-1728. There is another station at the Atlanta airport; call 404-765-9598. LaGrange, which is southwest of Newnan, also has a station at 101 Hoffman Drive; call 706-882-1897.

By car: The towns described in this chapter are clustered around I-85 south of Atlanta.

By train: The nearest **AMTRAK** station (see "What's Where in Georgia") is in Atlanta.

MEDICAL EMERGENCY Call 911.

VILLAGES AND NEIGHBORHOODS **Newnan** was founded in 1828 and named for Gen. Daniel Newnan, a War of 1812 veteran and Georgia General Assemblyman, after the area was opened up for settlement in the Land Lottery of 1827. Newnan later became known as the "Hospital City of the Confederacy" because six field hospitals, which served as many as 10,000 wounded soldiers from both the South and North, were located in churches, homes, and other buildings there. A monument erected in 1885 on the east side of the courthouse square honors the Confederate soldiers lost in that war, 63 of whom were laid to rest in Oak Hill Cemetery. The city is renowned for its historic homes built before the Civil War and during the Victorian era, so much so that the motto "the City of Homes" is emblazoned in lights on the old Carnegie Library building in downtown Newnan.

There are numerous historic districts in and around Newnan. The **Newnan Historic District,** a nine-square-block area, was laid out in 1828 in the Washington plan, which includes wide avenues and a public square. This district contains the neo–Greek Revival 1904 courthouse, the first Carnegie-endowed library in Georgia, four religious structures, and the historic black commercial district along Broad Street.

The **Cole Town Historic District,** founded in 1854, is a residential neighborhood with a wide variety of architectural styles.

The **College-Temple Historic District,** laid out in 1828, is an example of a well-planned residential neighborhood where walkways, fences, formal gardens, open lawns, and hedges accent the varied architectural styles. The academy lot was the site of seven schools between 1829 and 1975. The last of those schools now houses the **Male Academy Museum** (see *To See—Museums*).

In contrast to the planned residential neighborhoods, the **Greenville Street–LaGrange Street Historic District** is a patterned development where the principal streets have the oldest and grandest homes, while the infill streets have newer, smaller houses. One of the houses, Buena Vista, served as a Confederate headquarters during the Battle of Brown's Mill in July 1864.

Although it began in 1895, a collection of homes known as the **Platinum Point Historic District** that was built by wealthy Newnan citizens really developed with increased use of automobiles. Built in a parklike atmosphere, the district contains a variety of the revival architecture popular at the turn of the 20th century.

Roscoe–Dunaway Gardens Historic District is actually in Roscoe, a small crossroads community surrounded by farmsteads. The hamlet, which is listed on the National Register of Historic Places, features antebellum homes as well as architectural styles representing the late 19th and early 20th centuries. These farmhouses, large wood-framed barns, and fields depict the prominent role agriculture played and still plays in Coweta County. The only retail establishment left in town is the Roscoe General Store. A mural depicting Roscoe's busier times—when it had eight steam gins, five sawmills, four gristmills, four stores, six churches, and five schools—is painted on the side of the building. **Dunaway Gardens** reopened in 2005 (see *Green Space—Gardens*).

The town of **Grantville,** which was originally named Calico Corners, was renamed in 1852 for L. P. Grant, president of the Atlantic and LaGrange Railroad. In the late 19th and early

20th centuries, the town flourished with three factories, two banks, a theater, a civic auditorium, and a telephone and telegraph office—all of which earned it the name "Gem of Coweta County." Unfortunately, Grantville declined, and today it is a very small but friendly town.

The **Grantville Historic District** represents a small railroad town that grew up along the tracks. Two historic mills and mill villages remain within the district, along with several churches and the passenger and freight depot. One of the most significant homes is Bonnie Castle, an elaborate Romanesque brick home built in 1896 using a variety of styles.

Moreland, originally a railroad stop called Puckett's Station, was once a booming cotton town with a hosiery mill. It was the birthplace of two famous authors: novelist Erskine Caldwell and humorist Lewis Grizzard. Today the small town boasts two museums (see *To See— Museums*), a bike/pedestrian path that winds through town, and a huge Fourth of July weekend celebration.

Senoia was developed from a cluster of farms in 1827. When the coming of the railroads brought about the need for an organized community, the town was founded in 1860, then incorporated in 1864. Two railroads intersected in Senoia, and cotton and peaches were shipped from there. It is believed that the town was named for the wife of Chief William McIntosh, Senoya He-ne-ha, who was also his cousin. Much of the original town remains intact as a nationally designated historic district (see *To See—Scenic Drives*). No trip to Senoia would be complete without a visit to the **Buggy Shop Museum** (see *To See— Museums*) or a stay at the **Culpepper House Bed and Breakfast** or the **Veranda Historic Bed and Breakfast** (see *Lodging—Bed & Breakfasts*). The **Senoia Historic District** contains 150 historic structures representing architectural styles from Greek Revival to Queen Anne. It also includes several antebellum homes that predate the town's development. Most, however, are from the turn of the 20th century. **Old Town Sharpsburg** features antiques and craft shops housed in turn-of-the-20th-century buildings.

Whitesburg is known for the **McIntosh Reserve** (see *Green Space—Nature Preserves and Parks*), a recreation area on the site of the plantation of Chief McIntosh, and a superior inn located on the site of a historic mill (see *Lodging—Resorts*).

✳ To See

MUSEUMS ✿ ♂ ♿ **Buggy Shop Museum** (770-253-1018; www.senoiabuggyshop.com), 74 Main Street, Senoia. Open 1–4 the third Saturday of the month or by appointment. Relive history by viewing buggies, old-time tools and machinery, antique cars, player pianos, Coca-Cola memorabilia, and collectibles from a bygone era. The rustic building that houses the museum was built in 1867. Small admission fee.

✿ ♂ ♿ **Coweta County African American Alliance Museum and Research Center** (770-683-7055; www.africanamericanalliance.net), 92 Farmer Street, Newnan. Open 10–4 weekdays. The shotgun house in which the museum is located is an excellent example of historical African American architecture. The museum serves as a repository for artifacts concerning Newnan's African American history and an active research center with a genealogy workroom. A slave cemetery, the largest slave cemetery in the state, sits under centuries-old giant oak trees on the grounds. An authentic slave cabin is being relocated on the property and will be restored. Free; donations accepted.

✿ **Erskine Caldwell Birthplace and Museum** (1-800-826-9382; www.coweta .ga.us), East Camp Street on town square,

Moreland. Open 11–3 Tuesday–Saturday. "The Little Manse" was the birthplace of native son and world-famous author Erskine Caldwell. The small wooden house has been restored to its 1903 appearance and relocated to the town square to serve as a house museum documenting Caldwell's life and accomplishments and reflecting life when the mill dominated the South. The museum features biographical exhibits, personal items, and copies of his books in different languages. Although Caldwell penned 25 novels, he is best remembered for his compelling depictions of the rural South during the Great Depression in *Tobacco Road* and *God's Little Acre.* Adults $2, children $1.

MALE ACADEMY MUSEUM

♿ **Lewis Grizzard Museum** (770-304-1490 or 1-800-826-9382; www.cowetaga.com), 2769 US 29 South, Moreland. Call for hours. Native son Lewis Grizzard, who died from heart disease in 1994 at age 47, was beloved as a Southern humorist, author, and entertainer, sometimes called the poor man's Faulkner. Grizzard put Moreland on the map with his syndicated columns and books such as *Don't Sit Under the Grits Tree with Anyone Else but Me* and *Elvis Is Dead and I Don't Feel So Good Myself,* in which he fondly told about his childhood in the small rural town. The museum showcases old typewriters, family photos, mementos, and manuscripts. $1. (There are plans to move to a location on Main Street, so be sure to check ahead.)

♿ **Male Academy Museum** (770-251-0207; www.nchistoricalsociety.org), 30 Temple Avenue, Newnan. Open 10–noon and 1–3 Tuesday–Saturday, 2–5 Sunday. Housed in an 1840s building that once served as a school for boys, the museum features a Civil War exhibit with an authentic Confederate battle flag, uniforms, soldiers' personal items, artifacts, weaponry, maps, and paintings of the Battle of Brown's Mill. The museum is noted for its extensive collection of 19th- and early-20th-century clothing. Adults $5, students $2, children younger than 12 free.

♿ **Oak Hill Cemetery,** Highway 34 (Bullsboro Drive), Newnan. Open daylight hours. The peaceful cemetery is the final resting place of 269 Confederate soldiers who were buried here in 1863 and 1864. Every state in the Confederacy is represented, and only two of the soldiers are unknown. Revolutionary War soldiers and two Georgia governors rest here as well. Free.

A HISTORIC HOME IN ONE OF NEWNAN'S HISTORIC DISTRICTS

SCENIC DRIVES Pick up the brochures for all these tours from the **Coweta County Convention and Visitors Bureau and Welcome Center** (see *Guidance*).

The **Chattahoochee-Flint Heritage Highway** runs through Coweta, Troup, Harris, and Meriwether counties from Roscoe to St. Marks. The Creek Indians originally inhabited this land. Today the scenic highway and bike route is filled with historic sites.

Historic Grantville Driving Tour takes you past lovely homes, among them the Smith-Wilson House and Bonnie Castle. The Renaissance Revival home with its round battlement-like tower is surrounded by an original decorative wrought-iron fence. The original hitching post is still in place as well.

Moreland Driving Tour takes visitors past the restored history of the town, including the **Old Mill Building** (1894), the **Old Moreland Post Office** (1876), **Founders Cemetery**, and historic homes. Browse for antiques in the old general store.

Newnan Driving Tour includes five historic districts. Antebellum and Victorian-era houses, which are marked with black metal signs, represent Gothic, Queen Anne, Eastlake, Second Empire, and Colonial Revival styles. Particularly interesting are the painted ladies, those Victorian-era houses painted in three or more colors.

Senoia Driving Tour of Homes points out historic homes, businesses, and churches amid the town's tree-lined streets, 150 historic structures, and a commercial district.

✷ To Do

AUTO RACING 🏵 ✐ ♿ **New Senoia Raceway** (770-599-6161; www.newsenoiaraceway.com), 171 Brown Road, Senoia. Check the website or call for a schedule of events and ticket prices. Events at the speedway include many classes and series: the O'Reilly United Sprint Car Series, the Georgia Asphalt Series, Pro Challenge, Bandoleros, Street Stock, Legends-Pro, Legends-Semi-Pro, Sportsman, and IceMan classes. The demolition derby is another popular event.

BICYCLING 🏵 ✐ **McIntosh Reserve** (770-830-5879; www.carrollcountyga.com), 1046 West McIntosh Circle, Whitesburg. Open 8–dusk daily. (*Note:* The park is gated, and gates close promptly at sundown. Be sure to be out by then if you are not camping there.) Several interconnecting mountain biking trails in the reserve provide 15 miles of riding. Good places to start are the park station and Council Bluff. The trails provide a variety of flat and hilly terrain for beginning and intermediate riders, but there are some sandy, rocky, and eroded areas. And look out: Horses also use the trails and often leave a calling card behind. There is a yearly mountain bike race in August. $3 trail use fee for bikes or horses.

CANOEING, KAYAKING, AND RAFTING 🏵 ✐ **McIntosh Reserve** (770-830-5879; www.carrollcountyga.com), 1046 West McIntosh Circle, Whitesburg. Open 8–dusk daily. (See the warning under *Bicycling* about the gates closing at sundown.) The Chattahoochee River, which forms the southern boundary of the reserve, provides an excellent venue for these paddling sports. $3.

FRIGHTS 🏵 ✐ ♿ **Horror Hill Haunted Trails** (770-253-4983; www.horrorhill.com), 181 Ware Road, Newnan. Open Friday–Sunday evenings late September–Halloween. In operation since 1984 and considered to be the largest haunted trail in the Southeast, the route features buildings, cabins, mazes, tunnels, bridges, trapdoors, fog machines, lasers, and strobe lights to create spooky effects. The Vertigo, Mortuary, and Clown House attractions are 3-D. Use the directions on the website because GPS and map search websites aren't always accurate. $25, but there are many coupons and discounts available on the website.

✷ Green Space

GARDENS 🏵 ✐ ♿ **Dunaway Gardens** (678-423-4050; www.dunawaygardens.com), 3218 Roscoe Road/Highway 70, Newnan. Open 10–4 Friday–Saturday, noon–4 Sunday, June–October. One of the South's largest natural rock and floral gardens, 25-acre Dunaway

Gardens features spring-fed pools, stone waterfalls, and extensive rock paths, walls, and staircases. Dunaway Gardens was created on a former cotton plantation by vaudeville Chautauqua actress Hetty Jane Dunaway and her husband, Wayne Sewell, as part of a larger complex that included a theatrical training center, said to be one of the largest in the 1920s. Many of the company's ballet and theatrical productions were originally previewed at the 1,000-seat amphitheater. Walt and Roy Disney were frequent visitors, and Sarah Ophelia Colley created her Minnie Pearl character here in the 1930s. The gardens remained popular up until the 1950s, when the tearoom was often used for parties and plays were produced in the Patchwork Barn. Dunaway died in 1961, and the gardens were abandoned. Over the years of neglect the historic buildings disappeared, but the walls, walkways, patios, pools, ponds, and waterfalls were salvageable. Jennifer Rae Bingham bought the property in 2000 and spent three years reclaiming the gardens. Today visitors can enjoy the numerous pools, an amphitheater, rockery, many themed gardens, and patios. Little Stone Mountain is a huge outcropping of exposed granite, the base of which underlies the entire garden. It was said to be a favorite campsite of Chief William McIntosh. Adults $10, children $8.

🦎 ♿ **Oak Grove Plantation Bed and Breakfast and Gardens** (770-463-3010 or 770-841-0789; www.oakgrovega.com), 4537 US 29 North, Newnan. Open periodically for tours. Central to the plantation is the 1830s four-over-four house, which reflects early Plantation Plain and Federal styles. The owners live in the house and it is open only on special occasions, but visitors can admire the exterior architectural details. A restored carriage house offers bed & breakfast accommodations (see *Lodging—Bed & Breakfasts*). Twenty acres of gardens feature old-fashioned flowers and shrubs as well as herbs and vegetables. There are also other themed areas, such as the pool, meditation, secret, formal, patience, shade, rhododendron, sunken, and *sin el agua* (without water) gardens. A historic family cemetery created by former owners that is on the property is attractively planted as well. Oak Grove Plantation Nursery specializes in old-fashioned flowers and shrubs. $5.

NATURE PRESERVES AND PARKS 🦎 ✈ ♿ **Chattahoochee Bend State Park**
(770-254-7271; lodging reservations: 1-800-864-7275; www.gastateparks.org/Chattahoochee Bend), 425 Bobwhite Way, Newnan. Open 7 AM–10 PM daily. Georgia's newest state park, the 2,910-acre wilderness park boasts 5 miles of river frontage, 6 miles of wooded trails, and an observation platform. It is a haven for paddlers, anglers, and campers (see *Lodging—Campgrounds*). $5.

✈ ♿ **Coweta County Fairgrounds** (770-254-2685; www.coweta.ga.us), 275 Pine Road, Newnan. The 61-acre facility hosts the five-day **Coweta County Fair** in September, 4-H events, horse shows, rodeos, dog shows, circuses, and other events. Check the website or call for a schedule of events and prices. The **Walker Horne Outdoor Theater** is a popular site for concerts, stage performances, and weddings. Also within the facility is the **James E. McGuffey Nature Center** (open Tuesday–Sunday), which includes 30 acres of green space with a small pond, wetland environment, forest, and nearly 3 miles of nature trails—some of which are soft surfaced and some of which are hard surfaced, making them wheelchair accessible.

DUNAWAY GARDENS IN NEWNAN IS ONE OF THE SOUTH'S LARGEST GARDENS.

CHIEF WILLIAM MCINTOSH

McIntosh, a Lower Creek chief, served America as a distinguished soldier in several battles—including Autossee, Horseshoe Bend, the Creek Indian War, and the Seminole Wars—for which he was awarded the rank of brigadier general in the U.S. Army (the only Indian to ever reach that rank). He fought with Andrew Jackson and even dined with President Thomas Jefferson at the White House. Raised as an Indian, he never knew his Tory father, but since descent was determined through the mother, that was of little importance to the Creeks. He owned a plantation and operated an inn, two taverns, a trading post, and a ferry across the Chattahoochee River. He also owned 72 slaves and had Indians and white men working for him. McIntosh and other Lower Creeks ceded all Creek lands in Georgia west of the Flint River to the U.S. government. He then planned to leave for lands he had been promised in Arkansas. Before he could do that, however, the Upper Creeks killed him, burned the plantation, and destroyed what stock they didn't take, but they spared the lives of the women and children.

♦ ✦ ♿ **McIntosh Reserve** (770-830-5879; www.carrollcountyga.com), 1046 West McIntosh Circle, Whitesburg. Open 8–dusk daily. (*Note:* The reserve is a gated facility and is closed at sundown unless camping arrangements have been made.) The reserve is named for Chief William McIntosh Jr., the son of a Scottish captain in the British Army and a full-blooded Creek Indian woman who belonged to the Wind Clan of the Creek Nation. The park contains part of his plantation, which he called Lochau Talofau, or "Acorn Bluff." McIntosh rose to the rank of chief in the Coweta tribe of the Lower Creeks but was killed May 1, 1825, by his own people, who were angered that he had ceded land to the white settlers.

This area is called a "reserve" because McIntosh reserved some of it for himself. His simple grave is here, as well as a reproduction of his rustic dogtrot-style house. Today, the 527-acre property—which combines recreational activities, preservation of cultural heritage, education, fish and wildlife management, and conservation of the Chattahoochee River corridor—is used for camping, hiking, fishing, canoeing, rafting, and picnicking. More than 14 miles of trails, enjoyed by hikers, cyclists, and equestrians, wind through the reserve and along the Chattahoochee River, which forms the southern boundary. Model-airplane enthusiasts enjoy the grass airstrip in the lower park near the camping area. Primitive camping can be arranged for weekends only. During the summer, the **Spray and Splash Water Park** is open daily ($1). Annual events include the **Easter Festival, Fall Festival, Native American Pow Wow, Halloween Carnival,** and **Chattahoochee Challenge Car Show.** Entrance/parking $3, additional $3 for use of the bike and horse trails, $15 camping.

✳ Lodging

BED & BREAKFASTS

In Newnan

Oak Grove Plantation Bed and Breakfast and Gardens (770-463-3010 or 770-841-0789; www.oakgrovega.com), 4537 US 29 North. Located on 20 acres, the plantation is listed on the National Register of Historic Places (see *Green Space—Gardens*). Guest accommodations are offered in the restored tin-roofed carriage house, where two suites boast antique furnishings and private baths with Jacuzzi tubs. There is also a vintage kitchen, which guests are free to use. The cottage also features a common room stocked with diversions such as games, puzzles, TV, a video and DVD player, and books. In addition to enjoying the many different gardens, guests can use the outdoor pool and the playhouse area. Homemade cookies are served in the evening, and the day begins with a hearty breakfast. No smoking. Not wheelchair accessible. $175–250.

In Senoia

Culpepper House (770-599-8182; www.culpepperhouse.com), 35 Broad Street. The house was built in 1871 by Dr. John Addy, a Confederate veteran. The oak trees he planted during that era continue to shade the house and property. The house later belonged to Dr. Wilbur Culpepper and has retained his name. Twelve-foot ceilings and other architectural elements of the period create gracious public rooms and three guest rooms with private baths. Guests particularly enjoy the wraparound porch. A generous buffet breakfast is included in the nightly rate. No smoking. Not wheelchair accessible. From $95.

The Veranda Historic Bed and Breakfast Inn (770-599-3905 or 1-866-598-3905; www.verandabandbinn.com), 252 Seavey Street. Listed on the National Register of Historic Places, this 1906 Greek Revival structure began life as the Holberg Hotel and has been offering accommodations most of the time ever since then. Many famous people, from William Jennings Bryan to Marilyn Monroe, have stayed here. Today's visitors will enjoy the fine architectural features and the period decor in the nine guest rooms, as well as the rocking chair porches, the gardens, a full breakfast, the weekly teas, the gift shop, and the art gallery. Not wheelchair accessible. $125–155.

CULPEPPER HOUSE'S WRAPAROUND PORCH IS POPULAR WITH GUESTS.

CAMPGROUNDS

In Newnan

Chattahoochee Bend State Park (camping reservations: 1-800-864-7275). Provisions are made for all types of camping. There are 24 RV sites, 11 walk-in tent sites, 9 pop-up tent sites, 7 platform tent sites, and 4 Adirondack sites, as well as a bathhouse with hot showers and a playground. See *Green Space—Nature Preserves and Parks.* $20–35.

In Whitesburg

McIntosh Reserve (770-830-5879; www.carrollcountyga.com), 1046 West McIntosh Circle. Reservations for primitive camping are restricted to weekends only and can be arranged by calling the office between 9 and 5 weekdays. See also *Green Space—Nature Preserves and Parks.* $10 for county residents, $15 for nonresidents.

RESORTS

In Whitesburg

The Lodges at Historic Banning Mills Adventure Country Inn, Executive Retreat and Conservation Center (770-834-9149 or 1-866-447-8688; www.HistoricBanningMills.com), 205 Horseshoe Dam Road. The retreat is nestled on 700 wooded acres overlooking the Snake Creek Gorge. Guest accommodations are rooms in the lodge, log cabin suites, and cozy cottages. There is a campground as well. Many rooms feature a Jacuzzi, gas-log fireplace, refrigerator, microwave, and a deck with a spectacular view. Dining includes a full breakfast. A deli box lunch/gourmet picnic basket and dinner can be arranged at an additional fee. Amenities at the resort include an Olympic-size swimming pool; tennis, basketball, and sand volleyball courts; an 18-hole putting green; a baseball field; and a horseshoe pit. There's a catch-and-release fishing lake. Hiking along old town trails, Creek Indian paths, old water raceways, and along the Snake River can range from mild to moderately strenuous. Other activities, which are charged separately and range in price from $10 to $70, include fly-fishing, hayrides, skeet shooting, pistol shooting, kayaking, and kayak and pedal boat rentals. The newest attraction is the **Extreme Eco Canopy Tour** zip line, which is one of the longest and highest in the world. Check to see when there are periodic birds of prey shows at the amphitheater. An on-site spa offers numerous packages and body treatments ranging in price from $30 to $235. No smoking. Not wheelchair accessible. $99–189; ask about special packages. RV camping $22–29 (does not include breakfast).

✳ Where to Eat

DINING OUT

In Newnan

&. **Andre's Off the Square** (770-304-3557), 11 Jefferson Street. Open 5–9:30 Tuesday–Saturday. Serving creative American cuisine, the upscale restaurant features fresh seafood every night. No smoking. $14–26.

&. **Brick Yard Restaurant** (770-252-6000), 9 East Court Square. Open from 5 PM Tuesday–Saturday. Newnan's newest fine-dining establishment, which is located on the square, serves steaks, seafood, and chef's specials. The restaurant has an extensive wine list and often sponsors wine tastings. Reservations are recommended. No smoking. $18–28.

&. **Ten East Washington** (770-502-9100; www.teneastwashington.com), 10 East Washington Street. Open 5–9 Tuesday–Saturday. Brunch is served on the first Sunday of the month. Located just off the square, one of Newnan's finest restaurants has earned a reputation for superbly prepared seafood, steaks, and Continental cuisine. Chef George Rasovsky concentrates on refinement and fresh products. Live entertainment is offered once a month. No smoking. Dinner $14–30, brunch $10–16.

EATING OUT

In Newnan

♨ ✍ &. **Catfish Hollow** (770-502-1223), 2826 GA 154/Sharpsburg McCullum Road. Open 4:30–9 Tuesday–Thursday, 4:30–10

Friday and Saturday. Naturally, the restaurant serves a multitude of seafood choices, but diners also can choose among steaks, burgers, veggie plates, and more. No smoking. $8.75–19.

♨ ✍ &. **Golden's on the Square** (770-251-4300), 9 East Gordon Street. Open 11–9 Tuesday–Sunday. Located in a historic downtown building, Golden's has been feeding the citizenry of Newnan since the late '70s. Every day, the kitchen staff prepares six to eight made-from-scratch entrées, 12 to 14 freshly steamed vegetables, six to eight salads, and a variety of desserts. All meals are the same price and include a beverage, roll, and butter. No smoking. $7–16.

♨ ✍ &. **Redneck Gourmet Corner Cafe** (770-251-0092; www.redneckgourmet.com), 11 North Court Square. Open 7 AM–9 PM Monday–Saturday. Breakfast is cooked to order and includes anything you could want, from eggs and breakfast meats to pancakes and French toast. For lunch and dinner, diners can enjoy hot and cold sandwiches, salads, soups, daily specials, as well as homemade desserts and cookies. The café, which has been operated by the Smith family since 1998, is noted for its wide array of hot sauces. There is also Redneck-without-the-wait take-out. Call 770-683-NECK to place your order. No smoking. There's a second location in Senoia at 42 Main Street (678-723-0235). Breakfast $5–8, lunch and dinner $5–12.

♨ ✍ &. **Sprayberry's Barbecue** (770-253-4421; www.sprayberrysbbq.com), 229 Jackson Street (second location at GA 34 West [exit 47 off I-85]; 770-253-5080). Open 10:30–9 Monday–Saturday. Sprayberry's was humorist Lewis Grizzard's favorite place to eat, and there's even a dish named after him. Using a vinegar-based sauce and slow roasting meat over an oak and hickory fire, Sprayberry's offers BBQ chicken and slow-roasted pork, Brunswick stew, and baby-back ribs. Grilled fish tacos, steaks, chicken, and a full menu are also featured at the original 1926 location in a former gas station on Jackson Street, as well as at the new location on GA 34 West. Diners don't want to leave without purchasing some logo merchandise and bottled barbecue sauce. Sprayberry's is also renowned for its home-made pies—especially its fried pies. No smoking. $5–18.

✳ Entertainment

THEATER **Newnan Community Theatre Company** (770-683-NCTC; www.newnantheatre.org), 24 First Avenue, Newnan. The troupe, which has been in existence since 1975, produces comedies, dramas, musicals, works by Shakespeare, experimental pieces, and children's productions. Although the company has performed in converted warehouses, old cotton mills, churches, and even open fields, it now has a home in the former Johnson Hardware Building. The company also offers NITWITS, an improv troupe, and interactive murder mysteries. Call for a schedule of performances and ticket prices, which generally run about $12 for adults, $10 for seniors and students for the MainStage Series, $5 for NITWITS.

✳ Selective Shopping

ANTIQUES **Re-Use the Past** (770-583-3111; www.ReUseThePast.com), 98 Moreland Street, Grantville. Open noon–5 Wednesday–Saturday. The firm's motto is "If it's old, we probably have it." Located in an 1895 hosiery mill, the company serves as an architectural salvage and antiques store. If you're remodeling a historic house, this is the place to get antique heart-pine floor-boards, ceiling tin, doors, Victorian-era stained glass, bricks, pavers, hinges, door-knobs, chair rails, and molding, just to name a few items. If you simply want to add to your furnishings and decor, the store carries mirrors, coat hangers, wall sconces, antique furniture, and regional pottery.

BOOKS **Scott's Book Store** (770-253-2960), 28 South Court Square, Newnan. Open 9–5 weekdays, 9–4 Saturday. A true rarity, this independent bookstore has been operating since 1975. In addition to a wide selection of books and an extensive children's section, the store carries plush toys, American Girl dolls, and other items. You can purchase tickets here for local events as well.

GIFTS **Collector's Corner** (770-251-6835; www.collectors-corner.net), 8861 GA 54, Sharpsburg. Open 10–6 Monday–Saturday, 1–5 Sunday. This vast shop features antiques, collectibles, gifts, furniture, heritage lace, home and garden accessories, lamps, pictures, mirrors, custom florals, baby and toddler clothing, an art gallery, and much more. Take a break from shopping with a bite in the Jasmine Tea Room and Restaurant. The store has several special events throughout the year.

✳ Special Events

March or April: **Charles Wadsworth and Friends Concert** (770-253-2270). The native-son pianist, Spoleto musical director, and concert host performs at the named-

---

SPRAYBERRY'S BBQ

The now legendary eatery had its beginning as Houston Sprayberry's gas station. Sprayberry began selling BBQ sandwiches made on-site with his special sauce, and soon he was selling so many he closed the pumps and opened a restaurant. Politicians from U.S. presidents to governors have campaigned here, and entertainers and athletes stop in as well. Country music star Alan Jackson waited tables here when he was in high school, so whenever he's in the area, he stops in for BBQ, Brunswick stew, and lemon pie. Lewis Grizzard proclaimed Sprayberry's "merely the best barbecue joint on earth." His choice of meal was a BBQ sandwich, Brunswick stew, and onion—a combination now known as the Lewis Grizzard Special. Check it out at www.sprayberrysbbq.com.

for-him Wadsworth Auditorium in Newnan with some of his famous musical friends. Adults $20, students $15.

September: **Grantville Days Crosstie Festival** (770-583-9013; www.grantville days.com). Grantville Days is celebrated with live bands and other entertainment, food, and shopping bargains. Expect amusement rides, games, vendors, crafts, antiques, a parade, and a street dance. Free; some activities have a fee.

December: **Newnan Candlelight Tour of Homes** (678-854-2487). Sponsored by the Piedmont-Newnan Hospital Auxiliary, the walking tour features homes, churches, and businesses decorated in all their Christmas finery along with lavish refreshments and evening entertainment. $15.

Senoia Candlelight Tour of Homes (770-599-8182). Call for dates; tours 5–8. The Senoia Downtown Development Authority presents this much-anticipated event, which allows visitors to get a glimpse into several historic homes decked out for the holidays. $12 in advance; $15 that day.

NORTHERN SUBURBS (NORTHSIDE)
TALLAPOOSA TO SOCIAL CIRCLE

Atlanta was once surrounded by small municipalities, some of which predated the city, as well as by seemingly endless rural regions of fields and forests. As the metropolitan area grew—and grew—these towns appeared to be swallowed up. Although it's sometimes hard to distinguish one from another, many still exist as governmental entities, and each has its own distinct personality. More than simply bedroom communities for Atlanta, these municipalities offer numerous activities, attractions, lodgings, restaurants, and special events to draw the visitor.

All the towns described in this chapter lie north of I-20, stretching from the Alabama-Georgia state line to Covington, which is east of Atlanta. In fact, the vast majority of these towns lie right along I-20. A few of them are a bit farther north. Marietta and Kennesaw are easily reached from I-75, and Roswell and Alpharetta from GA 400. A traveler interested in visiting some of these towns could start on one side of the city and spend a couple days and nights exploring the area on the east or west side of Atlanta, stay overnight in the city, and then take a few days to explore the area on the other side of the city. Another alternative would be to use Atlanta as a hub and make day trips to the east and west of the city.

The most recognizable natural landmark in the region is Stone Mountain. About 300 million years ago, intense heat and pressure forced molten rock upward. When it cooled, the lava coalesced into compact granite crystals—an unusual mixture of feldspar, mica, and quartz—but it still remained 2 miles beneath the earth's surface. Over the next 200 million years, erosion not only exposed the mass but left 583 acres uncovered at a height of 825 feet above the surface: what we know today as Stone Mountain. Pieces of soapstone bowls and dishes found at the base of the mountain indicate that Native Americans lived around the mountain as long as 5,000 years ago. Long used as a landmark and gathering place by Native Americans and early American settlers, the massive mountain is now the centerpiece of Stone Mountain Park.

In 1909 C. Helen Plane had the idea of memorializing the Confederacy with a carving on the mountain. After several false starts, the carving was finally completed in 1970. It depicts Confederate president Jefferson Davis and generals Robert E. Lee and Thomas "Stonewall" Jackson astride their steeds. The area of the figures measures 90 by 190 feet and is surrounded by a 3-acre carved surface that is 400 feet above the ground and recessed 42 feet into the mountain. With the carving as a centerpiece, the ever-evolving park has developed.

The second most significant landmark is Kennesaw Mountain. A major Civil War battle occurred here, and the area is now a national battlefield park (see *To See—Historic Homes and Sites*).

For more information about Alpharetta, contact the **Alpharetta Convention and Visitors Bureau** (678-297-0102 or 1-800-294-0923; www.awesomealpharetta .com), Park Plaza, 178 South Main Street, Suite 200, Alpharetta 30009. Open 9–5 Monday–Friday, 10–4 Saturday.

To learn more about Conyers, contact the **Conyers Convention and Visitors Bureau–Conyers Welcome Center** (770-602-2606 or 1-800-CONYERS; www.conyersga.com), 901 Railroad Street, Conyers 30012. Open 8–5 weekdays.

Those planning a trip to the Decatur–DeKalb County area should contact the **DeKalb Convention and Visitors Bureau** (770-492-5000 or 1-800-999-6055; www.dcvb.org), 1957 Lakeside Parkway, Suite 510, Tucker 30084. Open 8–4:30 weekdays.

To find out more about Kennesaw, call the **City of Kennesaw** (770-422-9714; www .kennesaw-ga.gov). For information on all of Cobb County, contact the **Cobb County Convention and Visitors Bureau** (678-303-2622 or 1-800-451-3480; www.travelcobb.org), One Galleria Parkway, Atlanta 30339. Open 8–5 weekdays.

When planning a trip to the Marietta area, contact the **Marietta Welcome Center and Visitors Bureau** (770-429-1115 or 1-800-835-0445; www.mariettasquare.com), 4 Depot Street, Marietta 30060. Open 9–5 weekdays, 10–4 Saturday, 1–4 Sunday. Located in the charming 1898 Nashville, Chattanooga, and St. Louis Railway Company passenger train depot, the welcome center features the video *Marietta, My Hometown*, narrated by former Marietta resident Joanne Woodward. The depot was built on the site of the 1840s Western and Atlantic Railroad depot, which was destroyed by Union troops in 1864.

When planning a trip to the Roswell area, contact the **Historic Roswell Convention and Visitors Bureau–Visitor Center** (770-640-3253 or 1-800-776-7935; www.visitroswellga .com), 617 Atlanta Street, Roswell 30075. Open 9–5 weekdays, 10–4 Saturday, noon–3 Sunday. Stop here to watch a film, examine historic exhibits, and get pamphlets and advice. A brochure for a self-guided walking/driving tour is also available. Several tour options are available. Visitors can either download the Civil War/Roswell Mill Village Audio Tour or stop by the visitors center to borrow one. The Self-Guided Walking Tour can also be downloaded. The visitors center can lend an audio tour player provided you leave your driver's license or a $50 deposit. **Roswell Ghost Tours** (see *To See—Guided Tours*) offers guided tours, and Civil War historian and author Michael Hitt (770-712-8653; www.michaelhitt.com) does as well. Tours can also be arranged with the **Roswell Historical Society** (770-992-1665; www.roswellhs.org).

To learn more about Social Circle, contact the **Social Circle Visitors Center** (770-464-1866), 129 East Hightower Trail, Social Circle 30025. The center is staffed by volunteers, so be sure to call ahead to make sure someone is there.

To find out more about **Stone Mountain Park,** US 78 in Stone Mountain, call 770-498-5690 or 1-800-401-2407, or visit the website at www.stonemountainpark.com. The park and its attractions are featured many times throughout this chapter, so we list the contact information, hours, and admission fees only once—here. The park is open 6 AM–midnight daily; the individual attractions generally operate 10–8 daily in summer, with shorter hours the remainder of the year. A $10 parking fee per vehicle is required for entrance to the park (bicyclists and pedestrians can enter for free). Other attractions are priced at $5–14 each, so you can pay for only what you use. If you intend to visit more than three attractions, it would be wise to purchase a One-Day All Attractions Pass combination ticket, which covers most of the activities. Ride the Ducks is an additional add-on to the All Attractions Pass. Entrance to the 4-D theater and live entertainment cannot be purchased separately and are accessible only with the All Attractions Pass. Because some attractions are open seasonally, there is a Limited Attraction Pass.

For information about Stone Mountain Village, contact the **Stone Mountain Village Visitor's Center** (770-879-4971; www.stonemountainvillage.com), 891 Main Street, Stone Mountain 30083. Open 10–4 Tuesday–Friday, 10–6 Saturday, 1–4 Sunday.

As you cross the state line from Alabama into Georgia, there is the **Georgia Visitor Information Center—Tallapoosa** (770-574-2621; www.exploregeorgia.org), I-20 East, Tallapoosa 30176. Open 8:30–5:30 daily.

GETTING THERE *By air:* Visitors to the northern suburbs fly into Atlanta. Several companies offer shuttle service to various towns. See "What's Where in Georgia."

By bus: **Greyhound Lines** (see "What's Where in Georgia") provides service to downtown Atlanta. There is also a station in Marietta (770-427-3011 or 1-800-231-2222; www.greyhound .com), 1250 South Marietta Parkway SE, Marietta.

By car: North–south I-75 and I-85, which meet in downtown Atlanta, make access from the Northeast and Midwest easy. East–west I-20 traverses downtown as well and connects Birmingham and Augusta. I-285 serves as the circular bypass of the city.

By train: The nearest **AMTRAK** (see "What's Where in Georgia") station is in Atlanta.

GETTING AROUND Visitors to the northern suburbs need a car to get around—their own or a rental. There is some mass transportation. (See "What's Where in Georgia.")

MEDICAL EMERGENCY Call 911.

VILLAGES AND NEIGHBORHOODS **Alpharetta,** just a few miles to the north of Roswell on US 19, is a fashionable bedroom community, although it is also the home of many international companies. With nearly 200 restaurants featuring practically every cuisine imaginable, Alpharetta has become a premier dining destination in metro Atlanta. Evening entertainment includes live music ranging from rock to jazz, as well as coffeehouses with poetry readings and their own music.

Conyers is the little railroad village that grew and grew. The community has produced country singer Brenda Lee, Academy Award–winning actress Holly Hunter, former federal budget director James Miller, and three Pulitzer Prize winners. Now revitalized, Conyers's Olde Towne district features numerous historic sites as well as a botanical garden, pavilion, streetscapes, shops, and restaurants. In addition, Conyers is home to the **Georgia International Horse Park** (see *To See—Equestrian Events*) and the **Haralson Mill Covered Bridge** (see *To See—Covered Bridges*), as well as the annual **Conyers Cherry Blossom Festival** (see *Special Events*).

Decatur, named after naval hero Stephen Decatur, was formed on a rise where two Indian trails intersected, then chartered in 1823. The town predates Atlanta, and, in fact, if Decatur hadn't turned down a railroad's proposal to build a major station there, Atlanta might never have existed at all. Although the city limits of Decatur are barely perceptible from neighboring Atlanta, today's Decatur is still imbued with small-town charm, characterized by tree-lined streets, historic attractions, and international culture and cuisine. Delightfully walkable downtown Decatur boasts numerous restaurants, many with outdoor seating, and more than 120 retail shops. On the serious side, the city is the home of the Centers for Disease Control, Emory University, Agnes Scott College, and several significant museums.

Historic Decatur has several historic districts. The tree-lined **Clairmont Historic District,** the northern entryway to Decatur, features architecturally interesting homes from the 1920s. **Historic Sycamore Street,** originally known as Covington Road, was part of a stagecoach route to Augusta. It is the location of some of the grandest houses in town, including the High House, where Gen. William Tecumseh Sherman stopped during the Civil War. The

M.A.K. Local Historic District, named for McDonough Street, Adams Street, and Kings Highway, was Decatur's first residential subdivision. The neighborhood offers excellent examples of Craftsman-style homes that were popular during the first three decades of the 20th century. **Oakhurst,** one of the oldest sections in Decatur, was actually an independent town known as the City of Oakhurst. Annexed by Decatur in the 1920s, it features many examples of bungalow-style residences. **South Candler Street**—called "the road to the depot" in Caroline McKinney Clarke's *The Story of Decatur 1823–1899*—is home to Agnes Scott College and some of the loveliest Victorian-era homes in the city. Agnes Scott College was established in 1889 as the Decatur Female Academy and in 1907 was the first fully accredited school in Georgia. The campus covers eight blocks and includes many historic residential properties as well as the Bradley Observatory, which is open to the public on the second Friday of each month.

Kennesaw, just north of Marietta, was originally called Big Shanty because it was a construction camp for Irish railroad workers who lived in shanty houses there in the 1830s and 1840s. During the Civil War, Union raiders stole the General from here and attempted to flee to Chattanooga—an episode known as the Great Locomotive Chase. Their intent was to tear up tracks behind them to disrupt rail service to the Atlanta area, but they failed. At nearby Kennesaw Mountain, Confederate troops held off Union troops for several weeks. After the war, the name of the town was changed to commemorate the battle. Today the town has five historic districts and the **Southern Museum of Civil War and Locomotive History** (see *To See—Museums*). Kennesaw's 1908 railroad depot has been restored and is often the site of fairs and festivals. The town is also a site on the Blue and Gray Trail and the Dixie Highway Trail.

Marietta (pronounced MAY-retta by locals), founded in 1834, became a summer resort town for south Georgia planters seeking relief from the heat and malaria of the coastal region. The town's location at the foothills of the mountains contributed to its milder, very appealing climate. Fine hotels like the Kennesaw House, which now houses the **Marietta Museum of History** (see *To See—Museums*), welcomed visitors, many of whom stayed for months.

During the Civil War, Andrews's Raiders stayed in Marietta the night before they stole a train pulled by a locomotive called the General, thus beginning the famous Great Locomotive Chase. General Sherman ordered most of the buildings around the town square burned during the war, but he spared most of the residential areas. It was from Marietta that Sherman had the captured women and children mill workers from Roswell and Lithia Springs charged with treason shipped to the North to be imprisoned or placed in servitude.

In the 20th century, the Dixie Highway, which passes through Marietta, was a major route for Northerners on their way to and from Florida. Until the construction of the interstate highways, many travelers stayed, ate, or went sight-seeing in Marietta or Kennesaw during their trips.

Today Marietta has a population of 67,000 and is the state's ninth-largest city. Because Marietta's residential areas survived the Civil War, the city is blessed with five historic districts. **Northwest Marietta Historic District,** the city's oldest designated historic district, runs from Kennesaw Avenue to Powder Springs Road and includes numerous historic Greek Revival–style homes. **Whitlock Avenue Historic District,** which borders the Kennesaw Mountain National Battlefield Park, includes several historic homes. **Atlanta/Frazier Street Historic District,** Marietta's most recently designated district, borders the railroad tracks near the Confederate Cemetery and includes several more historic homes. **Washington Avenue Historic District,** on the east side of the city, includes the Marietta National Cemetery and "Lawyer's Row," mid- to late-19th-century houses now adapted for use as attorneys' offices. **Church/Cherokee Historic District** includes two parallel tree-lined streets that head north from the square. This neighborhood includes Victorian-era homes and several historic churches.

Pick up a copy of the *Historic Marietta Walking/Driving Tour* brochure from the **Marietta Welcome Center** (see *Guidance*). It describes 57 historic structures you can walk or drive by, most of which are private homes. The charming turn-of-the-20th-century town square is the prettiest in Georgia. More than 70 antiques and specialty shops, restaurants, theaters, and museums surround the square, and several bed & breakfasts are located nearby. Marietta is also the gateway to the state-designated Blue and Gray Trail and Georgia's Dixie Highway Trail, as well as the northwest Georgia mountains.

Roswell was a textile mill town before and during the Civil War. On July 5, 1864, as Union troops advanced, retreating Confederate troops burned the covered bridge at the Chattahoochee River to slow their progress. Not so easily deterred, Union troops found a place to ford the river and entered Roswell anyway. Although Theophile Roche, the French foreman of the mill, tried to claim neutrality by flying the French flag, he fooled no one, and on July 7 the mills were burned. Fortunately, the town and homes were spared.

All the mill workers, who were primarily young women and children, were charged with treason by orders from General Sherman. Apparently he feared that these plucky women would somehow find a way to make the things the Confederacy needed, so also by his orders, they were marched west to Marietta (a railhead the Union had already captured) and put on trains for the North. Many were imprisoned for the duration of the war, while others were forced into servitude to Northern families and businesses until they could escape or the war ended. Although many returned to Roswell after the war or at least let their families know where they were, others were never seen or heard from again, giving rise to the legend of the missing Roswell women and children. Several factual and fictional accounts of this story have been written for adults and children, including *Roswell Women* by Frances Patton Statham and *Turn Homeward, Hannalee* by Patricia Beatty.

After the war, the mills were rebuilt, and Roswell remained a small but successful textile town until the mid-1970s, when the mills closed for good. The town's proximity to Atlanta, however, guaranteed that rather than dying, as most Southern textile towns had done, Roswell prospered. Now, although Roswell has grown to be the seventh most populous city in Georgia and the home of offices of many national companies, it is primarily a very affluent bedroom community for Atlanta.

Because the town was spared during the Civil War, Roswell's 640-acre historic district, of which 122 acres are listed on the National Register of Historic Places, is filled with period homes, churches, and businesses—many of which serve as museum houses, museums, restaurants, and shops. Among those open to the public as house museums are **Bulloch Hall, Barrington Hall,** and the **Archibald Smith Plantation Home** (see *To See—Historic Homes and Sites*).

Stone Mountain Village, the gateway to Stone Mountain Park, is located just outside the park's West Gate. Established in 1845 and first named New Gibraltar, the village that is now Stone Mountain was a railroad community, center for Georgia's granite industry, and a popular tourist spot from the earliest days. In fact, Stone Mountain Depot was a strategic point for General Sherman's Union troops in their campaign to destroy Atlanta during the Civil War. The Union army destroyed much of the village and 5 miles of rail line, although buildings used as hospitals were spared. The village's historic commercial buildings once housed hotels, banks, and general stores that served the granite workers. Today, these same structures house 50 specialty stores, antiques shops, galleries, and restaurants. Streets surrounding the commercial area are filled with antebellum mansions, Victorian-era cottages, and bungalows. Two of these operate as bed & breakfasts. In all, the National Register of Historic Places Historic District (1830–1940) contains 275 properties and two historic cemeteries.

COVERED BRIDGES ✤ ✐ **Concord Covered Bridge,** Concord Road between Hicks Road and South Cobb Drive, Smyrna. Available to view daily. Listed on the National Register of Historic Places, the bridge is the centerpiece of the Concord Covered Bridge Historic District, which also contains four historic homes, a railroad trestle bridge, and a gristmill. The bridge, which was built around 1840, was burned during the Civil War but was reconstructed in 1872. The only covered bridge still in use on a public highway in metropolitan Atlanta, it is 133 feet long, 16 feet wide, and 13 feet high. Ruff's Mill, which was built in 1850, saw action during the Civil War Battle of Atlanta and operated until the 1930s. The Rock House, a fieldstone structure built in 1910 as a summer residence for a wealthy Atlanta family, is particularly interesting because no two windows are alike. Free.

✤ ✐ **Haralson Mill Covered Bridge,** 4400 Haralson Mill Road off Bethel Road, Conyers. Open daily. Visitors can actually drive through this covered bridge, also known as the Rockdale County Covered Bridge, the first of its kind built in Georgia since the late 1890s. The bridge, which is located at the northeast corner of Randy Poynter Lake at Black Shoals Park, replicates covered bridge design similar to the 1820s Town Lattice Truss design. The bridge, which consists of three 50-foot spans with solid concrete piers and spill-through abutments, was built with Georgia wood products and labor in 1997. Surrounding the bridge is the Haralson Mill Historic District, which includes the Haralson Mill House, a general store, the old mill site, and a blacksmith shop. Free.

CULTURAL SITES ✤ ♿ **Callanwolde Fine Arts Center** (404-872-5338; www.callanwolde.org), 980 Briarcliff Road NE, Atlanta. Office open 9–5 weekdays, 9–4 Saturday. Although this is primarily a center for art, literary, music, and dance classes, the home itself is worthy of a visit. The sprawling 27,000-square-foot Gothic-Tudor mansion in the historic Druid Hills neighborhood was built in 1920 for Charles Howard Candler, the oldest son of Coca-Cola Company founder Asa Candler. The designer was Henry Hornbostle, the architect who designed Emory University. One of the most outstanding features is a magnificent 3,742-pipe Aeolian organ, the largest in existence in playable condition in a residence. It's astounding that anyone would ever consider destroying this magnificent house, but it was slated for demolition in 1971 when concerned citizens organized to save it. Now listed on the National Register of Historic Places, the mansion is surrounded by 12 lush acres and several outbuildings. An on-site conservatory is the headquarters of the DeKalb County Federation of Garden Clubs. Many exhibits and performances occur during the year, the most widely anticipated of which is **Christmas at Callanwolde,** when the home is dressed up in holiday finery by local decorators and opened for tours. There are also monthly poetry readings, family storytelling evenings, Friday-night jazz concerts, and Sunday-afternoon classical piano concerts. Free concerts by the Callanwolde Concert Band and performances by the Atlanta Young Singers of Callanwolde are also on the schedule. The Callan Café serves beverages, pastries, and snacks. Free except for special events.

EQUESTRIAN EVENTS ✤ ✐ ♿ **Georgia International Horse Park** (770-860-4190; www.georgiahorsepark.com), 1996 Centennial Olympic Parkway, Conyers. Office open 8–5 weekdays. Call or consult the website for a schedule of events and ticket prices. Best known as the scene of the equestrian and mountain biking competitions and the final two events of the modern pentathlon at the 1996 Centennial Olympic Summer Games, the sprawling 1,400-acre multiuse park now hosts events such as rodeos, barrel-racing competitions, dressage shows, fairs, concerts, and festivals almost every day of the year. Some of the festivals include the Conyers Cherry Blossom Festival, Fabulous Fourth, and the Big Haynes Creek Wildlife Festival. In addition to barns and stalls, the park also boasts RV camping, the **Hawthorn Suites Golf Resort Hotel** (see *Lodging—Resorts*), **Cherokee Run Golf Club**

(see *To Do—Golf*), **Big Haynes Creek Nature Center** (see *Green Space—Nature Preserves and Parks*), and trails for mountain biking and horseback riding (see separate entries in *To Do*).

✿ ✍ ♿ **Wills Park Equestrian Center** (678-297-6120; www.willspark.com), 11915 Wills Road, Alpharetta. Outdoor and covered show rings provide the backdrop for an astounding array of English and Western horse shows, dressage events, rodeos, dog shows, dog agility trials, concerts, and festivals such as the ever-popular Fourth of July Fireworks and the Taste of Alpharetta. Call for a schedule of events and prices (office hours 8:30–5 Monday–Thursday, 8:30–4 Friday).

GUIDED TOURS ✍ **Ghosts of Marietta** (770-425-1006; www.ghostsofmarietta.com), 131 Church Street, Marietta. These lantern-led 1-mile tours, which stroll through the historic district streets past memorials and opulent mansions, blend storytelling, history, and the supernatural for a compelling experience. Tours, which last about one and a half hours, depart rain or shine. Space is limited, and reservations are strongly recommended. Adults $17, children 12 and younger $12.

✍ **Historic Marietta Trolley** (770-425-1006; www.mariettatrolley.com), 131 Church Street, Marietta. Two to three tours per day Thursday–Sunday. Check the website or call for exact departure hours. The one-hour tour explores Marietta's rich heritage by traveling around the vibrant downtown square, past antebellum mansions in the historic district, and then on to the Civil War battlefields of Kennesaw Mountain. Adults $20, seniors and students $18, children 4–12 $12.

✍ **Roswell Ghost Tour** (770-649-9922; www.roswellghosttour.com), Roswell. Tours at 7:30 Friday and Saturday; reservations required (check the website for the possibility of Sunday-night tours). Tours are more frequent in October. The one-and-a-half-hour easy walking tour of Roswell's Historic District includes plenty of chills and thrills concerning the spirits that are said to live behind the walls of the mansions and workers' dwellings in the mill village. The majority of the places on the tour are private homes, so there is no entry. Many ghost tours regale visitors with stories of long-ago residents. This tour focuses on current paranormal activity. Meet at the bandstand in the square, 610 Atlanta Street, 15 minutes prior to the tour and bring a flashlight (also, depending on weather conditions, bring bug spray or an umbrella). Adults $15, children younger than 10 $10 cash.

HISTORIC HOMES AND SITES ✿ ✍ ♿ **Archibald Smith Plantation Home** (770-641-3978; www.archibaldsmithplantation.org), 935 Alpharetta Street, Roswell. Tours hourly 10–3 Monday–Saturday, 1–3 Sunday. The original 300-acre farm was created by Archibald Smith, who had migrated to Roswell from coastal Georgia. Built in 1845, the house was lived in for 150 years by three successive generations of the Smith family until they donated the property to the city. All the furnishings, therefore, are original, which is very unusual. What is even more interesting, considering that the remaining 3-acre property is now completely surrounded by the bustling city of Roswell, is that 10 original outbuildings survive, including barns, the carriage house, corncrib, greenhouse, kitchen building, slave cabin, springhouse, and well. Wheelchair accessible on the first floor only. Adults $8, seniors $7, children 6–12 $6. The Trilogy Pass combination ticket (adults $18, children $15) includes admission to **Barrington Hall** and **Bulloch Hall** (see entries that follow).

✿ ✍ ♿ **Barrington Hall** (770-640-3855; www.barringtonhall-roswell.com), 535 Barrington Drive, Roswell. Tours on the hour 10–3 Monday–Saturday, 1–3 Sunday. The house, considered to be one of the finest examples of Greek Revival Temple architecture in the United States, was completed in 1842 for Barrington King, son of Roswell founder Roswell King, and lived in by four generations of the same family: Kings, Bakers, and Simpsons. The house is furnished with many original pieces. Several original outbuildings survive, including the smokehouse, icehouse, and kitchen building, as well as two wells. Limited wheelchair accessibility. Adults $8, seniors $7, children 6–12 $6. The Trilogy Pass combination ticket (adults $18, children $15) includes admission to the **Archibald Smith Plantation House** (see previous entry) and **Bulloch Hall** (see next entry).

🐾 ✿ ♿ **Bulloch Hall** (770-992-1731; www.bullochhall.org), 180 Bulloch Avenue, Roswell. Tours 10–3 Monday–Saturday, 1–3 Sunday. The most significant historic site in Roswell, Bulloch Hall, which was built in 1840, was the home of Maj. James Stephens Bulloch, one of the town's first settlers and the grandson of an early Georgia governor, Archibald Bulloch. Major Bulloch's daughter, Martha "Mittie" Bulloch, married Theodore Roosevelt Sr. in the dining room of Bulloch Hall on December 22, 1853. They went on to become the parents of President Theodore Roosevelt Jr. and, through their other son, Elliott, the grandparents of first lady Eleanor Roosevelt. In 1905, President Teddy Roosevelt visited his mother's former home and spoke to Roswell residents from the bandstand in the town square. Bulloch Hall was constructed of heart pine in the Greek temple style with a full pedimented portico and is considered one of the best examples of the style in Georgia. The interior style, typical of the period, was called "four-square"—four principal rooms and a central hall on each floor. The kitchen is in the basement rather than in a separate building (as was more common at the time), and it features a beehive oven. Osage orange trees were planted near the house because of their ability to discourage flies and rodents, and many of them still survive today, along with shade and fruit trees. In fact, 142 trees on the property are listed on the Historic Tree Register. Today the lovingly restored home is filled with gracious period pieces, including some original china used by the Bullochs. The dogtrot-style slave quarters, which were reconstructed on the original site, include a period room and an exhibit, *Slave Life in the Piedmont.* Bulloch Hall is home to many active guilds—quilting, sampler (needlework), gardening, basketry, docent, and archaeology—which demonstrate old-time skills at special events. Several special events—the monthlong **Christmas at Bulloch Hall,** Civil War encampments, **Osage Orange Festival, Garden Faire, Sip of the South, Halloween at the Hall,** storytelling programs, the annual **Quilt Show,** and summer camps for children—occur throughout the year. For visitors whose schedule doesn't permit them to tour the house during regular hours, there is a cell phone tour of the grounds. Wheelchair accessible on the main floor only. Adults $8, seniors $7, children 6–12 $6. The Trilogy Pass combination ticket (adults $18, children $15) includes admission to the **Archibald Smith Plantation House and Barrington Hall** (see preceding entry).

🐾 ✿ ♿ **Kennesaw Mountain National Battlefield Park** (770-427-4686; www .nps.gov/kemo), 900 Kennesaw Mountain Drive, off Old US 41 and Stilesboro Road, Kennesaw. Open dawn–dusk daily; visitors center open 8:30–5 daily. Hours extended in the summer. The site of a major Civil War battle where 5,350 men died on June 27, 1864, which temporarily thwarted the advance of Union troops from Chattanooga to Atlanta, the 2,884-acre park commemorates the Atlanta Campaign. A film at the visitors center describes the battle, and exhibits depict the life of Civil War soldiers. Living-history programs and ranger talks

BULLOCH HALL IS THE MOST SIGNIFICANT HISTORIC SITE IN ROSWELL.

are presented in the summer. For those who like to wander around on their own, there is a Self-Guided Cell Phone Audio Tour. The park features 16 miles of hiking trails, monuments, and re-created military positions, as well as recreation areas and picnicking facilities. On summer weekends a shuttle bus carries visitors almost to the summit of the mountain. From there they can walk the rest of the way to the top, where, on a clear day, they'll be rewarded with the best view of downtown Atlanta. Free. Shuttle: adults $2, children $1.

McDaniel-Tichenor House (770-267-5602; www.mcdaniel-tichenor.org), 319 McDaniel Street, Monroe. Open 10–2 Monday–Friday. This gracious mansion on 11 acres was the retirement home of Governor Henry Dickerson McDaniel, wounded Civil War veteran, lawyer, businessman, and governor of Georgia during Reconstruction. The house was originally designed in the Victorian Italianate Villa style, but it was extensively renovated in the 1930s in the neoclassical style you see today. Original period features such as original woodwork, doors, and faux marbleized fireplace mantels have been beautifully restored. The eclectically furnished interior features pieces from the late-18th to the mid-20th centuries and includes the governor's carved mahogany bed. One of the interesting things about this house is that it was occupied by several generations of only one family. $3.

Michael C. Carlos Museum of Emory University (404-727-4282; www.carlos .emory.edu), 571 South Kilgo Street NE, Atlanta. Open 10–4 weekdays, 10–5 Saturday, noon–5 Sunday; docent-led tours at 2 Sunday. Visitors can get wrapped up in the art and architecture of ancient civilizations as they view the large collection at the South's largest archaeological museum. The facility's 16,000 objects offer a glimpse of 9,000 years of art history and include extremely rare ancient Egyptian, Greek, and Roman pieces as well as works on paper from the Middle Ages through the present. Other present-day works come from the Middle East, Near East, Asia, sub-Saharan Africa, and Oceania. From the Western Hemisphere, the collection includes ceramics from Nicaragua and Costa Rica, and burial urns from Colombia. Adults $8; students, seniors, and children 6–17 $6; audio tours (recommended) can be rented for $2. Call or check the website for the one free day per month.

Monastery of the Holy Spirit (770-438-8705; www.trappist.net), 2625 US 212 SW, Conyers. Grounds open 7:30 AM–9 PM daily. Abbey Church open daily. Check for the hours for morning prayer and Mass, evening prayer, and night prayer. The monastery was begun in 1944 by a group of Cistercian monks. Sitting amid 2,000 acres of woodlands and lakes, the retreat offers peaceful walking paths and picnic areas. Sights to see at the monastery include the beautiful **Abbey Church, Welcome Center, Retreat House, Bonsai Greenhouse,** and **gift shop.** In the gift shop you'll find Monk's Fruitcake, Monk's Fudge, Monk's Coffee from a sister monastery in Venezuela, and other food items, as well as 14-carat and sterling silver jewelry and a wide variety of books. In the greenhouse, bonsai novices and enthusiasts can purchase pottery from among the largest selection of Tokoname pots in the United States. Korean mica pots, books, videos, accessories, tools, wire, and fertilizer are also available. Free.

Pickett's Mill Battlefield Historic Site (770-443-7850; www.gastateparks.org /PickettsMillBattlefield), 4432 Mount Tabor Church Road, Dallas. Open 9–5 Thursday–Saturday. On May 27, 1864, a Confederate victory here by 10,000 soldiers under the command of Gen. Patrick Cleburne slowed down the Union advance on Atlanta by a week. Today the battlefield is one of the best preserved in the nation. Located on 760 acres, the historic site has preserved earthworks; an interpretive center with an introductory film and exhibits of artifacts; 4 miles of hiking trails divided into Red, White, and Blue Trails to coincide with troop movements; and picnicking areas. Check the website or call for a schedule of living-history programs. $3–5.

The Root House Museum (770-426-4982; www.cobblandmarks.com/root-house.php), 145 Denmead Street, Marietta. Open 11–4 Tuesday–Saturday. One of the oldest surviving frame houses in Marietta, the 1845 Plantation Plain–style Root House offers a glimpse into the life of a middle-class merchant family. The simple frame house is furnished with period pieces typical of the 1850s. Also on the property is a re-created kitchen house with a working 1850s cookstove, as well as flower beds and vegetable plots with plants that were available in Cobb County before 1860. Wheelchair accessible on first floor only. Adults $7, seniors and students $6, children $5.

🦌 ♂ ♿ **Stone Mountain Park Antebellum Plantation and Farmyard.** The plantation, created by moving 19 buildings constructed between 1783 and 1875 to this site, portrays the lifestyle of 19th-century Georgians. In addition to the graceful manor house, other typical plantation outbuildings include a cookhouse, slave cabins, overseer's house, and blacksmith shop. Period gardens and a petting farmyard with live animals lend an air of authenticity. Several special events—such as **military drills by the 42nd Georgia unit,** an **Indian Festival and Pow-Wow, Tour of Southern Ghosts,** and **A Homespun Christmas**—occur on the grounds throughout the year. (See *Guidance* for prices and other details.) Limited wheelchair accessibility. Free with park admission.

MUSEUMS 🦌 ♂ ♿ **Bud Jones Taxidermy Wildlife Museum** (770-574-7480; www .budjonestaxidermy.com), 359 GA 120 East, Tallapoosa. Open 8–5 weekdays, 9–noon Saturday. Bud Jones's expertise is so well-known, he has mounted a full-size elephant for the Alabama Museum of Natural History in nearby Anniston and has created a full-size American mastodon and a giant beaver for the South Carolina State Museum in Columbia. At this museum, off US 78 near the Georgia/Alabama border, visitors will see exotic North American and African mammal, fish, bird, and reptile mounts as well as an extensive fossil collection. Free.

🦌 ♂ ♿ **Confederate Hall Historical and Environmental Education Center.** At Confederate Hall, located at the base of Stone Mountain's walk-up trail, visitors can learn about the geological and ecological history of the mountain, explore interactive exhibits, and view *The Battle for Georgia—A History of the Civil War in Georgia,* a 25-minute documentary narrated by Hal Holbrook. Exhibits include a life-size cave with a video about the origin of the mountain. A huge three-dimensional map enhanced by lights and sound effects depicts the Battle of Atlanta and the March to the Sea. Other exhibits include Civil War uniforms and other artifacts. Free with park admission.

🦌 ♂ ♿ **Discovering Stone Mountain Museum at Memorial Hall** (770-413-5086; www .stonemountainpark.com), US 78 East, Stone Mountain Park. Open 10–8 daily in summer, shorter hours remainder of year. This museum tells the story behind Stone Mountain from 12,000 years ago through ancient civilizations, Native American and pioneer times, the Civil War, and to the present. Displays include the original designs for the carving and true-to-scale elements from the world's largest relief carving. There's also an 11-minute film describing the creation of the carving. Free with park admission.

🦌 ♿ **Marietta/Cobb Museum of Art** (770-528-1444; www.mariettacobbmuseum.org), 30 Atlanta Street, Marietta. Open 11–5 Tuesday–Friday, 11–4 Saturday, 1–4 Sunday. The only all-American art museum in the metro area, this repository features 19th- and 20th-century national and regional art from Warhol to Wyeth and sponsors four annual special exhibits and children's activities. It is housed in an imposing many-columned Classical Revival building that was originally constructed to serve as a federal post office and was later used as a library. Adults $8, seniors and children $5.

🦌 ♂ ♿ **Marietta Fire Museum** (770-794-5491), 112 Haynes Street, Marietta. Open 8–5 weekdays. Housed at the Marietta Fire Station and featuring fire-fighting equipment from the 1800s to the present, the museum is the home of *Aurora,* a horse-drawn Silsby Steamer fire engine in service from 1879 to 1921. It is one of only five in existence. Other exhibits include firefighter clothing and apparatus, fire helmets from around the world, and equipment such as hoses, nozzles, and bells. Free.

🖐 ✎ ♿ **Marietta Gone with the Wind Museum/Scarlett on the Square** (770-794-5576; www.gwtwmarietta.com), 18 Whitlock Avenue, Marietta. Open 10–5 Monday–Saturday. Housed in an 1880s warehouse just off the town square, the museum features a privately owned collection of movie memorabilia, including original costumes, conceptual artwork, scripts, props, photographs, rare press and publicity books, premiere programs, promotional items, and more. Among the treasures are the original Bengaline silk honeymoon gown worn by Vivien Leigh, some of Margaret Mitchell's personal volumes of the novel, contracts, foreign versions of the novel, and foreign film posters. One display is dedicated to the African American members of the cast. Adults $7, seniors and students $6, children younger than eight free.

🖐 ✎ ♿ **Marietta Museum of History** (770-794-5710; www.mariettahistory.org), 1 Depot Street, Marietta. Open 10–4 Monday–Saturday. The second floor of the old 1855 Kennesaw House hotel provides a home for the local history museum and its collection of artifacts that tell Marietta's story from the time of the Native Americans to the present. Operating under the name Fletcher House in 1862, the hotel was the base from which Andrews's Raiders launched their bold move to steal the General—the event that set off the Great Locomotive Chase. Other displays include antique quilts and furnishings, mannequins in vintage clothing from various periods, and sewing arts. The Homelife Gallery houses 19th- and 20th-century clothing and accessories, inventions from the turn of the 20th century, a complete 1940s kitchen, and a vignette featuring the bachelor suite of Yankee spy Henry Green Cole. The Civil War Gallery features uniforms, weapons, a battle flag, one of General Sherman's hairpins (a twisted rail), and a military document signed by Abraham Lincoln. The General History Gallery tells the story of Native Americans, the gold rush, local businesses, influential Mariettans, the growth of the Bell Bomber Plant (which became Lockheed Martin), and displays from all of America's wars. Adults $7, seniors and students $5, children younger than five free.

🖐 ✎ ♿ **Southern Museum of Civil War and Locomotive History** (770-427-2117; www .southernmuseum.org), 2829 Cherokee Street, Kennesaw. Open 9:30–5 Monday–Saturday, 11–6 Sunday. This Smithsonian-affiliated museum describes how the locomotive has shaped history. Visitors learn the crucial role railroads played during the Civil War and how a locomotive factory aided in rebuilding the South after the war. On display is one of the most famous locomotives in the South: the General, which was hijacked by Union raiders during the Civil War but recaptured by Southerners after an 86-mile chase. The museum also displays a multimillion-dollar collection of Civil War relics, as well as the Glover Machine Works collection and traveling Smithsonian exhibits. Adults $7.50, seniors $6.50, children 4–12 $5.50.

🖐 ✎ ♿ **West Georgia Museum of Tallapoosa** (770-574-3125; www.tallapoosa.gov/museum), 185 Mann Street, Tallapoosa. Open 9–4 Tuesday–Friday, 9–5 Saturday. Extensive displays focus on local history and paleontology. From the prehistoric area visitors see a 30-foot *Tyrannosaurus rex,* seven smaller dinosaurs, a real dinosaur egg from China, and a 300-million-year-old fossilized tree from Alabama. Natural history is traced through mounted animals native to Haralson County. Native American displays include arrowheads and other artifacts, while early American history is described through a fully stocked general store and a fully furnished log cabin. The evolution of transportation over the past 100 years or so is shown through buggies, wagons, and early automobiles. The Lithia Springs Hotel in Tallapoosa, built between 1890 and 1892, was the largest wooden building east of the Mississippi. Although the hotel no longer exists, numerous items from the hotel, including a registration book with George Vanderbilt's signature, are exhibited here. Each month a special changing display keeps visitors coming back. Adults $2, children $1.

SCENIC DRIVES For a driving tour of Marietta's Civil War sites, the **Cannonball Trail,** or the **Historic Marietta Self-Guided Walking/Driving Tour,** pick up a brochure from the **Marietta Welcome Center and Visitors Bureau** (770-429-1115; www.marietta square.com), 4 Depot Street, Marietta.

❦ ✍ ♿ **Kennesaw Mountain National Battlefield Park** (see *Historic Homes and Sites*). The visitors center provides a brochure for a self-guided walking/driving tour of the park. The four sites on the trail are the overlook at the summit of Kennesaw Mountain, where visitors can get a panoramic view of north Georgia, including the Atlanta skyline; Pigeon Hill entrenchments, reached by a foot trail; Cheatham Hill, known as the Dead Angle, where fierce fighting occurred during the Civil War; and Kolb's Farm, where an 1836 log house has been restored but is not open to the public. The visitors center has cell phone audio tours to lend.

WINERY TOUR ❦ ♿ **Fox Vineyards Winery** (770-787-5402; www.foxvineyards winery.com), 225 GA 11 South, Social Circle. Open for tours and tastings 10–6 Wednesday– Saturday, 1–6 Sunday. The local award-winning winery grows seven varieties of European *vinifera* and French-American hybrids, as well as muscadine and scuppernong grapes, on its 15-acre vineyard and produces transitional wines. Tours, tastings, and sales of wine and wine gifts are available.

✳ To Do

BALLOONING **Magic Carpet Ride Balloon Adventure** (404-808-6132; www.magic ballooning.com). Call for flight schedules, prices, and launch locations. What better way to see the area than by getting a bird's-eye view from a hot-air balloon? Flights are conducted at dawn and about two hours after sunset, weather permitting.

BICYCLING ❦ ✍ The **PATH Foundation** (404-875-7284; www.pathfoundation.org), mailing address: P.O. Box 14327, Atlanta 30324, has been instrumental in developing bike paths in the metropolitan Atlanta area. The most ambitious of these trails is the **Silver Comet Trail** (see *Hiking*), which begins in Smyrna and ends 60 miles later at the Alabama line, where it connects with the 33-mile Chief Ladiga Trail. For information on renting regular and three-wheel recumbent bikes and skates or obtaining other related services, visit **Silver Comet Cycles** (770-819-3279; www.silvercometdepot.com), 4342 Floyd Road, Mableton. Open 11–5 Sunday and Monday, 11–6 Tuesday–Friday, 9–6 Saturday. The company also sponsors group walks and rides and provides some shuttle service. The **Stone Mountain Trail,** a portion of the Atlanta-DeKalb Trail System, extends 18 miles from Georgia Tech (see the Atlanta chapter) to Stone Mountain Park. To learn more about the trail system, including places to park, hospitals, restrooms, water, MARTA access, and other points of interest, purchase the *Silver Comet Guidebook* or the *Metro Atlanta Trails Guidebook* from the PATH Foundation for $7 plus Georgia tax.

BOAT EXCURSIONS ❦ ✍ **Ride the Ducks Adventure at Stone Mountain Park.** The amphibious sight-seeing experience makes a 40-minute tour of the park by road and then plunges into Stone Mountain Lake. These unusual vehicles are modeled after the World War II amphibious DUKWS. $15 per person in addition to park admission.

BOATING ❦ ✍ **Rental Boats at Stone Mountain Park.** The country store at the campground offers rowboats and pedal boats for use on Stone Mountain Lake. No private boats are permitted after 11 AM on weekends and on holidays between May 1 and September 30. Private boats are limited to 10-horsepower motors. Boat rental $25–35 per day.

CANOEING, KAYAKING, AND RAFTING On a hot summer day, there's nothing more refreshing than floating down the Chattahoochee River in a raft. This popular activity is known as "Shootin' the Hooch." The water stays about 50 degrees, so if you get too hot, all you have to do is splash yourself with water.

Chattahoochee Outfitters (770-650-1008; www.shootthehooch.com). Rentals and return shuttle service are available seasonally from their Johnson Ferry and Powers Island outposts. Bring your own picnic, because the leisurely trip takes between two and a half and six hours, depending on the outpost location and the speed of the river flow. U.S. Coast Guard–approved life jackets are required, and anyone younger than 18 must be accompanied by an adult. Call for prices.

🦐 🍸 **Chattahoochee River Outfitters** (404-650-1008), Chattahoochee River Park, 203 Azalea Drive, Roswell. Open 10–8 daily. Canoe, kayak, or raft the Chattahoochee River as it flows through Roswell. The company provides return shuttle service for rafters who have floated down the river. Call for prices.

FOR FAMILIES 🦐 🍸 ♿ **Crossroads at Stone Mountain.** Some stores may stay open until the laser show begins at 9:30. Visitors travel back in time to a 1870s Southern village at this park-within-a-park. Here they'll meet fascinating costumed characters and skilled crafts-people who demonstrate such old-time skills as glassblowing, candle making, candy and ice-cream making, blacksmithing, and grinding meal at the gristmill. Crossroads Village includes Yogi Bear's 4-D Adventure, Georgia's only 4-D theater, and the Great Barn, Atlanta's largest indoor play experience (see separate entry that follows). Admission to the Crossroads Village is free with park admission. Some of the individual attractions have a fee or are included in the One-Day All Attractions Pass.

🦐 🍸 **The Great Barn at Stone Mountain.** The gigantic barnlike structure features a series of interactive games geared toward teaching children ages 5–12 about harvest time. They'll also enjoy the super slides, trampoline floors, and climbing structures. Included in the One-Day Adventure Pass.

🍸 ♿ **Six Flags Over Georgia** (770-948-9290; www.sixflags.com/overgeorgia), 275 Riverside Parkway SW, Austell. Open weekends March–Memorial Day and Labor Day–end of October; daily in summer. Hours vary widely, so call ahead or consult the website. It's always playtime at this family-oriented theme park, which features 100 rides, including 12 white-knuckle coasters such as the Georgia Scorcher, one of the Southeast's tallest and fastest stand-up coasters; the Georgia Cyclone, the South's only twister coaster; and Acrophobia, a 200-foot rotating tower drop. Other family and not-for-the-faint-of-heart thrill coasters include the massive Goliath roller coaster, Superman—Ultimate Flight, and Batman the Ride. A variety of shows and other entertainment extravaganzas last late into the night on 10 stages. The park's newest additions are Skull Island, the world's largest interactive water-play structure, and Wile E. Coyote Canyon Blaster, a roller coaster. Numerous special events occur throughout the year, such as Fright Fest in October. Adults $54.99, children $39.99. Parking $16. Check for specials.

🍸 ♿ **Six Flags White Water** (770-948-9290; www.sixflags.com/ whitewater), 250 Cobb Parkway North, Marietta. Open weekends in May and week before Memorial Day, then daily Memorial Day weekend–early August, then weekends through Labor Day. Check the website or call for exact hours when you want to visit. The 35-acre site contains all the necessary ingredients for cooling off on hot summer days. Named one of the top 10 water parks in America as well as the Most Scenic Water Park in the country by *USA Today*, the complex offers 50 "splash-tastic" water rides that are fun for the whole family. The 90-foot-tall Cliffhanger provides one of the world's largest free falls, and the Tornado sends thrill seekers down a 132-foot-long tunnel, throws them into a giant open-ended funnel, and drenches them under a waterfall. The park also features tree-shaded waterfalls, a lazy Little Hooch River, the Atlanta Ocean wave pool, a family raft ride, and the four-story Tree House Island.

Five food concessions and a gift shop are on-site. Adults $37.99, children shorter than 48 inches $26.99; parking $12.

🐾 🎣 **Sky Hike at Stone Mountain Park.** The four-story outdoor attraction located at Crossroads Village is a trek through the treetops on suspended wooden bridges, leaps from one wooden slat to another, balancing on a single rope, and climbing vertical net bridges. There are three 0.25-mile routes: a 12-foot-high trail for beginners, a 24-foot-high trail for the more courageous, and 40-foot-high trail for daredevils. There are minimum height and maximum weight restrictions as well as age restrictions. Included in the One-Day Adventure Pass or $14 in addition to park admission.

🐾 🎣 ♿ **Stone Mountain Park.** Check the website or call for event schedules and fees, as they vary seasonally. The park, Georgia's most-visited attraction, has something for everyone in the way of outdoor entertainment and recreation. Central to the park is the world's largest exposed mass of granite as well as the world's largest bas-relief sculpture, which depicts Confederate president Jefferson Davis and generals Robert E. Lee and Stonewall Jackson on horseback. Surrounding the 825-foot mountain are 3,300 acres of forests, lakes, and parkland. Attractions include an antebellum plantation (*To See—Historic Homes and Sites*), Confederate Hall Historical and Environmental Center (*To See—Museums*), the 1870s town of Crossroads, a 4-D theater, the Great Barn, Ride the Ducks sight-seeing tour, mountaintop skyride, scenic train ride, and the Lasershow Spectacular—a 40-minute extravaganza of colorful lasers, surround sound, and fantastic fireworks (see separate entries throughout this section). Recreation includes canoeing, boating, golf, hiking, miniature golf, and a water slide complex (see separate entries in this section). Festivals and other special events occur year-round (see *Special Events*). Accommodations are offered in two hotels and at a campground (see *Lodging*), and numerous restaurants to please any palate (see *Where to Eat*).

🐾 🎣 ♿ **Summit Skyride at Stone Mountain Park.** Swiss-cable cars dangling 825 feet above the ground whisk visitors from the base of the mountain to the summit and afford a close-up view of the carving. Many visitors choose to take the Skyride to the summit and then walk down, although you don't come down to the same place from which you departed. $5.50 one-way or $9 round-trip per person in addition to park admission.

🐾 🎣 ♿ **Yellow River Game Ranch** (770-972-6643; www.yellowrivergameranch.com), 4525 US 78, Lilburn. Open 10–6 daily, shorter hours in winter (last tickets sold at one hour prior to closing). The most acclaimed resident of this 25-acre game preserve is General Beauregard Lee, Georgia's weather prognosticator. The famous groundhog comes out of his Tara-like abode on February 2 and foretells the weather in the South just as Punxsutawney Phil does in the North, though General Lee correctly predicts an early spring much more often than his Northern cousin does. Visitors to the ranch can see 600 animals, including black bears, bobcats, the largest herd of buffalo east of the Mississippi, cougars, coyotes, foxes, goats, mountain lions, pigs, raccoons, sheep and lambs, white-tailed deer, and other animals indigenous to Georgia. Little ones (and even jaded adults) are won over by feeding the deer with specially purchased feed. Spring and summer, when there are babies, are favorite months to visit. Adults $8, children 2–11 $7.

FRIGHTS 🎣 **Tour of Southern Ghosts.** Held after dark until 9 or 9:30 PM Thursday–Sunday on 13 evenings during the Halloween season, the tour consists of tales told by costumed tellers as they guide groups around the lantern-lit grounds of Stone Mountain Park's Antebellum Plantation (see *To See—Historic Homes and Sites*). Stories are a little scary, often humorous, but never so frightening that they're inappropriate for young audiences. Reservations and tickets are strongly recommended to avoid standing in long lines and perhaps being disappointed. Adults $12 in advance or $15 at the gate, children $7, in addition to park admission.

GOLF **Cherokee Run Golf Course at Georgia International Horse Park** (770-785-7904; www.cherokeerungolfclub.com), 1595 Centennial Olympic Parkway, Conyers. Tee times 8–6:30. The Arnold Palmer and Ed Seay–designed 7,016 yard, par-72, mountain-style course features terrain as varied as wetlands and granite outcroppings. Other amenities include a clubhouse with a pro shop and a restaurant. $15–25 walking, $25–41.50 riding.

Stone Mountain Golf Club at Stone Mountain Park (770-465-3278; www.stone mountaingolf.com), Stonewall Jackson Drive, Stone Mountain Park. Open 7 AM–to dusk daily. Managed by Marriott Golf, the club offers 36 championship holes on the Lakemont and Stonemont courses. The Stonemont Course has been named one of the top 25 public courses in the country by *Golf Digest*. A driving range, putting green, practice facilities, pro shop, PGA instruction, clubhouse with locker rooms, and the Commons Restaurant are also available. $35–59.

HIKING 🐾 ✎ **Arabia Mountain Trails** (770-484-3060), 3787 Klondike Road, Lithonia. Open daylight hours daily. The Davidson–Arabia Mountain Nature Preserve features a paved path for walking, biking, and skating, as well as several unpaved marked and unmarked paths varying in length from a half mile to a mile. These paths can be combined for a longer hike of 3.3 miles. The most challenging path is the Bradley Peak Trail, which leads to the top of the 954-foot mountain. Hikers will enjoy arched granite bridges, wooden boardwalks, and waterfalls. Free.

🐾 ✎ 🐦 **Chattahoochee River National Recreation Area** (678-538-1200; www.nps.gov /chat), headquarters office: 1978 Island Ford Drive, Sandy Springs. The Sope Creek unit of the 48-mile-long park is located on Paper Mill Road between Terrell Mill Road and Johnson Ferry Road in Marietta. It offers several miles of easy to difficult hiking trails, and mountain biking is allowed on designated stretches of the trails. A moderate hike takes you to the ruins of the Marietta Manufacturing Mill. The Powers Island unit has an easy 1-mile trail, the Johnson Ferry South unit has a 1.5-mile trail, and the Johnson Ferry North unit has 2.5 miles of easy trails. The Cochran Shoals unit contains easy to difficult trails, including a 3-mile fitness trail and a 3-mile bike loop. See the Atlanta chapter for more information about the recreation area.

🐾 ✎ **Georgia Wildlife Federation** (770-787-7887; www.gwf.org), 11600 Hazelbrand Road, Covington. Open daylight hours daily. The 115-acre grounds of the federation's headquarters offer woodlands, wetlands, meadow habitats, and demonstration wildlife habitat gardens. Visitors enjoy ambling along the Dogwood Trail as it meanders past the tupelo gum river swamp and along the Alcovy River. The center is popular for bird-watching and picnicking. Deer, fox squirrels, otters, and a variety of songbirds are just a few of the year-round residents. Free.

🐾 ✎ **Kennesaw Mountain National Battlefield Park** (see *To See—Historic Homes and Sites*). The park's trails offer short walks and long hikes. Various starting points on the trails create 2-, 5-, 10-, and 16-mile round-trip hikes. All the trails require moderately steep climbing. There is limited water and no shelter or food along the trails.

🐾 ✎ **Nature Trails of Stone Mountain Park.** The park is filled with 10 miles of easy to difficult trails that encourage visitors to enjoy the beauty of the seasons, the natural wonders, and the striking vistas while they get their exercise. The most difficult trail is the steep 1.3-mile **Walk-Up Trail** to the 1,683-feet-above-sea-level summit. Our suggestion is that, unless you're in very good shape, you take the Skyride ($5.50 one-way) to the top and walk down. If you walk up and ride down, there is no transportation back to the parking lot from which you started. Along the Walk-Up Trail visitors will see the 2-inch-tall red stonecrop, golden ragweed, and the Confederate yellow daisy. Fifteen other genera of rare plants grow on the mountain outcrops and along the trails. The short loop **Nature Trail** is associated with the

Nature Garden, where visitors can wander among native plants, flowering shrubs, and mountain streams. The lengthy 7-mile-plus **Cherokee Trail** with two connecting trails wraps all the way around the mountain. The site of the 1996 Centennial Olympic Summer Games archery and cycling events, the area encompasses the **Songbird Habitat and Trail,** a 1-mile trail with a variety of plant life and food for a wide array of birds. Along many of these paths, visitors can see vegetation that is native to Georgia and/or Stone Mountain Park. Trail use free with park admission.

🐾 ✐ ♿ 🐾 **Silver Comet Trail** (www.silvercometga.com). The trail connects the Atlanta metropolitan area to the Alabama state line—a 60-mile journey. A former railroad route for the *Silver Comet* passenger train, which ran from Boston to Birmingham between 1947 and 1968, the track has been taken up and paved so that the roadbed provides opportunities for walking, jogging, hiking, cycling, and skating. The trail is also suitable for baby strollers and wheelchairs. Those with their own horse can avail themselves of portions of the trail, and leashed pets are welcome. No motorized vehicles are allowed. The trail, which crosses six trestles and bridges, offers scenic views and access to Heritage Park, a 105-acre nature preserve. A 1.7-mile spur trail goes to the ruins of a woolen mill. Six trailheads offer parking, restrooms, and water fountains. The trail also can be accessed from several cross streets. It is patrolled by bicycle-mounted Cobb County police officers. The trail connects to the Wild Horse Creek Trail (see entry that follows) in Powder Springs and to the 33-mile Chief Ladiga Trail at the Georgia-Alabama state line, then continues on to Anniston, Alabama, which creates even more possibilities. See *Bicycling* for information about the shuttle service (reservations required) provided by **Silver Comet Cycles,** a year-round Volksmarch center.

🐾 ✐ 🐾 **Vickery Creek Unit, Chattahoochee River National Recreation Area** (678-538-1200; www.nps.gov/chat), Roswell. The topography of the heavily wooded park includes steep cliffs and rocky outcroppings as well as level terrain. A total of 11.5 miles of trails for all abilities crisscross the park along the creek or provide rigorous climbs over ridges. Within the park are the ruins of several mill buildings and a 1860s man-made mill dam that creates a cascading waterfall. Access at several locations. Free; $3 if parking off Riverside Drive.

🐾 ✐ ♿ 🐾 **Wild Horse Creek Trail** (770-439-2500), Powder Springs. Open daylight hours daily; closed immediately after a rainstorm. This area saw a lot of action as Union troops advanced on Atlanta in 1864. Today, a 10-foot-wide, 2-mile paved trail is used by cyclists, skaters, runners, and walkers. The trail, which begins at Macedonia Road and ends at Carter Road, is the first in a proposed citywide network of trails. It is appropriate for baby strollers, wheelchairs, and pets on leashes. Motorized vehicles and horses are not permitted. Along the way, users can see the largest red maple tree in the state or view the wetlands from an observation tower. Amenities include a rest area near Powder Springs Road, two emergency call boxes, and parking and restroom facilities at Wild Horse Creek Park. The trail also connects to the Silver Comet Trail (see preceding entry). Free.

HORSEBACK RIDING 🐾 ✐ **Georgia International Horse Park** (see *To See— Equestrian Events*). Open daylight–dusk daily, but closed occasionally for special events, so check the website. For those who can BYOH (bring your own horse), the park features more than 15 miles of horse trails that offer scenic views of the former Olympic Endurance Course as they wind through wooded areas and open pastureland and past streams. Varied trail lengths and links between trails allow riders to choose their own route and tailor their own ride. A large map of the trails is posted at each check-in shelter, and there are individual take-away maps as well. Free.

MOUNTAIN BIKING 🐾 ✐ **Georgia International Horse Park** (see *To See— Equestrian Events*). Open daylight–dusk daily, but closed occasionally for special events, so check the website. The park offers 8 miles of riding trails and 1,032 feet of elevation change on the first-ever Olympic mountain biking course in the world. A large map of the trails is posted at each check-in shelter, and there are individual take-away maps as well. Free.

SKYDIVING Skydive Monroe (770-207-1122; www.skydivemonroe.com), Monroe Municipal Airport, 535 Tower Street, Monroe. Open weekends. There are only four skydiving drop zones in Georgia, and this is the closest one to metro Atlanta. Skydive Monroe serves a mix of new jumpers, belly-fliers, and free-fliers. The company belongs to the U.S. Parachute Association and follows that organization's safety standards. Courses are taught by USPA-rated staff. $190–270.

SPORTS EXPERIENCES Andretti Indoor Karting and Games (770-992-5688; www.andrettikarting.com), 11000 Alpharetta Highway, Roswell. Open at 11 AM daily, closing varies from 11 PM to 2 AM. This indoor complex boasts racing-related entertainment for adventure seekers. Visitors can suit up in authentic racing gear and get behind the wheel of a high-performance, Italian-designed SuperKart. Two indoor courses were patterned after famous European courses. The Game Lab is an interactive arcade with the latest in video and virtual-reality games, including football, basketball, soccer, and racing simulators. The high-energy facility also offers a three-story rock-climbing wall, an Extreme Ropes Course, billiards, bowling, and 100 satellite-linked televisions, as well as Adrenaline Skybar and Andretti Grill restaurant. Racing is not suitable for preteen children. $7 for a license, $23 for one race, $40 for three races; $9 for three climbs on rock wall; $0.50–1.50 for arcade games.

TRAIN EXCURSIONS 🐾 ✑ **Scenic Railroad at Stone Mountain Park.** Riding aboard vintage 1940s open-air rail cars, passengers enjoy the 5-mile, 30-minute journey around the base of the mountain. Board the train in Crossroads Village (where tickets can be purchased). Adults $9, children $7, in addition to park admission.

✳ Green Space

NATURE PRESERVES AND PARKS 🐾 ✑ **Autrey Mill Nature Preserve and Heritage Center** (678-366-3511; www.autreymill.org), 9770 Autrey Mill Road, Johns Creek. Grounds open 8–dusk daily; center open 10–4 Monday–Saturday. Located on 46 acres of ravine forest and the site of an old cotton plantation, Autrey Mill offers scenic creeks, rocky shoals, spring seeps, picturesque cliffs, mature trees, wildflowers, native plants, wildlife, and 2 miles of hiking trails. Several circa late-1800s farmhouses from the plantation days remain, and several others have been moved there, for a total of nine. These are open only for special events. The rustic visitors center displays exhibits. The park offers special programs and events, including an Easter egg hunt, environmental activities, music programs, summer camp, trail walks, and Young Artist Days. Free.

🐾 ✑ **Big Haynes Creek Nature Center** (see *To See—Equestrian Events*). Within the **Georgia International Horse Park,** 173 acres are designated as a preserve dedicated to the preservation and study of native plants and wildlife. The preserve features 1.4 miles of riding trails and 5 miles of walking trails, a boardwalk, observation platform, and canoe launch. Interpretive signage as well as touch and audio stations enhance the experience with information about the ecosystem, plants, and animals. No fishing. Free.

🐾 ♿ **Black Shoals Park** (770-278-7529 or 770-761-1611; www.rockdalecounty.org), 3001 Black Shoals Road, Conyers. Open daily, 7 AM–9 PM summer, 7–6 winter; boats must be off the water a half hour before closing. No gasoline motors of any kind are permitted. Fishing, boating, and canoeing are the primary activities in this park surrounding Randy Poynter Lake, a 650-acre reservoir, but hiking and picnicking are popular as well. The Georgia

Department of Natural Resources stocks the lake with largemouth bass, assorted bream, and catfish. The park features a boat ramp, fishing pier, and picnic pavilion. A **Veterans Memorial Park** honors veterans and their families (www.walkofheroes.com). $5 per person, $5 per boat or canoe.

🐾 ᴓ ♿ **Chattahoochee Nature Center** (770-992-2055; www.chattnaturecenter.com), 9135 Willeo Road, Roswell. Open 10–5 Monday–Saturday, noon–5 Sunday. Visitors can get in touch with nature at this facility, where boardwalks and nature trails allow access to the 127-acre site and miles of freshwater ponds, river marshes, and wooded uplands that hug the Chattahoochee River. More than 30 species of wildlife call the nature center home. Among the popular exhibits is a beaver dam complete with beavers. Raptor aviaries display birds of prey that have been rehabilitated here and can't be returned to the wild. The nature center offers tours and hosts educational programs and special events throughout the year, including seasonal canoe trips on the river. Adults $8, seniors $6, children 3–12 $5.

🐾 ᴓ ♿ **Sweetwater Creek State Conservation Park** (770-732-5871; www.gastateparks .org/SweetwaterCreek), 1750 Mount Vernon Road, Lithia Springs. Park open 7 AM–10 PM; visitors center open 8–5; trails close at dark. This is the third most visited park in the state system and the most visited park without overnight facilities. More than 2,549 acres of peaceful wilderness and 9 miles of trails are located just west of Atlanta. A forest trail follows a stream to the ruins of the New Manchester Manufacturing Company, a textile mill that was burned during the Civil War. Its workers (mostly women and children) were charged with treason, marched to Marietta, and put on trains for the North, where they were either imprisoned or forced into servitude to Northern families and businesses for the duration of the war. From the mills, the trail climbs rocky bluffs and affords views of the shoals below. The park's streams and 215-acre George Sparks Reservoir provide recreation for anglers. (Electric motors only are allowed.) Fishing supplies and snacks are available in the park's Trading Post bait and gift shop, along with canoe, kayak, and fishing-boat rentals in season. The park also features picnicking facilities, a butterfly garden, and periodic interpretive programs and night hikes. Children love to feed the ducks in the pond. Maps and park information can be found at the visitors center. Parking $5.

RECREATION AREAS 🐾 ᴓ The **Chattahoochee River National Recreation Area** (678-538-1200) is a 48-mile stretch of the Chattahoochee River. Along the way are numerous day-use parks where visitors can enjoy boating, fishing, hiking, and wildlife observation. The units in the area described in various sections of this chapter include Cochran Shoals, Sope Creek, Powers Island, Johnson Ferry North, Johnson Ferry South, and Vickery Creek. Cochran Shoals offers several trails, including one that is wheelchair accessible. Sope Creek has stone ruins from a paper manufacturing company that produced much of the South's paper from 1855 to 1902. Powers Island is named for James Powers, who ferried travelers across the river before there were bridges.

RIVERS 🐾 ᴓ **Chattahoochee River.** The mighty Chattahoochee, which is the Cherokee word for "River of the Painted Rock," begins as Chattahoochee Spring in the northeast Georgia mountains near the White-Union County line and wends its way to Lake Seminole at the Georgia-Florida border. On the way it creates the border between Georgia and Alabama as well as several lakes. The river and its banks offer opportunities for fishing, hiking, picnicking, canoeing, and rafting. Visitors may see wildflowers, wildlife, and waterfowl. The City of Roswell created a River Parkway, an important link in the Roswell Trail System, along several miles of the river. Dotted along the River Parkway are the **Chattahoochee River Park** on Azalea Drive, **Riverside Park** on Riverside Road, and the **Don White Memorial Park** on Riverside Drive.

✳ Lodging

BED & BREAKFASTS

In Decatur

🐾 🐱 **Garden House Bed and Breakfast** (404-377-3057; www.gardenhousebedand breakfastdecatur.com), 135 Garden Lane. Located just four blocks from downtown Decatur, this B&B offers a second-floor suite in a home that was built in the 1940s. Guests can choose any type breakfast: continental, full, low-carb, or whatever they'd like. Small dogs accepted. No smoking. Not wheelchair accessible. $100.

In Marietta

The Stanley House Bed and Breakfast (770-426-1881; www.thestanleyhouse.com), 236 Church Street NE. When visitors see this large, stately Queen Anne Victorian, they find it hard to imagine that the house was built in 1895 as a summer "cottage" by Mrs. Felie Woodrow, an aunt of Woodrow Wilson. Now an elegant bed & breakfast, the inn offers five guest rooms and executive apartments. A full breakfast is included. No smoking. Not wheelchair accessible. Call for rates.

In Stone Mountain Village

♿ **Village Inn Bed and Breakfast** (770-469-3459; www.villageinnbb.com), 992 Ridge Avenue. Located in a stately home built in the 1820s as a roadside inn, the structure is the oldest building in Stone Mountain Village. It served as a Confederate hospital during the Civil War and was therefore spared during Sherman's March to the Sea. The inn has six guest rooms, including Scarlett's Room and Rhett's Room, each with two-person whirlpool tubs. Some guest chambers also boast a gas fireplace and/or a veranda. The Ballroom Suite has a sitting area with a daybed and a trundle bed, a refrigerator, a microwave, and a shower and whirlpool therapy tub. Full breakfast is included. Smoking outdoors only. Limited wheelchair accessibility. $139–179.

CAMPGROUNDS

In Conyers

🐾 **Georgia International Horse Park** (see *To See—Equestrian Events*). Office

THE VILLAGE INN BED AND BREAKFAST SERVED AS A CONFEDERATE HOSPITAL DURING THE CIVL WAR.

open 8–5 weekdays. Reservations required. The full-service park near the stable complex and Walker Arena complex offers 140 sites with full water, electric, and sewer hookups. The park also offers shower facilities. Reservations required. Call for price ranges.

In Stone Mountain Park

🐾 🐾 **Stone Mountain Park Campground** (770-498-5710 or 1-800-385-9807; www.stonemountainpark.com), 4003 Stonewall Jackson Drive, off US 78 East. Situated on 363-acre Stone Mountain Lake, the campground features 250 full-hookup and 191 partial-hookup sites as well as 56 primitive tent sites. Amenities include heated comfort stations, a campground store, laundry facilities, a playground, swimming pool, horseshoes, and volleyball court. Rowboat, pedal boat, and golf cart rentals available. $25–67.

INNS AND HOTELS

In Atlanta

🐾 ♿ **Renaissance Atlanta Waverly Hotel** (770-953-4500), 2450 Galleria Parkway. The Renaissance Waverly is one of the only AAA four-diamond hostelries in the northwest quadrant of metro Atlanta and one of the most luxurious hotels in the immediate area. The 14-floor hotel features 497 upscale guest rooms, 24 elegant suites, and a concierge level, as well as indoor and outdoor pools, a fitness center, and spa services. Restaurants include the Atrium Café and Medici for dinner. No smoking, no pets. $99–209.

  ↕ ☀ **University Inn at Emory** (1-800-654-8591; www.univinn.com), 1767 North Decatur Road. Guest accommodations are located in several buildings on the Emory University campus. Most rooms are spacious and have a microwave/refrigerator combination. The Guest House features the most economical accommodations, and many of its rooms have a kitchen. Oxford Hall offers long-term housing for those who do not require daily services. For all guests, the inn offers a complimentary continental breakfast and afternoon refreshments daily. Rooms are equipped with high-speed Internet access or modem connections and voice mail; the inn's business center offers fax, printing, and Internet access. Guests have access to the Emory fitness center. Pet friendly. No smoking. Some rooms are wheelchair accessible. Guest House: $79–189; inn: $79–109; Oxford Hall: $40 without private bath, $60 with private bath, 10-night minimum.

RESORTS

In Conyers

✈ ↕ ☀ **Hawthorn Suites Golf Resort** (770-761-9155 or 1-800-527-1133; www.georgiahorsepark.com), 1659 Centennial Olympic Parkway. Overlooking the seventh hole of the Cherokee Run Golf Club, the hotel boasts 77 one-, two-, and three-bedroom suites with kitchens, as well as an outdoor heated pool and whirlpool, bar, guest laundry facilities, fitness center, convenience and gift shop, and business center. A hot breakfast is served daily, and there's a manager's reception Monday–Thursday evenings. Pets allowed. Smoking and non-smoking rooms available. Some rooms are $70–119.

In Marietta

✈ ↕ **Hilton Atlanta/Marietta Conference Center and Resort** (770-427-2500 or 1-888-685-2500; www.hilton.com), 500 Powder Springs Road. This magnificent AAA four-diamond hotel, which resembles

the world-famous Greenbrier in West Virginia, sits on the site of the old Georgia Military Institute, which was destroyed by Union troops during the Civil War. Choose from 199 elegantly furnished guest rooms or nine parlor suites. Each offers a spectacular view of the Atlanta skyline or the golf course and Kennesaw Mountain. Other amenities include a restaurant, bar, billiards room, outdoor pool, fitness club, golf course, and lighted tennis courts. On the grounds is the historic **Antebellum Brumby Hall and Gardens,** the only surviving building from the school era. Smoking and nonsmoking rooms available; no smoking in restaurant or pub. $109–169.

In Stone Mountain

Stone Mountain Park offers two accommodations: the **Evergreen Marriott Conference Resort,** 4021 Lakeview Drive, and the **Marriott Stone Mountain Inn,** 1058 Robert E. Lee Drive. For reservations at either call 1-888-670-2250. The newer of the two properties, Evergreen, features a spa, indoor/outdoor pool, and four restaurants. From $169. The Stone Mountain Inn, which is in walking distance of some of the park's attractions, has a pool, restaurant, and pub. From $129. Both hotels have access to the golf course and all the amenities of the park.

✳ Where to Eat

DINING OUT

In Alpharetta

↕ **Cabernet** (770-777-5955; www.cabernetsteakhouse.com), 5575 Windward Parkway. Open 11:30–2:30 weekdays, 5:30–10 Monday–Thursday, 5–11 Friday and Saturday. Walk in the front doors, and you'll be reminded of grand steakhouses and watering holes in New York. Chef Richard Holley's menus feature the highest grade of prime aged beef and fresh seafood flown in daily. Smoking in bar and on the patio only. Lunch $9–37, dinner $22–45.

↕ **Ray's at Killer Creek** (770-649-0064; www.raysrestaurants.com/raysatkillercreek), 1700 Mansell Road. Open 11–10 Monday–Thursday, 5–11 Friday and Saturday, 11–9

Sunday. Voted one of the best steakhouses in Atlanta and a Taste of Alpharetta winner, this upscale restaurant offers premium steaks and fresh seafood. In addition, Killer Creek features signature cocktails and live entertainment on Friday and Saturday nights. No smoking. Lunch $7–29, dinner $14–33.

& **Sage** (770-569-9199; www.sagewoodfire tavern.com), 11405 Haynes Bridge Road. Open 11–10 Monday–Thursday, 11–11 Friday, 5–11 Saturday. Casual ambience paired with city chic serves as a pleasant backdrop for contemporary American cuisine with global influences. Fresh fish, hand-cut steaks, chops, and chicken are prepared over a hickory-oak wood-fire grill. Live samba and jazz is offered 6–10 Wednesday–Saturday. No smoking. Lunch about $10, dinner $15–39.

& **Village Tavern** (770-777-6490; www .villagetavern.com), 11555 Rainwater Drive. Open 11–9 Sunday and Monday, 11–10 Tuesday–Thursday, 11–11 Friday, 4–11 Saturday; Sunday brunch served 11–3. In this upscale yet casual restaurant, exposed timber beams, warm colors, and a stone fireplace set the stage for traditional and modern fare and an award-winning wine list. No smoking. Lunch $9–18, dinner $10–24, Sunday brunch $14–18; special-occasion Sunday brunch (such as Easter and Mother's Day) $20 adults, $11 children 12 and younger.

& **Vinny's** (770-772-4644; www.knowwhere togogh.com), 5355 Windward Parkway. Open 11–10:30 Monday–Thursday, 11–11 Friday, 5–11 Saturday, 5–10 Sunday. A sibling to the original Bistro VG in Roswell (see following entry), Vinny's is also a salute to Vincent van Gogh. Italian-inspired entrées range from sea bass to lamb to cowboy rib eye, with many other meat and seafood choices filling out the menu. No smoking. Lunch entrées average $10–15, dinner entrées $10–30.

In Atlanta

& **Ray's on the River** (770-955-1187; www.raysrestaurants.com), 6700 Powers Ferry Road. Open 11–10 Monday–Thursday, 11–11 Friday, 5–11 Saturday, 5–9 Sunday; 9:30–3 Sunday for brunch. Ray's is one of a very few restaurants in metro Atlanta blessed with a location on the banks of the languid Chattahoochee River. Diners vie for window or patio seating to couple a fine meal with a beautiful view. Seafood is prominently featured, and guests also can choose among pork chops, chicken, prime rib, steak, and lobster. The award-winning Sunday brunch features 80 items from peel-and-eat shrimp to mussels marinated in vinaigrette, a carving station, made-to-order omelets, a waffle station, and a vast assortment of desserts. Enjoy live music Thursday–Saturday evenings. No smoking (even outside). Lunch $10–20, dinner $15–50, Sunday brunch $30 adults, $15 children 5–10 (holiday Sundays $40 adults, $20 children).

In Chamblee

✈ & **57th Fighter Group** (770-234-0057; www.the57threstaurant.com), 3829 Clairmont Road. Open 11–2:30 Tuesday–Saturday, 10–2:30 Sunday for brunch, 5–9 Tuesday–Thursday and Sunday, until 10 on Friday and Saturday. World War II nostalgia and splendid views of small planes taking off and landing at DeKalb-Peachtree Airport are the major attractions here. The scene is set with a seemingly bombed-out French farmhouse and WWII planes and vehicles outside, and black-and-white photos of wartime scenes inside. The food includes favorites such as calamari, beer cheese soup, steak, and seafood. DJs spin tunes on the weekends, and there is often live entertainment. No smoking except on patio. Lunch $6–19, dinner $13–24, brunch $27.

In Decatur

& **Floataway Café** (404-892-1414; www.starprovisions.com), 1123 Zonolite Road. Open 6–whenever Tuesday–Saturday; reservations recommended. Operated by the same team as Midtown's Bacchanalia, the restaurant serves fresh Mediterranean cuisine reminiscent of Napa Valley and Italian countryside dishes embellished with local produce. Many dishes are cooked in a wood-fire oven or grill. The restaurant, located in a former warehouse along a purely industrial street, is named for the former tenant, the Floataway Door Company. The last time we were there, it was raining so hard we thought we would float away, but we enjoyed a wonderful dinner amid the chic decor. No smoking. $10–25.

In Marietta

♂ & **Hamilton's** and the **Pub** (770-427-2500), 500 Powder Springs Road. Hamilton's open 6:30–2 weekdays and 7–2 weekends; the Pub open 2–10 daily—bar open until midnight. Located at the **Hilton Atlanta/Marietta Conference Center and Resort** (see *Lodging—Resorts*), Hamilton's is an elegant restaurant fashioned after Southern estates of the 1800s. The New South breakfast buffet at Hamilton's features 80 items. A lunch buffet is served as well. The Pub serves soups, salads, sandwiches, pizza, English pub grub, and a wide variety of entrées. No smoking. Hamilton's breakfast $11, lunch $13; the Pub dinner $17–24.

Shillings Top of the Square (770-428-9520; www.shillingsonthesquare.net), 19 North Park Square. Open 5:30–11 Tuesday–Saturday. The restaurant offers formal dining with crisp table linens and candlelight, while its large windows provide a romantic view of Marietta Square. Dinner choices might include seafood, steaks, chops, chicken, or lamb. Live piano music and a full bar add to the ambience. No smoking. Not wheelchair accessible. $17–27.

In Roswell

& **Amalfi Ristorante Italiano** (770-645-9983), 292 South Atlanta Street. Open 5:30–9 Monday–Saturday; reservations not accepted. Anna Avino serves Neapolitan-influenced Italian cuisine here. Some specialties include scaloppine in many forms, linguine with seafood, veal, pasta fagioli, calamari with marinara sauce and yellow peppers, penne all'amatriciana, and homemade cannoli. Smoking at bar only. $13–20.

& **Bistro VG** (770-993-1156; www.knowwheretogogh.com), 70 West Crossville Road. Open 11:30–11 weekdays, 5–11 Saturday, 5–9 Sunday; Sunday brunch 11:30–2:30. The Zagat Survey considers Bistro VG to be one of the best restaurants in the entire metropolitan Atlanta area. The contemporary stone and rustic wood structure once housed a California-style restaurant. These days, the sophisticated contemporary decor is somewhat at odds with the casual structure, but nothing takes away from the fabulous cuisine or the extensive wine list. VG's wine cellar, which features more than 500 selections representing the world's greatest wine regions, has received *Wine Spectator*'s Award of Excellence several years running—one of only five such awards in the state. Lunch might include such delicacies as seared sea scallops, a grilled salmon BLT, a grilled bison burger, or a crabcake sandwich. Dinner choices include grilled chipotle-marinated pork tenderloin, roast rack of lamb, or confit and crisp-seared breast of duck. Save room for the to-die-for desserts. No smoking. Lunch $8–23, dinner $18–30, Sunday brunch $10–23.

& **Pastis** (770-640-3870), 928 Canton Street. Open 11:30–2:30 and 5:30–9:30 daily, until 10:30 Friday and Saturday. This trendy little restaurant in the heart of the Roswell art gallery district has an award-winning wine list and menu featuring French cuisine. Among the accolades heaped on Pastis by various Atlanta publications are Best Steaks, Best French Food, Best Live Music, Best Neighborhood Bar, Best Trendy Hangout, Best Romantic Restaurant, and Best Overall Restaurant. Live music Wednesday, Friday, and Saturday. No smoking. $10–30.

In Social Circle

♣ ♂ & **Blue Willow Inn** (770-464-2131 or 1-800-552-8813; www.bluewillowinn.com), 294 North Cherokee Road/GA 11. Open Tuesday–Sunday for lunch and dinner (call for exact hours); reservations recommended. Located in an imposing turn-of-the-20th-century Greek Revival mansion, the elegantly furnished restaurant earned the *Southern Living* Readers' Choice Award as Best Small Town Restaurant from 1996 until the award was retired in 2000. In 2001 and 2002, the restaurant earned the magazine's Best Country Cooking award, and it's also been recognized by *USA Today, Gourmet* magazine, *Food and Wine* magazine, *Guideposts,* CNN Travel Series, and the Food Network. The restaurant serves a traditional, upscale Southern buffet that includes 4 to 5 meats, 9 to 10 vegetables, soups, salads, biscuits, muffins, corn bread, and desserts, all served with "the Champagne of the South"—sweet tea. No smoking. Wheelchair accessible downstairs only. Lunch $14.95–18.95, dinner $16.95–23.95, Sunday brunch $19.95 all day.

EATING OUT

In Atlanta
🍴 ✏ ♿ **Fernbank Café** (404-929-6300; www.fernbankmuseum.org), 767 Clifton Road NE. Open 11–4 Monday–Saturday, noon–4 Sunday. Located within the Fernbank Museum of Natural History, the eatery serves soups, sandwiches, salads, pizza, specialty entrées, light snacks, kid meals, and refreshing beverages in comfortable surroundings with a spectacular view of Fernbank Forest. No smoking. $3–13.

In Conyers
✏ ♿ **Seven Gables Restaurant** (770-922-8824; www.sevengablesrestaurant.com), 1897 GA 20 SE. Open 5–10 Monday–Saturday. This fine-dining restaurant, a longtime favorite, occupies a Swiss chalet situated on 2.5 acres of oaks and cedars. As delightful as the setting is, the eatery is deservedly famous for its Dover sole, filet mignon béarnaise, rack of lamb, New York Ribeye Madagascar, duck, pheasant, quail, homemade breads and pasta, scrumptious desserts, and fresh dressings, soups, and sauces. In addition, there's a full bar and an extensive wine list. No smoking. $13–29.

In Decatur
🍴 ✏ ♿ **Café Alsace** (404-373-5622; www.cafealsace.com), 121 East Ponce de Leon Avenue. Open 11:30–2:15 Tuesday–Friday, 6–10 Tuesday–Saturday; 10–2 Sunday for brunch. This small, cozy, traditional French bistro has only 12 tables, but it's big on flavor. The French cuisine has a German twist with specialties such as spatzle with Alsatian

noodles, as well as a wide array of quiches, seafood, soups, salads, and sandwiches. Outdoor seating as well. No smoking. Lunch $7–14, dinner $7–23, brunch $7–8.

🍴 ✏ ♿ **Café Lily** (404-371-9119; www.cafelily.com), 308 West Ponce de Leon Avenue. Open 11:30–2:30 weekdays, 5:30–close Monday–Saturday, 11–close Sunday. This friendly neighborhood bistro offers a variety of Mediterranean dishes. You could make an entire dinner from appetizers such as Prince Edward Island mussels Posillipo or crab beignets. No smoking. All meals $8–16.

In Kennesaw
✏ ♿ **The Trackside Grill** (770-499-0874; www.tracksidegrill.com), 2840 South Main Street. Open 11–10 Tuesday–Thursday, 11–11 Friday and Saturday; 10–3 Sunday for brunch. The restaurant advertises "New South Flavor, Old South Charm," and that's what you get here—classic Southern comfort food. No smoking. Lunch and dinner $7–24, brunch $9–14.

In Marietta
🍴 ✏ ♿ **Dave and Buster's** (770-951-5554; www.daveandbusters.com), 2215 Dave and Buster's Drive. Open 11:30 AM daily; closes at midnight Sunday–Thursday, 1 AM Friday and Saturday. Food, while plentiful and good, takes second place to the state-of-the-art interactive video games, virtual-reality simulators, pocket billiards, shuffleboard, and entertainment to be found here. Fine dining is offered in the Grand Dining Room. Children are allowed when accompanied by adults. No smoking. $8–20.

In Roswell
🍴 ✏ ♿ **Dreamland Barbecue** (678-352-7999; www.dreamlandbbq.com), 10730 Alpharetta Highway. Open 10–10 Monday–Saturday, 11–9 Sunday. The one-of-a-kind Dreamland has been an institution in Tuscaloosa, Alabama, where it was a favorite of local citizens, University of Alabama students, Crimson Tide football players and coaches, and tourists. But it was a bit of a drive if Roswellians got a hankering for Dreamland barbecue, so it was exciting when a sister restaurant opened here. The

choices are primarily ribs, wings, quesadillas, and sandwiches served with side dishes such as coleslaw and baked beans, and a pile of napkins. No smoking. $3–20.

♠ ♂ ⌕ **Greenwood's on Green Street** (770-992-5383; www.greenwoodsongreen street.com), 1087 Green Street. Open 11:30–9 Wednesday, Thursday, and Sunday, until 10 Friday and Saturday. At this casual, down-home Southern eatery, owner Bill Greenwood creates signature dishes such as meat loaf, pork chops, chicken potpie, and luscious homemade pies, but even items as fine as duck are featured. No smoking. Limited wheelchair accessibility in one area of restaurant; restrooms not wheelchair accessible. $14–20.

✱ Entertainment

Arts at Emory (box office: 404-727-5050; www.emory.edu/ARTS), box office: 1700 North Decatur Road. Box office open 10–6 weekdays. Emory University offers a wide range of arts programs open to the public, including Theater Emory, Music at Emory, Emory Dance, Creative Writing Series, and visual arts exhibitions.

D A N C E Atlanta Chinese Dance Company (770-449-9953; www.atlantachinese dance.org), Chamblee. The company was created to promote the development, advancement, and appreciation of Chinese dance and culture, and has performed all over the metropolitan Atlanta area. Performances include classic Chinese dance styles, ethnic folk dances, and adaptations of modern dance drama performed in authentic, historically accurate costumes. Audiences delight in the colorful fabrics, platform shoes, tall headdresses, and other adornments. Call for a schedule of events, performance venues, and ticket prices.

M U S I C ♂ ⌕ Mable House Barnes Amphitheatre (box office: 770-819-7765; www.mablehouse.com), 5239 Floyd Road, Mableton. Box office open noon–6 Tuesday–Saturday (3–9 Saturday when there's a show). One of the Atlanta metro

area's most popular outdoor performance venues, the amphitheater has 2,200 covered seats located in a wooded setting on the property of the historic Mable House. The publicly owned venue provides all kinds of entertainment, including concerts, musical theater, dance, symphonic music, plays, and multidiscipline performances. It offers tables for four, fixed seats, and lawn seating. Call for a schedule of performances and ticket prices. Tickets can also be purchased through Ticketmaster.

N I G H T L I F E ♠ ⌕ Cowboy's Nightclub and Bar (770-420-1565; www.electric cowboy.com/kennesaw), 1750 North Roberts Road, Kennesaw. Open 7 PM–4 AM Wednesday–Saturday. Cowboy's is a mega country-music venue with a huge dance floor and local and nationally known bands. You'll find everyone here, from boot-scootin' rednecks to city slickers—often decked out in rhinestones and fringe. Over 18 only. Smoking is allowed throughout the facility at all times. $7 Thursday–Saturday (ladies free on Wednesday). Free cover until 9 PM.

♠ **Eddie's Attic** (404-377-4976; www.eddies attic.com), 515-B North McDonough Street, Decatur. Bar open 5 PM–12:30 AM Monday–Friday, 6:30 PM–2 PM Saturday and Sunday; kitchen open 6–10:30 Monday–Thursday, 5–10:30 Friday, 6–10:30 Saturday and Sunday. This venue is for those 21 and up. The center of Atlanta's singer-songwriter scene, the club features the finest acoustic players most nights. The club also has billiards and a popular covered Rooftop Garden Patio. Monday is open mic night, with 20 acts performing two songs each. No smoking in music room; patio and pool room allow smoking. Not wheelchair accessible. Cover charge $6–10 for music room, no cover for use of other facilities; dining $4–7.75.

♠ ⌕ **Twain's Billiards and Tap** (404-373-0063; www.twains.net), 211 East Trinity Place, Decatur. Open 11:30 AM–2 AM Monday–Saturday, 11:30 AM–12:30 AM Sunday. Not your pool room of old, Twain's features 20 Brunswick gold-crown tables as well as shuffleboard. Typical bar fare is served. No smoking. $6.

OUTDOOR DRAMA 🐾 🎗 ♿ **Laser-show Spectacular in Mountain Vision at Stone Mountain Park.** The seasonal laser show begins at 9:30 nightly in the summer, earlier on Saturdays in September and October. The world's largest laser show features a flame cannon and laser canopy, as well as surround sound and 3-D special effects choreographed to popular and patriotic music. The event culminates with a spectacular fireworks display. Free with park admission. VIP Laser Show terrace seating available with popcorn and a Coke for $10. Advance reservations required.

SPECIAL ENTERTAINMENT
Medieval Times (1-866-543-9637; www .medievaltimes.com/atlanta.aspx), 5900 Sugarloaf Parkway, Lawrenceville (attached to **Discover Mills Mall**—see *Selective Shopping*). Check the website or call for a schedule of shows. Transport yourself to 11th-century Spain and join the fun of a royal feast and jousting tournament. Guests enjoy a four-course dinner while cheering on their favorite knight competing in hand-to-hand combat, extraordinary horsemanship astride pure Spanish horses, and falconry. Before or after the show, visit the Hall of Arms and the medieval torture museum. Reservations are strongly recommended. Adults $52–72, children $36–56.

THEATER 🐾 🎗 ♿ **ART Station** (770-469-1105; www.artstation.org), 5384 Manor Drive, Stone Mountain Village. Gallery open 10–5 Tuesday–Friday, 10–3 Saturday. Call for schedule of theatrical performances. The contemporary, multidisciplinary arts center—housed in a historic trolley barn and power station that was active until 1948— stages six or seven productions each year. The group provides the storytellers for the **Tour of Southern Ghosts** in October at Stone Mountain Park. Galleries feature the works of prominent artists, and the center sponsors numerous other events for adults and children. Gallery free; donations appreciated. Prices for theatrical events vary.

♿ **Georgia Ensemble Theater** (770-641-1260; www.get.org), 950 Forrest Street, Roswell. Performed at the **Roswell Cultural Arts Center** (see entry that follows), the season of professional dramas, comedies, and musicals lasts September–April. Check the website or call for a schedule and ticket prices.

🎗 **Onstage Atlanta and Abracadabra Children's Theatre** (404-378-9901; www .onstageatlanta.com), 2597 North Decatur Road, Decatur. The company presents five dramas, musicals, and comedies, and also boasts an interactive, educational theater for children. Call for a schedule of events and ticket prices.

🎗 **PushPush Theater/SmallTall Theater** (404-377-6332; www.pushpushtheater.com), 121 New Street, Decatur. Not surprisingly, PushPush Theater, which produces films, theatrical productions, improv, and musical performances, pushes the envelope when it comes to exploring new ideas and encouraging artists to take risks that more traditional organizations would not. Twelve major professional productions are presented each year, as well as youth programs by the SmallTall Theater. Call for a schedule of events and ticket prices.

♿ **Roswell Cultural Arts Center** (770-594-6232 or 770-641-1260; www.roswell gov.com), 950 Forrest Street, Roswell. Box office open 12:30–6 Tuesday–Saturday. The center hosts theater, dance, musicals, and puppet show performances, as well as cultural events such as pageants, celebrations, and exhibits year-round. It is the home of the **Georgia Ensemble Theater** (see preceding entry) as well as the **Roswell Historical Society** and the **City of Roswell Archives and Research Library.** Call for a schedule of performances and prices.

✳ Selective Shopping

BICYCLE SHOPS **Bone Shakers Bicycle Shop** (770-222-BONE; www .boneshakersbicycles.com), 3267 New MacLand Road, Powder Springs. Open 11–6:30 weekdays, 11–5 Saturday. Located within riding distance of the Silver Comet

Trail, the Wild Horse Creek Trail, and the BMX track at Wild Horse Creek Park, the shop offers sales, repairs, and a limited number of rentals.

FOOD Harry's Farmer's Market (770-664-6300; www.wholefoodsmarket.com /stores/alpharetta), 1180 Upper Hembree Road, Roswell. Open 8 AM–9 PM Monday–Saturday, 8–8 Sunday; Coffee/Gelato Bar open 7–7 daily. Residents of the northern suburbs don't have to go to Decatur or south of the airport to shop at a farmer's market. Some visitors have likened Harry's to a culinary theme park or a chef's playground. You can get all kinds of exotic ingredients from around the world here.

Your DeKalb Farmers Market (404-377-6400; www.dekalbfarmersmarket.com), 3000 East Ponce de Leon Avenue, Decatur. Open 9–9 daily. Just about every fresh-grown ingredient you can think of is available at the world's largest indoor farmer's market. Without ever leaving the metro area, you have a passport to exotic places and delicious corners of the world. The market boasts a dizzying array of selections from more than 50 countries: cheese, coffee, deli items, fish, fruits, meat, produce, regional snacks, seafood, spices, vegetables, wine, and other foodstuffs. A restaurant and bakery are on-site, and tours are available.

OTHER GOODS The Brumby Chair Company (770-425-1875; www.brumby rocker.com), 37 West Park Square, Marietta. Open 10–5 Tuesday–Saturday. In 1875, the Brumby family began to make generous oak rocking chairs for Southern verandas. Over time, the popularity of the jumbo rockers led the company to produce other sizes: a double-courting rocker, a smaller lady rocker, a baby rocker, a footstool, and now, in the age of laptop computers, a lap desk rocker. The solid Appalachian red oak rockers come in six stained finishes and two paint colors. No matter what size you choose, the rocker is bound to become a family heirloom. Craftspeople actually assemble the chairs and cane the seats at the store, where visitors

also can examine antique Brumby rockers and photographs of famous Georgians with their Brumby rockers. When Jimmy Carter was president, he took them to the White House.

OUTLET MALLS Discover Mills (678-847-5000; www.discovermills.com), 5900 Sugarloaf Parkway, Lawrenceville. Open 10–9 Monday–Saturday, noon–6 Sunday. Among the 200 retailers are Last Call from Neiman Marcus, Kenneth Cole New York Outlet, and Bass Pro Shops Outdoor World. The mall also has several restaurants and offers periodic entertainment such as talent shows, concerts, and other family-oriented events. Other attractions include Lunar Mini Golf and **Medieval Times Dinner and Tournament** (see preceding entry).

✳ Special Events

March: **Conyers Cherry Blossom Festival** (770-602-2606; www.conyerscherry blossomfest.com). The festival, which is held at the Georgia International Horse Park in Conyers, features 300 food and arts and crafts booths. Other activities include international music, dance, games, croquet and golf tournaments, the Ultimate Air Dog Show of dock diving competition, a queen's pageant, hot dog– and cherry pie–eating contests, and an Easter egg hunt. Admission free; $5 parking fee or $8 for both days.

Easter: **Annual Easter Sunrise Service at Stone Mountain Park** (770-498-5690; www.stonemountainpark.com). The park gates and the Skyride open at 4 AM, services begin at approximately 7 AM. Allow an extra hour for lines waiting for the cable car. The park sponsors two simultaneous, nondenominational Easter sunrise services—one on top of the mountain and one on the Memorial Lawn at the base of the mountain. Parking is available at the Skyride or Crossroads lots (and Confederate Hall lot for those walking to the top). Skyride costs $9 per person for those who wish to ride to the top of the mountain and back; otherwise, visitors can attend the Memorial

Lawn service at no additional charge, and visitors who hike to the mountaintop service can do so for free.

April–August: **Concerts on the Square** (404-370-4100 or 404-553-6547; www.visit decaturgeorgia.com). Every Saturday night during these months, live bands entertain picnicking concertgoers on the square in Decatur. Free, but tables can be purchased for $45–65.

May: **Decatur Arts Festival** (404-371-9583; www.decaturartsfestival.org). This festival, held annually since 1988, includes performances by the Decatur Civic Chorus, theater and literary arts festival, juried fine art exhibition, Kids and Teens arts festival, New Dance Festival, Performing Arts Stage, artists' market, an Art Walk, and more. Most events are free.

May–October: **Roswell Riverside Sounds** (770-641-3705; www.roswellgov.com), Riverside Park, 575 Riverside Road, Roswell. Held at 7:30 PM on first Saturday of each month, May–October. The outdoor concert series features a wide variety of musical genres that might include roots rock, country, rock and roll, jazz, rhythm and blues, soul, swing, or Latin American. Food concessions are available, as are free parking and restrooms. Free.

June: **Beach Party** (404-371-9583). The Courthouse Square in landlocked Decatur is transformed into a tropical paradise when the city brings in 60 tons of sand and turns the square into a beach, complete with wading pools, a lighthouse, flamingos, and palm trees. Activities include a street dance, children's boardwalk games, a special beach movie on a giant inflatable screen, face painting, and more. Some events free; some have a small charge.

September: **Great Decatur Craft Beer Tasting Festival** (404-371-9583 or 404-371-8262; www.decaturbeerfestival.org). Hundreds of local and international beers are available on the square during the city's most popular event. The festival also includes music and food. The $40 entry fee includes a special tasting glass; proceeds benefit community charities. Children and pets not allowed.

Highland Games (770-521-0228; www.smhg.org). Two days of Scottish fun at Stone Mountain Park include Highland athletic events; Highland dancing; competitions in piping, drumming, and harping; kirking of the tartans; clan challenge events; a parade of the tartans; border collie herding demonstrations; clan and tartan information tents; many colorful Scottish shops; and traditional Scottish food. All events occur rain or shine. Admission charged in addition to park admission.

Yellow Daisy Festival (770-498-5690; www.stonemountainpark.com). The festival runs Thursday–Sunday at Stone Mountain Park; call for exact dates and times. The festival is considered to be America's top arts and crafts show. More than 400 artists and crafters from 38 states and two foreign countries display and sell their wares. The festival also includes daily live entertainment, children's corner activities, clogging and craft demonstrations, and fabulous food. Festival admission is free with park admission.

November: **Decatur Wine Festival** (404-371-9583 or 404-371-8262; www.decatur winefestival.org). More than 500 wines from around the world are available for tasting at this event on Decatur's square, held the first Saturday in November. Claiming to be Atlanta's largest outdoor festival, the event also includes samples from many of Decatur's eateries, live music, and an ArtWalk. The $30 entry fee, which benefits the Decatur Arts Alliance, includes a commemorative wine glass.

Pow Wow and Indian Festival (770-498-5690; www.stonemountainpark.com). This festival at Stone Mountain Park is the largest gathering of Native Americans in Georgia, drawing Native American dancers from across the country and Central America. During the four-day festival, visitors explore a living-history tepee village with tepee styles dating back to the late 1800s and witness dance, music, crafts, cooking, storytelling, and wildlife presentations. Native American demonstrations include fire starting, brain tanning, hide scraping, flint knapping, pottery making, and primitive tool technology. Visitors watch high-energy dance and drum competitions while warriors on horseback do battle in the Shield Dance. A marketplace provides visitors the opportunity to buy Native American jewelry and other arts and crafts. Admission charged in addition to park admission. Admission is included in the All-Activity Adventure Pass if purchased separately.

Roswell Tellabration (770-640-3253 or 1-800-776-7935), Roswell Adult Recreation Center, 830 Grimes Bridge Road, Roswell. The Friday before Thanksgiving at 7 PM. Stories not only entertain, they pass along culture and impart wisdom. As part of a worldwide event, regional storytellers gather for a fun night of family-friendly stories geared toward adults. $5.

November and December: **A Merry Olde Marietta Christmas** (770-429-1115 or 1-800-835-0445; www.mariettasquare.com). Two months of special events include holiday theater performances and the much-anticipated **Marietta Pilgrimage Christmas Home Tour** (www.marietta pilgrimage.com), which is held on the first full weekend in December with both daytime and candlelight options (three–four houses). The tour visits six historic private homes ranging in style from antebellum mansions to 1920s cottages and eight public buildings. It's said that 3,000 ornaments,

thousands of magnolia leaves, 500-plus strands of lights, and more than 100 poinsettias are used in decorating the houses. Shuttle service is provided along the route for the day tour but not the candlelight tour. Pilgrimage hours are 9–6 Saturday, 10–6 Sunday; Saturday candlelight tour runs 7–9:30. $20 in advance, $25 at the door.

Stone Mountain Christmas (770-498-5690; www.stonemountainpark.com). Yes, you can have a white Christmas in Atlanta. The festival at Stone Mountain Park features "snow" and fireworks, the Christmas story aboard the train, several lively holiday shows, millions of lights in the Crossroads Village, parades, pictures with the Snow Angel and with Santa, storytelling from Mrs. Claus at the Gingerbread House, and more. Call for specific dates and prices.

December: **Decatur Holiday Candlelight Tour of Homes** (404-371-9583; www .decaturtourofhomes.com). Held 5:30–9:30 the first weekend in December. Held every year since 1982, this much-anticipated Decatur event offers an opportunity to get a peek into a variety of Decatur's beautiful homes and other important points of interest decked out in their holiday best. A shuttle is available to take visitors from house to house. $20.

SOUTHERN SUBURBS (SOUTHSIDE)
CARROLLTON TO MORROW

With the exception of Carrollton, the primary area described in this chapter is called the Southern Crescent because it hugs the south side of Atlanta. To the casual observer, these municipalities seem to blend imperceptibly with each other and with the city of Atlanta, but in reality each is distinct from the others and is imbued with civic pride. This was also *Gone with the Wind* territory. Margaret Mitchell's grandparents lived here, and when young Peggy visited them, she met their neighbors and heard fascinating stories that inspired her to create the characters in her book. Don't come looking for Tara, however, or you'll be disappointed. It never actually existed. However, there are homes from the period that are open for tours.

It's somewhat surprising, considering the proximity to Atlanta, that there are so many parks, nature preserves, and green spaces here, but nature lovers who visit the Southern Crescent will not be disappointed. Farther west, in fact almost to the Georgia-Alabama state line, is Carrollton, the home of the University of West Georgia and John Tanner Park.

GUIDANCE Before planning a trip to the Carrollton area, contact the **Carrollton Area Convention and Visitors Bureau** (770-214-9746 or 1-800-292-0871; www.visitcarrollton .com), 102 North Lakeshore Drive, Carrollton 30117. Open 8:30–5 weekdays.

To learn more about Fayetteville and Peachtree City, consult the **Fayette County Chamber of Commerce** (770-461-9983; www.fayettechamber.org), 200 Courthouse Square, Fayetteville 30214. Open 8–5 weekdays.

When planning a trip to the Jonesboro, College Park, Forest Park, Hampton, Lovejoy, Morrow, or Riverdale area, contact the **Clayton County Convention and Visitors Bureau–Jonesboro Depot Welcome Center** (770-478-4800 or 1-800-662-7829; wwwvisitscarlett .com), 104 North Main Street, Jonesboro 30236. Open 8:30–5:30 weekdays, 10–4 Saturday. Pick up a brochure for the *Gone with the Wind* Historic District Driving Tour here.

To find out more about Morrow, contact the **Morrow Tourist Center** (770-968-1623; www .morrowtourism.com), 6475 Jonesboro Road, Morrow 30260. Open 9–5 Tuesday–Saturday.

GETTING THERE *By air:* Visitors to this area fly into Atlanta. There are also numerous shuttle companies, and several hotels have free shuttles to their properties; check ahead when you make your hotel reservation. For airport, airline, and car rental information, see "What's Where in Georgia."

By bus: The nearest **Greyhound Lines** (404-762-9581; www.greyhound.com) station is in Atlanta (see "What's Where in Georgia").

By car: The interstate system makes access to these municipalities easy. North–south routes I-75 and I-85 as well as east–west route I-20 meet in downtown Atlanta. The bypass I-285 circles the entire city. After I-75 and I-85 meet, they branch off south of the city, with I-85 continuing to the southwest through Fairburn and Palmetto and I-75 continuing to the southeast through Morrow. Most of the municipalities in this chapter can be reached easily from I-75, I-85, and I-285. Carrollton is south of I-20 on US 27.

By train: The nearest **AMTRAK** (see "What's Where in Georgia") station is in Atlanta.

GETTING AROUND Two companies offer mass transit (see "What's Where in Georgia").

MEDICAL EMERGENCIES For life-threatening emergencies, call 911.

VILLAGES In **Carrollton,** the University of West Georgia offers numerous gallery shows, sporting events, and cultural performances. Outdoors enthusiasts enjoy John Tanner Park, which has a lake with a large sand swimming beach, boat rentals, hiking trails, miniature golf, a campground, and motel rooms.

Fairburn's slogan is "History Lives Here." The historic downtown is a cluster of antiques shops, boutiques, and restaurants. Visitors should see the Confederate flag monument, the Confederate soldiers monument, the Fairburn cemetery, the grave of the first female sheriff, and the World War I monument. The **Georgia Renaissance Festival** (see *Special Events*) brings a quarter million visitors to Fairburn each spring.

Jonesboro is the legendary land of *Gone with the Wind.* More than 70 years after the burning of Atlanta, Margaret Mitchell spun a tale about her relatives and local characters in Clayton County. Her book became the best-selling novel of all time and was made into a movie in 1939, introducing Jonesboro and Clayton County to people all over the world. Thousands of visitors from around the globe come searching for Mitchell's mythical Tara. Although they are disappointed not to find it, there are plenty of other attractions connected with the author and her opus.

Morrow began as Morrow Station in 1846, a stop on the railroad line between Jonesboro and Atlanta. Known as the "Whistle Stop," the area gained popularity and was transformed from a farming community to a business and retail center. Today Morrow is the home of Spivey Hall and Clayton College and State University.

✳ To See

GUIDED TOURS *✐* **Gone with the Wind—The Tour** and **Southern Belles and Whistle Tour** (Jonesboro Welcome Center: 1-800-662-7829; www.peterbonner.com), 104 North Main Street, Jonesboro. Make arrangements with Peter Bonner for one of his Historical and Hysterical Tours from the 1867 train depot in the center of Jonesboro. Pete, costumed as a common Confederate soldier, is a font of local knowledge. He spins tales about the Battle of Jonesboro and about the local true stories that influenced Margaret Mitchell to write *Gone with the Wind* as he guides visitors around town for 90 minutes. He's in such demand these days, however, that he's often not available, so he's prerecorded a tour that you can take in the comfort of the Tour Trolley, sponsored in a partnership with the **Clayton County CVB** (see *Guidance*) and the **Road to Tara Museum** (see *Museums*). Offered Monday–Saturday; call for times. Walking tour with Peter Bonner: $15; Tour Trolley: adults $24.95, seniors and students $21.95, children 12 and younger $13.95.

HISTORIC HOMES AND SITES 🌸 *✐* ♿ **Stately Oaks** (770-473-0197; www.historical jonesboro.org), 100 Carriage Lane, Jonesboro. Open 10–4 weekdays and most Saturdays.

The grand, white-columned planter's home was built in 1839. Soldiers camped on the lawns during the Civil War. Tours of the home are conducted by costumed docents who interpret customs and lifestyles of the rural South. Also on the grounds are a log cookhouse, the old-fashioned 1894 Juddy's Country Store, and a one-room schoolhouse. Living-history demonstrations are conducted periodically, and many festivals and special events occur year-round. Limited wheelchair accessibility. Adults $12, seniors and military $9, children and retired military $6.

TOURS OF STATELY OAKS IN JONESBORO REVEAL WHAT LIFE WAS LIKE IN THE RURAL SOUTH IN THE MID-1800S.

MUSEUMS ✿ ♿ **Holliday-Dorsey-Fife House** (770-716-5332; www.hdfhouse .com), 140 West Lamar Avenue, Fayetteville. Open 10–3 Thursday–Saturday. Located in an 1855 Greek Revival house built by the uncle of infamous outlaw Doc Holliday, the museum features *Gone with the Wind* memorabilia; Civil War relics and documents, particularly from the Fayette Rifle Greys, Company I, 10th Georgia Volunteers; local Fayetteville history artifacts; and genealogical information about the three families who owned the house, which Doc Holliday actually visited. Margaret Mitchell's grandmother stayed in this house when it was used as a dormitory for the Fayetteville Academy. Be sure to stop at the Down South Treasures Museum Shop. Adults $5, seniors and students $4.

✿ ✍ ♿ **Road to Tara Museum** (770-478-4800 or 1-800-662-7829; www.visitscarlett.com), 104 North Main Street, Jonesboro. Open 8:30–5:30 weekdays, 10–4 Saturday; last ticket sold 45 minutes before closing. Located in the warehouse portion of the historic Jonesboro depot, which also houses the town's welcome center, the museum focuses on Jonesboro's part in the Civil War and the book *Gone with the Wind*. The museum boasts the largest collection of *Gone with the Wind* book and movie memorabilia in the country, including seats from the Lowe's Grand Theater in Atlanta, where the 1939 premiere was held. An original mural depicts scenes from the movie. Adults $7, students and seniors $6.

✷ To Do

FOR FAMILIES ✿ ✍ ♿ **The Beach at Clayton County International Park** (770-603-4005; www.claytonparks.com/InternationalPark/index.htm), 2300 GA 138 SE, Jonesboro. Park open 8–8 daily year-round; beach open 8–8 daily except Monday, Memorial Day weekend–Labor Day weekend; open weekends only after school starts, usually in early August. This multiuse park offers a little bit of everything to keep families busy. The **Beach Waterpark** (770-477-3766) is a spring-fed lake with a sandy beach, an adventure kiddie pool, water slides, a water trampoline, and a sundeck. In the same area, the **Nassau Arcade Center** features an indoor playground, snack bar, beach store, and changing facilities. The **Tennis Center** (678-479-5016) offers 17 hard courts, a pro shop with showers, lessons, and league play. There are often drills and round robins, too. Open Monday–Saturday, **Muscle Beach Fitness** (770-472-8093) is a full gym with strength machines, free weights, cardio equipment, and International Sports Science Association trainers. Classes include body sculpting, cardio, kickboxing, and yoga. A park-within-a-park, the **Hiking and Biking Trails** (770-477-3766) offer paved and naturalized trails accessible 8–8 year-round. Eleven **Volleyball Courts** (770-477-3766) allow beach volleyball play where the world's greatest athletes competed during the 1996 Centennial Olympic Summer Games. Or bring your own gear and drop a line into the **Fishing Lakes** (770-477-3766) for bass, bream, or catfish. A proper fishing license is required. Several concession stands are available. Check the website or call for the exact schedule, hours, and prices.

TREE CLIMBING **Tree Top Excursions at Panola Mountain State Conservation Park** (see *Green Space—Nature Preserves and Parks*), Stockbridge. The groves of magnificent oaks at this park make perfect vehicles for safely reliving the childhood joys of tree climbing or introducing that pleasure to your children. Experts assist climbers using rope-assisted methods known as CARE TTC (Canopy-Adventure-Research-Educational Technical Tree Climbing). Adventures include Introductory Climbs ($15) on the first Saturday of the month, Night Climbs ($25), Wild Climbs ($50), and even *ZZZ's in the Trees* ($125). For that adventure, after a day of climbing, participants actually sleep in a treeboat (a chairlike sling) suspended in the trees.

✳ Green Space

NATURE PRESERVES AND PARKS 🐾 ⊘ ♿ **Cochran Mill Nature Preserve** (770-306-0914; www.cochranmillnaturecenter.org), 6300 Cochran Mill Road, Palmetto. Open 9–3 Monday–Saturday. Fifty heavily wooded acres provide opportunities for hiking, wildlife observation, and environmental education programs. The center has many reptiles, birds, and amphibians. All have been injured and rehabilitated but can't be released back into the wild. Several special events include Snake Day in August, the Wild Trail Trot 5K Run in September, and the Halloween Hayride and Family Festival in October. Adults $3, children $2.

🐾 ⊘ ♿ **Cochran Mill Park** (770-463-8881), 6875 Cochran Mill Road, Palmetto. The park, operated by Chattahoochee Hills and located adjacent to the nature preserve (see preceding entry), offers hiking, jogging, horse trails (BYOH—bring your own horse), a playground, a picnic shelter, wildlife habitats, and primitive camping.

🐾 ⊘ ♿ **Flat Creek Nature Center** (770-486-7774; www.sctlandtrust.org/community -preserves/flat-creek-nature-area), 201 McIntosh Trail, Peachtree City. Open daylight hours daily. The 513-acre center, operated by the Southern Conservation Trust, is adjacent to 3.5 miles of paved paths, a 1,200-foot boardwalk, and two viewing platforms extending into the wetlands. The area sustains a wide variety of trees and plants. The educational center offers classes, camps, workshops, and programs throughout the year. Free.

🐾 ⊘ ♿ ✲ **John Tanner Park** (770-830-2222; www.carrollcountyga.com), 354 Tanner's Beach Road/GA 16, Carrollton. The park features two lakes, a beach, and a playground; 31 tent, trailer, and RV sites; a group lodge; and six motel units. Parking $5, camping $27–30, motel $80.

🐾 ⊘ ♿ **Panola Mountain State Conservation Park** (770-389-7801; www.gastateparks.org /PanolaMountain), 2600 GA 155 SW, Stockbridge. Open 7–dusk daily; interpretive center open 8:30–5 Friday–Monday. The 100-acre granite mountain, designated a National Natural Landmark, is located within a 1,026-acre park. The conservation park provides a home for rare plants and animals. Visitors can explore 2 miles of nature trails and a 1-mile fitness trail on their own or join ranger-led nature programs and 3.5-mile guided hikes of the restricted-access mountain Wednesday–Saturday (reservations required). The interpretive center features animal exhibits. The park also features archery, fishing, and a playground. The most unusual activity is tree climbing. Visitors can actually sleep in a tree (see *To Do—Tree Climbing*). Parking $5.

🐾 ⊘ ♿ **W. H. Reynolds Memorial Nature Preserve** (770-603-4188; www.reynoldsnature preserve.org), 5665 Reynolds Road, Morrow. Visitors center open 8–5 weekdays; park open

8–dusk daily. The 146-acre woodland and wetland preserve is dedicated to conservation. The center began with the donation of 130 acres by Judge William "Bill" Huie Reynolds in 1976. Sixteen acres were added to that in 1997. Among the park's attributes are ponds, streams, hardwood forests, piers, pavilions, bridges, a demonstration heritage herb and vegetable garden featuring varieties from the late 1800s, a butterfly and hummingbird garden, and a historic barn with displays of late-19th- and early-20th-century farm implements. The Nature Center houses a collection of native reptiles and amphibians as well as an observation honeybee hive and environmental education exhibits. Visitors can enjoy 3 miles of well-defined trails that run in half-mile loops to bring hikers back to their starting point. The Georgia Native Plants Trail is wheelchair accessible and also features Braille trail markers. Free.

✴ Lodging
BED & BREAKFASTS

In Palmetto
✿ ♿ **The Inn at Serenbe** (770-463-2610; www.serenbe.com), 10950 Hutcheson Ferry Road. Guests experience farm life with an elegant twist at this B&B, where accommodations and cuisine are decidedly upscale. Guest rooms are in the 1905 farmhouse; a restored 1930s horse barn; a lake house; two recently constructed, environmentally friendly cottages; and a private 1940s two-bedroom cottage. More than 100 animals live at Serenbe: chickens, bunnies, goats, pigs, and horses. Yes, you can feed the animals or gather eggs, but you also can enjoy afternoon tea, bedtime snacks, and a full country breakfast. Swim in the pool or soak in the outdoor hot tub, both of which are surrounded by glorious gardens. Play croquet or hike the trails to streams, water-

falls, or a lake, then take some time to laze in the cabana's twin-bed-size swings. Hayrides and roasting marshmallows around a campfire are sometime highlights. Dining options include the **Farmhouse at Serenbe,** the **Blue-Eyed Daisy Bake Shop,** and the **Hil on the Hill.** No smoking. Limited wheelchair accessibility. $200–400.

CAMPGROUNDS

In Carrollton
☀ ✿ ♿ 🐾 **John Tanner Park** (770-830-2222). The park features 31 tent, trailer, and RV sites ($27–30) as well as six motel units ($80). One of those units is dog friendly ($40 per dog; maximum of two). See *Green Space—Nature Preserves and Parks.*

✴ Where to Eat
DINING OUT

In College Park
✿ ♿ **The Feed Store** (404-209-7979; www.thefeedstorerestaurant.com), 3841 Main Street. Open 11–2 weekdays, 5–10 Monday–Thursday, 5–11 Friday and Saturday. Look for the mural of a horse on the side of the historic building, which actually was a feed store operated well into the 1980s by the current owner's grandmother. Many rustic architectural elements, such as exposed brick, have been retained and combined with sleek modern touches for an eclectic look. Antique farm implements grace the walls. The cuisine is described as artful New American. No smoking. Lunch $8–14, dinner $13–29.

THE MAIN HOUSE AT THE INN AT SERENBE IN PALMETTO ALSO HOUSES THE FARMHOUSE RESTAURANT.

EATING OUT

In Carrollton

🦐 🍸 ♿ **The Lazy Donkey** (770-834-6002; www.thelazydonkeyrestaurant.com/index .htm), 334 Bankhead Highway. Open 11–10 Tuesday–Thursday, 11–11 Friday and Saturday, noon–9 Sunday. This understated eatery serves Mexican and Latin cuisine in simple rooms and an outdoor eating area decorated with Mexican art to set the mood. The lunch menu features salads, black bean soup, nachos, quesadillas, enchiladas, chili, fajitas, Cuban sandwiches, and chicken, beef, and fish entrées. Many of the luncheon selections are available for dinner as well, including pork medallions, beef tenderloin, chicken dishes, and pasta. If you're not absolutely stuffed, try the butter pecan ice cream tostada or the sopaipillas, a fried tortilla pastry served with cinnamon and honey. No smoking. Limited wheelchair accessibility. Lunch $5–9, dinner $8–14.

In College Park

🦐 🍸 ♿ **The Brake Pad** (404-766-1515; www.brakepadatlanta.com), 3403 Main Street. Open 11 AM–midnight Sunday–Thursday; 11 AM–1 AM Friday and Saturday. An old gas station has been transformed into a funky bar and eatery where you can fuel up with appetizers, burgers, quesadillas, sandwiches, salads, and other pub food. In nice weather, diners enjoy eating and drinking on the patio. The Brake Pad has an extensive selection of beers, and you can get late-night fare until closing. Smoking on patio only. $7–15.

✳ Entertainment

MUSIC 🎵 ♿ **Aaron's Amphitheatre at Lakewood** (404-627-9704), 2002 Lakewood Way, East Point. This outdoor performance venue, built in 1989, is designed to offer a state-of-the-art musical experience for artists and patrons alike. Some seats are under a covered area, and there's plenty of lawn seating. Nationally renowned acts stop by regularly. Call for a schedule of performances and ticket prices.

🎵 ♿ **Frederick Brown Jr. Amphitheater** (770-631-0630; www.amphitheater.org), 201

McIntosh Trail, Peachtree City. Affectionately known as the Fred (as opposed to the Atlanta sports stadium, which is known as the Ted), the amphitheater is an intimate setting in which to enjoy a wide variety of entertainment, including a summer concert series with a variety of top acts. Call for a schedule of events and ticket prices.

🎵 ♿ **Spivey Hall** (box office: 678-466-4200; www.spiveyhall.org), 2000 Clayton State Boulevard, Morrow. Box office open 9–5 weekdays. Located on the campus of Clayton College and State University, this magnificent performance hall is the scene of the finest in piano, vocal, chamber, choral, classical, jazz, organ, string, and other musical entertainment. The acoustically perfect Spivey Hall is also the home of the magnificent Albert Schweitzer Memorial Pipe Organ, a 4,413-pipe organ built in Italy. The hall's acclaimed concert series receives national attention thanks to frequent appearances on National Public Radio's *Performance Today.* There is also a summer jazz and pops series, the Spivey Hall Children's Choir, the Spivey Hall Young Artists, and the Children's Concert Series. Call for a schedule of performances and ticket prices.

🎵 ♿ **The Villages Amphitheater** (770-719-4173; www.villagesamphitheater.com), 301 Lafayette Avenue, Fayetteville. In the heart of downtown Fayetteville is a state-of-the-art venue that provides a setting for a full schedule of local, regional, and national entertainment and concerts. Orchestra tables and tiered table areas are popular choices for enjoying the shows. Call for a schedule of events and ticket prices.

✳ Selective Shopping

BOOKS **Horton's Books and Gifts** (770-832-8021; www.hortonsbooks.com), 410 Adamson Square, Carrollton. Open 9–7 Monday–Thursday, 9–8 Friday, 10–8 Saturday, 1–6 Sunday. Opened in 1892 and certified by the American Booksellers Association, Horton's is the oldest bookstore in Georgia, the 3rd-oldest in the South, and the 10th-oldest in America. Antique cases display new books for sale, and shoppers can find used books and books on tape in the basement. Sales of books, cards, and gifts are rung up on the store's original 1892 cash register. Shoppers enjoy interacting with Chloe the cat, who lives in the shop and sponsors Chloe's Kids, a book club for children.

FOOD 🍴 ✎ ♿ **Atlanta State Farmer's Market** (404-366-8767 or 404-366-6910), 16 Forest Parkway, Forest Park. Open 24/7 except Christmas Day. The best time for retail shopping is 7–3. The South's largest farmer's market and one of the biggest in the world, the 150-acre site offers a dizzying array of produce; fruit; plants and flowers; homemade items such as pickles, jams, and relishes; and seasonal items such as pumpkins in October and Christmas trees at holiday time. Take a tour of the farmer's

THE TOWN OF FAIRBURN HOSTS A
RENAISSANCE FESTIVAL EVERY SPRING.

ATLANTA STATE FARMER'S MARKET FACTS
- Ninety tractor-trailer loads of goods are unloaded every day.
- The market has a $3 billion impact on the area each year.
- Thirty-five hundred vendors, purchasers, and other visitors visit the market daily.

market via the **Fresh Express Trolley Tour** ($3 per person). The open-sided trolley operates Tuesday and Thursday in good weather. **Georgia Grown Visitors Center and Gifts,** which is located on the grounds of the farmer's market, sells a variety of Georgia foodstuffs and souvenirs. The facility also dispenses travel information for the entire state of Georgia. Events at the market are listed on the market's Facebook page.

✳ Special Events

Mid-April–early June: **Georgia Renaissance Festival** (770-964-8575; www.ga renfest.com). Open 10:30–6 Saturday and Sunday, plus Memorial Day, rain or shine. The multiacre kingdom in Fairburn re-creates a 16th-century European country faire in a village of Tudor homes and enchanting cottages. There you can shop like a queen for handcrafted treasures, watch demonstrations of age-old arts, feast like a king on treats like steak on a stake or smoked turkey legs, rollick on dozens of games and rides for all ages in the medieval amusement park, and revel with a cast of costumed characters (costumes are even available for rent if you want to participate). Ten stages present music and comedy acts, rope walking, balancing stunts, magic shows, sword swallowing, and juggling. You also can cheer on your favorite in the joust or the Hack and Slash sword fight. Wheelchair accessible. Adults $19.95, seniors $17.95, children 6–12 $8.95; games and rides $1–5.

The Coast 2

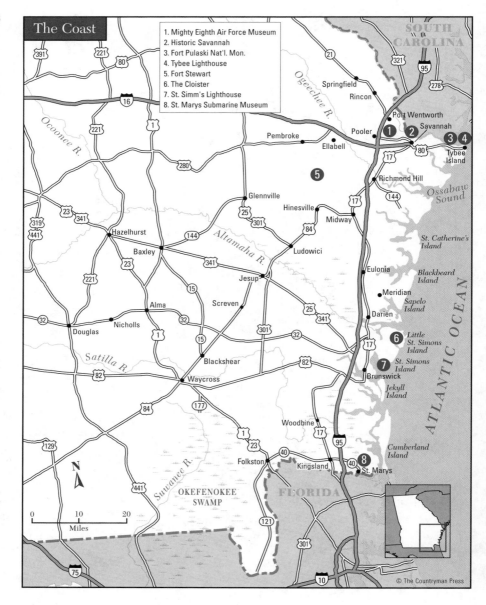

The Coast

1. Mighty Eighth Air Force Museum
2. Historic Savannah
3. Fort Pulaski Nat'l. Mon.
4. Tybee Lighthouse
5. Fort Stewart
6. The Cloister
7. St. Simm's Lighthouse
8. St. Marys Submarine Museum

SOUTH CAROLINA

Ogeechee R.
Springfield
Rincon
Pooler
Port Wentworth
Savannah
Pembroke
Ellabell
Tybee Island
Richmond Hill
Ossabaw Sound
Oconee R.
Glennville
Hinesville
Midway
St. Catherine's Island
Hazelhurst
Altamaha R.
Baxley
Ludowici
Eulonia
Blackbeard Island
Jesup
Meridian
Sapelo Island
Alma
Screven
Darien
Nicholls
Douglas
Blackshear
Little St. Simons Island
Waycross
St. Simons Island
Brunswick
Jekyll Island
Satilla R.
Woodbine
ATLANTIC OCEAN
Cumberland Island
Folkston
Kingsland
St. Marys
Suwanee R.
OKEFENOKEE SWAMP
FLORIDA

N

0   10   20
Miles

© The Countryman Press

INTRODUCTION

P ristine barrier islands with dunes and maritime forests, hushed mysterious swamps, unspoiled beaches rimmed with swaying sea oats, untouched tidal marshes, and abundant wildlife characterize the coastal region of the state, as do historic towns and villages, glamorous resorts, and outdoor recreation.

The coast is the cradle of Georgia history. It is here that Spanish monks set up missions in areas inhabited by Guale Indians. This is where Gen. James Oglethorpe established the colony of Georgia—making it the 13th colony—and where several forts were built, stretching along the coast. The coast is where the Spanish were defeated by the British and where some relatively insignificant Revolutionary War battles occurred. The coastal region is also where slaves were imported to work the rice and cotton plantations. During the Civil War, the capture of Savannah was the culmination of Union general William Tecumseh Sherman's March to the Sea in 1864, which hastened the war's end a few months later. The area continues to make history: In 2004, Sea Island played host to the G8 Summit.

Savannah, America's first planned city, is the centerpiece of the region. It was, after all, the colony's first city and first capital. Most of the historic squares laid out by General Oglethorpe still exist, surrounded by magnificently restored Greek Revival and Regency homes, many of which now operate as bed & breakfasts, small inns, restaurants, museums, and shops. Savannah's historic district is one of the largest in the country. Walking, horse and carriage, trolley, and van tours of the historic district are offered. Savannah is also reputed to be the most haunted city in America, and visitors enjoy a choice of several ghost tours of the historic district.

Other important colonial towns include Brunswick, Darien, Midway, and St. Marys. Sites with important African American history include Seabrook Village near Midway and Hog Hammock on Sapelo Island, where the Gullah culture survives along with its Geechee language, a Creole form of pidgin English. Although steeped in history, Brunswick and Savannah are active and important ports, as they always have

RESIDENT OF THE GEORGIA COAST

been. Brunswick, which claims to be the Shrimp Capital of the World, is the home of Brunswick stew.

The barrier islands, each of which has a distinct personality, are accessible by causeway, ferry, or private boat. Cumberland Island, where wild horses gallop on the beach, is designated as a national seashore. Jekyll Island, once the winter retreat of 100 millionaires and their families, is now a resort island, as are Sea Island—the home of the famed resort the Cloister at Sea Island—Tybee Island, and St. Simons Island. Little St. Simons, although privately owned, welcomes overnight guests. Several other islands are national wildlife refuges.

The region is dotted with nine state parks and historic sites. With so much of the area bordered by or surrounded by water, it's no wonder that water-based activities—boating, canoeing, kayaking, dolphin watching, fresh- and saltwater fishing, sailing, and scuba diving—are so popular. Naturally, seafood is prominently featured on the menus of numerous restaurants.

Alligators, snakes, wading birds, bobcats, and the cast of the *Pogo* comic strip are the residents of the murky Okefenokee Swamp, which Native Americans called "the land of the trembling earth." One of the last wild places in America, the preserve is a perfect place for canoeing and wildlife observation. Several sites in or near the park depict the difficulties and dangers endured by early settlers.

BRUNSWICK AND
THE GOLDEN ISLES

The Spanish pushed north from Florida looking for gold, but they didn't find the precious metal. Instead, they found the coastal barrier-island treasures they called Islas de Oro—the Golden Isles. In fact, if the Spanish hadn't lost a battle to the English on St. Simons Island in 1742, Spanish might be the primary language in Georgia today.

Brunswick and the Golden Isles—as Jekyll, St. Simons, Little St. Simons, and Sea islands are known—are ideal destinations for relaxed getaways. Lush natural beauty, a quiet atmosphere, countless outdoor sports pursuits, and abundant wildlife to observe combine to provide the ideal vacation. Sun-drenched beaches, dolphin tours, turtle walks, 216 holes of golf, fishing, canoeing and kayaking, surfing, windsurfing, scuba diving, boating, bicycling, and numerous other outdoor activities attract both the visitor who wants to do little or nothing and the visitor who craves action. Historic treasures include forts, homes, and a lighthouse, while romance abounds at the beaches and resorts as well as on carriage rides and sunset cruises.

The 486-foot-tall, 7,780-foot-long Sidney Lanier Bridge, US 17, spanning the Brunswick River is Georgia's tallest cable-stayed bridge. Connecting Brunswick on the mainland to St. Simons and Sea islands, it resembles a huge sailing ship and is a beautiful sight to see. Meanwhile, Cumberland Island, which is accessible only by boat, survives in its almost natural state, which makes it attractive to outdoors enthusiasts and travelers interested in ecotourism.

Accommodations of all kinds include bed & breakfasts, intimate inns, condominiums, resort hotels, chain hotels, and campgrounds. Four of *Condé Nast Traveler's* nine Georgia properties on its Gold List of Best Places to Stay are located along the state's coast: the Cloister at Sea Island, Greyfield Inn on Cumberland Island, the Lodge on Little St. Simons Island, and the Lodge at Sea Island. Eateries run the gamut from fine-dining establishments specializing in seafood to casual delis where you can get a sandwich. Visitors also have fun exploring several small mainland towns such as St. Marys, the gateway to Cumberland Island, and Folkston, the gateway to the mysterious Okefenokee Swamp.

GUIDANCE When planning a trip to Brunswick and the Golden Isles, contact the **Brunswick and the Golden Isles Convention and Visitors Bureau and Chamber of Commerce** (1-800-933-2627; www.comecoastawhile.com), 4 Glynn Avenue, Brunswick 31520. Open 10–5 daily. Once you arrive in the area, stop in at the **Brunswick I-95 Welcome Center,** 200 I-95, Brunswick 31525 (between exits 38 and 42), or the **Brunswick US 17 Welcome Center,** 2000 Glynn Avenue at the F. J. Torras Causeway, Brunswick 31520.

Both open 10–5 daily. At the US 17 location, visitors can see the original Brunswick stew pot as well as a short video about the area.

For information specific to Jekyll Island, contact the **Jekyll Island Convention and Visitors Bureau** (912-635-4155 or 1-877-4-JEKYLL; www.jekyllisland.com), 1 Beachview Drive, Jekyll Island 31527. Open 8–5 weekdays. When in the area, stop by the **Jekyll Island Welcome Center** (912-635-3636), 901 Downing Musgrove Causeway, Jekyll Island 31527. Open 10–5 Monday–Saturday, noon–5 Sunday.

Information about Folkston can be obtained from the **Okefenokee Chamber of Commerce, Folkston–Charlton County Development Authority** (912-496-2536; www.folkston.com), 5795 West Main Street, Folkston 31537. Open 8:30–5 weekdays, 10–3 Saturday.

For information about Kingsland, Cumberland Island, and the Okefenokee National Wildlife Refuge, consult the **City of Kingsland Welcome Center and Convention and Visitors Bureau** (912-729-5999 or 1-800-433-0225; www.visitkingsland.com), 1190 East Boone Street, Kingsland 31548. Open 9–5 weekdays, 10–5 Saturday. When in the area, stop by the **Georgia Visitor Information Center–Kingsland** (912-729-3253; www.georgia onmymind.org), 1501 St. Marys Road South (exit 1 off I-95), Kingsland 31548. Open 8:30–5:30 daily.

For information about St. Marys, consult the **St. Marys Welcome Center and Tourism Council** (912-882-4000; www.stmaryswelcome.com), 111 Osborne Street, St. Marys 31558. Open 8:30–5 Monday–Saturday, 1–4 Sunday. While at the welcome center, pick up a brochure for the **Historic District Braille Trail,** which has Braille markers describing 38 historic sites. Trolley Tours available at 11 and 2 Monday–Saturday and 2 Sunday. Adults $5, children $3. For more information about this area, contact the **Camden–Kings Bay Chamber of Commerce** (912-729-5840 or 1-800-868-8687; www.camdenchamber.com), 2603 Osborne Road, Suite R, St. Marys 31558. Open 8–noon and 1–5 weekdays.

When visiting St. Simons Island, stop by the **St. Simons Island Visitors Center,** located in the old Casino next to the pier (912-638-9014 or 1-800-933-2627), 530-B Beachview Drive. Open 10–5 daily.

GETTING THERE *By air:* **Brunswick Golden Isles Airport** (see "What's Where in Georgia") offers direct flights to and from Atlanta four times daily. Jekyll Island and St. Simons Island are less than a half hour from the airport. Otherwise, visitors can fly into Savannah, just an hour's drive north, or Jacksonville (an hour to an hour and a half south) in Florida (see "What's Where in Georgia"). See "What's Where in Georgia" for car rental information at each.

By bus: **Greyhound Lines** (912-265-2800 or 1-800-231-2222; www.greyhound.com) has a terminal at 1101 Gloucester Street in Brunswick.

THE ORIGINAL BRUNSWICK STEW POT

By car: The two major north–south routes are US 17 and I-95. The major east–west route into Brunswick is US 82 and into St. Marys is GA 40.

By train: The nearest **AMTRAK** (1-800-USA-RAIL) stations are in Savannah (see the Savannah chapter) and in Jacksonville, Florida, at 3570 Clifford Lane.

GETTING AROUND In addition to car rentals at the airport in Brunswick, rentals are also available from **Auto Rentals of Brunswick** (912-264-0530), 3576 Darien Highway.

Cumberland Island and Little St. Simons are reached only by ferry, and vehicles are not available for visitors, although there are bike rentals and beach wheelchairs. For ferry service to Cumberland Island, see *Green Space—Nature Preserves and Parks.*

MEDICAL EMERGENCY Call 911.

VILLAGES Brunswick, the gateway to the Golden Isles, has an extensive historic district. One of the most special events that takes place there is the annual Blessing of the Fleet on Mother's Day at Mary Ross Waterfront Park. The Portuguese tradition, held yearly, features a parade of brightly decorated shrimp boats passing the park for the blessing.

On **Cumberland Island,** wild horses frolic along vast stretches of pristine beaches. Cumberland, which is the nation's largest wilderness island, is 18 miles long and 3 miles wide, with a total of 36,415 acres, of which 16,850 are marsh, mudflats, and tidal creeks. The national seashore island is accessible only by ferry from St. Marys, and the number of visitors per day is limited to 300. The island was owned at one time by Thomas Carnegie, younger brother and business partner of financier Andrew Carnegie. Thomas and his wife, Lucy, built a mansion they called Dungeness in the late 1800s, although Thomas died before it was completed. Lucy finished the home and went on to acquire 90 percent of the island. She built four additional mansions for her children. Dungeness is now only a ruin. Among the other mansions, Plum Orchard is occasionally open for tours, and Greyfield is now a luxury inn. The only other accommodations on the island are campgrounds. Cumberland is a living laboratory of Georgia's treasured resources. In addition to a huge expanse of unspoiled beach, the island features marshlands, palmetto stands, tall pines, and moss-draped live-oak forests inhabited by wild horses, deer, bobcats, boars, turkeys, armadillos, sea turtles, and many species of birds. Visitors must carry in and out everything they might need, including water, a lunch, suntan lotion, and insect repellent.

Jekyll Island has a unique history. It was once described as "the richest, the most exclusive, and the most inaccessible club in the world" (*Munsey's Magazine,* 1904). The Jekyll Island Club was founded in 1886 as the private winter retreat of 100 of America's richest and most elite families—Morgans, Astors, Rockefellers, Pulitzers, and Vanderbilts among them. The ornate Queen Anne–style clubhouse was the center of activity. Some families stayed there; others built grand mansions they called "cottages" because they had no kitchens: Everyone ate at the club. They played golf, tennis, and croquet, and hunted for game birds. This idyllic lifestyle lasted for 40 years. When the railroads extended into Florida, the wealthy families moved on to other trendy locations. The island was purchased by the state of Georgia for $675,000, which ensures that 35 percent of it will remain in its natural state. The Jekyll Island National Historic Landmark District, the 240-acre riverfront compound used by the millionaires, has been preserved and is one of the largest ongoing restoration projects in the Southeast, if not the country. The Jekyll Island Club has become a luxury hotel (see *Lodging—Inns and Resorts*), and several of the Victorian-era homes are open for tours (see *To See—Historic Homes and Sites*). Other hotels, inns, bed & breakfasts, restaurants, shops, and sporting options make Jekyll Island an ideal family vacation spot. You don't even have to be a millionaire.

Kingsland was once owned by King George II of England. After the colony of Georgia was granted a charter from King George, another king, John King, acquired enough land to become the largest plantation owner in the area. Today Kingsland is the home of the Naval Submarine Base Kings Bay.

Little St. Simons is a privately owned 10,000-acre barrier island with 7 miles of undeveloped beach. It is reached only by private ferry from Hampton Marina on St. Simons Island. The beach is designated an Important Bird Area; 286 species have been seen there. Hiking, fishing, canoeing, kayaking, and other nature-based activities are popular pursuits. Most guests stay in the island's lodge, but a limited number of day trips are available, too.

Okefenokee Swamp is a dark, brooding swamp that can be accessed from the sleepy little town of **Folkston.** Known as the Land of the Trembling Earth, the wilderness encompasses 396,000 acres, or 700 square miles, making it the largest swamp in North America. The swamp is home to the American alligator, 234 species of birds, and many other examples of flora and fauna. It has been the site of several movies, including *Swamp Water* (1941) and *Lure of the Wilderness* (1952).

St. Marys, a small coastal village that serves as the gateway to Cumberland Island, is one of Georgia's best-kept secrets. After the Timicuan Indians, Spanish occupation began here in 1566, so St. Marys claims to be the second-oldest town in the United States after St. Augustine, Florida. The charming town boasts 38 National Register of Historic Places sites within walking distance of each other, a waterfront pavilion, and numerous bed & breakfasts located in historic homes and buildings. The Historic Braille Trail, located in downtown St. Marys, features Braille markers at 18 historic sites.

St. Simons is the largest and most populated of Georgia's barrier islands. Its approximately 27,000 acres include 4 miles of beaches, uplands, and marshes. Among its noted visitors was author Eugenia Price, who was so enthralled with the island, she moved there and set *Beloved Invader, Lighthouse, New Moon Rising,* and several other books on the island.

Ritzy **Sea Island** was the vision of early automobile mogul Howard Carl Coffin, who built up the island as a kind of residential-resort club for the wealthy. Management has remained in the family for four generations. The gated enclave offers 5 miles of scenic beach as well as multimillion-dollar private homes and the posh, historic Cloister at Sea Island resort, which features a hotel and elegant villas in the Spanish-Mediterranean style, as well as golf facilities and a top-notch spa (see *Lodging—Inns and Resorts*). Over the years, Sea Island has been visited by five presidents, was the site of Winston Churchill's daughter's wedding, and hosted a G8 Summit. George H. W. and Barbara Bush spent their honeymoon at the Cloister. Today the island is accessible only to overnight guests.

✳ To See

FOR FAMILIES ✿ ♬ �& **Georgia Sea Turtle Center** (912-635-4444; www.georgiasea turtlecenter.org), 214 Stable Road, Jekyll Island. Open 10–2 Monday, 9–5 Tuesday–Sunday, March–November; closed on Monday December–February. Jekyll Island is unique among developed islands for the significance of its annual turtle nesting. In nature things don't always go well, so this facility was developed for rehabilitation, research, and education into the life of the sea turtle from egg to adult. Many eggs are saved and eventually hatch, and numerous injured turtles are rehabilitated so that they can be released into the sea. See exhibits and live turtles. The center sponsors Turtle Walks, Nest Walks, camps, and special events. Adults $7; seniors, military, college students, and teachers $6; children $5.

✿ ♬ �& **Tidelands Nature Center** (912-635-5032; www.tidelands4h.org), 100 South Riverview Drive, Jekyll Island. Open 9–4 Monday–Friday, 10–2 Saturday and Sunday. Nature walks at 9 Monday, Wednesday, Thursday, and Friday, March–October. The center, which is operated by the University of Georgia Cooperative Extension Service, provides hands-on marine science exhibits, live animal displays, marsh kayak tours, and nature walks. Visitors observe native species of fish, turtles, crabs, snakes, alligators, and other coastal critters. Among the exhibits are an underwater dock–touch tank display, an alligator tank–freshwater display, a 1,100-gallon sea-turtle tank, and a marsh model. Ninety-minute public nature walks led by experienced guides explore the beach, maritime forest, and/or marsh. Be sure to call ahead, as walks leave from different locations. Three-hour guided kayak tours of Jekyll Creek are available, or visitors may rent a canoe and explore on their own. Admission to nature center: $2; nature walks: adults $5, children 8–17 $3; kayak tours: adults $50, tandem $80.

HISTORIC HOMES AND SITES ❦ ✿ ♿ **Fort Frederica National Monument** (912-638-3639; www.nps.gov/fofr), 6515 Frederica Road, St. Simons Island. Open 9–5 daily; movies shown every half hour. In the 18th century, the land that is now Georgia lay between British South Carolina and Spanish Florida, and was known as debatable land. It was the epicenter of a centuries-old imperial conflict between those two countries. In 1736, just three years after Georgia's first settlement was begun in Savannah, this fort was built by Gen. James Oglethorpe to protect the southern boundary of the new colony of Georgia. After the British repulsed the Spanish attempt to retake St. Simons Island, the garrison was disbanded and the community fell into decline. The ruins of the fortress—built with tabby, an oyster-shell cement—remain, and there are historical tours as well as hiking and nature trails. $3 walk-ins or cyclists, $5 vehicles.

❦ ✿ **Hofwyl-Broadfield Plantation State Historic Site** (912-264-7333; www.gastateparks .org/HofwylBroadfield), 5556 US 17 North, Brunswick. Open 9–5 Thursday–Saturday. Last main house tour at 4. A visit to Hofwyl-Broadfield Plantation provides a glimpse into life on a former rice plantation converted to a dairy farm when the rice economy failed. Begin at the visitors center by watching a film about the history of the plantation and the families who lived there. You also can see fine silver and a model of a working rice plantation. The pleasant walk from the visitors center to the historic house provides glimpses of salt marsh along the Altamaha River, magnolias, Spanish moss–draped live oaks, and playful goats. The simple 1850s home is filled with family antiques and books. $3.75–6.50.

❦ ✿ ♿ **Jekyll Island National Historic Landmark District** (912-635-4036; museum: 912-635-4052), Jekyll Island History Center, 100 Stable Road. Open 9–5 daily; tours leave at 11, 1, and 3. As described in the introduction to this chapter, Jekyll Island was the exclusive elite winter conclave of 100 wealthy families from 1886 through the beginning of World War II. Tour the 240-acre site by tram beginning at the **Jekyll Island History Center** (see *Museums*), where you can purchase tickets, watch an orientation video, and shop. The tram tour includes admission to two of the island's "cottages." Periodically there are special tours that focus on restoration, folklore, and families. In addition, **Mistletoe Cottage** showcases the work of nationally renowned Jekyll Island sculptor Rosario Fiore. Exhibit hours are

THE JEKYLL ISLAND CLUB WAS FOUNDED AS A PRIVATE RETREAT OF THE WEALTHY.

JEKYLL ISLAND FUN FACTS

- Gen. James Oglethorpe, founder of the colony of Georgia, named the island for Sir Joseph Jekyll, Master of the Rolls in Parliament, who had supported the founding of the colony.
- Horton House, now a tabby ruin, was constructed in 1743 and is one of the oldest structures in Georgia.
- The first golf course on the island was constructed in 1898.
- In 1910, leaders in banking finance met on Jekyll Island to discuss ways to address financial panic. This meeting led to the Aldrich Act and the establishment of the Federal Reserve System.
- During the 1910s and 1920s, the Red Bug, an early version of the dune buggy, was the main mode of transportation on the island.
- In 1915, AT&T president Theodore Vail placed the first transcontinental telephone call—from Jekyll Island.
- In 1954, the Jekyll Island Causeway was completed, linking the island to the mainland for the first time. Previous transportation was by ferry.
- Jekyll Island has been recognized as an Important Bird Area by the Audubon Society.
- In 2003, 204 sea turtles laid their eggs on the island's beaches.

2–4 weekends. Some special events and themed tours during the year include Folklore Rumor and Myth in October and Holidays in History in December. Museum free. Tram: adults $16, children 6–18 $7. Visitors who prefer to tour on their own can rent a Multi-Media Self-Guided Tour for $8.

MUSEUMS 🐾 🐕 ♿ **Cumberland Island National Seashore Museum** (912-882-4336, ext. 254 or 1-888-817-3421; www.nps.gov/cuis or www.stmaryswelcome.com), visitors center: 113 West St. Marys Street, St. Marys; museum: Osborne Street, St. Marys; mailing address: 101 Wheeler Street, St. Marys 31558. Visitors center open 8–4:30 daily; museum open 1–4 Wednesday–Sunday. The museum in St. Marys was created to provide a glimpse of the island for the benefit of those who are unable to visit it in person. It contains artifacts from the Native Americans, African Americans, and Carnegie family members who inhabited Cumberland Island. The visitors center at the ferry landing features exhibits about the island's ecosystem. The ferry schedule is extremely complicated depending on the season, so consult the website or call ahead to avoid disappointment. Museum and visitors center free. Ferry: adults $20, seniors $18, children $14. Park day-use fee $4.

🐾 🐕 ♿ **Jekyll Island History Center** (912-635-4036), 100 Stable Road, Jekyll Island. Open 9–5 daily. Begin a tour of the Jekyll Island National Historic Landmark District at this center, where you can see an orientation film about the island's inhabitants from Native Americans to the present. Tram tours leave from here (see **Jekyll Island National Historic Landmark District** under *Historic Homes and Sites*). Free.

🐾 🐕 ♿ **Maritime Center at the Historic Coast Guard Station** (Coastal Georgia Historical Society: 912-638-4666; www.saintsimonslighthouse.org/maritime.html), 4201 First Street, East Beach, St. Simons Island. Open 10–5 Monday–Saturday (closed noon–1 for lunch), 1:30–5 Sunday. Located in the 1935 Coast Guard Station on East Beach, the museum interprets the region's natural assets and maritime and War of 1812 military history through the letters and field journal entries of Ollie, a fictitious Coast Guardsman, and his dog, Scuttle. Seven galleries are filled with hands-on exhibits. Adults $10, children 6–11 $5; family discount and combination tickets, which also include St. Simons Lighthouse (see following entry), are available.

MARITIME CENTER, ST. SIMONS ISLAND

🐚 **Orange Hall House Museum** (912-576-3644 for automated information; www.orangehall.org or www.stmaryswelcome.com), 311 Osborne Street, St. Marys. Open 11–3 Monday–Friday, 1–4 Saturday and Sunday. The stately, stereotypical Southern Greek Revival mansion with its massive fluted columns and Doric capitals was built in the early to mid-1800s and is filled with artifacts from the area. During the Civil War it served as a headquarters for Union troops and remained relatively unharmed. Adults $3, children $1.

🐚 🦀 ♿ **St. Marys Submarine Museum** (912-882-2782; www.stmaryssubmuseum.com), 102 St. Marys Street West, St. Marys. Open 10–5 Tuesday–Saturday, noon–5 Sunday. Nearby Kingsland is the home of the Naval Submarine Base Kings Bay. The base is not open for tours, but this submarine museum tells the story of the submarine force in the United States and abroad. The self-guided tour takes one to two hours and includes an operational periscope, a submarine helm station, models of torpedoes, deep-sea fishing suits, uniforms, models of submarines, memorabilia, photos, patrol reports, films, and books. The small, unassuming building can be readily identified by the submarine periscope jutting from the roof. Visitors can peer at the waterfront through the periscope. Adults $5, seniors and active-duty military $4, children 6–18 $3.

🐚 🦀 ♿ **St. Simons Island Lighthouse Museum** (912-638-4666; www.saintsimonslighthouse.org), 101 12th Street, St. Simons Island. Open 10–5 Monday–Saturday, 1:30–5 Sunday (last climb to the top at 4:30). The restored, 104-foot, 1872 lighthouse remains a navigational aid for St. Simons Sound. The tower is open for climbing, and the 1872 keeper's cottage houses a museum with exhibits about this and other lighthouses, which interpret the lives of lighthouse keepers and their families. Limited wheelchair accessibility. Adults $10, children 6–11 $5.

SPECIAL PLACES 🐚 🦀 ♿ **Brunswick Shrimp Docks–Mary Ross Waterfront Park–Liberty Ship Memorial,** Bay and Gloucester streets, Brunswick. Open daily. The park along the docks is a perfect place from which to watch the butterfly-netted shrimp boats come and go. Early morning and late afternoon are the best times. When the boats return, they are usually laden with the day's shrimp catch and the treasures of the sea that may be on the dinner table that evening in one of Brunswick's restaurants. Shop at the **Brunswick Harbor Market,** a farmer's market, at the park. Also in the park is the **Liberty Ship Memorial Plaza,** where visitors can see a scale model of a Liberty ship similar to those built in Brunswick's shipyards during

THE ORANGE HALL HOUSE MUSEUM IS FILLED WITH ARTIFACTS FROM THE EARLY AND MID-1800S.

World War II. The multipurpose park also features an outdoor musical playscape for children and an amphitheater where a wide variety of festivals and events occur throughout the year. In addition, the park is a romantic place to watch a spectacular sunset. Free.

🦐 ✒ ♿ **Folkston Funnel Train Watching Platform** (912-496-2536; www.folkston.com), 103 North First Street, Folkston. Open daily. Train buffs are finding it harder and harder to find places to watch the magnificent behemoths. Folkston is located on CSXT's double-track main line, known as the CSXT Funnel out of Florida. This covered viewing platform with benches allows train watchers to see up to 70 trains per day, including six AMTRAK trains and intermodal and mixed freight trains. Visitors can activate a scanner to listen to train engineers as they pass through the town. The site is set up so that visitors can spend as long as they want and make a day of it. There are restrooms, a grill, and picnic tables. A special event is the Annual Rail Watch in April. During Folkston's Okefenokee Festival in October, the Orlando Society of Model Railroaders sets up an elaborate train layout. Free.

✴ To Do

BICYCLING On Jekyll Island, visitors can explore more than 20 miles of paved, winding trails that are perfect for cycling, walking, and jogging. Trails pass historic sites, beaches, marshes, and maritime forests. Rentals of 16-, 20-, 24-, and 26-inch bikes are available by the hour, day, or week next to the miniature golf course on North Beachview Drive. Helmets and child seats are also available. Open 9–5 daily. Bike rentals are also available at the **Jekyll Island Campground** (see *Lodging—Campgrounds*), from the **Jekyll Island State Park Authority** (912-635-2648), and at many hotels.

On St. Simons, bike paths wind around the airport, through the village, and along the marsh at East Beach as well as the entire length of Frederica Road. Rentals and purchases of equipment are available at a number of locations.

🦐 ✒ **Benjy's Bike Shop** (912-638-6766), 130 Retreat Plaza, St. Simons Island. Open 10–6 Monday–Saturday. The full-service bike shop offers rentals of adult and child beach cruisers and mountain bikes, baby seats, training wheels, and tag-alongs, as well as repairs, bike accessories, and apparel. $10 for four hours; $45 for a full week.

BIRDING 🦐 ✒ **Colonial Coast Birding Trail** (912-882-4000; downloadable map available at www.georgiawildlife.com). Southeast Georgia is a birder's paradise, offering a wide variety of habitats and species. Along the 18-site trail, which stretches from Savannah south to St. Marys and the Okefenokee Swamp, shorelines, salt marshes, old rice fields, woodlands, tidal rivers, and freshwater wetlands are just a few of the habitats to explore. In addition to a plentiful year-round bird population, Jekyll Island is a resting place in the spring and fall for migrating species on the Atlantic Flyway. The trail sponsors the annual **Colonial Coast Birding and Nature Festival** in September (see *Special Events*). Free.

BOAT EXCURSIONS ✒ **Okefenokee Adventures** (912-496-7156 or 1-866-THESWAMP; www.okefenokeeadventures.com), 4159 Suwannee Canal Road, off GA 121, Folkston. Call for schedules and fees. The visitor-services partner of the Okefenokee National Wildlife Refuge (see *Green Space—Nature Preserves and Parks*) offers guided interpretive tours, including multiday excursions. Sunset tours are particularly popular. The outfitter also rents bicycles, canoes, motorboats, and kayaks. While there, enjoy a light lunch at the Camp Cornelia Café.

✒ **Up the Creek Xpeditions and Outfitters** (912-882-0911 or 1-877-UPTHECREEK; www.upthecreekx.com), 111 Osborne Street, St. Marys. Call for schedules and fees. The company offers guided half-day, full-day, and overnight kayak trips, rentals, and instruction.

CANOEING AND KAYAKING The ocean and marshes provide ideal locations for this mode of exploration. Rentals, instruction, and guided excursions are available. For those who have never tried ocean kayaking, these vessels are lightweight, easily maneuverable, and more stable than their freshwater counterparts.

✐ **SouthEast Adventure Outfitters** (912-265-5292; www.southeastadventure.com), Brunswick Boathouse, 1200 Glynn Avenue, Brunswick; St. Simons Store, 313 Mallory Street, and Village Creek Landing, South Harrington Road north of the Sea Island Causeway, both on St. Simons. Call for a schedule of trips and prices. The company offers year-round guided kayak tours around the offshore islands as well as inland marsh and Altamaha and Satilla river tours.

CARRIAGE RIDES ✐ **Victoria's Carriages and Beach Trail Rid**es (912-635-9500), 100 Stable Road, Jekyll Island. Call for hours and fees; reservations required. The company offers narrated carriage tours of the historic district, trail rides on the beach and in maritime forests, hayrides, sunset rides, and couple rides. Moonlit rides depart from the Jekyll Island Club Hotel (see *Lodging—Inns and Resorts*) Monday–Saturday evenings.

DIVING Although Georgia's waters are murky near the shore, they are clear to crystal blue offshore. Many artificial reefs have been developed around sunken ships, and a variety of scuba services are available. Gray's Reef is an outstanding diving area.

✐ **Island Dive Center and Tours** (912-638-6590 or 1-800-940-3483), Golden Isles Marina, 101 Marina Drive, St. Simons Island. Call for schedules. The full-service facility offers snorkeling and scuba classes, guided dives, air fills, tours, and equipment rentals, sales, and service. Fees vary by activity.

FISHING The Georgia coast boasts access to deep-sea fishing as well as 700,000 acres of salt marsh, tidal creeks, and freshwater rivers. Opportunities for deep-sea, surf, inshore river, and lake fishing abound here. There are also numerous bridges and piers from which to fish. Anglers catch tarpon, whiting, red drum, sea trout, triple tail, spotted sea trout, striped mullet, sheepshank, black drum, and many others. Numerous marinas and experienced guides are available. A Georgia fishing license is required, and there may be limitations on the size and number of some species.

Public fishing is available at the St. Simons Island fishing pier, along the Torras Causeway, and at older bridgeheads. Good shore fishing can be found at Gould's Inlet on East Beach. Crabbing is also a popular activity, using hand lines from low docks or with crab pots and traps from bridges and piers. The Golden Isles Marina adjacent to the Torras Causeway on the Frederica River and the Hampton Point Marina at the north end of the island offer a full range of services, including charters. The St. Simons Boating and Fishing Club is a public facility.

✐ **Coastal Expeditions Charter Fishing and Dolphin Tours** (912-265-0392; www.coastalcharterfishing.com), One Harbor Road, at Jekyll Island Marina. Call for schedules and prices. Fishing, dolphin watching, and birding tours are offered daily. Specialties include inshore charters for trout and bass, near-shore charters for shark and tarpon, and deep-sea charters.

FRIGHTS ✐ ♿ **Ghost Walk of St. Simons** (912-638-2756; www.ghostwalksofstsimons.com), St. Simons Island. Call for a schedule of tours. All tours depart at 9 PM from St. Simons Village near the pier. The fun and informative one-and-a-half-hour lamplight walking tour explores Olde St. Simons. Participants experience frightful tales of folklore, mystery, legends, lovers, and the lost while discovering more about the island and its history. Bringing your own flashlight is recommended. Adults $13–16, children 5–12 $8.

GOLF Jekyll Island offers 63 holes of golf with three 18-hole courses and a historic 9-hole course, making the island Georgia's largest public golf resort. Jekyll Island hotels offer all-inclusive golf passport packages that allow players to experience these four courses and six others along the coast.

Great Dunes Golf Course (912-635-2170), Shell Road and Beachview Drive, Jekyll Island. Open 7–5 daily; earlier closing in winter. The historic nine-hole course, which was originally built in the late 1800s, lies along the ocean. Today the course still attracts and challenges golfers with its alternating simple and difficult holes. $25 riding, $18 walking; discounts for juniors, replay, and twilight hours.

Jekyll Island Golf Club (912-635-2368), 322 Captain Wylly Road, Jekyll Island. First tee time at 8 AM, last tee time two hours before dark. The club actually includes three 18-hole championship courses from a central clubhouse: **Indian Mounds, Oleander** (which is considered the most difficult), and **Pine Lake.** The facility also includes a putting green, driving range, practice bunker, pro shop, and restaurant. $45 riding, $30 walking; discounts for juniors, replay, and twilight play.

HIKING 🐦 ✿ **Earth Day Nature Trail** (912-264-7218), Coastal Resources Office, One Conservation Way, off US 17 at Sidney Lanier Bridge, Brunswick. The self-guided trail through salt marshes, tidal ponds, and coastal hammock high ground provides endless opportunities for bird-watching and wildlife observation. Wading birds are abundant, and visitors may catch a glimpse of an eagle or osprey on the nesting platform provided for them. There are observation decks and an observation tower, and binoculars are available for checkout. Maps can be downloaded from www.coastalgadnr.org/maps. Call ahead to access the trail. Free.

MINIATURE GOLF 🐦 ✿ ♿ **Jekyll Island Mini Golf** (912-635-2648), North Beachview Drive at Shell Road, Jekyll Island. Call for hours, as they vary widely by season. Two lighted, old-time, 18-hole courses are located across from the beach. $6.08 per person per game, $15 three-game pass, $45 10-game pass.

NATURE TOURS ✿ ♿ **Salt Marsh Nature Tours** (912-638-9354; www.marshtours .com), 1000 Hampton River Club Drive, at Hampton River Club Marina, St. Simons Island. Call for schedules. Captain Jeanne and Captain Jim offer nature tours and dolphin tours of the marshes and tidal creeks between St. Simons Island and Little St. Simons Island aboard *Marsh Hen,* their pontoon boat. They impart historical information as well as pointing out vegetation, birds, and mammals. $50 per person, minimum of four.

NATURE WALKS ✿ **Sea Turtle Walks** (912-635-4444), 214 Stable Road, Jekyll Island. Call for schedules and prices. Guides conduct walks that teach about sea turtles and their habitats, and participants search for turtle tracks and nesting loggerhead turtle mothers. Tours leave from the Georgia Sea Turtle Center (see *To See—For Families*).

SUMMER YOUTH PROGRAMS ✿ **Camp Cloister and Club Sea Island at the Cloister at Sea Island** (912-638-3611 or 1-888-732-4752; www.seaisland.com), 100 First Street, Sea Island. The resort has earned many accolades from readers of *Condé Nast Traveler* and *Travel + Leisure,* including being named the Best Resort for Families in the United States and Canada. The superior Children's Activity Center contains table tennis, air hockey, and other games. Special children's programs are conducted during the summer, spring break, and other holidays. Camp Cloister is available for children ages 3–8; Club Sea Island is for youngsters 9–12. Activities might include turtle walks, dunes discovery, fishing, sand sculpture, contests, tie-dye on the beach, boat rides, and more. Older youth can participate

FAMILIES FLOCK TO THE SUMMER WAVES
WATER PARK ON JEKYLL ISLAND.

in tennis and golf clinics and round robins. The resort also offers movies, teen bowling, Jeep safaris, and much more. $50 for a half day; some fees charged by activity; participation by reservation only.

TENNIS ✄ **Jekyll Island Tennis Center** (912-635-3154; www.jekyllisland.com/tennis), 400 Captain Wylly Road, Jekyll Island. Open 9–6 daily for open play; evening and night play until 10 PM available by reservation only prior to 6 PM day of play. Recognized as one of the finest municipal facilities in the country, the center offers 13 award-winning, fast-dry clay courts, of which seven are lighted, as well as a pro shop, racquet stringing, and instruction for every level of play. The center is the site of six USTA tournaments, junior tennis camps, clinics, and round-robin tournaments from October through March, so even visitors who aren't playing can usually find something to watch. $6 per person per hour for play; ball machine $10 per hour; racquet and hopper rental $3.

On St. Simons, there are tennis courts at Sea Palms Golf and Tennis Resort and the King and Prince Beach and Golf Resort (see *Lodging—Inns and Resorts*), as well as public courts at Mallory Park and Epworth Park.

TROLLEY RIDES ✄ **St. Simons Trolley Company** (912-638-8954; www.stsimons tours.com), 117 Mallory Street at the Village Pier, St. Simons Island. There are generally two tours daily in summer and one tour daily in winter, but hours vary by season, so consult the website or call ahead to avoid disappointment. Getting around St. Simons can be fun aboard one of the antique trolleys operated by the St. Simons Transit Company. The 90-minute narrated tours pass all the important sites on the island—the lighthouse, Bloody Marsh, Fort Frederica, and Retreat Plantation, to name just a few—and make a stop at Christ Church. Adults $22, children 4–12 $10; advance tickets and reservations not required.

WATER PARKS ✄ ♿ **Summer Waves Water Park** (912-635-2074; www.summer waves.com), 210 South Riverview Drive, Jekyll Island. Open daily May–early August when school starts, through Labor Day weekend, and a few more weekends in September; call for exact days and hours. The 11-acre, family-oriented water park features more than a million gallons of water used for a lazy river, a wave pool the size of a football field, a kiddie pool, and several exciting water slides with names such as Pirate's Passage, Nature's Revenge, and Thunder and Lightning. There are height restrictions on some rides. Locker rentals and concessions are available, and lifejackets are provided for small children. Those above 4 feet tall $19.95, seniors $10.95, those under 4 feet tall $15.95, ages three and younger free; two-day pass for adults $24.95.

✳ Green Space

BEACHES This coastal area and its barrier islands are rich in beaches: St. Simons offers 10 miles of beaches, Little St. Simons has more than 7 miles of sand, Cumberland Island boasts more than 17 miles of pristine beach, and Jekyll Island offers 10 miles of uncrowded, unspoiled beaches.

NATURE PRESERVES AND PARKS ♞ ✄ ♿ ❀ **Crooked River State Park** (912-882-5256; lodging reservations: 1-800-864-7275; www.gastateparks.org/CrookedRiver), 6222

Charlie Smith Sr. Highway, St. Marys. Open 7 AM–10 PM daily. The 500-acre park on the Crooked River features maritime forest and salt marshes. Water sports such as saltwater fishing, boating, and kayaking are the primary activities, but 4 miles of trails attract hikers, and the park offers an Olympic-size swimming pool, playground, and miniature golf course. Accommodations are offered in cottages (some of which are dog friendly) and campgrounds (see *Lodging—Campgrounds*). Parking $5.

✍ **Cumberland Island National Seashore** (912-882-4335 or 1-888-817-3421; www.nps .gov/cuis), landside office: 113 West St. Marys Street, St. Marys. Visitors center open 8–4:30 daily. Access is by ferry only, and reservations are strongly recommended to avoid disappointment. The ferry schedule is complicated and varies by season and day of the week, so it's best to consult the website or to call ahead. In general there are two morning departures and two afternoon returns. In all cases, the last ferry back to the mainland leaves the island at 4:45, so make sure not to get left there. The majority of Cumberland Island, the largest and southernmost of Georgia's barrier islands, is preserved as a national seashore. Secluded white, sandy beaches and a complex ecological system characterize the island. Popular travel guides have rated the island beaches A+ for beaches and sand quality, and the site has been named one of America's top beaches by the Travel Channel. Popular activities include beachcombing and shell gathering, swimming, sunning, walking and hiking (no vehicles allowed), fishing (a license is required and can be purchased in St. Marys; light tackle only can be used, and you must bring your own), camping (see *Lodging—Campgrounds*), and seasonal ranger-led programs. There are also several man-made sites to see on the island. Dungeness Ruins is the remains of a home built in 1884 by Thomas Carnegie. The simple First African Baptist Church served as a church, community hall, and school for the island's early African Americans. It gained worldwide recognition when it served as the site of John F. Kennedy Jr.'s marriage to Carolyn Bessette. Plum Orchard Mansion, which was built by the Carnegie family in 1898, is sometimes open for ranger-guided tours. The Ice House Museum is open daily. Most of these attractions are too widely scattered to visit on foot in the time allotted before the return ferry. There are several NPS guided interpretive tours by passenger van or open-air tram at an additional cost. These tours, which leave from Sea Camp and last five to six hours, include Land and Legacies, Plum Orchard Mansion, the old settlement and First African Baptist Church, and the Wharf. Call ahead to reserve these tours. Shorter walking tours include the one-hour, 1-mile Footsteps tour of Dungeness Historic District, the 30-minute Dockside Tour, and a Just for Kids Tour in summer. *Note:* There are no stores on Cumberland Island. St. Marys businesses and the ferry carry sandwiches, snacks, beverages, and souvenirs. Visitors should wear comfortable clothing and shoes, and bring food, drinks, sunblock, insect repellent, rain gear, sunglasses, and perhaps an umbrella. You must carry out what you bring in. No pets or bicycles are permitted on the ferry. Bikes and beach wheelchairs can be rented at Sea Camp. For those whose idea of roughing it is room service, luxurious accommodations are available at the privately operated **Greyfield Inn** (see *Lodging—Inns and Resorts*). Park day-use fee $4, in addition to ferry service: adults $20, seniors $18, children 12 and younger $14.

🦆 ✍ **Okefenokee National Wildlife Refuge, East Entrance–Suwannee Canal Recreation Area** (912-496-7836; www.fws.gov/okefenokee), 2700 Suwannee Canal Road, Folkston. Open sunrise–7:30 PM daily, March 1–November 1; until 5:30 the remainder of the year. The Okefenokee NWR is the largest wildlife refuge in the eastern United States as well as being one of the oldest and best-preserved freshwater areas in America. It is a vast bog occupying a saucer-shaped depression that was once an ocean floor. The swamp, which boasts 120 miles of canoe trails, is made up of upland islands, moss-draped cypress forests, scrub-shrub vegetation, prairie wetlands, waterways, and open lakes. In addition to alligators, the swamp is home to other reptiles, amphibians, bobcats, white-tailed deer, black bears, songbirds, birds of prey, wading birds, and migrating waterfowl. Winter is an excellent time

ALLIGATORS PASS THE TIME AT THE
OKEFENOKEE NATIONAL WILDLIFE REFUGE.

to see the endangered Florida sandhill crane, and spring is the time to catch a glimpse of red-cockaded woodpeckers. Human habitation has included Native Americans, early settlers, canal builders, and lumbermen. Visit the preserved Chesser Island Homestead, the hardscrabble home place of the Chesser family for more than 100 years, to see the primitive conditions in which the family eked out an existence. The Swamp's Edge Information Center offers interpretive nature exhibits. Activities at the park include a driving tour, biking, walking and hiking, boating, fishing, hunting, wildlife observation, interpretive programs, and special events. One recommended short jaunt is the 1.5-mile round-trip boardwalk trail to Seagrove Lake and the Owl's Roost observation tower. There are several other half-mile to mile-long hiking trials, and canoe trails range from 12 to 55 miles long. Wilderness canoeing and camping on raised platforms are offered by permit only. Guided boat tours are offered, and canoe, kayak, motorboat, and bike rentals are available. There is also a snack bar and gift shop. (See also the Waycross chapter, and the Valdosta chapter in part 5, Southern Rivers, for more information about the swamp.) $5; overnight wilderness canoe permit $10 per night.

✳ Lodging
BED & BREAKFASTS

In Brunswick

🐾 **Brunswick Manor** (912-265-6889; www.brunswickmanor.com), 825 Egmont Street. The stately 1886 home, which overlooks an original 1771 park in the Old Town residential district, offers three elegant guest rooms with private baths and plenty of luxurious amenities. Outside, guests are invited to enjoy the wraparound veranda, the arbored patio, and the hot tub. A delicious breakfast is included. Special Events Dinners are scheduled from time to time at an additional cost. Smoking outdoors only. One accommodation pet friendly. Not wheelchair accessible. $99–139.

McKinnin House (912-261-9100 or 1-866-261-9100; www.mckinnonhousebandb .com), 1001 Egmont Street. Located in the heart of Old Town Brunswick, the imposing home was built in 1902 for a lumber magnate. Seventeen Corinthian columns support the upstairs and downstairs verandas,

where guests often enjoy afternoon refreshments. Family heirlooms and period reproductions characterize the public and guest rooms. Guests enjoy private baths, sweeping verandas, a Southern gourmet breakfast, and afternoon tea. Smoking outdoors only. Not wheelchair accessible. $125.

WatersHill Bed and Breakfast (912-264-4262; www.watershill.com), 728 Union Street. The intimate retreat with modern amenities is located in a historic home in Old Town Brunswick. Five elegantly appointed guest rooms feature private baths. Porches, gardens, fountains, and a koi pond entice guests outdoors. No smoking. Not wheelchair accessible. Not child or pet friendly. $85–125.

In Folkston

🐾 ♿ **Inn at Folkston Bed and Breakfast** (912-496-6256 or 1-888-509-6246; www.inn atfolkston.com), 3576 Main Street. The fully restored 1920s Craftsman-style bungalow features four antiques-filled guest rooms, each uniquely decorated with an individual theme. All feature amenities you'd expect to find in an upscale hotel: feather beds, down comforters, robes, hair dryers, and more. Some rooms boast a gas-log fireplace, a private screened porch, and/or a whirlpool tub. The inn also features a large porch, a six-person hot tub, an herb garden, and 2 acres on which to wander. Nightly rates include a full hot breakfast and an evening social hour. Children of all ages welcome. Smoking outdoors only. One room wheelchair accessible. $120–160.

In St. Marys

Emma's Bed and Breakfast (912-882-4199 or 1-877-749-5974; www.emmasbed andbreakfast.com), 300 West Conyers Street. Located in a lovely, traditional-style home on 4 tranquil acres in downtown St. Marys, Emma's is named for Emma Bealey, who came here as a bride in 1911. The nine individually themed guest rooms and suites in the main house and an additional building have private baths. The grounds feature beautiful gardens. No smoking. Not wheelchair accessible. $119–189; two-night minimum during holidays or special events.

& **Goodbread House Bed and Breakfast** (912-882-7490 or 1-877-205-1453; www.goodbreadhouse.com), 209 Osborne Street. Located in a historic house on the main thoroughfare in St. Marys, Goodbread House, with its attractive upstairs and downstairs verandas, features guest rooms whimsically named for famous couples— Rhett and Scarlett, Guinevere and Lancelot, Gabriel and Evangeline, Gable and Lombard, Bogie and Bacall, and Lucy and Ricky—each with a private bath. No smoking. Ask about pets. $99–139.

✧ & **Spencer House Inn** (912-882-1872 or 1-888-840-1872; www.spencerhouse inn.com), 200 Osborne Street. Spencer House has a long history as a hotel. It was built in 1872 by Capt. William T. Spencer and was known as the finest hotel in St. Marys and southeast Georgia. The stately pink building with upstairs and downstairs verandas features 14 rooms and suites with private baths. Fine antiques and reproductions furnish public spaces and guest

rooms. A full buffet breakfast is served in the cheery breakfast room. No smoking. $135–245; minimum stay may be required during holidays or special events.

On St. Simons Island

✧ & **Village Inn and Pub** (912-634-6056 or 1-888-635-6111; www.villageinnandpub .com), 500 Mallory Street. A restored 1930s beach cottage serves as the heart of this inn. Designed around the original cottage, the newly constructed inn integrates the architecture of the neighborhood and the facade of the cottage. Accommodations, decorated to celebrate the luxury and tastes of the '30s with modern amenities, range from standard rooms to junior suites and deluxe rooms, most with private balconies. In the evening, enjoy the pub's wild-orchid martini or other libations in an Old English atmosphere. The inn also has a pool and gardens, and therapeutic massages are available by reservation. Continental breakfast, served on the pub's sunporch, is included. Accommodations are also available at the Village Retreat and the Beach House (ask about those rates). No smoking except on balconies or other outdoor locations. $99–210; peak season March 1–Labor Day weekend.

CAMPGROUNDS

In Brunswick

✦ ✧ & **Blythe Island Regional Park** (912-279-2812 or 1-800-343-7855; www .glynncounty.org), 6616 Blythe Island Highway. The 1,100-acre public park offers a full-service campground, excellent freshwater and saltwater fishing, a marina, boat ramp, boat rental, freshwater swimming lake, bait sales, walking and biking trails, two lighted tennis courts, field archery range, playground, volleyball courts, boat hoist, and laundry facilities. $38.63 for full hookups.

On Cumberland Island

✦ ✧ **Backcountry and Sea Camps** (912-882-4335 or 1-888-817-3421; www.nps .gov/cuis). Two types of camping are offered on Cumberland Island. Developed sea campgrounds offer restrooms, cold-water showers, and drinking water, and campfires are permitted. Backcountry camps offer only drinking water. Campfires are not permitted, so a camp stove is required. Keep in mind that backcountry campsites may be up to 10 miles from the dock; campers must walk both ways while carrying all their equipment. There are no stores, so you must pack in and out everything you need. $2 per person per day for backcountry primitive camping, $4 per person per day for sea camp developed camping; $4 day-use fee in addition to camping fee, plus the cost of ferry passage to and from the island (see **Cumberland Island National Seashore** under *Green Space— Nature Preserves and Parks*); reservations required.

On Jekyll Island

🐾 ♪ **Jekyll Island Campground** (912-635-3021 or 1-866-658-3021; www.jekyll island.com/wheretostay/campground.aspx), 1197 North Riverview Drive. Eighteen wooded acres on the island's north end provide the site for 206 tent and RV campsites—some with full hookups, others with partial hookups—and some primitive sites. The campground also features a camp store, coin laundry, restrooms with showers, and bicycle rentals. $21 for tent sites; $26 for water and electric sites; $32 for back-in, full-service sites; $35 for pull-through, full-service sites. All higher on holiday weekends.

In St. Marys

🐾 ♪ 🐾 **Crooked River State Park** (lodging reservations: 1-800-864-7275). The park offers 62 tent, trailer, and RV sites shaded by Spanish moss–draped oaks. See *Green Space—Nature Preserves and Parks.* $25–28.

CONDOS

On St. Simons Island
♪ **The Beach Club** (rental agency: 912-638-5450; 1-888-306-1396; www.beachclub stsimons.com), 1440 Ocean Boulevard. The oceanfront condominium complex features 106 fully furnished, one- to three-bedroom, one- to two-bath units with complete

kitchens and laundry facilities. Amenities include an oceanside pool, kids' pool, playground, hot tubs, tennis courts, a fitness center, an observation deck, and a boardwalk. $170–275.

♪ **North Breakers Condominiums** (rental agency: 912-638-1244; www.north breakersstsimons.com), 1470 Wood Avenue. The oceanfront condominium complex features fully furnished, one- to three-bedroom, two-bath units with complete kitchens and laundry facilities. Amenities include an oceanside pool, a Jacuzzi, and a children's pool. $153–180.

COTTAGES AND CABINS

In Folkston
🐾 ♪ **Okefenokee Pastimes Cabins** (912-496-4472 or 1-800-230-4134; www .okefenokee.com), GA 121 South. Okefenokee Adventures (see *To Do—Boat Excursions*) offers three levels of cabins. All have heat and air-conditioning, but none have phones or televisions. Deluxe cabins feature a double bed and a bunk bed, a private bath, equipped kitchenette with a microwave and small refrigerator, and screened porch. Log cabins are similar but do not have a bathroom; guests use the communal bathroom. Linens are provided for the deluxe and log cabins. Camping cabins are basically a climate-controlled roof over your head. There are no bathrooms, kitchenettes, or linens, and you must clean the cabin when you leave. $110 for deluxe cabins, $85 for log cabins, $50 for camping cabins; multinight discounts available for all.

On Jekyll Island
♪ **Jekyll Realty Vacation Rentals** (912-635-3301 or 1-888-333-5055; www.jekyll-island.com), Jekyll Shopping Center. Fully furnished and equipped one- to five-bedroom homes, apartments, and villas are available by the week and month or for shorter periods when available.

♪ **Parker-Kaufman, Realtors** (912-635-2512 or 1-888-453-5955; www.parker-kaufman.com/jekyll), 561 North Beachview Drive. More than 100 accommodations are available in one- to six-bedroom cottages and condos. Weekly and monthly rates are available, as well as shorter stays when available.

In St. Marys

🦐 🐾 🐚 **Crooked River State Park** (lodging reservations: 1-800-864-7275). Eleven cottages overlook the river at this state park. Several allow dogs ($40 per dog/ maximum two). $125–150. See *Green Space—Nature Preserves and Parks.*

INNS AND RESORTS

On Cumberland Island

🐾 ♿ **Greyfield Inn** (904-261-6408 or 1-866-401-8051; www.greyfieldinn.com), mailing address: 4 North Second Street, Fernandina Beach, FL 32035. Although the majority of Cumberland Island is national seashore, some areas remain in private hands. Greyfield, a historic 1901 mansion built as a wedding present for Lucy and Thomas Carnegie's daughter, Margaret Ricketson, is still in the hands of descendants of the Carnegie family. Decorated with family heirlooms and antiques, the inn provides an elegant, private retreat from the busy daily world. Eleven guest rooms and suites feature private, adjacent, or shared baths. The daily rate includes accommodations; ferry transportation to the island; a full Southern breakfast, picnic lunch, and formal candlelit gourmet dinner; naturalist-led Jeep tours of the island; and unlimited use of bicycles and sports, fishing, and beach equipment. Children six and older welcome. No smoking. Limited wheelchair accessibility. $395–595; two-night minimum stay required, except three-night minimum on holidays.

On Jekyll Island

🐾 ♿ **Jekyll Island Club Hotel** (912-635-2600 or 1-855-535-9547; www.jekyllclub .com), 371 Riverview Drive. Built in 1887, the main structure was the clubhouse for the private Jekyll Island Club (see *To See— Historic Homes and Sites*). A National Historic Landmark, the hotel offers 157 first-class accommodations in five historic settings: the main hotel in the clubhouse, the 1901 Clubhouse Annex, the 1896 Sans

Souci apartments, 1917 Crane Cottage, and 1904 Cherokee Cottage. Guest rooms and suites are nicely appointed with period reproductions. Amenities include fine dining at the **Grand Dining Room** and the **Courtyard at Crane** (see *Dining Out— Jekyll Island*) as well as casual dining at **Café Solterra** (see *Eating Out—On Jekyll Island*), an outdoor heated pool, a croquet lawn, seasonal children's programs, room service, five gift shops, and concierge service. Smoking and nonsmoking rooms available. $169–479; American Plan or Modified American Plan available at additional cost.

On Little St. Simons Island

🐾 ♿ **The Lodge on Little St. Simons** (912-638-7472 or 1-888-733-5774; www .littlestsimonsisland.com), depart from 1000 Hampton Point Drive on St. Simons Island. In addition to being named to *Condé Nast Traveler*'s prestigious Gold List of Best Places to Stay in 2006, the resort has been honored by other publications. *Southern Living* has recognized the island resort for having one of the best beaches in the South, and the *Robb Report* has named it one of the World's 10 Great Escapes. The island, which is accessible only by the lodge's private boat, comprises 10,000 acres with 7 miles of pristine beach. Overnight guests are limited to 32 guests, who are housed in 15 guest rooms located in 5 rustic cottages that were constructed in 1917, 1926, the 1930s, and the 1970s. The Hunting Lodge, the heart of the island, is where guests meet for meals, cocktail hour, games, and socializing. The nightly rate includes three meals, accommodations, horseback riding, guided interpretive programs, boating, biking, bird-watching, fishing, and use of sports equipment. There's also a pool. No smoking. All-inclusive room rates $600–1,200; entire cottages $1,650–2,500; entire island $8,000–8,500.

On St. Simons Island

🐾 ♿ **King and Prince Beach and Golf Resort** (912-638-3631 or 1-800-342-0212; www.kingandprince.com), 201 Arnold Road. Located directly on the beach, the elegant, Mediterranean-style hotel, a member of Historic Hotels of America, offers handsomely decorated guest rooms and suites—many of them oceanfront—as well as oceanfront cabanas, villas, and residences. Amenities include the Royal Treatment Cottage Spa, an indoor heated pool and hot tub in the atrium lobby, four outdoor pools, two clay tennis courts, a fitness room, and a full-service oceanfront restaurant noted for its Friday-night seafood buffet and Sunday brunch. Seasonal poolside dining also is offered. Golfers can play at the King and Prince Golf Course. Only four smoking rooms available; remainder are nonsmoking. $104–699.

✦ ♿ **Ocean Inn and Suites** (912-634-2122 or 1-877-OCEAN-INN; www.ocean innsuites.com), 599 Beachview Drive. The island's newest luxury-suite hotel, located across from the lighthouse, beach, and Neptune Park, boasts a saltwater jetted outdoor pool, a daily complimentary breakfast, and an evening manager's reception with an ice cream social. Units feature a microwave and refrigerator. No smoking. $119–389.

✦ ♿ **Sea Palms Golf and Tennis Resort** (912-638-3351 or 1-800-841-6268; www.sea palms.com), 5445 Frederica Road. Luxurious guest rooms, suites, and one- to four-bedroom villas overlook the Marshes of Glynn. Amenities include 27 holes of championship golf on three courses, a private beach club, full-service restaurants, a health and racquet club, three clay tennis courts, three outdoor pools, a children's wading pool, volleyball court, and horseshoe pits. A personal trainer is available, as are bike rentals. The St. Simons Beach Club offers private beach access, a pool, Jacuzzi tub, beach chair rentals, and a snack bar. Only seven smoking rooms; remainder are nonsmoking. $159–499 February 1–Thanksgiving; $119–489 off-season.

On Sea Island

✦ ♿ **The Cloister at Sea Island** (912-638-3611 or 1-800-732-4752; www.sea island.com), 100 First Street. The legendary resort began in 1928 with a Spanish-style building on beautifully landscaped grounds. After a multiyear renovation completed in 2005, the historic building was replaced with a new one. Ranked Number One Resort in the U.S. by the readers of *Condé*

Nast Traveler, the resort's $200 million improvement plan included the complete rebuilding of the main building, new River House wings, new dining and lounge facilities, and a new spa. Those who are appalled at the idea of demolishing the original hotel should be relieved to know that the look of the original design remains. The specialty woods, fixtures, stained glass, and mantels from the renowned Spanish Lounge were salvaged so the room could be reconstructed in the new building. Elegantly appointed guest rooms and suites with all the most luxurious amenities are found in the Cloister hotel, the Cloister Beach Club, the Cloister Ocean Villas, and the Cottages. Extras at the resort include 5 miles of private beach, three championship golf courses and a Golf Learning Center, a five-star spa, 25 tennis courts, golf and tennis pro shops, a shooting school, five gift shops, five restaurants, three swimming pools, a private beach, children's programs (see *To Do—Summer Youth Programs*), and many special themed events throughout the year. The equestrian program offers ring rides, trail rides, beach rides, lessons, clinics, stable tours, and a petting zoo. Hobie Cat sailboats, sea kayaks, beach funcycles, and boogie boards are available for rent. The main dining room is a throwback to a truly elegant era: Jackets for gentlemen and boys older than 12, and slacks and a collared shirt for boys 12 and younger, are required for dinner. *Note:* Travelers must be overnight guests at the Cloister to enjoy the activities or restaurants. No smoking. $300–2,000.

✦ ♿ **The Lodge at Sea Island** (912-634-4300 or 1-866-465-3563; www.seaisland .com), 100 Retreat Avenue. Part of the Cloister complex, the Lodge at Sea Island is geared to golfers. It's one of only 24 properties worldwide to have earned both Mobil five stars and AAA five diamonds, and it's also been named the Best Golf Resort in the U.S. by the *Robb Report*. The 40-room English Country Manor hotel is luxurious in the style of a private estate, with butlers available 24 hours a day to attend to any need or wish. Guests also have use of all the amenities at the Cloister. No smoking. $450–650.

On St. Simons Island

🍽 🍷 ♿ **Epworth-by-the-Sea** (912-638-8688; www.epworthbythesea.com), 100 Arthur J. Moore Drive. This Methodist Retreat Center (open to all) was named in honor of John and Charles Wesley's boyhood home. The 83-acre retreat located on the banks of the historic Frederica River features 10 motels (from basic 1950s style to upscale new construction), 12 family apartments, and 13 youth buildings—all told accommodating 1,000 people. Exceptional accommodations are offered in the VIP House, which was originally built in 1880 as the office for a sawmill. Meals are served cafeteria-style in several dining rooms. Guests can use the outdoor pool (open seasonally), lighted tennis courts, two fishing piers, and covered basketball courts. The newest attraction is the Epworth Adventure Challenge Ropes Course, which is ideal for team building. Dolphin tours and a museum are also available. No smoking. $65–123.

✴ Where to Eat

DINING OUT

On Jekyll Island

🍽 🍷 ♿ **Fins on the Beach** (912-635-3522), 200 North Beachview Drive. Open 4–9 Wednesday and Thursday, 11–9 Friday through Sunday. This casual, nautically themed beachfront family restaurant (the only restaurant on the island directly on the beach) offers authentic island, lowcountry, and traditional American cuisine, specializing in fresh seafood in addition to a wide variety of appetizers, entrées, nightly specials, and desserts. Dine inside or out on the deck overlooking the beach. No smoking. $9–26.

🍷 ♿ **Jekyll Island Club Hotel** (912-635-2600; www.jekyllclub.com), 375 Riverview Drive. Grand Dining Room (912-635-5155) open 7–11 AM Monday–Saturday (until 10 Sunday), 11:30–2 Monday–Saturday, and 6–10 daily; Sunday brunch 10:45–2 (reservations requested, ext. 1002). Courtyard at Crane open 11–4 Sunday–Friday, 11–2 Sat-

urday. The elite historic hotel offers several dining options, including the **Grand Dining Room** and the **Courtyard at Crane.** The palatial Grand Dining Room in the main hotel offers lunch with appetizers, soups, salads, sandwiches, and specialties, while dinner features seafood, duck, pork, chicken, quail, and beef dishes. Jackets are requested for gentlemen at the evening meal. The Grand Dining Room's Sunday Brunch features seafood, meats, pâtés, cheeses, breads, omelets, entrées that change weekly, and a dessert buffet. The Courtyard at Crane is located adjacent to the hotel in one of the restored "cottages," now used as additional lodging. The cuisine there is Mediterranean influenced, with Spanish and Moroccan specialties. Alfresco dining in the courtyard is a popular option. Lunch features salads, seafood, burgers, sandwiches, and chicken. Dinner choices include salads, chicken, steak, veal, lobster, pastas, steaks, and vegetarian entrées. In addition, the hotel offers casual dining at **Café Solterra** and **Vincent's Pub** (see *Eating Out*). No smoking. Grand Dining Room: breakfast $9–14, lunch $10–16, dinner $25–35; Sunday brunch $28.95 for adults, $14.95 for children younger than 12. Courtyard at Crane: lunch $10–16, dinner $10–35. Victorian Tea $14.95; once-monthly Sunday Dinner Dance $38.95.

In St. Marys

🍷 ♿ **Borrell Creek Landing** (912-673-6300), 2715 Osborne Road. Open 11:30–2:30 and 5–10 weekdays. The restaurant is noted for a variety of entrées, many of which feature steaks and seafood, and a view of the creek. No smoking. Lunch $8–12, dinner $15–30.

On St. Simons Island

🍽 🍷 ♿ **Barbara Jean's** (912-634-6500; www.barbara-jeans.com), 214 Mallory Street. Open 11–8:30 Sunday–Thursday, 11–9:30 Friday and Saturday. The restaurant features Southern dining specializing in signature crab dishes. In fact, the restaurant's motto is, "If you don't have anything else, try the crab cakes!" These Eastern Shore of Maryland–style crabcakes are prepared different ways and in different sizes.

You can have them as appetizers, on sandwiches, or as an entrée. Numerous other kinds of seafood are offered, along with meat loaf, pot roast, turkey, pork chops, chicken, steaks, homemade soups, sandwiches, and desserts. No smoking. $10–20.

& **Halyard's** (912-638-9100; www.halyards restaurant.com), Shops at Sea Island, 55 Cinema Lane, Suite 19. Open 6–10 PM Monday–Saturday. Superbly prepared and presented island cuisine ranges from Maine lobster to prime New York strip steak. The restaurant is also renowned for its exceptional service and good wine list. No smoking. $18–38; special three-course dinner for $33.

✈ & **The King and Prince Beach and Golf Resort** (912-638-3631, ext. 5321; www.kingandprince.com), 201 Arnold Road. Several dining venues: The **King's Tavern** serves breakfast, lunch, and dinner; the **Delegal Room** serves the Friday Seafood Buffet and the Sunday Brunch Buffet; the **Atrium** café serves a light early breakfast; and the **Paradise Beach Bar and Grill** serves a casual lunch and dinner seasonally. An island tradition for more than 75 years, the oceanfront hotel's famous Friday Seafood Buffet (February–November) features more than 30 items, including authentic lowcountry boil, a vast variety of other seafood, and a "cornucopia of decadent desserts." The gargantuan Sunday Brunch Buffet features a seafood table, a complete breakfast buffet, cooked-to-order omelets and Belgian waffles, a carving station with four meats, and desserts galore. No smoking. Breakfast $8–12, lunch $4–15, dinner $8–33; Friday Seafood Buffet $24.95 (children's menu available); Sunday Brunch Buffet $21.95 for adults, $10 for children 6–10.

EATING OUT

In Folkston

♨ ✈ & **Okefenokee Restaurant** (912-496-3263), 1507 Third Street. Open 7 AM–9 PM Monday–Saturday Local folks gather here for batter-fried bacon and catfish dinners and other real Southern home cooking. Out-of-towners are always impressed by the large portions and reasonable prices. Breakfast and lunch are served, and there is a buffet dinner featuring steaks, seafood, and freshwater fish. No smoking. Breakfast $4–5, lunch and dinner $9–15.

On Jekyll Island

♨ ✈ & **Café Solterra** (912-635-2500; www.jekyllclub.com), 371 Riverview Drive. Open 7 AM–10 PM daily. For casual dining at the Jekyll Island Club Hotel, the bakery/deli café serves muffins and pastries, deli sandwiches, soups, and pizza. Also at the hotel, **Vincent's Pub** serves cocktails and light fare from 5:30 until late night. No smoking. $7–13.

In St. Marys

♨ ✈ & **Riverside Café** (912-882-3466; www.riversidecafesaintmarys.com), 106 St. Marys Street. Open 7:30 AM–9 PM daily. Located on the waterfront in the historic district, the restaurant serves three meals daily. Luncheon choices include homemade soups, pita and other sandwiches, and a wide variety of salads. Dinner from the grill includes charbroiled steaks and lamb chops. Smoking outdoors only. Breakfast $3–14, lunch $6–13, dinner $10–20.

On St. Simons Island

♨ ✈ & **The 4th of May Deli and Café** (912-638-5444; www.4thofmay.net), 321 Mallory Street. Open 8 AM–9 PM daily. Get your day off to a good start with eye-opening omelets, breakfast burritos, griddle goodies, and à la carte items. If you don't want to get up and get dressed to come in, delivery is available. There are different luncheon and dinner specials daily, as well as seafood, salads, deli sandwiches, fresh-baked breads, home-cooked vegetables, and desserts. There's a children's menu, too. No smoking. $6–7 for breakfast, $7–15 for lunch and dinner.

✳ Entertainment

GAMBLING CRUISES *Emerald Princess II* Casino Cruises (912-265-3558 or 1-800-842-0115; www.emerald princesscasino.com), One GISCO Point Drive, Brunswick. Cruises at 7 PM Monday–Saturday; additional cruises at

11 Friday and Saturday, and 1 Sunday. Reservations are preferred; guests must be at least 18 years old. Passengers can enjoy light snacks and gambling. Once the boat reaches international waters, gamblers can choose from blackjack, stud poker, slot machines, craps, Texas Hold Em poker, and roulette. Free 15-minute lessons are provided prior to the casino opening. $10 (higher on holidays and for special events) for the cruise; gambling, food, and beverages extra.

THEATER The Island Players (912-638-0338; www.theislandplayers.com), at the Casino Theater, 530 Beachview Drive at the Pier Village, St. Simons. Call for a schedule of performances and ticket prices. Local thespians present four live productions year-round at the theater. Children's theater and camps also are offered.

Ritz Theater (912-262-6934; www.golden islesarts.org), 1530 Newcastle Street, Brunswick. Office hours 10–6 Thursday and Friday, 10–2 Saturday. Call for a schedule of productions and prices. Live productions with local, regional, national, and international artists are performed year-round at this renovated theater in Old Town Brunswick. Art exhibits also are staged. Built in 1898 as the Grand Opera House, the structure also houses shops and offices.

✳ Selective Shopping

BOOKS Jekyll Books at the Old Infirmary (912-635-3077; www.jekyllbooks .com), 101 Old Plantation Road, Jekyll Island. Open 9:30–5:30 Monday–Saturday, 10–5 Sunday. The shop offers new and used books, antiques, collectibles, and gift items, as well as an opportunity to see Furness Cottage, one of the cottages in the Jekyll Island National Historic Landmark District (see *To See—Historic Homes and Sites*). It was once used as the infirmary building.

GIFTS Jekyll Island Museum Store (912-635-4168), 100 Stable Road, Jekyll Island. Open 9–5 daily. The shop, located in the Jekyll Island History Center (see *To*

See—Museums), carries quality reproduction historical gifts and books about the island.

OTHER GOODS Santa's Christmas Shoppe (912-635-3804), 17-A Pier Road, Jekyll Island. Open 10–5 daily. The year-round emporium offers a wide variety of fine gifts, holiday decorations, and name-brand collectibles such as Christopher Radko, Byers' Choice, Fontanini nativities, and Possible Dreams.

✳ Special Events

August: **Sea Islands Black Heritage Festival** (912-230-2834; www.seaislands blackheritagefestival.org; e-mail: apca004 @aol.com). Enjoy Gullah and Geechee craft demonstrations, artists, authors, poets, a live performance by the famed Georgia Sea Island Singers, native Georgia cuisine, and more at this event on St. Simons Island. Free.

September: **Catfish Festival** (1-800-433-0225; www.visitkingsland.com/festivals .html). The annual three-day Labor Day weekend festival in Kingsland features crispy, Southern-fried, and Cajun catfish and other foods; country music; entertainment by nationally known artists; a parade; arts and crafts; a children's amusement area; a classic car and tractor exhibition; food booths; a pancake breakfast; a 5K run; and other activities. Free; some activities have a small charge.

Colonial Coast Birding and Nature Festival (912-729-5999; www.jekyllisland .com). Participants see how many species they can spot in a one-day period. During the festival on Jekyll Island there are exhibitions by vendors and conservation groups, children's activities, arts and crafts, and a raptor show. Festival free; some activities have a small charge.

Okefenokee Festival (912-496-2536; www.folkston.com). The festival, held on the second Saturday at the old train depot in Jesse Crews Sr. Memorial Park and Main Street, Folkston, features a parade, entertainment, food, arts and crafts, clogging, line dancing, and a street dance. Festival free; some activities have a small charge.

November: **Brunswick Rockin' Stewbilee** (912-729-5999 or 1-800-933-2627; www.brunswickstewbilee.com). Held in Brunswick's Mary Ross Waterfront Park, the event is a Brunswick stew cook-off. In addition, the festival features a concert by one or more nationally known groups ($25 in advance, $35 at the gate), Pooch Parade, antique car show, road race, and children's activities. Walking tours of the historic district are also available: $15–20; no tour tickets sold day of festival. Festival: adults $6, children $3 in advance; at the gate adults $9, children $4.

DARIEN AND THE COAST

B eing sandwiched as it is between Savannah to the north and the Golden Isles to the south, the unsung Georgia coast is full of treasures that are often overlooked by travelers but well worth the effort to seek out and explore. Georgia has 100 miles of coastline on the Atlantic Ocean, but if bays, islands, and river mouths are counted, the state boasts 2,344 miles of coastline. Soldiers, sailors, Native Americans, timber barons, and even pirates once flourished here, as did forts and rice plantations.

The coast, where the serene and natural surroundings promote a slower pace of life, is dotted with small towns (see *Villages*), historic sites, picturesque waterfronts, shopping enclaves, myriad seafood restaurants, and accommodations that vary from campgrounds to bed & breakfasts to chain hotels. Nature lovers find deserted stretches of beach, marsh, or forest where they are the only inhabitants besides the turtles, alligators, or shorebirds. Historians can trace the events of colonial days, the American Revolution, the Civil War and Sherman's March to the Sea, and postwar and turn-of-the-20th-century African American history. The Gullah-Geechee culture, that of descendants of freed plantation slaves, survives on Sapelo Island.

Quaint shrimp boats line the waterfronts, and area restaurants serve freshly caught shrimp, oysters, fish, crab, and other delicacies of the sea prepared from favorite regional recipes. Barbecue and other traditional Southern cuisine also are prominently featured. During the shrimp season, fresh sweet Georgia shrimp can be purchased from local markets.

GUIDANCE For information about Darien and Eulonia, contact the **McIntosh County Chamber of Commerce–Welcome Center** (912-437-6684; www.mcintoshcounty.com), 105 Fort King George Drive, Darien 31305. Open 9–5 Monday–Friday. The welcome center is located in a park right on the waterfront where shrimp boats dock. Picnic facilities and public fishing docks are available. There's a visitors center at the **Darien Outlet Center** (912-437-4837), 1111 Magnolia Bluff Way SW, Suite 255, Darien 31305. Open 10–8 Monday–Saturday, 11–6 Sunday. In addition, there's a visitors center in the **Old Jail Art Center and Museum** (912-437-7711), 404 Northway/US 17, Darien 31305. Open 10–5 Tuesday–Friday and 10–4 Saturday.

To find out more about Hinesville and Midway, consult the **Liberty County Chamber** (912-368-4445; www.libertycounty.org), 425 West Oglethorpe Highway, Hinesville 31313. Open 9–5 weekdays.

To learn more about Ellabelle and Richmond Hill, contact **Richmond Hill–Bryan County Chamber of Commerce** (912-756-3444 or 1-800-834-3960; www.bryancoga.org), 2591 US 17, Suite 100, Richmond Hill 31324. For more specific information about Richmond Hill, contact the **Richmond Hill Convention and Visitors Bureau** (912-756-2676; www

.richmondhillvisit.com), 520 Cedar Street, Richmond Hill 31324. Open 8:30–5 weekdays. Stop by the **Richmond Hill Local Welcome Center** (912-756-3697), GA 144 and Timber Trail Road, Richmond Hill 31324. Open 10–4 Monday–Saturday.

To learn more about Sapelo Island and the Sapelo Island National Estuarine Research Reserve, consult the **Sapelo Island Visitors Center** (912-437-3224; www.sapelonerr.org), 1766 Landing Road, Darien 31305. Open 7:30–5:30 Tuesday–Friday, 8:30–8:30 Saturday, 1:30–5 Sunday.

GETTING THERE *By air:* The closest airports to this region are in Brunswick, Savannah, and Jacksonville, Florida. See "What's Where in Georgia" for airport, airline, and car rental information.

By bus: **Greyhound Lines** (912-876-3855), in the Thrift Shop at 1439-A West Oglethorpe Highway, Hinesville. Otherwise, the nearest stops are in Savannah or Brunswick (see those chapters).

By car: Travel up and down the Georgia coast is easy. For the quickest route, use I-95; for the most scenic route, use US 17.

By train: **AMTRAK** (1-800-USA-RAIL) stops in Jesup (176 Northwest Broad Street), Savannah (see the Savannah chapter), and Jacksonville, Florida (see the Brunswick chapter).

GETTING AROUND A car is necessary to explore this region—either your own or a rental. Rental cars are available in Savannah, Brunswick, and Jacksonville, Florida, if you arrive in any of those cities by air, bus, or train (see the Savannah and Brunswick chapters).

MEDICAL EMERGENCY Call 911.

VILLAGES The area that became **Darien** began humbly as the home of Guale (pronounced Wally) Indians. The Spaniards briefly had a mission there called Santo Domingo de Talaje. When the English and Scottish Highlanders arrived, they built Fort King George (see *To See—Historic Homes and Sites*) in 1736—just three years after Savannah and the colony of Georgia were founded. In fact, Darien is the second-oldest planned town in Georgia. Darien eventually became a major seaport on the East Coast and the Southeast's foremost exporter of lumber, a title it retained until 1925, when the industry died due to overcutting. Today, commercial fishing and forestry are the area's largest employers.

Originally called Ways Station, **Richmond Hill** was in the center of rice plantation country. These plantations, which were heavily dependent on slave labor, were ravaged at the end of the Civil War by Sherman's troops, which destroyed the area's economic livelihood and residents' way of life. The desperate years from 1865 to 1925 were mostly noted for malaria and moonshine. Then Henry Ford and his wife, Clara, decided to build a winter retreat on the site of the former Richmond Plantation. The philanthropist, who eventually owned 85,000 acres, also constructed a sawmill, drained the swamps, and subsidized health care. He started the first kindergarten and built schools, a church, commissary, trade school, community house, and homes for 600 employees. Along with Thomas Edison and Harvey Firestone, he formed the Edison Botanic Society and attempted to transform agricultural products into goods for the auto industry. Ford Farms changed the former rice plantations into truck gardens, which produced iceberg lettuce and 365 varieties of soybeans. The town was renamed Richmond Hill in 1941.

Georgia's fourth-largest barrier island, **Sapelo Island** is rich in human history. Located 5 miles off the mainland, it was inhabited by Paleo-Indians as long as 4,000 years ago. They left several shell middens, including a shell ring 15 feet high and 200 feet in diameter. The ruins of a French plantation known as Chocolate, which was built more than 200 years ago, also remain. In the early 1800s, Thomas Spalding introduced plantations that cultivated Sea Island cotton, corn, and sugarcane. These plantations were dependent on the labor of 400 slaves imported from Charleston and the West Indies, so the island has significant African American history and culture. Freed slaves from the island's plantations found peace in isolated communities such as Hog Hammock—a 434-acre area deeded to African Americans by Spalding—where the Gullah culture is still rich today. Their culture, customs, and songs have been preserved along with the unique Geechee or Gullah language, a Creole form of pidgin English.

Several other white men have added to the island's history. Howard Coffin, the founder of the Hudson Motor Company, bought Sapelo and renovated and enlarged the Spalding home, adding both indoor and outdoor swimming pools and a bowling alley. Beginning in 1934, R. J. Reynolds, tobacco magnate of the Reynolds Tobacco Company, owned the island for more than 30 years and conducted agricultural experimentation. He established the Sapelo Island Research Foundation in 1949 and donated a portion of the island to the University of Georgia to use as a marine research laboratory. In 1969, the northern part of the island was sold to the state and became a wildlife refuge, while the southern part was acquired by the state and the National Oceanic and Atmospheric Administration for the Sapelo Island National Estuarine Research Reserve. Today the island's pine and hardwood forests, salt marsh, and 2 miles of wide beach are protected from development, and the restored lighthouse is once again wearing its original red-and-white-striped pattern. Sapelo Island is reached only by ferry from Meridian (see **Sapelo Island Visitor Center** under *To See—Guided Tours*).

✴ To See

FOR FAMILIES 🦐 ✐ ♿ **Cay Creek Wetlands Interpretive Center** (contact Midway City Hall: 912-884-3344), 189 Charlie Butler Road, Midway. Open 9–dusk weekdays. The saltwater marsh area is an excellent example of tidal, freshwater wetlands, with several different ecosystems amid sites that are either permanently wet or alternate between wet and dry conditions. A variety of trees, birds, mammals, reptiles, amphibians, and insects make their homes here. The center offers trails, an elevated boardwalk, a dock, and a 15-foot observation tower. Free.

GUIDED TOURS ✐ ♿ **Harris Neck Cultural and Eco Tours** (912-437-7821), P.O. Box 2355, Darien 31305. Call for a schedule and tour prices. Heritage and history tours focus on the African American community of Harris Neck (now a 2,688-acre wildlife refuge).

✐ ♿ **Sapelo Island Visitor Center–Sapelo Island Reserve and Reynolds Mansion** (mainland visitors center: 912-437-3224; park: 912-485-2299; www.gastateparks.org/Sapelo IslandReynoldsMansion), visitors center, Darien. Visitors center open 7:30–5:30 Tuesday–Friday, 8–5:30 Saturday, 1:30–5 Sunday; public tours 8:30–12:30 Wednesday (mansion and island) and 9–1 Saturday (lighthouse and island); check the website or call for schedules of additional and extended tours in spring and summer. Transportation to the island is by a 30-minute ferry ride through tidal creeks and marshes for those on guided tours only; reservations required for tours, Reynolds Mansion, and camping. Nature trails are available at the visitors center. The island boasts a beach boardwalk, nature trail, and wildlife observation tower. Popular activities include fishing, bird-watching, beachcombing, hiking, and kayaking. The reserve is a 6,100-acre coastal plain estuary protected on its seaward side by a 16,006-acre Pleistocene barrier island.

The restored lighthouse was built in 1820 to serve as a guide for mariners transiting Doboy Sound to and from the port of Darien. It was in service until 1905. After years of neglect, it was restored in 1998 with its original red-and-white-striped day mark and is once again working as an aid to navigation. Visitors can climb to the top for a view of the island and see exhibits in the oil house. For more information about the lighthouse, refer to www .lighthousefriends.com.

Accommodations for individual travelers are offered in private cottages not associated with the state park. Accommodations at the Reynolds Mansion and a pioneer campground are available for groups only. *Note:* Insect repellent is recommended spring through fall. $6–10 for guided tour, which includes ferry fee of $1 each way.

✍ ♿ **Spirit of Sapelo Tours** (912-485-2170; www.gacoast.com/geecheetours.html), Sapelo Island. Call for reservations and fees (tour fees are in addition to ferry fee to reach the island). The company, operated by descendants of slaves, offers three-hour tours of the island, including their community of Hog Hammock, aboard handicapped-accessible minibuses. Hog Hammock, 434 acres deeded to them by Thomas Spalding, was named for Sampson Hog, who served as caretaker of the Spalding hogs. Picnic lunches and hayrides can be arranged for an additional fee.

HISTORIC HOMES AND SITES ♣ ✍ **Dorchester Academy National Historic Site** (912-884-2347; www.dorchesteracademy.com), US 84, Midway. Open 11–2 Tuesday, Saturday, and Sunday. The academy was founded after the Civil War as a school for freed slaves. By 1917, it was accredited and had eight buildings and 300 students. The academy ceased to function as a school in the 1940s; the remaining Georgian Revival building now serves as a community center and museum. Dr. Martin Luther King Jr. prepared here for the 1963 Birmingham campaign. Special events include a Black Expo and A Day at Old Dorchester. Free.

♣ ✍ ♿ **Fort King George Historic Site** (912-437-4770; www.gastateparks.org/FortKing George), 302 McIntosh Road SE, Darien. Open 9–5 Tuesday–Sunday. From 1721 to 1736, this small Altamaha River fort garrisoned by His Majesty's Independent Company was the southernmost outpost of the British Empire in North America. At the palisaded earthen fort, soldiers endured hardships from disease, threats from the Spanish and Native Americans, and the harsh environment. Eventually the fort was abandoned, but then Gen. James Oglethorpe, founder of Georgia, brought Scottish Highlanders to the site in 1736. They called the settlement Darien. The fort and several buildings are reconstructions built using old records and drawings. A remains of three sawmills and tabby (oyster-shell cement) ruins are visible. The interpretive center has a film that traces the history of the area. Numerous special events during the year include living-history demonstrations, battle reenactments, walking tours, Scottish Heritage Days Encampment in March, **Winter Muster and Candle Lantern Tour** and **Drums along the Altamaha** in November (see *Special Events*), and Colonial Christmas in December. Parking $5; admission $3.75–6.50.

♣ ✍ ♿ **Fort McAllister State Historic Park** (912-727-2339 or 1-800-864-7275; www.ga stateparks.org/FortMcAllister), 3894 Fort McAllister Road, Richmond Hill. Park open 7 AM–10 PM daily; museum open 8–5. Noted for the best preserved sand and mud earthwork fortifications surviving from the Confederacy, the 1,725-acre park is located on the south bank of the Great Ogeechee River. The fort was attacked seven times by Union forces but withstood these assaults until it was captured in 1864 by Union general William Tecumseh Sherman at the end of his infamous March to the Sea. Henry Ford once owned the site and was instrumental in restoring it in the 1930s. The Civil War museum inside the visitors center is designed to resemble a bombproof and contains Civil War exhibits, artifacts relating to many periods in the fort's history, a video for viewing, and a gift shop. A covered outdoor display is dedicated to the recovered artifacts of the CSS *Nashville*, a blockade runner that was sunk in the Ogeechee River. There is a well-developed and signed nature trail through the Redbird Creek area. To learn more about the park's recreational facilities, see *Green Space—Nature Preserves and Parks.* Accommodations are available at campgrounds and cottages (see *Lodging—Campgrounds* and *Lodging—Cottages and Cabins*). Admission $3.75–6.50; parking $5.

🦐 ✒ ♿ **Fort Morris State Historic Site** (912-884-5999 or 1-800-864-7275; www.gastate parks.org/FortMorris), 2559 Fort Morris Road, Midway. Open 9–5 Thursday–Saturday. The principal attraction at this 70-acre park is the historic fort, but there is also a 1-mile nature trail, part of the Colonial Coast Birding Trail. The importance of the site was apparent from the time of the Continental Congress in 1776. The participants saw the strategic advantage of protecting the growing seaport of Sunbury from the British, so the bluff on the Medway River was fortified and garrisoned by a small group of patriots. When the British first tried to get the fort to surrender, Col. John McIntosh is reported to have replied, "Come and take it!" Although the British withdrew at that time, they returned 45 days later and captured the fort. Later renamed Fort Defiance, it was used during the War of 1812 and the Civil War. Today earthworks remain, and the visitors center offers a film called *Sunbury Sleeps.* Exhibits chronicle the history of the fort, military and civilian life from the colonial to ante-bellum periods, and the lost town of Sunbury. A trail leads to the cemetery, which is the only vestige of the once bustling town. Firing of period weapons is often demonstrated. Special events feature reenactments with costumed interpreters, including the **Independence Day Colonial Faire** on July Fourth and **"Come and Take It!"** in November (see *Special Events*). Admission $3–4.50; parking $5.

🦐 ✒ **LeConte Woodmanston Plantation and Botanical Gardens** (912-884-6500; www .leconte-woodmanston.org), off US 17 at 4918 Barrington Ferry Road, Riceboro. Open 10–3 Tuesday–Sunday; special tours by appointment. Once the home of Dr. Louis LeConte, the property was one of the state's first inland-swamp rice plantations and is now a nature preserve. Its once world-famous 18th-century gardens are being re-created with heirloom plants. Visitors can see the cypress forest, stroll through the Avenue of Oaks, and walk along the interpretive trail through the Bulltown Swamp blackwater ecosystem. Admission $2 per person; $5 family rate for up to four people.

THE HISTORIC MIDWAY CHURCH WAS BUILT IN 1792.

🦐 **Midway National Historic District** (912-884-5837), Old Sunbury Road near the intersection of US 17 and GA 38, Midway. Cemetery open at all times; museum open 10–4 Tuesday–Saturday, 2–4 Sunday. The 18th-century district contains a church built in 1792, a museum in a raised cottage (see *Museums*), and a cemetery. The simple white-frame New England–style church served as Union general William Tecumseh Sherman's cavalry foraging headquarters during the Civil War. The cavalrymen plundered area plantations and corralled animals in the cemetery. Among the 1,200 graves are those of two Revolutionary War generals (one was Daniel Stewart, the great-grandfather of Theodore Roosevelt) and a state governor. The cemetery, which was laid out in the 1750s, also is reputed to house the ghost of a slave. To this day, the church has no heating system or artificial lights. Special events in the Midway Historic District include a church service on the last Sunday in April and an annual Christmas tea at the museum. (*Note:* Visitors can obtain a key for the church from the museum or from the service station across the street from the church.) Adults $3, students $1.

🕊 ✍ ♿ **Seabrook Village** (912-884-7008), 660 Trade Hill Road, Midway. Open 10–4 Tuesday–Saturday and by appointment. The remnants of this African American village contain eight turn-of-the-20th-century buildings, including a one-room school that operated from 1895 to 1940. Costumed living-history interpreters are on hand only for groups of 15 or more or for special events. During these times, visitors are presented with aspects of old-time village life through interactive activities such as grinding corn or washing using a scrub board. View the grave art of Cyrus Bowens and the Willis Hakim J. Hones Material Culture Collection of handmade items. Walking tours $5 for adults.

MUSEUMS 🕊 ✍ ♿ **Fort Stewart Military Museum** (912-767-7885; www.stewart.army .mil), Building T904, 2022 Frank Cochran Drive, Hinesville. Open 10–4 Tuesday–Saturday. Group tours are given on request. The museum traces the history of the fort—the largest military post east of the Mississippi River—from its inception in 1940 to the present, as well as presenting the story of the Third Infantry Division (Mechanized), which makes its home there. Changing exhibits taken from the museum's 5,000 objects feature objects from World War I, World War II, the Korean War, Desert Storm, and current military activities. Especially popular with the little ones are tanks, helicopters, and weapons. *Note:* Due to heightened security, visitors are required to stop at the main gate and provide proof of auto registration, insurance, and a driver's license to receive a visitor's pass. Free.

🕊 **Midway Museum** (912-884-5837; www.themidwaymuseum.org), US 17, Midway. Open 10–4 Tuesday–Saturday. The museum, which is located in a typical 18th-century raised plantation cottage, contains documents and exhibits as well as furniture and art typical of early coastal homes from colonial days to the Civil War. The museum's gift shop carries a good selection of books about local history. Adults $3, students $1.

🕊 ♿ **Old Jail Art Center and Museum** (912-437-7711), 404 Northway, Darien. Open 10–4 Tuesday–Saturday. The 1888 jail is one of the three oldest buildings in Darien. Today it houses exhibits of historic artifacts in the old cells. Also housed there are the six galleries of the McIntosh Art Association, as well as a gift shop and outdoor gardens. Free.

🕊 ♿ **Richmond Hill Historical Society and Museum** (912-756-3697; www.richmondhill historicalsociety.com), GA 144 at the corner of Ford Avenue and Timber Trail Road, Richmond Hill. Open 10–3 Monday–Saturday. Housed in the old Ford kindergarten building, the museum's photographs, displays, and artifacts focus on colonial, Revolutionary, and Civil War history, as well as Henry Ford's development of the town of Richmond Hill. Other exhibits depict the plantation era. A one-room schoolhouse and country store of the early 1900s are re-created. Free, but donations accepted.

SCENIC DRIVES 🕊 ✍ **The Historic Liberty Trail** (www.discoverlibertyga.com/liberty trail.asp). The driving tour offers history, culture, and ecology. Beginning at exit 76 on I-95, the trail has nine major attractions: the Midway National Historic District, Dorchester Academy National Historic Place, LeConte Woodmanston Plantation and Botanical Gardens, Seabrook Village, Fort Morris State Historic Site (see *Historic Homes and Sites*), Melon Bluff birding trail (see *Green Space—Nature Preserves and Parks*), Cay Creek Wetlands Interpretive Center (see *For Families*), Fort Stewart Military Museum (see *Museums*), and Sunbury Cemetery. A map is available on the website.

SPECIAL PLACES 🕊 ✍ ♿ **Smallest Church in America** (912-832-5922), US 17 South (exit 67 off I-95), Eulonia. Open daylight hours daily. Services are held the third

Sunday of each month at this diminutive church, actually named Christ's Chapel in Memory Park, which is only 10 feet wide by 15 feet long and seats only 12. Little larger than a child's playhouse, albeit with stained-glass windows from England, the church was built in 1949. Mrs. Agnes Harper wanted it to serve as a place of meditation and rest for weary travelers. Free.

WALKS ✿ ✐ *A Walk through Historic Downtown Darien* **Walking Tours** (912-437-4837; www.mcintoshcounty.com), Darien. The free brochure, which is available at the Welcome Center (see *Guidance*), describes a self-guided tour of the scenic waterfront, historic squares, and important landmarks. The brochure also describes the 7-mile pedestrian-biking trail, which stretches to Fort King George Historic Site.

✳ To Do

BALLOONING ✐ **Feather Air Hot-Air Balloons** (912-858-2529), 4326 Wilma Edwards Road, Ellabelle. Call for schedules, reservations, and prices. The company offers 45-minute to one-hour flights that float over 10 miles of country, field, and swamps.

BICYCLING ✿ ✐ ♿ **Darien Walking and Bike Paths.** A series of paths lined with Spanish moss–laden live oaks connect the downtown waterfront with Fort King George.

BOAT EXCURSIONS ✐ **Altamaha Coastal Tours** (912-437-6010; www.altamaha .com), 229 Fort King George Road, Darien. Call for a schedule. Guided canoe and sea kayak tours are offered. Day trips $50, overnight trips $150, rentals $15–40.

BOATING ✐ **Fort McAllister Marina** (912-727-2632), 3203 Fort McAllister Road, Richmond Hill. Open 7–7 daily. The marina offers fishing charters and tours by the fort. There is a large boat show each year, too.

✐ **Ogeechee Outpost** (912-748-6716; www.ogeecheeoutpost.com), 182 Rose Drive, Ellabelle. Call for schedules and reservations. The company offers guided overnight trips, instruction, and canoe and kayak rentals. Rentals $25 per day, $40 with return shuttle; guided tours $50 additional.

FISHING An abundance of rivers and proximity to the ocean have attracted anglers for years. Charter boats, public marinas and boat ramps, fishing piers and docks, bait and tackle shops, and guide services are available. Fishing licenses are required.

Liquid Assets Offshore Fishing (912-264-8860; www.liquidassetfishing.com) offers half- and full-day fishing charters as well as sight-seeing charters. For an entire list of charters, consult the **University of Georgia Marine Extension Service** website, www.marex.uga .edu/advisory/Charter.html.

✳ Green Space

BEACHES Those on Blackbeard Island and Sapelo Island are among the most pristine in the state.

NATURE PRESERVES AND PARKS ✿ ✐ **Altamaha Waterfowl Management Area** (contact Game Management in Brunswick: 912-262-3173), US 17 South, Darien. Open daylight hours daily. Visitors can learn about the role of managed wetlands in the conservation of wildlife through the Ansley-Hodges M.A.R.S.H. Project. Georgia Outdoor Recreation Pass (GORP) required for anyone 16–64 who does not already have a hunting or fishing license: $3.50 for three days.

🦐 ✒ **Blackbeard Island National Wildlife Refuge** (regional office in South Carolina: 843-784-2468; www.fws.gov/blackbeardisland), Alligator Alley, Blackbeard Island. Open sunrise–sunset daily. Blackbeard Island, which is accessible only by boat, serves as a preserve and breeding ground for wildlife and migratory birds. More than 3,000 acres are designated as a national wilderness area. The preserve is popular for bird-watching and wildlife observation, hiking along existing scenic trails and roads, and fishing in the saltwater creeks. Endangered species such as loggerhead sea turtles, American bald eagles, wood storks, and piping plovers are often seen here, along with large concentrations of waterfowl, wading birds, shorebirds, songbirds, raptors, deer, and alligators. Island free; fee for private ferry from Shellman Bluff on mainland.

🦐 ✒ **Butler Island Rice Plantation** (contact the Darien Visitors Center: 912-437-6684), US 17 South, Butler Island. Open 9–dusk daily. Once one of the largest plantations in the South, the property was purchased by Capt. Pierce Butler of Philadelphia to grow rice. He married famous British actress Fanny Kemble, who was horrified by the treatment of slaves when she visited the plantation. Her book, *Journal of a Residence on a Georgia Plantation,* is believed to have swayed the British to oppose slavery and the Civil War. Owned by the Nature Conservancy, today the property is open for picnicking, fishing, and bird-watching. Visitors can explore the property via an elevated boardwalk and get a bird's-eye view from the observation tower. Free.

🦐 ✒ ♿ **Cay Creek Wetland Interpretive Center** (912-884-3344; www.historicmidway.com), 189 Charlie Butler Road, Midway. Open 8–4 weekdays. Paths along the marsh wetlands permit visitors to view 100 native plants and various kinds of wildlife in several different ecosystems. Earthen berms are actually the remnants of dikes used when the area was a rice plantation. Plans are under way for a boardwalk and an interpretive center. Free.

🦐 ✒ ♿ **Darien Waterfront Park** (912-437-6684; www.mcintoshcounty.com), Darien. Open daily. During the 19th century, this area, which was the busiest port in the Southeast, was the commercial, cultural, social, and religious center of Darien. Today, the park is a popular place to come for biking, fishing, and picnicking, and to enjoy the pavilion, docks, and playground. The popular **Blessing of the Fleet Festival** (see *Special Events*) takes place here. Free.

🦐 ✒ ♿ **Fort McAllister State Historic Park** (912-727-2339; lodging reservations: 1-800-864-7275; www.gastateparks.org/FortMcAllister), 3894 Fort McAllister Road, Richmond Hill. Park open 7 AM–10 PM daily; museum open 8–5. Giant live oaks and surrounding salt marsh create a quiet haven where visitors enjoy outdoor recreation. Boat ramps, a dock, and a fishing pier attract anglers, while hikers and bikers enjoy 4.3 miles of trails. Canoe and kayak rentals are available seasonally. Admission $3.75–6.50; rentals additional. Parking $5.

🦐 ✒ ♿ **Harris Neck Wildlife Refuge** (regional office in South Carolina: 843-784-2468; www.fws.gov/harrisneck), US 17 and Harris Neck Road, Eulonia. Open daylight hours daily; access by personal boat from public boat ramp on Barbour River at termination of GA 131 or through outfitter company tours (see, for example, **Harris Neck Cultural and Eco Tours** under *To See—Guided Tours*). Enjoy nature at this 2,762-acre preserve with salt marshes, grasslands, mixed deciduous forest, and cropland. Many species of birds can be observed, including hundreds of egrets,

THE TREASURE OF BLACKBEARD ISLAND

Blackbeard Island was named for the infamous pirate Edward Teach, alias Blackbeard, who plied the waters off the coast of the Southeast. Rumor has it that some of his ill-gotten gains are buried here, but no trace of his booty has ever been found. Instead, the treasures of the island are pristine beaches and dunes, freshwater and salt marshes, maritime forests, and abundant wildlife.

wood storks, and herons in the summer and ducks in the winter. The refuge contains part of the Colonial Coast Birding Trail. There are 15 miles of paved roads and trails, a boat ramp and fishing pier, biking trails, and observation decks. Fishing in the tidal creeks is excellent. Free to individual visitors for self-guided tours and use; fees charged for guided tours.

🦐 🐚 ♿ **Melon Bluff Nature and Heritage Reserve** (912-884-5779), 2999 Islands Highway, Midway. Open 9–4 daily, September 15–May 15. Parking is at the Melon Bluff Nature Center trailhead. This 3,000-acre, privately owned preserve is located on land that was once a rice plantation and is now in the heart of the Colonial Coast Birding Trail. Habitats, which range from pine forests to salt marsh to woodlands and creek swamps crisscrossed by rivers and dotted with lakes, support a wide variety of birds and wildlife. Twenty-five miles of all-season unpaved trails crisscross the property. Biking, birding, hiking, and canoe and kayak expeditions are available. The nature center features exhibits and sponsors educational programs. The gift shop–bookstore also sells snacks and offers equipment rental. No smoking, pets, alcohol, or firearms. Day-use fee $3; $15 per horse per day trail riding fee—BYOH (bring your own horse; for prearranged groups of 10 or more); other fees vary by activity.

RIVERS 🦐 🐚 **Altamaha River** (www.altamahariver.net). Dubbed one of the 75 "Last Great Places" in the world by the Nature Conservancy, the 100-mile river, which winds through cypress swamps and tidal marshes and empties into the sea near Darien, flows freely with no dams. The river's banks are dotted with boat ramps and landings, bait and tackle shops, and marked hiking trails for those who enjoy boating, fishing, water sports, and wildlife observation. The *Altamaha River Canoe Trail Map* is available on the website. Numerous other contacts for various city and county organizations and outfitters that line the river can be found by searching "Altamaha River" on the Internet.

🦐 🐚 **Ogeechee River.** Part of the 294-mile blackwater river, which begins in the Piedmont region, flows through the lower coastal plain and tidal marsh of this area before emptying into the sea at Ossabaw Sound. Wildlife often sighted includes raccoons, deer, otters, beavers, mink, water snakes, alligators, wading birds, wood storks, southern bald eagles, and occasionally manatees. The river is particularly popular with canoeists and anglers.

✴ Lodging
BED & BREAKFASTS
In Darien
🦆 **Blue Heron Inn** (912-437-1346), One Blue Heron Lane SE. Located in a contemporary home at the edge of a marsh and tidal creek, the bed & breakfast offers four guest rooms with private baths, three floors of porches and decks from which to admire the scenery, and a full breakfast. Accommodations are also offered in Marsh House, Seabreeze Island Cottage, and Hideaway on Cotton Field Farm. Those require a two-night minimum. Blue Heron Inn offers the closest accommodations to Shellman Bluff and the ferry to Sapelo Island. No smoking. Not wheelchair accessible. Pets are welcome in one room with an additional fee of $20 per pet per night. Rooms $110–149, cottages $100–250.

Open Gates Bed and Breakfast (912-437-6985; www.opengatesbnb.com), 301 Franklin Street. The huge Victorian home overlooking historic Vernon Square was built in 1876 by a local timber baron. Today the home offers five guest rooms—four with private baths—each distinctively decorated. Overnight rates include a full Southern breakfast. Guests enjoy the elegant common rooms and the outdoor pool. No smoking. Not wheelchair accessible. $90–125.

In Eulonia
🦐 ♿ **McIntosh Manor** (912-816-1112; www.mcintoshmanorga.com), US 17. The eclectically furnished 1905 house provides a homey, comfortable ambience. Two of the five guest rooms share a bath, which makes them desirable for a family or two couples

traveling together. The B&B's suite has a private bath. A full breakfast is served. No smoking. Limited wheelchair accessibility (one bedroom on first floor, but steps to climb to get into house). $90.

In Midway

✧ ♿ **Dunham Farms Exclusive Country Inn** (912-880-4500; www.dunhamfarms .com), 5836 Islands Highway. The inn is actually two quite different accommodations—Palmyra Plantation Barn and Palmyra Plantation Cottage at Melon Bluff. Horses and mules were once housed in the barn, along with corn in the corncrib, grain in the feed room, and hay in the second-story loft. Now the barn has been transformed into a comfortable B&B with nine guest rooms and suites decorated with country charm. The nightly rate for rooms in the Palmyra Plantation Barn includes a full breakfast, afternoon hors d'oeuvres, daily guest activities, free movies, and use of the pool, trails, and bikes, as well as admission to the Melon Bluff Nature and Heritage Reserve and discounts for kayaking. The fully equipped 1840 cottage with a kitchen is ideal for two to six people in the same party. Meal and maid service are not included with stays in the cottage but can be arranged for an additional fee. No smoking; no pets; children 8 and older welcome. One room on first floor of the barn is wheelchair accessible. B&B rooms $165–205, cottage $300.

CAMPGROUNDS

In Richmond Hill

♨ ✧ ♿ ☀ **Fort McAllister State Historic Park** (camping reservations: 1-800-864-7275). Located amid giant live oaks and alongside a beautiful salt marsh, camping facilities include 65 tent, trailer, and RV sites with water and electric hookups, as well as backcountry primitive campsites and a pioneer campground. Amenities include two comfort stations with toilets, heated showers, and laundry facilities; a playground; and a dock and boat ramp. Campers have access to all the park's amenities. See *Green Space—Nature Preserves and Parks*. $25–28; backcountry sites $9 per person.

In Ellabelle

♨ ✧ **Ogeechee Outpost Camping** (912-748-6716; www.ogeecheeoutpost.com), 182 Rose Drive. Cabin rentals include use of a boat or canoe. $80.

In Richmond Hill

✧ ☀ **Fort McAllister State Historic Park** (cottage reservations: 1-800-864-7275). The park offers three traditional cottages and new two-bedroom cottages that sit on 14-foot stilts and have beautiful views of the sunrise and the salt marsh. One cottage is designated pet friendly ($40 per pet per night, maximum two). See *Green Space—Nature Preserves and Parks*. $130.

✴ Where to Eat

DINING OUT In this laid-back area of the coast, few restaurants are so elegant they fit our definition of fine dining, and, indeed, locals concur. Rather, there are dozens of popular casual eateries—many specializing in all types of seafood prepared a variety of ways. Using our price definition for fine dining entrées being more than $20, however, these restaurants fit the category.

In Crescent

✧ ♿ **Pelican Point** (912-832-4295; www .pelicanpointseafood.com), 1398 Sapelo Avenue NE. Open 5–10 Wednesday–Friday, noon–close Saturday and Sunday. A local favorite since 1986, the restaurant overlooks the Sapelo River. The family's six shrimp boats are docked next door, guaranteeing the freshest, biggest, and highest-quality catch. The family also raises littleneck clams. Although diners can order from the à la carte menu, many prefer the enormous 100-item seafood buffet, which features a variety of seafood as well as prime rib and chicken, a 30-item salad bar, and a dessert station. There's entertainment in the piano bar on Friday and Saturday evenings. Smoking allowed. $16.95–23.95, buffet $26.95.

In Darien

🌮 ♿ **Skipper's Fish Camp Restaurant and Oyster Bar** (912-437-FISH; www .skippersfishcamp.com), 85 Screven Street. Open 11–9 daily. The fish-camp theme and open-air oyster bar set just the right tone for dining on local seafood like Georgia white shrimp and flounder, as well as steaks and slow-smoked barbecue ribs, while enjoying the views of the Darien River. No smoking. $10–29.

In Midway

🌮 ♿ **Sunbury Crab Company** (912-884-8640; www.sunburycrabco.com), 541 Brigantine Dunmore Road. Open 5–10 Wednesday–Friday, noon–10 Saturday, noon–8 Sunday. Overlooking the Medway River and exuding a Key West atmosphere, the restaurant features specialties like crabcakes, crab stew, burgers, and Cuban sandwiches. No smoking. $8–30.

In Richmond Hill

🌮 ♿ **Steamers Restaurant and Raw Bar** (912-756-3979), 4040 US 17 South. Open 4–9 Sunday–Thursday, 4–10 Friday and Saturday. Although it doesn't overlook the water, this popular eatery has a fish-camp ambience. In addition to a raw bar to die for, the restaurant offers all kinds of seafood, including local fish caught fresh every day, lowcountry boil, ribs, and more. Happy hour and early-bird specials. No smoking. $10–30.

In Townsend

🌮 ♿ **Buccaneer Club** (912-832-5171; www.thebuccaneerclub.com), Buccaneer Club Road. Open 5–10 Tuesday–Thursday, 5–11 Friday and Saturday, noon–10 Sunday. This seafood restaurant is located on the banks of the Sapelo River near Eulonia, where diners can watch the picturesque shrimp boats come and go. The eatery takes its name from an old bar and private club that once stood on this spot. Particularly known for its heaping platters of many kinds of fresh seafood and 20-ounce T-bone steaks, the eatery's menu choices also include sandwiches and salads. No smoking. $17.50–38.

EATING OUT

In Darien

🦐 🌮 ♿ **B&J's Family Restaurant and Pizza Place** (912-437-2122), 901 North Wall Street/US 17. Open 7 AM–9 PM Monday–Saturday, 7–4 Sunday. This is where the locals go to eat. The eatery is noted for its breakfast, lunch, and dinner buffets—particularly the Friday Seafood Buffet. No smoking. Breakfast $6, lunch $7, dinner $19–33.

✳ Entertainment

MUSIC Hinesville Area Arts Council Series (www.hinesvillearts.com). Contact the organization or check the website for a schedule of events and prices, which average $7. The council sponsors a series of performances at the Brewton-Parker College Auditorium, 2140 East Oglethorpe Highway, Hinesville.

✳ Selective Shopping

For the most part, specialized shopping isn't part of life in these small towns. For out-of-the-ordinary shopping, residents go to Savannah, Brunswick, or the Golden Isles. Darien is an exception, as it has quaint shops and an outlet mall.

Historic Darien Shopping (visitors center: 912-437-6684; www.visitdarien.com /shopping), US 17, Darien. Open 9–5 Monday–Saturday. The shops of the historic district contain antiques and gift shops as well as a restaurant.

OUTLET MALLS Darien Outlet Center (912-437-8360 or 1-888-545-7224; www.visitdarien.com/shopping), 1111 Magnolia Bluff Way, Darien. Open 10–8 Monday–Saturday, 11–6 Sunday. Located at I-95's exit 49, the outlet mall boasts more than 35 stores, from Bass to Zales.

✳ Special Events

Spring: **Blessing of the Fleet Festival** (visitors center: 912-437-6684; chamber of commerce: 912-437-2683; www.blessing

ofthefleet.com). Activities begin Friday with a parade, fish fry, and Art in the Park festival in Darien. On Sunday morning, elaborately decorated boats parade by while clerics from several denominations bless them from the bridge as they pass. Other activities include a 5K River Run, live entertainment, children's activities, beauty pageants, a car show, and a community worship service. The weekend may occur in March, April, or May, so call for exact dates. Admission $5 for those 13 years of age and older on Friday and Saturday, free on Sunday.

July: **Independence Day Colonial Faire** (912-884-5999; www.gastateparks.org/Fort Morris). Held at Fort Morris State Historic Site in Midway, the celebration includes cannon, musket, and black-powder demonstrations; colonial games of skill; colonial music; and reenactors. Free.

October: **Great Ogeechee Seafood Festival** (Richmond Hill–Bryan County Chamber of Commerce: 912-756-3444; www .goseafoodfestival.com). Held Friday evening through Sunday afternoon the third weekend in October, the Richmond Hill festival at J. F. Gregory Park, 521 Cedar Street, features great Southern seafood, arts and crafts, a carnival, a classic car show, the 5K Crab Crawl, and live entertainment from bands and pop singers, dancers, fencers, cheerleaders, and more. The finale features fireworks. $2–5.

November: **"Come and Take It!"** (912-884-5999). Colonial demonstrations, musket and cannon drills, a tactical skirmish, and costumed interpreters discussing soldier and civilian life pay homage to Fort

Morris's role in the American Revolution. Held in Midway. $1.50–3.

Drums along the Altamaha (912-437-4770). This event at the Fort King George Historic Site in Darien features a battle reenactment, artillery and musket firings, baking and brewing demonstrations, arts and crafts, coastal maritime history, and Native American skills. Festival activities included with regular admission. (See **Fort King George Historic Site** under *To See—Historic Homes and Sites.*)

Winter Muster and Candle Lantern Tour (912-727-2339). At this event at Fort McAllister State Historic Park in Richmond Hill, you will learn about the last days of the fort before it was captured by Union forces. The battle begins at 4 PM and the tour at 6. Adults $4, seniors $3.50, children $2.50, plus regular $3 parking fee.

DEMONSTRATIONS OF PERIOD WEAPONS ARE PART OF "COME AND TAKE IT!"

SAVANNAH AND TYBEE ISLAND

Savannah, literally Georgia's first city, is also known as the "Queen City of the South." This gracious town was wrenched from raw wilderness in 1733 when English general James Oglethorpe founded the colony of Georgia and its first settlement. A bluff overlooking the Savannah River upriver from the coast was chosen because it created a strategic buffer between South Carolina and the Spanish in northern Florida. Savannah served as the capital of the colony, then of the state, from 1733 to 1782 and prospered as a port city for the exportation of cotton.

One of Oglethorpe's greatest legacies was his city plan, which was laid out on a grid with 24 parklike squares, most of which remain to this day. The squares have burgeoned with now-mature live oak trees draped with gently swaying Spanish moss. Over the years, the city has added monuments and fountains as well as lush landscaping featuring azaleas, oleanders, and magnolias, among other Southern favorites. These oases serve as resting and gathering places and are often the scenes of festivals and other events.

Around the squares, gracious neighborhoods of stately homes developed, some areas punctuated by majestic churches and genteel businesses. During the Civil War, Union general William Tecumseh Sherman captured the city at Christmastime in 1864 but refrained from destroying it. By contrast, in the 1950s, some of these structural treasures were being destroyed and disappearing at an alarming rate—being replaced by insignificant buildings in the name of "progress."

Fortunately, Savannah's citizens woke up to what they were losing, and preservationists banded together to save what was left. In 1966 a 2.2-square-mile area was designated as a National Landmark Historic District by the National Trust for Historic Preservation. Today this area remains one of the largest such districts in the country. More than 1,800 structures have been saved and restored, and they now serve as private homes, museum houses, inns, bed & breakfasts, and other businesses that attract scores of visitors.

The compact area and orderly arrangement of streets make Savannah a particularly easy walking city—another plus for tourism. In recent years, the cultlike following created by the fame of John Berendt's book *Midnight in the Garden of Good and Evil* (known locally and frequently referred to in this chapter as "the Book") and the subsequent movie have brought thousands of new visitors to Savannah. Once there, they share the many charms of the state's fourth-largest city.

Many experts in the paranormal consider Savannah the most haunted city in America. Long-dead abandoned lovers, children who died before their time, Civil War and Revolutionary War soldiers, pirates, sailors, and yellow fever victims allegedly still populate Savannah. Because so many tourist attractions, restaurants, and lodgings are located in historic buildings, visitors are just as likely as not to encounter some of these spirits. Several tour companies offer trolley or walking tours that teach visitors about these restless spirits.

Located just 20 minutes away, off the coast of Savannah, is Tybee Island, where bathing suits, shorts, and flip-flops are de rigueur. With its 3 miles of pristine beach, the family-oriented beach is still lost in the '50s, although it gets more posh every year. A low-key attitude, quaint rental cottages—many as old as 100 years—mom-and-pop motels, and casual eateries coupled with a lack of high-rises and amusement parks create an appealing destination for a laid-back vacation for all ages. Sunbathing, all kinds of boating and water sports, surf fishing, sand-castle building, crabbing, shelling, and bird-watching are just a few of the delights awaiting visitors to this island paradise. Just in case you don't have the opportunity to see a live sea turtle while you're visiting the island, the Tybee Arts Association is helping save the endangered creature through ecological education in public art. So far 10 huge fiberglass sea turtles have been whimsically decorated by local artists and placed around the island.

GUIDANCE There are several excellent sources of information about Savannah and Tybee Island. When planning your trip from home, you can contact the **Savannah Area Convention and Visitors Bureau and Chamber of Commerce** (912-644-6400 or 1-877-SAVAN-NAH; www.savannahvisit.com or www.savannahchamber.com), P.O. Box 1628, Savannah 31402, for a Savannah Travel Planner and other information. The street address is 101 East Bay Street. Open 8:30–5 Monday–Friday.

There's no shortage of information and assistance in Savannah. When you arrive in Savannah, there are several visitor information centers with staff and brochures to help you. The **Savannah Visitor Information Center** (912-944-0455), 301 Martin Luther King Jr. Boulevard, Savannah 31401, is open 8:30–5 weekdays, 9–5 Saturday, Sunday, and holidays. There is an introductory movie at this location, and you can leave your car here, joining one of the many tours offered by different companies or taking advantage of the public transportation available. The **River Street Visitor Information Center** (912-651-6662), One River Street, Savannah 31401, is open 10–5 daily, December and January; until 8 in February and November; until 9 August–October; until 10 March–July. Another **visitor information center** is located at 20 Barnard Street (912-525-3100, ext. 1343). Open at least 10–6 daily, open later spring and fall, and even later in summer. Located at Forsyth Park, 621 Drayton Street, is yet another **visitors center,** which is open 8–7 Monday–Saturday.

If you are arriving by air, the **Savannah Airport Visitor Information Center** (912-966-3743), 400 Airways Avenue, Savannah 31401, is open 9 AM–10 PM daily. On the way into the city on I-95, there is the **Georgia Visitor Information Center at Savannah** (912-963-2546; www.exploregeorgia.org), I-95, mile marker 111, Garden City 31407. Open 8:30–5:30 daily.

The **Tybee Island Visitors Information Center** (912-786-5444 or 1-800-868-BEACH; www.tybeevisit.com, www.tybeeonline.com, or www.tybeeisland.com), US 80 at Campbell Avenue, Tybee Island 31328, is open 9–5:30 daily.

GETTING THERE *By air:* Five airlines fly into **Savannah/Hilton Head International Airport,** located off I-95 at exit 104, just 10 miles west of downtown. Numerous car rental companies, public transportation, hotel shuttles, and taxis offer transportation from the airport to Savannah and Tybee Island. (See "What's Where in Georgia" for airport, airline, and car rental information.)

By bus: Savannah is a regular stop on **Greyhound Lines** (912-232-2135) routes. Buses arrive at the terminal at 610 West Oglethorpe Avenue.

By car: Along the coast of the eastern United States, take I-95, getting off at exit 99 onto I-16 East, which ends in downtown Savannah at Montgomery Street. If continuing to Tybee Island, take US 80 from East Liberty Street in downtown Savannah to the island.

By train: **AMTRAK** (912-234-2611), 2611 Seaboard Coastline Drive, uses Savannah as a major stop on its Atlantic coast Silver Service/Palmetto service between New York and Miami.

GETTING AROUND Numerous options make getting around Savannah easy. Because of the parking problems in the historic district, you might want to take advantage of these alternatives. If you're staying in the historic district, walking is by far the most pleasant choice. Free and convenient, the ❀ **CAT dot Express Shuttle** operated by **Chatham Area Transit** (912-233-5767; www.catchacat.org), headquarters at CAT Central, 124 Bull Street, makes 32 stops throughout the historic district, including shops, attractions, and hotels. CAT also offers free transportation on a trolley as well as ferry service between River Street and Hutchinson Island. The former, the **River Street Streetcar**, operates Thursday–Sunday. Outside the historic district, regular fares are $1.50 per ride or $3 all day. Multiride passes are available for 10 rides or 7 or 31 days.

Savannah has a plethora of tour company options. At last count, there were 53 offering general tours and/or specializing in subjects as diverse as African American history, "the Book" (*Midnight in the Garden of Good and Evil* for the uninitiated), the Civil War, ghosts, pirates, and pubs. Many tour companies offer guided tours via trolleys and/or buses, some with on-and-off privileges. Among them, just a few include **Gray Line Trolley Tours** (912-234-8687; www.grayline.com/savannah), which offers eight tours; **Old Savannah Tours** (912-234-8128 or 1-800-517-9007; oldsavannahtours.com), which offers six tours; and **Old Town Trolley** (912-233-0083; www.oldtowntrolley.com), which offers four tours. All depart from the Savannah Visitor Information Center and pick up at some hotels.

What's more romantic than touring the city to the clip-clop of a horse-drawn carriage? Several companies offer day and nighttime tours, among them **Carriage Tours of Savannah** (912-236-6756) and **Historic Savannah Carriage Tours** (912-443-9333 or 1-888-837-1011).

Some of the most popular tours are walking tours, and some of these are given after dark. Most tour guides meet participants in a central location rather than at their offices, so we supply only the telephone and website information here. **Savannah by Foot** (912-238-3843; www.savannahtours.com) and the **Savannah Walks** (912-238-WALKS; www.savannahwalks.com) are just two of many. (See *Entertainment* for ghost tours.)

If you are staying outside the historic district or want to explore outside it, **Chatham Area Transit** (see previous entry) also offers for-fee ($1.50 per ride) bus routes within the city and Chatham County.

Car rentals are available from **Alamo** (1-877-222-9075), **Avis** (912-964-1781), **Budget** (912-964-4600), **Dollar** (1-866-957-0118), **Enterprise Rent-a-Car** (912-920-1093), **Hertz** (912-964-9595), **Thrifty** (912-966-2277), and **Vanguard** (912-964-1771).

CARRIAGE TOURS ARE A CHARMING WAY TO SEE SAVANNAH.

The easiest and most pleasant way to travel across the river from River Street in the historic district to the Westin Savannah Harbor Golf Resort and Spa and the Savannah International Trade and Convention Center on Hutchinson Island is by way of the **Savannah Belles Ferry,** operated by **Chatham Area Transit** (912-233-5767; www.catchacat.org), which leaves from the City Hall dock or the Waving Girl Statue. The taxis operate every half hour between 7 AM and 11 PM daily. Free.

On Tybee Island, trolley tours are available May–September.

PARKING On-street parking in the Savannah Historic District is practically all metered and can be extremely difficult for sightseers to find. Even many inns and bed & breakfasts have little off-street parking, and guests must park at meters on the street. The good news is that metered parking is free on weekends, and city-owned parking lots are free on Sunday. But don't let your vacation be ruined at other times by getting a ticket or having your car booted or towed. One of the easiest solutions is to park at the visitors center on Martin Luther King Boulevard and take free public transportation (see *Getting Around*). There are several convenient for-fee parking lots and garages, both public and private, within easy walking distances of most tourist sites, accommodations, restaurants, and nightspots.

Tourists who make the choice to park in the historic district may purchase a $7 one-day parking pass or a $12 48-hour parking pass from the Savannah Visitor Information Center, the Parking Services Division, and various hotels and inns. The pass allows one hour or more of free parking on meters, free parking in the city lots and garages, and extended time in time-limit zones. During the St. Patrick's Day parade, parking on the parade route is prohibited, so be sure to learn the route in advance. Also, be aware of schedules for street cleaning, when parking may be prohibited or may be changed from one side of the street to another. If you have questions about parking, Parking Services (912-651-6470) officers can answer them.

On-street parking in the commercial and beach areas on Tybee Island is also metered and can be scarce in the high season, especially on weekends and holidays. Parking is enforced 8–8 daily, year-round. There are numerous Pay and Display kiosks where visitors can purchase parking privileges for $1.20 per hour. Several for-fee parking lots a few blocks from the beach are available. In contrast to the situation with some accommodations in Savannah, most accommodations on Tybee Island have adequate off-street parking.

WHEN TO GO Savannah is a year-round destination, though it's particularly beautiful in the spring when the azaleas are blooming and at Christmas, when many of the homes and inns are beautifully decorated and open for tours. A visit during the St. Patrick's celebration requires advance planning. Accommodations for the popular St. Patrick's event often need to be booked a year in advance and usually require a several-night minimum stay and full non-refundable payment in advance.

As a beach destination, Tybee Island is most sought out during the summer months. September and October are ideal—the air and water temperatures are delightful, and the crowds are gone. If swimming is not your primary reason for visiting, Tybee can be enchanting for walking, biking, bird-watching, and shelling in the off-season months. Because Tybee Island is more heavily visited in the summer, some establishments have restricted hours or may even close in the winter, so call ahead.

MEDICAL EMERGENCY Call 911.

✳ To See

FOR FAMILIES 🐾 🧿 ♿ **Tybee Island Light Station and Museum** (912-786-5801; www.tybeelighthouse.org), 30 Meddin Drive, Tybee Island. Open 9–5:30 daily except Tuesday. Last tickets sold at 4:30. This light station is one of this country's most intact, still having most of its historic support buildings—several keeper's cottages, the summer kitchen, garage, and fuel storage building—in addition to the lighthouse. Some kind of light on this spot has been guiding mariners safely into the Savannah River for more than two centuries. The first was built in 1736; Georgia's first public structure, at that time it was the tallest lighthouse in America. A later lighthouse, the first with interior stairs, had to have George Washington's approval. The current 154-foot, 178-step lighthouse was built in 1867 on the base of one from 1773. It wears its 1916 day-mark color scheme and is one of the few surviving American lighthouses to have its original first-order Fresnel lens. The Head Keeper's Cottage has been restored and furnished to reflect an earlier era. The adjacent museum in the summer kitchen displays lighthouse artifacts and local Tybee historical items. Limited wheelchair accessibility. Adults $8; children 6–17, seniors, and military $6; children five and younger free.

♠ ♂ ♿ **Tybee Island Marine Science Center** (912-786-5917 or 1-866-557-9172; www.tybeemarinescience.org), 1510 the Strand at 14th Street, Tybee Island. Open 11–5 daily. This small center interprets marine life with touch tanks, aquariums, and other exhibits. There are monthly Discovery Beach Walks and other programs throughout the year, as well as a summer Sea Camp for children 3–12. Adults $4, children $3.

♠ ♂ ♿ **University of Georgia Marine Science Complex and Aquarium** (912-598-2496; www.marex.uga.edu/aquarium), 30 Ocean Science Circle, Savannah. Open 9–4 weekdays, 10–5 Saturday. Part of the university's Marine Extension Service, the complex conducts studies on coastal sea life found in the tidal creeks of salt marshes, ocean beaches, and open waters of the continental shelf, including live bottom areas such as Gray's Reef National Marine Sanctuary off Sapelo Island. The 14-tank aquarium exhibit shows 200 live examples that represent 50 species of fish, turtles, and invertebrates, including some of the more spectacular Georgia marine life, such as *Octopus vulgaris,* the loggerhead turtle, the shark sucker, and the longnose gar. Among the other permanent and traveling exhibits are archaeological finds such as the fossils of sharks, giant armadillos, whales, mastodons, and woolly mammoths dredged from the Skidaway River. Other exhibits showcase Native American and Gullah cultures as well as the works of local artists. Alongside the Intracoastal Waterway are a nature trail and a picnic area, while the Jay Wolf Nature Trail meanders through the ruins of the old Roebling plantation. Summer camps offer fun and education to children age 6–15. Several special events include the **Coastweeks Celebration** open house in the fall and the annual **Underwater and Coastal Georgia Art and Photography Contest.** Adults $6; children 3–12, seniors, and military $3; children younger than three free.

FORTS ♠ ♂ ♿ **Fort Pulaski National Monument** (912-786-5787; www.nps.gov/fopu), US 80 East, Savannah. Open 9–5 daily, September–May; 9–6:30 daily, June–August. The star-shaped fort, located on Cockspur Island between Savannah and Tybee Island, was once a masterpiece among brick-and-masonry forts. In fact, when Confederate forces occupied it during the early Civil War, they thought it was invincible. Unfortunately, it fell to the Union's rifled artillery in less than 30 hours, and that defeat marked the end of masonry forts. Today the fort is interpreted through a film and exhibits in the visitors center, as well as ranger-led programs in the fort. See towering walls, artillery tunnels, the drawbridge, and two moats. Nature trails and picnic grounds round out the offerings. $5, children younger than 16 free.

♠ ♂ ♿ **Old Fort Jackson** (912-232-3945; www.chsgeorgia.org), One Fort Jackson Road, Savannah. Open 9–5 daily. The oldest standing fort in Georgia, Old Fort Jackson perches on a bluff above the Savannah River. Once a Revolutionary War fort, it saw action during the War of 1812 and the Civil War. Cannons, small arms, tools, and machinery are among the interpretive exhibits, along with artifacts from the sunken ironclad CSS *Georgia,* which rests 40 feet below the surface of the Savannah River in front of the fort. Between June 15 and August 15, weapons are demonstrated and cannon fired at 11 AM and 2 PM daily. Among the cannons is the largest black-powder cannon ever fired in America. Battlefield reenactments and special events are ongoing throughout the year, and the fort is also a great place from which to watch the ships sailing up and down the Savannah River. Adults $6; children, seniors, and military $5.50; children younger than six free.

(912-233-6854;
www.andrewlowhouse.com), 329 Abercorn Street, Savannah. Open 10–4 Monday–Saturday,
noon–4 Sunday. This gracious Greek Revival– and Italianate-style home was the site where
the first Girl Scout troop in America was organized: in 1912 by Juliette Gordon Low, a
Savannah native. (For more about the founder, see the Juliette Gordon Low National Birthplace entry that follows.) This 1848 structure had been the home of Mrs. Low's father-in-law,
Andrew Low, who was a cotton merchant. The young couple inherited the house upon his
death. The classical design of the structure also shows West Indian plantation-style influences. The property also contains what is considered to be Savannah's most notable collection of classical furnishings from the period 1800–1850. Purchased by the Colonial Dames in
1928, the Andrew Low House was Savannah's first historic house museum. Limited wheelchair accessibility. Adults $8, students $6, and Girl Scouts $5.

🐌 ♿ **Bonaventure Cemetery** (912-651-6843; www.bonaventurehistorical.org), 330
Bonaventure Road, Thunderbolt. Open 8–5 daily. The visitors center in the Administration
Building at the front gates is open 10–4 Saturday and Sunday. Visitors can get free maps and
directions there. Massive moss-draped oaks stand guard over elegant statuary and headstones
dating back more than two centuries in this cemetery on the banks of the Wilmington River.
The cemetery is the final resting place of some of Savannah's most famous former residents,
such as Pulitzer Prize–winning poet Conrad Aiken and lyricist and Academy Award winner
Johnny Mercer, as well as Confederate generals, plantation owners, and lesser-knowns such
as a little girl named Gracie whose likeness tops her tomb. The cemetery also figured prominently in the book *Midnight in the Garden of Good and Evil* and the movie version. It was
here that the narrator sipped martinis and learned about Savannah society. In fact, so many
visitors come because of "the Book" that the famous Bird Girl statue had to be removed and
now reposes at the Telfair Academy of Arts and Sciences (see *Museums*). Danny Hansford,
whose murder is the central theme of the book, is buried in nearby Greenwich Cemetery.
Tours are given at 2, 2:30, and 3 on the second Sunday. Visitors meet the guide at the intersection of Mullryne and Wiltberger ways, and the tour lasts about one to two hours. Free,
but donations appreciated. (At least one private tour company offers guided tours of
Bonaventure Cemetery for a fee.)

🐌 ♿ **Colonial Park Cemetery** (912-651-6843), 201 Abercorn Street and Oglethorpe
Avenue, Savannah. Open 8–8 daily. Filled with fascinating markers and tombs watched over
by ancient magnolias, Colonial Park Cemetery, the oldest graveyard in Savannah, entombed
many of Savannah's early colonists from 1750 to 1853. Among those resting here are
Archibald Bulloch, the first governor of Georgia, and Button Gwinnett, a Revolutionary War
hero and signer of the Declaration of Independence. A point of interest is the hand-carved
graffiti on many of the headstones, the work of Union soldiers camped in the cemetery during the Civil War. Look for deaths dated before births and other oddities. Free. As is no surprise, several walking ghost tours stop at the cemetery.

🐌 **Flannery O'Connor Childhood Home** (912-233-6014; www.flanneryoconnor.org), 207
East Charlton Street, Lafayette Square, Savannah. Open 1–4 Friday–Wednesday. Closed in
February. Get a glimpse into the early life of the famous Georgia novelist and short-story
writer at this house, where she lived until she was 13. Built in 1856, the home is furnished as
it might have been when the O'Connor family lived there in the 1920s and 1930s, and contains rare books. In addition, the gardens, where the six-year-old Flannery once taught a
chicken to walk backwards, have been restored and offer a quiet place to sit a spell. The center offers special literary programs in the fall and spring. Adults $6, students $5.

🐌 **Green-Meldrim House** (912-232-1251), 14 West Macon Street near Madison Square,
Savannah. Open 10–12:30 and 1–4 Tuesday and Thursday, 10–1 Friday and Saturday (last
tour 30 minutes before closing). Closed Veterans Day week and from mid-December to
mid-January. Considered to be one of Georgia's finest examples of neo–Gothic Revival

architecture, this circa 1850 house serves as the parish house of St. John's Episcopal Church. During the Civil War occupation by Union troops, the house was the headquarters of Gen. William Tecumseh Sherman. It was in one of the bedrooms that Sherman wrote his famous telegram telling President Lincoln that he was presenting Savannah to him as a Christmas gift. Today the house has been fully restored and appropriately furnished. Adults $8, children and seniors $3.

Isaiah Davenport House Museum (912-236-8097; www.davenporthousemuseum.com), 324 East State Street, Columbia Square, Savannah. Open 10–4 Monday–Saturday, 1–4 Sunday. Built between 1815 and 1820 by master builder Isaiah Davenport, the house is a stellar example of Federal architecture and features outstanding architectural details such as delicate plasterwork, an elliptical cantilevered staircase, and Ionic-Tuscan columns. Furnishings include a fine collection of Davenport china, Chippendale and Sheraton furnishings, and period decorative arts. This house was the first restoration project of the Historic Savannah Foundation. In fact, it was the threatened demolition of this house that served as the catalyst for the preservation movement in Savannah and led to the foundation's formation. Numerous exhibitions and special events occur throughout the year. Adults $8, children $5.

Juliette Gordon Low National Birthplace (912-233-4501; www.juliettegordon lowbirthplace.org), 10 East Oglethorpe Avenue, Savannah. Open 10–4 Monday, Tuesday, and Thursday–Saturday; 11–4 Sunday. Shorter days and hours November–February, so be sure to check ahead. Closed New Year's Day–January 14; check for hours near major holidays. The home, which was Savannah's first designated National Historic Landmark, is of interest whether you've ever had any association with the Girl Scouts of America or not. This lovely 1820 Regency-style town house was the childhood home of the founder of the girls' organization and has been restored to the period of her residency, 1860 to 1886. In addition to the fine classical interior details, visitors will be interested in many original family pieces. In May, the birthplace sponsors the **Celebrate Girl Scouting** festival, which spills out into Wright Square. Limited wheelchair accessibility. Adults $8, children and students $7. Discounts for Girl Scouts.

King-Tisdell Cottage (912-234-8000; www.kingtisdell.org), 514 East Huntingdon Street, Savannah. Open noon–5 Tuesday–Saturday. A beautifully restored 1896 cottage with unusually intricate gingerbread trim on the porch and dormers, the house is a museum highlighting the contributions of African Americans. Among the exhibits are 19th-century art objects, documents, and furniture. Adults $1.50, seniors and children $0.75.

The Mercer Williams House Museum (912-236-6352 or 1-877-430-6352; www.mercer house.com), 429 Bull Street, Savannah. Open 10:30–4 Monday–Saturday, noon–4 Sunday. Closed in January. Originally built in the 1860s for Gen. Hugh W. Mercer, the great-grandfather of songster Johnny Mercer, this stately house was purchased in 1969 by antiques dealer and preservationist Jim Williams. During his career, Williams saved more than 50 historic homes in the area. Opulently restored, the Monterey Square home is furnished with 17th- through 19th-century furniture and art he collected. Although you won't hear a word about it on the tour, this house and the late Mr. Williams played pivotal roles in the real-life saga that inspired the book and movie *Midnight in the Garden of Good and Evil.* Today it is owned and is the residence of his sister Dr. Dorothy Kingery. Before leaving, be sure to stop in at the Carriage House Shop, 430 Whitaker Street; open 10–5 Monday–Saturday, 10:30–4:30 Sunday. Adults $12.50, students $8.

Owens-Thomas House (Telfair Museums: 912-790-8800; www.telfair.org/owens-thomas -house), 124 Abercorn Street, Savannah. Open noon–5 Monday, 10–5 Tuesday–Saturday, 1–5 Sunday; tours every 30 minutes, with the last at 4:30. This National Historic Landmark mansion, considered to be one of the finest examples of the Regency style in America, was designed by Englishman William Jay, one of the first professionally trained architects to practice in America, and built between 1816 and 1819. The Marquis de Lafayette stayed in the home in 1825 and addressed the citizens of Savannah from the unusual cast-iron balcony on the south facade. Many of the furnishings are original to the Thomas family and represent the period 1750–1830. In 1830 the house was sold to the Owens family and remained in their hands until 1951, when it was bequeathed to the Telfair Academy of Arts and Sciences. Today the house is operated under the auspices of the Telfair Museums. In the Owens-Thomas Carriage House, the lives and stories of Savannah slaves are told through items in the Acacia Collection. A $20 three-site combo ticket allows a one-time admission not only to this house, but to the **Telfair Academy of Arts and Sciences and the Jepson Center for the Arts** (see *Museums*) for one week after the date of purchase; $20 for adults, $18 for seniors and military; a family pass is available for $40. Students K–college can purchase a one-site ticket for $5.

🔆 ✒ ♿ **Wormsloe Historic Site** (912-353-3023; www.gastateparks.org/Wormsloe), 7601 Skidaway Road, Savannah. Open 9–5 Tuesday–Sunday. Located on the Isle of Hope, Wormsloe was a royal grant to Noble Jones, one of Georgia's first colonists, in 1756. It remained in the same family until 1974, when it was given to the Georgia Heritage Trust. A beautiful oak-lined drive leads visitors to the ruins of the home. The site is interpreted at the visitors center with exhibits of items excavated at Wormsloe and audiovisual programming about the founding of the 13th colony. Make a day of it by wandering along the nature trails to see the tabby (oyster-shell cement) fortification and the Fort Wimberly earthworks. The living-history area is the scene of periodic special programs by costumed staff who demonstrate skills and crafts necessary to early settlers. Call for a schedule of these special events. In February, the **Colonial Faire and Muster** highlights 18th-century life with military drills, crafts demonstrations, music, and dance. Admission $4.50–8; parking $5.

MUSEUMS 🔆 ♿ **Effingham Museum and Living History Site** (912-826-4705 or 912-754-2170; www.historiceffinghamsociety.org), 1002 Pine Street, Springfield. Open 9–1 Monday–Friday, 2–5 Sunday. Almost three-quarters of a century old, the old jail houses Revolutionary War and Civil War artifacts, Native American artifacts, and displays as varied as the contents of an old-time general store, turpentine production, and a 1940s kitchen. The Seckinger-Bridgers House log cabin has been moved to the property. Free.

🔆 ♿ **Massie Heritage Interpretation Center** (912-395-5070; www.massieschool.com), 207 East Gordon Street, Savannah. Open 9–4 weekdays. The center, housed in the only remaining structure of Georgia's oldest chartered school system, is the repository of exhibits explaining Savannah's outstanding architecture from 1865 to 1974. Exhibits include *Oglethorpe's City Plan, Architectural Treasures,* the *Victorian Era,* and *North America in Coastal Georgia.* Young people are especially interested in the Heritage Classroom. Self-guided tours: adults $5 (guided tours $8), children 3–12 $3, children younger than three free.

🔆 ✒ ♿ **Mighty Eighth Air Force Museum** (912-748-8888; www.mightyeighth.org), 175 Bourne Avenue, Pooler. Open 9–5 daily. Exhibits range from World War II to the present. One of the highlights is a simulated B-17 bombing mission where visitors can experience a bomber crew's harrowing flight over Nazi Germany. At another exhibit, visitors can test their skills as a waist gunner. *The Fly Girls of World War II* exhibit is devoted to women in aviation, particularly the unsung heroes of the Women's Airforce Service Pilots. Outdoors, the Chapel of the Fallen Eagles occupies a replica of a 15th-century English church sitting amid the Memorial Gardens. Thirteen stained-glass windows honor World War II airmen. Conflicts in Vietnam and Korea are also represented. Aircraft on view include an F-4 Phantom, B-47 Stratojet, MiG-17 Fresco, Boeing-Stearman PT-17 Kaydet, and Messerschmitt ME-163 B Komet. The museum is an affiliate of the Smithsonian Institution. Spending a day here is bound to work up an appetite. Miss Sophie's Marketplace features Southern cuisine and British fare. Open 11–6 Monday–Friday, 1–2 Saturday. Adults $10, seniors $9, children 6–12 and active military $6, children younger than six free.

🐾 ⚐ Ralph Mark Gilbert Civil Rights Museum (912-231-8900), 460 Martin Luther King Jr. Boulevard, Savannah. Open 9–5 Monday–Saturday. The museum explores Savannah's African American history and culture, with special emphasis on Savannah's struggle against segregation. While you're at the museum, pick up a *Negro Heritage Trail* brochure, which details three separate walking or driving tours pertinent to black history. Adults $4, seniors $3, children $2.

🐾 ⚐ Roundhouse Railroad Museum (912-651-6823; www.chsgeorgia.org), 601 West Harris Street, Savannah. Open 9–5

B-52 ON DISPLAY AT THE MIGHTY EIGHTH AIR FORCE MUSEUM

daily. This complex, which actually contains 13 original structures, includes the oldest and most complete antebellum locomotive repair shop and roundhouse still in existence in the country. Exhibits include two of the oldest surviving steam engines, as well as other antique locomotives, machinery, and rolling stock. Adults $10, children $4.50. Admission includes a train ride and other activities such as rail car tours, a hand car, and children's activities in the baggage car. When available, visitors can ride in a diesel or steam locomotive ($20).

🐾 ⚐ Saltzburger Museum and Jerusalem Church (912-754-7001; www.georgia saltzburgers.com), 2980 Ebenezer Road, Rincon. Open 3–5 Wednesday, Saturday, and Sunday. In 1734, 60 Lutheran religious exiles from the Principality and Archbishopric of Salzburg arrived in Georgia, where they founded the town of Ebenezer on the Savannah River. The museum, which traces the history of this group, is located on the site of the Ebenezer Orphanage, the first in the state. The church, which was built between 1767 and 1769, still holds services Sunday at 11. Free.

🐾 ⚐ ⚐ Savannah History Museum (912-651-6825; www.chsgeorgia.org), 303 Martin Luther King Jr. Boulevard, Savannah. Open 8:30–5 weekdays, 9–5 weekends. Among the 10,000 artifacts, numerous exhibits and a film detail the city's history since its founding in 1733. The building, which was the passenger station for the Central of Georgia Railway, also houses a prop from the movie *Forrest Gump:* the bench on which the hero sat while waiting for the bus in Chippewa Square. Adults $5, children under six free.

REFLECTING POOL AND MEDITATION GARDEN AT THE MIGHTY EIGHTH AIR FORCE MUSEUM

🐾 ⚐ Ships of the Sea Maritime Museum (912-232-1511; www.shipsofthe sea.org), 41 Martin Luther King Jr. Boulevard, Savannah. Open 10–5 Tuesday–Sunday. Housed in the elegant William Scarborough House, the museum displays ship models and maritime antiques representing 2,000 years of seagoing history, with primary focus on the 18th and 19th centuries. Intricate models represent sail steamers, warships, tugs, supertankers, and more. Among the other exhibits are scrimshaw art and maritime paintings. Scarborough was the principal owner of the *Savannah*, the first steamship to cross the Atlantic. In addition to the outstanding exhibits inside, at the rear of the house there is a lovely garden—the largest in the historic district. Adults $8; children, seniors, and military $6; a family of up to two adults and two children $20.

🐾 ✍ ♿ **Telfair Academy of Arts and Sciences and Jepson Center for the Arts** (912-790-8800; www.telfair.org), Telfair: 121 Barnard Street, Savannah; Jepson Center: 207 West York Street, Savannah. Open noon–5 Monday, 10–5 Tuesday–Saturday, 1–5 Sunday. Docent-led tours at 2 PM daily; additional tours at 1 PM Thursday and Friday, 11 AM Saturday. The South's oldest public art museum, the Telfair Academy of Arts and Sciences is housed in a magnificent mansion designed and built by William Jay, also the designer of the **Owens-Thomas House** (see *Historic Homes and Sites*), in 1818. Opulent period rooms are meticulously restored to their 1819 appearance to serve as an elegant backdrop for the extensive collection of fine and decorative arts, including original family furnishings. A large wing added in 1883 contains superb American and European paintings and sculpture. Aficionados of *Midnight in the Garden of Good and Evil* enjoy seeing the famous Bird Girl statue from the cover of "the Book." Although it once graced Bonaventure Cemetery, it had to be moved for its own protection. A few years ago the museum opened the state-of-the-art **Jepson Center for the Arts** in a striking modern Moshe Safdie–designed building located catty-corner across the street. The Jepson displays 20th- and 21st-century art as well as Southern and African American art, photography, works on paper, and outdoor sculpture. The Jepson's children's gallery displays interactive exhibits inspired by works in the museum's collection. The Jepson Center features multilevel interactive galleries, an auditorium, museum store, café, and sculpture gardens. A three-site combo ticket allows a one-time visit to the Telfair Academy, the Jepson Center, and the Owens-Thomas House for seven days from the date of purchase: adults $20, seniors and military $18, family $40. A single-site ticket is available for students for $5.

SPECIAL PLACES 🐾 ✍ ♿ Savannah Riverfront, Riverfront Plaza, and Factors Walk,

River Street between Martin Luther King Jr. Boulevard and East Broad Street. The Savannah River is the heart of the historic district, and on its south bank is River Street. In past centuries, the street was lined with cotton warehouses and offices of the factors (cotton brokers). The streets were paved with ballast stones, which had been carried in ships to distribute the weight and then discarded. Today River Street is still paved with ballast stones, but the cotton warehouses contain inns, restaurants, nightspots, shops, boutiques, galleries, and artists' studios. **Riverfront Plaza,** a nine-block brick-paved esplanade stretching between City Hall and the Savannah Marriott Riverfront, is dotted with fountains, landscaping, benches, and a children's play area. Always hopping with activity, the plaza is often the scene of festivals, special events, and entertainment. At the far end of the plaza is the **Waving Girl Statue,** which depicts Florence Martus, a young woman whose sailor boyfriend went off to sea and never returned. No one knows whether he died

SAVANNAH'S TELFAIR ACADEMY OF ARTS AND SCIENCES IS THE COUNTRY'S OLDEST PUBLIC ART MUSEUM.

or just changed his mind, but Florence greeted every ship that entered the port of Savannah from 1887 to 1931, anticipating his return. Nearby, the **Olympic Cauldron Sculpture** commemorates the sailing events from the 1996 Summer Olympic Games, which were held off the coast of Savannah. First-Saturday festivals are held on Riverfront Plaza each month. **Factors Walk** is located between River and Bay streets on the bluff above the river. This area was a 19th-century center of commerce for cotton merchants. Offices were on the upper level, warehouses on the lower level. Bridgeways connect the buildings. Riverfront Plaza is wheelchair accessi-

SAVANNAH'S JEPSON CENTER FOR THE ARTS HOUSES CONTEMPORARY ART.

ble, as is Factors Walk. The ballast stone paving makes crossing River Street difficult. Chatham Area Transit offers a free trolley along River Street on weekends.

✳ To Do

AUTO RACING ✈ ♿ **Oglethorpe Speedway Park** (912-964-8200; www.ospracing.net), 200 Jesup Road, Pooler. The park sponsors NASCAR-sanctioned events and Go-Kart Races on weekends. Call for a schedule of events and ticket prices.

BICYCLING One of the most pleasant ways to get around Tybee Island is by bicycle, and the hard-packed beach is even conducive to bike riding. Bring your own or rent one when you get there.

Both single and tandem bikes are available from **Fat Tire Bike Rental** (912-786-4013), 1403 Butler Avenue, Tybee Island. Single $15 per day; tandem $25 per day.

Tim's Beach Gear (912-786-TIMS), Tybee Island, delivers bikes; umbrellas, beach chairs, beach carts, towels, and horseshoe and boccie ball sets; and baby gear such as cribs and high chairs. Single bike $12 per day; tandem $25 per day.

THE PLAYGROUND AT RIVERFRONT PLAZA

BIRDING Numerous locations are excellent for bird-watching, from the beaches to the state park to the national wildlife refuge.

✿ ✈ **Colonial Coast Birding Trail,** measuring more than 112 miles along the coast of Georgia, has 18 stops—some with 18th- and 19th-century sites that were once part of plantations. The northern portion of the trail is near Savannah. Free.

BOATING ✈ **Ogeechee River Canoe and Kayak Rentals** (912-748-8893; cell 912-633-0442; http://ogeecheecanoe.net), Bloomingdale. The company also offers guided and unguided canoe trips, return shuttle service, and training. Call for schedules and fees.

CRUISES ⚓ ♿ **River Street Riverboat Company** (912-232-6404 or 1-800-786-6404; www.savannahriverboat.com), 9 East River Street, Savannah. Rates and schedules vary by activity and between winter and summer, so call for prices and a timetable of narrated sight-seeing, lunch, brunch, dinner, and moonlight cruises. Make a voyage of discovery aboard the *Savannah River Queen* or the *Georgia Queen,* replicas of old-fashioned paddle-wheelers. In addition to the types of cruises already mentioned, the company also provides nine themed specialty cruises, such as gospel, murder-mystery, Civil War slave, and Valentine cruises. Wheelchair access on first deck, but restrooms not accessible. Smoking outdoors only. Basic sight-seeing cruise: adults $16.95, children 4–11 $14.95, children three and younger free. Call for prices of other cruises.

DOLPHIN WATCHING ⚓ **Capt. Mike's Dolphin Adventure Tours** (912-786-5858 or 1-800-242-0166; www.tybeedolphins.com), Lazaretto Creek Marina, Tybee Island. Mailing address: P.O. Box 787, Tybee Island 31328. Open 9–5 daily. Tours offered at different times depending on season. Reservations recommended. The SS *Dolphin,* a small *African Queen*–like vessel, provides a magical cruise to catch sight of playful bottlenose dolphins. Even on a bad day when no dolphins appear, you'll still enjoy the sight-seeing, which passes Old Cockspur Lighthouse, Fort Pulaski, and the north beach of the island. Not wheelchair accessible. Adults $15, children 12 and younger $8; Sunset Cruise adults $18, children $11.

⚓ **Dolphin Magic** (912-897-4990 or 1-800-721-1240; www.reelemn.com/dolphinmagic), mailing address: P.O. Box 30247, Savannah 31401. Offered seasonally March–November, the two-hour dolphin tour aboard Savannah's largest dolphin-watching vessel leaves daily from River Street behind the Hyatt, glides along the Riverfront and past the Waving Girl Statue, then proceeds past Fort Jackson and Fort Pulaski on its way past Cockspur Lighthouse, until it finally reaches Tybee Island, which is prime dolphin territory. Not wheelchair accessible. Adults $27, children 3–12 $13.75, children younger than three free.

FISHING An area bounded by the ocean and crisscrossed with rivers is a fisherman's heaven. You can throw a line in almost anywhere, but be aware of fishing laws. Numerous companies offer guided inland fishing trips and deep-sea charters. See "What's Where in Georgia" for fishing regulations.

GOLF Mild year-round weather makes for perfect golfing, and the Savannah area boasts 30 golf courses within 30 miles of town. Savannah is also the home of the Senior PGA's Liberty Mutual Legends of Golf tournament.

Henderson Golf Course (912-920-4653; www.hendersongolfclub.com), One Al Henderson Drive, Savannah. Considered Savannah's best public course, Henderson has 18 holes, a practice facility, and a lighted driving range. Call for hours and prices.

KAYAKING The rivers and marshes that abound around Savannah and Tybee Island are perfect for still-water kayaking, while the ocean provides challenges for sea kayakers. Several companies provide kayaks, lessons, and guides.

Sea Kayak Georgia (912-786-8732 or 1-888-529-2542; www.seakayakgeorgia.com), 1102 US 80, Tybee Island. Open year-round. Sea Kayak Georgia provides experiential education and adventure travel. Basic and advanced kayak instruction and certifications sanctioned by the American Canoe Association and the British Canoe Union are offered. Half-day to multi-day trips with camping or overnights at a bed & breakfast take paddlers to places steeped in scenic beauty as well as cultural and natural history. Sea Kayak Georgia also offers kayak and equipment rentals, as well as the largest selection of composite sea kayaks for sale in the Southeast. Half-day guided tours $55 adults, $45 children; full-day tours $110. Call for schedules and prices for instruction and overnight trips.

OUTDOOR ADVENTURES 🎣 ✿ ♿ **Oatland Island Wildlife Center** (912-395-1212; www.oatlandisland.org), 711 Sandtown Road, Oatland Island. Open 10–5 daily. Among the 175 acres of oaks, pines, and magnolias is a 1.75-mile nature trail that provides opportunities to observe large enclosures with more than 50 indigenous species of wildlife native to the state—shorebirds, alligators, wolves, gopher tortoises, armadillos, indigo snakes, cougars, bobcats, foxes, and diverse raptors among them. Exhibits are divided into *Wolf Wilderness, Alligator Wetlands, Predators of Georgia,* and *Birds of Prey.* Youngsters can see and feed farm animals in the barnyard. The facility is owned by the Savannah–Chatham County School System as an environmental education center, but it is open to the public. Adults $5; children, seniors, and military $3.

🎣 ✿ **Old Savannah-Tybee Railroad Historic and Scenic Trail,** US 80 East, Tybee Island. Open daily. At the turn of the 20th century, visitors were transported from Savannah to Tybee Island by train. In fact, it was the only way between the mainland and the island until 1933. With the construction of bridges and roadways, the railroad was no longer needed, and the tracks fell into disuse and disrepair. Eventually the tracks were taken up and the 6.5-mile roadbed converted to a crushed-stone walking-jogging-bicycling trail. The tree-lined trail provides excellent views of the Savannah River and marshes, along with glimpses of native wildlife—brown pelicans, red-tailed hawks, box turtles, and alligators. Free.

✿ **Wilderness Southeast** (912-236-8115; www.wilderness-southeast.org), 711 Sandtown Road, Savannah. Open year-round. This outdoor school offers overnight wilderness discovery adventures including canoeing, hiking, and sailing. Transportation might include walking, driving, motorboating, and paddling. Call for a schedule of events. Price dependent on the activity.

SWIMMING With the beaches and other water around Savannah and Tybee Island, there are limitless places to swim. On the occasional rainy day, check out the 🎣 ✿ ♿ **Chatham County Aquatic Center** (912-652-6793; www.aquatic.chathamcounty.org), 7240 Sallie Mood Drive, Savannah. Open 6 AM–8 PM weekdays, 8–6 Saturday. A state-of-the-art swimming complex, the 50,000-square-foot facility contains an Olympic-size pool, therapeutic pool, and Nautilus weight equipment. Programs include water aerobics, swimming lessons, and general recreational swimming. Adults $5, seniors $4, children 3–10 $3.

✳ Green Space

BEACHES The beaches of Tybee Island are wide and usually hard packed. Protected by dunes covered with gently swaying sea oats, these beaches provide endless hours of fun in the sun. Not only can you just lie on the beach and read or vegetate, you can walk or jog, hunt for shells, build sand castles, bury someone in the sand, fly a kite, scoot across the waves on a boogie board, wind surf, fish in the surf, and even ride a bike. The beaches are public, and there are numerous access points.

GARDENS 🎣 ♿ **Chatham County Garden Center and Botanical Gardens** (912-355-3883), 1388 Eisenhower Drive, Savannah. Gardens open 9:30–4:30 daily; garden center open 10–2 weekdays. The Savannah Area Council of Garden Clubs maintains 10 acres of gardens on an old prison farm featuring roses, perennials, herbs and vegetables, and seasonal beds. The garden center is housed in a 1840s-era farmhouse. Free, but $3 donation encouraged.

EAT YOUR PICNIC LUNCH WITH A VIEW OF THE TYBEE PIER.

♀ ♿ **Georgia Botanical Gardens at the Historic Bamboo Farm** (912-921-5460; www.bamboo.caes.uga.edu), 2 Canebrake Road, Savannah. Open 8–5 Monday–Friday, 10–5 Saturday, noon–5 Sunday. Operated by the University of Georgia's College of Agricultural and Environmental Sciences, the 52-acre experimental station contains many plant collections and gardens. The gardens began on this site with three plants more than 100 years ago. Today, the farm boasts the largest collections of bamboo in North America, with more than 140 varieties of both shade- and sun-loving bamboos—some of which are the only specimens in this hemisphere. In the Cottage Garden, old and new varieties of perennials, annuals, and bulbs are tested. The Xeriscape Garden demonstrates water-wise landscaping and is used to teach water conservation practices. Collections of butterfly plants, ornamental grasses, crape myrtles, ferns, ornamental vines, 16 varieties of Southern magnolias, and 600 varieties of daylilies are also exhibited. Of further interest to gardeners are projects demonstrating composting, vegetables, fruits, flowers, shrubs, and turf varieties. A palm collection also has been started. Special events throughout the year include a wild-game supper, spring and fall gardening festivals, and an annual Sunday supper in the strawberry patch. Check the website or call for a schedule of special events.

NATURE PRESERVES AND PARKS ♀ ✿ ♿ ☘ **Bacon Regional Park** (912-652-6780), 6262 Skidaway Road, Savannah. The largest regional park in Chatham County covers 500 acres and boasts a municipal golf course (912-354-2625; 1 Shorty Cooper Drive), tennis courts, soccer fields, ball fields, the **Chatham County Aquatic Center** (see *To Do— Swimming*), a weight-lifting center, and **Lake Mayer Community Park** (912-652-6782). The park-within-a-park has a 35-acre fishing lake, a jogging-walking track with fitness stations, picnic areas, basketball and tennis courts, a remote-control auto racetrack, an outdoor skating rink designed for in-line hockey, boat ramps, a pier, a dog park, playground, and volleyball. This park also offers a conditioning course for people in wheelchairs.

♀ ♿ **Emmet Park,** along East Bay Street above Factors Walk and along River Street between Lincoln and Houston streets, Savannah. In addition to ancient live-oak trees, the park contains the Old Harbor Light, which dates to 1852 and warned mariners of British vessels scuttled off the coast in 1779; a fountain commemorating three ships named for Savannah; a Vietnam Memorial; the Oglethorpe Bench, which marks the site of Georgia founding father Gen. James Oglethorpe's landing; and the Celtic Cross, also known as the Irish Monument.

♀ ✿ ♿ **Forsyth Park** (912-351-3852), bounded by Gaston, Whitaker, Drayton, and Hall streets, Savannah. Always open. Forsyth Park, created as a park in 1851 on the oldest and largest of Savannah's squares, is 20 acres of green punctuated with wide sidewalks, an ornate fountain, a Confederate monument and other monuments and memorials, and the Fragrant Garden for the Blind. In addition, the park offers many athletic facilities, including two playgrounds, lighted tennis and basketball courts, playing fields, a 1-mile jogging course, and a summer wading fountain. Many festivals occur in the park during the year. Free.

🦐 🌊 ♿ **Historic Savannah-Ogeechee Barge Canal Nature Center** (www.savannahogeecheecanal.com), 681 Fort Argyle Road, Savannah. Open daylight hours daily. Although it has not been in use for more than 100 years, the canal features four lift locks that are being restored. The 184-acre nature center encompasses river swamp, pine flatland, and sandhill habitats supporting a diversity of migratory birds, reptiles, and other animal life such as the endangered gopher tortoise. Walk alongside the 16.5-mile canal, which links the Savannah and Ogeechee rivers.

🦐 🌊 ♿ **Savannah National Wildlife Refuge** (regional office in South Carolina: 843-784-2468; www.fws.gov/savannah), access from GA 25 north of Port Wentworth, or SC 170 south of Hardeeville, South Carolina. Open sunrise–sunset; visitors center open 9–4:30 Monday–Saturday.

FOUNTAIN AT FORSYTH PARK, SAVANNAH'S LARGEST PARK

The 26,349-acre refuge, which lies on both the Georgia and South Carolina sides of the Savannah River just upriver from Savannah, is a haven for wildlife. Fish, fowl, and alligators call the refuge home. Its position on the Atlantic Flyway brings in thousands of migratory birds and ducks during the winter, followed by songbirds during the spring and fall. Among the endangered species that call the refuge home are bald eagles, wood storks, manatees, and shortnose sturgeon. The 4-mile Laurel Hill Wildlife Drive off SC 170 is open to vehicular traffic throughout the year. The refuge also offers short hiking trails along which you can see remnants of old plantations with small cemeteries and foundations of slave cabins. The Cistern Trail leads to a huge brick circle where the plantation collected fresh water. Picnicking facilities are available. Call for hunting and fishing times and regulations. Don't forget the bug spray. Free.

🦐 🌊 ♿ **Skidaway Island State Park** (912-598-2300; lodging reservations: 1-800-864-7275; www.gastateparks.org/Skidaway), 52 Diamond Causeway, Savannah. Open 7 AM–10 PM daily. This 588-acre barrier island has both salt water and fresh water due to estuaries and marshes that flow through the area. The park borders Skidaway Narrows, a part of the Intracoastal Waterway. In addition to 1- and 3-mile nature and hiking trails that showcase local flora and fauna, the park has earthworks and a lookout tower, a museum and interpretive center, a giant ground sloth exhibit, and a birding station. The park also offers tent and trailer sites, a playground, picnic shelters, fishing, and a Junior Olympic–size swimming pool. Most facilities handicapped accessible. Parking $5.

✳ Lodging

Most visitors to Savannah prefer to stay in the historic district, which is home to several new and historic award-winning hotels, as well as numerous historic inns and bed & breakfasts where luxury abounds. These hostelries may be positioned along the Savannah River overlooking River Street or located in delightful neighborhoods of 18th- and 19th-century homes, but all are within walking distance of Savannah's primary sights. In addition to the lodgings described here, you might want to check out these websites: www.romanticinnsofsavannah.com and www.historicinns-savannah.com.

Sun, sand, sea, and salty breezes draw visitors to Tybee Island, where accommodations are found in small hotels and motels, condos, small inns and bed & breakfasts, and rental cottages—some beachfront. Many of the inns and bed & breakfasts offer extras such as afternoon tea or a cocktail hour.

BED & BREAKFASTS

In Savannah

♿ **Ballastone Inn** (912-236-1484 or 1-800-822-4553; www.ballastone.com), 14 East Oglethorpe Avenue. Named one of the most romantic inns in the country by *Brides* magazine and *Glamour*, the four-diamond Ballastone Inn, housed in an 1853 mansion, is truly a diamond among Savannah's many gems. Guest rooms and suites, many of which sport working fireplaces and/or whirlpool tubs, are exquisitely furnished with ornately carved rice poster or canopy beds and other antiques. Among the many amenities are breakfast, high afternoon tea, late night tea and refreshments, robes, and turndown service. Smoking in courtyard only. Wheelchair accessible by elevator. $179–365.

♿ **Dresser-Palmer House** (912-238-3294), 211 East Gaston Street. The elegant Italianate town house was built in 1876 and has been meticulously restored and furnished with antiques and period reproductions. Among its premier features are its long verandas and second-story galleries,

both of which invite sitting in a rocker with a book or a cool drink. A full breakfast and evening hors d'oeuvres are included. No smoking. Some whirlpool tubs, and some rooms wheelchair accessible. $199–329.

✎ ♿ **Eliza Thompson House** (912-236-3620 or 1-800-348-9378; www.eliza thompsonhouse.com), 5 West Jones Street. The 1847 town house and carriage house have been lovingly restored to house 25 spacious rooms and suites with all the amenities a modern traveler could want. The beautifully landscaped courtyard, exuding Old South formality, provides a quiet oasis in which guests can relax. Other niceties include a deluxe continental breakfast, afternoon wine and cheese, and evening desserts. No smoking. One wheelchair-accessible room. $119–289.

♨ **Foley House** (912-232-6622 or 1-800-647-3708; www.foleyinn.com), 14 West Hull Street, Chippewa Square. Foley House occupies two 1896 Federal-style town houses restored in minute detail. Each of the 18 guest rooms is a handsomely appointed masterpiece. Many guest chambers boast a working fireplace and/or a whirlpool tub. Throughout the day, guests are pampered with a hearty full breakfast, formal afternoon tea, early evening hors d'oeuvres, and late evening cordials. The inn has earned a AAA four-diamond rating. Smoking allowed on porches and balconies only. Not wheelchair accessible. Some pet-friendly rooms ($50). $199–389.

♨ **Forsyth Park Inn** (912-233-6800 or 1-866-670-6800; www.forsythparkinn.com), 102 West Hall Street. This wonderful old mansion sits on a lushly landscaped lot across the street from Forsyth Park. Elegantly furnished with period antiques, guest rooms feature fireplaces and all the modern amenities. Guests are indulged with a high level of service as well as evening beverages and hors d'oeuvres, plus turndown service with cordials and dessert. Pets welcome in cottage only. No smoking. Not wheelchair accessible. $131–275.

♿ **The Gastonian** (912-232-2869 or 1-800-322-6603; www.gastonian.com), 220 East

Gaston Street. This AAA four-diamond inn, recognized as one of the most romantic inns in the Southeast, offers 17 luxurious guest rooms as well as three two-room suites—all with a working fireplace, some with a whirlpool tub—in two historic 1868 homes and a carriage house. Public and guest rooms are lavishly decorated and furnished in Georgian and Regency styles. Guests enjoy a full Southern breakfast, afternoon tea, evening desserts, and nightly turndown service. Ask about the ghost of Eleanor Richardson, whose portrait hangs over the mantelpiece in the front parlor. No smoking. One room with wheelchair access. $159–355.

& **Hamilton-Turner Inn** (912-233-1833 or 1-888-448-8849; www.hamiltonturner inn.com), 330 Abercorn Street, Lafayette Square. This AAA four-diamond property is one of the most beautiful and luxurious inns in Savannah. Known around town as the "Grand Victorian Lady," the Second Empire–style residence was built in 1873 and features public rooms and guest chambers furnished with Empire, Eastlake, and Renaissance Revival antiques. Guests enjoy a full Southern breakfast and afternoon tea. Smoking in courtyard only. Some rooms wheelchair accessible. $169–389; carriage house $549–659.

& **Kehoe House** (912-232-1020 or 1-800-820-1020; www.kehoehouse.com), 123 Habersham Street. This magnificent Renaissance Revival mansion was built in 1892 on Columbia Square. Listed on the National Register of Historic Places, Kehoe House has been exquisitely restored and enhanced with antiques and period reproductions. Sumptuous guest rooms feature luxurious beds, and some boast a private or shared porch. An experienced staff pampers guests with a full gourmet breakfast, afternoon tea and hors d'oeuvres, nightly turndown, a concierge, laundry, and limited room service. No smoking. Elevator makes most rooms wheelchair accessible; one bathroom fully adapted for handicapped. $139.

✎ & ❀ **The President's Quarters Inn** (912-233-1600 or 1-800-233-1776; www

.presidentsquarters.com), 225 East President Street, Oglethorpe Square. Many of the elegant rooms and suites in these twin 1855 Federal-style town houses feature a whirlpool tub, steam shower, and/or a gas-log fireplace. Amenities include a gourmet continental-plus breakfast, afternoon refreshments, plush robes, nightly turndown service, room service, 24-hour concierge, an elevator, courtyard, lap pool, outdoor hot tub, and off-street parking. Children welcome. Pet friendly. No smoking. Many rooms wheelchair accessible. $189–325.

17 Hundred 90 Inn (912-236-7122; www.17hundred90.com), 307 East President Street. Built in the year for which it is named, this is Savannah's oldest inn. Among 14 guest rooms handsomely decorated with antiques and Scalamandre fabrics in old Savannah designs, 12 of the rooms feature a fireplace. Room 204 is said to be inhabited by the ghost of the original owner, to which we can attest since she visited us there. The inn also boasts an award-winning restaurant and lounge (see *Where to Eat—Dining Out*) that is one of the locals' favorite places to eat and drink. No smoking. Not wheelchair accessible. $119–179.

On Tybee Island

Lighthouse Inn Bed and Breakfast (912-786-0901 or 1-866-786-0901; www.tybeebb.com), 16 Meddin Drive. Cute as a button, this intimate inn is located near the beach, the lighthouse, and the **North Beach Grill** (see *Where to Eat—Eating Out*). Get to know Susie and Stuart, the friendly owners, while rocking on the shady veranda. No smoking. Not wheelchair accessible. $179–199.

Tybee Island Bed and Breakfast Inn (912-786-9255 or 1-866-892-4667; www.tybeeislandinn.com), 24 Van Horn Street. Once the recreation hall of Fort Screven, the building has been cleverly renovated to accommodate an intimate bed & breakfast located near the beach and lighthouse. Enjoy the porches and the tropical gardens. No smoking. Not wheelchair accessible. $119–179.

CAMPGROUNDS

In Savannah

🦐 **Bellaire Woods Campground** (912-748-4000), 805 Fort Argyle Road. Twenty-four shaded acres along the Ogeechee River offer shady, pull-through sites, a bathhouse, convenience store, children's playground, outdoor pool, boat ramp, fishing and boating, laundry facilities, and on-site RV repairs. $39–44.

On Tybee Island

🦐 🏊 **River's End Campground and RV Park** (912-786-5518 or 1-800-786-1016; www.cityoftybee.org/campground.aspx), 5 Fort Avenue at Polk Street. Conveniently located within walking distance of the lighthouse, Fort Screven, and the beach, River's End has 100 shady primitive tent sites and RV sites with full or partial hookups, as well as a laundry, dumping site, fuel, picnic tables, bathhouse, a pool, and a camp store. $34–39; cabin rentals $60–100.

COTTAGES

On Tybee Island

🏊 **Tybee Cottages** (912-786-6746 or 1-877-524-9819; www.tybeecottages.com), mailing address: P.O. Box 1226, Tybee Island 31328. Offers daily and weekly rentals of one- and two-bedroom condos or cottages with up to five bedrooms—many waterfront. $875–4,500 per week with accommodations for 4–17.

EFFICIENCIES

In Savannah

🏊 ♿ **Suites on Lafayette** (912-596-1500; www.suitesonlafayette.com), 201 East Charlton Street, Lafayette Square. Centrally located in the historic district, these one- to four-bedroom apartments feature gourmet kitchens, fireplaces in every room, a washer and dryer, and private porches. No smoking. One four-bedroom suite wheelchair accessible. $149–239.

On Tybee Island

17th Street Inn (912-786-0607 or 1-888-909-0607; www.tybeeinn.com), 12 17th Street. Located just a half block from the beach, this small inn offers efficiency apartments with kitchenettes and private porches. Smoking on porches or decks only. Not wheelchair accessible. $125–210.

HISTORIC INNS AND HOTELS

In Savannah

🏊 ♿ 🏨 **East Bay Inn** (912-238-1225 or 1-800-500-1225; www.eastbayinn.com), 225 East Bay Street. The location alone, just across from Factors Walk and River Street, makes this historic hotel—housed in a former cotton warehouse—an attractive place to stay. Charm, romance, elegant decor, and personalized service are important as well. Travelers with a pet, however, choose the East Bay Inn because their four-legged friends are also welcome in specified rooms. Other amenities include a restaurant, deluxe continental breakfast, evening reception, and turndown service with a sweet treat. No smoking. Elevator makes inn fully wheelchair accessible. $119–259.

🏊 ♿ **Marshall House** (912-644-7896 or 1-800-589-6304; www.marshallhouse.com), 123 East Broughton Street. Originally built as a hotel in 1851, the Marshall House declined along with Broughton Street and was closed and decaying for many years. With the renaissance of Broughton Street, however, the hotel was fully restored, reopening in 1999 with a 45 Bistro restaurant and lounge. Today the four-star hotel, which was named the Best Hotel in Savannah by *Connect Savannah* magazine in 2004, blends Savannah's past with stylish decor and all the modern amenities and conveniences. Among them: an elevator for wheelchair access, off-street parking—a premium in Savannah—robes, turndown service, complimentary continental breakfast, an evening reception Sunday–Thursday, and health-club privileges. Artifacts discovered during the renovation are displayed throughout the hotel. No smoking. $99–183.

🏊 ♿ 🏨 **Mulberry Inn** (912-238-1200 or 1-877-488-1200; www.savannahhotel.com), 601 East Bay Street. Located in an elegantly restored former Coca-Cola Bottling Works, this award-winning, full-service hotel features gracious rooms and suites furnished with period reproductions; a charming courtyard and café where breakfast and brunch are served; Sgt. Jasper's Tavern, where dinner is served; afternoon tea with a live pianist; an evening reception Monday–Friday; concierge services; a fitness center; and an outdoor pool and hot tub. Most rooms nonsmoking, but eight rooms reserved for smokers. Rooms are wheelchair accessible, but only four of the bathrooms are fully accessible. Pet friendly up to two pets 50 pounds or less ($75 nonrefundable deposit). $149–389.

𝄢 ☀ **Olde Harbour Inn** (912-234-4100 or 1-800-553-6533; www.oldeharbourinn .com), 508 East Factors Walk. Olde Harbour Inn offers one of the city's best views of the Savannah River and River Street. Built in 1892, the building began life as a cotton warehouse and shipping center. After a brief life as a condominium complex, the structure became an all-suites hotel. Now, each guest chamber is either an efficiency or a full apartment with one or more bedrooms—all furnished in period reproductions. Deluxe continental breakfast and afternoon candlelight wine and hors d'oeuvres provide opportunities for guests to mingle. Pets welcome. No smoking. Not wheelchair accessible. $119–200.

𝄢 ₺ **Planters Inn** (912-232-5678 or 1-800-554-1187; www.plantersinnsavannah), 29 Abercorn Street, Reynolds Square. An intimate historic hotel built in 1912, Planters Inn blends the warmth and charm of a small inn with the services of a large hotel. High-ceilinged guest rooms feature four-poster beds and lavish bed and window coverings done in reproductions of old Savannah fabrics. In-room continental breakfast, afternoon wine and cheese, nightly turndown service, robes, and valet parking round out the amenities. No smoking. An elevator makes accommodations wheelchair accessible. $211–400.

𝄢 ₺ **River Street Inn** (912-234-6400 or 1-800-253-4229; www.riverstreetinn.com), 124 East Bay Street. Offering riverfront hospitality at its best, the historic River Street Inn, built in 1817 as a cotton warehouse, boasts spacious rooms—many with balconies overlooking the river and River Street. With themes that range from sea captain to English chintz, guest chambers feature all the modern conveniences. The hotel also offers three restaurants (Bernie's, Huey's, and Tubby's), an elevator, billiards room, concierge service, hors d'oeuvres reception, and nightly turndown service with a chocolate. Children younger than 16 stay free in the room with parents and using existing bedding. Located on Factors Walk, the hotel has easy access onto East Bay Street and River Street. No smoking. $129–279.

INNS AND HOTELS

In Savannah

₺ **Mansion on Forsyth Park** (912-238-5158 or 1-888-213-3671; www.mansionon forsythpark.com), 700 Drayton Street. This chic and luxurious four-diamond hostelry offers irresistible accommodations, culinary experiences, and spa services in a restored 1888 historic property around which an addition was built. A successful blend of old and new, the property features dramatic architecture, lavish interiors, and lush gardens. Some guest rooms feature whirlpool tubs. Amenities include the four-star full-service Poseidon Spa, fitness center, 700 Drayton gourmet restaurant, 700 Kitchen cooking school, a lounge with live entertainment, Grand Bohemian Art Gallery, outdoor pool, 24-hour concierge, and business services. No smoking. Some rooms wheelchair accessible. $229–349.

𝄢 ₺ **Savannah Marriott Riverfront** (912-233-7722 or 1-800-228-9290; www .marriott.com/hotels/travel/savrf-savannah -marriott-riverfront/), 100 General McIntosh Boulevard. Overlook the Savannah River from your spacious room. The 346-room, 41-suite hotel offers a concierge level, indoor and outdoor pools, whirlpool, fitness facility, a spa, and two restaurants. The hotel is just a short stroll from River Street and Riverwalk. No smoking. No pets. $219–279.

RESORTS

In Savannah

⚓ ♿ ❀ **Westin Savannah Harbor Golf Resort and Spa** (912-201-2000 or 1-800-937-8461; www.westinsavannah.com), One Resort Drive. A AAA four-diamond resort located on Hutchinson Island on the Savannah River across from the historic district, the Westin is Savannah's newest luxury hotel. In addition to more than 400 rooms with Westin's signature beds and baths, the resort hotel features a restaurant and lounge, fitness center, riverside Jacuzzi, cabanas, heated pool, four lighted tennis courts, and a 400-foot water dock. The property also boasts a championship golf course designed by Sam Snead and Robert Cupp, as well as the renowned Greenbrier Spa. Water-taxi service is available to River Street and downtown Savannah. The hotel is adjacent to the Savannah International Trade and Convention Center. No smoking. Pet friendly. $299–409.

On Tybee Island

⚓ ♿ **Ocean Plaza Resort** (912-786-7777; www.oceanplaza.com), 1401 Strand Avenue. Tybee Island's only large hotel, the Ocean Plaza features 215 rooms and suites, many of them oceanfront. The hotel also features two swimming pools and a poolside bar in season. The hotel's Dolphin Reef Restaurant and Lounge, which is open daily for breakfast, lunch, and dinner, specializes in seafood and steaks. No smoking. Free parking for guests—a premium on Tybee Island. $79–299.

✳ Where to Eat

Savannah is a virtual cornucopia of award-winning restaurants featuring eclectic cuisines ranging from lowcountry and other Southern traditional favorites to ethnic cuisines such as Asian, Caribbean, English, French, Greek, Irish, Italian, Moroccan, and Southwestern, to name a few. Tybee Island is noted for its plentitude of casual seafood eateries, although it also has several outstanding upscale restaurants. When eating out in Savannah and Tybee Island, it's best to forget the diet and leave the calorie counter at home.

DINING OUT

In Savannah

⚓ ♿ **Chart House Restaurant** (912-234-6686; www.chart-house.com), 202 West Bay Street. Open 11–close daily. Although part of a national chain, each Chart House Restaurant is located in a historically significant building that has been lovingly restored. The Savannah location is no different, occupying a converted sugar and cotton warehouse reputed to be the oldest masonry building in Georgia. Proceed from raw-bar selections to appetizers, soups, and salads—including the signature Chart House Salad—then move on to fresh fish and seafood specialties or prime rib, steaks, and chicken. Top off your gastronomic delight with a dessert such as Hot Chocolate Lava Cake. No smoking. Wheelchair ramp on Bay Street side. $18–46.

Elizabeth on 37th (912-236-5547; www.elizabethon37th.net), 105 East 37th Street. Open 6–9 daily, until 9:30 on Friday and Saturday. Located in a lavish Greek Revival–style Southern mansion built in 1900, the restaurant was the creation of chef Elizabeth Terry, winner of the prestigious James Beard Award. Terry's devotion to classic Southern cooking led her to extensively research 18th- and 19th-century Savannah cooking in order to create her contemporary recipes. Although she is no longer involved in the restaurant, Terry's culinary legacy is still evident under the direction of her brothers Greg and Gary Butch and head chef Kelly Yambor. Spacious dining rooms exquisitely embellished with beautiful architectural details and a palette of historic Savannah colors and patterns serve as an elegant backdrop for your epicurean delights. Seasonal menus showcase the bounty of local seafood and produce, including herbs and edible flowers from the restaurant's own gardens. Reservations by phone required (e-mail reservations not accepted). No smoking. Not wheelchair accessible. $30–40.

& **Garibaldi** (912-232-7118; www.garibaldi savannah.com), 315 West Congress Street. Open 5:30–10:30 Monday–Thursday, 5–midnight Friday and Saturday, 5–10:30 Sunday. Garibaldi serves local seafood specialties such as flounder and tuna, creative chicken and veal entrées, and other European dishes with an Italian flair. Blending the old with the new, the restaurant is housed in a historic 1871 firehouse filled with colorful impressionistic murals. The crowd tends to be young and lively. Start with the house favorite, calamari, and finish with a sinful dessert. No smoking. $14–40.

Olde Pink House (912-232-4286), 23 Abercorn Street. Open 5:30–10 Sunday–Thursday, 5:30–11 Friday and Saturday. Contemporary and colonial Georgian and Caribbean-influenced cuisine is served in one of Savannah's oldest mansions, built in 1771. Signature dishes include crispy scorched flounder, crab-stuffed grouper, and rack of lamb. Reservations are essential. No smoking. Not wheelchair accessible. $16–28.

& ♪ & **The Pirates' House** (912-233-5757; www.thepirateshouse.com), 20 East Broad Street. Open 6–9 Monday–Thursday, 6–9:30 Friday and Saturday. Originally an inn for seafarers, this 1753 tavern reportedly became a rendezvous for bloodthirsty pirates. In fact, rumors persist that a tunnel extends from the old rum cellar under the Captain's Room to the river and that drunken sailors were carried unconscious through the tunnel to ships waiting in the harbor. What's more, some of the action in Robert Louis Stevenson's *Treasure Island* is supposed to have occurred at the Pirates' House. Old Captain Flint, who originally buried the treasure, is supposed to have died here with cohort Billy Bones at his side. Pages from a rare early edition of the book decorate the walls in some of the 15 dining rooms. Today, the site's treasure is its delicious food—particularly its seafood and Southern specialties—drink, and rousing good times. No smoking. Wheelchair ramp into restaurant, but may be small steps inside. $15–30; Southern buffet $13.95.

& & **The River House** (912-234-1900 or 1-800-317-1912; www.riverhouseseafood .com), 125 West River Street. Open 11–10 daily, until 11 Friday and Saturday, opens at 11:30 Sunday. This popular restaurant is located in a converted 1850s cotton warehouse, where you can sit riverside and watch the ships and tugs sail by while savoring genuine Savannah flavors, fresh seafood dishes, steaks, chops, chicken, and home-baked breads and desserts. Some signature dishes include pecan-encrusted tilapia and lowcountry grits, yellowfin tuna, or veal chop au poivre, as well as po'boys and pizzettas. No smoking. For wheelchair access, ask staff to open special door. Lunch $10–15, dinner $10–30.

17 Hundred 90 Restaurant (912-236-7122; www.17hundred90.com), 307 East President Street. Restaurant open 11:30–2 weekdays, 5:30–10 nightly. Pub open 11–11; happy hour with hors d'oeuvres 4–7. This restaurant delivers a fine-dining experience: wonderful entrées and professional service in an elegant setting with original brick floors and fireplaces. Lunch menus feature soups, salads, sandwiches, and entrées such as crabcakes, pasta, catch of the day, and chicken. Dinner entrées feature seafood, veal, rack of lamb, and beef. *Georgia Trend* singled out the restaurant as a favorite spot for "financiers, business people, and professionals." *Gourmet* and *Travelhost* magazines have heaped accolades on it as well. The restaurant's pub has been a local hangout for years—especially with its popular happy hour. No smoking. Not wheelchair accessible. Lunch under $10, dinner $20–32.

On Tybee Island

& & **Sundae Café and Deli** (912-786-7694), 304 First Street/US 80 East. Open 11–9 Monday–Saturday. Tucked in an unassuming strip center is a fine-dining restaurant that serves lunch and dinner. Tablecloths, cloth napkins, and flickering candlelight set the stage for entrées such as black and white sesame–encrusted yellowfin tuna, char-grilled filet mignon, bacon-wrapped and crab-stuffed jumbo shrimp, and other delicacies. No smoking.

Lunch $6.50–23, lunch specials $8, dinner $16–29.

EATING OUT

In Savannah

🦐 ♿ **Crystal Beer Parlor** (912-349-1000; www.crystalbeerparlor.com), 301 West Jones Street. Open 11–10 Sunday–Thursday, 11–11 Friday and Saturday. Locals and visitors frequent the Crystal Beer Parlor for American fare and laid-back entertainment on Friday nights. The old speakeasy-style restaurant began during Prohibition in the 1930s, and it is the second-oldest restaurant/bar in Savannah. No smoking. $10–25.

🦐 ♿ **Huey's** (912-234-7385), 115 River Street. Open 7 AM–10 PM Monday–Thursday, 7 AM–11 PM Friday, 8 AM–11 PM Saturday, 8 AM–10 PM Sunday. Whether you just want a beignet (a square, holeless doughnut covered in powdered sugar) or a New Orleans–inspired meal of po'boys, red beans and rice, jambalaya, or other Cajun favorites, this fun eatery is the place to go. A table outside or by the window allows diners to people-watch while getting a glimpse of the ships and other boats plying the river. If you eat outside, you can bring your dog. When we asked for a bowl of water for our two cocker spaniels, they were supplied with a porcelain bowl with a lemon wedge on the edge. No smoking. Lunch $8–12, dinner $14–32.

🦐 ♿ **The Lady & Sons** (912-233-2600; www.ladyandsons.com), 102 West Congress Street. Open 11–whenever Monday–Saturday, 11–5 Sunday. There probably isn't a person in America now who doesn't know who Paula Deen is. This is her original restaurant, which she started with her sons. Voted the best buffet in Savannah by *Connect Savannah* magazine, this restaurant serves Southern cuisine some call Georgia Coastal and others call Plantation Country. We just call it good. Favorites include Southern fried chicken, collard greens, barbecued pork ribs, lowcountry boil, and macaroni and cheese, but there's much more comfort food from which to choose. Reservations aren't taken, but they start taking names on a first-come, first-

served basis at 9:30 AM. No smoking. Lunch and dinner buffet $15.99, à la carte entrées $18–28.

🦐 ♿ **Mrs. Wilkes Dining Room** (912-232-5997; www.mrswilkes.com), 107 Jones Street. Open for lunch 11–2 weekdays. Although the inimitable Mrs. Wilkes passed on to culinary heaven in 2002 at age 95, family members still operate the famous restaurant where folks come from all over for a bountiful, all-you-can-eat, down-home Southern feast served family-style. Your guaranteed-to-be-interesting table mates may be from anywhere in the world. Neither credit cards nor reservations are accepted. Get in line early if you don't want to be disappointed. No smoking. $16 flat fee, $8 for children 12 and younger.

On Tybee Island

♿ **A-J's Dockside Restaurant** (912-786-9533; www.devivohosting1.com/ajs docksidetybee), 1315 Chatham Avenue. Open 4–10 Monday–Thursday, until 11 Friday and Saturday, lunch only 11–4 on Sunday. Don't be discouraged by the unimpressive streetside facade of this delightful eatery—all the action is on the dock jutting out into the Back River, where you can watch the glorious sunsets (there are a few tables inside and on a covered deck for the occasional rainy day). A wide variety of appetizers, soups, salads, sandwiches, and entrées such as shrimp Creole, jambalaya pasta, rib eye, pork chops, and more satisfy any appetite. Diners may come by car or boat, and there is live entertainment in season. No smoking inside. Wheelchair accessible (if arriving by boat, ramp from boat dock very steep at low tide). Lunch $7–16, dinner $13–33.

🦐 ♿ **The Breakfast Club** (912-786-5984), 1500 Butler Avenue. Open 7–1 daily. Frequented by locals and consistently voted the best place for breakfast in the Savannah area, this very casual restaurant offers simple, hearty breakfast and lunch fare for the budget-conscious traveler. Primary to the menu are ice-cold, fresh-squeezed orange juice, and eggs just about any way you like them—including a variety of omelets with names such as Father Guido Sarducci—

accompanied by grits and toast. Hash browns and waffles also figure prominently. Lunch items include burgers, sandwiches, and specials. After such a huge meal, you'll have plenty of energy for a long walk on the beach or a bike ride. No smoking. $6–14.

✿ ✍ ✦ **The Crab Shack at Chimney Creek** (912-786-9857; www.thecrabshack .com), 40-A Estill Hammock Road. Open 11:30–10 daily. Billed as "Where the Elite Eat in Their Bare Feet," the Crab Shack has been a local tradition since 1983. What began as a fishing camp is now a popular, casual, indoor-outdoor eatery that serves all kinds of seafood. Naturally, crabs of all types top the menu, but you can feast on clams, oysters, shrimp, and lowcountry boil. The occasional diner who doesn't care for seafood can choose from chicken, ribs, pork, chili, and hot dogs. Picnic tables have a hole in the middle and a trash can underneath so you can dispose of your shells.

Paper towels serve as napkins. You get the picture. A gift shop and a pool of tiny alligators offer some distractions for those waiting in line, a given in season. Food pellets for the gators $3. You also can have your boat put in or taken out of the water here. No smoking inside. $4–40.

✿ ✍ ✦ **Huc-A-Poo's Bites and Booze** (912-786-5900; www.hucapoos.com), 1213 US 80 in the Shops at Tybee Oaks. Open 4–midnight weekdays, 11 AM–midnight Saturday and Sunday. Tucked away in a shady grove, Huc-A-Poo's (named after a race-horse) is a casual eatery that specializes in build-your-own pizzas, wraps, nachos, hot dogs, gyros, chili, and a large selection of beers. There's some inside seating, but most folks elect to sit on the huge deck. A full bar, live entertainment, children's play area, and some games of skill make this a fun place to spend an afternoon or evening. No smoking allowed. $15–18.

THE CRAB SHACK

The ramshackle appearance of the building and grounds—the name, after all, is "Shack"—just points out that this is an old fishing camp grown up. Since the 1930s, there has been some kind of fish camp on these 4 acres of high ground overlooking Chimney Creek. In the beginning, locals put their boats in the water here and bought bait and simple "necessaries"—which included cold beer. Then spaces were rented out for a few small camper trailers, and the Chimney Creek Fishing Camp was born.

Jack and Belinda Flanigan, displaced locals who had left the area for the frenetic pace of Atlanta, decided to return to their roots when the fish camp was for sale in 1983. At first they ran the camp and marina while studying for their captain's licenses. Soon Jack was running off-shore charters and Belinda was running inshore fishing trips, and both were hearing that their guests wanted a place to gather and cook the crabs, shrimp, and fish they had caught. So a table appeared here and there, and locals, friends, and strangers soon followed.

A business license was obtained in 1987, and the Crab Shack was born. Jack did the cooking, and Belinda waited tables. Then folks wanted a libation with their meal. A liquor license came next, and the Flanigans and their friends had an old-fashioned barn raising, but this one was a "bar raising." (No longer married, Jack and Belinda are still business partners in the enterprise.)

Now picnic tables cover several decks and fill screened buildings where folks can still enjoy a meal on a rainy day. Relics from the old days—including the marina and bait-shop building from the '30s, which now houses the Gift Shack, and the restroom building from the '50s—contribute to the overall dilapidated look. But they don't detract from the picturesque location where you can watch dolphins play or gaze at the stunning sunsets as you dine alfresco amid hundred-year-old live oaks. Come by boat or car, in your shorts or your bathing suit, and you'll be perfectly at home at the Crab Shack.

🦐 🍴 ♿ **North Beach Grill** (912-786-4442; www.NorthBeachBarandGrill.net), 33 Meddin Drive. Open 11:30–10 daily in season; call ahead for winter hours. Don't be put off by the shanty appearance; there's good food and good times in store. The cuisine is innovative, Caribbean-inspired fare such as grilled plantains with chutney, conch fritters and fish tacos, or a chunky crabmeat sandwich. The menu also offers the usual burgers, hot dogs, and wings for lunch, and jerk pork or chicken, duck, and rib eye for dinner. Top off your meal with a Red Stripe beer, and you'd swear you were in the islands. No smoking inside. Lunch $7–13, dinner $15–19.

🦐 🍴 **Sunrise** (912-786-7473), 1511 Butler Avenue. Open 6–2 daily. While tourists are lined up to get into the Breakfast Club, locals stroll on over to the less-crowded Sunrise for a hearty breakfast or lunch. All kinds of eggs, omelets, pancakes, waffles, and French toast fill the breakfast menu. Sandwiches, burgers, steaks, chicken, and salads make up the lunch menu. A breakfast buffet is served on weekends and holidays, and a lunch buffet on weekdays. No smoking. Not wheelchair accessible. $2–10.

TEAROOMS

In Savannah

🦐 🍴 ♿ **Gryphon Tea Room** (912-525-5880), 337 Bull Street. Open 8:30 AM–9:30 PM weekdays, 10–9:30 Saturday. Owned by the Savannah College of Art and Design, the Gryphon is located in the meticulously restored former A. A. Solomon's and Company drugstore, which has been converted to resemble a Parisian tearoom while retaining many of the architectural features of the old apothecary, such as the Tiffany glass globes featuring the gryphons that lend the tearoom its name. The Gryphon serves breakfast and lunch, but the pièce de résistance is afternoon tea served from 4 to 6. There is also a selection of specialty coffees. Selections range from scones, tea sandwiches, and pastries and other sweet delights to deli sandwiches and salads. No smoking. $5–15.

✳ Entertainment

HAUNTED TOURS Savannah claims to be the most haunted city in America, and plenty of strange occurrences have been documented there. Whether or not you believe in the supernatural, these tours, which usually gather after dark in a central location, are mesmerizing. One is offered by **Hauntings Tours** (912-441-9277; www.hauntingstour.com). Adults $20, children 6–14 $7.

Another is the **Creepy Crawl: Haunted Pub Tour,** operated by Savannah by Foot Tours (912-238-3843; www.savannahtours .com/CreepyCrawl.htm). Voted Savannah's Best Tour by *Connect Savannah* magazine, the Creepy Crawl is an enjoyable after-dark walk with spirited tales of ghosts, witchery, and voodoo, along with stops (and drinks) at some of Savannah's most interesting pubs. Reservations required. $20 per person, not including gratuities; $18 online.

MUSIC Jazz has been a tradition in Savannah since Reconstruction-era brass bands were popular in the city. Vaudeville, ragtime, and rhythm and blues followed. Today, contemporary jazz stylings can be heard at various venues, and a plentitude of musical performances can be heard at theaters, houses of worship, and festivals. Music is integral to the **St. Patrick's Day** celebration as well as the **Savannah Music Festival** and **Savannah Jazz Festival** (see *Special Events*).

Savannah is also part of the **Georgia Music Trail,** which includes Atlanta, Athens, and Macon, too. For more information on the trail, consult www.georgia.org /tourism/music_trail/index.asp.

🍴 ♿ **Savannah Theatre** (box office: 912-233-7764; www.savannahtheatre.com), Savannah Theatre, 222 Bull Street, Chippewa Square, Savannah. The restored theater is a perfect venue for an annual season of five plays, the majority of which are musicals. Check the website or call for a schedule of performances. Adults generally $35, children $16.

& **Savannah Philharmonic Orchestra** (tickets: 912-525-5050; information: 912-232-6002; www.savannahphilharmonic.org), 225 Abercorn Street, Savannah. Box office open 9–5 weekdays. Check the website or call for a schedule of events and prices. Savannah's orchestra is one of only two fully professional orchestras in Georgia (Atlanta's is the other). The yearly nine-concert Masterworks series is performed at the historic **Lucas Theatre** (see *Theater*).

NIGHTSPOTS As much as there is to do in Savannah during the day, the city really sparkles at night, with a variety of clubs featuring jazz and blues, Latin salsa, bluegrass, swing, oldies, and every genre in between.

Club 1 (912-232-0200; www.clubone-online.com), One Jefferson Street, Savannah. Open 5 PM–3 AM Monday–Saturday, until 2 AM Sunday. Club 1 has been voted Savannah's top dance club since 1997 by readers of *Connect Savannah* magazine. Activities include trivia night, talent night, Gothic and show night, karaoke, and bingo, but the premier event is a not-to-be-missed monthly appearance by the one-and-only Lady Chablis of *Midnight in the Garden of Good and Evil* fame (check the website or call for her schedule). Smoking permitted. Wheelchair accessible on first floor only. *Note:* Shows are on the second floor, which is not wheelchair accessible. $6 general admission, $10 for a show, $27 for Lady Chablis.

& **Savannah Smiles Dueling Pianos Saloon** (912-527-6453; www.savannah smilesduelingpianos.com), 314-B Williamson Street, Savannah. Open 5 PM–3 AM Wednesday–Friday, 5:30 PM–3 AM Saturday, 5:30 PM–2 AM Sunday. Piano entertainment 8:45 PM–1:30 AM Wednesday, 8:30 PM–2:30 AM Thursday–Saturday. Get there early, because this nightspot with continuous dueling piano music is so popular that parking is at a premium and the venue fills up fast. Pub grub is served. Smoking allowed. $5 cover charge; food $5–10.

& **Tubby's Tank House** (912-233-0770), 115 East River Street, Savannah. Open 11–10 Monday–Thursday and Sunday, 11–11 Friday and Saturday. Tubby's offers a happy hour and live entertainment (weather permitting) daily on River Street's largest balcony, as well as seafood, sandwiches, and the like. Smoking outside only. $11–30.

& **Wet Willie's** (912-233-5650; www.wetwillies.com/locations/Savannah.html), 101 East River Street, Savannah. Open 11 AM–1 AM Monday–Thursday, 11 AM–2 AM Friday and Saturday, 12:30 PM–1 AM Sunday. Now with several locations nationwide, Wet Willie's started right here on Savannah's River Street in 1989. Famous for its daiquiris and other frozen drinks with names such as Sex on the Beach, Shock Treatment, and Willie's Electric Tea, the establishment also offers live entertainment including disc jockeys, karaoke, dancing, and trivia contests. A location on Tybee Island is in the works. No smoking. $2–7.

PROFESSIONAL SPORTS

& **Savannah Sand Gnats** (912-351-9150; www.sandgnats.com), 140 East Victory Drive at Bee Road, Savannah (mailing address: P.O. Box 3783, Savannah 31414). The minor-league team, an affiliate of the New York Mets, competes in the Class-A South Atlantic League. The team plays about 70 home games at Grayson Stadium in Daffin Park between April and Labor Day. Tickets can be purchased at the gate, online, or by calling ahead.

THEATER & **The Lucas Theatre** (912-525-5040; www.lucastheatre.com), 32 Abercorn Street, Reynolds Square, Savannah. Guided tours of the theater 10–4 Tuesday–Friday. The Lucas Theatre is an icon of a bygone era. Built in 1921 as the first and only movie palace in Savannah, the opulent Italian Renaissance theater contains 1,250 seats. It closed in 1976, and although it was once slated for demolition, the theater was saved and fully restored, including its majestic 40-foot-wide ceiling dome, intricately detailed Adam-style plasterwork, Wedgwood-inspired colors, and gold-leaf accents. It reopened in 2000 and today is a premier performing arts center offering musical theater, classic performances, and concerts by the Savannah Philharmonic and touring top artists. Check the website or call for a schedule of events and prices.

♭ **Trustees Theater** (box office: 912-525-5050; www2.scad.edu/venues/trustees), 216 East Broughton Street, Savannah. Formerly the Weis Theater, Trustees was once part of Savannah's thriving post–World War II theater district. It claimed to be fireproof, had one of the largest movie screens in the Southeast, had air-conditioning, and was lavishly decorated in the Art Moderne style. As in other cities, the theater and others nearby failed as movie theaters followed residents to the suburbs, and it closed in 1980. Fortunately, it was bought and restored by the Savannah College of Art and Design and now plays host to the school's productions, student film screenings, national headline acts, concerts, lectures, and the annual Savannah Film and Video Festival. Check the website or call for a schedule of events and prices.

✱ Selective Shopping

Quaint ballast stone streets along Savannah's River Street and Factors Walk are lined with shops and boutiques purveying everything from pralines to kites to nautical-themed apparel and gifts. Several blocks away, but still within the historic district, City Market—known as the "Art and Soul of Savannah"—is a four-block courtyard alive with art studios, galleries, specialty shops, restaurants, and nightspots. Bull and Broughton streets are the heart of Savannah's antiques district.

Tybee Island has a growing number of upscale galleries and shops, but shopping there is primarily limited to beach clothing, equipment, and souvenirs.

ANTIQUES Clipper Trading Company, Inc. (912-238-3660 or 1-800-390-0498; www.clippertrading.com), 201 West Broughton Street, Savannah. Open 10–6 Monday–Saturday. Clipper Trading imports artwork, antique furniture, china, collectibles, crafts, and home accent pieces from Southeast Asia and China.

ART GALLERIES City Market Art Center (912-232-4903; www.savannahcitymarket.com/art), 204 West St. Julian Street, City Market, Savannah. Hours vary on weekdays; open most weekends. The center is actually a community of 21 working artists who make and sell their work in studio and gallery lofts.

Gallery by the Sea (912-786-7979; www.gallerybythesea.com), 1016 US 80 East at Campbell Avenue, Tybee Island. Open 9–5:30 daily. Home to the artists of the Tybee Arts Association, the gallery shows the work of local and regional artists.

Ray Ellis Gallery (1-800-752-4865; www.rayellis.com), 205 West Congress Street, Savannah. Open 10–4 Monday–Saturday. The gallery exhibits the watercolors, oils, and bronzes of Ray Ellis exclusively, as well as limited- and open-edition prints and books.

BOOKS E. Shaver, Bookseller (912-234-7257), 326 Bull Street, Savannah. Open 9:30–5:30 Monday–Saturday. With 12 rooms of books, this exceptional bookstore offers an extensive collection of hardbacks and paperbacks, specializing in architecture, decorative arts, and regional history. The shop also carries antique maps.

FLEA MARKETS ♭ Keller's Flea Market (912-927-4848; www.ilovefleas.com), 5901 Ogeechee Road, Savannah. Open 8–6 every weekend year-round. The full-service flea market includes 600 stalls where you can find just about anything. Look for the giant cow. The site also includes restaurants and camping facilities for the serious shopper. No pets allowed. Free parking and admission.

FOOD Savannah is known for its pralines and other sweets. The following stores sell everything your sweet tooth could desire.

River Street Sweets (912-234-4608 or 1-800-793-3876; www.riverstreetsweets.com), 13 East River Street, Savannah. Open

9 AM–11 PM daily. This is Savannah's original candy store, and it's where you can find its world-famous pralines as well as gourmet Southern candies and gift baskets.

Savannah Candy Kitchen (912-233-8411; www.savannahcandy.com), 225 East River Street, Savannah. Open 9:30 AM–10 PM daily, until 11 Friday and Saturday. Pecan pralines and fudge are specialties, but the sweetshop also sells cakes, pies, and gift baskets. There's another location at City Market.

OUTLET MALLS Savannah Festival Factory Stores (912-925-3089), 11 Gateway Boulevard, Savannah. Open 10 AM–9 PM Monday–Saturday, 11–6 Sunday. The facility features a restaurant and 30 brand-name outlet stores, including Bass Outlet, Bon Worth, Book Warehouse, Dress Barn, Paper Factory, Rack Room Shoes, Samsonite, and Van Heusen.

SPECIAL STORES "The Book" Gift Shop and Midnight Museum (912-233-3867; www.midnightinsavannah.com), 127 East Gordon Street, Calhoun Square, Savannah. Open 10:30–5 Monday–through Saturday, 12:30–4:30 Sunday. Your one-stop shop for fine Savannah gifts is the city's only official headquarters for *Midnight* information, products, and memorabilia, including autographed books. The shop also offers daily bus and walking tours to sites described in "the Book."

The Christmas Shop (912-234-5343; www.the-christmas-shop.com), 307 Bull Street, Savannah. Open 9:30–6 Monday–Saturday, noon–3 Sunday. Shop here for the finest in Christmas collectibles, ornaments, and decorations, as well as designer jewelry and handbags, and infant and children's clothing.

Saints and Shamrocks (912-233-8858; www.saintsandshamrocks.com), 309 Bull Street, Savannah. Open 9:30–5:30 Monday–Saturday. The city is so Irish, it's only natural that an Irish-themed store would find its home there. The family-owned Saints and Shamrocks is a tasteful, upscale book, gift, and religious gift shop. No trashy souvenirs cluttering the shelves here.

✳ Special Events

Known as the "Hostess City of the South," Savannah boasts more than 200 citywide festivals and events each year, so there's bound to be something to appeal to every traveler, no matter what your age group or interests. Among the premier events in the city and on Tybee Island are these:

February: The **Savannah Black Heritage Festival** (912-358-4309; www.savannah blackheritagefestival.com) includes a variety of cultural activities presented by Savannah State University and the City of Savannah's Department of Cultural Affairs. Grand Festival Day features music, dance, youth talent shows, visual arts, drama, tours, and more. Free.

The **Savannah Irish Festival** (information: 912-604-8298; box office: 1-800-351-7469; www.savannahirish.org) celebrates everything Irish and features Irish music and Irish step dancing. Check the website for a schedule of events. $12.

March: A Savannah tradition since 1824, the annual **St. Patrick's Day Parade** (912-233-4804; www.savannahsaintpatricksday.com) is the second largest in the nation. In addition to the parade, three days of activities create a nonstop party. Be prepared for green water in the fountains, green fireworks, pets adorned in green costumes, and green food and beverages. Parade and most activities free. Be sure to book lodging far

EVEN PETS CELEBRATE AT SAVANNAH'S ANNUAL ST. PATRICK'S DAY PARADE.

in advance. Some lodgings are booked a year in advance. Most require a three-night minimum, and their rates are higher than normal.

Truly "Southern, Soulful, and Sophisticated," the **Savannah Music Festival** (912-234-3378; box office: 912-525-5050; www.savannahmusicfestival.org) is a two-week musical feast offering one-time-only performances and world premieres showcasing blues, jazz, and other indigenous music from the Deep South; newly composed chamber music; ballet; and internationally renowned musicians in concert. Some events free; other events $5–75. Check the website or call for a schedule and prices.

The annual **Tour of Homes and Gardens** (912-234-8054; www.savannahtourofhomes .org) offers self-guided walking tours of private homes and gardens in the historic district. Walking tour $35, special events and seminars $45, other activities vary.

April or May: **Fine Arts on the River Festival** (912-234-0295; www.riverstreet savannah.com), sponsored by the Savannah Art Association, showcases the best in Savannah's visual and performing arts. This major arts festival includes a juried art exhibit, an arts and crafts show, performances by the Savannah Philharmonic and other groups, food, a wine tasting, and children's activities. Fireworks serve as a grand finale. Free.

May: The **SCAD Sand Arts Festival** (912-525-5225; www.scad.edu), held near the lighthouse on Tybee Island, features competitions among students from the Savannah College of Art and Design (SCAD) using sand and natural beach objects such as shells, pebbles, driftwood, and seaweed to create sand castles, sand sculptures, sand reliefs, wind sculptures, and the best representation of an underwater sea creature.

The only binding agent permitted is water. As many as 155 teams and 450 students have competed for the $5,000 in prizes. The competition regularly draws 5,000 spectators. Free.

September: The **Savannah Jazz Festival** (www.savannahjazzzfestival.org or www .coastal-jazz.org) showcases the best in local and regional jazz artists at venues in City Market and Forsyth Park. Free.

October: **Tybee Island Pirate Festival** (www.tybeepiratefest.com). Well shiver me timbers! Ahoy there, mateys. Held in the South Beach parking lot at Tybrisa and the Strand near the pier, this popular event features a parade; separate costume contests for adults, children, and pets; a dance—in costume, of course; grog and grub; Little Matey's Cove, an area for children's activities; and more. Tickets are $15 in advance, $20 at the gate; children 12 and younger free.

December: **Savannah Holly Days Festival** (912-944-0455; www.savannahholly days.com) includes a festival of trees, open houses at shops and artists' studios, tours of homes and inns, a holiday door contest, parade, arts and crafts festival, live performances, Holly Jolly Trolley Tours, a Gingerbread Village, a Santa Train, and more. Among the much-anticipated events is the **Christmas Lighted Boat Parade** (1-800-786-6404). Some activities free; others have a fee. Check the website or call for a schedule of events and prices.

The annual **Tybee Island Christmas Boat Parade** (912-786-5444; www.tybeeforthe holidays.com) features whimsically decorated boats. Other holiday festivities include the Christmas Parade, with Santa and Mrs. Claus arriving on a fire engine. The season closes with the annual Polar Bear Plunge on New Year's Day. Most activities free.

WAYCROSS

Waycross, at the northern end of the 450,000-acre Okefenokee National Wildlife Refuge, offers something for everyone. History buffs will be enthralled by the Okefenokee Heritage Center and the Southern Forest World museums. For the nature-minded, the Okefenokee Swamp offers a glimpse of a one-of-a-kind ecosystem. Catch all the history and cultural exhibits at Obediah's Okefenok and the Okefenokee Swamp Park's pioneer area, where you can see what life was like for the early settlers of this unusual area. Train enthusiasts will be dumbstruck by "Rice Yard," the second-largest computerized rail yard for CSX in the United States. It can be studied in comfort from the patio area at the visitors center in downtown Waycross. While there, be sure to pick up a copy of the *Historic Walking Tour* guide, which will lead visitors on a tour that details the pioneer, Native American, and environmental history of this area.

Waycross owes its development to the Plant System Railroad, which laid tracks in this area in the mid-1800s. As railroad traffic increased, the prosperity of the town grew. Today, the railroad is still the number-one employer in the county. The Waycross Tourism Bureau and Visitor Center, the Waycross–Ware County Chamber of Commerce, and other local businesses are housed in the restored train depot.

Waycross is also home to the Green Frog, a restaurant built in the 1930s by the Dardin brothers, who went on to found the Red Lobster restaurant chain. Other famous natives include Pernell Roberts, Gram Parsons, Ozzie Davis, and Burt Reynolds. Interestingly, alligators outnumber people in this fascinating region. Do not touch, taunt, or feed them, especially the babies. The mother is always nearby, and they are very fast, even on land.

GUIDANCE When planning a trip to the Waycross area, contact the **Waycross Tourism Bureau and Visitor Center** (912-283-3744; www.swampgeorgia.com), 315-A Plant Avenue, Waycross 31501. Open 9–5 weekdays.

Visitors planning a trip to Baxley should contact the **Baxley–Appling County Board of Tourism** (912-367-7731; www.baxley.org), 305 West Parker Street, Baxley 31513. Open 8–5 weekdays.

For information about Douglas, contact the **Douglas–Coffee County Chamber of Commerce and Welcome Center** (912-384-1873 or 1-888-426-3334; www.douglasga.org), 212 South Gaskin Avenue, Douglas 31533. Open 8–5 weekdays.

GETTING THERE *By air:* Fly into **Macon** or **Atlanta** (for either, see "What's Where in Georgia").

By car: Waycross is located at the junctions of US 1, 82, and 84 in the southeastern corner of Georgia, situated at the northern edge of the Okefenokee National Park and Wilderness

Area. Jesup is located off I-95 about 60 miles south of Savannah and about 60 miles north of Jacksonville, Florida.

By train: **AMTRAK** (1-800-872-7245; www.amtrak.com), 176 NW Broad Street, has been stopping in Jesup since the 1980s. The station is open 30 minutes prior to arrival, but there is no staff at this station. Contact AMTRAK directly or see a local travel agent for tickets.

MEDICAL EMERGENCY Call 911.

VILLAGES Alma got its name by combining the first three letters of four of Georgia's past and current capitals: Augusta, Louisville, Milledgeville, and, of course, Atlanta. The people of this agrarian community are truly friendly, perhaps due to the slower pace of life here. When driving the winding country roads, however, you'll see more soybeans, corn, tobacco, cotton, and blueberries than people.

Tiny **Baxley** is the county seat of Appling County. Like Waycross, Baxley, once known as "Station Number Seven," came into being largely due to the railroad. Caroline Miller (Georgia's first Pulitzer Prize winner) was living here when she wrote *Lamb in His Bosom* in the early 1930s, and it was in this community that she learned about the dignity and courage of the state's early settlers. Adventurers will enjoy exploring the undimmed Altamaha River, the second-largest watershed on the eastern seaboard. The Nature Conservancy has dubbed it "Georgia's Natural Treasure, One of America's Last Great Places."

Douglas, the county seat of Coffee County, was founded in 1858 and named for Stephen A. Douglas, who challenged Abraham Lincoln for the presidency. Its economy was originally based on the railroads and agriculture. It was a major tobacco market in the 1920s and 1930s. Today agriculture remains important, along with some light manufacturing. The town is located in some of the most beautiful land in Georgia. Broxton Rocks, one of the 30 Natural Wonders of Georgia, is just one of the attractions. Several others have been named Georgia Hidden Treasures. Hiking, hunting, fishing, horseback riding, and relaxing are popular pastimes, but there are numerous other diversions.

Modern downtown **Hazlehurst** features a historic district with many specialty stores. The city also hosts the state's largest horse auction every Friday.

Jesup's local economy has always been heavily influenced by the proximity of the Altamaha River, the railroads, and the timber industry. It has long marked the intersection of the Atlantic and Gulf Railroad (now CXS) and the Macon and Brunswick Railroad (now Norfolk Southern). To this day, these industries are the number-one employers in the county.

✳ To See

FOR FAMILIES ✤ ✿ ♿ **Southern Forest World Museum** (912-285-4056), 1440 North Augusta Avenue, Waycross. Open 10–4 Tuesday–Saturday. Museum visitors can listen to the "talking tree," a model of a loblolly pine tree that tells the story of this species, which dominated the economy of the area for more than a century. Then they can climb the winding stairway built inside a huge pine-tree replica and later get their picture taken inside a huge cypress tree or atop the Agent Lumber Company's No. 3 steam engine. The star attraction is Stuckie, the Petrified Dog (see the "Mummies in America?" sidebar). Free, but donations appreciated.

HISTORIC HOMES AND SITES

✤ ♿ **Ashley-Slater House** (912-384-1873; www.cityofdouglas.com), 212 South Gaskin Avenue, Douglas. Open 8–5 weekdays. One of the most opulent homes in Douglas, the Ashley-Slater House, built in 1912, is a prime example of the Italianate style. Today it serves as a Georgia Regional Information Center. In addition to obtaining tourism information

MUMMIES IN AMERICA?

One of the most fascinating items on exhibit at the Southern Forest World Museum is a mummified dog called Stuckie. Nature, not Egyptian priests, created this mummy. No one knows how long ago it happened, but the dog apparently chased a small animal into a hollow tree and actually climbed up inside the chimneylike space, where he got stuck and died. Instead of decomposing, the dog was mummified by a combination of updrafts, which prevented the scent from attracting predators; the dry environment; and tannic acid in the tree. He was discovered, almost perfectly preserved, when loggers cut down the tree and were cutting it into pulpwood lengths.

about the area, visitors can tour the house and view an original mural, antique furnishings, and a collection of family items including World War II memorabilia, love letters, and photos. Then they can stroll through the gardens and grounds. The home's tragic past includes three deaths, and there's reputed to be a ghost. Limited wheelchair accessibility. Free.

🐾 ♂ ♿ **Obediah's Okefenok** (912-287-0090; www.okefenokeeswamp.com), 5115 Swamp Road, Waycross. Open 10–5 daily. 'Round about 130 years ago, the legendary Obediah Barber was known as the King of the Okefenokee. His homestead, including the original cabin, syrup boiler shelter, smokehouse, potato crib, eight-stall livestock barn, cotton gin, blacksmith's shop, and gristmill, has been preserved as a National Historic Site. Scattered around the site are several small museums containing historic exhibits and artifacts from that time period. The park is also home to animals that are native to the Okefenokee area, and they can be seen along the trails and boardwalk. Adults $6.50, seniors $5.50, children 6–17 $5, children five and younger free.

MUSEUMS 🐾 ♂ ♿ **Appling County Heritage Center** (912-367-8133), 137 Thomas Street, Baxley. Open noon–4:30 Tuesday, Thursday, and Friday. The facility is the repository of the county's historical and genealogical records, as well as an extensive collection of artifacts pertaining to the turpentine industry and exhibits about agriculture, African American history, and war history. Among the displays are 19th- and 20th-century memorabilia, county architectural items, and collections and publications by local historians. Free.

🐾 ♂ **Glennville-Tattnall Museum** (912-654-3756 or 912-654-2823), South Hillman Street, Glennville. Open 9–4 Monday–Friday. This museum houses a collection of exhibits relating to art, science, and local culture and history. Its goal is to teach "young people to learn from the past, live in the present, and plan for the future." Favorite exhibits include a turpentine still, Native American artifacts, and an old-time kitchen. Youngsters particularly enjoy the old-fashioned classroom. Free, but donations accepted.

🐾 ♂ ♿ **Heritage Station Museum** (912-389-3461; www.cityofdouglas.com), 219 West Ward Street, Douglas. Open 10–4 Thursday–Saturday. Located in the historic 1905 Georgia & Florida Railroad Depot, the museum displays railroad history through original G&F documents, furnishings, and period clothing. In addition, the center exhibits Douglas and Coffee County history. Adults $1.

🐾 ♂ **Little Red Caboose** (912-427-3233), 101 East Cherry Street, Jesup. Open 1–5 weekdays. The caboose is used as a museum to exhibit Wayne County history from Gen. "Mad" Anthony Wayne to the railroad boom. Free.

🐾 ♂ ♿ **Okefenokee Heritage Center** (912-285-4260; www.okefenokeeheritagecenter.org), 1460 North Augusta Avenue, Waycross. Open 10–4:30 Tuesday–Sunday. The first thing that catches your eye is the 1912 steam locomotive No. 9 sitting outside of the museum. Visitors are encouraged to climb aboard the locomotive as well as the passenger cars. The old train depot and an 1800s cabin are filled with all the necessities of pioneer life, while the museum houses a large Native American exhibit that includes the requisite arrowhead collection, pottery, a campsite display, and tools. Other exhibits focus on African Americans and pioneers, and include walk-through displays of an old Colonial-style home, an early-1900s schoolhouse, and a church. The one-of-a-kind *Sacred Heart Gospel Sing* exhibit is an interactive musical display. $3.

🦐 🌿 ♿ **Pierce County Heritage Museum and Depot** (912-449-7044), 200 South Central Avenue, Blackshear. Open 8–4 weekdays. The 1902 depot houses a museum that exhibits Civil War and local history artifacts. Exhibits pertain to tobacco, farm tools, and a Civil War prison camp. On display are the contents of an early-1900s store and antique courthouse furniture. A genealogical library is also on-site. Free.

🦐 🌿 ♿ **WWII Flight Training Museum** (912-383-9111; www.ww2flighttrainingmuseum .org), 3 Airport Circle, Douglas. Open 11–4 Friday and Saturday. At the outbreak of World War II, the Army Air Corps quickly and drastically expanded its pilot training. With America's entry into the war, training was further expanded by contracting with 45 civilian flying schools to provide primary training. One of those schools was Raymond-Richardson Aviation School in Douglas, where the 63rd Flight Training Detachment received instruction. Numerous improvements were made to the small airport, including the construction of several buildings, most of which survive, making the site the most intact, independent, and freestanding WWII Primary Flight School in the nation. The museum is located in one of the 1941 barracks. The exhibits, which include period military artifacts and homefront memorabilia, are divided into the *Barracks Room, Training, War in the Air,* the *Home Front,* and the library. $1 donation appreciated.

✳ To Do

BIRDING The east entrance to the Okefenokee Swamp has 2.5 miles of hiking trails and a 4,000-foot boardwalk. These wilderness walkways attract hundreds of birdwatchers right about sunset.

CANOE TRIPS See **Canoe Canoe Outfitters** under *To Do—Boating* in the Statesboro chapter in part 3, "Historical South," for guided tours in the Okefenokee Swamp to visit the cypress forests, scrub areas, lakes, and wet prairies. For the really adventurous, arrange an overnight trip where you'll camp on raised wooden platforms by night and during the day visit the islands where Native Americans and early settlers lived. This is a one-of-a-kind chance to visit nature in one of its most unusual environments.

FOR FAMILIES 🦐 🌿 ♿ **Okefenokee Swamp Park** (912-283-0583; www .okeswamp.com), US 1 South, Waycross. Open 9–5:30 daily. Located on the northern edge of the Okefenokee National Wildlife Refuge, the park acts as one of the gateways into the "Land of Trembling Earth"—the Great Okefenokee Swamp— via guided boat tour, train excursion, or on foot. Visitors get a glimpse of the original

CYPRESS TREES, OKEFENOKEE SWAMP PARK

Native American waterways and have a chance to see local wildlife in its natural habitat. The most famous inhabitant of the Okefenokee Swamp was the cartoon character Pogo, created by Walt Kelly. There's an exhibit devoted to them. Guests are also invited to visit Pioneer Island, a re-creation of pioneer life in the swamp, to see the Wildes Cabin Museum. Adults $12; children 3–11, seniors, and military $11; children younger than three free.

GOLF ♘ **The Lakes at Laura Walker Golf Course** (912-285-6154; www.ga stateparks.org/LauraSWalker), 5653 Laura Walker Road, Waycross. This Steve Burns–designed championship golf course uses natural sand for the bunkers. In addition to being a challenging 18-hole course, its proximity to the swamps make it the habitat for local wildlife, including deer, herons, box turtles, quail, red-tailed foxes, and alligators. The course also features a clubhouse, golf pro, unlimited weekday play, and junior/senior discounts. $31–38.50.

THE CARTS ARE READY TO GO AT THE LAKES AT LAURA WALKER GOLF COURSE.

TRAIN EXCURSION ♘ ✎ **Okefenokee Railroad Tour** (912-283-0583; www.okeswamp.com), US 1 South, Waycross. The Lady Suwanee, a 36-gauge replica steam engine with three coaches, operates 9–5 daily except Thanksgiving and Christmas. A 1.5-mile-long train ride takes visitors into the swamp, where they can hear stories about swamp life and see a honeybee farm, turpentine farm, Seminole Indian village, and moonshine still. A stop at Pioneer Island gives visitors a glimpse into the world of this area's early settlers and also features native animals in their own habitat. It also includes a tour of Wildes Cabin Museum and a visit to the country store. Interestingly, the Seminole Indians named this area Okefenokee, or "land of the trembling earth," because of the many floating islands in the swamp. Many of them will support the weight of a person, but when you step on them, they shake. The cost of this unique excursion is included in the admission to Okefenokee Swamp Park (see *For Families*). Adults $12; children 3–11, seniors, and military $11; children three and younger free.

✳ Green Space

LAKES ♘ ✎ **Lake Lindsay Grace** (on US 84, Screven). Open daily. The lake provides numerous opportunities for all water sports. Free.

NATURE PRESERVES AND PARKS ♘ ✎ ♿ **General Coffee State Park** (912-384-7082; lodging reservations: 1-800-864-7275; www.gastateparks.org/GeneralCoffee), 46 John Coffee Road, Nicholls. Open 7 AM–10 PM daily. The 1,511-acre park features a lake, a pitcher-plant bog, and a 4-mile nature trail and boardwalk. Recreational opportunities include boating and fishing. Farm buildings and live animals impart agricultural history.

Children love interacting with the goats, sheep, chickens, pigs, and donkeys. Horseback riding trails are popular; BYOH (bring your own horse). There are seasonal canoe and bike rentals. Camping available (see *Lodging—Campgrounds*). Parking $5; fee for horseback riding trails.

🐾 ✎ ♿ **Laura S. Walker State Park** (912-287-4900; lodging reservations: 1-800-864-7275; www.gastateparks.org/LauraSWalker), 5653 Laura Walker Road, off GA 177, Waycross. Open 7 AM–10 PM daily. One of Georgia's few parks named for a woman, this one honors the Georgia writer, teacher, civic leader, and naturalist who worked for the preservation of trees. The park covers 626 acres, including a 120-acre lake known for its great bass fishing as well as for canoeing, boating, and waterskiing. For those who prefer to stay on land, the park includes 3 miles of nature trails that meander through the loblolly pines and show off the natural beauty of the area. Keep an eye out for carnivorous pitcher plants, saw palmettos, and various oaks, as well as wildlife such as the shy gopher tortoise, yellow-shafted flickers, warblers, owls, great blue herons, and even alligators. The park also features a golf course (see *To Do—Golf*). Other recreational opportunities include a fishing dock, boat ramp, and canoe rentals. Accommodations are offered at the campground (see *Lodging—Campgrounds*). Parking $5.

NATURAL WONDERS 🐾 ✎ **Broxton Rocks** (contact the Nature Conservancy at 404-253-7216 or the City of Douglas Tourism Office at 912-384-4555). Tours are limited to a few times a year and must be prearranged. Broxton Rocks, which has been named "One of Georgia's Hidden Treasures" by WSB-TV and one of the "30 Natural Wonders of Georgia to See Before You Die" by the *Atlanta Journal-Constitution,* is a waterfall cascading over a rocky dropoff. What makes the area unique is that such a formation comes as a complete surprise in the sandy coastal plains. Botanists come from all over the country to study the fragile ecosystem, which features 530 species of plants—some of them endangered—native to the tropics and to the Appalachian Mountains, as well as indigo snakes, gopher tortoises, 100 bird species, and other mammals and reptiles. To preserve the environment, access to the area is limited.

RECREATION AREAS 🐾 ✎ ♿ **Lake Mayers Public Recreation Area** (Board of Tourism: 912-367-7731), 100 Oak Street, Baxley. Open during daylight hours daily. Lake Mayers offers fishing for largemouth bass, bream, crappie, bluegill, shellcracker, and catfish. Facilities include a swimming beach, boat launch, restrooms, and picnicking facilities. Free.

RIVERS 🐾 ✎ **Altamaha River–Altamaha Canoe Trail** (912-437-8765; www.altamaha river.org or www.altamahariverkeeper.org), Baxley. Open daily. The Nature Conservancy has proclaimed the Altamaha River "Georgia's Natural Treasure, One of America's Last Great Places." The river, which borders Appling County, is the second-largest watershed on the eastern seaboard. Completely undammed, it is crossed only five times by roads and twice by rail lines, so its natural beauty is largely undisturbed. It flows 137 miles through 11 counties from its head, where the Oconee and Ocmulgee rivers come together north of Baxley, to its delta on the coast. The river flows through Jeff Davis, Tattnall, and Wayne counties (discussed in this chapter). Surrounded by more than 2 million acres of forest land, the river provides a habitat for more than 130 species of birds, plants, and animals, including many that are rare and endangered, and it is a mecca for canoeing, kayaking, fishing, and birdwatching. A popular biannual event is the Altamaha River Rat Run, a canoe and kayak excursion in the spring and fall. Free.

✴ Lodging

BED & BREAKFASTS

In Waycross

Pond View Inn (912-283-9300 or 1-866-582-5149; www.pondviewinn.com), 311 Pendleton Street. Very well-known for its upscale restaurant (see *Where to Eat—Dining Out*), this B&B has four elegantly decorated guest rooms on the second floor. All the upscale amenities are featured, including private baths—some with whirlpool tubs—and silver tray breakfast service. No smoking. Not wheelchair accessible. $81–129.

CAMPGROUNDS

In Nicholls

🍴 🐾 ♿ ⛺ **General Coffee State Park** (lodging reservations: 1-800-864-7275). This park features 50 tent, trailer, and RV sites, as well as equestrian campsites. See *Green Space—Nature Preserves and Parks.* $24–26; equestrian sites $8–18, including the trail fee.

In Waycross

🍴 🐾 ♿ ⛺ **Laura S. Walker State Park** (lodging reservations: 1-800-864-7275). The park offers 44 tent, trailer, and RV sites. See *Green Space—Nature Preserves and Parks.* $24–26.

COTTAGES AND CABINS

In Nicholls

🍴 🐾 ♿ ⛺ **General Coffee State Park** (lodging reservations: 1-800-864-7275). The park offers six fully equipped cottages for rent. See *Green Space—Nature Preserves and Parks.* One cottage is dog friendly ($40 per pet; maximum two). $105–165.

✴ Where to Eat

DINING OUT

In Waycross

♿ **Andrew's Café and Grill** (912-285-1545), 412 Elizabeth Street. Open 5:30–10 Thursday–Saturday. Andrew's is one of Waycross's best dining experiences, a place where guests can get steaks, seafood, salads,

pasta, and homemade soups and desserts. No smoking. $8–24.

♿ **Pond View Inn** (912-283-9300 or 1-866-582-5149; www.pondviewinn.com), 311 Pendleton Street. Open 6–10 Wednesday–Saturday. Perfect for an intimate and romantic evening of fine dining, the restaurant serves favorites such as crabcakes, rib eye, duck, a variety of seafood, and melt-in-your-mouth desserts. No smoking. $19–27.

EATING OUT

In Baxley

🍴 🐾 ♿ **B & F Restaurant** (912-367-4766), 500 West Parker Street. Open 5 AM–9 PM Monday–Saturday. This popular eatery serves homemade breakfasts, sandwiches, and traditional Southern dinners. No smoking. Around $5.

🍴 🐾 ♿ **Fuji Express Japanese Steakhouse** (912-366-9444), 201 West Parker Street. Open 11–9 Monday–Thursday, 11–10 Friday–Sunday. The restaurant serves steak, chicken, seafood, fried rice, and vegetables. No smoking. $6–12.

In Jesup

🍴 🐾 ♿ **Jones Kitchen** (912-427-4100), 526 West Cherry Street. Open 11–2 Monday–Saturday. This restaurant offers good old-fashioned country cooking buffets, including fried chicken, pork chops, and an assortment of vegetables. No smoking. $8.

🍴 🐾 ♿ **Overpass Steak & Ribs** (912-530-6900), 123 East Pine Street. Open 11–9:30 Monday–Saturday. The restaurant offers steaks, chicken, pork, seafood, and ribs with your choice of vegetable and a salad. No smoking. $5–30.

🍴 🐾 ♿ **Sugar 'N Spice Bake Shop** (912-427-9956), 74 West Walnut Street. Open 6 AM–2 PM Tuesday and Wednesday, 6–6 Thursday and Friday, 6–1 Saturday. Homemade chicken and tuna salads, sandwiches, and sweets round out the menu here. No smoking. $3–4.50.

In Waycross

🍴 🐾 ♿ **Cavagnaro's** (912-285-4000; www.cavagnaros.com), South Georgia Parkway

West. Open 11–10 Monday–Thursday, 11–11 Friday and Saturday, 11–9 Sunday. An interesting combination of restaurant and sports bar, this eatery serves good Italian entrées. It has a good wine list, too. No smoking. $7–14.

🦐 🍴 ♿ **Cedar River Seafood** (912-338-0074), 2456 Memorial Drive. Open 11–9 daily. The popular eatery has been serving seafood, steak, chicken breasts, pastas, and other favorites since 1977. No smoking. $8–25.

🦐 🍴 ♿ **Jerry J's Country Café** (912-287-1303), 1406 Plant Avenue. Open 6 AM–8 PM Monday–Thursday, 6 AM–9 PM Friday and Saturday. This is the place to go for big meals in Waycross. The restaurant serves breakfast, lunch, and dinner. Menu favorites include huge handmade biscuits and all the other breakfast staples, as well as meat and vegetable plates like your grandmother used to make. The hardest thing is narrowing down your choices. No smoking. Breakfast $4–5, lunch $5–7, dinner $7–13.

COFFEEHOUSES

In Baxley

🦐 🍴 ♿ **Common Ground Coffee and Eatery** (912-366-9997), 20 NW Park Avenue. Open at 7 AM for breakfast and lunch Monday–Saturday. Open for dinner Saturday. The coffeehouse offers specialty coffees along with soups, salads, and sandwiches. No smoking. $4–8.

✳ Entertainment

Appling County Arts Council (912-367-7731). Events take place primarily at the Appling County Elementary Complex in Baxley or the City Auditorium. Call for schedule of performances, information on the particular venue, and ticket prices. This group exists to enhance appreciation for the arts in Appling County and hosts numerous programs each year, including performances by the South Georgia Ballet and the Valdosta Symphony Orchestra, piano concerts, madrigal singers, and art shows.

THEATER Martin Centre (912-383-0277; www.cityofdouglas.com), 109 East Ashley Street, Douglas. The historic 1940s art deco–style theater has been restored as a multiuse performance venue where numerous theatrical and musical programs are presented. Call for a schedule of performances and ticket prices.

✳ Selective Shopping

ANTIQUES Honest Al's Antique Emporium (912-367-0808), 906 East Parker Street, Baxley. Open 10–6 weekdays, 9–5 Saturday. Rare finds include tobacco memorabilia, reproduction pieces, and furnishings from the 1700s to the 1950s.

McCurdy's on Main (912-654-4004; www.mccurdysonmain.com), 208 South Main Street, Glennville. Open 8:30–5:30 weekdays, 8:30–1 Saturday. This spacious establishment has been in business for more than 30 years, specializing in antiques and unique gifts.

✳ Special Events

March: **Annual Dogwood Festival** (chamber of commerce: 912-427-2028). Activities include a 1-mile/5K Family Fun Run, SPAR Bike Ride, Wayne County Young Farmers Truck Pull, arts and crafts, barbecue, and more fun-filled events for the whole family are held throughout Jesup. This event takes place on the fourth Saturday in March. Free.

Peaches to Beaches Yard Sale (912-367-7731; www.peachestobeaches.com). Those die-hard shoppers looking for bargains in Baxley, Hazlehurst, and Jesup will want to check out some sections of the 172-mile yard sale, which follows US 341/Golden Isles Parkway from Culloden to Brunswick and the Golden Isles. The sale, held the second Friday and Saturday of March, is Georgia's longest yard sale. Free.

April: **Baxley Tree Fest** (chamber of commerce: 912-367-7731). A celebration of the forestry industry and outdoor recreation, this three-day festival's highlights include a street dance, outdoor expo, parade, arts and crafts, entertainment, sports events,

"Treeography" photo contest, motorcycle show, petting zoo, and much more. Free, except $2 for street dance.

Swamp Fest (912-287-2969; www.swamp fest.us). The annual Swamp Fest is held the first weekend in April. Activities include a parade, street dance, concert, arts and crafts, great Southern cooking, a beauty pageant, live theater, a BMX bike show, appearances by Okefenokee Joe, and children's entertainment. The festival takes place in downtown Waycross, although some events are held at the Waycross fairgrounds. Free.

June: **Shriners' Annual All-Night Gospel Sing** (912-283-3744; Ware County: 912-287-4300; www.warecounty.com). For more than 45 years the Shriners have sponsored an event that includes nationally known gospel groups and a talent search that showcases performers from all over the Southeast. This annual event at the Okefenokee Fairgrounds in Waycross usually takes place the last weekend in June, beginning on Friday night and lasting until the wee hours of Saturday morning. $13 in advance; $15 at the door.

August: **South Georgia Outdoor Expo** (City of Douglas Central Services: 912-383-0277; www.cityofdouglas.com). Held at the Central Square Complex in downtown Douglas (200 South Madison Avenue), the Expo highlights hunting, fishing, and the outdoors. Events include a Wild Game Supper, Wild Game and BBQ Cook Off, Make A Break Sporting Clays Competition (at another location), DNR Hunter Safety Education Workshops, and numerous other events. Adults $5, children 12 and younger free.

October: **Guysie Mule Roundup** (Alma Chamber of Commerce: 912-632-5859). The two-day event held on a Friday and Saturday on GA 32 between Alma and Nicholls features displays of antique barn implements and old-fashioned tools. Demonstrations show the way farm chores were once accomplished. The roundup also features a rodeo, parade, food, and wagon rides. Adults $4, children 12 and younger free.

November: **Smokin' on the Square/ National Barbecue Festival** (912-381-0006 or 1-800-385-0002; www.cityof douglas.com). After three years of hosting the Smokin' on the Square barbecue festival downtown, Douglas expanded this event to the National Barbecue Festival Best of the Best in 2004, and it now occurs at the Waycross Fairgrounds (2401 Knight Avenue). Representatives from more than 38 states compete to determine the best barbecue in the nation. $5 at the gate allows attendees to sample five of the Best of the Best entries.

December: **Christmas Lights in the Park** (912-283-0583; www.okeswamp.com). Ride the Lady Suwannee train on a 30- to 40-minute trip through the Okefenokee Swamp Park in Waycross to see this spectacular Christmas light show and other decorations. Every Friday through Sunday evening from Thanksgiving to the weekend after Christmas. Last train at 9. Adults $8, children 3–11 $6.

Historical South 3

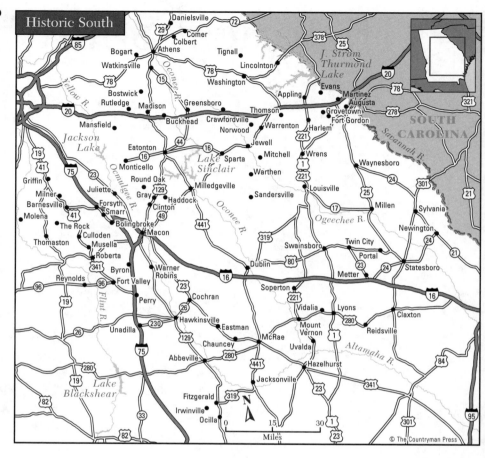

Historic South

Danielsville · 72
29 · Comer
Colbert
Bogart · Athens · Tignall · 378 · 25
85 · Watkinsville · J. Strom Thurmond Lake
Oconee R. · 78 · Lincolnton · 20 · 78
78 · Washington · Evans · Martinez
Bostwick · 15 · Appling · Augusta
Rutledge · Madison · Greensboro · Thomson · Grovetown · 278 · 321
20 · Buckhead · Crawfordville · Warrenton · Fort Gordon · SOUTH CAROLINA
Mansfield · Norwood · Harlem
Jackson Lake · 44 · 221 · Savannah R.
Eatonton · 16 · Jewell · Wrens
19 · 16 · Lake Sinclair · Sparta · Mitchell · 1 · Waynesboro
41 · Monticello · Warthen · 221 · 24 · 301
Griffin · Round Oak · Milledgeville · Louisville · 25 · 21
75 · 23 · 129 · Sandersville · 17 · Millen · Sylvania
Milner · Juliette · Gray · Haddock · Oconee R. · Ogeechee R. · Newington
Barnesville · Forsyth · Clinton · 49 · Swainsboro · Twin City · 24
Molena · 41 · Smarr · 441 · 319 · Portal · 21
The Rock · Bolingbroke · Macon · 80 · 23 · 24 · Statesboro
Culloden · Musella · Dublin · Metter · 16
Thomaston · Roberta · Warner Robins · 16 · Soperton · 221
341 · Byron · 23 · Vidalia · Lyons · Claxton
Reynolds · 96 · Fort Valley · Cochran · 221 · 280 · Reidsville
96 · Perry · 26 · Mount Vernon · 1
19 · Hawkinsville · Eastman · McRae · Uvalda
26 · Unadilla · 129 · Chauncey · 280 · Hazelhurst · 84
75 · Abbeville · 441 · Jacksonville · 23 · 341
280 · Flint R. · Lake Blackshear · Fitzgerald · 319 · N · 1
19 · Irwinville · 82
82 · Ocilla · 0 · 15 · 30 · 1 · 95
33 · Miles · 23
82 · © The Countryman Press

© The Countryman Press

INTRODUCTION

The Historic South area of the state is, indeed, Georgia's heartland. In some ways, the region is the most stereotypically Southern, with lots of small towns and white-columned mansions, but the area is also quite diverse.

The region in the rolling hills of the Piedmont contains several small cities, each of which has a very distinct personality. Among these are Athens, home of the University of Georgia; Augusta, home of the Masters golf tournament, the Augusta Futurity cutting-horse competition, and several important boating events; Macon, home of several major museums and a state hall of fame as well as the annual International Cherry Blossom Festival; Milledgeville, Georgia's capital at the time of secession; Statesboro, home of Georgia Southern University; and Warner Robins, home of Robins Air Force Base and the Museum of Aviation.

The region also contains many charming small towns, a national forest, some major rivers, several significant lakes, 15 state parks, historic sites, and some interesting special events. The Historic South is the only area touched by all of Georgia's other tourism regions—Atlanta Metro, the Coast, the Mountains, and the Southern Rivers—and it's also bordered on the east by South Carolina.

One would expect such a large area to be far from homogeneous. Thus the region is further subdivided into the state-designated Classic South, represented by Augusta, Thomson, Washington, and several smaller towns; Historic Heartland, represented by Athens, Barnesville, Conyers, Covington, Eatonton, Fort Valley, Juliette, Macon, Milledgeville, Monroe, Monticello, Perry, Social Circle, Warner Robins, Watkinsville, and other small towns; and Magnolia Midlands, represented by Dublin, Eastman, Fitzgerald, Hawkinsville, Statesboro, Vidalia, and a few other towns.

The entire region is famous for its peaches, pecans, and coveted sweet Vidalia onions, but it's also well-known for fruitcake produced by two companies in the small town of Claxton.

Golf is synonymous with the Masters golf tournament in Augusta, but the sport is widely available at several state parks and resorts such as those around Lake Oconee. This is also horse country, and different events are held at the Georgia International Horse Park in Conyers and the Lawrence Bennett Harness Horse Training Facility in Hawkinsville.

The region's multifaceted history is represented by such sites as the Tubman African American Museum in Macon; the Ocmulgee National Monument, also in Macon; the Governor's Mansion in Milledgeville; Callaway Plantation in Washington; Jarrell Plantation in Juliette; and the Boyhood Home of President Woodrow Wilson in Augusta.

Outdoor recreation is not neglected. The lakes and the rivers provide ample opportunities for various types of boating, fishing, and other water sports. The Altamaha River, formed by the confluence of the Ocmulgee, Oconee, and Ohoopee rivers, is the largest river system east of the Mississippi and supports more than 100 species of endangered plants and animals.

ATHENS

I t's not for its name only that Athens—named for its old-world predecessor, the Greek center of higher learning—is known as "the Classic City." Even its tree-lined neighborhoods are showcases of antebellum Greek Revival architecture.

The city was founded in 1806 concurrently with the University of Georgia (UGA), the nation's first state-chartered university. For various reasons, the city was spared during the Civil War, leaving much to admire today. For one thing, Union troops who were directed to destroy rail lines around Athens were ambushed and taken prisoner by Confederate troops. Additionally, after the fall of Atlanta, Union general William Tecumseh Sherman's March to the Sea moved southeast toward Milledgeville and thus bypassed Athens.

Although the city suffered during the Civil War and Reconstruction, it bounced back quickly. Athens's antebellum economy was based on cotton, railroad transportation, and textiles. Its flourishing textile mills created growth unparalleled in the New South.

Today Athens is the fifth-largest city in the state and the largest city in the northeast Georgia Piedmont region, with a population of 102,000. It is dominated by the ever-growing university. As with all college towns, the presence of the university means there is a healthy variety of museums, cultural events, sports venues, restaurants, and nightspots. In fact, Athens has been named one of America's Top 25 Arts Destinations by *AmericanStyle* magazine.

With its bohemian allure and downtown district filled with enough clubs to earn the city the title "Live Music Central" from the *New York Times* and the "#1 Music Mecca/College Music Scene in America" by *Rolling Stone* magazine, Athens is a major site on the **Georgia Music Trail,** which also includes Atlanta, Macon, and Savannah. From a long history of folk music to the advent of bands such as the B-52s and R.E.M. in the early 1980s, to present-day bands such as Widespread Panic and Drive-By Truckers, Athens has long cultivated musicians and other artists. (Just a little piece of trivia: On April 18, 1998, downtown Athens hosted the largest CD release party in history when local band Widespread Panic gave a free concert attended by 100,000 fans.) With blues, classical, country, hip-hop, rock, and every alternative genre playing on a continuous basis, Athens provides one of the most eclectic and affordable music scenes in the world.

GUIDANCE Before your trip, consult the **Athens Convention and Visitors Bureau** (706-357-4430 or 1-800-653-0603; www.visitathensga.com), 300 North Thomas Street, Athens 30601, for information. Open 8–5 weekdays.

Once you arrive in Athens, stop by the **Athens Welcome Center** (706-353-1820 or 1-866-455-1820; www.visitathensga.com), 280 East Dougherty Street, Athens 30601. Open 10–5 Monday–Saturday, noon–5 Sunday in fall and winter, until 6 in spring and summer. Housed in the historic Federal-style **Church-Waddell-Brumby House,** the center provides maps, brochures, self-guided tours of more than 50 sites, audio tours, and visitor information. For more information about the house, see *To See—Historic Homes and Sites.* Before leaving the welcome center, pick up the brochures *Athens Music Walking Tour,* a 28-stop self-guided tour to some of the most significant spots in the city's rich musical history; *A Walking Tour of Downtown Athens; Georgia's Antebellum Trail,* a 100-mile trail of pre–Civil War sites that stretches south to Macon and for which Athens is the northern gateway; and *Heartland of the Confederacy Trail,* a Civil War heritage trail. Guided tours given by **Classic City Tours** (706-208-TOUR) depart from the center at 2 PM daily. On Wednesday and Friday there are also tours at 10:30. See *To See—Guided Tours.*

For more information about the University of Georgia campus, consult the following organizations. The **UGA Visitors Center** (706-542-0842; www.visit.uga.edu), Four Towers Building, 405 College Station Road, Athens 30602. Open 8–5 weekdays, 10–3 Saturday; closed on official university holidays. The visitors center, housed in a former dairy barn called the Four Towers Building because of its four silos, provides assistance and information about the university. Stay awhile to see the displays that focus on university history, campus life, and distinguished alumni. The *Campus Arboretum Walking Tour of Trees* brochure is available at the UGA Visitors Center, too. The **UGA Alumni Association** (706-542-2251 or 1-800-606-8786; www.alumni.uga.edu), 298 Hull Street, is housed in the historic 1825 Wray-Nicholson House, one of the oldest structures in Athens and Clarke County, which is open for tours. Open 8–5 weekdays.

For information about Watkinsville, consult the **Oconee County Visitors Bureau** (706-769-5197; www.visitoconee.com), 21 North Main Street/US 441, Watkinsville 30677. Open 10–4 Monday–Saturday.

GETTING THERE *By air:* Air transportation is into **Athens–Ben Epps Airport,** named for Georgia's first aviator, Ben Epps, who began building and flying planes in Athens in 1907. Many visitors may prefer to fly into Atlanta. See "What's Where in Georgia" for airport, airline, and car rental information.

By bus: **Southeastern Stages/Greyhound Lines** (706-549-2255; www.southeasternstages .com), 220 West Broad Street, provides direct service.

By car: The major highway routes into Athens are GA 15, US 78, and US 129/441; GA Loop 10 goes around the city.

GETTING AROUND The **Athens Transit System** (706-613-3434; www.athenstransit .com) provides public transit transportation throughout the Athens area. Downtown, rental cars are available from **Budget Rent-A-Car** (706-353-0600), 1870 West Broad Street, and **Enterprise Rent-A-Car** (706-546-8067), 368 Oak Road.

PARKING Adequate parking (except for UGA football home-game weekends) is available at four for-fee parking decks downtown, and there is also on-street, metered parking. There are new parking decks at the Classic Center and one at College Avenue. At the University of Georgia, there is a free lot for short-term parking adjacent to the visitors center (obtain a pass inside the center). Additional visitor parking is available in for-fee lots and parking decks around the campus. The one at North Campus is very convenient to downtown.

WHEN TO GO In the autumn, if you aren't attending a UGA football home game, we strongly urge you avoid the city, which will be crowded, traffic-choked, and expensive. Graduation weekend is a similar story. In addition, Athens is not totally friendly to the weekend visitor. Many of the major attractions are open only on weekdays, although the situation is gradually being resolved. The Georgia Museum of Art and the State Botanical Garden of Georgia, for example, are open on weekends.

MEDICAL EMERGENCY Call 911.

VILLAGES AND NEIGHBORHOODS Athens is teeming with National Register of Historic Places–designated neighborhoods: **Athens Warehouse,** a commercial area on Foundry Street; **Bloomfield Street,** a residential area of Craftsman bungalows; **Boulevard,** a turn-of-the-20th-century streetcar district; **Buena Vista Heights,** a neighborhood of small cottages; **Cobbham,** an area of imposing Queen Anne Victorian homes; **Old North Campus–UGA,** where the first permanent college buildings were erected in 1806; the **Prince Avenue** corridor, with the best examples of Greek Revival homes; and **Shotgun Row,** a collection of narrow shotgun cottages. Other historic districts include Dearing Street, Downtown Athens, Milledge Avenue, Milledge Circle, Oglethorpe Avenue, Reese Street, Rocksprings, and West Hancock Avenue. All these neighborhoods make excellent walking tours. Get information from the welcome center.

When visiting sleepy little nearby **Watkinsville,** it's hard to believe that the town was once considered for the site of the University of Georgia. It was decided, however, that the existence of the Eagle Tavern made the town "too frivolous an atmosphere for studious young gentlemen." Those who made the decision to locate the school in Athens must be turning over in their graves, because over the years UGA has earned the dubious reputation of being a party school. Today Watkinsville is known as the ARTland of Georgia because it boasts a plethora of artists' studios and galleries, and is also the home of the Oconee Cultural Arts Foundation, which hosts exhibits in a 1902 schoolhouse.

✵ To See and Do

COVERED BRIDGES ♨ ♂ ♿ **Elder's Mill Covered Bridge,** Elders Mill Road/GA 15 over Rose Creek, Watkinsville. Located in Herman Michael Park, the bridge is always accessible. Not only is this one of just 16 covered bridges remaining in the state, it is one of the last still in use on a public road. The bridge was originally constructed in 1897 in the Town Lattice design over Calls Creek between Athens and Watkinsville, but in 1924 it was relocated by wagon to cross Big Rose Creek. It's truly amazing that the bridge is able to carry traffic without the support of underlying steel beams. The local garden club maintains the grounds, and an individual who lives nearby decorates the bridge with Christmas lights every year. Free.

CULTURAL SITES ♨ ♂ ♿ **Lyndon House Arts Center, Ware-Lyndon House** (706-613-3623; www.visitathensga.com), 293 Hoyt Street, Athens. Open noon–9 Tuesday and Thursday, 9–5 Wednesday, Friday, and Saturday. Guided tours are available with 48-hour advance reservations. Originally located in a circa-1850 house considered to be one of the most historically significant homes in the city, the community visual arts center has been renovated and expanded to feature galleries, a children's wing, artists' workshops, a gift shop, and a perennial garden. The **Visual Arts Guild of Athens** (706-546-7580) is based at the arts center. Now that its rooms are no longer needed as galleries, the completely restored Ware-Lyndon House, one of the few antebellum homes in Athens with Italianate elements, is open as a house museum filled with decorative arts. Free.

♨ ♿ **University of Georgia Historic North Campus** lies between Lumpkin, Jackson, Broad, and Baldwin streets. Despite the fact that the bulldog, Uga, may appear to be the most familiar representation of the university, the landmark cast-iron arch, through which students and visitors enter the North Campus, is officially featured as the logo of the university. The cast-iron fencing around the area was originally not just for decorative purposes; it kept grazing animals out of the quadrangle. This section of the university, the location of the original campus in the early 1800s, features Greek Revival architecture, handsome gardens, and majestic trees. Among the historically significant buildings is the UGA Chapel, home of George Cooke's painting of St. Peter's Cathedral. Measuring 17 by 23.5 feet, it was the largest framed oil painting in the world at the time of its completion in 1847.

GUIDED TOURS Guided tours given by ✍ **Classic City Tours** (706-208-TOUR) depart from the Athens Welcome Center at 2 PM daily, and on Wednesday and Friday at 10:30. Tours are $15. Although the four Athens house museums listed in *To See* (Church-Waddell-Brumby House, Taylor-Grady House, Ware-Lyndon House, and T.R.R. Cobb House) are open to the public for tours by individuals, Classic City Tours offers a guided tour of historic interiors of these museums at 4 PM Tuesday and Thursday. The price of $20 per person includes the price of admission to each museum.

🌺 ✍ **UGA Visitors Center Tours** (706-542-0842; www.visit.uga.edu). Open 8–5 weekdays, 10–3 Saturday; closed on official university holidays. The center provides guided walking and van tours (reservations required)—three on weekdays, two on Saturday, one on Sunday. These tours via minibus last one hour and involve walking as well as riding. Free.

HISTORIC HOMES AND SITES 🌺 **Church-Waddell-Brumby House** (706-353-1820; www.visitathensga.com). Open 10–5 Monday–Saturday, noon–5 Sunday in fall and winter, until 6 in spring and summer. The historic Federal-style house serves as the city's welcome center (see *Guidance*). Built in 1820, the house itself is considered to be the oldest house in Athens. It was built for UGA mathematics professor Alonzo Church and later became the home of university president Moses Waddell. The rescue and restoration of this house in the 1970s sparked the historic preservation movement in Athens. Besides serving as the welcome center, the house is a museum filled with period furniture and decorative arts. Free.

🌺 ✍ ♿ **Double-Barreled Cannon,** Cannon Park on City Hall lawn at College and Hancock streets, Athens. Accessible daily. Probably the most unusual weapon from the Civil War, this unique cannon was built in 1863 at a local foundry when the uneasy citizenry dreaded an attack by invading Union armies. This one-of-a-kind weapon designed by Athenian house builder John Gilleland was a prototype for a hoped-for superweapon. The theory was that two cannonballs attached by a chain would be fired simultaneously and would mow down everything in their path, including wide swaths of the enemy, before striking their target. Unfortunately, the first firing was spectacularly unsuccessful. An observer noted that the cannonballs "plowed up an acre of ground, tore up a cornfield, mowed down saplings, and the chain broke, the balls going in opposite directions, one of the balls killed a cow in a distant field, while the other knocked down the chimney from a log cabin. The observers scattered as though the entire Yankee army had turned loose in that vicinity." Although no other copy was ever built, the original sits on the Court House lawn, facing north—just in case. The unusual weapon has been featured on *Ripley's Believe It or Not!* Free.

THIS UNIQUE DOUBLE-BARRELED CANNON WAS BUILT IN ATHENS IN 1863 TO PROTECT THE TOWN FROM UNION FORCES.

🐾 ♿ **Taylor-Grady House** (706-549-8688), 634 Prince Avenue, Athens. Open 9–1 and 2:30–5 weekdays. Guided tours available through Athens Welcome Center/Classic City Tours. Looking at this imposing 1844 Greek Revival mansion, it's hard to realize that it was built as a summer home by Gen. Robert Taylor. The exterior is bordered by 13 columns representing the 13 original states. Admire how these soaring columns are connected by delicate ironwork. Famed journalist, orator, and editor of the *Atlanta Constitution,* Henry Grady, who was credited with reuniting the North and South and establishing the concept of the New South after the Civil War, lived here during his collegiate career. Operated by the Junior League, the site is filled with graceful period pieces. Limited wheelchair accessibility. Adults $3, children younger than 12 free.

🐾 ✂ ♿ **Tree That Owns Itself,** Deering and Finley streets, Athens. If you simply drive by without knowing what you're seeing, you'd think this was just an ordinary tree—gigantic though it is. You'd be wrong, however. Professor William H. Jackson loved the shade of the great white oak on his property so much that in the 1890s he deeded the tree to itself along with 8 feet of land on all four sides. Unfortunately, the 100-foot-tall, 15-foot-diameter tree blew down in a 1942 windstorm, but what was considered a tragedy by the fond citizenry had a happy ending. A new tree grew from one of the acorns of the original, and today Jackson Oak Jr. rivals its parent in size.

🐾 **T.R.R. Cobb House** (706-369-3513; www.trrcobbhouse.org), 175 Hill Street, Athens. Open 10–4 Tuesday–Saturday. Thomas Reade Root Cobb was an UGA graduate, the founder of the school of law there, and a principal author of the Constitution of the Confederate States of America (CSA). Although he was a lawyer and an advocate of education and religion, he was also a Southern nationalist who advocated states' rights and slavery, and he was an officer in the CSA. Once abandoned, the house was moved to Stone Mountain Park near Atlanta, where there were plans to restore it and add it to the re-created plantation. That never happened, however, and the house languished for 20 years. Moved back to Athens, it sits only two blocks from its original location. Finally fully restored, it is filled with period antiques and memorabilia from Cobb's life. $2 donation.

MUSEUMS 🐾 ✂ ♿ **Butts-Mehre Heritage Hall and Sports Museum** (706-542-9036; www.georgiadogs.com), Selig Circle off Pinecrest Drive and Lumpkin Street, Athens. Open 8–5 weekdays, limited hours on days of home football games. Named for two former coaches, Wallace Butts and Harry Mehre, the museum is housed in a striking building constructed of red granite accentuated with black glass, which serves as the home of UGA Football and the UGA Athletic Association. It was recently renovated and expanded to the tune of $33 million. Inside, the museum displays showcase more than 100 years of athletic accomplishments of UGA students such as Herschel Walker and Frankie Sinkwich, whose Heisman Trophies are on display. Exhibits, memorabilia, and touchscreen displays tell the stories of all UGA sports—both men's and women's. Outdoors, visit the 11-acre Dooley Sculpture Garden, named for one of the most beloved coaches in UGA's history. Free.

THE BUTTS-MEHRE HERITAGE HALL AND SPORTS MUSEUM FOCUSES ON THE ATHLETIC ACCOMPLISHMENTS OF UNIVERSITY OF GEORGIA STUDENTS.

🐾 ✂ ♿ **Eagle Tavern Museum and Welcome Center** (706-769-5197, www.visit oconee.com), 26 North Main Street, Watkinsville. Open 10–4 Monday–Saturday.

SIMPLE ITEMS FROM THE 1700S FURNISH THE EAGLE TAVERN MUSEUM AND WELCOME CENTER.

This humble building, one of the oldest structures in Oconee County, began life in 1789 as a fort, built to protect settlers from Indians. It remained a fort until 1801, when it opened as a stagecoach stop and tavern. The structure has been restored to its Federal Plain–style appearance. The "two up, two down" interior is furnished with simple 1700s pieces to replicate a tavern downstairs and stagecoach-stop hostelry upstairs. Among the exhibits are artifacts excavated on the property. Free, but donations appreciated.

🐾 ♿ **Georgia Museum of Art** (706-542-4662; www.georgiamuseum.org), 90 Carlton Street, Athens. Open noon–5 Wednesday, Friday, and Saturday; noon–9 Thursday; 1–5 Sunday. Located in the East Campus Triangle in the Performing and Visual Arts Complex, the museum is the Official State Art Museum. The permanent collection features more than 8,000 works that focus primarily on 19th- and early-20th-century American paintings. Other collections include the Kress Collection of Italian Renaissance paintings; a significant collection of American, European, and Asian prints from the Renaissance to the present; and a growing collection of decorative arts. Obviously all these works can't be displayed at once, so the museum produces 20 culturally and artistically diverse shows each year featuring pieces from the permanent collection and works from traveling and private collections. Self-guided; guided tours available by reservation with two weeks' notice. $3 suggested donation. Plan to lunch or have some light refreshments at the museum's **Ike & Jane** (see *Where to Eat—Eating Out*). Don't leave without viewing the Jane and Harry Willson Sculpture Garden.

WHO LET THE DAWGS OUT?

The *We Let the Dawgs Out* public art exhibit (www.weletthedawgsout.com) can be found at various locations throughout Athens. Always accessible. Even before the internationally known Cow Parade (painted fiberglass bovines as public art) came to Atlanta temporarily, Athens was the first city in Georgia to create such public art with an animal theme, turning the entire area into an outdoor museum. The project was sponsored by the Athens-Oconee Junior Woman's Club and funded by city, art, and private sectors. Naturally, the animal of choice was not as mundane as a cow but, rather, was the Athens icon—the bulldog. That's "dawg" to the uninitiated. More than three dozen larger-than-life bulldawgs were created, and each is a unique representation of the vision of a different local artist. Just a few of these fine whimsical canines include Caesar Dawgustus, Carmen Mirandawg, Dawgwood, the Blue Dawg of Happiness, and A-pooch-ecary. You get the idea. Rather than auctioning off the pooches as other such projects have done, the bulldawgs are on permanent display around the city. Finding them makes a pleasant and amusing walking and/or driving tour. Don't forget your camera. More than a dozen dawgs are clustered in the downtown area and another 10 in the Five Points area; others are scattered farther afield. To find them, go to the aforementioned website and print a map showing the locations of all the dawgs, or pick up a map from the Athens Welcome Center. This is one tour that will guarantee a smile. Free.

🦐 ✿ **Georgia Museum of Natural History** (706-542-1663; http://museum.nhm.uga.edu), Natural History Building, East Campus Drive and Cedar Street, UGA campus, Athens. Visitors may park in lot adjacent to building; request a parking permit from museum office. Open for tours at 10–4 weekdays, noon–3 Saturday. Fourteen separate collections of objects, artifacts, and specimens relating to the natural history of Georgia and the Southeast are housed at the museum, ranked as ninth in the nation among natural history museums. It is the Official State Museum of Natural History for Georgia. The Archaeology Laboratory houses more than 3 million artifacts and specimens chronicling 12,000 years of human settlement and includes stone tools, plant and skeletal remains, and pottery. $2.

🦐 ✿ ⚅ **ITA Collegiate Tennis Hall of Fame** (706-542-8064), Dan Magill Tennis Complex at Henry Field Stadium on the UGA South Campus, Athens. Open 9–noon and 2–5 weekdays. Guided tours by reservation. Using photographs and equipment of legends of the Intercollegiate Tennis Association, the hall of fame honors more than 170 players, coaches, and contributors dating back to 1883, including Arthur Ashe, Jimmy Connors, and Stan Smith. Free.

SELF-GUIDED TOURS **Heartland of the Confederacy Civil War Trail** (www.civil waringeorgia.com). The Leader's Trail section of this regional self-guided heritage trail, which stretches from Gainesville to Crawfordville, features 45 historic sites, 24 of which are located within Athens and Clarke County. The local sites include historical monuments, homes belonging to Confederate leaders, and unusual relics. Maps are available at the Athens Welcome Center (see *Guidance*) or can be downloaded from the website.

SPECIAL PLACES 🦐 ✿ ⚅ **Uga Memorial,** western end of Sanford Stadium, UGA campus, 310 Sanford Drive, Athens. Fans of the University of Georgia football teams worship Uga (pronounced Ug-ah), the English bulldog mascot, named the nation's best mascot by *Sports Illustrated.* For more than 60 years, one after another of these eight (so far) "damn good dogs" has presided over regular-season games and postseason bowl games. When Ugas depart for doggie heaven, they are interred at the stadium in a marble vault and memorialized with a plaque presided over by a bronze statue of a previous mascot named Mike. Fans place flowers and other tributes on the vaults and, just like rubbing a Buddha's tummy for good luck, pat the muzzle of the statue for good fortune. Visitors can see the memorial during home games or during campus tours from the UGA Visitors Center (see *Guidance*). Free.

WALKING TOUR 🦐 **Athens Music History Walking Tour** (contact the Athens Welcome Center at 706-353-1820; www.visitathensga.com/musictour). This 28-stop self-guided tour of Athens's music heritage will tell you everything you ever wanted to know about the local music scene, including the humble spots where many famous bands got their start. At some of the stops, such as **Weaver D's Fine Foods, the Grit, Copper Creek Brewing Company, 40 Watt Club,** or **Georgia Theatre,** you can get a meal or a drink or enjoy live entertainment. Free. You can pick up a brochure from the welcome center or download it from the website.

✳ Green Space

GARDENS 🦐 ⚅ **Founders Memorial Garden** (706-542-1816; www.uga.edu/garden club/foundersgarden.html), 325 South Lumpkin Street, Athens. Open daily during daylight hours, except during events. The first garden club in America was begun by 12 ladies in Athens in 1891. In 1946, this small formal garden on the North University Campus behind Brooks Hall was created to commemorate that event. The garden serves not only as a museum of landscape design but also as a natural laboratory for botany, forestry, and related

THE FOUNDERS MEMORIAL GARDEN IN ATHENS COMMEMORATES THE FOUNDING OF THE FIRST GARDEN CLUB IN AMERICA.

disciplines. The layout of the 1.5-acre garden consists of winding walkways, a formal boxwood garden, two courtyards, a fountain, a perennial garden, and an arboretum. A centerpiece of the garden, the early-1800s house, is used by the School of Environmental Design. Free.

🌸 🏵 ♿ **State Botanical Garden of Georgia** (706-542-1244; www.botgarden.uga .edu), 2450 South Milledge Avenue, Athens. Open year-round. Grounds open 8–8 daily, April–September; 8–6 daily, October–March. Conservatory/visitors center open 9–4:30 Tuesday–Saturday, 11:30–4:30 Sunday. Guided tours by reservation. Encompassing 313 acres, the complex features dramatic gorges and spring-fed streams in addition to the formal gardens. Five miles of trails wander along wooded, flower-lined vistas, providing plenty of opportunities to enjoy native flora and fauna. Most of these trails are wheelchair friendly, but not all. Special collections include magnolias, native and adapted trees and shrubs including shade and ornamental trees, poisonous and medicinal plants, a bog garden, and herbaceous flower gardens. In the **Dunson Native Flora Garden,** more than 300 native Southeastern species are showcased. In addition, a dazzling three-story **tropical conservatory** houses a rain forest of tropical and semitropical plants and seasonal annuals. Of special interest is the magnificent collection of orchids. Allow at least 30 minutes to see the conservatory. For family fun, visitors to the garden can rent a **Garden Adventure Pack** filled with hands-on activities for children. Call ahead to reserve a pack.

Clute's Kugel, located in the pavilion overlooking the international garden, is a perfectly balanced 816-pound black granite sphere that floats and revolves on a thin sheet of water. It was named for a young boy, Clute Barrow Nelson, who died from a brain tumor. Also on the grounds is the lovely **Day Chapel** and the headquarters of the Garden Club of Georgia (706-227-5369; www.gardenclub.uga.edu), which occupies a neoclassical structure situated on a hill overlooking the Heritage Garden. It contains a decorative arts museum and an impressive collection of museum-quality antiques. Tours can be arranged and cost $5. Admission to gardens free.

NATURE PRESERVES AND PARKS 🌸 🏵 ♿ **Memorial Park and Bear Hollow Wildlife Trail** (park: 706-613-3580; zoo: 706-613-3616; www.athensclarkecounty.com /bearhollow), 293 Gran Ellen Drive, Athens. Open 8–sunset weekdays, 9–sunset weekends and holidays; zoo open 9–5 daily; exhibit hall open 1–4 Sunday. Guided trail tours by reservation. The 72-acre park contains nature trails, a recreation building, a lake for fishing and paddleboating, basketball court, pool, picnic areas, and playground. More than 120 species of native animals, including black bears, bobcats, white-tailed deer, river otters, owls, and others, may be viewed on the Bear Hollow Wildlife Trail. Memorial Day features living history. Free.

🍴 🚲 ♿ ☎ **North Oconee River Greenway and Heritage Trail** (706-613-3615, ext. 242; www.athensgreenway.com), Athens. Open sunrise–sunset daily. Seven miles of paved and dirt trails enjoyed by hikers, bikers, skaters, and joggers connect Sandy Creek Park, Sandy Creek Nature Center, North Oconee River Park, Dudley Park, and the UGA campus. A 4-mile section of the trail system consists of a 10-foot-wide paved, lighted trail. Fifty interpretive panels along a section of the Heritage Trail illustrate the rich history of Athens. The park also offers boating, canoe launches and landings, fishing, and a picnic area. Leashed dogs are welcome. Free.

🍴 🚲 ☎ **Oconee Forest Park** (706-542-1571; www.warnell.forestry.uga.edu/ofp), UGA Recreational Sports Complex, College Station and East Campus roads, Athens. Open daily during daylight hours. With 60 acres, the 100-year-old forest park features 15-acre Lake Herrick, lakeshore hiking trails, a 1.2-mile mountain biking trail, a picnic area, and the Teaching Tree Trail—actually a network of trails with more than 100 identified native trees and shrubs. Mature oak and hickory trees mingle with tulip poplars and the largest scarlet oak tree in Georgia. There's an off-leash area for dogs and a pond where they can swim. Free.

🍴 🚲 ♿ **Sandy Creek Nature Center** (706-613-3615; www.sandycreeknaturecenter.com), 205 Old Commerce Road, Athens. Trails open sunrise–sunset daily; center open 8:30–5:30 Tuesday–Friday. In addition to 225 acres of pristine woodland, fields, and marshlands that are home to numerous native species, the center also features 4 miles of trails, a wildlife observation area, interactive exhibits, and environmental education programs. A wide variety of activities range from stargazing to salamander searches. The newest addition to the center is **ENSAT** (Environment, Natural Science, and Appropriate Technology) **Center,** a state-of-the-art learning laboratory that features live animal exhibits and handicapped-accessible trails. Some trails connect with the North Oconee River Greenway as well as with Cook's Trail. The center highlights energy-saving and "green" technology, construction, and architecture. Free.

🍴 🚲 ☎ **Sandy Creek Park** (706-613-3631; www.sandycreekpark.com), 400 Bob Holman Road, Athens. Open 7 AM–9 PM daily in summer, 8–6 daily in winter. Centered on 260-acre **Lake Chapman,** the 782-acre park offers a visitors center, boat rentals, picnicking, fishing, camping, and swimming at the beach area, as well as playgrounds. There are also private dog runs and a group play area for your four-legged friends. The lake is fully stocked with bass, bream, and crappie, though you must have a valid fishing license. You can bring your own boat, but no gas motors are allowed. Sports areas feature tennis courts, a basketball court, disc golf ($1), and all kinds of ball fields. There's a 4-mile trail to the Sandy Creek Nature Center and a 3-mile trail alongside the lake. Some of the trails are available for horseback riding. Adults $2, younger than 4 and older than 64 free. Primitive camping available for $5 per night.

✳ Lodging

BED & BREAKFASTS

In Athens

The **Colonels B&B,** a distinguished country manor on **Angel Oaks Farm** (706-559-9595; www.thecolonels.net), 3890 Barnett Shoals Road, Athens. Located in a quintessential antebellum 1860s Greek Revival mansion on a 30-acre estate, the B&B is named for the owners: Both husband and wife are retired lieutenant colonels. Opulent accommodations are offered in six guest rooms, each in pairs with a Jack and Jill bath. Some boast a working fireplace and/or a whirlpool tub. A sumptuous full breakfast accompanies your stay. For those who bring their own horse, stalls are available for $30 per night. No smoking. Not wheelchair accessible. $115–175 (higher weekends of UGA home games).

In Watkinsville

♿ ☎ **Ashford Manor Bed and Breakfast** (706-769-2633, www.ambedandbreakfast

.com), 5 Harden Hill Road. The 5-acre Ashford Estate overlooks Watkinsville's distinguished Main Street, with its antiques shops and art galleries, but it is still secluded by its border of magnolias, redbuds, and pines. What's truly amazing is that the ornate Victorian house, which was built in 1893, was occupied by the same family for 100 years. Six gracious guest rooms, a bridal suite, and a two-story penthouse feature private baths. Sunday through Thursday breakfast is room-service continental; Saturday a full breakfast is served. Among the landscaped gardens you can enjoy a gazebo, a pool, and paths leading to woods and a creek. Special events include the Ashford Manor Concert Series on the lawn and Shakespeare on the Lawn. Dogs accepted. In June, **Grace's Doggie Birthday Party** is a party for dogs and the people who love them, and benefits needy clients of the UGA Vet School (see *Special Events*). No smoking. Limited wheelchair accessibility. Two-night minimum for UGA games and graduation. $89–199.

INNS AND HOTELS

In Athens

*✔ ♿ **The Foundry Park Inn and Spa** (706-549-7020 or 1-866-9ATHENS; www.foundryparkinn.com), 295 East Dougherty Street. Built on the 4-acre site of the former 1850s foundry, which created the UGA Arch and the Double-Barreled Cannon, this upscale boutique property features 119 luxurious rooms and suites. In addition, the inn offers meeting facilities, a full-service spa, dining at the historic 1829 **Nathan Hoyt House Restaurant** (see *Where to Eat—Eating Out*), and food and live music at the **Melting Point Lounge. The Day Spa** (706-425-9700) showcases a wide variety of treatments. Smoking rooms available. $100–150; on home game weekends there is a two-night minimum and the rate is $225 per night.

*✔ ♿ **Georgia Gameday Center** (706-583-4500; www.gamedaycenter.com), 250 West Broad Street. This unique college-market property offers 65 UGA-themed suites with one, two, or three bedrooms. The fully furnished suites, which even have a washer and dryer, are within walking distance of restaurants, shopping, and entertainment. The facility offers a fitness center, covered parking, concierge service, high-speed Internet access, and a club room. No smoking. $139–229.

✳ Where to Eat

DINING OUT

In Athens

♿ **East-West Bistro** (706-546-9378; www.eastwestbistro.net), 351 East Broad Street. Open 11–9 Monday—Saturday, 11–8 Sunday; brunch served 11–3 Sunday. The restaurant serves Asian-Mediterranean fusion cuisine and has a lively bar scene. The Northern Italian cuisine is considered by many to be the best in Athens. No smoking. Lunch $5–10, dinner $12–22, brunch $6–8.

♿ **Five and Ten** (706-546-7300; www.fiveandten.com), 1653 South Lumpkin Street. Open 5:30–10 Monday–Thursday, 5:30–11 Friday and Saturday; brunch 10:30–2:30 Sunday. Considered by many to be the best fine-dining venue in Athens, the trendy Five and Ten is under the direction of nationally acclaimed chef Hugh Acheson, who is known for putting fun twists on old standards on the seasonally changing menu. (Acheson earned national acclaim as one of *Food and Wine* magazine's Top 10 New Chefs in America in 2002.) No smoking. Brunch $8–17, dinner $14–32.

*✔ ♿ **NONA—New Orleans 'N Athens** (706-353-7065; www.neworleansnathens.com), 279 East Broad Street. Open 11–whenever daily. Located just across the street from UGA's arch in a converted historic drugstore with a skylit atrium, this upscale jazz- and Mardi Gras–themed restaurant specializes in Cajun and Creole cuisine but also offers steak, veal, quail, and seafood. Try the weekend brunch. No smoking. Lunch and brunch $8–10, dinner $18–29.

In Athens

🦐 🍴 ♿ **Big City Bread** (706-353-0029; www.bigcitybreadcafe.net), 393 North Finley Street. Open 7 AM–9:30 PM Monday–Saturday, 7–3 Sunday. A great place for a leisurely breakfast, this laid-back bakery/restaurant/coffeehouse specializes in an array of fresh breads and fabulous pastries. The eatery serves lunch and dinner as well, using organic produce, meats, and cheeses. Smoking on patio only. $3–11.

🦐 🍴 **Donderos' Kitchen at the Botanical Gardens** (706-542-6359; www.botgarden.uga.edu), 2450 South Milledgeville Avenue. Open 10–4 Tuesday–Saturday, 11:30–4 Sunday. Located in the conservatory of the **State Botanical Garden of Georgia** (see *Green Space—Gardens*), this casual eatery offers light meals along with a beautiful view of the outdoors. You also can enjoy the monthly art exhibits. No smoking. Not wheelchair accessible. $5–6.

🦐 🍴 ♿ **The Grit** (706-543-6592; www.thegrit.com), 199 Prince Avenue. Open 11–10 weekdays, 10–3 for brunch, and 5–10 Saturday and Sunday. Although you can get grits in this dinerlike eatery, the primary focus is on good, healthful Southern vegetarian cuisine. No smoking. $3–10.

🦐 ♿ **Hoyt House Restaurant** (706-425-0444; www.foundryparkinn.com), 295 East Dougherty Street. Open for breakfast 7–11 and for lunch 11:30–2:30 daily. The on-site restaurant of the **Foundry Park Inn and Spa** (see *Lodging—Inns and Hotels*), the Hoyt House Restaurant, housed in the 1829 Nathan Hoyt home, serves traditional Southern fare for breakfast and small bites, salads, burgers, fish, and chicken for lunch. No smoking. Breakfast $6–9, lunch $5–11.

🦐 ♿ **Ike & Jane** (706-542-4662; www.georgiamuseum.org), 90 Carlton Street. Open 10–4 Tuesday–Friday. Although most diners are **Georgia Museum of Art** patrons (see *To See—Museums*), the gourmet sandwich- and rotating soup-based menu is worth the trip. Save room for dessert. No smoking. $4.50–5.50.

🦐 ♿ **Last Resort Grill** (706-549-0810; www.lastresortgrill.com), 184 West Clayton Street. Open 11–3 Monday–Saturday, 5–10 Sunday–Thursday, 5–11 Friday and Saturday, brunch 10–3 Sunday. Nouvelle Southern cuisine is served in a building that was once a nightclub where R.E.M. and the B-52s got their start. The ambience is casual and the prices affordable. Specialties such as the cornmeal-battered fried green tomato sandwich topped with Vidalia-bacon dressing, grilled salmon, or north Georgia trout top the menu. No smoking before 11 PM. Wheelchair accessible on lower-level bar and patio only. Brunch and lunch $9, dinner $14–32.

🦐 🍴 ♿ **Weaver D's Fine Foods** (706-353-7797), 1016 East Broad Street. Open 7:30–6 Monday–Saturday. "The fried chicken's on and we're waitin' for ya" is the friendly invitation at this restaurant. This Athens institution looks pretty inauspicious in its white concrete building, but it was made famous by R.E.M.'s *Automatic for the People* album—named for a sign that hangs outside the eatery. The sign refers to good food and quick, efficient service with a smile. Weaver D's serves up "soul food that rocks," and a typical lunch might consist of fried chicken, pork chops, catfish, barbecue, steak and gravy, or meat loaf. No smoking. $4.50–11.

SNACKS

In Athens

🦐 🍴 ♿ **The Grill** (706-543-4770), 171 College Avenue. Open 24/7. In this downtown diner oozing '50s nostalgia, you can get burgers, fries, and a milk shake. Started in 1981, it's the second-oldest restaurant in Athens. If you're in the mood for something more substantial, the menu includes hot sandwiches; crinkle-cut fries with feta dressing, the local specialty; and vegetarian offerings. You can get an ample breakfast from midnight to noon. No smoking. $2.50–8.

🦐 🍴 ♿ **The Varsity** (706-548-2880 or 1-800-273-4690; www.thevarsity.com), 1000 West Broad Street. Open 10–10 Sunday–Thursday, 10–midnight Friday and Saturday. Opened in 1928, the original location in Atlanta is still in operation. At all Varsity outlets, including the one in Athens, the hot dogs, onion rings, greasy fries, and frosted orange drinks are beloved by Georgians. No smoking. $1–6.25 (cash only).

COFFEEHOUSES

In Athens

🍴 🎵 ♿ **Jittery Joe's Coffee Roasting Company–Five Points** (706-208-1979; www.jitteryjoes.com), 1210 South Milledge Avenue (with two other locations in the city). Open 6:30 AM–midnight weekdays, 7:30 AM–midnight weekends. Athens's favorite coffee shop, now a national chain, began in Athens next to the 40 Watt Club. Joe's slogan is "Jittery Joe's—Because life is too short to drink grocery store coffee." True to the company philosophy, Jittery Joe's claims to serve the freshest coffee in town, with several varieties of locally roasted coffees served hot, cold, or frozen. In addition, you can get tea, soft drinks, bagels, pastries, and desserts. No smoking. Coffee $1.65–3.75, pastries $2–4.

✳ Entertainment

COLLEGE SPORTS **University of Georgia** (UGA Visitors Center: 706-542-0842; www.visit.uga.edu). For schedules and tickets to UGA games and sporting events, contact the **UGA Athletic Association** (706-542-1515; www.georgiadogs .com). The university boasts 21 Division 1-A sports teams that have won 10 national championships and 22 Southeastern Conference championships since 1998. Football is played at **Sanford Stadium** (706-542-9036), Sanford Drive; basketball and gymnastics use **Stegeman Coliseum** (706-542-1231), Smith Street; swim meets and volleyball tournaments occur at the **Ramsey Student Center for Physical Activities** (706-542-5060), River Road.

MUSIC **Athens Symphony Orchestra** (706-425-4205; www.athenssymphony.org), mailing address: P.O. Box 5244, Athens 30604. For ticket information, contact the box office at the **Classic Center Theatre** (706-357-4444), 300 North Thomas Street. Since 1979, the community orchestra has been entertaining Athenians with winter, spring, pops, and Christmas concerts. Most performances are held at the Classic Center Theatre. Free, but tickets required. They can be picked up at Classic Center box office Monday two weeks prior to concert; maximum four tickets per family.

NIGHTLIFE ♿ **40 Watt Club** (706-549-7871; www.40watt.com), 285 West Washington Street, Athens. Open 10 PM–2:45 AM daily unless nationally touring band is performing, at which time opening is 8 PM. The world-famous nightclub, named for the single 40-watt bulb that barely provided the illumination in the original location on opening night in 1978, offers live music six nights a week and a DJ on the seventh night. Although the club is best known for rock, it also books some R&B. No smoking. Wheelchair accessible, including restrooms. Cover $5–6. Admission cash only; bars take credit cards. Some bands require ticketed admission. Ticket may be purchased at the club; online at the club's website; at **Low Yo Yo Stuff Records** (706-227-6199), 285 West Washington Street, Athens; and at **Schoolkids Records** (706-353-1666), 264 East Clayton Street, Athens. Call or check the website for a schedule of performances and ticket prices.

Georgia Theatre (706-850-7670; www .georgiatheatre.com), 215 North Lumpkin Street, Athens. Call or consult website for a schedule of events and prices. One of the city's most revered venues, this theater helped launch the careers of numerous local musicians and bands, such as R.E.M., Widespread Panic, and the B-52s, which achieved national fame. The theater was built in 1889, but extensive renovations in 1935 resulted in the art deco facade. Tragically the building was heavily damaged by fire in 2009. In partnership with the Georgia Trust for Historic Preservation, the theater was restored and reopened in 2011. Today it is used as a nightclub venue for popular bands. Call for a schedule of events and ticket prices. The box office is open 11:30 AM–midnight daily.

Melting Point Live Music Venue (706-254-6909; www.foundryparkinn.com), 295 East Dougherty Street, Athens. Opens at 6 PM for evening entertainment and shows; dining begins at 3 PM. Artists as diverse as the Old Crow Medicine Show, Sean Lennon, Preservation Hall Jazz Band, and Francine Reed have performed here. A full menu is served. Call for a schedule of performances and ticket prices.

THEATER Classic Center Theatre (box office: 706-357-4444; www.classiccenter .com), 300 North Thomas Street, Athens. Box office open 10–6 Monday–Friday, 9–1 Saturday (weekdays only in summer). Call for a schedule of events and prices. The state-of-the-art, 2,050-seat theater is the venue for national Broadway touring companies, a country music series, headline entertainers, the **Athens Symphony Orchestra** (see *Music*), and other productions.

Morton Theatre (706-613-3770; events line: 706-613-3771; www.mortontheatre .com), 195 West Washington Street, Athens. Box office open 10–1 and 3–6 weekdays. Call for a schedule of events and prices. Free tours by reservation. One of the country's first and oldest surviving vaudeville theaters, the Morton was built in 1910 and owned and operated by African American politician and businessman M. B. Morton. During its heyday, it hosted performers such as Louis Armstrong, Cab Calloway, Duke Ellington, and Bessie Smith. Now listed on the National Register of Historic Places, the theater serves as a community performing arts venue with a wide range of dramatic and musical performances, including national touring groups.

University of Georgia Performing Arts Center (box office: 706-542-4400 or 1-888-289-8497; www.pac.uga.edu), 230 River Road, Athens. Box office open 9–5 Monday–Friday. Call for a schedule of events and prices. Actually several venues, the center is home to the **Athens Symphony Orchestra** (see *Music*), Dance Fest, the Showtime Series, Traditions Series, and the Ramsey Hall Concert Series, as well as

an outstanding lineup of award-winning local, regional, and national talent. The center has two theaters: the 1,100-seat Hogdson Hall and the 360-seat Ramsey Hall. Last-minute tickets frequently available.

✴ Selective Shopping

ANTIQUES Athens Antique Mall (706-354-0108; www.theathensantique mall.com), 4615 Atlanta Highway, Bogart. Open 10–5:30 Monday–Saturday, 12:30–5:30 Sunday. The largest antiques emporium in the Athens area, the mall has 25 dealers who offer European and American antiques including silver, fine arts, and home furnishings.

Athens Five Points District, centered on Milledge Avenue, Milledge Circle, and Lumpkin Street in Athens, is an area of 1920s and 1930s homes now teeming with antiques and other shops, such as Appointments at Five and the Garden Gate.

ART GALLERIES Fire Hall No. 2 (706-353-1801), 489 Prince Avenue, Athens. Call for hours. Located in a triangular 1901 structure, the two-story Romanesque firehouse at Hill and Prince avenues anchors one end of the Cobbham Historic District. In its newest incarnation, the old fire hall contains an art gallery and is also the home of the Athens-Clark Heritage Foundation.

Oconee Cultural Arts Foundation (706-769-4565; www.ocaf.com), 34 School Street, Watkinsville. Open 10–4 Tuesday–Saturday. Several nationally recognized artists live and work in Oconee County. The Oconee Cultural Arts Center, located in a 1902 four-room brick schoolhouse, provides exhibition space for contemporary art, folk art, and various crafts, as well as musical and theatrical performances and other events.

CRAFTS Chappelle Gallery in the Historic Haygood House (706-310-0985; www.chapellegallery.net), 25 South Main Street, Watkinsville. Open 10–5:30 Monday–Saturday. The gallery showcases American crafts including drawings, paintings, pottery, blown glass, stained glass, wood, wrought iron, candles, and other works by local, regional, and national artists.

Happy Valley Pottery (706-769-5922), 1210 Carson Graves Road, Watkinsville. Open 9–4 daily. Founded in 1970 and named after a Walt Disney production, the facility features on-site pottery-making and glass-blowing demonstrations.

FLEA MARKETS J&J Flea Market (706-613-2410), 11661 Commerce Road, Athens. Open 8–5 daily. An astounding 750 outside tables and 400 inside booths are crammed with bargains in antiques, crafts, collectibles, and everything from boiled peanuts to live chickens to tube socks. During the summer months, farmers sell their homegrown produce. Five dining options, including the Flea Bite Café, keep hungry shoppers on the property.

RECORDS Wuxtry Records Buy and Sell and Bizarro Wuxtry Comics (706-369-9428; www.wuxtry-records.com), 225 East Clayton Street, Athens. Open 10–8 Monday and Tuesday, 10–10 Wednesday–Saturday, noon–6 Sunday. A locally owned music shop established in 1975, Wuxtry Records was the first-of-its-kind used-record outlet and has been named one of the Top 25 Record Stores in the U.S. by *Rolling Stone* in 2010. Considered part museum and part record shop, it has offered mainstream and obscure albums as well as a vast array of CDs, cassettes, and publications. R.E.M.'s Peter Buck worked here, and, in fact, he and fellow band member Michael Stipe met here. Other merchandise includes toys, models, cards, clothes, and vintage delights.

SPECIAL STORES & **The Junkman's Daughter's Brother** (706-543-4454), 458 East Clayton Street, Athens. Open 11–7 Monday–Saturday, noon–6 Sunday. A sibling to the trendy Junkman's Daughter in Atlanta's funky Little Five Points neighborhood, the emporium carries cool clothes, leather and studs, costumes, posters, pop-culture collectibles, hilarious novelties, and used, vintage, and consignment items.

✻ Special Events

April or May: **Athens Human Rights Festival** (706-208-8674; www.athens humanrightsfest.org), College Square downtown. For more than a quarter century, the two-day festival has been an activist tradition that combines politics, music, outdoor fun, and a full lineup of local musicians, as well as art and entertainment interspersed with speakers and political activists from around the world. Free.

June: **AthFest Music and Arts Festival** (www.athfest.com), downtown Athens at outside stages and in clubs. The four-day music and arts festival showcases local talent and includes as many as 150 bands, a juried artists' market, a nighttime "Club Crawl," a music seminar, and activities for children at KidsFest. A compilation CD is released each year to showcase new music and groups. Performances at outdoor stages free; all-venue weekend wristbands that include performances in clubs $10–15. If you have questions, use the website to determine the proper e-mail contact.

❦ **Grace's Doggie Birthday Party** (706-769-2633; www.gracesbirthday.com). Held on the grounds of the **Ashford Manor Bed and Breakfast** (see *Lodging—Bed & Breakfasts*), 5 Harden Hill Road in Watkinsville, the party for pooches and their human guests features entertainment, a silent auction, and contests. The fun-filled event, which raises money for needy clients of the UGA Vet School, has been featured in *Southern Living* magazine. $15.

October 31: **Wild Rumpus, Halloween, Athens Style** (www.wildrumpus.org). Bands and thousands of fans alike dress in wild costumes for a parade through downtown ending at the Georgia Theatre for an After Party. It's a fright to behold. Athens's version of Mardi Gras consists of floats and motorized vehicles as well as participants organized into brigades such as Zombies, Pythons (Monty, that is), movie characters, dead and famous, leather and lace, and the like. For more information, consult the website or send an e-mail to wild rumpus@gmail.com.

November and December: **Christmas in Athens** (convention and visitors bureau: 706-357-4430; www.visitathensga.com /holiday). A compilation of almost 150 events throughout November and December. One of the premier Christmas in Athens activities is the **Downtown Athens Christmas Parade of Lights** (706-613-3620), traditionally held the first Saturday evening in December. The festivities begin with the tree lighting by Santa and Mrs.

Claus at City Hall, followed by the parade that features 60 floats and bands. Another popular Christmas in Athens event is the **Georgia Club Foundation Christmas Tour of Homes** (770-725-8100), an opportunity to visit six private homes decked out in all their holiday glory. $25 in advance, $28 the day of the tour (usually the second Sunday in December). Some Christmas in Athens events free; individual events $8–25.

AUGUSTA

Augusta is Georgia's second-oldest city (dating from 1736) as well as its second largest, with a population of 193,000. Once Savannah had been settled in 1733, explorers and settlers followed the Savannah River north and developed a remote trading post at what is now Augusta—named for Princess Augusta, the mother of King George III. St. Paul's Church sits on the site of Fort Augusta, the original location of the city.

The area first served as a fur trading outpost. Settlers then attempted unsuccessfully to grow tobacco, so cotton was tried next. In 100 years, Augusta developed into the second-largest inland cotton market in the world. The city served as the state capital from 1783 to 1795 and saw action in the French and Indian, Revolutionary, and Civil wars. Despite the fact that Confederate ammunition was made here, the city was spared.

The Augusta Canal, which was built in 1846 and expanded in 1872 to harness the power of the Savannah River and to attract manufacturing to the South, was constructed by Irish, Italians, Chinese, slaves, and free blacks—all of whose influence can still be seen today. The canal saw 25,000 bales of cotton a year moved along its banks. During this era of "White Gold," it was reported that when cotton bales were stacked ready for shipping, a person could walk from bale to bale for more than a mile without ever putting a foot on the ground. Reaching from the headgates in Columbia County to downtown Augusta, the canal is a nationally designated heritage area. The canal and its associated towpath, where mules used to pull the barges, offer opportunities for hiking, cycling, fishing, and canoeing or kayaking.

Although the Savannah River was the instrument of the city's commercial and industrial success, it hasn't always been a hospitable neighbor. Several great floods left residents getting around the streets by boat. A levee was built to hold back the river, but even it was breached in 1929, when the river crested at more than 45 feet. Unfortunately, the city also suffered a great fire in 1916 that devastated 32 blocks.

Located on the Piedmont Fall Line, Augusta was considered upcountry by coastal residents who fled there in the summer for the cooler temperatures. Augusta's prosperity, coupled with the felicitous weather and the fact that the city was the end of the line for north–south railroads for many years, made Augusta a playground for the rich and famous. President William Howard Taft, John D. Rockefeller, and Harvey Firestone were only a few of the elite who wintered in Augusta's luxury hotels. Sadly, none of those hotels survives today.

It was during the resort era that the first golf courses were laid out. Golf legend Bobby Jones built his dream course in the 1930s on the site of the Fruitlands Nursery. Today, golf legends play the Augusta National Golf Club each April during the annual Masters golf tournament. Be forewarned, however, that the Augusta National Golf Club, where the Masters is played, is a private club and does not allow visitors on the grounds at any time. Admission to the tournament is by a special badge for which there is a lengthy waiting list.

In addition to golf, Augusta is also known for other sporting events, such as the Augusta Futurity, a cutting-horse event, and the Barrel Horse World Championships. Known as "the Watersports Capital of the Southeast," Augusta also hosts several rowing and racing events.

NOW A BANK, THE AUGUSTA COTTON EXCHANGE WAS ONCE THE SECOND-LARGEST COTTON MARKET IN THE WORLD.

GUIDANCE When planning a trip to the Augusta area, contact the **Augusta Metropolitan Convention and Visitors Bureau** (706-823-6600 or 1-800-726-0243; www.augustaga.org), 1450 Greene Street, Suite 310, Enterprise Mill, Augusta 30901. (Mailing address: P.O. Box 1331, Augusta 30903-1331.) Open 8:30–5 weekdays.

The **Augusta Visitor Information Center** (706-724-4067 or 1-877-284-8782), 5608 Reynolds Street, Augusta 30901, is located inside the **Augusta Museum of History** (see *To See—Museums*). Open 10–5 Monday–Saturday, 1–5 Sunday.

There is also a **Georgia State Visitor Center** (706-737-1446) on I-20 westbound just inside the Georgia–South Carolina state line in Martinez. Open 8:30–5:30 daily.

Additional sources of information are the **Augusta Canal Authority** (706-823-0440 or 1-888-659-8926; www.augustacanal.com), 1458 Greene Street, Suite 400, Augusta 30901, for facts about the canal and its recreational opportunities, and **Historic Augusta** (706-724-0436; www.historicaugusta.org), 415 Seventh Street, Augusta 30901, for historical details about the city and tour information.

For Masters golf credentials, housing, hospitality, and transportation services, contact **Ticket Daddy LLC** (706-364-4250 or 1-888-642-4200; www.TicketDaddy.com), the Atrium Building, 3633 Wheeler Road, Suite 270, Augusta 30901.

GETTING THERE *By air:* Visitors will fly into **Augusta Regional Airport** or into Atlanta and take a shuttle or rental car to Augusta. In either case, see "What's Where in Georgia" for airport, airline, and car rental information.

By bus: **Southeastern Stages** (706-722-6411; www.southeasternstages.com), 1128 Greene Street, serves Augusta directly and connects to **Greyhound Lines** (1-800-229-9424; www.greyhound.com), 1128 Greene Street.

By car: Major highways that serve Augusta are I-20 and I-520 (which circles the city), US 1, US 25, US 78, and US 278.

GETTING AROUND Car rentals can be obtained from **Alamo, Avis, Budget, Economy, Enterprise, Hertz, National,** and **Thrifty.** Local bus service with numerous routes is offered by **Augusta Public Transit** (706-821-1719).

WHEN TO GO The **Masters** golf tournament is a ticketed event, and tickets are almost impossible to obtain (see *Special Events*). If you are not one of the privileged few with tickets, we strongly urge you not to visit Augusta during the first week in April. Not only are accommodations almost impossible to find, they are outrageously expensive and require a minimum stay. Traffic is heavy, and restaurants are crowded. With 51 other glorious weeks in which to visit, why subject yourself to the aggravation? If you are one of the lucky few, then all the inconveniences won't bother you at all.

VILLAGES AND NEIGHBORHOODS Augusta boasts several historic neighborhoods of tree-lined streets and majestic mansions that are appropriate for walking and/or driving tours. The **Summerville–Gould's Corner** neighborhood, locally known as "the Hill" because of its lofty location above the city, is a time warp where Greek Revival mansions vie for attention with Italian Renaissance Victorians. The **Olde Town Pinch Gut Historic District** also features many historical styles popular at the turn of the 20th century. The neighborhood derived its unusual name from the corsets with which ladies cinched themselves in those days. The **Laney-Walker Historic District** is the heart of what was the African American business district in the days of segregation.

✳ To See

Purchase an 🎨 **Augusta Gallery Pass** from the visitor information center and other venues. The pass allows entrance to seven attractions and galleries including the Augusta Canal, Meadow Garden, Augusta Museum of History, Morris Museum of Art, Ezekiel Harris House, the Boyhood Home of Woodrow Wilson, and the Lucy Laney Museum. The cost is $20, and if you visit at least four places, you'll have paid for the pass and can enjoy all the other attractions gratis.

CULTURAL SITES Augusta boasts several interesting monuments. For more information about any of them, consult the **Augusta Metropolitan Convention and Visitors Bureau** (see *Guidance*).

🎨 ✎ ♿ **Confederate Monument,** between Seventh and Eighth streets at Broad Street, is unusual in that it honors the common soldier with a Confederate private featured on the top, while generals Robert E. Lee, Stonewall Jackson, T. R. R. Cobb, and W. H. T. Walker encircle the base.

🎨 ✎ ♿ **Confederate Powderworks Chimney,** 1717 Gooodrich Street. The only permanent structure ever built by the Confederate States of America was the Confederate Powderworks in Augusta, created to manufacture ammunition. During its brief operation, the Powderworks manufactured 2 million pounds of gunpowder. Although the building is long gone, the chimney remains and is a visible, if silent, reminder of the Confederacy.

🎨 ✎ ♿ **Haunted Pillar,** Fifth and Broad streets, is a local legend. The pillar was part of the Lower City Market. The story goes that an itinerant evangelist was refused permission to preach at the market, so he put a curse on it. In 1878 a cyclone destroyed the market, with the exception of this pillar. Legend has it that several attempts have been made to remove or move the pillar, all to no avail.

🎨 ✎ ♿ **Signers Monument,** Greene and Monument streets. The obelisk marks the burial spot of two of three Georgia signers of the Declaration of Independence: Lyman Hall and George Walton.

In addition to these significant historical monuments, there's another monument in Augusta that's just plain fun. That's the life-size **statue of James Brown**—the Godfather of Soul, aka Mr. Dynamite, an Augusta native—that stands in the middle of Broad Street across from Augusta Commons between Eight and Ninth streets. The James Brown CAM allows you to have your picture taken with Soul Brother Number One by dialing a special number on your cell phone. The picture of you and the Hardest Working Man in Show Business posts in 10 minutes.

In Thomson, the **Women of the Confederacy Monument,** 111 Railroad Street, is one of the few such monuments in the South. It was created from Italian marble sometime between 1910 and 1920 in Florence, Italy. The base contains the names of Confederate soldiers from Thomson.

GUIDED TOURS 🏛 ♂ **Saturday Guided Historic Tours** (706-724-4067). Tours depart at 1 from outside Augusta Visitor Information Center in the Augusta Museum of History, Sixth and Reynolds streets. By reservation only at least 24 hours in advance. Taking one of these fascinating driving tours is an opportunity to see Augusta in the company of local guides who impart their love of the city's rich history. To tour on your own, request a copy of *Discover Augusta on Foot* or any of four other tours from the Augusta Metropolitan Convention and Visitors Bureau (see *Guidance*). These tours are also downloadable from the website www.wilsonboyhoodhome.computerone.us/walking-tours.cfm. Guided tour: all seats $12.

HISTORIC HOMES AND SITES 🏛 ♂ ♿ **The Boyhood Home of President Woodrow Wilson** (706-722-9828; www.wilsonboyhoodhome.org), 419 Seventh Street, Augusta. Open 10–5 Tuesday–Saturday; tours on the hour until 4. This is the oldest presidential site in Georgia. From 1860 to 1870, the future 28th president of the United States, Thomas "Tommy" Woodrow Wilson, lived in the manse of the First Presbyterian Church while his father served as the church's pastor. The house has been restored by Historic Augusta and opened to the public. Wilson's sojourn here, which lasted from age 3 to 13, occurred during the Civil War, and the wounded soldiers he saw on the lawns of the church undoubtedly affected his later views about war. The house museum shows 14 rooms, including Tommy's bedroom, each furnished with original and period pieces, as well as the Carriage House–Stable, where the future president played with his friends. Look for the place where he signed his name in the house. Wilson visited while he was president and reminisced about how that period had affected his life. Next door is the **Joseph Rucker Lamar Boyhood Home** (706-722-9828), 415 Seventh Street, which serves as the headquarters of Historic Augusta and the visitors center of the Wilson Home. Open 8:30–5 Monday–Friday, 10–5 Saturday. A friend of Wilson's when the two were boys, Lamar later became a Supreme Court Justice, but not during Wilson's presidency. Four downtown walking tours are downloadable from the website www.wilsonboyhoodhome.computerone.us/walking-tours.cfm. *Note:* Only the first floor of the Wilson Home is wheelchair accessible. Adults $5, seniors $4, children through 12th grade $3.

🏛 **Ezekiel Harris House** (706-737-8454; www.augustamuseum.org/harrishouse.php), 1822 Broad Street, Augusta. Open 10–5 Saturday. Built in 1797, the house is a reminder of the days when tobacco, not cotton, was king. It is the second-oldest building in Augusta. Ezekiel Harris established a tobacco inspection station and warehouse, and laid out a town he called Harrisburg, which he hoped would rival Augusta. He also offered accommodations in his house. Considered to be the finest 18th-century house in Georgia, it is an outstanding example of early Federal-style architecture. Adults $2, children $1.

🏛 **Meadow Garden, George Walton Historic Site** (706-724-4174; www.historicmeadow garden.org), 1320 Independence Way (13th Street at Walton Way), Augusta. Open 10–4 weekdays; last tour at 3:30. The oldest documented house in Augusta, Meadow Garden was built in 1792. It was the home of George Walton, one of Georgia's signers of the Declaration of Independence, who, at 35, was the youngest signer. Walton went on to have distinguished careers as a soldier, a legislator, a judge, and eventually the governor of Georgia. The house was saved from demolition by the Georgia State Society of the Daughters of the American Revolution in 1900 and opened as a house museum in 1901. As such it is the oldest house museum in Georgia. The house you will see includes additions made between 1825 and 1840 and is filled with simple colonial-era furnishings. Take some time outside to enjoy the herb, kitchen, and weavers gardens. Adults $4, seniors $3.50, college students $3, children $1.

🏛 ♿ **Sacred Heart Cultural Center** (706-826-4700; www.sacredheartaugusta.org), 1301 Greene Street, Augusta. Open 9–5 weekdays. An architectural masterpiece built between

1897 and 1900, this graceful building was once a Catholic church. Deconsecrated when the congregation moved to the suburbs, the building was in danger of demolition before it was saved and restored to have a new life as the heart of Augusta's cultural community, with offices of the ballet, opera, symphony, and other arts organizations. The redbrick, double-spired Romanesque church features no less than 15 brick patterns. Inside, feast your eyes on the stained-glass windows, elaborate altar, and Italian columns, among other fine examples of old-world craftsmanship. Many concerts, six art exhibitions, and other special events, such as the Garden Festival in April and holiday events in December, are held here throughout the year. Donations accepted for self-guided tours.

♥ **Ware's Folly, Gertrude Herbert Institute of Art** (706-722-5495), 506 Telfair Street, Augusta. Open 10–5 Tuesday–Friday, Saturday by appointment. So exorbitant ($40,000) was the cost of Nicholas Ware's Federal-style home in 1818 that locals called it Ware's Folly. Itself a work of art, the mansion has among its features a double exterior stairway, fluted pilasters, a three-story elliptical staircase, and elegant bay windows. Mrs. Olivia A. Herbert, a New Yorker who wintered in Augusta, bought the mansion and renovated it. In 1937 she gifted it as a permanent home for the Augusta Art Club in memory of her daughter, Gertrude Herbert Dunn. Today the institute offers art classes and workshops, and presents several major art exhibitions each year. Free.

♥ **Watson Homes** (706-595-7777 or 1-879-595-9777; www.hickory-hill.org), 502 Hickory Hill Drive, Thomson. Open 10–5 weekdays; tours on the hour until 4, but call ahead to make sure the house isn't closed for a school group. Thomson was the home of controversial lawyer, statesman, senator, author, and publisher Thomas E. Watson. He was best known for founding the Georgia People's Party in 1891 and running unsuccessfully as the party's vice presidential candidate, but he is also acknowledged as the father of the rural free mail delivery system. His birthplace and two of his later homes are owned and operated by the Watson-Brown Foundation. The simple **Thomas E. Watson Birthplace** is a cabin built in 1830 and moved here from its original location 3 miles away. The **Thomas E. Watson House** was built in 1865 and acquired by Watson in 1881. Today the house serves as the administrative headquarters of the foundation but is open for tours. Filled with photographs, memorabilia, and period furniture, it is surrounded by 6 acres of gardens. Lastly, in 1900 Watson acquired **Hickory Hill,** which was built around 1864. He added impressive Greek Revival elements, enlarged the house, and added modern conveniences such as electricity and indoor plumbing. After extensive renovation, it has been restored to its 1920 appearance and features original furnishings throughout as well as memorabilia depicting the senator's life and career. Surrounding the house are support structures such as the corncrib, smokehouse, pigeon cote, garage, and even a one-room schoolhouse. There are gardens and orchards, too. Adults $3, seniors $2, children 5–18 $1.

MUSEUMS ♥ ✍ ♿ **Augusta Canal National Heritage Area Interpretive Center** (706-823-0440; www.augustacanal.com), 1450 Greene Street, Augusta. Open 9:30–5:30 Monday–Saturday, 1–5:30 Sunday; closed Monday, December–February. One of the pivotal factors in the development of Augusta was the Augusta Canal. Now designated as the Augusta Canal National Heritage Area—Georgia's only officially designated National Heritage Area—the 8-mile waterway is the only intact industrial canal in the country in continuous use since its construction in the 1840s. The interpretive center is appropriately housed in the renovated 19th-century **Enterprise Mill,** an important landmark itself. Built in 1877, by 1900 it had 33,000 spindles and 928 looms. It employed more than 400 workers, who manufactured more than 10.8 million yards of cloth yearly, the equivalent of 6,200 miles of fabric. The center narrates the story of the canal and the Southern textile industry it made possible. Begin a tour with the movie *The Power of a Canal* and then see the exhibits, which include models, working mill machinery, and more. Many of the exhibits are interactive. In season, a highlight of any visit to the center can be a **Petersburg Boat Guided Tour,** which glides past natural and historic sites. The only Petersburg tour boats in the world, the shallow-draft, 49-passenger boats were modeled on the long wooden vessels powered by six-man African American crews that carried cargo on the river and canal. These boats are the largest electrically powered boats in America. Boat tours are held weather permitting. The towpath and nature trails along the canal are also worth exploring. Get a free self-guided tour map of the canal from the **Augusta Canal Authority** offices (see *Guidance*) or the interpretative center. Admission to center: adults $6, seniors and military $5, children 4–12 $4. One-hour guided boat tour with admission to center: $12.50. Saturday sunset boat tour and admission to center: $25; Friday Moonlight Tour: $25.

🐾 ✍ ♿ **Augusta Museum of History** (706-722-8454; www.augustamuseum.org), 560 Reynolds Street, Augusta. Open 10–5 Tuesday–Saturday, 1–5 Sunday. Filled with fascinating exhibits, some of them interactive, the museum has 15,000 artifacts that chronicle Augusta's 12,000-year history from its prehistoric physical geography to the Paleo-Indian period to the present, concentrating on the area's transformation from a trading post to an industrial and commercial center. The Confederate collection features uniforms, flags, and weapons. Among other interesting artifacts are Edgefield pottery from nearby South Carolina, Masters golf tournament memorabilia, and an exhibit centered around the Godfather of Soul James Brown, which includes an array of costumes, family photos, programs from his memorial services, and audiovisual stations showcasing performance footage, studio recordings, and interviews. Other displays center on railroading and banking. This museum allows visitors to clean cotton in a replica cotton gin, as well as view a Petersburg boat, a restored 1917 steam locomotive, and a reconstructed 1930s gas station. In the Susan L. Still Children's Discovery Gallery, named for the astronaut, youngsters can pack a canoe, sit at the controls of a space shuttle, and dress up and play games of children from throughout Augusta's history. Documentaries are shown continuously in the History Theater. Adults $4, seniors $3, children 6–18 $2.

🐾 ✍ ♿ **Laurel and Hardy Museum** (706-556-0401 or 1-888-288-9108; www.laurel andhardymuseum.org), 250 North Louisville Street, Harlem. Open 10–4 Tuesday–Saturday. Visitors can yuck it up as they watch old Laurel and Hardy films and see other memorabilia concerning Oliver Hardy, the more rotund of the duo, who entered the world's stage in Harlem in 1892. Although he attended Georgia Military College in Milledgeville, the Atlanta Conservatory of Music, and even the University of Georgia School of Law, entertainment was in his blood. He left for Hollywood in 1918 and paired up with Englishman Stan Laurel. Together they made more than 100 films and worked on the stage and in radio and television. In addition to the film clips, visitors can see movie posters, photographs, and souvenirs related to Hardy's career. In October, the town keeps his legacy alive by sponsoring the **Oliver Hardy Festival** (see *Special Events*). Free.

AN EXHIBIT AT THE AUGUSTA CANAL INTERPRETIVE CENTER

🐾 ✍ ♿ **Lucy Craft Laney Museum of Black History** (706-724-3576; www.lucy craftlaneymuseum.com), 1116 Phillips Street, Augusta. Open 9–5 Tuesday–Friday, 10–4 Saturday. Serving an important function in the central Savannah River area, the museum is the only one in the area focusing on African Americans. The museum is housed in the modest house of Lucy Craft Laney, who, although born a slave, graduated from Atlanta University and became a famous educator. Among her many accomplishments were Augusta's first kindergarten for African Americans, the first nurse's

THE FOUNTAIN AT THE ENTRANCE TO
RIVERWALK AUGUSTA

training classes for black women, and the Haines Normal and Industrial Institute, which educated thousands of African American students. Artifacts from Laney's life and exhibits about notable Augustans are among several permanent exhibits and collections. While you're visiting the museum, save enough time to stroll through the Period Garden. Adults $5, seniors $3, children $2.

🐾 ♿ **Morris Museum of Art** (706-724-7501; www.themorris.org), One Tenth Street, Augusta. Open 10–5 Tuesday–Saturday, noon–5 Sunday. This site, known as the Museum of Painting in the South, exhibits the work of Southern artists from the antebellum period to the present, with some of the exhibits focusing on Civil War art, the black presence in Southern art, and Southern impressionism. The museum, located on Riverwalk downtown, is an affiliate of the Smithsonian Institution. Adults $5; military, students, youth, and seniors $3; children 12 and younger free. Free on Sunday.

🐾 ✒ **Savannah Rapids Visitor Center** (706-868-3373), 3300 Lock-and-Dam Road, Augusta. Open 10–4 Tuesday–Thursday, 11–3 Sunday. Located in a historic lockkeeper's home, the center offers not only information and brochures, but also serves as a museum depicting the history of Columbia County and describing the significance of the Augusta Canal through pictures and exhibits. The lockkeeper's bedroom has been re-created to interpret the lives of those who once lived and worked there. Free.

🐾 ✒ ♿ **U.S. Army Signal Corps Museum** (706-791-2818; www.signal.army.mil/ocos /museum), Conrad Hall, Building 29807, Fort Gordon. Open 8–4 Tuesday–Friday. Exhibits trace the development of the Signal Corps from its beginning in 1860 to the present. The museum has more than 10,000 objects in its collections. Among the interesting exhibits are those focusing on Signal Corps aviation and the World War I "Hello Girls." The Signal Corps winter flight school was located in Augusta from 1911 to 1913. Free.

SPECIAL PLACES 🐾 ✒ ♿ **Riverwalk Augusta,** which hugs the river between Seventh and 10th streets, is a jewel in Augusta's crown. The wonderful park is created along and on top of a flood-protection levee. A paved walkway allows visitors to stroll at their own pace while enjoying the landscaped slopes, inspect markers chronicling important events in Augusta's past, and see Hero's Overlook, which is dedicated to members of the armed forces. In addition, visitors see flags that have flown over the region, a children's playground, and **Takarazuka,** a waterfall and miniature Japanese garden display donated by the people of Augusta's sister city. Entrances at Eighth Street and 10th Street have granite markers that show the height and date of Augusta's most devastating floods. Erupting from the antique brickwork that paves the courtyard of the Eighth Street entrance is a dancing fountain that is an irresistible draw to kids of all ages—whether they're dressed for getting wet or not. The position of the **Jessye Norman Amphitheater** on the banks of the river allows spectators to enjoy concerts and other local, regional, and national entertainment from land or water. Riverwalk hosts many festivals and other events throughout the year. Free.

✳ To Do

BICYCLING 🐾 ✒ **Augusta Canal Trail,** along the old towpath, offers the best cycling in the area. Another good spot is the challenging 8-mile **Rock Dam Trail** at **Mistletoe State**

Park (see *Green Space—Nature Preserves and Parks*). It's best to bring your own bikes, because rentals are very limited.

🐾 ✏ **The Bicycle Peddler at Savannah Rapids Park** (706-373-4519), 3300 Evans to Lock Road, Martinez. Open 10–7 weekends. $20 for four hours.

✏ **Chain Reaction Cycling** (706-855-2024), 3920 Roberts Road, Augusta, offers comfort and mountain bikes. Rental $20 per day.

BOATING 🐾 ✏ ♿ **Augusta Riverwalk Marina** (706-722-1388), One Fifth Street, Augusta. Open 11–5 weekdays, 10–5 Saturday, noon–5 Sunday. The marina offers the only full service for boaters along the Savannah River between Savannah and Augusta. There are 68 slips with full hookups, a store with supplies and refreshments, pontoon boat rentals, and public restrooms.

CANOEING AND KAYAKING Canoeing and kayaking are available on both the Savannah River and the canal. Augusta outfitters such as **Broadway Tackle and Canoe Rentals** (706-738-8848), 1730 Broad Street, have drop-off and pickup points on both.

GOLF Jones Creek Golf Club (706-860-4228; www.jonescreekgolfclub.com), 777 Jones Creek Drive, Evans. Open 7:30–6 daily, until 7 PM during daylight saving time. Considered by many to be the best public course in America and consistently rated as one of *Golf Digest's* premier public courses, Jones Creek, a Rees Jones–designed, 18-hole, 6,900-yard course, is often called "the poor man's Augusta National." Tom Fazio was involved in a recent renovation of the course, making it even better. It also has a practice facility, driving range, instruction, a pool, and tennis courts. $45 Monday–Thursday, $55 Friday–Sunday, carts included.

HIKING Most hiking trails in these parts are easy walking—the only difference is the length. For a short, easy hike, try the 1.2-mile **Turkey Trot Trail,** the 1.3-mile **Clatt Creek Trail,** or the 1.9-mile **Twin Oaks Trail** in **Mistletoe State Park** (see *Green Space—Nature Preserves and Parks*). For longer hikes, try the 8.5-mile **Augusta Canal Trail** that runs between Martinez and downtown (see *To See—Museums*). (Keep in mind that this distance is one-way.) Modern technology has come to the Augusta Canal Trail with a new DigiTrail: At about half-mile intervals along the canal's first level are 18 signs sporting QR tags. Point your smartphone at the tag to link to mobi pages with information about history, wildlife, and natural features, as well as links to maps, phone numbers, and more. Set to launch in spring 2012 is an Augmented Reality (AR) program called Layar, which uses the smartphone's camera and GPS capabilities to digitally re-create in 3-D the long-lost buildings of the Confederate Powderworks along a 2-mile stretch of the trail.

HORSEBACK RIDING 🐾 ✏ **Hilltop Riding Stable** (706-791-4864; www.fortgordon .com/hilltop_riding_stable.php), North Range Road, Building 508, Fort Gordon. Open 9–3 Saturday, 9–noon Sunday, 11 AM Wednesday–Friday with reservations 24 hours in advance. Miniature ponies as well as beginner, intermediate, and advanced horses are available. The stable also offers youth horse camps, family fun days, and riding lessons. One-hour trail ride, unsponsored civilians, $30.

RIVERBOAT TOUR ✏ ♿ **Augusta Patriot Riverboat Tours** (office in South Carolina: 803-730-9739; www.patriottourboat.com) depart from the Tenth Street dock at the Marriott at 2:45 Wednesday–Sunday. What better way to see and hear about Augusta, the Savannah River, the surrounding undeveloped countryside, and wildlife than aboard a leisurely riverboat. Check about two-hour Saturday Sunset Cruises. Smoking outside only. Limited wheelchair accessibility. No food or beverages sold onboard. Daytime cruise: adults $12, children $6; sunset cruise: $20. Cash or check only.

GARDENS Augusta's slogan, "Garden City of the South," was chosen in the early 20th century because the city had so many large private gardens. An emphasis on gardens is still evident today.

🌿 ♂ ♿ **Monroe Kimbrel Gardens** (706-595-8886; www.watson-brown.org), 310 Tom Watson Way, Thomson. Open 8–5 weekdays, weekends by appointment. Operated as an outdoor classroom by the Watson-Brown Foundation, the gardens cover 4 acres and encompass lawns, ponds, and wetlands. Flora and fauna are Georgia natives found in the Piedmont region. Free.

LAKES 🌿 ♂ ♿ **Clarks Hill Lake–Thurmond Lake.** This schizophrenic lake straddles the border of two states and is called Clarks Hill Lake on the Georgia side and Strom Thurmond Lake on the South Carolina side (although Congress passed a bill in 1988 to change its official name to Thurmond). No matter what you call it, with 70,000 surface acres, it is the largest man-made Corps of Engineers lake east of the Mississippi River. The lake also boasts 1,200 miles of shoreline, six state parks, two county parks, and numerous Corps of Engineers and private campgrounds. Boating, swimming, hunting, fishing, and picnicking opportunities abound. Hikers can enjoy 15 miles of the Bartram Trail. Several marinas offer boat rentals and more.

NATURE PRESERVES AND PARKS 🌿 ♂ ♿ **Augusta Common,** mid-900 block of Broad Street, Augusta. The city's newest park links Broad Street to the Riverwalk and serves as the scene of many festivals, such as **Arts in the Heart of Augusta,** which is held in September. The James Brown statue is in the middle of Broad Street (see *To See—Cultural Sites*). Free.

🌿 ♂ ♿ **Mistletoe State Park** (706-541-0321; lodging reservations: 1-800-864-7275; www.gastateparks.org/Mistletoe), 3725 Mistletoe Road, Appling. Open 7 AM–10 PM daily. Located on the shores of Clarks Hill Lake, the park is known as one of the best bass-fishing spots in the country. The lake itself has no limit on boats, and three boat ramps make access easy. The park was named for Mistletoe Junction, a nearby place where folks gathered mistletoe at the turn of the 20th century. In addition to fishing, the park offers a swimming beach, 3.5 miles of nature and bike trails, a 12-mile backpacking trail, and canoe and fishing-boat rentals in season. For overnight guests, lodging is available in cottages and at campsites (see *Lodging—Campgrounds* and *Lodging—Cottages*). The park is the scene of several special events. Parking $5.

🌿 ♂ ♿ **Phinizy Swamp Nature Park** (706-828-2109; www.phinizyswamp.org), office at 1858 Lock-and-Dam Road, Augusta. Open noon–dusk weekdays, dawn–dusk weekends. Although it's located near the city, this Southeastern Natural Sciences Academy park boasts more than 1,100 acres of swampland, which provide a haven for birds and wildlife. Miles of nature trails and boardwalks as well as observation towers allow visitors to view a variety of wildlife, including blue herons, bobcats, red-shouldered hawks, otters, and alligators. Free.

🌿 ♂ ♿ **Savannah Rapids Park** (706-868-3349), 3300 Evans-to-Lock Road, Martinez. Open daylight hours. Bull Sluice identifies the first of the rapids that stretch more than 4 miles downstream and mark the fall line between the Piedmont Plateau and the Coastal Plain as well as the end of navigation up the Savannah River from the ocean. A breathtaking view of the turbulent rapids is just one reason to visit this park, because it also offers opportunities for hiking, canoeing, kayaking, fishing, and bicycling. A $1.5 million improvement project includes new launching areas for canoes and kayaks, additional walking and biking trails, additional parking, and pedestrian access. Bike rentals are available seasonally (see *To Do—Bicycling*). From here the scenic 7-mile trail extends to downtown. The park is the scene of several festivals during the year. Free.

♠ ♂ ♿ **Wildwood Park** (706-541-0586), 3780 Dogwood lane, Appling. Open 8 AM–11 PM daily. Located on Clarks Hill Lake, the 975-acre park offers beaches, eight boat ramps, a 12-mile horse trail, a nature trail, biking trails, fishing, campsites, picnicking, and volleyball. It is also the home of the International Disc Golf Center and Hall of Fame. Day use $3; $6 if pulling a boat or horse trailer.

✳ Lodging

BED & BREAKFASTS

In Augusta

♠ **Queen Anne Inn** (706-723-0045; www .queenanneaugusta.com), 406 Greene Street. Located in an imposing three-story Victorian house in Olde Town, the inn offers seven antiques-filled guest accommodations, most with a fireplace. One particularly romantic suite features a heart-shaped two-person whirlpool tub. Amenities include an outdoor Jacuzzi. No smoking. Not wheelchair accessible. $89–149; $300–600 Masters Week.

CAMPGROUNDS

In Appling

♠ ♂ ♿ ✿ **Mistletoe State Park** (lodging reservations: 1-800-864-7275; www.gastate parks.org/Mistletoe). The park features 96 tent, trailer, and RV sites; 4 walk-in sites; and 3 backcountry sites. See *Green Space— Nature Preserves and Parks.* $25–28 for tent, trailer, RV sites; $15 for primitive walk-in sites; $10 for backcountry sites.

COTTAGES

In Appling

♠ ♂ ♿ ✿ **Mistletoe State Park** (706-541-0321; lodging reservations: 1-800-864-7275; www.gastateparks.org/Mistletoe). The park offers 10 fully equipped lakeside cottages, five of which are log cabins, as well as a camper cabin that sleeps four. $45 for camper cabin, $135–145 for cottages (higher during Masters Week). Two cottages are dog friendly ($40 per dog; maximum two). See *Green Space—Nature Preserves and Parks.*

INNS AND HOTELS

In Augusta

♂ ♿ **Partridge Inn** (706-737-8888 or 1-800-476-6888; www.partridgeinn.com), 2110 Walton Way. This stately inn, the "grand dame" of Augusta hostelries, began as a private residence in 1879. Perched on a hillside overlooking downtown, the structure grew and grew over the years and eventually became a hotel. Although it was never as big as some of the hotels from the city's golden resort era from 1889 to 1930, it is the only one to survive. Today, beautifully restored and elegantly furnished, the inn offers 156 rooms, suites, and studios. One of the inn's most entrancing features is the wide expanse of verandas and balconies (a quarter mile in total)—perfect places to relax in a rocking chair with a cool drink. In addition to luxurious accommodations, the inn boasts a restaurant (see *Where to Eat— Dining Out*), lounge, pool, elevator, and exercise facility. The lobby is a mini museum in itself, with old photographs, postcards, newspaper clippings, letters, and other artifacts from the inn's long history. No smoking. $107–139.

♂ ♿ ✿ **Augusta Marriott at the Convention Center** (706-722-8900 or 1-888-868-5354; www.marriott.com), 2 10th Street. Although the hotel is fairly new, its construction blends well with the historic warehouses along the Riverwalk. Among its many attributes are river and Riverwalk views. The 349-room, 23-suite hotel features all the modern conveniences, along with a riverside pool, restaurant, and lounge. No smoking. Eleven guest rooms and all public areas fully wheelchair accessible. Small pets welcome; $25 nonrefundable deposit. $154–279.

✳ Where to Eat

DINING OUT

In Augusta

♿ **French Market Grille** (706-737-4865; www.frenchmarketaugusta.com), 425 Highland Avenue, in the Surrey Center. Open 11–10 Monday–Thursday, 11–11 Friday and Saturday. Consistently voted the best restaurant in Augusta, the eatery serves spicy Louisiana cuisine as well as a large variety of wines and beers from around the world. Smoking and nonsmoking sections. Lunch $10–14, dinner $19–28.

& **La Maison on Telfair and VERITAS Wine and Tapas Bar** (706-722-4805; www.lamaisontelfair.com), 404 Telfair Street. Open 6–9:30 daily; VERITAS open 5–whenever. Occupying a beautifully restored home built in 1853 in Olde Town, the restaurant is a perfect place for a romantic dinner. The eatery serves such specialties as wild game and seafood with French, German, and Swiss influences. A seven-course tasting dinner is available. For a lighter meal, dine on appetizers in VERI-TAS. Reservations recommended. No smoking. Appetizers $8–12, tasting dinner $49, entrées $2–40.

& **The P.I. Inn Bar and Grill** (706-737-8888 or 1-800-476-6888; www.partridge inn.com), 2110 Walton Way. Open 11–10 weekdays, 11–11 weekends; brunch 11–2 Sunday. P.I. stands for Partridge Inn, where the restaurant is located. Dinner specialties include prime rib and red snapper. The bar is a hot place for jazz on Friday and Saturday nights, and the Sunday brunch buffet is both gargantuan and accompanied by a live pianist. A lunch buffet is served weekdays. Smoking permitted after 9 PM. Lunch $6–10, dinner $14–29, Sunday brunch $22.

🍴 & **T-Bonz** (706-737-8325), 2856 Washington Road. Open 11–10 weekdays, 11–11 weekends. There's no doubt why the restaurant has been named the Best Steak in Augusta by the readers of *Augusta Magazine* every year since 1987. There's a band on Friday and Saturday nights, but no cover charge. No smoking. $11–22.

EATING OUT

In Augusta
🍴 ✒ & **Boll Weevil Café and Sweetery** (706-722-7772; www.thebollweevil.com), 10 Ninth Street. Open 11–10 Sunday–Thursday, 11–11 Friday and Saturday. A great place for a quick lunch or snack, the eatery serves a variety of Southern and Southwestern cuisine, as well as wings, soups, salads, sandwiches, pizzas, and a staggering array of desserts. No smoking. Lunch about $10, dinner $8–15.

🍴 ✒ & **Fat Man's Mill Cafe** (706-733-1740), 1450 Greene Street, Enterprise Mill Courtyard. Open 10:30–4 weekdays. Refuel with a meal of Southern comfort/soul food at this down-home restaurant. Local favorites include squash casserole, turnip greens, candied yams, macaroni and cheese, barbecue, ham, liver, and fried chicken finished off with banana pudding. The restaurant also serves hamburgers, hot dogs, and numerous varieties of sand-wiches, soups, and salads. No smoking. Under $10.

🍴 ✒ & **Sunshine Bakery** (706-724-2302), 1209 Broad Street. Open 9–3:30 weekdays. Sunshine Bakery's been a favorite for lunch with locals since the 1950s, and for good reason. Sandwiches such as Reubens, Dutch Rhubuns, pastrami, and other choices get folks lining up early to get in, to say nothing of the potato soup and brats. Lunch is served all day, so it's best not to go around noon. Whatever your luncheon choice, wash it down with a lemony Sun-shine Tea. Take home some freshly baked breads and pastries. No smoking. Under $10.

✳ Entertainment

DANCE Augusta Ballet (706-261-0555; www.augustaballet.org), offices at Sacred Heart Cultural Arts Center, 1301 Greene Street, Augusta. Four productions a year are performed at the Imperial Theatre (745 Broad Street) between October and May. Call for a schedule of performances and prices.

MUSIC Augusta Choral Society (706-826-4713; www.augustachoralsociety.org), offices at Sacred Heart Cultural Center, 1301 Greene Street, Augusta. The choral society performs major choral works, new compositions, holiday favorites, and lighter classical works—often accompanied by members of the Augusta Symphony. Single tickets: adults $25, seniors $20, and students $10.

Augusta Symphony (706-826-4705; www .augustasymphony.org), box office at Sacred Heart Cultural Center, 1301 Greene Street, Suite 200, Augusta; open 9–5 weekdays. The symphony, which celebrated its 50th anniversary in 2005, performs classical, pops, family, world premiere, and chamber concerts at various venues around the city. Tickets generally $10–40.

NIGHTLIFE & **Fox's Lair** (706-828-5600; www.thefoxslair.com), 349 Telfair Street, Augusta. Open 4 PM–midnight Tuesday–Thursday, 4 PM–2 AM Friday, 7 PM–2 AM Saturday. This English-style neighborhood pub, located on the basement level of a historic house, is an old favorite of locals and visitors alike. There is live Irish music Friday and Saturday evenings. Smoking area. No cover charge.

& **Soul Bar** (706-724-8880; www.soulbar .com), 984 Broad Street, Augusta. Open 8 PM–3 AM Monday–Saturday. A mecca for James Brown fans, this soul and funk bar offers live entertainment and dancing. Smoking area. No cover charge.

PROFESSIONAL SPORTS Augusta GreenJackets (706-736-7889; www.green jackets.net), Lake Olmstead Stadium, 78 Milledge Road, Augusta. The minor-league baseball team is a class-A affiliate of the San Francisco Giants. The season runs early April through September. Call for a schedule and prices (generally $7–13).

Augusta Riverhawks Pro Hockey (706-993-2645; www.augustariverhawks.com), office at 712 Telfair Street, Augusta. A member of the very popular and fast-growing Southern Professional Hockey League, the AA hockey Lynx play in the Augusta–Richmond County Civic Center. The season runs October through early April. Call for a schedule. $10–18.

THEATER The Fort Gordon Dinner Theatre (706-791-4389; box office: 706-793-8552; www.fortgordon.com/theatre .php), Third Avenue, Building 32100, Fort Gordon. Dinner at 7, followed by show at 8. A six-show season features plays such as *Barefoot in the Park, Caught in the Net, Passing the Buck, Pippin,* and *Wait Until Dark.* Civilians $40, $25 for show only.

The Imperial Theatre (706-722-8293; box office: 706-722-8341; www.imperial theatre.com), 745 Broad Street, Augusta. Box office open 10–4 Tuesday–Friday. The theater was built in 1917 after a terrible fire that devastated much of downtown Augusta. It hosted vaudeville, silent movies, and then "talkies." Today it hosts live stage performances such as concerts, touring Broadway shows, and movies, and is the home of the Augusta Opera and Augusta Ballet. Call for a schedule of events and prices.

✳ Selective Shopping

ART GALLERIES Artists Row (www.artistsrowaugusta.com), 700–1200 blocks of Broad Street, Augusta. Centered on the 1100 block, this is really a collection of two dozen art galleries, working studios, specialty boutiques, and one-of-a-kind bistros and cafés housed in restored 19th- and early-20th-century storefronts. There's something for everyone, including original works, prints, posters, golf prints, jewelry, and crafts. Demonstrations, artists' chats, and receptions take place monthly during First Friday gatherings (see *Special Events*). Numerous other special events take place here throughout the year.

Gertrude Herbert Institute of Art (706-722-5495), in Ware's Folly, 506 Telfair Street, Augusta. Open 10–5 Tuesday–Friday, Saturday by appointment. (See *To See—Historic Homes and Sites* for more information about the mansion.) The institute sponsors at least six major exhibitions a year, showcasing the works of students as well as local and regional artists. Each exhibition lasts six to eight weeks, and many works are for sale.

Sacred Heart Cultural Center (706-826-4700; www.sacredheartaugusta.org), 1301 Greene Street, Augusta. Open 9–5 weekdays. The gift shop features works by regional artists as well as other quality gifts and books. See *To See—Historic Homes and Sites.*

FLEA MARKETS **The Barnyard Flea Market** (706-793-8800 or 1-866-993-8800; www.barnyardfleamarkets.com), 1625 Doug Barnard Parkway, Augusta. Open 7–4:30 Saturday, 8–4:30 Sunday. The ultimate garage sale features 600 dealers.

✳ Special Events

Monthly: **First Friday Artists Row,** on Broad Street between 10th and 11th streets, Augusta. This event features art exhibitions, demonstrations, and an opportunity to meet various artists in an outdoor setting (see *Selective Shopping—Art Galleries*). Free.

January: **Augusta Futurity** (contact the Atlantic Coast Cutting Horse Association: 706-823-3417; during Futurity week call 706-722-1059; www.augustafuturity.com), held at James Brown Arena, 601 Seventh Street, Augusta. This is the largest cutting-horse tournament east of the Mississippi and one of the top 10 in the world. The fast-paced event features the country's foremost professional riders and horses competing for hundreds of thousands of dollars in prizes. Totally Western in flavor, the event features working broncs, bull riding, a horse-and-wagon parade, evening shows, an exposition of Western wear and gear, the Wrangler Family Fun Fest, seminars, and horse sales. Tickets $9–16.50 per event. Call for a schedule.

April: Practice-round tickets for the **Masters** golf tournament (706-667-6000; www.masters.com), Augusta National Golf Club, Augusta, are available through a lottery system. Online you would go to "Tickets," then go to the year, then set up your account. If

you're a lucky winner, they'll notify you by e-mail. Call for details.

May: **Blind Willie McTell Blues Festival** (706-597-1000; www.blindwillie.com). Held the third week in May in Thomson, the festival honors the pioneer and all-time great country blues 12-string guitarist William Samuel "Blind Willie" McTell, who was born south of Thomson in 1901. McTell was posthumously inducted into the Georgia Music Hall of Fame in 1990 for his more than 120 songs, including "Statesboro Blues," which was made famous by the Allman Brothers Band. The festival features a variety of local and national talent. $25 in advance, $35 at the gate.

July: **Augusta Southern Nationals Dragboat Races** (www.augustasouthern nationals.org), centered on Augusta Riverwalk Marina (see *To Do—Boating*). Gates open at 8 AM, races occur 9–6. This is a weekend of supercharged hydroplane and flat-bottomed boats competing in nine classes. Considered the world's richest dragboat race, the event carries more than $120,000 in prizes. Purchase tickets online at www.Tix-On-Line.com or call 803-278-4849. $25 per day in advance, $30 at the gate.

October: **Oliver Hardy Festival** (706-556-0401 or 1-888-288-9108; www.laureland hardymuseum.org), Harlem. The highlight of the festival is the look-alike contest, during which dozens of fussbudget Laurels roam the streets, wringing their hands and declaring, "This is a fine mess you've gotten us into." Crafts, a carnival, kids' rides and games, entertainment including skits featuring the famous duo, a parade, more movies, and a street dance keep the town hopping. Free; a fee for some activities.

BARNESVILLE

This charming, laid-back area of central Georgia is characterized by small towns, dairy farms, the timber industry, and antiques shops. In the past, Barnesville was the Buggy Capital of the World, and Forsyth served as a Civil War hospital town.

Today visitors can enjoy a historic plantation, museums, two covered bridges, numerous bed & breakfasts in grand historic homes, and a wide variety of festivals that celebrate everything from buggies to barbecue, forsythias to fried green tomatoes. The Flint River, Lake Juliette, many parks, and wide-open spaces provide endless opportunities for canoeing and kayaking, mountain biking, off-road excursions, hiking, and even skydiving.

GUIDANCE When planning a trip to Barnesville, contact the **Barnesville–Lamar County Chamber of Commerce** (770-358-5884; www.barnesville.org), 100 Commerce Place, Barnesville 30204. Open 9–5 weekdays. Get information here for the self-guided **Barnesville Walking Tour.**

For more information about Forsyth and Juliette, contact the **Forsyth–Monroe County Chamber of Commerce** (478-994-9239 or 1-888-642-4628; www.forsyth-monroechamber .com), 68 North Lee Street, Forsyth 31029. Open 8–5 weekdays. Ask about brochures for the self-guided **Historic Forsyth Walking Tour** and the **Monroe County Driving Tour.** Both tours begin at the courthouse and feature Civil War monuments, landmarks, and antebellum homes. The driving tour also includes the McCowen Cemetery, the towns of Bolingbroke and Culloden, Ham's Store, and Russellville Baptist Church. For more specific information about Juliette, consult the website at www.juliettega.com.

For information about Clinton, contact the **Jones County–Gray Chamber of Commerce** (478-986-1123; www.jonescounty.org), 161 West Clinton Street, Gray 31032.

To learn more about Thomaston, consult the **Thomaston–Upson County Chamber of Commerce** (706-647-9686; www.thomastonchamber.com), 110 West Main Street, Thomaston 30286. Open 8:30–5 Monday–Thursday, 8–4:30 Friday. You can pick up information for a self-guided driving or walking tour past Thomaston's historic homes (many of which are private residences).

GETTING THERE *By air:* The nearest airport to this region is in Macon. Because Atlanta is also close by, it is often easier to fly into there. In either case, see "What's Where in Georgia" for airport, airline, and rental car information.

By bus: The nearest **Greyhound Lines** station is in Macon (see the Macon chapter).

By car: Most of the towns in this chapter lie between I-85 and I-75, south of Atlanta and north of Macon.

By train: The nearest **AMTRAK** station is in Atlanta (see "What's Where in Georgia").

GETTING AROUND Car rentals are available at both the Atlanta and Macon airports. (See "What's Where in Georgia.")

MEDICAL EMERGENCY Call 911.

VILLAGES AND NEIGHBORHOODS Barnesville enjoyed its heyday from before the Civil War until the 1880s. During that time the small town had four buggy factories and produced 16,000 horse-drawn buggies annually, along with wagons, carts, and hearses, which earned the town the title "Buggy Capital of the World." Today Barnesville boasts a museum, an art gallery–studio, gift shops, and many restaurants. The town celebrates its history with the annual **Barnesville Buggy Days** (see *Special Events*).

Clinton was once one of the fastest-growing centers of trade and culture in this part of Georgia. Today it is a sleepy village known as "the town that time forgot." Part of the small town is designated as the Old Clinton Historic District, which is listed on the National Register of Historic Places to preserve a dozen homes built between 1808 and 1830. A brochure for a self-guided tour is available from the Jones County–Gray Chamber of Commerce (see *Guidance*). Clinton also offers several yearly and monthly events, including tours of the historic homes sponsored by the Clinton Historical Society, **Old Clinton War Days** (see *Special Events*), and the **Ole Clinton Opry** (see *Entertainment—Music*).

Forsyth became a hospital center during the Civil War. After the battles of Atlanta, Stone Mountain, and Jonesboro, 20,000 wounded soldiers were sent here. The Monroe County Courthouse, Monroe Female College, Hilliard Institute, Lumpkin Hotel, stores, and private homes were pressed into service, and there were still so many wounded, tents had to be used. After the boll weevil decimated the cotton economy, the county turned to dairy farms and timber. Forsyth's historical mid- to late-1800s commercial district is centered by 1896 Courthouse Square, where the **Forsythia Festival** is held each spring (see *Special Events*).

Griffin is called the Iris City because the Flint River Iris Society promotes and grows irises, sponsors an iris show in the spring, and offers an iris sale in the late summer. Another of Griffin's claims to fame is that it was the birthplace of the infamous outlaw Doc Holliday. Today Griffin has several museums and historic sites open to the public.

Jones County is the site of **Jarrell Plantation Historic Site** and the **Piedmont National Wildlife Refuge,** while **Gray,** the county seat, has a magnificent 1905 courthouse surrounded by a park with a gazebo and fountain.

Juliette was a thriving Monroe County community along the railroad tracks and the Ocmulgee River in the early 1900s. Unfortunately, time and changes in the economy left Juliette a virtual ghost town. In 1991, however, its river, railroad line, abandoned mill, and quaint old buildings brought Juliette a new prosperity. The small town's abandoned air was made famous as the site where the film *Fried Green Tomatoes* was filmed. Although the fictional story takes place in Alabama, author Fanny Flagg thought Juliette perfectly represented the town she envisioned. Fans of the movie will want to have lunch and some fried green tomatoes at the real **Whistle Stop Café** (see *Where to Eat—Eating Out*) and then shop up and down McCrackin Street for gifts and souvenirs.

Thomaston, imbued with small-town charm, has twice been listed in the book *100 Best Small Towns in America.* Thomaston boasts several museums and historic houses, a restored art deco theater, a covered bridge, and quaint antiques and gift shops around the courthouse square. The city also hosts an Emancipation Proclamation Celebration each May, the nation's oldest and longest running such event. It includes speeches, a parade, and a candlelight prayer service. **Sprewell Bluff Wildlife Management Area** is nearby (see *Green Space—Nature Preserves and Parks*).

✴ To See

COVERED BRIDGES 🐾 ✒ ♿ **Auchumpkee Creek Covered Bridge,** on Allen Road off US 19 South, Thomaston. Open daily. Covered bridges are so precious that when one is lost, it's a great tragedy. The original 96-foot-long Town Lattice–design bridge in this location was built in 1892. Unfortunately, it was destroyed by the devastating south Georgia floods of 1994 but has since been authentically rebuilt by a nationally renowned covered-bridge craftsman using portions of the original bridge. Many of the original building techniques were used, including the use of a team of draft horses to help pull the structure across the creek. Free.

HISTORIC HOMES AND SITES 🐾 ✒ ♿ **Jarrell Plantation Historic Site** (478-986-5172; www.gastateparks.org/JarrellPlantation), 711 Jarrell Plantation Road, Juliette. Open 9–5 Thursday–Saturday; last tour at 4. This is not the grand plantation of the stereotypical Old South, but rather a self-contained, self-supporting working farm depicting the period from the 1840s to the 1940s. Generations of the Jarrell family lived and worked here from 1847, when John Fitz Jarrell built the first simple heart-pine house and made many of the furnishings. In 1895, his son Dick built another house for his family. In 1974, the buildings and artifacts were willed to the state and constitute one of the largest and most complete collections of original family relics in Georgia. Several rustic homes on the site contain looms, spinning wheels, quilting frames, a cobbler's bench, and a wood-burning stove. A small museum in the visitors center includes exhibits and a film. Many other buildings are scattered around the grounds, including a sawmill, cotton gin, gristmill, sugarcane press, syrup evaporator, carpenter shop, blacksmith shop, shingle mill, smokehouses, wheat houses, and barn. Farm animals and equipment, a garden, and grape arbors lend an air of authenticity. Special events and exhibitions, which feature sheep shearing, spinning, weaving, blacksmithing, and woodstove cooking, occur throughout the year. Wheelchair access is limited. An adjacent Jarrell home retained by family members offers bed & breakfast accommodations (see **Jarrell 1920 House** under *Lodging—Bed & Breakfasts*). $3.50–6.

MUSEUMS 🐾 ✒ **Old Jail Museum and Archives** (770-358-3855), 326 Thomaston Street, Barnesville. Open 10–5 Wednesday, 10–2 Saturday, 2–5 Sunday. The museum, which is located in the old Lamar County Jail, chronicles Barnesville's history as the Buggy Capital of the World. In addition to buggies and buggy memorabilia, artifacts include uniforms, dresses, antique toys and dolls, and household items. The Old Crowder Brothers Gin House on the property houses a collection of buggies and carriages, while the archives house materials back to the early 1800s. Suggested donation $1.

✴ To Do

SHOOTING SPORTS ♿ **Meadows National Gun Club** (478-994-9910), 1064 Rumble Road, Forsyth. Open 10–6 Wednesday–Sunday. The 400-acre world-class gun club facility, which was the site of the 1998 U.S. Open Sporting Clays Championship, offers a 100-bird sporting clays course with 12 stations and a 25-bird five-stand sporting clays course.

SKYDIVING **Skydive Atlanta** (706-647-9701 or 1-800-950-JUMP; www.skydiveatlanta.com), 2333 Delray Road, Thomaston. Open 8–sunset weekends, by appointment weekdays. Whether you're an expert thrill seeker or a wannabe, Skydive Atlanta has a certified instructor appropriate for your experience level. Call for fees.

✴ Green Space

GARDENS 🐾 ✒ ♿ **University of Georgia Research and Education Garden** (770-229-6107; www.griffin.uga.edu), Georgia Station, 1109 Experiment Street, Griffin. Open 8–5 weekdays, year-round; 1–4 Sunday, May–September. Encompassing 65 acres, the College of Agriculture and Environmental Sciences garden demonstrates new approaches to environmental gardening, including the latest landscape and turf grass findings. The gardens consist of 17 theme gardens, including a garden for the disabled, a children's garden, rock garden, water garden, butterfly garden, bog garden, Xeriscape (plants that need little water), and gardens devoted to perennials, native plants, herbs, ornamental grasses, heirloom plants and flowers, antique roses, irises and daylilies, turf, and wildflowers. Free.

LAKES ❀ ✿ ♿ **Lake Juliette** (land management office in Jackson: 478-954-4040; www .georgiapower.com/lakes/Juliette.asp), US 23/GA 87, Juliette. Open 7 AM–10 PM daily. Operated in cooperation with the Georgia Department of Natural Resources, this 3,600-acre lake is strictly for fishing, whether along its banks or by boat. Boats with engines greater than 25 horsepower are prohibited, as are waterskiing and Jet Skiing. In the surrounding lands, a public boat ramp, picnicking, primitive campsites, and developed campsites with hookups are available (call 1-888-GPCLAKE). Access free; fees for some activities.

NATURE PRESERVES AND PARKS ❀ ✿ ♿ **Piedmont National Wildlife Refuge** (478-986-5441; www.fws.gov.piedmont), 718 Juliette Road, Round Oak. Open daylight hours daily; visitors center open 7:30–5. The 35,000-acre refuge, administered by the U.S. Fish and Wildlife Service, offers fishing, 18 miles of hiking trails, and a wildlife drive. Loblolly pines on the ridges, hardwoods along creek bottoms, coves, streams, and beaver ponds all combine to create an ideal habitat for 200 species of migrating birds and waterfowl, as well as beavers, raccoons, opossums, turkeys, and deer. Educational programs, fishing, and hunting are available. Transportation through the preserve is primarily by way of gravel roads and footpaths. Three trails range from 0.9 mile to 2.9 miles. The best time to catch a glimpse of the red-cockaded woodpecker, by the way, is April through July. The Allison Lake Trail is the best place to view wintering waterfowl and wading birds. Free.

SPREWELL BLUFF IS ALONG THE BANKS OF THE FLINT RIVER.

❀ ✿ ♿ **Sprewell Bluff Outdoor Recreation Area** (706-825-6354; www.gastate parks.org/SprewellBluff), 740 Sprewell Bluff Road, Thomaston. Open 7–sunset daily. This little-known and undeveloped 1,372-acre park on the banks of the Flint River is truly a spot to get away from it all. There's a ramp for those who want to put canoes, kayaks, and rafts into the river, and fishing for bass and catfish is a popular pastime. A 3-mile trail hugs the riverbank and climbs among rocky bluffs from which visitors can get excellent views of the river. Picnicking, horseshoes, a playground, and volleyball round out the activities. Parking $5.

RIVERS **Flint River.** One of the major rivers in Georgia, the Flint flows from the Atlanta metropolitan area to the Florida border, providing scenic beauty and many recreational opportunities, including canoe and kayak trips, tubing, white-water rafting trips, and fishing.

✳ Lodging

BED & BREAKFASTS

In Barnesville

♿ **Antebellum Oaks Bed and Breakfast**
(678-359-1116; www.antebellumoaksbb
.com), 643 Greenwood Street. The 1849
Greek Revival house, which sits amid 3
acres of lawns and gardens, served as a
Confederate headquarters and hospital during the Civil War. Many people believe that
the house was the inspiration for the fictional plantation home of the Tarleton twins
in *Gone with the Wind.* In fact, for many
years it was the home of Fred Crane, who
played Brent Tarleton in the movie. Guest
rooms, which are named for Rhett, Scarlett,
Melanie, and Ashley, are spacious and furnished with period antiques. Each features
a private bath, sitting area, fireplace, and
cable television, A gourmet breakfast is
served in the Tara Dining Room. It's obvious that Southern hospitality is not gone
with the wind at Antebellum Oaks. No
smoking. $109.

In Juliette

🌿 **Jarrell 1920 House** (478-986-3972 or
1-888-574-5434, ext. 1920; www.jarrell
house.com), 715 Jarrell Plantation Road.
This circa 1920 home was originally part
of the **Jarrell Plantation** (see *To See—
Historic Homes and Sites*) and was the third
home built on the farm as well as the fanci-
est, though it is still a simple plantation
country house. The floors, walls, and ceilings are rare heart pine—felled, milled, and
assembled by the family on-site at the plantation. The bed & breakfast enjoys a quiet,
wooded setting just 30 minutes north of
Macon. Accommodations are offered in
Dick and Mamie's Room, which has an
adjoining bath, or in the Guest Room,
which has a bath down the hall. Weeknight
guests are treated to a full buffet breakfast;
weekend guests enjoy a continental breakfast on Saturday and coupon for a free
order of fried green tomatoes at the **Whistle Stop Café** (see *Where to Eat—Eating
Out*). A full breakfast buffet is served on
Sunday. Also part of a stay at the bed &
breakfast is a free pass to the **Jarrell Plan-**

THE JARRELL 1920 HOUSE BED &
BREAKFAST OCCUPIES A QUIET SPOT NEXT
TO JARRELL PLANTATION.

tation Historic Site (open Thursday–
Saturday). The B&B is only suitable for
well-behaved children older than 12. No
smoking. No pets. Not wheelchair accessible. $115 Sunday–Thursday; two-night min-
imum for Friday and Saturday nights; $215
for the weekend.

In Thomaston

🌿 **Woodall House Bed and Breakfast**
(706-647-7044), 324 West Main Street. This
large 1910 residence with a wide wraparound veranda sits on an expansive shaded
lot. Inside, much of the original gingerbread survives. Victorian-era antiques create an elegant but comfortable ambience in
the four guest rooms. Guests are within
easy walking distances to the courthouse
and 22 other historic structures. No smoking. Not wheelchair accessible. $74–84.

CAMPGROUNDS

In Juliette

🌿 ✵ **Dames Ferry Park** (478-994-5253;
camping reservations: 1-888-GPC-LAKE;
www.georgiapower.com/lakes/juliette.asp),
9546 US 23/GA 87. This all-service campground on the shores of Lake Juliette provides RV and tent sites, a dump station,
restroom and shower facilities, a public
boat launch, and a beach. $3–16.

✳ Where to Eat
DINING OUT

In Forsyth

🦞 🍴 ♿ **Grits Café** (478-994-8325; www
.gritscafe.com), 17 West Johnston Street.
Open 11–2 Tuesday–Saturday, 5:30–9
Tuesday–Thursday, 5:30–10 Friday and
Saturday. The Grits Café offers contemporary Southern cuisine with Cajun, Southwestern, and Asian flair. Located in a
restored century-old building, the café provides upscale but casual dining in a comfortable environment. Menu items include
dishes with grits and Vidalia onions, barbecue, fried green tomatoes, a wide array of
salads, sandwiches, daily specials, wraps,
quesadillas, seafood, lamb, duck, chicken,
pork, and beef. Look for special events such
as wine tastings, wine dinners, guest speakers, and theme dinners. No smoking.
Lunch $7–16, dinner $17–25.

In Griffin

♿ **Manhattan's Restaurant** (770-228-
5442), 1707 North Expressway. Open
11–10 Monday–Thursday, 11–11 Friday
and Saturday, 11–9 Sunday. Menu items at
the upscale restaurant run the gamut from
prime rib, steak, and seafood to pasta and
even take-out. Smoking permitted in a
completely separate bar area. $12–22.

JULIETTE IS HOME TO THE WHISTLE STOP
CAFÉ, MADE FAMOUS BY THE MOVIE *FRIED
GREEN TOMATOES*.

In Forsyth

🦞 🍴 ♿ **This Little Piggy Bar-B-Q** (478-
994-0618), 866 Indian Springs Drive. Open
11–6 Monday–Wednesday, 11–7 Thursday
and Friday, 11–4 Saturday. The casual
eatery serves pulled pork and chicken barbecue, as well as ribs and fish. No smoking.
$7–10.

In Juliette

🦞 🍴 ♿ **Whistle Stop Café** (478-992-8886
or 1-888-642-4628; www.thewhistlestopcafe
.com), 443 McCracken Street. Open 11–4
daily. Just step inside the screen door, and
you'll be transported to the *Fried Green
Tomatoes* movie set. Furniture and memorabilia re-create the 1930s and 1940s
depicted in the movie. The 1927 general-
merchandise store operated until 1972 and
then served as a real estate office, timber
consulting firm, and antiques shop before
being "discovered" and turned into the
café. Naturally, green tomatoes, lightly bat-
tered and fried, top the menu choices
($7–8), but you can find plenty of other
Southern favorites, such as polk salit, barbecue, burgers, and sandwiches for lunch. An
early dinner usually consists of chicken,
pork, chopped steak, country fried steak,
pork chops, ham, or ribs. Make room for a
fruit cobbler or pound cake and fruit for
dessert. No smoking. Lunch $6–8, dinner
$8–20.

✳ Entertainment

MUSIC **The Ole Clinton Opry** (call
Paul Moncrief at 478-461-3544; www.ole
clintonopry.com), 215 Old GA 18, Gray.
Held 6–9:30 every Friday. The event, which
attracts 200 to 250 people, showcases
regional bluegrass, country, and gospel talent. Admission free, but donations
accepted.

THEATER **Main Street Players** (770-
229-9916; www.mainstreetplayers.org), 115
North Hill Street, Griffin. After six years of
planning, the community theater group
presented its first play in 2001. The old
Woolworth's building has been renovated to

serve as the 100-seat, black-box theater, where a full season of plays is presented each year. Call for a schedule of performances. Adults $18, seniors $15, students $10.

Ritz Theater (706-647-2749 or 706-647-7022 for showtimes; 706-647-5372 for Ritz Cafe), 114 South Church Street, Thomaston. The beautifully restored 1930s art deco–style theater, which boasts the largest screen in the area, shows first-run and classic movies throughout the year and also hosts live performances. Redesigned for the comfort of today's audiences, the theater's seats feature retractable armrests with cup holders and folding countertop-style tables. A few of the original seats are on display as mementos. The renovated VIP balcony for adults age 21 and up serves wine and beer. The facility operates as the Ritz Café during the day and offers coffee and desserts to moviegoers at night. Call for a schedule. All seats $6.

✳ Special Events

March: **Forsythia Festival** (478-994-9239 or 1-888-642-4628; www.forsythiafestival .com). The family-oriented festival on the Courthouse Square in Forsyth features arts and crafts, a children's fair, 5K and fun runs, sporting tournaments, live entertainment, a chili cook-off and yellow dessert contest, foods, a beauty pageant, classic car show, treasure hunt, and a pancake breakfast. Free; some activities have a fee.

April: **Barnesville BBQ and Blues Festival** (770-358-5884; www.barnesville.org). This Florida BBQ Association–sanctioned event, held Friday night and Saturday in Barnesville, features entertainment by live blues bands, a classic car show, and a horseshoe-pitching tournament. $5 in advance, $7 at the gate.

May: **Old Clinton War Days** (478-986-6403; www.jonescounty.gov). This Clinton

FORSYTHIA

All seven varieties of forsythia shrubs—known for their bright yellow, star-shaped flowers—are related to the olive family. The flowers appear in the early spring before the leaves. The shrub was named for the Scottish horticulturist William Forsyth (1737–1804).

Historical Society and Sons of Confederate Veterans–sponsored weekend event features a reenactment of the Federal occupation of Clinton including the Battle of Sunshine Church, the Griswoldville Battle, and on Saturday evening at twilight a Candlelight Memorial Service at Clinton UMC Cemetery. Adults $5 per day, children $3 per day.

September: **Barnesville Buggy Days** (chamber of commerce: 770-358-5884; www.barnesville.org). The celebration of Barnesville's glory days as a preeminent buggy-manufacturing center features 150 artists and craftspeople, as well as historic buggies on display outdoors and at the Old Jail Museum; food; 10K, 5K, and 2-mile fun runs; tennis and softball tournaments; and the Buggy Blast Fun Park, an attraction with a rock-climbing wall, racetrack, pony rides, and a spider jump, as well as a concert and street dance. A gala parade features buggies, floats, 250 horses, and civic groups. Park at Lamar County High School and ride the free Buggy Days van. The van operates 9–6 Saturday, 1–5 Sunday. Festival free; some activities have a small charge.

October: **Green Tomato Festival** (1-888-642-4628; www.juliettega.com). This festival in Juliette is filled with arts and crafts vendors, live entertainment, antiques and collectibles, children's pony rides, hayrides, and games. Naturally, fried green tomatoes are featured, along with other food. Free; some activities have a fee.

HAWKINSVILLE, EASTMAN, AND FITZGERALD

L ocated in the heart of Georgia, this area of rural countryside and small towns has some interesting Civil War history, including the capture of fleeing Confederate president Jefferson Davis near Irwinville and the creation of a village settled by former soldiers from the North and South.

Hawkinsville and Pulaski County's love affair with harness racing began in 1894, when the Pulaski County Fair Association held its first official harness races and Northerners realized that Georgia's mild climate and red clay track surfaces provided an excellent combination for conditioning young horses. Now known as "the Harness Horse Capital," Hawkinsville has been a winter home for American and Canadian harness horses since 1920. Several world champions have been trained on Hawkinsville tracks.

The region is also popular for outdoor recreational pursuits such as canoeing and kayaking, boating, fishing, hunting, and wildlife observation.

The area is home to some unusual festivals, too, including those dedicated to harness racing, wild chickens, and wild hogs.

GUIDANCE To learn more about Eastman, call the **Eastman–Dodge County Chamber of Commerce and Local Welcome Center** (478-374-4723; www.eastman-georgia.com), 1646 College Street, Eastman 31023. Open 8:30–5 weekdays, 9–noon Saturday.

To find out more about Fitzgerald, contact the **Fitzgerald Tourism Office** (229-426-5033 or 1-800-386-4642; www.fitzgeraldga.org), 115 South Main Street, Fitzgerald 31750. Open 8–5 weekdays. Get information on the town's self-guided Architectural Treasures Tour, A Captured President Tour, and A Tale of Two Cities Tour here. Information also can be obtained from the **Fitzgerald–Ben Hill County Chamber of Commerce** (229-423-9357 or 1-800-225-7899; www.fitzgeraldchamber.org), 805 Grant Street, Fitzgerald 31750.

Information about Hawkinsville, including the Hawkinsville Historic Driving Tour, can be obtained from the **Hawkinsville–Pulaski County Chamber of Commerce** (478-783-1717; www.hawkinsville.org), 46 Lumpkin Street, Hawkinsville 31036. Open 9–5 weekdays.

GETTING THERE *By air:* This area is served by **Hartsfield-Jackson Atlanta International Airport.** See "What's Where in Georgia" for airport, airline, and car rental information.

By bus: The nearest **Greyhound** stations are in Macon (see the Macon chapter) or Dublin (see the Statesboro chapter). A bus passenger arriving in either of those towns would need to rent a car to get around.

By car: Hawkinsville lies between the north–south route I-75 and the east–west route I-16. The primary U.S. highways through the area are 23, 129, and 341.

By train: The nearest **AMTRAK** stations are in Atlanta or Columbus (see "What's Where in Georgia" and the Columbus chapter). An arriving rail passenger would then need a rental car.

MEDICAL EMERGENCY Call 911.

VILLAGES Dodge County was created in 1870 as the 134th Georgia county and was named for William E. Dodge, a New Yorker who owned vast tracks of timberland in Georgia. He was instrumental in getting Congress to remove taxation from timber, and when he learned that a county was being named in his honor, he built the county's first courthouse in 1908 as a gift.

Eastman, the largest town, is the home of the original Stuckey Candy Plant, renowned for its pecan roll, and is known as "the Candy Capital of Georgia." At one time Stuckey had 320 outlets along U.S. highways and employed 1,000 people. After dwindling to 100 outlets, the company was sold to Standard Candy, which is famous for its Goo Goo Cluster. The plant in Eastman continues to operate.

Fitzgerald is a Southern town with a Yankee foundation. In the 1890s, P. H. Fitzgerald, an Indianapolis newspaperman and veterans' pension attorney who was a Union drummer boy in his youth, decided that as part of the healing process between North and South, a colony should be created where former soldiers from both sides could live together. He thought the colony should be in the South so aging Union soldiers could escape harsh winters and drought.

More than just an idea, the American Tribune Soldiers Colony, also known as the Old Soldiers Colony Company, actually came into fruition in 1895 on 50,000 acres purchased for that purpose. It was rather ironic that the area chosen was so close to the place where Confederate president Jefferson Davis was captured. Nearly 3,000 former soldiers from both sides came from 38 states to fulfill the dream. These soldiers were able to conquer their painful feelings and forge lifelong friendships. They named the streets for Ulysses S. Grant and William T. Sherman as well as Robert E. Lee and Stonewall Jackson. Other streets are named for both Northern and Southern trees and flowers. In the early years, a harvest celebration was planned that would include both Union and Confederate parades, but on the day of the event all marched together as one.

The experiment seems to have worked. The town continues to prosper and is known as "Where North and South Reunited." Its Evergreen Cemetery is filled with the graves of the town's early Rebel and Yank settlers.

Today Fitzgerald's historic downtown is a 16-block area on the National Register of Historic Places with venerable buildings, brick streets, sidewalks paved in blue and gray bricks, and landscaped parks. The 1902 railroad depot houses the **Blue and Gray Museum** (see *To See—Museums*).

Hawkinsville is home to the 86-acre Lawrence Bennett Harness Training Facility, which can be toured, and sponsors the **Hawkinsville Harness Festival and Spring Celebration** (see *Special Events*).

Irwin County, the 45th county created in Georgia, was formed in 1818 and encompassed all of south-central Georgia. Several other counties were created from this area, and today Irwin County contains the upper reaches of the Alapaha, Satilla, and Willachoochee rivers. Irwinville was the county seat during the Civil War, but that honor is now held by Ocilla. Several endangered species still survive in Irwin County: the Florida panther, the peregrine falcon, and the southern bald eagle.

The area between what is now **Irwinville** and Fitzgerald became an important footnote to history on May 9, 1865, when Confederate president Jefferson Davis, his family, and some of his staff were captured here by Union troops. Although the Civil War was officially over and the Confederate cabinet had been dissolved, Davis was headed to Louisiana and Texas, where he hoped to reunite rebel forces and continue the fight. As they were camping in this pine forest, they had no idea that two groups of Union soldiers were in close pursuit. As it happened, neither of the Union detachments knew of the existence of the other, so they began firing at each other. Davis and his party were caught between them and captured.

✴ To See

HISTORIC HOMES AND SITES ✿ ⬥ **Evergreen Cemetery,** Benjamin Hill Drive East, Fitzgerald. Open 8–5 daily. Brochures are available for a self-guided tour. Among the notable Fitzgerald citizens buried here is Lewis Clute, who is credited with capturing Jefferson Davis. This is also the final resting place for Civil War soldiers William J. Bush, who lived to be the oldest Georgia veteran, and Jerome Moss, who was Union general William Tecumseh Sherman's drummer boy. The cemetery took its name from the Gettysburg cemetery over which the famous battle was fought. Street names within the cemetery take their names from the Gettysburg cemetery as well: Cemetery Ridge Road, Emmitsburg Road, Little Round Top Lane, and Seminary Ridge Road. Other streets include Confederate Lane and Union Road. Free.

✿ ⌁ ⬥ **Jefferson Davis Memorial State Historic Site** (229-831-2335; www.gastateparks .org/JeffDavis), 338 Jeff Davis Park Road, Fitzgerald. Open 9–5 Wednesday–Sunday. This 13-acre park marks the spot where Confederate president Jefferson Davis and some of his staff were captured on May 9, 1865, after the official end of the Civil War. At the museum, visitors can watch a video about the event and see Civil War memorabilia, including a preserved piece of the tree where Davis was standing when he was captured. The park also features a small nature trail and picnic facilities. Several special events occur throughout the year, including "1860s Christmas," the first or second weekend in December, when visitors can enjoy candlelit tours, period refreshments, caroling, crafts, decorations, and a visit from Santa. $2.75–4.

✿ ⌁ ⬥ **Liberty Square,** downtown McRae. Open daily. The grounds of the quaint square are adorned with miniature monuments, including a ½th size Statue of Liberty and a replica of the Liberty Bell. The square also contains a memorial to fallen soldiers from the area. Free.

✿ ⬥ **Orphans Cemetery, Williamson Mausoleum,** Orphan Cemetery Road, Eastman. Cemetery open daylight hours daily. This 1887 cemetery is dedicated to a young man who was orphaned and left to raise his five younger brothers. A. G. Williamson commissioned this impressive mausoleum with life-size figures of himself, his wife, and his nephew, J. G. Williamson. The elder Mr. Williamson sent a photograph of what he wanted to an Italian sculptor in 1887, and the mausoleum was rendered in marble, then sent to Eastman. The cemetery also contains other ornate memorials from the Victorian era. Free.

MUSEUMS ✿ ⌁ ⬥ **Blue and Gray Museum** (229-426-5069; www.fitzgerald.ga.org), 116 North Johnston Street, Fitzgerald. Open year-round, 10–4 Tuesday–Saturday, 1–5 Sunday. The museum, which is housed in a historic railroad depot, chronicles the history of Fitzgerald's creation as a haven for soldiers from both sides of the Civil War. Among the exhibits are photos and mementos from the colony's beginnings, as well as Union and Confederate battle relics and other artifacts. Among the interesting artifacts are a key from Andersonville Prison, a war drum dated 1861 and used in Fitzgerald parades for more than a century, and a Southern Cross of Honor medal. The Hall of Honor lists the names of Fitzgerald's pioneers, and the film *Marching as One* tells the story of the town's founding. Other exhibits include uniforms, arms, and medals used in all of this country's major conflicts. One section is dedicated to Fitzgerald native son and Congressional Medal of Honor winner Gen. Raymond G. Davis. Adults $3, students $2.

🐾 ♫ ♿ **Fitzgerald Fire Engine Museum** (229-426-5030), 315 East Pine Street, Fitzgerald. Open 9–5 daily. The Fitzgerald Fire Department began way back in 1895. The current department displays a collection of antique equipment, including hand-drawn and horse-drawn apparatus and the first gasoline engine the department acquired in 1915. Kids can slide down the original brass firefighter's pole and take home a red hat of their own. Visitors also can view sparkling up-to-the-minute engines and equipment next door. Free.

> **SOUTHERN CROSS OF HONOR**
> Although the Union created the Congressional Medal of Honor during the Civil War, the Confederacy had nothing similar. After the war, the United Daughters of the Confederacy created the Southern Cross of Honor to award the service of every soldier who had fought for the Confederate States of America. In all, they presented 78,000 medals.

✳ To Do

BOATING 🐾 ♫ ♿ **Telfair County Boat Landing,** Ocmulgee River at the US 341 Bridge, Lumber City (east of Hawkinsville). Open daily. Several boat landings permit easy access to the river for boaters and anglers. Free.

FISHING 🐾 ♫ ♿ **Georgia DNR Dodge County Public Fishing Area** (478-374-6765; www.gofishgeorgia.com), 325 Dodge Lake Road, Eastman. A Georgia fishing license is required. Open sunrise–sunset Wednesday–Sunday. The 104-acre lake is stocked with bluegill, bream, channel catfish, crappie, redear sunfish, and largemouth bass. The facility also features a boat ramp, fish-cleaning station, pier, restrooms, an interpretive nature trail, and a picnic area. Some facilities wheelchair accessible. A Georgia Outdoor Recreation Pass (GORP) is required for anyone 16–64 who does not already have a fishing license: $3.50 for three days.

GOLF **Southern Hills Golf Club** (478-783-0600; www.southernhillsgolf.com), 360 Warner Robins Highway, Hawkinsville. Generally open full daylight–two hours before dusk, weather permitting. Call to be sure. The semiprivate, 18-hole course is 6,741 yards, par 72. The rolling terrain features a change in elevation of 131 feet. *Golf Digest* readers voted it one of the top five golfing values in the country, and the service as the third best. $28 weekdays, $37 weekends.

🐾 ♫ **Wallace Adams Golf Course at Little Ocmulgee State Park** (pro shop: 229-868-6651; 1-888-882-8906; tee times: 1-800-434-0982; www.gastateparks.org/LittleOcmulgee or www.golfgeorgia.org), 55 Spanish Moss Drive, Helena. Open 8–dusk daily. The state park boasts an 18-hole, 6,625-yard, par-72 course, along with clubhouse, pro shop, instruction, and snack bar. The course is characterized by loblolly pines, magnolias, and willows. The older back nine is wider open than the newer front nine. $30 weekdays, $37 weekends and holidays.

HORSE RACING 🐾 ♫ ♿ **Lawrence Bennett Harness Training Facility** (478-892-9463; www.hawkinsvilletrainingcenter.com), 290 Abbeville Highway/US 129 South, Hawkinsville. Open daily during daylight hours, October–May. The South's only training facility for harness racing trains trotters and pacers on half-mile and mile tracks. Visitors are welcome to watch the training or simply visit with the horses. The annual **Hawkinsville Harness Festival and Spring Celebration** (see *Special Events*) is held each March, and rodeos occur once a month. Free.

www.gastateparks.org/LittleOcmulgee), 80 Live Oak Trail, Helena. Open sunup–10 PM daily.
The mini golf course replicates the state park's **Wallace Adams Golf Course** (see *Golf*). $2.

✳ Green Space

NATURE PRESERVES AND PARKS ✸ ✧ ⚲ **Grand Plaza Park** (229-426-5033 or
1-800-386-4642; www.fitzgeraldga.org), Fitzgerald. Open daily. Green space located in the
heart of downtown across from the Grand Theatre (see *Entertainment*) celebrates Fitzgerald's heritage. Landscaped with flowers, trees, and other greenery, the park's central attractions include topiaries of Union and Confederate generals shaking hands and a giant
Burmese chicken. A fountain, an original hitching post, granite benches, brick arches from
Monitor High School, and ironwork columns from the Empire hotel, which once stood on
the spot, punctuate the park. Outdoor performances are often held here, and chess aficionados can make use of the park's life-size chessboard and pieces. Free.

✸ ✧ **Horse Creek Wildlife Management Area** (229-426-5267), GA Highway 117, Jacksonville. Open dawn–dusk daily. The preserve offers fishing, hiking, and hunting. There's also
an area set aside for training bird dogs. Free; check for hunting fees.

✸ ✧ ⚲ ❉ **Little Ocmulgee State Park and Lodge** (229-868-7474; lodge reservations:
1-877-591-5572; camping and cottage reservations: 1-800-864-7275; www.gastateparks.org
/LittleOcmulgee), 80 Live Oak Trail, Helena. This 1,265-acre park of sand hills and pine
forests has a plethora of recreational amenities, including a golf course (see *To Do—Golf*),
miniature golf (see *To Do—Miniature Golf;* additional fee), a 265-acre lake with a swimming
beach, a swimming pool for lodge and cottage guests only, boat ramp, canoe and pedal boat
rentals in season, two lighted tennis courts, and an amphitheater. Fishing, boating, and
waterskiing are popular pursuits, and the park has a water-ski ramp. A seasonal splash pool is
open 1–6 Wednesday–Sunday at an additional fee. The 2.5-mile Oak Ridge Trail meanders
through scrub oaks and pine toward a buzzard roost and boardwalk. Wildlife seen along the
trail might include the harmless indigo snake or the endangered gopher tortoise. Accommodations include a lodge, campground, and cottages (see *Lodging*). Pets are permitted in the
campground and cottages but not the lodge. Parking $5.

RIVERS Ocmulgee River. The river provides countless opportunities for boating, tubing,
fishing, wildlife observation, and camping. Anglers try their luck fishing for largemouth bass,
bream, catfish, and trout. In fact, the world-record 22-pound largemouth bass was caught
near Ben Hill County Landing (near Fitzgerald). The area surrounding the river abounds
with deer, wild turkey, quail, and other wildlife. Camping is available on the honor system.

THE FITZGERALD CHICKENS

One of Fitzgerald's more amusing and endearing present-day idiosyncrasies is the presence of
wild Burmese chickens. Visitors see the brilliantly plumed fowl wandering around town, greeting
locals and visitors, roosting in trees, and guiding their biddies around. Traffic stops to let them
cross the streets. They were originally introduced all over the state by the Department of Natural
Resources in the 1960s as an additional game bird to be hunted like pheasant or quail. For whatever reason, the chickens never took hold anywhere in Georgia but here. Soon the chickens realized they could get free handouts by venturing into town. They've multiplied, of course, so at one
time removing them was discussed, but the majority of the citizenry has become so attached to
them that the idea was quickly dropped. The annual Fitzgerald Wild Chicken Festival celebrates
these wild residents (see *Special Events*).

✳ Lodging

BED & BREAKFASTS

In Eastman

🦐 ♿ **Dodge Hill Inn** (478-374-2644; www.dodgehillinn.com), 5021 Ninth Avenue. The experience here is described as "Like coming home to Mother, but without the guilt." This gracious home was built in 1912 by N. W. Hurst, the town's first school superintendent. During the 1920s, the Cooke family owned the house, and Mrs. Cooke planted hundreds of camellias and other flowering bushes, many of which are still flourishing. The inn is furnished with antiques and accessorized with bisque figurines, oil paintings, antique toys, and old glass and china. Guest accommodations are offered in two suites, two guest rooms, and two nearby guesthouses. All rooms offer refrigerators, and the guesthouses boast a full kitchen. A full Southern breakfast is included in the nightly rate. No smoking. $80–85 for rooms, $90 for suites, $95–125 for guesthouses.

In Fitzgerald

🦐 **Dorminy-Massee House Bed and Breakfast Inn** (229-423-3123; www .dorminymasseehouse.com), 516 West Central Avenue. The opulent mansion, which is within walking distance of the historic downtown, was built in 1915 by J. J. "Captain Jack" Dorminy, who personally picked the heart pine used in the construction. He lived there until his death in 1952, after which his daughter Eulalie Dorminy Massee inherited the house and lived there until her death in 1995. Today it is owned and operated by her grandson Mark and his wife, Sherry. The house features spacious rooms with high ceilings and lavish furnishings and decor. Six luxurious guest rooms are offered. The landscaped grounds boast a goldfish pond, smokehouse, and gazebo. A full breakfast is included in the nightly rate. No smoking. Not wheelchair accessible. $95.

In Unadilla

🦐 **Sugar Hill Bed and Breakfast** (478-627-3557; www.sugarhillbedandbreakfast .com), 2540 Sugar Hill Road. This mid-1800s farmhouse is located just 4 miles from I-75, but a world and a century away. Its idyllic country setting offers solitude, peace, and quiet. Family antiques, three fireplaces, two common rooms, a rocker-filled front porch, and a swimming pool entice guests to unwind. Mom and Pop's Room boasts a two-person whirlpool tub, a sitting area, and a gas-log fireplace. Four other rooms are offered. Full country breakfast included. Ask about children. No alcohol. No smoking. Not wheelchair accessible. $60–80.

CAMPGROUNDS

In Helena

🦐 🐾 ♿ 🎪 **Little Ocmulgee State Park and Lodge** (camping reservations: 1-800-864-7275). The state park offers 55 tent, trailer, and RV sites with cable TV hookups. See *Green Space—Nature Preserves and Parks*. $25–28.

COTTAGES AND CABINS

In Helena

🦐 🐾 ♿ 🎪 **Little Ocmulgee State Park and Lodge** (cottage reservations: 1-800-864-7275). The park features 10 fully equipped one- and two-bedroom lakeside cottages. Some are dog friendly ($40 per dog, maximum two). See *Green Space—Nature Preserves and Parks*. $80–105.

INNS AND RESORTS

In McRae

🦐 🐾 ♿ **The Lodge at Little Ocmulgee State Park** (lodge reservations: 1-877-591-5572). The state park's 60-room, two-junior-suite lodge features a restaurant with a golf-course view. Visitors enjoy all the amenities of a resort state park. See *Green Space—Nature Preserves and Parks*. $70–135.

✳ Where to Eat

DINING OUT

In Hawkinsville

🦐 🐾 ♿ **Steakhouse Restaurant** (478-892-3383), 9 Bucahn Drive/US 341 Bypass. Open 11–9 Monday–Saturday, 11–2:30

Sunday. This is where locals go for lunch and dinner, and the best steaks in town. No smoking. $5–33, buffets $9–22.

EATING OUT

In Hawkinsville

🦐 🍴 ♿ **Tom and Sandy's Horseshoe Restaurant** (478-892-3526), 194 Broad Street. Open 6 AM–2 PM Monday–Saturday, 11 AM–2 PM Sunday. Country cooking is the staple here, and the full country breakfast is a great way to start the day. No smoking. Breakfast $6–10, lunch buffet $9.

In Helena

🦐 🍴 ♿ **Fairway Grill** (229-868-7474; www.gastateparks.org/LittleOcmulgee), at the Lodge at Little Ocmulgee State Park, 80 Live Oak Trail, off US 441. Open 7–10 and 11–2 daily, 5–9 Monday–Saturday. Overlooking the sixth and seventh holes on the Wallace Adams Golf Course, the restaurant offers buffets and à la carte selections. Beer and wine are offered. No smoking. Breakfast buffet $8, lunch buffet $9, dinner buffet $15.

✳ Entertainment

MUSIC **Colony City Opry** (229-426-5060 or 1-800-386-4642), 217 East Pine Street, Fitzgerald. Open 6–midnight Saturday. Either bring your own fiddle, guitar, or other instrument to join in with local musicians on stage, or sit back and listen. Gospel and country-western are the specialties, but you might hear blues or oldies, too. Free.

THEATER **Grand Theatre** (229-426-5090), 119 South Main Street, Fitzgerald. Box office open 8–5 weekdays. Built in the 1930s in the art deco style, this theater has been restored to serve as a venue for movies and the performing arts. It has been gifted with a 1926 three manual/eight rank Barton Theatre organ to enhance performances. On movie nights, the theater opens at 6:30 for organ performances, and the movie begins at 7. Call for a schedule of events and prices for live performances.

Historic Opera House (478-783-1884; www.hawkinsvilleoperahouse.com), 100 North Lumpkin Street, Hawkinsville. The restored 1908 opera house, which boasts near-perfect acoustics, stages concerts and other live performances of all kinds. Be sure to admire the hand-painted canvas stage curtain. Call for a schedule of performances and ticket prices. Free tours 10–4 daily by reservation.

✳ Selective Shopping

ANTIQUES **Hawkinsville Antique Mall** (478-783-3607), 76 North Lumpkin Street, Hawkinsville. Open 10–5 Monday–Saturday. Multiple dealers sell antiques and collectibles.

✳ Special Events

March: **Fitzgerald Wild Chicken Festival** (1-800-386-4642; www.wildchicken festival.com). Fitzgerald's wild Burmese chickens are celebrated with wildlife displays, street dance, pancake breakfast, car show, 5K Fun Run, Pine Wood Derby, magic show, pageant, and children's activities. One of the highlights is the crowing contest. Free; some activities have a fee.

Hawkinsville Harness Festival and Spring Celebration (478-783-1717; www.hawkinsvilleharnessfestival.com). The main attraction is the harness racing, but in addition, this two-day festival at the Lawrence Bennett Harness Training Facility includes arts and crafts, fireworks, concerts, beauty pageants, a golf tournament,

RACES ARE JUST ONE PART OF THE HAWKINSVILLE HARNESS FESTIVAL.

hayrides, a reptile show, carnival rides, clowns, magic, rides, cartoon characters, and food. Adults $5, children $2.

May: **Ocmulgee Wild Hog Festival** (229-467-2144; www.hogfestival.com). Abbeville's festival in Lion's Park features food, arts and crafts, live musical entertainment, horse and carriage rides, an antique car and tractor show, a Saturday-night dance, and various contests such as hog baying and a kids' pig chase. Of course, wild boars are displayed, too. $2.

MACON

Known as the "City of White Columns and Cherry Blossoms," Macon is one of the most gracious cities in the South. Blessedly spared during the Civil War, it still showcases its profusion of significant historic structures. Macon boasts 5,500 individual structures in 11 historic districts listed on the National Register of Historic Places, including 70 antebellum and 19 plantation homes. In all, the city has more acreage on the prestigious register than any other city in Georgia.

Something else it has in profusion is cherry trees. Although anytime is a good time to visit, the best time is in the spring, when the city is canopied by the pink blossoms of 285,000 Yoshino cherry trees—more than any other city in the world. Washington, D.C., so well-known for its cherry trees, has a mere 5,000.

Georgians have left their stamp on every genre of music, from ragtime and blues to smooth soul and punk rock. Many of these musicians called Macon home. During the 1950s and 1960s, nightclubs flourished up and down Broadway. R&B radio personalities commanded the airwaves, and the careers of Little Richard, Otis Redding, and James Brown were launched. In the 1970s, the combination of Capricorn Records and the Allman Brothers Band made Macon the home of Southern Rock.

The city is a site on the Georgia Music Trail, along with Atlanta, Athens, and Savannah.

Georgians also have made an indelible mark on virtually every sport. Olympic champions, professional superstars, and legendary coaches are native sons and daughters. Macon was tapped as the site of the **Georgia Sports Hall of Fame** (see *To See—Museums*).

A plethora of small towns around Macon each have one or more attractions to keep visitors in the region.

GUIDANCE Before making a trip to the Macon area, contact the **Macon–Bibb County Convention and Visitors Bureau** (478-743-1074 or 1-800-768-3401; www.maconga.org), 450 Martin Luther King Jr. Boulevard, Macon 31201. Open 9–5 weekdays, 10–4 Saturday. Located in the old Trailways bus station, The CVB's Welcome Center dispenses brochures and advice, and visitors can pick up a self-guided tour map.

Visitors also can get information from the **Macon I-75 Welcome Center** (478-994-9191), I-75 at mile marker 179, Macon 31201. Open 10–5:30 daily.

To learn more about Fort Valley and Peach County, contact the **Peach County Chamber of Commerce–Welcome Center** (478-825-2535; www.peachcounty.net), 205 West Church Street, Suite 204, Fort Valley 31030.

To learn more about Perry, contact the **Perry Area Convention and Visitors Bureau–Perry Welcome Center** (478-988-8000; www.perryga.com), 101 General

Courtney Hodges Boulevard, Perry 31069. Open 8:30–5 weekdays, 10–4 Saturday; Memorial Day through Labor Day, also 1–5 Sunday. Pick up a brochure for the self-guided *Historic Perry Walking-Driving Tour* of more than 50 historic locations in Perry.

For information about Warner Robins, contact **Warner Robins Convention and Visitors Bureau–E. L. Greenway Welcome Center** (478-922-5100 or 1-888-288-WRGA; www .wrga.gov), 99 North First Street, Warner Robins 31093, located in the historic train depot. To learn more about visiting the air force base, contact the **Robins Air Force Base** (478-926-1001 or 478-327-7605; www.robins.af.mil).

GETTING THERE *By air:* Visitors to this area can fly into Macon, but because Macon is so close to Atlanta, most travelers would prefer to fly into the latter in order to avoid a connection and time wasted. In either case, see "What's Where in Georgia" for airport, airline, and car rental information.

By bus: **Greyhound Lines** (478-743-5411; www.greyhound.com) provides service to Macon at 65 Spring Street.

By car: Access to Macon is extremely easy by either I-75 from the north and south or I-16 from the east—both of which intersect in Macon.

By train: The closest **AMTRAK** (see "What's Where in Georgia") station is in Atlanta. Greyhound, however, does have connecting service to AMTRAK from its station (see *By bus*).

GETTING AROUND Intracity bus service is offered by **Macon–Bibb County Transit Authority** (478-746-1354; www.mta-mac.com), which operates 20 buses in the city.

MEDICAL EMERGENCY For life-threatening emergencies, call 911.

VILLAGES AND NEIGHBORHOODS Macon has numerous historic neighborhoods. **Ingleside Village,** Ingleside Avenue between Rogers and Corbin avenues, is becoming known as Antiques Alley with its collection of quaint shops (see *Selective Shopping*).

Pleasant Hill Historic District, bounded by College, Neal, Rogers, and Vineville streets, was one of the first African American neighborhoods in the country to be listed on the National Register of Historic Places. It was the childhood home of "Little Richard" Penniman, the "Architect of Rock and Roll."

Fort Valley, the county seat of Peach County, Georgia's youngest county, is known for camellias, peaches, and pecans. In fact, Fort Valley—which would be named Fox Valley if not for a mistake made by the U.S. Postal Service in Washington—is known as "the Peach Capital of Georgia." Peach season is May through August, while pecan season runs October through January. William Tecumseh Sherman and his Union troops bypassed Fort Valley on the March to the Sea, so the historic district features homes from that period. The city's cemetery contains grave markers of both Confederate and Union soldiers.

Perry, named for naval hero Oliver Hazard Perry, is known as the crossroads of Georgia because of its central location, where three major state and federal highways (I-75, US 341, and US 41, which parallels I-75) intersect and the Golden Isles Parkway begins. The small city, three hours from the north Georgia mountains and three hours from the coast, is featured on three state tourism trails: the **Antiques Trail,** the **Peachblossom Trail,** and the **Andersonville Trail.** An agricultural center, Perry is also the site of the **Georgia National Fair** (see *Special Events*) and numerous sporting competitions.

Warner Robins is the home of the Air Logistics Center at Robins Air Force Base, Georgia's largest single employer. The center is Georgia's largest industrial complex and one of only three such centers in the country. Both the town and Air Force base were named for Brig. Gen. Augustine Warner Robins. A fast-growing aviation museum also calls the town home.

FOR FAMILIES 🐾 🍃 ⚘ **Georgia National Fairgrounds and Agricenter** (478-987-3247 or 1-800-987-3247; www.gnfa.com), 401 Larry Walker Parkway, Perry. Call for a schedule of events and prices. The premier event at this vast multipurpose facility is October's **Georgia National Fair** (see *Special Events*), which attracts 360,000 visitors, but other events include concerts, horse shows, livestock competitions, rodeos, RV rallies, and sporting events. The parklike setting, with a fountain, lakes, gardens, and picnic facilities, invites visitors to stop by even when no events are in progress. Admission to complex free; fees for some events.

HISTORIC HOMES AND SITES **Allman Brothers Band Museum at the Big House** (478-741-5551; www.thebighousemuseum.com), 2321 Vineville Avenue, Macon. Open 11–6 Thursday–Sunday (last tour at 5). The Allman Brothers Band formed in 1969, and they came to Macon to record for Capricorn Records. In 1970 Berry Oakley and his wife, Linda, rented the large Tudor-style house for $225 a month. Pretty soon most of the band members, along with family, friends, and roadies, were living there, too, and they remained until the band broke up in 1973 after the deaths of Berry Oakley and Duane Allman. The museum, which was created to "guarantee that the dreams, music, and legacy created then lives on," features guitars, other instruments, clothing, photos, posters, gold records, and other memorabilia. Adults $8, seniors and military $6, children 3–10 $4.

🐾 **Anderson House Museum and Welcome Center** (478-825-66211), 1005 State University Drive, Fort Valley. Open 8–11 Monday and Wednesday, 9–4 Tuesday and Thursday. Formerly the home for the president of Fort Valley State University, which began as a black land-grant school and is now a research institution, the 1800s residence is now a house museum furnished in the style of the late 1800s. The Biggs Collection is one of the finest accumulations from the turn of the 20th century—so fine, in fact, that it was sought by the Smithsonian. The collection, which spans the time period 1860 to 1900, includes period furnishings, silver, glassware, china, quilts, linens, and Civil War memorabilia. Free.

🐾 ⚘ **Cannonball House and Civil War Museum** (478-745-5982; www.cannonballhouse.org), 856 Mulberry Street, Macon. Open 10–5 Monday–Saturday; tours every half hour until 4:15. There's a lot to see here, but the house is named for the 12-pound nonexplosive cannonball that crashed into it during the Civil War in 1864, coming to rest on the hall floor, where you can still see it today. In fact, the house had the dubious distinction of being the only one hit in Macon during the halfhearted attack by Union troops. A stereotypical white-columned Southern Greek Revival, the gracious home, built in 1853, is filled with period antiques. Two rooms are furnished as replicas of chambers at Old Wesleyan College, the first woman's college in the country and home of the first national sorority. The adjacent brick kitchen and servants' quarters building is a repository for Civil War artifacts, including several that purportedly belonged to Mrs. Robert E. Lee. If wheelchair accessibility is needed, call ahead so that staff can set up ramp over back stairs; no access to second floor. Adults $6, seniors and military $5, students $4, children younger than four free. A combination ticket is available that also allows admission to the Hay House and the Sidney Lanier Cottage: adults $19, seniors and military $16, students, $10.

🐾 ⚘ **Hay House** (478-742-8155; www.hayhouse.org), 934 Georgia Avenue, Macon. Open 10–4 Tuesday–Saturday, 1–4 Sunday (last tour at 3). One of Macon's most magnificent houses, the 18,000-square-foot Hay House is a prime example of the Italian Renaissance Revival style. Known as the "Palace of the South," it was built between 1855 and 1859 by William Butler Johnston, who later became the keeper of the Confederate treasury. The mansion has been featured on the A&E Channel series *America's Castles*. Amazingly, the grand home was occupied by only two families throughout its history before it was acquired by the Georgia Trust for Historic Preservation. Nearly fully restored, the house displays numerous examples of the exquisite workmanship of the period when it was built, such as 12-foot-high, 500-pound front doors; 16- and 30-foot ceilings; carved Carerra marble mantelpieces; ornately embossed cornices, medallions, and moldings; stained glass; marbleized faux finishes; and intricate trompe l'oeil wall and ceiling paintings. At the time of its construction, the Hay House incorporated such then-unheard-of amenities as indoor plumbing, walk-in closets, an elevator, an intercom, and the best ventilation system ever designed for an American home until the invention of air-conditioning. Eighteen rooms are filled with sumptuous 18th- and 19th-century antiques and objets d'art. Limited wheelchair accessibility. Adults $9, seniors and military $8, children $5. Additional charge during the Cherry Blossom Festival and the Christmas holidays. A combination ticket is available that allows admission to the Cannonball House and the Sidney Lanier Cottage: adults $19, seniors and military $16, students $10.

THE HISTORIC HAY HOUSE IS OPEN FOR TOURS.

🐾 🎣 ♿ Ocmulgee National Monument

(478-752-8257; www.nps.gov/ocmu), 1207 Emery Highway, Macon. Open 9–5 daily. Seven impressive temple and burial mounds from the Mississippian Period (A.D. 900 to 1100), the tallest of which is 45 feet tall, remain on the 683-acre historic site. A ceremonial earth lodge where tribal political and religious meetings were held has been reconstructed on the original 1,000-year-old floor. The interpretive center features artifacts such as axes, clay pipes, beads, knives, and other weapons from the six distinct Native American groups that occupied the site, as well as later traders. A film traces Native American history in the area over 12,000 years. The park also features 5 miles of walking trails (see *To Do—Hiking*), and visitors can stomp their feet to the primitive beat of Native American ceremonial dances each September at the **Ocmulgee Indian Celebration** (see *Special Events*). Free, except during some special events.

EXPLORE NATIVE AMERICAN TRADITIONS AND SITES AT THE OCMULGEE NATIONAL MONUMENT.

🐾 **Sidney Lanier Cottage** (478-743-3851; www.historicmacon.org/sidney-lanier-cottage), 935 High Street, Macon. Open 10–4 Monday–Saturday (last tour at 3:30). Famous Southern poet and musician Sidney Lanier was born in 1842 in this house, the home of his grandparents. Despite his fame as the author of the poems *"The Marshes of Glynn"* and *"Song of the Chattahoochee,"* Lanier was also a linguist, mathematician, musician, and lawyer. He served in the Confederate Army and was captured and imprisoned by the Union. It was during his incarceration that he lost his health, which he never regained, and he died at age 31. At the cottage, see his writings, his flute, and even his bride's tiny wedding gown. Adults $5, seniors and active military $4, children 6–18 $3, children under six free. A combination ticket is available that allows admission to the Cannonball House and the Hay House. Adults $19, seniors and military $16, students $10.

MUSEUMS ☏ ✆ ♿ **Georgia Children's Museum** (478-755-9539; www.georgiachildrens museum.org), 382 Cherry Street and Martin Luther King Jr. Boulevard, Macon. Open 10:30–5 Tuesday–Saturday, noon–5 Sunday. Everywhere in the children's museum are colorful murals of children at play and engaged in learning activities, each painted by artist Arrin Freeman. What will be a six-floor museum already features the **Riverside Ford Theatre for Young Audiences**—a black-box theater where professional and amateur performances are held, as well as theatrical arts exhibits. Separate floors are devoted to interactive exhibits including dinosaurs, Creek Indians, puppets, and Legos. In addition, the Lost Parent Café and ice cream shop provides a welcome break. After-school, school break, and summer programs are offered. Admission $4, but subject to change.

☏ ✆ ♿ **Georgia Sports Hall of Fame** (478-752-1585; www.georgiasportshalloffame.com), 301 Cherry Street, Macon. Open 9–5 Tuesday–Saturday. Exhibits honor high school, college, amateur, professional, and Olympic teams and individuals, as well as legendary coaches. Baseball's Hank Aaron, boxing's Evander Holyfield, golf's Bobby Jones and Nancy Lopez, racing's Bill Elliott, and football's Herschel Walker are just a few athletic superstars to call Georgia home. Their exploits and those of many others are showcased at America's largest sports hall of fame. Displays, audiovisual presentations, and interactive games where you can exercise your body and your mind keep visitors busy. Adults $8, seniors and military $6, children younger than 16 $3.50.

☏ ✆ ♿ **Go Fish Education Center** (478-988-6701; www.gofisheducationcenter.com), 1255 Perry Parkway, Perry. Open 9–5 Friday and Saturday, 11–5 Sunday. Fishing has a huge impact on Georgia. Visitors take an educational journey through Georgia's watersheds to learn about the state's diverse wildlife, their habitats, the impact on water pollution, and how to be a good steward of our waterways. Exhibits include freshwater aquaria filled with trout and largemouth bass; live aquatic wildlife including alligators and turtles; interactive fishing, boating, and shooting simulators; and a fish hatchery. Anglers can walk the nature trails and catch a fish in the stocked pond. Adults $5, seniors $4, children 3–12 $3.

RACING SIMULATOR AT GEORGIA SPORTS HALL OF FAME

☏ ✆ ♿ **Museum of Arts and Sciences** (478-477-3232; www.masmacon.com), 4182 Forsyth Road, Macon. Open 9–5 Tuesday–Saturday, 1–5 Sunday; the last Monday of the month 10–8. Daily shows: live animals at 3, planetarium at 4; check about extra shows. This is a place for families—particularly those with young children—to discover the world. The "arts" side permits visitors to examine the beauty of original works of art in changing and permanent exhibits, including the Gunn Collection of Boehm Porcelains. On the "sciences" side, visitors can journey to outer space in the planetarium, which features new digital projection technology; see live tamarind monkeys and parrots in an enclosed animal habitat with a replica of a giant banyan tree; watch and identify birds at the bird-watching window; experience hands-on adventures in the three-story Discovery House, which includes an artist's garret, a humanist's study, a globe room, Poet's Corner, and a scientist's workshop; and hike the nature trails on the 18-acre property to see a turn-of-the-20th-century caboose, a historic cabin, and several outdoor sculptures. The star of the museum is a 40-million-year-old whale-skeleton fossil found in the area, which would indicate that Macon was once close to the sea. The **Mark Smith Planetarium** offers daily galaxy shows in a 40-foot dome. On clear Friday nights, visitors can view the real night sky from the **Observatory.** The museum's recent affiliation with the Smithsonian Institution will enable the facility to get important traveling exhibitions. Adults $8, seniors and military $6, students 12 and older $5, children 2–11 $4.

🍴 ♿ **Perry Area Historical Museum** (478-224-4442; www.perryhistoricalsociety.org), 901 Northside Drive, Perry. Open 10–noon and 2–4 Tuesday–Thursday; open some Saturdays (check the website or call). Artifacts and memorabilia describe the history of Perry's earliest days. Located in a historical cottage, the museum displays educational artifacts, vintage clothing, antique toys, art, furniture, vintage Christmas decorations, vintage appliances, and the like. Free.

🍴 🎖 ♿ **Tubman African American Museum** (478-743-8544; www.tubmanmuseum.com), 340 Walnut Street, Macon. Open 9–5 Tuesday–Friday, 11–5 Saturday. Named in honor of Harriett Tubman, mastermind of the Civil War Underground Railroad, the museum is the state's largest museum devoted to African American history and culture. What began as a grassroots effort to recognize the triumphs of blacks has grown to the extent that the museum garners international recognition. The museum devotes 14 exhibition galleries to the journey and accomplishments of African Americans from Africa to modern America and includes the esteemed Noel Collection of African Art. Among the most fascinating exhibits are those devoted to inventions of African Americans. In the Inventors Room, you'll learn about the African American creators of the automated traffic signal, barbed harpoon, corn planter, eye dropper, fire extinguisher, gas mask, goggles, horseshoes, ironing board, lawn sprinkler, linoleum, oxygen tanks, postal letter box, a precursor of the riding lawnmower, and the wildly popular Super Soaker. You'll also hear about African Americans who contributed to the invention of the first electric lights and the first open-heart surgery. Art includes paintings, tapestries, carved ivory, masks, and textiles from Africa. Permanent collections are augmented by touring national and international exhibitions. The museum is also home to the Pan African Festival. Adults $6, seniors and military $5, children and college students $4.

🍴 🎖 ♿ **U.S. Air Force Museum of Aviation–Georgia Aviation Hall of Fame** (478-926-6870; www.museumofaviation.org), US 129/GA 247 South and Russell Parkway, Warner Robins. Open 9–5 daily. Visitors' spirits will soar at the indoor-outdoor Museum of Aviation, the fastest-growing aviation museum in the Southeast and the country's fourth-largest aviation museum. It's "Just PLANE Fun!" to tour the more than 200,000 square feet of space in four buildings filled with interactive exhibits and historical displays of more than 90 military aircraft. The oldest aircraft is an 1896 glider; outstanding modern aircraft include the F-15A and the SR-71 Blackbird, the fastest plane on earth. The newest addition is an Air Force Sikorsky special operations helicopter, which was widely used in Iraq. Exhibits focus on World War II, Korea, Desert Storm, the Flying Tigers, Tuskegee Airmen, and China-Burma-India Hump pilots. In the *Footsteps of Giants* display, the lives of famous Georgians are examined: President Jimmy Carter, United Nations Ambassador Andrew Young, Congressman Carl Vinson, and Senators Walter F. George, Herman Tallmadge, and Sam Nunn. Films are shown continuously in the **Robert L. Scott Vistascope Theater.** The Hall of Fame commemorates the careers of distinguished men and women who have made significant contributions to aviation in Georgia, such as Ben Epps Sr., the first man to fly in Georgia;

Jacques Ballard, the first African American military aviator; and Robert L. Scott, World War II ace and author of *God Is My Co-Pilot*. In the Heritage Building, *Windows to the Distant Past*, a sight-and-sound exhibit, explores the cultures of Native Americans. Have lunch in the Victory Café and watch planes take off at Robins Air Force Base next door. Free.

SPECIAL PLACES ✿ Rose Hill Cemetery (478-751-9119; www.historic rosehillcemetery.org), 1091 Riverside Drive, Macon. Open daylight hours. A beautiful example of the Victorian park movement, the 65-acre cemetery is one of the oldest memorial parks in the nation, having been

CIVIL WAR GRAVE SITES, ROSE HILL CEMETERY

founded in 1840, just 17 years after the city of Macon. It is named for its founder, Simri Rose, whose ornate grave is in the cemetery. The burial ground's opulent monuments, mausoleums, and vaults mark the final resting places of many famous Macon residents, including three Georgia governors, two U.S. senators, a congressman, and 31 Macon mayors. The graveyard has Jewish, Catholic, Protestant, and African American sections. The Confederate section contains the remains of more than 600 Civil War soldiers, reinterred here from the places where they fell in battle.

The graves that attract the most interest, however, are those of rock and roll legends Duane Allman and Berry Oakley. Both members of the Allman Brothers Band, they were killed in separate motorcycle accidents in 1971 and 1972 near the same spot. They rest side by side on a tranquil terrace overlooking the Ocmulgee River, where they often came in life to smoke and drink and look for inspiration for their songs. In the past, visitors who came to pay their respects and read the flowery inscriptions on their gravestones often left liquor, cigarettes, and beer in tribute. Today, the grave sites are watched over and protected by Berry's sister, Candace, who is often there to make sure the graves are properly honored. Also in the cemetery are the graves of "Little Martha" and "Elizabeth Reed," both of whom were mentioned in the band's songs.

Also memorialized at the cemetery is Lieutenant Bobby, a dog that President Calvin Coolidge allowed to remain in the military with his master even after the little dog's useful military life was over. Tragically, Lieutenant Bobby met an unexpected demise when he fell down an elevator shaft in a Macon hotel in 1936. He's buried among the human dead with a proper

THE GRAVE OF JOHN B. ROSS JUHAN IS ONE OF THE POIGNANT MARKERS AT THE ROSE HILL CEMETERY.

headstone. Six years later, when his master, D. C. Harris Jr., died, he was laid to rest next to his dog.

One of the most poignant memorials is that of John B. Ross, the eight-year-old son of W. A. and Elizabeth Jane Juhan. Little John wanted to be a fireman when he grew up, and he spent so much time at Defiance Company No. 5 that he was made their mascot. His touching gravestone was created to look as though it is draped with his child-size fireman's cape, hat, and belt.

The steeply terraced cemetery gives beautiful views of the river and the Ocmulgee Heritage Trail on the other side. Guided walking tours are given periodically, but participants should be forewarned about how steep some of the hills are. Cars can drive around most of the cemetery, but the roads are narrow. Free.

✳ To Do

AUTO RACING ✇ ⅏ **Silver Dollar Raceway** (478-847-4414; www.silverdollarraceway .com), 42 Raceway Drive, off GA 96 West, Reynolds. Open weekends, January–November. The quarter-mile National Hot Rod Association–sanctioned drag strip sponsors turn-and-test events and quarter-mile points series races. Call for a schedule of events and prices.

FACTORY TOURS ☕ ✇ ⅏ **Lane Packing Company** (478-825-3662 or 1-800-27-PEACH; www.lanepacking.com), 50 Lane Road/GA 96 East, Fort Valley. Open 10–5 daily, Labor Day–Memorial Day; 9–7 daily, Memorial Day–Labor Day. The fourth-generation, family-owned company grows 30 varieties of peaches and 10 kinds of pecans, as well as strawberries and asparagus. During the peach season, mid-May through August, the state-of-the-art packing facility is bustling with activity as peaches are harvested, cleaned, sorted, boxed, and shipped. Inside, the self-guided plant tour shows how more than 300,000 peaches per hour are carefully weighed, counted, separated, and packed to prevent bruising. Visitors can get a bird's-eye view of the operation from overhead walkways. In June and July a guided tram tour takes visitors through acres and acres of peach and pecan orchards; reservations suggested. You may want to have lunch at the **Peachtree Café,** but for sure you'll want to enjoy some peach cobbler or peach ice cream. Shop for Southern gifts and Georgia food items in the **Just Peachy Gift Shop,** or buy some fruit or nuts to take home from the roadside market. Visitors can pick their own strawberries March through May; pecan season is October through January. A corn maze attracts visitors in October. Check the website or call for times and prices. The company also has a full-service mail order department. Facility wheelchair accessible, but tram difficult for those who can't stand or step up into it. Self-guided tours free; tram tours: adults $6, seniors and military $5, children 3–12 $4.

FOR FAMILIES ✇ ⅏ **DJ's Galaxy Quest** (478-329-8002), 815 Russell Parkway, Warner Robins. Open 11–8 Thursday, 11–10 Friday and Saturday, 1–8 Sunday. Other hours available for private parties. The facility's activities include miniature golf, laser tag, and a roller coaster, to name just a few. Rates are based on each child's age and activity level. Average for three hours of entertainment about $18 per child.

HIKING ☕ ✇ **Ocmulgee National Monument** (478-752-8257; www.nps.gov/ocmu), 1207 Emery Highway, Macon. Open 9–5 daily, year-round. Five easy trails, together covering almost 6 miles, crisscross the historic site and offer opportunities to view deer and other four-legged critters, as well as ducks and water birds. The longest path is the Human Cultural Trail. At 4 miles in length, it focuses on the Indian mounds (see *To See—Historic Homes and Sites*). The mile-long River Trail leads naturally enough to the Ocmulgee River.

Along the 0.4-mile Wildflower Trail, visitors may see wildlife as well as wildflowers. The 0.3-mile Loop Trail meets the 0.25-mile Opelofa Trail, which circles swampy lowland. Free.

WALKING TOURS ✎ ♿ **Lights on Macon–Historic Intown Illumination Tour** is a self-guided walking tour past 33 mansions dramatically lit in a nighttime display of Southern grandeur. Each mansion is bathed in a warm glow that brings back memories of a bygone front-porch culture. Get a walking tour brochure from the welcome center so you can follow the route and learn something about the various architectural gems. Free.

✳ Green Space

GARDENS ✎ ✿ ♿ **American Camellia Society–Massee Lane Gardens–Annabelle Lundy Fetterman Educational Museum** (478-967-2358 or 1-877-422-6355; www .camellias-acs.com), 100 Massee Lane, Fort Valley. Open 10–4:30 Tuesday–Saturday, 1–4:30 Sunday. Guided tours in February only (prime camellia blooming time) by reservation. Naturally, the stars in this 9-acre garden on the grounds of the headquarters of the American Camellia Society are the 2,000 camellia bushes that bloom from late fall to early spring. Red, white, pink, and variegated blooms are spectacular from October through March. Other flowers, however, are not neglected. Seasonal flora is found in the Kitty Frank Daffodil Garden, the Marvin Jernigan Native Azalea Garden, and the Scheibert Rose Garden. Daylilies, annuals, perennials, and chrysanthemums are featured in their seasons.

In addition, the Brown and Hall Environmental Garden showcases plants indigenous to the Southeast, and the peaceful Abendroth Japanese Garden features a koi pond. The landscaped greenhouse contains camellias, azaleas, and other plants.

This garden began in the 1930s as the private garden of David C. Strother. In addition to planting his flowers and flowering shrubs, he collected millstones from corn-grinding mills in middle Georgia and old wire mile markers, which can still be seen around the garden. He donated the property to the American Camellia Society in 1966. An orientation slide show informs visitors about camellias and the garden.

Within the gardens, the **Stevens-Taylor** and the **Fetterman Museum galleries** contain the world's largest public display of Edward Marshall Boehm porcelain sculptures of birds and flowers. Also on display are porcelains created by Connoisseur, Cybis, and other world-renowned studios.

The newest attraction is the Children's Garden, where little ones can dig for "fossils," play in the playground, or run to their heart's content while Mom and Dad relax in old-fashioned swings. Special events at the garden include the **Festival of Camellias** throughout February (see *Special Events*) and the Daylily Extravaganza throughout June. Adults $5, seniors $4, children younger than 12 free.

NATURE PRESERVES AND PARKS ✎ ✿ ♿ **Ocmulgee Heritage Trail, Gateway Park** (478-722-9909; www.ocmulgeeheritagetrail.com), New Town Macon, 479 Cherry Street, Macon. This 2-mile, flat, paved path on the banks of the Ocmulgee River is popular with walkers, joggers, bikers, in-line skaters, and birders. When complete, the trail will stretch 10 miles from the **Ocmulgee National Monument** (see *To See—Historic Homes and Sites*) to the Amerson Old Waterworks Park. At the entrance to Charles H. Jones Gateway Park, visitors will find the **Otis Redding Statue.** The life-size bronze statue of the legendary native son singer-songwriter of "Sittin' on the Dock of the Bay" fame sits on a set of pilings overlooking the river, holding a guitar, pen, and paper. It's not difficult to imagine where inspiration for this hit song came from. The park also offers an interactive fountain sure to attract the kids. Jazz on the Docks performances are held here periodically.

HISTORICAL SOUTH

www.co.bibb.ga.us/laketobesofkee), 6600 Mosely Dixon Road, Macon. Open dawn–dusk daily. Surrounding a 1,750-acre lake with 35 miles of shoreline boasting three white-sand beaches, the recreation area actually contains Arrowhead Park, Sandy Beach Park, and Claystone Park, which among them offer boat ramps, picnicking, playgrounds, and tennis. There is also a full-service marina and a lakeside restaurant. Fishing for several types of bass, bream, catfish, and crappie; boating; camping; and swimming are also popular pastimes. A well-liked annual event is the Arrowhead Arts and Crafts Festival each October. Day use $3, camping $18–25.

✳ Lodging

BED & BREAKFASTS

In Macon

♿ **1842 Inn** (478-741-1842 or 1-800-336-1842; www.1842inn.com), 353 College Avenue. Luxurious AAA four-diamond accommodations are offered in this antebellum Greek Revival mansion and its Victorian-era cottage. Set in one of the city's most beautiful and best preserved historic neighborhoods, the imposing residence boasts a huge veranda with 18 soaring columns. All of the opulent guest rooms feature antiques, artwork, ornate beds, and a writing desk. Some boast a working fireplace and/or a whirlpool tub. Afternoon refreshments and a delicious breakfast are highlights of each day. No smoking. Some rooms wheelchair accessible. $189–230.

CAMPGROUNDS

In Macon

🦐 🐾 ❀ **Lake Tobesofkee Recreation Area** (478-474-8770; www.co.bibb.ga.us /laketobesofkee), 6600 Moseley Dixon Road. Amenities include boating, fishing, lighted tennis courts, a playground, white-sand beach, covered picnic pavilions, and a softball field. Pets allowed, but must be kept leashed. $18–25 per campsite.

In Perry

🦐 🐾 **Fair Harbor RV Park** (478-988-8844 or 1-877-988-8844; www.fairharborrvpark .com), 515 Marshallville Road. Camp around a fishing pond among 100 shady acres located adjacent to the Georgia National Fairgrounds and Agricenter. $39 per campsite, additional $2.50 for high-speed Internet connection; discounts for multinight or long-term stay.

INNS AND HOTELS

In Macon

🐾 ♿ ❀ **Ramada Plaza Macon** (478-746-1461), 108 First Street. The upscale, high-rise Ramada offers 200 guest rooms with all the modern conveniences, as well as concierge services, a pool, sauna, fitness center, restaurant, café, bar, and lounge. Smoking and nonsmoking rooms available. Pet friendly ($10; one pet only). $59–109.

In Perry

🐾 ♿ **New Perry Hotel** (478-224-1000; www.newperryhotel.com), 800 Main Street. Although it was built in 1925 and the newest rooms added in 1956, it's still called the New Perry Hotel because it's built on the site of the original 1870s hostelry, Cox's Inn, which was built as a stagecoach stop. Before the advent of interstate highways, the hotel was on a major route to Florida, and travelers planned their itinerary to stay or eat a meal here. Guest rooms are offered in the main hotel and a poolside annex. Even today, for lots of folks, it's the dining room that brings them here (see *Where to Eat—Eating Out*). The hotel has been named a National Historic Site. Breakfast is served for hotel guests only. Smoking rooms available; no smoking in public areas or restaurants. $59–125.

RESORTS

In Perry

♿ **Henderson Village** (478-988-8696 or 1-888-615-9722; www.hendersonvillage .com), 125 South Langston Circle. Scattered around 18 shady acres on this AAA four-diamond and Select Registry property are four stately 19th-century homes with

GUESTS CAN RELAX IN LUXURIOUS ACCOMMODATIONS AT HENDERSON VILLAGE RESORT.

sprawling verandas and white columns, as well as six simple tenant cottages—each containing luxurious guest accommodations with antique or reproduction furnishings, a gas-log fireplace, a claw-foot or jetted tub, and beautiful decorative accents. Twenty-four guest suites are offered in all. Naturally, the guest chambers in the homes are more formal than those in the tenant cottages, but all feature amenities such as robes and nightly turndown service. Delicious haute cuisine is served in the historic Langston House Restaurant (see *Where to Eat—Dining Out*). A lovely formal garden and a swimming pool are among other amenities on the property. Many sporting excursions can be arranged on the **Gamelands at Henderson Village,** an exceptional 3,400-acre hunting preserve of timberlands, pastures, and croplands. In addition to bird and wild game hunting, the facility offers five-stand sporting clays, pond and creek fishing for bass and bream, horseback riding, mule-drawn wagon rides, and hiking. No smoking. $140–160 including breakfast; call for the prices of hunting and fishing packages.

✳ Where to Eat
DINING OUT

In Macon
& **Tic Toc Room** (478-744-0123), 408 Martin Luther King Jr. Boulevard. Open 4–10 Monday–Thursday, 4–11 Friday and Saturday. The upscale restaurant serves sophisticated Southern cuisine. Menu items include sushi, beef items, seafood, and creative

chef's specials. Other enticements include an elaborate wine and martini list. Dress is business casual. No smoking. $30–40.

In Perry
& **Langston House Restaurant** (478-988-8696 or 1-888-615-9722; www.henderson village.com), 125 South Langston Circle. Open 7:30–9:30 AM daily, 11–2:30 Tuesday–Saturday, 6–9 Tuesday–Thursday, 6–10 Friday and Saturday. Located in a 19th-century house in the historic Henderson Village resort (see *Lodging—Resorts*), the restaurant serves breakfast daily, as well as lunch and dinner, but not every day. For dinner, guests might be treated to such specialties as barbecued salmon, rack of lamb, duck, beef, veal, or sea bass. Breakfast and lunch favorites include breakfast sandwiches, fried catfish, and chicken specialties. No smoking. Breakfast and lunch about $5–14, dinner $21–29.

EATING OUT

In Macon
🍴 ✎ & **Fincher's Barbecue** (478-788-1900), 3947 Houston Avenue. Open 10–5 Monday–Thursday, 10–7 Friday and Saturday, 10–2 Sunday. Founded in 1935, Fincher's is the only restaurant whose barbecue went into space with NASA. Fincher's serves up the flavor of the South and even has curb service. No smoking. $8–10.

🍴 ✎ & **H&H Restaurant** (478-742-9810), 807 Forsyth Street. Open 6:30–4 Monday–Saturday. Meat-and-three soul-food plates include enough meat, vegetables, bread, and a beverage to appease even the most voracious appetite. Back when the Allman Brothers Band was getting started and the band members didn't have more than a few dollars, they'd come in and place one order, and they'd all share it. When they got famous, they'd fly Mama Louise out to California to cook for them. The casual eatery is complete with a funky jukebox and memorabilia-covered walls. No smoking. Breakfast $5.35, lunch and dinner $8.60.

🍴 ✎ & **Nu-Way Weiners** (478-743-1368; www.nu-wayweiners.com), 430 Cotton

Avenue. Open 6 AM–7 PM weekdays, 7 AM–6 PM Saturday. An institution in this location and sporting the same neon sign since 1916, this hot-doggery is one of the two oldest hot dog stands in the country. The restaurant purveys private-label pork and beef wieners, secret-recipe chili, burgers, and sandwiches. The signature dog is dressed with mustard, onions, the afore-mentioned chili, and barbecue sauce, but if that combination isn't to your liking, you can have it your way. It's obvious why their slogan, "I'd go a long way for a Nu-Way," has stuck since 1916. Note that the diction-ary spells franks *wiener,* but Nu-Way spells it *weiner.* Who can argue with success? Although the franks are the stars, the eatery serves a hearty breakfast as well. There are several other locations in Macon, as well as one in Fort Valley and one in Warner Robins. No smoking. Under $5.

In Perry

🍴 ♦ ♿ **The Restaurant at the New Perry Hotel** (478-224-1000), 800 Main Street. Open 11–2 and 5–9 Monday–Saturday, brunch 11–3 Sunday. Fresh flow-ers from the hotel's year-round gardens embellish the white starched tablecloths. The menu is typical Southern comfort food. Visitors can expect dishes such as chopped steak, mackerel, salmon croquettes, or turkey accompanied by a relish tray, salad, soup, and three vegetables. Save room for the pecan pie. No smoking. Lunch and din-ner $10–12.

For more casual dining, the hotel also offers the **Tavery.** Open 4–9:30 Monday–Saturday, with a happy hour 5–6:30 each of those days. The Tavery has a full bar, an extensive wine list, a bar menu, and patio dining on the terrace. No smoking.

✳ Entertainment

MUSIC Grand Opera House (478-301-5460; www.mercer.edu/thegrand), 651 Mul-berry Street, Macon. Open only for performances; box office open 10–5 week-days. Built in 1884 as the Academy of Music, the Grand Opera House boasts one of the largest stages in the South—it's seven stories high. Over its many-year history,

such superstars of the day as Burns and Allen, Houdini, Sarah Bernhardt, Bob Hope, and Will Rogers trod the boards here. Restored to its former opulence, the Grand now serves as the performing arts center for Mercer University and Wesleyan College and hosts performances by the **Macon Symphony Orchestra** (see follow-ing entry), Broadway touring companies, and other arts and cultural events. Call for a schedule of events and prices.

Macon City Auditorium (box office: 478-751-9232), 415 First Street, Macon. The auditorium has the world's largest copper dome, and its proscenium displays a mural depicting Macon's leaders through history. The facility hosts concerts and other per-formances. Call for a schedule of events and prices.

Macon Symphony Orchestra (478-301-5300; www.maconsymphony.com), offices: 400 Popular Street, Macon. The symphony presents six classical concerts, four pops concerts, and six Macon-Mercer Symphony Youth Orchestra concerts. The symphony often performs in outlying areas such as Milledgeville, Fort Valley, Eatonton, Grif-fin, Hawkinsville, Warner Robins, and Hen-derson Village, so check schedules if you are going to be in those towns. Call for a schedule of performances and ticket prices (usually adults $38, students with ID $18, children 12 and younger $13). Purchase tickets by calling the box office or by log-ging on to the symphony's website.

🍴 ♦ **Powersville Opry** (478-953-1406), 240 Powersville Road, Byron. Open for per-formances 5–9:30 Saturday, but there are jams on Monday and Tuesday evenings, and the house band practices on Thursday evenings. Bluegrass, country, and gospel are played to standing-room-only crowds. You never know who might sit in with the musi-cians at this old store turned concert venue. Admission free, but donations welcome.

THEATER Douglass Theatre (478-742-2000; www.douglasstheatre.org), 355 Mar-tin Luther King Jr. Boulevard, Macon. Open 10–5 weekdays. A significant African American theater built in 1921, the Dou-glass hosted such performers as Count

Basie, Cab Calloway, Ma Rainey, and Bessie Smith. Otis Redding was discovered here, and Little Richard and Godfather of Soul James Brown performed here as well, but the theater closed in 1972 and slumbered for 20 years before renovations began. Beautifully restored, the state-of-the-art theater now hosts 3-D films, live musical and theatrical performances, and meetings. Call for schedule and prices.

Macon Little Theatre (478-477-3342 or 478-471-7529; www.maconlittletheatre.org), 4220 Forsyth Road, Macon. Box office open 1–6 Monday–Friday. Located adjacent to the Museum of Arts and Sciences. Yearly productions include at least one musical. Call for a schedule of productions. Adults $18, seniors $15, students $10.

Perry Players Community Theatre (478-987-5354; www.perryplayers.org), 909 Main Street, Perry. The Perry Players, performing since 1962, put on three or four productions each year and are housed in a renovated horse barn. Open seating, so get there early. Adults $10, students and seniors $6.

Theatre Macon (478-746-9485; www.theatremacon.com), offices: 438 Cherry Street, Macon. During the regular season, the organization presents seven productions. Call for a performance schedule. Adults $20, seniors and students $18.

Warner Robins Little Theatre (478-929-4579; www.wrlt.org), 502 South Pleasant Hill Road, Warner Robins. This busy little theater hosts five performances per season. Call for schedule of performances. Adults $15; seniors, military, and children $12.

✳ Selective Shopping

Ingleside Village Shopping and Arts District (contact the CVB: 478-743-3401 or 1-800-768-3401), Ingleside Avenue, Macon. The district is a trendy area filled with art galleries and specialty shops that purvey antiques, books, clothing, gifts, and home accents.

ANTIQUES Big Peach Antique Mall and Welcome Center (478-956-1968), 119 Peachtree Parkway, Byron. Open 10–7 Monday–Saturday, noon–6 Sunday.

Instantly identifiable from I-75 because of its towering peach (not counting the pedestal, the giant peach measures 75 feet from stem to tip and is 28 feet in diameter), this mall offers 230 dealers selling antiques, collectibles, china, and other fine items in 40,000 square feet of retail space. Make time to stop for a picture of the Big Peach and slurp down a peach ice-cream cone.

ART GALLERIES Macon Arts Gallery (478-743-6940; www.maconarts.org), 468 First Street, Macon. Open 9–5 weekdays. Local artists show their one-of-a-kind creations, with new works added frequently.

FOOD Dickey Farms (478-836-4362 or 1-800-732-2442; www.gapeaches.com), 3440 Old US 341, Musella. Open 8–3 weekdays. Purchase peaches and other peachy treats from the oldest operating packinghouse in Georgia.

Priester's Pecans Candy Kitchen and Restaurant (478-987-6080 or 1-800-277-3226; www.priester.com), 106 Fairview Drive (exit 134 off I-75 at South Perry Parkway), Perry. Open 9–6 daily. Watch pecan pralines, divinity, fudge, sugared nuts, and other sweets being made, and sample all the homemade candies.

OUTLET MALLS Peach Festival Outlet Shops at Byron (478-956-1855; www.peachshopsatbyron.com), 331 GA 49 North, Byron. Open 10–9 Monday–Saturday, noon–6 Sunday. This center provides middle Georgia's only outlet shopping. The center features dozens of brand-name stores such as Bon Worth, Dress Barn, and Leggs/Hanes/Bali, purveying goods from kitchenware to clothing. Montana Steakhouse is also on-site.

✳ Special Events

Early February: **Festival of Camellias at the American Camellia Society–Massee Lane Gardens** (478-967-2358; www.camellias-acs.com). The monthlong celebration in Fort Valley includes senior days, deluxe tours, music Saturdays, box lunch days, a fashion show and luncheon, camellia sales, clinics, and workshops. Included with regular admission; free first Saturday in February. See *Green Space—Gardens.*

March: **International Cherry Blossom Festival** (478-751-7429; www.cherry blossom.com). For 10 days, visitors to Macon are treated to more than 400 activities, extravagant displays of springtime beauty, and exciting festivities—all situated under a pink canopy of blossoms. Among the activities are headliner concerts, old-fashioned dances, and daily performances in Central City Park. Festival free; some events have a charge.

Peaches to Beaches Antiques and Yard Sale (contact Golden Isles Parkway Association: 229-868-6365; www.peaches tobeaches.com). This 172-mile-long yard sale connects the peach-growing counties of middle Georgia to the Golden Isles of the coast, stopping in 17 communities along the way, including Perry. If you like to haggle, then this March event is the Super Bowl of yard sales for you. Free.

April and October: **Mossy Creek Barnyard Festival** (478-922-8265; www.mossy creekfestival.com). Held at 315M Lake Joy Road, 6 miles east of I-75, near Perry and Warner Robins. Open 10–5:30 Saturday and Sunday. The award-winning weekend fair, named one of the top 20 events in the Southeast and one of the top 100 events in North America, features pioneer demonstrations, continuous music and storytelling, arts and crafts, and hayrides. Adults $5, children $1. Parking free.

May: **Battle of Byron** (www.battleofbyron .com). Activities include a barbecue cook-off, arts and crafts, food vendors, hayrides, cake walks, games, karaoke, and jail 'n bail. Free; some activities have a fee.

Macon's Secret Garden Tour (contact Hay House for tickets: 478-742-8155; www.hayhouse.org). In addition to the opportunity to tour some of Macon's most sumptuous private gardens, the festival includes several free events, such as the three-day Garden Market plant sale at Central City Park, and seminars by noted gardeners. Call for a schedule of events and prices.

June: **Georgia Peach Festival** (478-825-4002 or 1-877-322-4371; www.gapeach festival.org). Some activities occur in Fort Valley and others in Byron. Georgia's Official Food Festival, the fair's highlight is the world's largest peach cobbler, a juicy 6-by-9-foot dessert. Other activities include a hat contest, street dance, barbecue cook-off, Glitz and Glamour Ball, Peach Queen Pageant, an art show, concerts, a parade, food vendors, arts and crafts, music and dancing, and an ice-cream making contest. Admission $1; some activities have an additional fee.

September: **Ocmulgee Indian Celebration** (478-752-8257; www.nps.gov/ocmu). Held 10–6 Saturday and Sunday the third weekend in September at the **Ocmulgee National Monument** (see *To See— Historic Homes and Sites*), this festival, the largest of its kind in the Southeast, is a gathering of 200 Creeks, Cherokees, Chickasaws, Choctaws, and Seminoles. They perform ancient ceremonial dances in colorful regalia and tell of Native American legends and lore. Among the food choices are roasted corn, buffalo burgers, and Indian tacos. Music, art, living history demonstrations, and native crafts round out the activities. Adults $5, active military and children 6–12 $2.

October: **Georgia National Fair** (478-987-3247; 1-800-YUR-FAIR in Georgia only; www.gnfa.com). Open 8 AM–10 PM daily. A 10-day fall exposition, this family-oriented festival includes a circus, games, home and fine arts competitions, horse shows, livestock events, midway rides, youth exhibits, and food. Nights are filled with concerts, entertainment, and fireworks. General admission: adults $8, seniors $7, children 10 and younger free. Rides charged individually.

Wings and Wheels Car Show (478-926-6870; www.museumofaviation.org). Held at the Museum of Aviation, US 129/GA 247 South and Russell Parkway, in Warner Robins. The annual show features more than 300 show vehicles on display, a "for sale" car corral, and special attractions. Call for exact date. Free.

MADISON TO WASHINGTON

The Piedmont country between Georgia's mountainous region and its coastal plain is the heart of the state's Historic South region. Not only is it centrally located, but it is also the most stereotypically Southern area of Georgia. Although Union general William Tecumseh Sherman's infamous March to the Sea came right through the heartland and resulted in immense destruction of plantations and towns, much was spared and survives to this day. In fact, Madison is known as the "town Sherman refused to burn." This entire area of Georgia's historic heartland is a living museum to a less harried time in U.S. history, and it contains shining examples of plantation architecture.

Many of the wonderful historic plantation and in-town properties are featured on much-anticipated annual tours of homes, which sell out early, so don't lollygag when making your reservations. Others are used as elegant bed & breakfasts. Outside of Savannah, this area has one of the largest concentrations of B&Bs in the state, and in a region where expansive front porches are de rigueur, it's no surprise that Southern hospitality is at its best here. Still other historic properties create homes for a variety of museums. The region is an important part of the **Georgia Antique Trail** and the **Antebellum Trail.** After you get off the interstate, scenic byways wind past pastoral fields and through quaint villages inviting visitors to stop by for a spell.

Cotton may have been king at one time, but recreation—and golf in particular—is king now. State parks and resorts offer outstanding opportunities for golfers of all abilities. Several lakes and state parks as well as a national forest provide innumerable choices for water sports and other outdoor recreation, including hiking, biking, swimming, bird-watching, boating, fishing, horseback riding, and shooting sports. Lake Oconee claims to have more fish per cubic yard than any other lake in Georgia.

GUIDANCE Before visiting Madison, Buckhead, or Rutledge, contact the **Madison–Morgan County Chamber of Commerce, Convention and Visitors Bureau, Madison Welcome Center** (706-342-4454 or 1-800-709-7406; www.madisonga.org), 115 East Jefferson Street, Madison 30650. Open 9–4:30 weekdays, 10–4 Saturday, 1–3 Sunday.

When planning a trip to the Eatonton area, contact the **Eatonton-Putnam Chamber of Commerce** (706-485-7701; www.eatonton.com), 305 North Madison Avenue, Eatonton 31024. Open 8:30–5 weekdays. Information is available here for the **Alice Walker Driving Tour, Historic Walking Tour of Eatonton,** and the **Antebellum Trail.**

For information about Greensboro, consult the **Greene County Chamber of Commerce** (706-453-7592 or 1-866-341-4466; www.greeneccoc.org or www.oconee.com), 111 North Main Street, Greensboro 30642. Open 9–5 weekdays.

When planning a trip to the Washington area, contact the **Washington–Wilkes County Chamber of Commerce** (706-678-5111; www.washingtonwilkes.org), 20 West Square, Washington 30673. Open 9–4 weekdays, 8–3 Saturday.

GETTING THERE *By air:* Most visitors to this area who are arriving by air fly into Atlanta but could also fly into Macon. See "What's Where in Georgia" for airport, airline, and car rental information at either.

By bus: **Greyhound Lines** (706-549-2255 or 1-800-231-2222; www.greyhound.com) operates service to Crawfordville, Greensboro, Madison, and Washington, but then a visitor would need a rental car.

By car: This chapter has two completely separate nodes, but all the towns are found just north or south of I-20. The western node contains Buckhead, Eatonton, Greensboro, Madison, and Rutledge. The eastern node contains Crawfordville, Lincolnton, Warrenton, and Washington. Various routes will take you to the charming towns, so get a good Georgia map.

By train: **AMTRAK** (see "What's Where in Georgia") operates service to Atlanta and Augusta (see the Augusta chapter). A visitor would need to rent a car at either of those locations to get to and around this area.

GETTING AROUND This area has no mass transit or taxi service, and rental cars are available only at the Atlanta or Macon airports (see "What's Where in Georgia").

MEDICAL EMERGENCY Call 911.

VILLAGES Before the Civil War, **Madison** was known as the most cultured and aristocratic town on the stage route from Charleston to New Orleans, but during the Civil War it became known as "the Town Sherman Refused to Burn." Madison was on the direct path of Sherman's March to the Sea from Atlanta to Savannah, and the expectation was that it would be put to the torch as so many other towns were. After more than a century, the question still remains unanswered: Why was Madison spared? According to one story, Senator Joshua Hill was a friend of Sherman's brother and had been an early foe of secession. It is reported that he was able to come to a gentleman's agreement with Sherman that would save the town from being burned. Whether there's any truth to this conjecture or not, this fortuitous fact that Madison and its outstanding architecture—a large portion of which was built between 1830 and 1860—was spared resulted in the town being named a designated historic district by the Department of the Interior in 1974. One of the first such districts in Georgia, it is also one of the largest in the country. A few historic homes are open for tours year-round, and several tours throughout the year allow visitors to get a glimpse into private residences.

Eatonton bills itself as "Close to Everything, Next to Perfect." The town has a rich storytelling and literary history. Two of Eatonton's most famous citizens are Joel Chandler Harris, creator of the Uncle Remus tales, and Alice Walker, author of *The Color Purple, The Temple of My Familiar,* and other books. Harris was born in Eatonton in 1848. His first collection of poems and proverbs was published in 1881 as *Uncle Remus: His Songs and Sayings.* Other famous Eatonians include Dr. Benjamin Hunt, a transplanted New Yorker who is credited with bringing the dairy industry to Georgia, and S. Truett Cathy, the founder of the Chick-fil-A fast food chain.

Greensboro was founded in 1786 and boasts five historic districts and seven historic sites, including Bethesda Baptist Church (organized in 1785), the original campus of Mercer University (1830), Jefferson Hall and Heard-Carpenter House (1830), and the Greensboro Old Gaol (1807). The area is a hub for family activities and events. In recent years the development of several luxury resorts around nearby Lake Oconee has fueled interest in the area.

Washington, which was the site of the Revolutionary War Battle of Kettle Creek, has several history museums and an intact plantation now open for tours.

✳ To See

CULTURAL SITES ✆ ✍ ᕓ **Madison-Morgan Cultural Arts Center** (706-342-4743 or 1-877-233-0598; www.mmcc-arts.org), 434 South Main Street, Madison. Open 10–5 Tuesday–Saturday, 2–5 Sunday. The majestic 1895 Romanesque Revival–style schoolhouse was one of the first graded schools in the South. The structure currently houses a history museum, a performing arts center, and several authentically restored and furnished turn-of-the-20th-century classrooms. In addition, the museum is filled with 19th-century decorative arts, historical artifacts, and information about the Piedmont region of Georgia, as well as permanent and traveling art exhibits. A variety of performances and special events are given in the apse-shaped auditorium (see *Entertainment—Theater*). Adults $3, seniors $2.50, children $2.

HISTORIC HOMES AND SITES ✆ ✍ ᕓ **Callaway Plantation** (706-678-7060; www.callaway.washingtongeorgia.net), 2160 Lexington Road/US 78, Washington. Open 10–5 Tuesday–Saturday. A living-history museum, the facility has three historic houses and primitive crafts, and even allows visitors to pick cotton. Sight-seers can follow the original family from its humble log cabin beginnings all the way to life in this beautiful Greek Revival manor house. Limited wheelchair accessibility. Adults $4, children 5–12 $2.

✆ ᕓ **Heritage Hall** (706-342-9627; www.friendsofheritagehall.org), 277 South Main Street, Madison. Open 11–4 Monday–Saturday, 1:30–4:30 Sunday. Built circa 1811, this gracious, many-columned structure is furnished with period pieces. Be sure to look for a unique feature of this historic home: Many windows have etchings on them. These were done by the daughters and granddaughters of Dr. Elijah Evans Jones, the home's second owner. The ghost of Virginia Nisbet, one of the daughters, who died in childbirth with her baby, is said to haunt the house. An image on the fireplace, which appears to be a woman holding a baby, is said to be the pair. All attempts to remove it have failed. Adults $5, students $2, children 12 and younger free. A $6 combo ticket also allows admission to Rogers House and Rose Cottage (see following entry).

✆ ✍ ᕓ **Liberty Hall, A. H. Stephens State Historic Park** (706-456-2602; www.gastate parks.org/AHStephens), 456 Alexander Street North, Crawfordville. Museum and Liberty Hall open 9–5 Friday–Sunday (last tour at 4). Liberty Hall was the home of A. H. Stephens, who served as the vice president of the Confederate States of America and later as governor of Georgia. The home, which was built after the Civil War in 1875, has been restored to that period and furnished with period pieces and Stephens memorabilia. The adjacent museum contains one of the finest collections of Civil War artifacts in the state. A statue of the "Little Giant" marks his grave site in the front yard. Admission to museum and Liberty Hall: $2.75–4.

✆ ✍ ᕓ **Rock Eagle Effigy** (706-484-2899; www.rockeagle4H.org), Rock Eagle 4-H Center, 350 Rock Eagle Road, Eatonton. Open dawn–dusk daily. The rock representation of an eagle is the second-oldest and most unusual attraction in the state (the oldest is the Sapelo Shell Ring Complex on Sapelo Island). The prone bird, which measures 102 feet from head to tail and 120 feet across the wingspan while rising 8 feet from the ground, is thought to have been created 2,000 years ago by Woodland Indians as a ceremonial meeting place. The milky quartz rocks used to construct the giant bird range from baseball-size stones to boulders and were brought from as far as 100 miles away in an era when there were no horses or wheeled vehicles on this continent. It is believed that they must have been dragged on deerskins. For the best view and photo op, climb the granite observation tower (not wheelchair accessible), which was built by the WPA in the 1930s. Boating and fishing are allowed on the 4-H center's 110-acre lake, but swimming is not permitted. (**Rock Hawk,** also located in Putnam County, is a sister mound of similar construction. This site is located at the entrance to Georgia Power's **Lawrence Shoals Park** on Lake Oconee. (See *To Do—Hiking.*) Free.

🦐 ♿ **Rogers House and Rose Cottage** (706-343-0190; www.madisonga.org /activities), 179 East Jefferson Street, Madison. Open 10–4:30 Monday–Saturday, 1–4 Sunday. Located on the same property, the two houses represent two different time periods. The Rogers House, circa 1810, is one of the oldest Piedmont Plain–style homes in the county and is filled with period furnishings. Rose Cottage, circa

THE ROCK EAGLE EFFIGY IS THOUGHT TO BE 2,000 YEARS OLD.

1891, was built by Adeline Rose, who was born into slavery. It has been moved to the site. $3 for both houses, students $2. A $6 combo ticket allows admittance to both houses and Heritage Hall (see previous entry).

MUSEUMS 🦐 ✎ ♿ **The Bruce Wiener Microcar Museum** (no phone; www.microcar museum.com), Double Bubble Acres, 2950 Eatonton Road/US 441, Madison. Open 10–4 Friday and Saturday. Bruce Wiener made his fortune from Double Bubble Gum, hence the name of his property. His passion for microcars led to the largest collection in the world. See 300 of them here spanning the time period from the late 1940s to the early 1960s. These amazing cars are even smaller than today's Smart Car. In addition, the collection includes thousands of models, toys, and memorabilia relating to the microcar. $5.

🦐 ♿ **Madison Museum of Fine Art** (706-485-4530; www.mmofa.org), 300 Hancock Street, Madison. Open 1–5 Sunday–Friday, 11–5 Saturday. Through the generosity of donors, the permanent collection includes works by Picasso, Dali, Calder, Chagall, Whistler, and Batistello, an Italian Old Master, as well as Asian art and African stone sculptures. Works are displayed in an intimate atmosphere with club chairs, a fireplace, and soft music. Changing exhibits entice visitors to return again and again. Visitors also enjoy the sculpture garden and café. Free. Some special exhibits have a fee.

🦐 ✎ ♿ **Morgan County African American Museum** (706-342-9191; www.mcaam.org), 156 Academy Street, Madison. Open 10–4 Tuesday–Saturday. This museum, dedicated to African American heritage and contributions to Southern culture, is located in the historic 1890s Moore House. Exhibits illustrate the African origins of Morgan County blacks and seek to preserve and promote a greater awareness of contributions African Americans have made to the South. Adults $5, children $3.

🦐 ✎ ♿ **Old School History Museum** (706-485-3156; www.theplazaartscenter.com), 305 North Madison Avenue, Eatonton. Open 9–5 weekdays for self-guided tours; docent-led tours 10–4 Saturday and 2–4 Sunday. Located in the Plaza Arts Center, which was once the original 1916 Eatonton School, the museum features exhibits in four of the old classrooms. One room is devoted to the contents of a vintage drugstore, complete with a marble-topped soda fountain and a 1940s jukebox. Another room portrays turn-of-the-20th-century downtown Eatonton storefronts with "windows in time" filled with period artifacts, memorabilia, and treasures. A 1900s classroom is re-created with a vintage blackboard, cloakroom, desks, and student memorabilia, as well as pictures of every graduating class from 1916 to 1970. The fourth classroom is the history gallery, which describes the history and heritage of Eatonton and Putnam County through displays of Native American artifacts, exhibits describing Sherman's March to the Sea through Putnam County, and an homage to several of the area's famous former residents, such as Joel Chandler Harris and Alice Walker. The facility is also the venue for theatrical and musical performances (see *Entertainment— Theater*). Free.

🐾 🎣 **Robert Toombs House Historic Site** (706-678-2226; www.gastateparks.org/Robert ToombsHouse), 216 East Robert Toombs Avenue, Washington. Open 9–5 Tuesday–Saturday, 2–5 Sunday. This stately, white-columned home was the residence of Confederate leader Robert Toombs. A legend in his own time, Toombs was a wealthy planter and lawyer who became a state legislator and U.S. senator, eventually evolving into a fiery secessionist. He served five months as the Confederate secretary of state, but he resigned to serve as a brigadier general in the Army of Northern Virginia. After the Civil War, he was one of only a few who refused to sign an oath of allegiance to the Union, calling himself an Unreconstructed Rebel. He helped create the Georgia state constitution in 1877. His home is filled with Toombs family furniture as well as Civil War exhibits. Visitors also should see the dramatic film about Toombs and tour the grounds. Several special events occur throughout the year. $2–3.

🐾 ♿ **Steffen Thomas Museum of Art** (706-342-7557; www.steffenthomas.org), 4200 Bethany Road, Buckhead. Open 11–4 Tuesday–Saturday. Inside a steel warehouse is a wondrous art museum filled floor to ceiling with expressionist oil paintings, watercolors, mosaics, and sculptures—all the work of the late Steffen Thomas. Thomas immigrated to Atlanta from Germany in the 1920s and lived there until his death in 1990. He is known for having created the statue of former governor Eugene Talmadge located on the grounds of the Georgia Capitol, the Alabama Memorial at Vicksburg National Military Park in Mississippi, and a bronze bust of George Washington Carver, which is displayed at the Tuskegee Institute in Alabama. The works he created for himself, including mosaics, ceramics, furniture, and works on paper, are displayed here. The subject matter ranges from women to landscapes, pets to farm animals. Adults $8, students $6, children free.

🐾 🎣 ♿ **Uncle Remus Museum** (706-485-6856; www.uncleremusmuseum.org), 2414 Oak Street Extension/US 441 South, Eatonton. Open 10–12 and 1–5 Monday–Saturday, 2–5 Sunday; closed Tuesday in January and February. The first thing visitors see is the Br'er Rabbit Statue. The large, sprightly, brightly dressed statue is a tribute to the star of the tales author Joel Chandler Harris heard from slaves. When stopping to take a photo here, imagine what devilment Br'er Rabbit is contemplating to inflict on Br'er Fox and Br'er Bear. Several authentic slave cabins were combined in Turner Park, part of the original homestead of Joseph Sidney Turner—who was the "Little Boy" in the tales—to create this museum dedicated to Harris and his critters. Among the displays are shadow-box scenes of the critters, first editions, and other Harris memorabilia. A portrait of Uncle Remus and the Little Boy as they appeared in the Disney movie *Song*

THE UNCLE REMUS MUSEUM IS DEDICATED TO JOEL CHANDLER HARRIS, CREATOR OF THE UNCLE REMUS TALES.

THE TALES OF UNCLE REMUS

Joel Chandler Harris was born into utter poverty in 1848, but through the care of others who recognized his potential, he received an education. The postmaster used to give him discarded papers and magazines to satisfy his hunger for learning. At age 13, Harris was hired as a printer's devil for the *Countryman,* a newspaper published by Joseph Addison Turner on his plantation, Turnwold. It was while working here that Harris began his lifelong friendship with the plantation's African Americans and the animals he later wrote about. Harris always insisted that he was not the author of the tales, but only the compiler. He eventually produced nine books with 183 different stories in which the lowly and enslaved always outwit their masters. These stories have been translated into 27 languages.

of the South hangs over the fireplace. The surrounding park contains historic outbuildings and old-fashioned farm tools. Adults $3, children younger than eight $2.

🐾 ✎ ⚐ **Washington Historical Museum** (706-678-2105), 308 East Robert Toombs Avenue, Washington. Open 10–5 Tuesday–Saturday, 12:30–3:30 Sunday. Visitors learn about the history of Washington and Wilkes County by viewing Native American and Civil War artifacts and other memorabilia contained in the antebellum Barnett-Slaton House, which was begun in 1835. This house museum is decorated with authentic period furnishings, has a replica of a plantation kitchen, and includes displays about prehistoric Indian life, the Battle of Kettle Creek, and Native American pottery. Adults $3, children 5–12 $2, children under five free.

SPECIAL PLACES 🐾 ✎ **Scull Shoals Archaeological Site** (chamber of commerce: 706-453-7592; www.scullshoals.org), Macedonia Church Road (consult the website for detailed directions), Greensboro. Open daily. Visitors may see active archaeological digs under way at these pre-Columbian–era Indian mounds on the site of the now-defunct village of Scull Shoals. The extinct 19th-century mill village once included Georgia's first paper mill and a water-powered cotton mill, as well as gristmills, sawmills, a four-story brick textile mill, stores, and homes. Flooding caused the demise of the mills in the 1880s, and the town was abandoned in the 1920s. The 2,200-acre site is now an experimental forest area, a hub for environmental education, and a research center for the study of the history of technology, economics, medicine, forestry, landscape use, and other subjects. **Scull Shoals Historical Area, Oconee National Forest,** is reached by a gravel road or a 1-mile hiking trail that leads past the ruins of this once-prosperous town. From there, the **Boarding House Trail** leads to the ruins of an old boardinghouse. The **Indian Mounds Trail** traverses the Oconee River floodplain to two prehistoric mounds. Occasional heritage festivals include living-history demonstrations. Free.

✳ To Do

BICYCLING 🐾 ✎ A brochure for a **self-guided bicycling tour of Eatonton** is available from the Eatonton-Putnam Chamber of Commerce (706-485-7701). A local biker has mapped out the community in a very scenic and energetic ride for the entire family. Call for details.

GOLF 🐾 **The Creek at Hard Labor** (706-557-3006 or 1-888-353-4592; www.gastate parks.org/HardLaborCreek or www.golfgeorgia.org), 1400 Knox Chapel Road, Social Circle. Open 7–7 daily. One of Georgia's best golf values, the 18-hole course is intersected by Hard Labor Creek, which creates water hazards on five holes. The course features a pro shop, driving range, unlimited weekday play, and junior and senior discounts. $36–46.

Golf Club at Cuscowilla (706-485-0094 or 1-800-458-5351; www.cuscowilla.com), 126
Cuscowilla Drive, Eatonton. Open 7–7 daily. Four championship courses blend with the
rolling meadows and pine forests that dot the shores of Lake Oconee. This highly acclaimed
course features a pro shop, practice green, driving range, swimming, tennis, and the Golf
House Grill, which serves breakfast and lunch. Guest accommodations are also available (see
Lodging—Inns and Resorts). Greens fees $89–130.

Harbor Club at Lake Oconee (pro shop: 706-453-4414; 1-800-505-4653; www.harbor
club.com), One Club Drive, Greensboro. Open 8–7 daily. This 18-hole course offers a challenge to golfers of all skill levels. Many holes border Lake Oconee or one of the facility's natural streams. $105–125.

Reynolds Plantation Golf Club (706-485-0235; www.reynoldsplantation.com), 112
Plantation Drive, Eatonton. Open 8–7 daily. This beautiful property boasts seven world-
class golf courses. Many holes enjoy breathtaking views of Lake Oconee. Amenities include
the Reynolds Golf Academy, Taylor Made Performance Lab, and Annika Boutique. The
courses are open only to guests staying at the **Ritz-Carlton Lodge, Reynolds Plantation**
(see *Lodging—Inns and Resorts*) or those with a temporary membership, of which there are
several types available to travelers (call for details). Greens fees $110 winter–$250 peak
weekends.

HIKING 🐾 🚲 ♿ **Rock Hawk Effigy Trails** (www.rockhawk.org/maps for directions),
located at the entrance to Lawrence Shoals Park on Lake Oconee. Open daylight hours. Also
known as Little Rock Eagle, this is the second of only two such effigies found east of the
Mississippi. The other is the **Rock Eagle Effigy** (see *To See—Historic Homes and Sites*).
The effigy is located along what was the ancient Native American Okfuskee Trail, which
linked the coast near present-day Charleston with the Mississippi River. The Historical Piedmont Scenic Byway (GA 16) roughly follows that trail. Smaller and less distinct than its larger
sibling, the effigy is still impressive when seen from observation towers. Georgia Power
maintains the property, which includes 15 miles of trails divided into five color-coded sections, a large lake, major river, wetlands, forests, and fields. Lockerly Arboretum has labeled
trees and plants on a 3-mile section. More than 200 species of birds have been observed
here. Free.

SPAS ♿ **The Ritz-Carlton Lodge, Reynolds Plantation** (706-467-0600; www.ritz
carltonlodge.com), 3000 Lake Oconee Trail, Greensboro. Open 8–8 daily. The spa, which is
ranked fourth on *Travel + Leisure's* list of Top Resort Spas in the United States and Canada,
offers an impressive variety of spa treatments. Many are inspired by Southern ingredients
such as magnolia, gardenia, primrose, eucalyptus oil, and Oconee mud. Reservations are
required two to three weeks in advance. Use of the facilities is free for resort guests; $50 for
nonguests. Spa treatments priced individually and vary widely. (For more information about
this resort, see *Golf, Lodging—Inns and Resorts, Where to Eat—Dining Out,* and *Where to
Eat—Eating Out.*)

TOURS 🐾 **Miss Fanny's Tours** (706-318-3128; www.missfanny.com), Washington. Tours
drive by 50 historical homes and sites while Miss Fanny regales visitors with tales of local
Revolutionary War and Civil War history as well as other local lore. $20.

WALKING TOURS 🐾 **The Walking Tour of Madison** (706-342-4450 or 1-800-709-
7406). Discover the unexpected in historic Madison by taking this self-guided walking tour,
which begins at the Madison Welcome Center on the Square. This 1.4-mile tour is a pleasant
and healthy way to see some of the finest architecture that the South has to offer. Driving
routes are available as well. Free.

WATER SPORTS Waterskiing opportunities abound on nearby **Lake Oconee, Clarks Hill Lake, Lake Jackson,** and **Lake Sinclair.** Fishing, swimming, and boating are other popular water sports. See *Green Space—Lakes.*

✳ Green Space

LAKES 🐾 ✂ ♿ **Clarks Hill Lake** (706-359-7970 or 1-800-533-3478; www.lincolncounty ga.org), office: 2959 McCormick Highway/US 378 East, Lincolnton. Open daily. A mecca for water-sports enthusiasts, Clarks Hill Lake straddles the Georgia–South Carolina border. It is known as Strom Thurmond Lake on the South Carolina side. The lake, which is the largest reservoir in the Southeast, boasts 1,200 miles of shoreline, of which 400 miles are in Lincoln County. With its 11 Corps of Engineers recreation areas, 13 Corps campgrounds, 5 commercial marinas, 6 state parks, and 4 county parks, it attracts 6 million visitors per year. Free.

🐾 ✂ ♿ **Lake Jackson** (706-468-6062; www.monticelloga.com), GA 16 and GA 212, Monticello. Open daily. The Alcovy, South, and Yellow rivers meet at Lloyd Shoals Dam, which was built in the early 1900s to create a lake for swimming, fishing, boating, and other water sports. Free.

🐾 ✂ ♿ **Lake Oconee** (706-453-7592 or 1-866-341-4466; www.oconee.org), GA 44 South/Lake Oconee Parkway, Greensboro. Open daily. In 1980 Georgia Power Company built Wallace Dam, creating a 19,000-acre lake to supply hydroelectric power for the region. The resulting Lake Oconee, the second-largest lake in Georgia, supports a world-class resort community with access from numerous places from Eatonton to Greensboro. The 374 miles of shoreline provide ideal locations for three Georgia Power Company parks, marinas, beaches, restaurants, lodging, and golf courses. Water sports include boating, fishing, swimming, and waterskiing. Camping, hiking, bird-watching, and picnicking are other popular activities. Access to lake free; some activities have fees. A brochure can be downloaded from the website.

🐾 ✂ ♿ **Lake Sinclair** (chamber of commerce: 706-485-7701; www.lakesinclair.org), Eatonton. Open daily. Numerous parks and marinas, public boat ramps, bird-watching, tailrace fishing, and other water activities are available at this 14,750-acre lake with 417 miles of shoreline formed by damming the Oconee River. Free.

NATURE PRESERVES AND PARKS 🐾 ✂ ♿ **A. H. Stephens State Historic Park** (706-456-2602; lodging reservations: 1-800-864-7275; www.gastateparks.org/AHStephens), 456 Alexander Street North, Crawfordville. Park open 7 AM–10 PM daily. This park combines Civil War history with outdoor recreation. Central to the park is **Liberty Hall,** the home of A. H. Stephens (see *To See—Historic Homes and Sites*). Surrounding the historic site is a 1,177-acre park with fishing lakes, a Junior Olympic–size swimming pool open seasonally, 4 miles of walking trails—one of which is ADA accessible—and 12 miles of horseback riding trails (BYOH—bring your own horse). Private boats with electric motors are permitted, and fishing and pedal boats are available for rent seasonally. Lodging is offered at the campground and in cottages (see *Lodging—Campgrounds* and *Lodging—Cottages and Cabins*). Parking $5.

🐾 ✂ ♿ **Elijah Clark State Park and Museum** (706-359-3458; lodging reservations: 1-800-864-7275; www.gastateparks.org/ElijahClark), 2959 McCormick Highway, Lincolnton. Park open 7 AM–10 PM daily; cabin open weekends April–November. Located on the western shores of Clarks Hill Lake, the 447-acre park is named for a frontiersman and war hero who led pioneers during the Revolutionary War. He and his wife, Hannah, are buried here. A renovated log cabin serves as a museum where furniture, utensils, and tools from the late 1780s are displayed. Recreational facilities include a swimming beach, playground, miniature golf (additional fee), shuffleboard courts, four boat ramps, an accessible fishing pier, a cleaning station, and 3.75 miles of hiking trails. Accommodations are available in cottages and campsites (see *Lodging—Campgrounds* and *Lodging—Cottages and Cabins*). Parking $5.

🦆 💧 ♿ **Hard Labor Creek State Park** (706-557-3001; lodging reservations: 1-800-864-7275; www.gastateparks.org/info/HardLaborCreek), 5 Hard Labor Creek Road, off US 278/Fairplay Road (parallels I-20), Rutledge. Open 7 AM–10 PM daily. The origin of this park's name is shrouded in mystery. Two possibilities seem likely. Some believe the area was named by Native Americans who found it difficult to ford the creek here. Others believe that the area was named by slaves who tilled the fields. Regardless of where it got its name, the wooded 5,804-acre park has a wide range of recreational opportunities. It is well-known for its golf course (see *To Do—Golf*) but is equally popular for its 24.5 miles of hiking trails and 22 miles of horseback riding trails (BYOH—bring your own horse), as well as lakes, fishing, and a lakeside beach open for swimming in the summer. Horseback riders will find 30 rental stalls for their equine friends, as well as a riding ring and 12 equestrian campsites. Canoes, fishing boats, and pedal boats are available to rent seasonally. Accommodations are available at campgrounds and in cottages (see *Lodging—Campgrounds* and *Lodging—Cottages and Cabins*). Parking $5.

🦆 💧 **Oconee National Forest** (Oconee District Ranger: 706-485- 7141; www.fs.usda.gov), office at 1199 Madison Road, Eatonton. Open daily. The forest consists of 16,000 acres of public lands with two wildlife management areas. Hiking, camping, bird-watching, and wildlife observation are popular activities. The forest includes the **Sinclair Recreational Area** on Lake Sinclair as well as two recreational areas with boat access on Lake Oconee. In addition to numerous hiking trails, five horseback riding trails meander through the woodlands (BYOH—bring your own horse; there are no rentals). Camping is permitted forest-wide. Stop by the office for the brochure *A Guide to the Chattahoochee-Oconee National Forests*. Free.

✳ Lodging

BED & BREAKFASTS

In Greensboro

♿ **Goodwin Manor** (706-453-6218; www.goodwinmanor.com), 306 South Main Street. This gracious home with the four soaring columns supporting the porch roof has been in the same family for more than 100 years. The core of the house was a one-story structure that was moved to the property in 1909. As the family grew, an upstairs was added in 1913. Today, fully restored, the bed & breakfast offers five sumptuously furnished guest rooms named for flowers. The downstairs bedroom is wheelchair accessible. A full multicourse Southern breakfast is included. The B&B is conveniently located two and a half blocks from downtown. $225–250.

In Madison

♿ **Brady Inn** (706-342-4400 or 1-866-770-0773; www.bradyinn.com), 250 North Second Street. Enjoy the charm of the Victorian era in this tastefully and lovingly restored 1885 home with heart-pine floors and original gingerbread trim. Besides the full breakfast with complimentary morning newspaper, a selection of homemade goodies and beverages is always available in the dining room. All seven antiques-filled guest rooms boast private baths. Guests enjoy the wedding gardens, bikes, boccie ball, croquet, horseshoes, and a hammock. No smoking. Two rooms wheelchair accessible, but baths not handicapped equipped. $125–300.

💧 ♿ **Farmhouse Inn** (706-342-7933 or 1-866-253-0023; www.thefarmhouseinn.com), 1051 Meadow Lane. Rediscover life's simple pleasures at this 100-acre farm. Families enjoy the inn's many farm animals, walking trails, and lake frontage. Canoeing on the Apalachee River is another option. Guest accommodations include five private rooms and two separate cottages. Smoking permitted on terrace outside Red Barn Meeting Room. Wheelchair accessible, but baths not handicapped equipped. $150–170.

Madison Oaks Inn and Gardens (706-343-9990; www.madisonoaksinn.com), 766 East Avenue. This 1905 Greek Revival mansion offers accommodations truly befitting the rich history, architecture, gardens, and antiques of Madison. Each of the four guest rooms features a private bath, superior linens, satellite TV, plush robes, and early morning coffee or tea service. A full gourmet breakfast is included. Smoking permitted outdoors. Not wheelchair accessible. $105–250.

✧ **Southern Cross Guest Ranch** (706-342-8027; www.southcross.com), 1670 Bethany Church Road. This ranch/B&B /horse farm, which is home to 200 paint and quarter horses, has been named one of America's Best Dude Ranches by *Travel + Leisure* magazine. Sixteen theme-decorated guest rooms, ranging from a rustic Western theme to traditional Southern decor, offer something for everyone. All rooms have private bath, air-conditioning, television, VCR, and state-of-the-art communication equipment. Some feature a whirlpool tub or fireplace. After a strenuous horseback ride, cool off in the outdoor pool or relax in the hot tub. Tours of the property also can be arranged for those not staying overnight (tour only: adults $10, children $8); see the website for additional offerings. English, French, and German are spoken here. Optional activities and services ranging from mountain bikes to aqua massage incur an additional cost. Smoking permitted outdoors. Not wheelchair accessible. $80–280 for a double room with breakfast, $120–330 for a double room with three meals, $135–250 per person for a room, three meals, and daily horseback riding.

In Washington

✧ ♿ ❀ **Babe's House Bed and Breakfast** (706-678-2083), 415 East Robert Toombs Avenue. This property offers a private two-bedroom guest cottage with its own kitchen, living and dining rooms, screened-in porch, and private bath. A full Southern breakfast buffet is served. The owners are delighted to welcome well-behaved children and pets. No smoking. $100–150.

✧ ❀ **Holly Ridge Country Inn** (706-285-2594), 2221 Sandtown Road. Two historical houses were joined on this quiet 100-acre property in 1985. After extensive renovation, the property opened in 1987 as a country inn. Guests can choose from eight authentically furnished rooms with private baths. Other amenities include a sunroom, parlor, extra-large dining room, and wraparound porch with swings, rockers, and wicker furniture. This exciting property also boasts a pond with an authentic log cabin, an old post office, and a country store, all of which are currently being renovated for use as guest cottages. The breakfast of your choice (from continental to a full Southern meal) is included in the price of your stay. Innkeepers Roger and Vivian Walker welcome well-behaved children and pets. No smoking. $125.

♿ **Southern Elegance B&B Inn** (1-877-678-4775; www.southernelegancebandb .com), 115 West Robert Toombs Avenue. Located in a lovely historic home set amid gracious grounds and gardens, the bed & breakfast is located just two blocks from downtown. Hospitality is on display with such attention to detail as plush robes and towels, fruit baskets, and fresh flowers. Complimentary champagne is included in the anniversary/honeymoon suite, which also boasts a fireplace and whirlpool tub. Guests enjoy the relaxation of the rocker-filled wraparound porches. A full country breakfast is served. Two-night minimum

HOLLY RIDGE COUNTRY INN

required on weekends. No smoking. One room wheelchair accessible. $99–225.

The Washington Plantation Bed and Breakfast (706-678-2006 or 1-877-405-9956; www.washingtonplantation.com), 15 Lexington Avenue. This lovely old Greek Revival home once ruled over a 3,000-acre plantation that saw encampments of both Union and Confederate soldiers during the Civil War. Today, sitting on 7 acres of lawns and gardens, it offers guests a glimpse of the South's gracious past and has been named one of the Top Ten Romantic Inns by American Historic Inns. Five spacious guest rooms with private baths are decorated with both comfort and elegance in mind. Each features crystal and brass chandeliers, Irish crystal glassware, 1,000-count Egyptian cotton sheets, and gas fireplaces. Bowing to the 21st century, all rooms have a television, telephone, and wireless Internet access. A formal full breakfast is served. Smoking permitted on veranda. Not wheelchair accessible. $162–232.

CAMPGROUNDS For contact details and a description of the amenities at all three parks, see *Green Space—Nature Preserves and Parks.*

In Crawfordville

🦐 🌲 ⚕ 🎋 **A. H. Stephens State Historic Park** (lodging reservations: 1-800-864-7275). Camping facilities include 25 tent, trailer, and RV sites, as well as 20 horse campsites with power and water. $21–25 for regular sites; $21–23 for horse campsites.

In Lincolnton

🦐 🌲 ⚕ 🎋 **Elijah Clark State Park and Museum** (lodging reservations: 1-800-864-7275). The park offers 165 tent, trailer, and RV sites nestled in the forest, as well as a country store. $25–28.

In Rutledge

🦐 🌲 ⚕ 🎋 **Hard Labor Creek State Park** (lodging reservations: 1-800-864-7275). Camping facilities include 48 tent, trailer, and RV sites. Amenities at the campground include a swimming beach, bathhouse, two lakes, horse stables and trails, four picnic shelters, and one barbecue pit. Reserva-

tions required for equestrian camping. $25–28; horse stalls $18.

COTTAGES AND CABINS For contact information and a description of the amenities at all three parks, see also *Green Space—Nature Preserves and Parks.*

In Crawfordville

🦐 🌲 🎋 **A. H. Stephens State Historic Park** (lodging reservations: 1-800-864-7275). The park offers four fully equipped cottages; one is dog friendly ($40 per dog; maximum two). $115–125 (higher during Masters Week).

In Lincolnton

🦐 🌲 🎋 **Elijah Clark State Park and Museum** (lodging reservations: 1-800-864-7275). The park has 20 cottages located at the water's edge; two are dog friendly ($40 per dog; maximum two). $120–130 (higher during Masters Week).

In Rutledge

🦐 🌲 🎋 **Hard Labor Creek State Park** (lodging reservations: 1-800-864-7275). The park offers 20 fully equipped cottages; two are dog friendly ($40 per dog; maximum two). $95–120 (higher during Masters Week).

HOTELS

In Washington

⚕ **The Fitzpatrick Hotel** (706-678-5900; www.thefitzpatrickhotel.com), 16 West Square. Built in 1898, the venerable hotel sat empty for 50 years, beginning in 1952, but was restored and reopened in 2004 with 17 guest rooms, dining room, and retail space. The current owners have furnished this Queen Anne Victorian property in period reproductions and antiques. All rooms have queen-size beds and private baths—some with claw-foot tubs and/or a fireplace. Continental breakfast is included. No smoking. $120–225.

INNS AND RESORTS

In Eatonton

🌲 ⚕ **Cuscowilla Resort on Lake Oconee** (706-484-0050 or 1-800458-5351; www.cuscowilla.com), 126 Cuscowilla Drive.

Accommodations are in golf cottages, lodge villas, or fabulous lakeside villas. Amenities at the resort include a golf course (see *To Do—Golf*), swimming pool, restaurant, two tennis courts, walking trails, and a spa. Call for a list of spa treatments, rates, and hours. No smoking. Limited wheelchair accessibility. $150–800.

In Greensboro

✍ ♿ **The Ritz-Carlton Lodge, Reynolds Plantation** (706-467-0600; www.ritz carltonlodge.com), 3000 Lake Oconee Trail. The AAA four-diamond property on the secluded shores of Lake Oconee in central Georgia, ranked fifth on the list of Top Hotels and Resorts in America by *Travel + Leisure*, is a new concept in Ritz-Carlton accommodations. Instead of a typical high-rise urban or beachfront hotel, the lodge is a 251-room facility that sprawls across a knoll in the manner of the great resorts of the early 20th century. What doesn't change from a traveler's expectations is the legendary Ritz-Carlton level of service. Sumptuous lodging is offered in hotel rooms and suites, Club Level rooms and suites, lakeside cottages, and a Presidential House. In addition, the resort offers a golf course (see *To Do—Golf*), an award-winning spa (see *To Do—Spas*), exemplary cuisine in restaurants including Georgia's Bistro, Linger Longer Steakhouse, Gaby's on the Lake (see *Where to Eat—Dining Out*), and the

THE RITZ-CARLTON LODGE, REYNOLDS PLANTATION

Lobby Lounge (see *Where to Eat—Eating Out*), and activities from fishing to waterskiing to canoeing. No smoking. Rooms $249–829, suites $1,200–1,500, houses $4,000–5,000.

✳ Where to Eat
DINING OUT

In Greensboro

✍ ♿ **Gaby's on the Lake** (706-467-0600), 3000 Lake Oconee Trail. Open 11–10 daily. This delightful poolside restaurant at the Ritz-Carlton Lodge offers splendid views of Lake Oconee, so guests can enjoy casual dining in a beautiful setting. Menu items for lunch include salads and traditional hot and cold sandwiches. Dinner enticements include rosemary-rubbed grilled chicken, blackened redfish, grilled fillet of beef, salmon, mussels steamed in white wine, barbecue ribs, and even pizza. A children's menu is available. No smoking. Lunch $8–10, dinner $15–29.

♿ **Troutdale at Harbor Club** (706-453-9690 or 1-800-505-4653), One Club Drive. Open 11–3 daily and 5–9 Thursday–Sunday. Both formal and informal dining rooms and a comfortable lounge can be found at this fine-dining restaurant, where specialties include lamb, veal, and beef tenderloin. No smoking. Lunch $6–10, dinner $12–26.

EATING OUT

In Eatonton

♿ **Waterside & Veranda Café at Cuscowilla** (706-484-2044), 126 Cuscowilla Drive. Open 5–9 Wednesday–Sunday, Sunday brunch 10:30–2. Poolside service offered 11:30–4 Wednesday–Sunday in season. This restaurant specializes in club cuisine with a Southern flair. Menu favorites include beef tenderloin, filet, Dover sole, stuffed sea bass, other seafood dishes, and pasta dishes. Smoking outside only. Around $17–27.

In Greensboro

✍ ♿ **The Lobby Lounge at the Ritz-Carlton Lodge, Reynolds Plantation**

(706-467-0600), 3000 Lake Oconee Trail. Open 5–10:30 Sunday–Thursday, 3–midnight Friday and Saturday. Enjoy a snifter of cognac as you look over the soothing shores of Lake Oconee from the fabulous veranda. Inside, enjoy light fare by the fireplace. Favorites include fried oysters, shrimp cocktail, crab, hush puppies, soups, and salads, but also more ambitious dishes such as trout, rib eye, and filet. The Lobby Lounge is the perfect place for a cocktail before dinner or a drink before bedtime. On Friday and Saturday nights, enjoy live entertainment 8 PM–midnight. No smoking. $10–38.

🍷 ♪ ♿ **The Plantation Grille at Reynolds Plantation** (706-467-0600), 100 Linger Longer Road. Open for breakfast daily, for dinner Wednesday–Sunday. Menu items range from salads to sandwiches, steaks to seafood. No smoking. Breakfast $9–12, dinner $14–25.

In Madison
🍷 ♪ ♿ **Adrian's Place** (706-342-1600), 325 West Washington Street. Open for lunch weekdays. The menu at this cafeteria-style restaurant changes daily. Try their vegetable plate. No smoking. $6–7.50.

🍷 ♪ ♿ **Amici Italian Café** (706-342-0000), 113 South Main Street. Open for lunch and dinner daily. Menu favorites include calzones, 25 varieties of pizza, hot and cold subs, wings, and salads. No smoking. About $10–15.

🍷 ♪ ♿ **Madison Chop House Grille** (706-342-9009), 202 South Main Street. Open for lunch and dinner daily. The specialty here is American cuisine. Menu favorites include pasta, salmon, steaks, and salads. No smoking. $8–24.

In Tignall
🍷 ♪ ♿ **Kumback Café** (706-285-2831), 112 Independence Street. Open for breakfast and lunch Tuesday–Saturday and dinner Friday. You'll find all your favorite breakfast and short-order items on the menu, as well as steaks, shrimp, and catfish at dinnertime. No smoking. Breakfast and lunch $3–7, dinner $10–15.

✳ **Entertainment**

THEATER Madison-Morgan Cultural Arts Center (706-342-4743; www.mmcc-arts.org; see *To See—Cultural Sites*). In addition to the museum housed here, this intimate 397-seat theater contains original woodwork, ceilings, seats, and chandeliers (circa 1895). Music, lectures, dance, film, and theater presentations feature such notables as the Alvin Ailey Dance Company, the Atlanta Symphony Orchestra, the Royal Shakespeare Company, and the Vienna Boys Choir. Among the annual events are the Mainstage Series and the Chamber Music Festival. Check the website or call for a schedule of events and ticket prices.

The Plaza Arts Center (706-925-1665; www.theplazaartscenter.com), 305 North Madison Avenue, Eatonton. Numerous performances of music and theater are held in the historic old school's auditorium. The summertime Meet Me at the Plaza series takes place outdoors in the plaza. A highly anticipated event each year is the *Holly, Jolly Murder Mystery* audience participation dinner theater in December. Art and photography and other exhibits are scheduled throughout the year as well. Check the website or call for a schedule of events and ticket prices.

✳ **Selective Shopping**

ANTIQUES Greensboro Antique Mall (706-453-9100; www.greensboroantiquemall.com), 101 South Main Street, Greensboro. Open 11–5 Monday–Thursday, 11–5:30 Friday and Saturday. Shop here not only for antiques, furniture, jewelry, and collectibles, but also for unusual items.

In High Cotton (706-342-7777), 158 West Jefferson Street, Madison. Open 10–5:30 Monday–Saturday, 1–5 Sunday. This charming store carries a little bit of everything. Merchandise includes but is not limited to furniture, mirrors, wrought iron, wicker, lamps, and candles.

ART GALLERIES Genuine Georgia, an Artist Marketplace (706 453-1440),

101 North Main Street, Greensboro. Open 10–5 Monday–Saturday. This artists' emporium features the work of more than 130 Georgia artisans. Items for sale include heritage crafts, Okefenokee palmetto dolls and fans, pine-needle baskets, folk art and fine art paintings, pottery (both utilitarian and decorative), birdhouses, silks, weavings, a genuine Georgia pantry section with gourmet foods from all over the state, and a book center that features Georgia authors.

Steffen Thomas Museum & Archives (706-342-7557; www.steffenthomas.org). Open 11–4 Tuesday–Saturday, noon–5 Sunday. Stop by the gift shop at this quirky museum (see *To See—Museums*) to see or to purchase original works of the late Steffen Thomas, as well as a selection of signed prints and other products featuring reproductions of his art.

C R A F T S Craftsman's Row (706-557-9020 or 1-800-709-7406; www.madison ga.org), US 278/Fairplay Street, Rutledge. Open 10–5 Monday–Saturday, 1–5 Sunday. This two-block area is filled with artisans' shops where craftspeople cane chairs, hook rugs, quilt, carve wood, and create other works of art.

FLEA MARKETS Madison Mall and Flea Market (706-342-0018), 1291 Eatonton Highway, Madison. Open 10–5 Monday–Thursday, 9–5:30 Friday and Saturday, noon–5 Sunday. More than 60 vendors participate in this massive enterprise. Treasure hunters will be delighted by the wide variety of merchandise on display.

✳ Special Events

Spring: **Antebellum Trail Pilgrimage** (1-800-768-3401; www.atpilgrimage.org). Visit gracious old homes and gardens not generally open to the public along the 100-mile trail's beautiful tree-lined streets and scenic byways between Macon and Athens (with a major section in the area covered by this chapter). This walking and driving tour is self-guided. With access from 10 to 4 over four days, the pilgrimage allows visitors to see any or all of the sites. Call for details, because dates vary from year to year. $25.

March: **Washington-Wilkes Tour of Homes** (706-678-2013; www.wwtourof homes.com). Held annually in Washington, this event features tours of at least six private homes not generally open to the public, as well as churches, public buildings, museums, and other sites. $30; single home $8 at the door.

April: **Southland Jubilee Festival** (chamber of commerce: 706-359-7970; www .southlandjubilee.com). The historic business district of Greensboro is the setting for this unique family festival. Activities include three different stages of live music, juried arts and crafts, heritage craft demonstrations, living-history interpreters, children's games, agricultural exhibits, an antique car show, a parade, cow milking, a petting zoo, pony rides, food, and more. Call for exact date. Free.

October: **Mule Day Southern Heritage Festival** (706-678-7060). Held on the second Saturday in October at Callaway Plantation in Washington, this event celebrates plantation life in the Old South with mule contests, primitive demonstrations, food, an arts and crafts show, and lots more fun. Free with regular admission.

December: **Christmas at Callaway Plantation** (706-678-7060). This event, held on the second Saturday in December, allows visitors to enjoy a plantation Christmas the way the first settlers of Wilkes County experienced it. The entire plantation in Washington is beautifully decorated, and music adds to the atmosphere. Free with regular admission.

MILLEDGEVILLE

T his area of Georgia is characterized by rolling hills, red clay, pine trees, and hardwoods. Native Americans lived here 12,000 years ago, as evidenced by earthen mounds, pottery, tools, and weapons that have survived. Several Indian trading trails converged near what is now Milledgeville.

The town, which served as the state capital from 1807 to 1868, is the only city in the country besides Washington, D.C., designed specifically to be a capital. When Union troops occupied Milledgeville, they burned the military arsenal and stabled their horses in St. Stephen's Episcopal Church while pouring molasses down the pipes of the organ. Although various romantic legends claim to know why Union general William Tecumseh Sherman spared the city on his March to the Sea from Atlanta to Savannah, the real, mundane reason was probably that the city had no military significance.

Because Milledgeville survived the Civil War, it is considered to be the only remaining example of a complete Federal-era city in America. As is not surprising in an old town with so much history, Milledgeville is well-known for its ghosts, among them Miss Sue and the banshee.

GUIDANCE When planning a trip to Milledgeville, contact the **Milledgeville–Baldwin County Convention and Visitors Bureau and Welcome Center** (478-452-4687 or 1-800-653-1804; www.visitmilledgeville.org), 200 West Hancock Street, Milledgeville 31061. Open 9–5 weekdays, 10–4 Saturday. After you arrive in town, you can pick up information on Andalusia tours and the Historic Trolley Tour, as well as brochures for self-guided walking-driving tours (see *To See—Guided Tours* and *To See—Historic Homes and Sites*). Check out the convention and visitors bureau website, which offers coupons and special packages.

GETTING THERE *By air:* The **Baldwin County Airport,** 216 Airport Road (off US 441), Milledgeville, has a 5,000-foot airstrip for private aircraft. Otherwise, visitors fly into Macon. See "What's Where in Georgia" for airport, airline, and car rental information.

By bus: The nearest **Greyhound Lines** (1-800-231-2222; www.greyhound.com) service is to Macon (see the Macon chapter), so a visitor would need a rental car to get around.

By car: The towns described in this chapter are clustered along US 441 and US 1/221 between I-20 and I-16.

By train: The nearest **AMTRAK** station is in Atlanta (see "What's Where in Georgia").

GETTING AROUND When visiting these small towns, it's imperative to have a car—either your own or a rental. There are few taxis and no public transit. The towns themselves are some distance apart.

MEDICAL EMERGENCY Call 911.

✷ To See

CULTURAL SITES ✿ ⅙ **Flannery O'Connor Memorial Room** (478-445-4391; www2.gcsu.edu/library/sc), 221 North Clarke Street, Ida Dillard Russell Library at Georgia College and State University, Clark and Montgomery streets, Milledgeville. Open 8–4 Monday–Saturday when school is in session. Furnished in the style of the 1870s, the room features pieces from Andalusia Farm (see *To See—Historic Homes and Sites*), the home where Flannery O'Connor wrote most of her fiction. Also on display are her personal library of more than 700 books and other memorabilia, including letters, manuscripts, and paintings by the author. A short film chronicles her life story and early death. Many papers are available only to scholars by reservation. Free.

✿ ⅙ **John Marlor Art Center** (478-452-3950; www.milledgevillealliedarts.com), 201 North Wayne Street, Milledgeville. Open 9–4:30 weekdays. This beautiful Federal-style house was built in the 1830s by John Marlor as a wedding present for his second wife. Today it houses the Allied Arts Center and the Elizabeth Marlor Bethune Art Gallery, which offers works by local artists and traveling exhibits throughout the year. In addition, the organization has taken over the 1911 Allen's Market Building across the street and adapted it for theater and studio space. Free.

GUIDED TOURS ✿ ♪ **Milledgeville Historic Trolley Tour** (478-452-4687 or 1-800-653-1804; www.milledgevillecvb.com), 200 West Hancock Street, Milledgeville. Leaves at 10 AM weekdays, 2 PM Saturday, from convention and visitors bureau. The tour makes rotating visits to the Old Capitol, St. Stephen's Episcopal Church, Lockerly Hall, or the Stetson-Sanford House. Stops vary daily. Visitors who purchase a trolley tour receive a discount on the Old Governor's Mansion tour (see *To See—Historic Homes and Sites*). Adults $10, children 6–16 $5.

HISTORIC HOMES AND SITES ✿ **Andalusia Farm** (478-454-4029; www.andalusia farm.org), 2628 Columbia Street/US 441 North, Milledgeville. Open 10–4 Tuesday and Thursday–Saturday or by appointment. This dairy farm–home of Flannery O'Connor is where the world-renowned author wrote two of her novels, *The Violent Bear It Away* and *Wise Blood,* as well as a number of the short stories for which she is so famous. Tours of the white, two-story main house from the 1850s include the PBS video *The Displaced Person;* Flannery's bedroom, where she did most of her writing; and the sitting room, the dining room, a guest room, kitchen, and addition. Visitors are then free to wander around the farm, where they can see various farm buildings, ponds, a creek, and several ecosystems, and perhaps catch a glimpse of some wildlife. The Lower Tabor Creek Trail is part of the Dr. Bernard Cline Outdoor Learning Center. $5.

✿ ♪ **Lockerly Hall** (478-452-2112; www.lockerlyarboretum.org), 1534 Irwinton Road, Milledgeville. Open 8:30–4:30 weekdays and for those taking the Monday, Tuesday, and Wednesday Milledgeville Historic Trolley Tour (see *Guided Tours*). The stately Greek Revival mansion is an outstanding example of plantation architecture. Built around 1839 and lived in by only six families, the house was once known as Rose Hill because such a profusion of wild Cherokee roses grew in the region. Gardens still surround the house today. Lockerly Hall is the centerpiece of **Lockerly Arboretum** (see *Green Space—Nature Preserves and Parks*). Donations appreciated.

✿ ⅙ **Market House,** center of Broad Street, Louisville. Tiny Louisville (pronounced Lewisville) was the state capital from 1795 to 1806. Named for France's Louis XVI, the entire town was laid out and its buildings, including the governor's mansion and the capitol, constructed before inhabitants moved in. Constructed in the late 1700s at the time of the town's founding at the intersection of two Native American trails, this timber, open-air structure contains a bronze bell that was made in France in 1772 for a New Orleans convent. The bell never made it to New Orleans, however, because it was captured by pirates off the coast of Savannah. When it was put on the auction block, it was purchased and brought to Louisville, the state capital at the time, where it was used as a community warning system in the event of a possible Indian attack. Later the bell rang out to celebrate the independence of the 13 colonies, and even later it announced Georgia's secession from the Union. Historians disagree about whether the market was ever used for the slave trade or whether it was simply a community market where farmers and craftsmen could sell their products. Free.

🐾 ♿ **Memory Hill Cemetery,** Franklin and Liberty streets, Milledgeville. Open daily daylight hours. Land for this cemetery was designated when the town plan was laid out in 1803 as one of four public squares of 20 acres each. It later became known as Cemetery Square. Several Revolutionary and Civil War soldiers are buried here. The cemetery is the final resting place of many patients of the Lunatic Asylum, which for many years was the largest hospital in the world for the mentally ill. In addition, the cemetery contains some interesting African American graves. In front of each headstone is a metal rod with hooks and chains attached to it. One link means the person was born into slavery, two means he or she was born and lived in slavery, and three means the person was born, lived, and died in slavery. Flannery O'Connor's grave site is here, as are those of U.S. congressman Carl Vinson and other Georgia statesmen. On the infamous side, notorious stagecoach and train robber Bill Miner is buried here as well. Free.

🐾 ♿ **Old Governor's Mansion** (478-445-4545; www.gcsu.edu/mansion), 120 South Clarke Street, Milledgeville. Open 10–4 Tuesday–Saturday, 2–4 Sunday. Guided tours are given on the hour. Built in 1839, the pink stucco-covered mansion was home to 10 Georgia governors through the antebellum, Civil War, and Reconstruction periods until the state capital was moved to Atlanta in 1868. Union general William Tecumseh Sherman used the mansion as his headquarters on November 22, 1864, during his March to the Sea. When the capital was moved to Atlanta, the building was given to Georgia Normal and Industrial College (now Georgia College and State University) as the founding building of that institution. The Old Governor's Mansion is considered to be one of the country's most outstanding examples of High Greek Revival–style residences. An extensive three-year renovation has returned the mansion to its 1850s appearance, complete with its original layout, colors, and lighting. The tour includes the main floor, the bedroom level, and the servants' area. One of the biggest surprises is the rotunda and 40-foot dome, which can't be seen from the street. Make sure to note the intricate gilding in the interior of the dome. Adults $10, seniors $7, students $2, children younger than six free.

MUSEUMS 🐾 ♿ **Brown House Museum** (478-552-1965), 268 North Harris Street, Sandersville. Open 2–5 Tuesday, Thursday, and Friday; 10–3 Saturday. Built in 1850, the house was considered part of the so-called Silk Stocking Street district, because the wealthy ladies who lived there hung their silk stockings on the porch rails to dry to show off their affluence. Union general William Tecumseh Sherman used this house as his headquarters when he and his army passed through Sandersville on the March to the Sea. Restored to its original condition, the house displays Sandersville and Civil War artifacts. Furnishings original to the house include the sofa that

THE OLD GOVERNOR'S MANSION WAS BUILT IN 1839.

General Sherman reportedly napped on during his brief stay. Donations accepted.

🐾 🐾 ♿ **Georgia College and State University Natural History Museum** (478-445-2395; www.gcsu.edu/biology/museum.htm), Herty Hall, Room 143, Wilkinson Street, Milledgeville. Open 8–4 weekdays, 10–4 on the first Saturday. See fossils from Georgia and around the world at this museum, which also offers sky shows in its planetarium (call for a schedule). Free.

🐾 ♿ **Museum and Archives of Georgia Education** (478-445-4391; www.library.gcsu.edu/~sc/magepages), 131 South Clarke Street, Milledgeville. Open 2–5 Monday–Friday. Corinthian columns and graceful Palladian windows characterize this circa 1900 Classical Revival building, which houses artifacts, memorabilia, and records

THE OLD STATE CAPITOL BUILDING IS NOW OCCUPIED BY GEORGIA MILITARY COLLEGE AND GEORGIA'S OLD CAPITOL MUSEUM.

chronicling the development of education in Georgia. One gallery features rotating exhibits. Free.

🐾 🐾 ♿ **Old State Capitol Building, Georgia's Old Capitol Museum** (478-453-1803; www.oldcapitolmuseum.org), 201 East Greene Street, Milledgeville. Open 10–3:30 Monday–Friday, noon–4 Saturday. Built around 1807, the Old Capitol Building is considered to be the finest example of the Gothic Revival style in America. It may also be the oldest public building in the country. It served as the seat of government for the state of Georgia from 1807 to 1868. It was here in the legislative chambers that the Secession Convention was held in 1861. During the brief time that Union troops held the town in November 1864, they conducted a mock assembly of the legislature here and "repealed" the Ordinance of Secession. The north and south gates were constructed from bricks recovered from the arsenal destroyed by Sherman's troops. Since 1879, the Georgia Military College has occupied the historic site, and today it serves primarily as a classroom building, but the House Chamber operates as **Georgia's Old Capitol Museum** with exhibits on area history and culture, including period furnishings and memorabilia. Each of the five galleries depicts a different era in the history of the former capital: prehistoric Georgia, early Milledgeville, pre Civil War, Civil War, and post Civil War. Adults $5.50, seniors $4.50, students $2.75.

✳ To Do

BIRDING Mississippi kites, osprey, waterfowl, great blue herons, snowy and common egrets, pine siskins, Carolina wrens, and a wide variety of woodpeckers, to name just a few, can be found at the **Baldwin Forest Public Fishing Area** (see *Fishing*).

FARM TOURS 🐾 🐾 **Olive Forge Herb Farm** (478-932-5737), 161 Brown's Crossing Road, Haddock. Open 9–5 Thursday–Saturday, other days by appointment. This unique attraction offers 360 varieties of culinary, medicinal, and wreath herbs, including 18 varieties of rosemary. Olive Forge also features a gift shop with culinary items and toiletries made at the farm. Herbal refreshments available. Free.

FISHING 🐾 🐾 ♿ **Baldwin Forest Public Fishing Area** (478-453-7832). From Milledgeville travel south on US 441, go approximately 3 miles south of GA 243 intersection to point where highway crosses Little Black Creek, and follow signs to entrance of public fishing area. Facility not staffed. This 2,500-acre park boasts five ponds covering 51 acres of water that provides angling for channel catfish, largemouth bass, and bream. Bird-watching is also excellent. No fees.

✳ Green Space

LAKES 🦆 ✍ ♿ **Lake Sinclair,** US 441, Milledgeville. Open daily year-round. Halfway between Atlanta and Augusta, this popular 15,300-acre lake with 417 miles of shoreline spans Oconee, Greene, Morgan, Putnam, Hancock, and Baldwin counties, and offers boating, fishing, and other water sports. In addition to several major fishing tournaments, visitors can find accommodations of all sorts, as well as several marinas, recreation areas, and restaurants. Lake Sinclair also claims to be the cleanest lake in the state. Free.

NATURE PRESERVES AND PARKS 🦆 ✍ ♿ **Bartram Educational Forest** (478-445-5164), 2892 US 441 South, Milledgeville. Open 8–4:30 weekdays. In prehistoric times, the area was a shallow sea, as evidenced by the soil found in an erosion ravine and by the remaining wetlands. In 1794, the area was inhabited by Native Americans. Today, three looping walking trails with educational stations provide opportunities for bird-watching and plant and wildlife observation. The facility also offers a pavilion, garden, and fishing. Free.

🦆 ✍ ♿ 🌼 **Hamburg State Outdoor Recreation Area** (for park information contact A. H. Stephens State Park: 706-456-2602; lodging reservations: 1-800-864-7275; www.gastate parks.org/Hamburg), 6071 Hamburg State Park Road, Mitchell. Open 7 AM–10 PM daily. It's not just outdoor adventures that await visitors to this park, although it is considered to be a fishing paradise. Sure, there's Little Ocmulgee River–fed 225-acre Hamburg Lake and its associated water sports, as well as a boat ramp, a fishing pier, and nature and hiking trails wandering through 741 acres. But the park also features the **Ogeechee River Mill,** a working water-powered gristmill. There has been a working gristmill on this site for 175 years. The current mill was built in 1921. During special events, the mill is open for tours, and visitors can see agricultural tools and appliances used in rural Georgia as well as seeing corn being ground. During those events, fresh cornmeal can be purchased. The park offers campsites available seasonally along the lake's edge (see *Lodging—Campgrounds*). Parking $5.

🦆 ✍ ♿ **Lockerly Arboretum** (478-452-2112; www.lockerly.org), 1534 Irwinton Road, Milledgeville. Open 8:30–4:30 weekdays, 9–1 Saturday. Fifty acres contain many types of native trees, shrubs, herb beds, flower gardens, and vineyards. The floral gardens feature iris, daylily, rhododendron, bulb, and perennial gardens, and there is also a tropical and desert greenhouse. In addition to educational exhibits, the arboretum features trails, a stream, and a tiny museum. Admission to arboretum free. The centerpiece of the property is **Lockerly Hall** (see *To See—Historic Homes and Sites*).

✳ Lodging

BED & BREAKFASTS

In Louisville

🦆 **Old Town Plantation and Retreat** (478-589-7814; www.oldtownplantation .com), 8910 GA 17 South. This 4,000-acre resort with three guesthouses is open year-round. Activities include tennis, swimming, and fishing. Guests are also invited to use the weight room or visit the old gristmill

(circa 1825) on the property. Closed June–August, except for groups or a three-night minimum stay. No smoking. Not wheelchair accessible. $125.

In Milledgeville

Antebellum Inn (478-453-3993; www .antebelluminn.com), 200 North Columbia Street. The inn occupies a late-1800s Greek Revival home with all the modern amenities. Verandas, lushly landscaped lawns, and a swimming pool create a restful oasis. Even more privacy is assured with a stay in the poolside cottage. No smoking. Not wheelchair accessible. $109–169.

CAMPGOUNDS

In Milledgeville

❦ ♪ ⎕ ❦ **Little River Park Campground** (478-452-1605; www.littleriverpark.com), 3069 North Columbia Street. Get there early, as sites are first-come, first-served at this campground on Lake Sinclair. Among the 130 RV campsites with all the modern amenities, 39 of them are waterfront. The campground also features a beach, bathhouse, laundry facilities, a playground, horseshoes, basketball, picnic tables, grills, a marina, and a restaurant. $30–40.

❦ ♪ ⎕ **Scenic Mountain RV Park and Campground** (478-453-8683 or 1-800-716-3015), 2686 Irwinton Road. This 108-acre facility offers full hookups on spacious lots. Amenities include five stocked ponds, a nature trail, phone, cable, a clubhouse, bathhouse, pool, and spa. $40 per night.

In Mitchell

❦ ♪ ⎕ ❦ **Hamburg State Outdoor Recreation Area** (see *Green Space—Nature Preserves and Parks*). Between March 15 and November 30, 30 campsites are available on a first-come, first-served, self-registration basis. The campground features electric hookups and hot showers. $25–28.

❋ Where to Eat

DINING OUT

In Milledgeville

❦ ♪ ⎕ **Jackson's Restaurant** (478-453-9744), 3065 North Columbia Street/US 441 North. Open 4:30–9 Monday–Thursday, 4:30–10 Friday and Saturday. This casual restaurant located at Little River Park on Lake Sinclair delights diners with burgers, seafood, freshwater fish, and steak. Come by car or boat. No smoking. $10–17.

EATING OUT

In Milledgeville

❦ ♪ ⎕ **Amici's Italian Café** (478-452-5003), 101 West Hancock Street. Open for lunch and dinner daily. Menu selections include salads, sandwiches, and pasta. No smoking until 11 PM. $6–24.

❋ Selective Shopping

OTHER GOODS ❦ ♪ **Braswell Farm** (706-547-6784), 1089 Hoyt Braswell Road, Wrens. Open 8 AM–dark daily. If you want any size gourd to use as a birdhouse or for any decorative purpose, this farm is the place to come. You can also buy homemade syrups and fresh produce.

❋ Special Events

October: **Deep Roots Festival** (478-414-4014; www.deeprootsfestival.com). Held in downtown Milledgeville, the festival includes something for everyone: a barbecue cook-off, arts and crafts, an antique car show, vendors, and the Little Roots Kid Zone activities for little ones. A music fest includes all kinds of music, from bluegrass to rock and roll, featuring local and national talent. $5.

Haunted Trolley Tours (478-452-4687). Take a ride on the spooky side and experience the thrills and chills of days gone by. Costumed actors play scary spirits, revealing lurid tales that have made Milledgeville one of the spookiest towns in Georgia. See where the ghosts live and hear stories about the spirits who still lurk in this world. Adults $15 in advance, $20 at the time of tour (don't take a chance on waiting until the last minute; tour may be full).

December: **Antebellum Christmas at the Old Governor's Mansion** (478-445-4545), 120 South Clarke Street, Milledgeville. Three first Saturdays in December at 6 and 7, candlelight tours are offered when the mansion is decorated in all its holiday finery. Adults up to age 61 $10 ($7 in advance), older than 61 $7.

STATESBORO TO WAYNESBORO TO DUBLIN

With a few exceptions, this tranquil area of central to eastern Georgia is characterized by rural agricultural areas and small towns with populations ranging from 500 to 3,500. Regardless of size, each municipality has something unique to offer.

One of the larger small towns is Statesboro in Bulloch County, with a population of nearly 23,000. Statesboro, which has been named one of the 100 best small towns in America by author Michael Crompton, is the home of Georgia Southern University. Like most universities, GSU offers many benefits to the general public, from theatrical and musical performances to museums, botanical gardens, and a renowned raptor center. Interestingly, the town, which is believed to have been named in honor of the statehood of Georgia, is the only Statesboro in America.

Bulloch County was named for Archibald Bulloch, who presided over the Provincial Congress on July 4, 1775, and became Georgia's first provincial governor in 1776. A traveler to early Statesboro (then spelled Statesborough) noted that the residents were hard workers, but also hard drinkers. Supposedly at that time there were only three public buildings: a log courthouse, a log whiskey shop, and a boardinghouse. One hundred years later, the Jaeckel Hotel opened and was renowned for having the finest accommodations in the area. Celebrities such as Henry Ford, William Jennings Bryan, and Cornelius Vanderbilt stayed at the hotel and enjoyed its Southern hospitality. Today, that structure serves as Statesboro City Hall.

Potential visitors to this area of Georgia may be very familiar with some of the products of the region without being aware of the towns or rural areas from which they come. The Vidalia area, for example, known around the world for its sweet onions, is blessed with the perfect climate and soil to produce this wonderful vegetable. The town of Vidalia and the others near it were settled at the turn of the 20th century along the Savannah, Americus & Montgomery Railroad.

Of further interest—and regardless of the fact that some comedians claim that there is only one fruitcake in the world, which just keeps getting passed around—the small town of Claxton has two famous fruitcake-baking companies that together produce more than 7 million pounds of the sweet treat annually.

Tattnall County is one of the largest and most diversified agricultural counties in the state. Besides producing more than half of the world's Vidalia onions, this area—also known as "the Breadbasket of Georgia" and the state's tomato capital—grows produce from blackberries to watermelon and everything in between. In this area near Vidalia is the tiny town of Santa Claus, Georgia (one of only two so named towns in the world). The streets have names

THE LADY OF 6,000 SONGS

Bulloch County native daughter Emma Kelly was renowned for her encyclopedic knowledge of the popular music of the late Johnny Mercer and others and her ability to play any of them on request without sheet music. In addition to playing and singing for local church services, civic clubs, graduations, proms, and recitals, she often played in clubs in Savannah. When author John Berendt wrote his famous book, *Midnight in the Garden of Good and Evil,* he dedicated an entire chapter to the talents of Mrs. Kelly, which resulted in her playing a cameo role as herself in the 1997 movie directed by Clint Eastwood. A national concert tour followed, and in 1998 Mrs. Kelly was inducted into the Georgia Music Hall of Fame. She died in January 2001 at the age of 83.

such as Candy Cane Lane and Reindeer Street. City Hall is located at 25 December Drive. Visitors can take their Christmas cards to City Hall to be postmarked by the elves.

GUIDANCE If you are planning a trip to the Statesboro area, contact the **Statesboro Convention and Visitors Bureau** (912-489-1869 or 1-800-568-3301; www.visit-statesboro .com), 332 South Main Street, Statesboro 30458. Open 8:30–5 weekdays.

For more information about Dublin, consult the **Dublin–Laurens County Chamber of Commerce** (478-272-5546; www.dublin-georgia.com), 1200 Bellevue Avenue, Dublin 31021. Open 8:30–5 weekdays. Pick up a *Dublin's Walking Tour of Historic Downtown* brochure from the chamber. Further information can be obtained from the **Dublin– Laurens County Welcome Center** (478-272-5766; www.dublin-georgia.com), 102 Travel Center Boulevard/I-16 at US 441, Dublin 31021. Open 8:30–5 Monday–Saturday.

To learn more about Vidalia, contact the **Vidalia Area Convention and Visitors Bureau** (912-538-8687; www.vidaliaarea.com), 100 Vidalia Sweet Onion Drive, Vidalia 30474. Open 8:30–5 weekdays. Get information here about Vidalia farm tours. You also can contact the **Toombs-Montgomery Chamber of Commerce and Development Authority** (912-537-4466; www.toombsmontgomerychamber.com), 2805 East First Street, Vidalia 30474. Open 8:30–5 weekdays.

GETTING THERE *By air:* The closest airport is 55 miles away in Savannah (see "What's Where in Georgia" for airport, airline, and car rental information).

By bus: **Greyhound Lines** (1-800-231-2222; www.greyhound.com) stops in Dublin at 620 East Jackson Street (478-272-2912). Any tourist arriving in the area by bus would need a rental car to get around.

By car: The towns in this chapter are stretched out to the north or south of I-16. North–south highways include US 301, 25, 1, and 221.

By train: **AMTRAK** provides service as far as Augusta and Savannah (see those chapters). A visitor would need a rental car to get around.

GETTING AROUND Getting around in these small towns requires a car—either your own or a rental. There is no mass transportation and no taxi service.

MEDICAL EMERGENCY Call 911.

VILLAGES AND NEIGHBORHOODS Statesboro's **Savannah Avenue Historic District** was the town's first suburb in the early 1900s. Many of the original homes and gardens have been preserved.

Claxton, which is world renowned for its fruitcakes, is also famed for its **Rattlesnake Roundup** (see *Special Events*), began in 1968 when a local boy was bitten several times by an eastern diamondback rattler as family members were picking vegetables on their farm. Fortunately, swift and skilled medical attention saved the child's life, but it took a year for him to recover, and even after that he had side effects. A group of residents decided to learn more about rattlesnakes, formed the Evans County Wildlife Club, and eventually sponsored the roundup—the purpose of which is to "educate, not eradicate."

The area around **Dublin,** "the Emerald City," is a haven for sportsmen who enjoy tennis, golf, fishing, and hunting. It is St. Patrick's Day, however, for which the small town is famous. While Savannah's St. Patrick's Day celebrations are the second largest in the nation, Dublin's are the second largest in Georgia.

When Col. Samuel H. Hawkins of Americus was building railroad depots along the route of the Savannah, Americus & Montgomery Railroad, he named some of the stations after places he'd visited in Europe. The **Lyons** depot was named after Lyons, France, and a town soon grew up around the station. Today Lyons, which possesses the only complete set of weights-and-measures scales in Georgia, boasts several hidden treasures, such as New Deal public art. Along the side of one block of stores is a large mural depicting scenes from the town's folk play, *Tales from the Altamaha* (see *Special Events*).

Metter, the county seat of Candler County, was established solely as a stop on the railroad and was incorporated in 1903. Legend has it that a railroad official named the town for his wife because he "met her" there. Today Metter is the home of **Guido Gardens,** located on the property of an evangelistic association (see *Green Space—Gardens*).

Soperton, named for Benjamin Franklin Soper, a construction engineer with the Macon, Dublin & Savannah Railroad, was incorporated in 1902. The only incorporated municipality in Treutlen County, it is known as "Million Pines City" but should actually be called "Seven Million Pines City" because James Fowler planted more than 7 million pine seedlings on 10,000 acres here. Pine by-products are an important part of the local economy, and the most important annual event is November's **Million Pines Arts and Crafts Festival** (see *Special Events*).

Vidalia is the home of Georgia's Official State Vegetable—the sweet Vidalia onion. They're so sweet, you can eat them like an apple. Use them in almost anything calling for onions. A popular way to cook them is to core them, drop in a dollop of butter and a spoonful of brown sugar (as if they need sweetening), and bake them.

Waynesboro is known as the "Bird Dog Capital of the World" because of the **annual bird-dog field trials** (see *Special Events*) held here every year. In fact, people come from all over the world to enter and observe these competitions to determine whose bird dog is the best of the best.

✳ To See

COVERED BRIDGES 🐾 ✐ ♿ **Parrish Mill Bridge** (478-763-2759; www.gastateparks .org/GeorgeLSmith), George L. Smith State Park, 371 George L. Smith State Park Road, Twin City. Open 7 AM–10 PM daily. George L. Smith State Park is located off GA 23 between Twin City and Metter, and within it lies a most unusual covered bridge. In fact, it is unique in the state of Georgia because the bridge, a gristmill, a sawmill, and a dam are all lodged under one roof. The structure was built in 1880 on beautiful Fifteen Mile Creek. The doors at each end can be opened to allow passage, but you'll have to walk through the bridge because it is closed to vehicular traffic. For more information about the park, see *Green Space—Nature Preserves and Parks*. Parking $5.

FOR FAMILIES ✿ ✐ ✆ **Center for Wildlife Education and Lamar Q. Ball Jr. Raptor Center** (912-681-0831 or 1-800-568-3301; http://welcome.georgiasouthern.edu/wildlife), Old Forest Drive, Georgia Southern University, Statesboro. Open 9–5 weekdays, 1–5 Saturday, September–May. Many species of native birds of prey live here among 4 acres of natural woodland habitats. The center also has a large collection of reptiles and amphibians. Sure to be a hit of any visit is a raptor show presented at 3 PM on Saturday, and those who aren't turned off by snakes enjoy the reptile show at 2. Children enjoy finding the 50 hidden animals in the Down-to-Earth Encounter and the 17 stations along the Children's Discovery Trail, where they can look for animal tracks, antlers, bird nests, eggshells, feathers, skeletons, snake skins, and turtle shells. They can even climb into a life-size eagle's nest for a photo opportunity. Adults $2; seniors, military, and children 3–11 $1.

MUSEUMS ✿ ✆ **Altama Museum of Art and History** (912-537-1911; www.vidaliaga .com), 611 Jackson Street, Vidalia. Open 10–4 Monday, Tuesday, Thursday, and Friday. Housed in the 1911 neoclassical Brazell House, the museum's permanent collection includes 18th- and 19th-century American and European prints, the 18th- and 19th-century Norma Damon Libby porcelain collection of 260 pieces of Staffordshire in 210 patterns, 24 John James Audubon first-edition hand-colored prints, and 200 20th-century Southern paintings. For the young and young-at-heart girl, the Girl Scout Room has scouting memorabilia back to 1929. The museum also shows the work of visiting artists. Free.

✿ ✆ **Dublin-Laurens Museum** (478-272-9242), 311 Academy Avenue, Dublin. Open 1–4:30 Tuesday–Friday. The graceful building, which serves as a repository for county memorabilia, was built as a library with a grant from Andrew Carnegie in 1904. Today it serves as the museum and the home of the Laurens County Historical Society. Exhibits include photos, paintings, and Native American relics. Free.

✿ ✐ ✆ **Georgia Southern University Museum** (912-478-5444; http://ceps.georgiasouthern .edu/museum), Rosenwald Building, 2142 Southern Drive, Georgia Southern University, Statesboro. Open 9–5 Tuesday–Friday, 2–5 Saturday and Sunday. The stars at this natural-history museum are a 26-foot fossil of a mosasaur, the prehistoric *T. Rex* of the sea, which is believed to be 78 million years old, and *Georgiacetus vogtlensis,* the oldest whale fossil found in North America, but there are many other skeletons and fossils. Kids Be a Paleontologist allows the little ones to dig for their own fossils. $2 for everyone three and older; last Saturday free; check the schedule for free Super Sundays.

✿ ✐ ✆ **Vidalia Onion Museum** (912-537-1918; www.vidaliaonionmuseum or www.vidalia onion.org/about_us/vidalia_onion_museum), 100 Vidalia Sweet Onion Drive. Vidalia. Open 9–5 Monday–Friday. Just to prove that there's a museum for everything under the sun, the town of Vidalia celebrates its most-famous product with a museum. The purpose of the museum is to provide an interactive, historical experience that highlights the economic, cultural, and culinary significance of the famous sweet onion and its exclusive 20-county growing area. Exhibits "unearth each unique layer of the Vidalia Onion story," just like peeling a real onion. *Pioneers, Problems, and Promises* describes the challenges local Depression-era farmers had in creating a new cash crop. Would you believe that some companies and individuals actually counterfeit the precious vegetable with false labeling? The struggles to protect the onion's integrity are recounted in the *Protecting the Name and Fame* exhibit. The story of getting Vidalia onions from planting to market is told in *A Year-Round Job.* As the onion became well-known and sought after, it entered our daily lives in many ways we might not realize. *Vidalias in Pop Culture* describes the onion's inclusion in current entertainment, such as *CSI Miami* and several works of popular fiction. So famous is the vegetable that DreamWorks Animation has entered into partnership for marketing promotion. *Onion Town* tells how the community celebrates its most-famous citizen with festivals (see *Special*

FUN FACTS ABOUT VIDALIA ONIONS

- The conditions to grow the sweet onions are ideal in only 20 Georgia counties. Onions grown anywhere else can't bear the name.
- It's something special about the soil and the number of minutes of sunlight in the winter that create the ideal conditions.
- When Georgian Jimmy Carter was president, he sometimes presented Vidalia onions as White House gifts.
- Vidalia onions are fat free, low calorie, and are a good source of vitamin C.
- Vidalia onions aren't used only in vegetable dishes. There's even a recipe for Happily Ever After Onion Chocolate Cake.

Other onion facts:

- Native Americans used onions in making dyes and also as toys.
- Roman gladiators rubbed their bodies with onions to firm their muscles.
- In ancient Egypt artists created images of onions in solid gold as a symbol of eternity.
- Egyptians believed onions had strength-building properties, so they were fed to the pyramid builders.

Events), cook-offs, pageants, and cookbooks. And *On the Menu* describes how chefs as diverse as Julia Child and Bobby Flay have incorporated the onions into their recipes. *Sweet World for Kids* introduces youngsters to the Yumion mascot. Free.

SPECIAL PLACES 🐾 ♿ **Meinhardt Vineyards Winery** (912-839-2458; www .meinhardtvineyards.com), 305 Kennedy Pond Road, Statesboro. Open 10–7 Tuesday–Thursday, 11–10 Friday and Saturday, 1–6 Sunday. Dinners are served 5–9 Friday and Saturday. Meinhardt Vineyards and Winery, southeast Georgia's first winery, specializes in muscadine wine. What was a 15-year family winemaking hobby became a business in 2004 with the opening of the winery. A relaxing atmosphere and scenic views are extra added features of a visit to the winery for complimentary tastings and tours. The tasting room sells food items and wine-related merchandise. Free.

✳ To Do

BICYCLING 🐾 🚲 **Yamassee Bicycle Trail** (contact Vidalia Area Convention and Visitors Bureau: 912-538-8687; www.vidaliaarea.com). This 17-mile "billboard-free" trail, which largely parallels the Oconee River, allows the whole family to pedal past beautiful farm country, historic churches, and huge pine forests. You'll also pass through the Long Pond, Alston, and Uvalda communities, where you can learn a little about their histories and purchase refreshments. Call for a trail map.

BOATING 🚣 **Canoe Canoe Outfitters** (912-786-8732 or 1-888-529-2542; www.canoe canoe.com), 3008 US 280 East, Lyons. The outfitter company knows the flat rivers of south Georgia as well as the camps and where the fish bite. Canoe Canoe furnishes everything from paddles to gourmet camp cuisine. Trips range from several hours to overnight trips to custom-designed excursions on Pendleton Creek and the Altamaha, Ocmulgee, Ohoopee, and Oconee rivers. Call for prices.

🚣 **Three Rivers Outdoors** (912-594-8379; www.explorethreerivers.com), 612 McNatt Falls Road, Uvalda. The outfitter offers services to the Altamaha, Ohoopee, Oconee, Ocmulgee, and Little Ocmulgee rivers, including trips of two hours to two weeks, as well as rentals, shuttle service, retail sales of boats and gear, and guide service. Call for prices.

FISHING 🐾 𝒮 ♿ **Evans County Public Fishing Area** (chamber of commerce: 912-739-1391; 912-594-1805; www.gofishgeorgia.com), US 280 East, Claxton. Open sunrise–sunset daily. Located on 372 gently rolling acres, the three-lake fishing compound features a boat ramp, fishing pier, boardwalk, picnicking facilities, and primitive campsites. A fishing license is required. A Georgia Outdoor Recreation Pass (GORP) is required for anyone 16–64 who does not already have a fishing license: $3.50 for three days.

FRUIT AND BERRY PICKING 🐾 𝒮 ♿ **Clark Farm and Produce** (912-865-3200), 526 Clark Farm Road, Twin City. Open 9–7 Monday–Saturday, April 1–October 31; call to verify availability. At this working farm, visitors can take a tour, pick their own strawberries in season, enjoy strawberry ice cream year-round, or choose a pumpkin and take a hayride in the autumn. Berries $1.50 per pound.

GOLF **Brazell's Creek Golf Course and Pro Shop at Gordonia-Alatamaha State Park** (912-557-7745; www.gastateparks.org/GordoniaAlatamaha). The signature 15th hole on this 18-hole, par 71, 7,000-yard course requires the golfer to hit over scenic wetlands to an island green. $30–36. (Also see *Green Space—Nature Preserves and Parks*.)

SWIMMING AND WATER PLAY 🐾 𝒮 ♿ **Splash in the Boro** (912-764-5637; www.splashintheboro.com), off GA 24, Statesboro. In late May and late August through Labor Day, open weekends. In June and July, open 10–6 Monday, Tuesday, Wednesday, and Friday; 10–8 Thursday and Saturday; noon–6 Sunday. Therapy and competition pools open year-round. This 5-acre family water park and aquatics center, located in **Mill Creek Regional Park**, features three water slides, zero-depth entry pools, water guns, valves that shoot water unexpectedly all over the pool, a bucket that dumps 600 gallons of water every three minutes, an 800-foot Lazy River, a four-lane therapy pool, and a 25-meter competition pool. A bubble dome covers the therapy and competition pools during colder months for year-round operation of those facilities. Winter activities include water aerobics, lap swimming, open recreational swimming, open exercise and therapy swimming, and swimming lessons. Adults $12, youth $10.

✳ Green Space

GARDENS 🐾 𝒮 ♿ **Georgia Southern University Botanical Garden** (office: 912-871-1149; Bland Cottage: 912-871-1114; www.georgiasouthern.edu/garden), 1505 Bland Avenue, Statesboro. Gardens open 9:30–7 Monday–Friday (cottage closes at 5:30), 1–4 Sunday. Amazingly enough, this preserve, set on an 11-acre early-20th-century farmstead, is located in the middle of Statesboro. It showcases native plants, unique and endangered plants, and microhabitats of the Coastal Plain. Among the seven Southern gardens are ones devoted to heritage plants, roses, camellias, native azaleas, and native plant landscapes. Others of special interest are the bog garden and the Children's Learning Garden. The original Bland Cottage now serves as the garden center. A new attraction is the Oak Grove one-room schoolhouse. Several woodland trails wind through the grounds. Free.

🐾 𝒮 ♿ **Guido Gardens** (912-685-2222; www.GuidoGardens.com), 600 North Lewis Street, Metter. Open for tours 8–noon and 1–5 weekdays; reservations suggested for guided tours. Located on the campus of Sowers Ministries, the gardens contain the Chapel in the Pines, as well as arbors, bridges, a boardwalk, a gazebo, topiaries, and water attractions such as waterfalls and fountains. Rest awhile in one of the many porch swings dotting the grounds and take in the beauty of your surroundings. During the Christmas season's Nights of Lights, the gardens are filled with a million lights and lighted sculptures. Open 6–9. Free.

NATURE PRESERVES AND PARKS 🐾 ✂ ♿ ☙ **George L. Smith State Park** (478-763-2759; lodging reservations: 1-800-864-7275; www.gastateparks.org/GeorgeLSmith), 371 George L. Smith State Park Road, Twin City. Open 7 AM–10 PM daily. Named for a Georgia legislator, this quiet, 1,634-acre park is popular with sports enthusiasts. Anglers and canoeists enjoy the lake, while birdwatchers look for blue herons and white ibis. Hikers stretch their legs on 7 miles of trails while they keep an eagle eye out for the endangered gopher tortoise. Bikers also use the trails. Located right on the water's edge of 412-acre Cypress Lake, the circa 1880 Parrish Mill at the park is a combination gristmill, sawmill, covered bridge, and dam (see **Parrish Mill Bridge** under *To See—Covered Bridges*). Private boats are permitted and there is a boat ramp, but motors are limited to 10 horsepower. Canoes and fishing and pedal-boat rentals are available in season. Accommodations are offered at tent, trailer, and RV sites, as well as at a primitive campground and in four cottages (see *Lodging—Campgrounds* and *Lodging—Cottages and Cabins*). $5.

🐾 ✂ ♿ ☙ **Gordonia-Alatamaha State Park** (912-557-7744; lodging reservations: 1-800-864-7275; www.gastateparks.org/GordoniaAlatamaha), 522 Park Lane, off US 280, Reidsville. Open 7 AM–10 PM daily. The park's unusual name comes from the rare Gordonia tree (a member of the bay family) and the original spelling of the Altamaha River. The 462-acre park is visited for golf (see *To Do—Golf*) and water sports. At the small 12-acre lake, visitors can fish or rent fishing and pedal boats seasonally. Private boats are not permitted. Land-loving anglers can fish from the docks, and children like looking for beaver dams from the observation deck. The park also features a swimming pool in season, tennis courts, miniature golf (additional fee), a large playground, basketball hoop, volleyball net, and camping (see *Lodging—Campgrounds*). Parking $5; swimming $3; mini golf $2.50; paddleboats $2.50 per hour.

🐾 ✂ ♿ ☙ **Magnolia Springs State Park** (478-982-1660; lodging reservations: 1-800-864-7275; www.gastateparks.org/MagnoliaSprings), 1053 Magnolia Springs Drive, Millen. Park open 7 AM–10 PM daily. The 1,071-acre park is best known for its crystal-clear springs, from which 7 million gallons of water flow each day. Visitors can admire the springs from a boardwalk that spans the water and offers a good place from which to view wildlife such as alligator, turtle, ibis, heron, and other species. A 28-acre lake is popular for boating and fishing. Other recreational amenities include three playgrounds, a swimming pool in season, 10 miles of hiking and biking trails, a wheelchair-accessible fishing dock, and a boat ramp. There are canoe and fishing boat rentals seasonally, and private boats are allowed. During the Civil War, a prison called Camp Lawton occupied the site, and the earthen breastworks that surrounded the prison remain today. Accommodations are available in cottages and campgrounds (see *Lodging—Campgrounds* and *Lodging—Cottages and Cabins*). $5.

RIVERS 🐾 ✂ ♿ **Canoochee River,** access at US 301 North, US 280 East, and GA 169 North, Claxton. Open daily. Public landings attract anglers (a fishing license is required), boaters, and swimmers to the shores of the river. Free. Other rivers worth exploring in the area include the Altamaha, Ocmulgee, Oconee, and Ohoopee—all of which offer similar activities and access at numerous points.

✳ Lodging

BED & BREAKFASTS

In Claxton

🐌 **Smith House Inn** (912-739-8095), 610 West Liberty Street. This quaint, circa 1910 B&B offers four comfortably decorated guest rooms with private baths. A full breakfast is included. No smoking. Not wheelchair accessible. $100.

In Dublin

🐌 ♿ **Dublin Farm** (478-275-8766; www .dublinfarm.com), 875 James Currie Road. This country-style B&B is located on a picturesque 30-acre farm where horses and donkeys roam the fields in the scenic and peaceful countryside of middle Georgia. It offers four guest rooms with private baths. Guests also enjoy the swimming pool. The hosts speak English, German, and Italian, making this an ideal retreat for visitors from other countries. Sumptuous breakfast included. Guests have a choice of either continental or full breakfast, and room service can even be arranged for those who want to stay in bed longer. In addition to offering accommodations, Dublin Farm is well-known in the area for its Friday and Saturday night dinners at **Ristorante da Maria,** which are open to the public with reservations (see *Where to Eat—Dining Out*). No smoking. $95.

♿ **Page House** (478-275-4551; www.page housebb.com), 711 Bellevue Avenue. This beautiful and elegant antebellum Greek Revival home is located on a street that used to be referred to as Millionaires Row because of all the opulent mansions cotton built. The B&B features five spacious guest rooms (one with a private balcony) and one honeymoon suite with a whirlpool tub and a kitchenette. Full gourmet breakfast included. No smoking. One room on the first floor is wheelchair accessible. $89–119.

In Statesboro

🐌 ♿ **Georgia's Bed and Breakfast** (912-489-6330), 123 South Zetterower Avenue. This historic home has four guest rooms, all with private baths. A full breakfast is included. No smoking. $105.

COLEMAN HOUSE BED AND BREAKFAST WAS BUILT IN 1904.

In Swainsboro

🐌 **Coleman House Bed and Breakfast** (478-237-2822), 323 North Main Street. This magnificent 1904 painted lady boasts 10,000 square feet of living space, 98 windows, 11 fireplaces, 500 spindles, 2,000 feet of porches, and a widow's walk. Luxurious guest rooms feature all the modern amenities. The B&B also has a popular restaurant (see *Where to Eat—Eating Out*). No smoking. Not wheelchair accessible. $75–85.

CAMPGROUNDS For contact information and a description of the amenities at all three state parks, see *Green Space—Nature Preserves and Parks.*

In Millen

🐌 ⚓ ♿ 🌳 **Magnolia Springs State Park** (lodging reservations: 1-800-864-7275). The park features 26 tent, trailer, and RV sites, as well as 3 walk-in sites and 2 pioneer campgrounds. $25–28.

In Reidsville

🐌 ⚓ ♿ 🌳 **Gordonia-Alatamaha State Park** (lodging reservations: 1-800-864-7275). This park campground offers 26 tent, trailer, and RV sites. $19–30.

In Twin City

🐌 ⚓ ♿ 🌳 **George L. Smith State Park** (lodging reservations: 1-800-864-7275). The park provides 25 tent, trailer, and RV sites right at the water's edge, as well as a pioneer campground. $19–25.

COTTAGES AND CABINS

For contact information and a description of the amenities at all three state parks, see *Green Space—Nature Preserves and Parks.*

In Millen
⚲ ❋ **Magnolia Springs State Park** (lodging reservations: 1-800-864-7275). The park offers eight fully equipped cottages. One is dog friendly ($40 per dog; maximum two). $125–150 (higher during Masters Week).

In Reidsville
⚲ ❋ **Gordonia-Alatamaha State Park** (lodging reservations: 1-800-864-7275). This park offers five fully equipped cottages with fireplaces and screened porches. One is dog friendly ($40 per dog; maximum two). $115.

In Twin City
⚲ ❋ **George L. Smith State Park** (lodging reservations: 1-800-864-7275). Eight fully equipped cottages with gas fireplaces and screened porches are nestled in the woods. One is dog friendly ($40 per dog; maximum two). $110–120.

RESORTS

In Swainsboro
♿ **Flat Creek Lodge Fish and Game** (478-237-3474 or 1-877-352-8275; www.flatcreeklodge.com), 367 Bishop Chapel Road. This east Georgia hunting and fishing reserve on the shores of Flat Creek offers the epitome in luxurious accommodations, dining, and spa services, in addition to many sporting activities. The almost 2,000-acre woodland preserve includes 19 ponds that occupy 250 acres in total, so anglers have the opportunity to fish for trophy-size largemouth bass, bream, bluegill, and crappie in the creek or in ponds. Wild boar, bobwhite quail, wild turkey, white-tailed deer, and other wildlife indigenous to the area inhabit the preserve and provide opportunities for hunting. Two hundred acres are devoted to organic farming, and the bounty of the gardens, orchards, bee-

hives, mushroom fields, and the dairy often appear on the dining table along with fish or game from the property (see *Where to Eat—Dining Out*). In fact, the dairy is one of the top producers in the state of artisanal cheeses. Behind the Scenes Dairy Tours are offered with cheese tastings. Accommodations are found in 12 individually themed lodge rooms with verandas overlooking the lake or in six two-bedroom cottages. The spa (478-237-3474) features a Japanese mineral bathhouse, steam room, sauna, whirlpools, a lap pool, and fitness center. Spa treatments include massages, facials, manicures, pedicures, and paraffin wraps ($20–100). Stumpknockers serves double duty as a shop featuring local arts and crafts and as a bar. Flat Creek Lodge Outfitters sells hunting and fishing apparel and equipment. In season the property is open to the public for pick-your-own strawberries, blueberries, and raspberries. Rounding out things to do, the resort offers five-stand sporting clays and paintball. You can even land your helicopter here. $185–400.

❋ Where to Eat
DINING OUT

In Dublin
♿ **Ristorante da Maria at Dublin Farm** (478-275-8766; www.dublinfarm.com), 875 James Currie Road. Open at 7 PM every Friday and Saturday; also on special occasions such as Mother's Day and Father's Day. Reservations required, as the restaurant offers only one seating for this

> ### YOU GO, GIRL
> The first female sheriff in Georgia and possibly the first in the entire nation was from Evans County. Her name was Josie Mae Rogers, and she was sworn in on June 24, 1940, to fill the unexpired term of her father, Jessie C. Durrence. Josie Mae carried her Smith & Wesson in her purse, not on her hip, because it has been noted that she had a "disdain for dramatics."

authentic fixed-price, five-course Italian meal. Wines can be purchased by the bottle. No smoking. $28–39.

In Statesboro

🦫 🍴 ♿ **Beaver House Inn Restaurant** (912-764-2821; www.beaverhouseinn.com), 121 South Main Street. Open for lunch daily and dinner Monday–Saturday. This antebellum home houses a fine restaurant. Reminiscent of Sunday dinner at Grandma's, the concept behind the restaurant was modeled on the famous Mrs. Wilkes Dining Room in Savannah. All-you-can-eat, family-style selections include fried chicken, scratch biscuits, black-eyed peas over rice, vegetables, casseroles, and sweet tea. À la carte choices are available, too. No smoking. Lunch $8.99, dinner $9.99.

In Swainsboro

The Dining Room at Flat Creek Lodge (dining reservations: 1-877-352-8273; see *Lodging—Resorts* for other details). Open 6:30–11:30 PM Thursday–Saturday. This upscale restaurant serves the best in farm-to-table cuisine and features not only fruits, vegetables, and cheeses from the property, but also fish and game caught there. Other choices include New York strip, rib eye, seafood, pork, and chicken. $19–30.

EATING OUT

In Lyons

🦫 🍴 ♿ **Chatters Restaurant** (912-526-8040), 674 NW Broad Street. Open 5 AM–9 PM Monday–Saturday, 11–3 Sunday. Don't miss the seafood buffet on Friday and Saturday nights. No smoking. Breakfast about $4, lunch about $8, dinner $7–14.

In Statesboro

🦫 🍴 ♿ **Ocean Galley Seafood** (912-489-4145), 503 Northside Drive East. Open 11–9 Sunday–Thursday, 11–10 Friday–Saturday. Menu favorites include seafood, steaks, hamburgers, chicken fingers, grilled chicken, and specialty salads. No smoking. Lunch $7–10, dinner $10–18.

In Swainsboro

🦫 🍴 ♿ **The Coleman House** (478-237-2822), 323 North Main Street. Open 11–2

daily; reservations recommended for holidays. Located in a gorgeous 1904 Queen Anne Victorian mansion with turrets, a wraparound porch, and a widow's walk, the restaurant serves a lunch buffet that changes daily and à la carte selections. The Coleman House also offers bed & breakfast accommodations (see *Lodging—Bed & Breakfasts*). No smoking. $10–13.50.

COFFEEHOUSES

In Statesboro

🦫 ♿ **Daily Grind** (912-489-5070), 124 Savannah Avenue, Suite #1-E. Open 7 AM–10 PM Monday–Thursday, 7 AM–11 PM Friday, 8 AM–11 PM Saturday. Traditional coffeehouse fare is served at a very reasonable price. No smoking. Lunch and dinner about $10, beverages $3–5.

✳ Entertainment

MUSIC Statesboro Georgia Southern Symphony (912-681-5396; www.georgia southern.edu/music), mailing address: P.O. Box 2311, Statesboro 30459. The semiprofessional orchestra presents three subscription concerts, two youth shows, one outdoor pops concert, and a holiday program each year. The Music Department of the university also offers a Symphonic Wind Ensemble, the Southern Chorale, a Wind Symphony, and a Jazz Combo. Call for a schedule of performances and ticket prices.

THEATER David H. Averitt Center for the Arts (912-212-2787; www.averitt centerforthearts.org), 33 East Main Street, Statesboro. Box office and galleries open 1–5:30 Tuesday–Friday. The center, which occupies the historic Old Bank of Statesboro (circa 1911) and the old Georgia Theater (circa 1936), provides a permanent home for the arts in Statesboro and features the Emma Kelly Theater and four art galleries. There are performances of one kind or another going on almost every weekend. $10–45, depending on performance.

Georgia Southern University Theater South (box office: 912-486-7999; 1-866-PAC-ARTS; www.georgiasouthern.edu/pac).

The university center presents 10 shows yearly with nationally and internationally known artists in music, dance, and theater at the school's Performing Arts Center. Call for a schedule of performances. $25–45.

Theatre Dublin (478-277-5074), 100 South Church Street, Dublin. The renovated 1934 theater serves as an arts center for a variety of performances, including music, comedy, and youth performances. Call for a schedule of performances and ticket prices.

✳ Selective Shopping

F O O D Claxton Bakery (912-739-3441 or 1-800-841-4211; www.claxtonfruitcake .com), 203 West Main Street, Claxton. Open 8–5 Monday–Saturday. Between September and December, millions of pounds of fruitcake are baked and shipped by this world-renowned bakery, but it's not the only fruitcake bakery in Claxton (see entry that follows).

Farm Fresh Tattnall (Co-op Extension Service: 912-557-6724), mailing address: P.O. Box 580, Reidsville 30453. This organization is a cooperative of 18 roadside and pick-your-own farms in Tattnall County. Visitors can find every fresh product from peaches and strawberries to Vidalia onions, sweet potatoes, and turnip greens.

Georgia Fruit Cake Company (912-739-2683; www.georgiafruitcakecompany.com), 5 South Duval Street, Claxton. Open 8–5 weekdays. This fourth-generation, family-owned bakery is famed for its homemade fruitcakes.

Vidalia Onion Factory and Gift Shop (912-526-3466 or 1-800-227-6646; www .vidalia.com), 3309 East First Street, Vidalia. Factory tours available by appointment only April through mid-June; gift shop open 9–6 Monday–Saturday, 1–5 Sunday, year-round. Stop by and get a behind-the-scenes glimpse into what happens to a Vidalia onion before it gets to the grocery store. The process is fascinating. Don't leave the Vidalia area without taking home some onion products—not only the sweet onions themselves, but steak and barbecue

sauces, dressings, relishes, pickles, salsas, and other delicacies made with them. The shop also offers onion ring mix, cookbooks, a microwave onion cooker, souvenirs, collectibles, and Christmas ornaments. The café specializes in fried onion rings.

✳ Special Events

January: **Annual Bird Dog Field Trials** (chamber of commerce: 706-554-5451). These field trials are among the oldest in the country. Georgia Open Shooting Dog Championship Field Trials, the Georgialina Field Trials, and the Southeastern Field Trials attract hundreds of dogs, handlers, horses, judges, field marshals, and spectators from all over the world for a month-long series of shooting dog championship events at Di-Lane Plantation Wildlife Management Area in Waynesboro. Free for spectators.

March: **Claxton Rattlesnake Roundup and Wildlife Festival** (912-739-3820; www.claxtonrattlesnakeroundup.com). This event, held in Claxton on the second weekend in March, features rattlesnakes on exhibit, prizes for hunters, live snake milking for venom, handling demonstrations, wildlife exhibits, a turkey-calling contest, a 100-unit parade, a 5K fun run, handmade arts and crafts, educational lectures, live music, cloggers, queen's coronation, gospel singing, children's activities, and food. Ages six and older $5.

Dublin St. Patrick's Day Celebrations (chamber of commerce: 478-272-5546; www.dublinstpatricks.com). Running the entire month of March, this fun-filled celebration, held annually since 1966, includes 45 separate events, including a hot-air balloon festival, several sports tournaments, beauty pageants, a barbecue cook-off, leprechaun contests, leprechaun races, bagpipe music, and, of course, corned beef and cabbage, Irish soda bread, and green beer. The highlight is the spectacular two-hour parade on the weekend after St. Patrick's Day and the arts and crafts festival at Southern Pines Park. Free; some activities have a fee.

April: **Tales from the Altamaha—A Georgia Folk Life Play** (912-526-8106 or 912-526-6445; www.lyonsga.org/tales-from-the-altamaha or www.talesfromthealtamaha .com). For two weeks, playgoers are transported back to a time when Southern traditions were just being forged. The unforgettable blend of comedy, music, and drama, based on the years of newspaper columns by Col. T. Ross Sharpe, is performed by a cast of 100 volunteers in the renovated 1936 Blue Marquee Theater in Lyons. The play describes the lives, loves, losses, scandals, and plain ol' gossip of the colorful characters who were the settlers within a five-county radius in this area of rural south Georgia. Reserved seating $20, general admission $15, Tuesday Family Discount Night $10 for all seats.

Vidalia Onion Festival (912-538-8687; www.vidaliaonionfestival.com). This annual four-day something-for-everyone event in Vidalia has been named One of the Five Don't Miss Festivals Across the U.S. by MSNBC. Going strong since 1978, the festival features arts and crafts; an antiques fair; a cooking school; recipe contest and public tasting; fireworks; street dance; Miss and Little Miss Vidalia Onion beauty pageants; carnival; Golden Onion Chef's Competition using Vidalia onions; several sports competitions; live entertainment; gospel fest; a rodeo; an antique car, truck, and motorcycle show; an onion-eating contest; lots of food; a Battle of the Bands; a Civil War reenactment; and so much more. Most activities take place at the Vidalia Regional Airport, but some take place downtown.

Free, but a charge for some events. Parking $5 on Thursday and Sunday, $10 on Friday and Saturday. Check the website or call for details and prices.

October: **The Real Squeal: Lyons Barbecue and Bluegrass Festival** (912-526-6445). The real attraction for barbecue aficionados are the Kansas City Barbecue Society–sanctioned professional and backyard cookoff events and thousands of dollars in prize money. Other attractions include live musical entertainment, primarily bluegrass; a car show; chainsaw carving competitions; an outdoor expo; and other events such as a show of Native American artifacts and demonstrations of primitive skills. $5 for 12 and older.

South Georgia Jaycee Fair (478-237-3986), Jaycee Fairgrounds, 324 Fairgrounds Road, Swainsboro. Held every year during the first week in October since 1918, the fair features commercial and 4-H exhibits, animal competitions, the Swine and Cattle Show, nightly beauty pageants, midway rides, great food, games, and live entertainment. Adults $4, children 6–12 $3.

November: **Million Pines Arts and Crafts Festival** (912-529-6611; www.million pines.com), at Iva Park, 421 Main Street East, Soperton. The festival features arts and crafts sales and demonstrations of how these skills were used in days gone by, live entertainment, and old-time fair food, including Georgia's famous boiled peanuts and pork rinds. Adults $4, children six and younger free; parking and shuttle free.

The Mountains   4

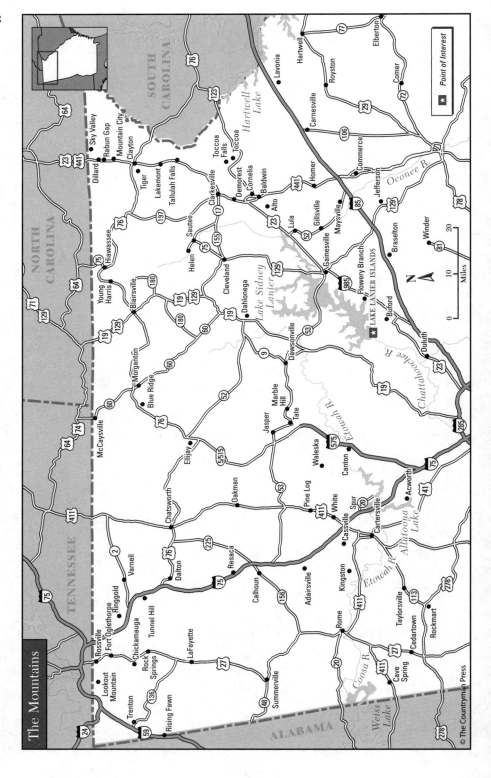

The Mountains

Point of Interest

© The Countryman Press

INTRODUCTION

Mountains cover the entire northern part of Georgia from Alabama to South Carolina and bordering Tennessee and North Carolina. Sensational scenery is one of the biggest draws for visitors to the mountainous area of northern Georgia. Crystal-clear blue skies permit visitors to enjoy long-range vistas from rugged mountaintops such as Brasstown Bald, one of the highest points in the East. Throughout the region, steep slopes are covered with brilliant wildflowers in the spring and flamboyantly hued leaves in the fall. The Chattahoochee National Forest encompasses 750,000 acres with 10 wilderness areas, 1,367 miles of trout streams, and 430 miles of hiking trails. The Appalachian Trail begins—or ends, depending how you look at it—in north Georgia.

Water plays a prominent role in north Georgia, whether it plummets over a rocky precipice to create a cascading waterfall, drifts serenely in a glassy-surfaced lake, or careens down a tumultuous white-water river such as the Chattooga or the Ocoee. Lakes Allatoona, Blue Ridge, Burton, Carters, Hartwell, Lanier, Rabun, Tallulah, Tugaloo, and several others provide plentiful opportunities for popular activities such as fishing, boating, swimming, and waterskiing. Although some of these lakes are the most visited in the nation, many of them didn't even exist 100 years ago. Because Georgia didn't experience glacial action during the last ice age, the scouring necessary to create lakes left the region with few large, naturally occurring lakes. It was only in the early years of the 20th century that the need for power generation, navigation, and flood control led the U.S. Army Corps of Engineers, Georgia Power, and the Tennessee Valley Authority to create dams and reservoirs—the by-product of which is waterborne recreation. In fact, Georgia doesn't have a single large natural lake.

With all these lakes, rivers, forests, and trails in the area, outdoor recreation is a major reason for tourists to flock to the mountains. In fact, this region is the cradle of tourism in the state. From early times, wealthy families from the coast and southern Georgia escaped to the mountains for the entire summer to avoid the heat of their homes and the diseases rampant in the hotter climes. Railroads later brought middle-class visitors from all over the state for prolonged stays. Nowadays auto travelers can make the trip for as little as a day. The region contains the highest concentration of Georgia's state parks and historic sites: 24 parks, which offer something for almost everyone.

History is not just a footnote in north Georgia. The area is imbued with Native American history. The Cherokee capital of New Echota that flourished near what is present-day Calhoun lasted until America's first gold rush in the hills around Dahlonega. After that event, the Native Americans were forced off their land and sent west along the Trail of Tears. Today's travelers can visit the Etowah Indian Mounds Historic Site and other important Native American sites along the Chieftains Trail. They also can stop by the Dahlonega Gold Museum Historic Site, tour a gold mine, or even pan for gold.

The first European settlers in this area were sturdy, self-sufficient mountaineers who led a hardscrabble life. Learn about them at the Foxfire Museum in Mountain City or the Northeast Georgia History Museum in Gainesville, among others. Northwest Georgia was the site of many important Civil War battles and the scene of the famous Great Locomotive Chase in which Union spies stole a locomotive called the General. Numerous Civil War sites can be seen along the Blue and Gray Trail, and several battles are reenacted annually.

Agriculture makes a different and less significant contribution to this area than it does to more southerly parts of the state, but apples play a major role, and the success of growing grapes has led to the creation of several wineries. Different types of farms are open for tours and other activities such as corn mazes and hayrides.

A few of the unusual or unexpected attractions in north Georgia include the Bavarian-style village of Helen, BabyLand General Hospital (the birthplace of the Cabbage Patch Kids), the Booth Western Art Museum, and Rock City Gardens.

CARTERSVILLE AND BLUE RIDGE

Northwest Georgia occupies the southern reach of the Blue Ridge Mountains. The area has more changes in topography than the lower two-thirds of the state and has, therefore, been attracting tourists since the 1800s. Early visitors, who came to escape the heat and diseases of the lowcountry, often stayed for months at a time. Before the first tourists, however, the area was inhabited by Native Americans, including Mississippian Mound Builders and Cherokees, and then by white settlers. Many historical attractions include Native American sites and Civil War battlefields and cemeteries. Historical trails include the **Blue and Gray Trail** and the **Chieftains Trail.**

Despite the modern-day existence of interstate highways, small cities, and other signs of "progress," the area remains very much as it was hundreds of years ago. Vast acreage, including the Cohutta Wilderness, is covered by the Chattahoochee National Forest. State parks and U.S. Forest Service recreation areas also keep much of northwest Georgia in its natural state. Lakes Allatoona, Acworth, and Blue Ridge as well as the Toccoa River provide fishing, boating, and other water sports. Other outdoor recreational opportunities range from hiking to mountain biking, horseback riding to white-water rafting.

In addition to natural beauty, northwest Georgia offers a covered bridge; Indian mounds; the world's first Coca-Cola sign; museums dedicated to geology, famous residents, Native Americans, African Americans, and even Western art; farm tours concentrating on everything from alpacas to apples; one of Georgia's last drive-in movie theaters; a scenic railroad ride; and an array of festivals and special events. Accommodations range from bed & breakfasts to cabins to campgrounds, while dining options range from casual eateries to fine restaurants.

GUIDANCE When planning a trip to the Cartersville area, including Adairsville, Cassville, and White, contact the **Cartersville–Bartow County Convention and Visitors Bureau, Georgia Local Welcome Center** (770-602-3748; www.notatlanta.org), in the Charles Brown Conference Center, 5450 GA 20 (exit 290 off I-75), Cartersville 30120. Open 8:30–5 weekdays, 11–4 Saturday.

To find out more about Acworth, contact the **Acworth Area Convention and Visitors Bureau** (770-974-7626; www.acworthtourism.org), 4415 Senator Russell Avenue, Acworth 30101. Open 8–5 weekdays. Pick up a brochure for a 30-site walking tour of historic Acworth here.

For information about Blue Ridge and McCaysville, contact the **Fannin County Chamber of Commerce and Local Welcome Center** (706-632-5680 or 1-800-899-MTNS; www.blueridgemountains.com), 152 Orvin Lance Drive, Blue Ridge 30513. Open 8–5 weekdays, 9–5 Saturday, 1–5 Sunday. The center provides information on **Fannin County Self-Guided Driving Tours, back-roads tours,** and other attractions.

For information about Ellijay and East Ellijay, consult the **Gilmer County Chamber of Commerce and Welcome Center** (706-635-7400; www.gilmerchamber.com), 369 Craig Street, East Ellijay 30540. Open 9–5 daily. There is a new **Downtown Welcome Center** (706-635-7400), 368 Craig Street, Suite 104, East Ellijay 30540. Open 9–5 Saturday and 1–5 Sunday.

GETTING THERE *By air:* The nearest airports to this region are in Atlanta and in Chattanooga, Tennessee. There is some shuttle service between the two. Visitors might decide it's easier to fly into Atlanta and rent a car rather than to make a connection into Chattanooga and still have to rent a car. For either, see "What's Where in Georgia" for airport, airline, or car rental information.

By bus: The nearest **Greyhound Lines** stations are in Dalton (see the Dalton chapter), Atlanta (see "What's Where in Georgia"), and Chattanooga, Tennessee, at 960 Airport Road (423-892-1277).

By car: I-75, US 441, I-575, and GA 5/515 run north–south through northwest Georgia. GA 53 and US 76 run east–west.

By train: The nearest **AMTRAK** stations are in Atlanta (see "What's Where in Georgia") and Toccoa (see the Clarkesville chapter). In either case, a traveler would need to rent a car to get to and around in this area.

GETTING AROUND In Cartersville, car rentals are available from **Enterprise** (770-607-2020), 804 Joe Frank Harris Parkway SE.

WHEN TO GO North Georgia is the only area of the state that gets much snow, although even here it is rare. Do plan accordingly in the winter. Due to colder temperatures and the possibility of severe weather, some campgrounds and other establishments that deal with outdoor activities close for a few months in the winter, so be sure to check ahead to avoid disappointment.

MEDICAL EMERGENCY Call 911.

VILLAGES During the Civil War, Union troops camped in the **Acworth** area, and homes and churches were used as field headquarters and hospitals. Union general William Tecumseh Sherman was headquartered in Acworth for several days. When the Union troops left Acworth, they burned much of the town. The cotton economy brought prosperity back to Acworth by the late 1870s, and new homes and businesses were built. These are the historic buildings visitors see today. The small town's **Collins Avenue Historic District** showcases 150 years of architecture. **Lake Allatoona** and **Lake Acworth** were built in the 1950s, earning Acworth the nickname "Lake City" and providing numerous recreational opportunities (see *Green Space—Lakes*).

Blue Ridge, in Fannin County, is considered the gateway to the Blue Ridge Mountains. During the early 1900s, the Marietta and North Georgia Railroad brought large numbers of tourists to Blue Ridge because of its pure mineral waters, which turned the small town into an elite health resort. Today visitors come to ride the scenic railroad (see *To Do—Train Excursions*) and to shop for Appalachian arts and crafts, antiques, mountain furnishings, apples, trout, and items made from alpaca wool. Art fairs, gallery tours, exhibitions, receptions, festivals, concerts, and plays occur throughout the year.

Cartersville is rich in history, culture, scenic beauty, and recreational opportunities. Evidence of human habitation here goes back as far as 10,000 B.C. The first historic documentation was written in 1540 by Hernando de Soto, who visited the area and described the Mound Builder civilization. Creeks and Cherokees later inhabited the area until driven out and sent along the Trail of Tears. The Civil War intruded upon Cartersville, though it suffered little damage compared to other nearby towns. After the war, the railroads and natural resources brought great prosperity to the area. Today one of its greatest assets is tourism.

Cassville was once the cultural center of north Georgia, with two colleges, four hotels, and a newspaper. The town even had wooden sidewalks. Georgia's first Supreme Court decision was delivered at Cassville in 1856, and many Cherokee legal battles took place at the Cassville Courthouse. The town was decimated by the Civil War, however. Residents were given only 20 minutes' notice to flee, and no images or official records survived. All that remained afterward were three houses, two churches, and a Confederate cemetery. In the 20th century, Cassville enjoyed being on the route of the Dixie Highway, the nation's first planned interstate highway. During the 1930s, the Works Progress Administration constructed an Atlanta Campaign Pocket Park there. The old post office, which operated until the 1990s, houses the Cassville History Museum.

McCaysville is schizophrenic. The town has a blue line painted down the middle of the main street. On one side of the line you are in McCaysville, Georgia; on the other side, you are in Copperhill, Tennessee. A favorite photo op is to pose with one foot in each state.

✳ To See

COVERED BRIDGES 🐾 🎣 ♿ **Euharlee Covered Bridge and History Museum** (770-607-2017), 116 Covered Bridge Road, Cartersville. Museum open 10–5 Tuesday–Saturday, 10–6 Sunday. One of only 16 covered bridges left in Georgia and part of the state's Covered Bridge Trail, the Euharlee Bridge was built by Washington King, an African American contractor who became quite famous as a bridge builder, in 1886. Although the town of Euharlee was bustling with several mills in the 1840s, it is now virtually a ghost town. Remains of the old town include a well, courthouse, blacksmith shop, gristmill ruins, and commissary. Buildings still in use include a store, Baptist and Presbyterian churches, and a parsonage. The museum, located in an 1850 cowshed next to the bridge, is a good source of information about the town. Pick up the *Historic Euharlee Georgia* brochure here. Free.

HISTORIC HOMES AND SITES 🐾 🎣 ♿ **Etowah Indian Mound Historic Site** (770-387-3747; www.gastateparks.org/EtowahMounds), 813 Indian Mounds Road SE, Cartersville. Open 9–5 Wednesday–Saturday, 2–5:30 Sunday. On the scenic banks of the Etowah River, this area, an important stop on the **Georgia Chieftains Trail,** was home to several thousand Native Americans between A.D. 1000 and 1550, a time period known as the Mississippian era. During this time their great achievement was a series of earthen mounds used socially and ceremonially for temples and tombs. The mounds were seen by De Soto on his exploration through the area in 1540, although the civilization was rapidly declining by then. Today the 54-acre site preserves the mounds as well as the area where there was a village surrounded by a defensive ditch. The interpretive center houses artifacts, beads, ornaments, pot shards, and other artifacts found on the site. "Ike" and "Mike," the two largest carved-stone effigies ever discovered at a

ONE OF THE EARTHEN MOUNDS CREATED BY NATIVE AMERICANS AT THE ETOWAH INDIAN MOUNDS HISTORIC SITE

Mound Builder site, also are on display. Wooden stairs permit visitors to climb to the top of the largest mound (63 feet tall and covering 3 acres) for a wonderful panoramic view of the surrounding area and a glimpse of the V-shaped, piled-stone traps the natives built to catch fish and mussels. Only 9 percent of the area has been excavated, so who knows what wonders are still to be unearthed. *Note:* Interpretive center and paths wheelchair accessible; top of mound is not. $3.50–5.50.

🔶 𝒞 ♿ **Kirby-Quinton Heritage Cabin and Old Pickens County Jail** (706-692-7793; www.marblevalley.org), 141 North Main Street, Jasper. Open 2–5 Saturday, mid-April–the end of November, as well as July 4th, Labor Day, and Marble Fest weekend. The jail/residence was constructed in 1906, with the living quarters for the jailer and his family on the first floor and the cellblocks on the second floor. It's hard to believe this arrangement served the county until 1982. Some of the antique furniture includes a rope bed, spinning wheel, and crib. $3.

MUSEUMS 🔶 𝒞 ♿ **Bartow History Museum** (770-382-3818; www.bartowhistory museum.org), 4 East Church Street, Cartersville. Open 10–5 Tuesday–Saturday (Thursday until 8), 1–5 Sunday. The museum, a site on Georgia's **Blue and Gray Trail,** preserves the cultural, industrial, and agricultural heritage of the county. Displays follow the footsteps of the Cherokee, march with Civil War soldiers, and visit a 20th-century dentist's office. Trade, politics, and transportation are examined through artifacts, archival material, and oral histories from pioneer settlements to the early 20th century. Adults $5.50, seniors and students $4.50, active military free.

🔶 𝒞 ♿ **Booth Western Art Museum** (770-387-1300; www.boothmuseum.org), 501 Museum Drive, Cartersville. Open 10–5 Tuesday–Saturday (Thursday until 8), 1–5 Sunday; tours at 1:30 daily; café open 10–3:30 Tuesday–Saturday. This stunning museum, the only one of its kind in the Southeast and the second-largest museum in Georgia, showcases contemporary Western art as well as Civil War art, presidential photographs and letters, and other items. The collection consists of paintings and sculptures by more than 200 of the 20th century's best-known Western artists—most of whom are still living. All U.S. presidents are represented by a painting or photograph and a typed or signed document in the Presidential Gallery. Another exhibit, *Illustration and Movie Star Art,* features Western movie posters. An orientation film, *The American West,* is shown continuously. The Sagebrush Ranch children's gallery features a replica of a stagecoach and a fiberglass horse youngsters can climb on; an artist's studio; a bunkhouse where they can dress up in costumes; "Tall Tales Barn," where they can watch vintage Western TV programs; a fully outfitted chuck wagon; and a puzzle corral, branding station, and barrel computer station. The museum's café serves sandwiches, salads, soups, chili, and desserts. Special events at the museum include the **Southeastern Cowboy Festival and Symposium** and **Cowboy Poetry Gathering** held each March and October (see *Special Events*). Limited number of wheelchairs available, and closed caption orientation film offered. Adults $10, seniors $8, students $7, active military and children 12 and younger free.

THE BOOTH WESTERN ART MUSEUM CONTAINS CONTEMPORARY WESTERN ART, PRESIDENTIAL PHOTOGRAPHS, AND MORE.

🐾 🦅 ♿ **Funk Heritage Center** (770-720-5970; www.reinhardt.edu/funk.htm), 7300 Reinhardt College Circle, Waleska. Open 9–4 Tuesday–Friday, 10–5 Saturday, 1–5 Sunday. Located on the campus of Reinhardt College and designated as the state's official Frontier and Southeastern Indian Interpretive Center, the museum is devoted to Native American history as well as the pioneer experience of early Appalachian settlers. The contemporary building was inspired by the Indian design of the Long House. Highlights include the Hall of Ancients, dioramas, interactive displays, artifacts, the Rogers Contemporary Native American Art Gallery, and the Sellers Gallery of Historic Hand Tools—thousands of tools from more than 100 crafts and trades from the 18th and 19th centuries. Visitors will want to see the films about Southeastern Indians and the Trail of Tears. On the grounds is a re-created 19th-century settlers village including pioneer log cabins, a blacksmith shop, and farm buildings, which are open only for guided tours and special events, and a nature trail. Adults $6, seniors $5.50, children $4.

🐾 🦅 **Lake Allatoona Visitors Center** (678-721-6700; www.sam.usace.army.mil/allatoona), 1138 GA Spur 20 at Allatoona Dam, Cartersville. Open 8–4:30 daily. A multimedia presentation and numerous exhibits tell the stories of Native American history and culture; the U.S. Army Corps of Engineers from its inception in the Revolutionary War; the Civil War, including the Battle of Allatoona Pass; the geology of Bartow County; and the building of Lake Allatoona. A short walk takes visitors to the Allatoona Dam overlook to view the dam and powerhouse. One of the other hiking trails—an easy, 0.7-mile trail that runs along a railroad bed once used by mining trains—leads to the **Cooper's Furnace Day Use Area** (see *Green Space—Nature Preserves and Parks*). The moderate, 1-mile Laurel Ridge Trail runs along slopes overlooking the Etowah River Valley. The museum is a site on Georgia's **Blue and Gray Trail.** Free.

ROSE LAWN MUSEUM OCCUPIES THE FORMER HOME OF 19TH-CENTURY EVANGELIST SAMUEL PORTER JONES.

🐾 ♿ **Noble Hill–Wheeler Memorial Center and Black Cultural Museum** (770-383-3392; www.noblehillwheeler.com), 2361 Joe Frank Harris Parkway, Cassville. Open 9–4 Tuesday–Saturday. This black history museum and cultural center is housed in the first school in north Georgia to be built with Rosenwald funds in 1923, which were specifically designated to be used for the education of African American children. Four special events are held each year. Free; donations accepted.

🐾 ♿ **Rose Lawn Museum** (770-387-5162; www.roselawnmuseum.com), 224 West Cherokee Avenue, Cartersville. Open 10–noon and 1–5 Tuesday–Thursday, 10–noon Friday. Samuel Porter Jones, a noted evangelist of the 1800s, lived in this now restored 1850 mansion, which today serves as a museum. It got its name because it was once surrounded by 200 rosebushes. The facility contains writings and memorabilia related to Jones as well as to Rebecca Latimer Felton, a Bartow County resident who became the first woman to serve in the U.S. Senate. Also on the property are a historic schoolhouse, a smokehouse, and a carriage house. Wheelchair accessible on the first floor. Adults $5, children 12 and younger $2.

✿ ✐ ♿ **Tellus Science Museum** (770-606-5700; www.tellusmuseum.org), 100 Tellus Drive, White. Open 10–5 daily. The museum, which features an extensive collection of minerals from Georgia and around the world as well as fossil displays and antique mining equipment, was built around the Weinman Mineral Gallery, which was considered to be the finest mineral museum in the Southeast. Gold and gemstones are still displayed, and youngsters particularly enjoy the simulated cave tunnel and hands-on exhibits. In recent years, however, the museum has morphed into a major science museum with numerous other exhibits, the Solar Decathlon House, and a planetarium. The Fossil Gallery features a full-scale cast of an apatosaurus dinosaur. At nearly 80 feet tall, it was one of the largest dinosaurs to ever walk in North America. Other ancient creatures include a sabertooth cat and the jaw of a megalodon shark. There's a Georgia underwater exhibit, as well as Science in Motion, which depicts changes in automotive manufacturing beginning in 1886 and features everything from vintage vehicles circa 1896 to replicas of the Apollo I capsule, a Mercury capsule, and Sputnik. The Collins Family My Big Backyard includes inventions, experiments, an interactive garden, and a walk-in tree. Outdoor activities include fossil hunting and gold and gem panning. Adults $12, seniors $10, children 3–17 $8. Planetarium shows $3 additional.

SCENIC DRIVES ✿ ✐ **Georgia Mountain Parkway Trail.** The 65-mile route stretches from Jasper to Hiawassee and includes Ellijay, Blue Ridge, Blairsville, and Young Harris. Along the trail are these nostalgic towns, beautiful scenery, wildflowers, apple orchards, antiques, galleries, seasonal festivals, and ample opportunities for outdoor pursuits such as camping, canoeing, fishing, kayaking, and white-water rafting.

✿ ✐ **Southern Highroads Trail** (706-633-6706; www.southernhighroads.org/georgia), headquarters mailing address: P.O. Box 1528, Blue Ridge 30513. This 360-mile scenic route goes through 13 counties in four states. The Georgia section stretches through eight counties from Blue Ridge to Clayton (see the Clarkesville chapter) and provides scenic beauty and Appalachian history and culture. Free.

✴ To Do

BICYCLING ✿ ✐ **Ridgeway Mountain Bike Trail** (U.S. Resource Manager: 706-334-2248), US 76/GA 282, Ellijay. Open daily. The 6-mile trail has advanced and intermediate sections to challenge riders of various skill levels. Trail use free; parking $4.

Ellijay Mountain Bike Association (www.ellijaymountainbike.org) recommends the Bear Creek Trail, the Doublehead Gap Ride, the 27-mile South Fannin Tour, and the 27.3-mile Tumbling Creek Loop.

BOATING ✿ ✐ **Toccoa River Canoe Trail** (chamber of commerce: 706-632-5680; 1-800-899-6867; www.blueridgemountains.com/toccoa_river_canoe_trail.htm), 3990 Appalachian Highway, Blue Ridge. A 17-mile class II river, its few rapids making it perfect for beginners, winds through the Chattahoochee National Forest with its beautiful scenery. Put in at Deep Hole Recreation Area on GA 60 South. Parking $5. Call for maps and suggested take-out points.

FARM TOURS ✿ ✐ **Apple Orchard Alley,** GA 52 East, East Ellijay. Open daily during apple season, August–December. Gilmer County is Georgia's apple capital. Eleven of the county's 18 apple orchards are along GA 52. Free.

✿ ✐ ♿ **Pettit Creek Farms** (770-386-8688; www.PettitCreekFarms.com), 337 Cassville Road, Cartersville. Open October–December; call for hours and admission fees. During

October, the farm offers the Pumpkin Pickin' Patch, where you can choose the perfect pumpkin for your jack-o'-lantern. During the second weekend of October, the **Pumpkinfest** arts and crafts festival is held. See a camel, zebra, Patagonian cavy, emu, ponies, buffalo, and a petting zoo with traditional farm animals. Beginning the day after Thanksgiving, you can choose your own Christmas tree, take a hayride tour of the farm, and enjoy a drive-through holiday lights display. Walk-about guided tour and a stop at the petting zoo to feed the animals: adults $10, children $8; a tour by pony ride: $25 (reservations required).

🐾 🐕 ♿ **Tanglewood Farms** (770-667-6464; www.tanglewoodfarmsminiatures.com), 171 Tanglewood Drive, Canton. Open year-round 10–2 Wednesday–Friday, 10–5 weekends (all days the last ticket is sold one hour prior to closing). Named one of Atlanta's best attractions by Turner South, *Atlanta Magazine,* and *Fodor's Around Atlanta with Kids,* this enchanting farm features a Wild West Town and 100 miniature farm animals to pet and feed. Set against a backdrop that includes an Old West bank, saloon, jail, trading post, mine shaft, and schoolhouse, the farm provides the opportunity for families to interact with child-size animals that aren't in any way frightening to young children: African pygmy goats, babydoll sheep, Shetland sheep, Nigerian dwarf goats, and miniature versions of cows, donkeys, horses, llamas, alpacas, pigs, and even Jack Russell terriers and Manx cats. As if being with these adorable animals isn't enough, visitors can participate in pony rides, hayrides, and panning for gold. Monthly events and riding lessons are offered, and in the summer months youngsters can participate in Cowpoke Classes (additional fees for riding lessons and Cowpoke Classes). Farm admission $10 per person for everyone age one and older.

FRUIT AND BERRY PICKING 🐾 🐕 ♿ **Hillcrest Orchards** (706-273-3838; www .hillcrestorchards.net), 9696 GA 52 East, Ellijay. Open September 1–December 31. In addition to pick-your-own fruit, the farm sells apples, cider, sorghum syrup, mountain honey, and apple butter. Activities include wagon rides, a nature trail, and a petting zoo. The **Apple Pickin' Jubilee** in September and October is packed with activities (see *Special Events*). Call for specifics. $5.

🐾 🐕 ♿ **Mercier Orchards** (706-632-3411 or 1-800-361-7731; www.mercier-orchards.com), 8600 Blue Ridge Drive/GA 5 North, Blue Ridge. Open 7–6 daily; pick-your-own apples 10–4 weekends mid-August–September; strawberries in mid-April, cherries in late May, and blueberries in mid-June. Mercier Orchards is one of the largest apple orchards in the Southeast. Since 1943, four generations of one family have been growing and selling more than 30 varieties of fruit, including 20 varieties of apples, as well as blueberries, blackberries, raspberries, and peaches. In addition, the property features a farmer's market that offers cider, jellies, jams, pickled okra, smoked trout, sourwood honey, and gift items; a bakery that produces apple cider doughnuts, apple bread, pies, cakes, apple dumplings, fritters, and fried pies; and a deli.

APPLES ARE THE STAR EVERY SEPTEMBER AT HILLCREST ORCHARDS IN ELLIJAY.

GOLF **Cobblestone Golf Course** (tee times and information: 770-917-5152, ext. 3; www.cobblestonegolf.com), 4200 Nance Road, Acworth. This course with seven holes along Lake Acworth is loaded with accolades: #1 Public Course in Georgia by *Golf Digest,* Top 100 Courses You Can Play by *Golf Magazine,* 2010 Best Municipal Courses by *Golfweek,* and four stars by

Golf Digest. $56.50–65 for 18 holes, $38–42 for nine holes, $10 for advance bookings of more than four days, and many other special rates.

HIKING ♠ ✍ **Allatoona Pass Trail** (Etowah Valley Historical Society: 770-606-8862), Old Allatoona Road, Cartersville. Open dawn–dusk daily. The 190-foot-deep pass was used as a railroad bed of the Western and Atlantic Railroad. A Civil War battle occurred here on October 5, 1864, and visitors can still see trenches and fortifications constructed by Union troops. Two and a half miles of interpretive signs explain the battle. Free.

♠ ✍ **Aska Trails** (chamber of commerce: 706-632-5680; 1-800-899-6867; www.blueridge mountains.com/aska_trails.html), 3990 Appalachian Highway, Blue Ridge. Open year-round. The Aska Trails area is a 17-mile hiking and mountain biking trail system through Chattahoochee National Forest lands near Deep Gap. Trail sections range from 1 to 5.5 miles, vary in difficulty, and run from the shores of Lake Blue Ridge to 3,200 feet in elevation. Free.

♠ ✍ **Benton MacKaye Trail** (www.bmta.org) extends nearly 300 miles through the Appalachian Mountains, part of it in Georgia beginning at Springer Mountain. The trail, which is rated strenuous, passes through some of the most remote backcountry in Georgia and crosses the Appalachian Trail several times. There are numerous access points and trailheads—including 16 in Georgia—which create many options for short or long, one-way or round-trip hikes. Permits are required only for backcountry camping. Free.

♠ ✍ **Riverside Park, Vineyard Mountain Trail,** Allatoona Dam Road, Cartersville. Open 8 AM–9:30 PM daily. Three difficult trails take hikers along steep slopes overlooking the Etowah River, Allatoona Dam, and Lake Allatoona. Free.

HORSEBACK RIDING ✍ **Adventure Trail Rides** (706-258-2276; www.adventuretrail rides.com), Blue Ridge. Open daily. The first ride leaves at 9:15, the last at 5:30 (earlier in winter). Call or consult the website for directions. Guided rides explore easy scenic trails, more advanced terrain, and steep terrain and winding trails suitable only for advanced riders. Special Fairy Cross and Sunset Rides are by reservation only. In all cases, please book at least 24 hours in advance. $30–45, depending on level of difficulty.

✍ **Blanche Manor Riding Stables** (706-455-RIDE or 423-496-1060; www.blanchemanor .com), office: 181 Deal Hollow Road, Blue Ridge. Call for hours. Guided trail rides wind through 350 acres in the north Georgia mountains and Copperhill, Tennessee. Hayrides, dinner rides, and bonfire rides are also available. Consult the website for directions because GPS units are often inaccurate. $30–50, depending on length; $10 for pony rides.

✍ **Mule Top Mountain Outfitters** (706-633-7055; www.mtmoutfitters.com), 319 Hells Hollow Road, Blue Ridge. Reservations required. Although there is one easy ride, most of these rides are not for the fainthearted—these adventurous rides are on steep trails with slow walking and tight turns. Consult the website for directions because GPS units are often inaccurate. $35–40.

MINIATURE GOLF ♠ ✍ ♿ **Gilmer Golf and Games** (706-847-9338), 7286 GA 515 North, Ellijay. Open 4–8 Friday, 1–8 Saturday, 1–6 Sunday, March 1–October. In addition to miniature golf, the facility offers indoor batting cages and video game rooms. $5.75–8.75.

TRAIN EXCURSIONS ✍ **Blue Ridge Scenic Railway** (706-632-9833 or 1-800-934-1898; www.brscenic.com), 241 Depot Street, Blue Ridge. Call for schedule. Generally the train doesn't operate from January to mid-March. The nostalgic train, which winds 26 miles through rolling hills alongside the Toccoa River to McCaysville, Georgia/Copperhill, Tennessee, has both open and closed cars. The layover in McCaysville allows time for lunch or shopping, but usually not both. Weekends in December, the railway offers the **Blue Ridge Scenic Railway Santa Express,** which includes visits from Santa and Mrs. Claus and the elves, Christmas stories, and caroling. Reservations are highly recommended, especially during leaf season and for the Santa Express. Rail and Raft tours are also provided. Call for more information. Adults $27–42, seniors $22–36, children 2–12 $14–22.

WHITE-WATER RAFTING ✒ Call the **Fannin County Welcome Center** (706-632-5680 or 1-800-899-6867) for information about experienced guides and outfitters.

✳ Green Space
GARDENS ✒ ♿ **Gibbs Gardens** (770-893-1880; www.gibbsgardens.com), 1998 Gibbs Drive, Ball Ground. Open 9:30–5 Thursday–Sunday, March–November; last entrance at 4. One of the most anticipated events in years was the March 1, 2012, opening of Gibbs Gardens, the largest residential estate garden in the country. The brainchild of Jim Gibbs, founder and retired president of the award-winning Gibbs Landscape Company, the gardens are the culmination of more than 30 years' preparation. Gibbs traveled the world for 15 years visiting gardens to get ideas. He spent six years looking for the ideal location and found 292 acres of rolling hills, streams, and springs here in north Georgia. He built his home in 1980 and started on the gardens. Visitors enter the grounds through an allee of 120 Red Sunset maples backed by Leyland cypresses. Within the grounds are 16 garden venues that provide a changing palette every two weeks as new flowers and shrubs come into bloom. Twenty-four ponds, 32 bridges, and 19 waterfalls have been created. The gardens are full of superlatives—the largest Japanese garden in the country, the largest collection of waterlilies (140 varieties), and the largest daffodil display. The Manor House Gardens drop in seven terraces over a 150-foot change in elevation from the house to the Valley Gardens. Visitors will see ferneries, azaleas, dogwoods, mountain laurels, Japanese maples, hollies, willows, and oaks, to name just a few. A tram is available to take visitors around the grounds ($5 additional). Other attractions include the Arbor Café, an art gallery, and a gift shop. The paths are wheelchair accessible unless there has been a prolonged period of heavy rain. Adults $20, seniors and children $18.

LAKES This area is dotted with lakes, including the following listings as well as Carter's Lake, Dockery Lake, and Lakes Black Rock, Burton, Chatuge, and Conasauga.

🎣 ✒ ♿ **Allatoona Lake** (678-721-6700; www.sam.usace.army.mil/allatoona). In addition to water sports, the lake and surrounding land offer hiking trails, an interpretive center (see *To See—Museums*), and camping (see *Lodging—Campgrounds*). Free.

🎣 ✒ ♿ **Lake Acworth** (770-974-3112; www.acworthtourism.org), Acworth. Open daylight hours daily. The 90-acre urban lake offers numerous recreational activities (see *Nature Preserves and Parks*). The lake is stocked with channel catfish, largemouth bass, bluegill, redear sunfish, crappie, carp, and bullhead. Free.

🎣 ✒ ♿ **Lake Blue Ridge** (chamber of commerce: 706-632-5680 or 1-800-899-MTNS; www.blueridgemountains.com/lake_blue_ridge.html), located within the Chattahoochee National Forest, Blue Ridge. Formed by a Tennessee Valley Authority dam, the 3,290-acre lake's crystal-clear blue waters contain the headwaters of the Toccoa River, one of the state's most pristine rivers. Boating, camping, hiking, picnicking, and waterskiing are popular pastimes. Trout fishing is particularly popular with anglers, but the lake also contains bass, bream, catfish, crappie, perch, and other species. There is an overlook near the dam as well as a canoe and kayak launch below it. When water is released, the river provides class I and II float trips.

NATURE PRESERVES AND PARKS 🎣 ✒ ♿ **Acworth Beach, Cauble Park** (770-917-1234; www.acworthtourism.org), Beach Street, Acworth. Park open 7 AM–11 PM daily year-round; beach open Memorial Day–Labor Day. Boat ramps, two playgrounds, concession stand, trails, pedal boat rental (seasonally), fishing dock, boating (electric motors only), fishing (license required), designated swimming area (in summer), occasional outdoor concerts, and fireworks on special occasions keep families busy here. Admission free; parking $5 8:30–6 on weekends (cash only).

🦐 ♊ ♿ **Cooper's Furnace Day Use Area** (678-382-4700), River Road, Cartersville. Open 8–dusk daily, March–October. The site, which is on Georgia's **Blue and Gray Trail** at the base of Allatoona Dam, is the last reminder of the town of Etowah (now under the waters of Lake Allatoona) and Cooper's Iron Works. Mark Anthony Cooper sold the iron manufacturing facilities to the Confederacy in 1863, and it was destroyed by Union forces in 1864. The town and most of the remnants of the iron industry were lost when the man-made lake was created in 1950. A lone cold-blast furnace is the only memorial to the iron empire. Visitors can hike the nature trail to an overlook atop the dam. Free.

🦐 ♊ ♿ 🎪 **Red Top Mountain State Park** (office: 770-975-0055; visitors center: 770-975-4226; lodging reservations: 1-800-864-7275; www.gastateparks.org/RedTopMountain), 50 Lodge Road, Cartersville. Open 7 AM–10 PM daily. This popular 1,776-acre state park on the shores of 12,000-acre Allatoona Lake features a swimming beach, a marina, two boat ramps, two docks, boating, fishing, hiking, picnicking, tennis, and miniature golf (additional fee). The mountain, once an important iron mining area, is named for the soil's rich red color. Twelve miles of wooded hiking trails wind through the park. The 4-mile Hill Trail is for hiking and biking. A 0.75-mile paved trail behind the office is suitable for wheelchairs and strollers. A special attraction is the reconstructed 1860s homestead, which is used for heritage events during **Spring Time at the Homestead** and **Harvest Time at the Homestead.** The Mountain Cove Discovery Room features nature exhibits and ranger programs. The park also hosts many other special activities, including an **Iron Pour,** in which molten iron ore is poured at 2,800 degrees Fahrenheit. Accommodations are offered in cottages or at a campground (see *Lodging—Campgrounds* and *Lodging—Cottages and Cabins*). Parking $5.

RIVERS 🦐 ♊ The **Toccoa River** is a popular destination for tubing, canoeing, kayaking, and trout fishing. It flows into Lake Blue Ridge, then journeys down a wide valley known as the McCaysville Basin. Trout fishermen favor this area of the river. After the river leaves McCaysville, it becomes the Ocoee, a world-class white-water river and the site of the 1996 Summer Olympic Games' white-water events.

✳ Lodging
BED & BREAKFASTS
In Blue Ridge
Blue Ridge Inn (706-632-0222; www.blueridgeinnbandb.com), 477 West First Street. One of the oldest residences in Blue Ridge, the three-story Victorian-era inn features 12-foot ceilings, heart-pine floors, original hand-carved woodwork, claw-foot tubs, eight fireplaces, and a rocking-chair porch. Accommodations are in three rooms and a suite with private en suite baths, and three other rooms with private hall baths. Room decor is based on themes such as roses, Marilyn Monroe, sports, garden, cabin, lighthouse, and safari. A full country breakfast is included in the nightly rate. The inn is within easy walking distance of the Blue Ridge Scenic Railway depot, shops, and restaurants. No smoking. Not wheelchair accessible. $95–165.

In Ellijay
Martyn House (706-635-4759; www.themartynhouse.com), 912 Flat Branch Road. Glam Camping, or Glamping, on the model of *Tales of the Arabian Nights* is offered on this 18-acre private haven. Accommodations are in secluded colorful luxury tented sleeping palaces from India. The commodious interiors are a fantasy of brightly patterned silks, rich hues, European antiques, and fine linens. Each is situated on a platform with an outside deck and features electric lights and chandeliers, hot water, and composting toilets.

Vegetable, herb, and flower gardens add to the peaceful ambience. Two artist studios are open for exploration. Massages and body treatments are available ($65–140). Several times a year Farm to Table candlelight dinners with wine are offered ($80). $180 per night Sunday–Thursday, $220 per night Friday and Saturday. Closed December–March.

CAMPGROUNDS

In Acworth

🐟 ✒ **Holiday Harbor Marina, Campsites, and Resort** (770-974-2575; www.lakeallatoona.net), 5989 Groovers Landing Road. The campground offers 20 campsites as well as a camp store, restaurant, and boat rentals. Campsites $25. Seven waterfront cabins each offer a kitchen, living room with fireplace, dining room, two bedrooms, one or two bathrooms, a deck, and a courtesy boat dock. No smoking. Not wheelchair accessible. Cabins $100–170.

In Blue Ridge

There are numerous **U.S. Forest Service campgrounds** (706-745-6928; www.fs.usda.gov) in this area. Check on reservations and rates for all of them.

In Cartersville

The area has numerous **U.S. Corps of Engineers campgrounds** (678-721-6700 or 1-877-444-6777; www.sam.usace.army.mil/Allatoona/camping). Check on information, reservations, and rates for all of them.

🐟 ✒ ♿ ❦ **Red Top Mountain State Park** (camping reservations: 1-800-864-7275), located on Lake Allatoona, offers 92 RV and tent sites, as well as a yurt. Sixty-eight sites have water and electrical hookups; the remainder are primitive sites. One site is wheelchair accessible. The RV pull-through sites are not waterfront. $19–28; yurt $60. For more information about the park's amenities, see *Green Space—Nature Preserves and Parks.*

COTTAGES AND CABINS

In Acworth

See **Holiday Harbor Marina, Campsites, and Resort** under *Campgrounds.*

In Cartersville

🐟 ✒ ♿ ❦ **Red Top Mountain State Park** (cottage reservations: 1-800-864-7275) offers 18 fully equipped cottages—two of which are wheelchair accessible and two of which are dog friendly ($40 per dog; maximum two). $90–160. For the park's other amenities, see *Green Space—Nature Preserves and Parks.*

INNS AND RESORTS

In Ellijay

✒ **Whitepath Lodge Mountain Resort** (706-276-7199; reservations: 706-669-6900; www.whitepathlodge.com), 987 Shenandoah Drive. Enjoy gorgeous mountain views and manicured gardens at this retreat. Accommodations are in 14 two-bedroom villas with fully equipped kitchens, gas fireplaces, and private porches and decks. Swimming in the pool and lawn games are laid-back pursuits. Golf and tennis can be found nearby. No smoking. Villas not wheelchair accessible, although common room in lodge is. $140–240; two-night minimum on weekends; some three-night minimums at peak times.

In Jasper

🐟 ✒ **Woodbridge Inn and Restaurant** (706-253-6293; www.woodbridgeinn.net), 44 Chambers Street. Most folks come to the hostelry, named for the historic wooden bridge leading to the inn, for the gourmet dining in the restaurant (see *Where to Eat—Dining Out*), but you can stay here as well, relaxing and enjoying the Blue Ridge mountain views, the landscaped lawns, two ornamental fish ponds, and the swimming pool. Eighteen modern rooms are offered, each with private bath and with either one or two queen-size beds. $60–80.

✳ Where to Eat
DINING OUT

In Blue Ridge

✒ ♿ **Blue Orleans Bistro** (706-258-2275; www.blueorleansbistro.com), 224 West Main Street. Open for lunch Monday, Tuesday, Sunday; for dinner Thursday–Saturday. New Orleans comes to the north Georgia mountains. The casual eatery serves Cajun cuisine including old stand-bys such as jambalaya, po'boys, muffalettas, and étouffée, and more daring choices such as gator tail. Smoking on covered patio only. Wheelchair accessible from rear of restaurant. Lunch $8–13, dinner $12–27.

In Cartersville

🍴 🎵 ♿ **Appalachian Grill** (770-607-5357), 14 East Church Street. Open 11–9 Monday–Friday, 11–10 Saturday, noon–10 Sunday. On the historic square "under the bridge" (a highway overpass), this casual yet upscale eatery is eclectic in decor and cuisine as well as in its choice of background music. The ambience is warmed by stone and brick walls and aged wood, while music ranges from bluegrass to country to blues to light rock. Dinner entrées include steaks, prime rib, seafood, chicken, and pork. No smoking. Wheelchair accessible, but all seating is in booths, so wheelchair must be set at end of table. Reservations not accepted. Lunch $10–16, dinner $16–27.

In Jasper

🎵 ♿ **Woodbridge Inn and Restaurant** (706-253-6293; see *Lodging—Inns and Resorts*). Open 11–2 Wednesday, Saturday, and Sunday; 5–9 Tuesday–Saturday. Renowned TV chef Hans Rueffert offers scrumptious seafood, rainbow trout, filet, New York strip, tournedos, duck, and veal dishes. $16–24.

EATING OUT

In Cartersville

🍴 🎵 ♿ **The Four Way** (no phone), Main and Gilmer streets. Open 6 AM–3 PM Monday–Saturday. For more than 80 years, this restaurant has been serving Southern specialties and ethnic delights such as hamburger with gravy, fries smothered in gravy, and the world's sloppiest chili dogs, as well as burgers, fries, fried pies, and peach cobbler. A hungry-man breakfast includes sawmill gravy. Don't be put off by the sign that says THIS IS NOT BURGER KING. YOU DON'T GET IT "YOUR WAY." YOU GET IT OUR WAY OR YOU DON'T GET IT AT ALL. The service is friendly and efficient. Notables such as Harrison Ford, Ricky Schroeder, and

Robert Duvall have eaten here. When the eatery burned down in 1993, citizens from near and far rallied and raised money to rebuild it as close to the original as possible. Today it's as popular as ever. Lines are often out the door because there are only about a dozen stools at the famous red counter. Take-out might be a better option. No smoking. $4–10.

🍴 🎵 ♿ **The Village Porch Café** (770-386-3100), 25 North Wall Street. Open 10:30–3 Tuesday–Friday, 7:30–3 Saturday. Choose from more than 20 sandwiches, Italian sodas, and ice cream. No smoking. $4.50–6.50.

✳ Entertainment

The **Blue Ridge Mountain Arts Association** (706-632-2144; www.blueridgearts.com) sponsors seasonal exhibits and gallery tours, as well as Concerts in the Park in July and August and the Arts in the Park Festival on Memorial Day weekend and in October. Under the organization's umbrella is the Art Center, Galleries on West Main, open 10–4 Tuesday–Thursday and 10–6 Friday and Saturday.

MOVIES 🍴 🎵 **Swan Drive-In** (1-888-469-1955; www.swan-drive-in.com), 651 Summit Street, Blue Ridge. Box office open Friday–Sunday evenings. One of four remaining drive-ins in Georgia, the family-oriented Swan began operation in 1955 and continues to offer first-run movies year-round. Full concessions available. Adults $7, children ages 4–11 $4; cash only.

THEATER Blue Ridge Community Theater (706-632-9223; www.blueridge communitytheater.com), 2591 East First Street, Blue Ridge. Shows are usually Friday and Saturday evenings and Sunday afternoons. The volunteer group presents a full calendar of seven dramas, comedies, and musicals. Traveling shows perform here as well. The Sunny D Children's Theater Workshop offers a summer camp and a Christmas production. Check the website or call for a schedule of productions. Tickets average adults $20, seniors $18, students $11.

Grand Theatre of Cartersville (information and ticketing: 770-386-7343; www.the grandtheatre.org), 7 North Wall Street, Cartersville. Built in the 1920s and fully restored, the theater hosts a wide variety of performing arts events throughout the year. Call for a schedule of performances and ticket prices.

Legion Theater and the Pumphouse Players (770-387-2610; www.pumphouse players.com), 114-C West Main Street, Cartersville. Formed in the 1960s, the troupe of community players performs a variety of genres from musicals to Shakespeare. Call for a schedule of performances and ticket prices.

✳ Selective Shopping

Cartersville Historic Downtown Shopping District (CVB: 770-387-1357; 1-800-733-2280; www.notatlanta.org), One Friendship Plaza, Cartersville. The area contains more than 46 shops and 15 restaurants.

ANTIQUES You'll be captivated by **Acworth's** Victorian village–style downtown, where you'll find many antiques shops.

HISTORIC GRAND THEATRE, DOWNTOWN CARTERSVILLE

✳ Special Events

March: **Cowboy Poetry Gathering** (770-387-1300; www.boothmuseum.org). Held in conjunction with Cartersville's Booth Western Art Museum, the event features artists' presentations and workshops; art and history programs; a concert at the Grand Theatre (additional cost); children's activities; a poetry- and song-writing workshop; blacksmithing demonstration; chuck wagon and Dutch-oven cooking contest; Cowboy Church; Writing through Art Literacy contest; and banjo, mandolin, guitar, and fiddle contests. Included with regular admission: adults $10, seniors $8, students $7, active military and children 12 and younger free; see **Booth Western Art Museum** under *To See—Museums.*

September and October: **Apple Pickin' Jubilee at Hillcrest Orchards** (706-273-3838), 9696 GA 52 East, Ellijay. General hours 9–6 weekends, last three weekends of September and all the weekends in October (call ahead to be sure of dates and times). Pick all the apples you can shake a stick at, and visit the petting zoo. Milk a cow, watch live pig races, take a wagon ride, and enjoy live bands and cloggers. Kids also enjoy the playground and giant slide. History buffs enjoy seeing the stills in the Moonshine Museum and the 1900 farmhouse. $5; additional $3 petting zoo.

October: **Southeastern Cowboy Festival and Symposium** (770-387-1300; www .boothmuseum.org), Cartersville. Activities include cowboy poetry and music, a reenactment of the Gunfight at the OK Corral, chuck-wagon cooking demonstrations, Native American programs and dance, children's activities, Western fashion shows, artists offering everything from jewelry to bows and arrows to leather goods, a frontier camp with pioneer demonstrations, an Indian encampment, concerts, and Cowboy Church on Sunday. Admission the same as museum admission; see **Booth Western Art Museum** under *To See—Museums* and the entry for the **Cowboy Poetry Gathering** in this section; nominal fee charged for children's activities; concerts $5–25.

CLARKESVILLE TO CLAYTON

L ocated at the southern end of the Blue Ridge Mountains—so named for the blue haze that covers them year-round—this area is widely visited thanks to the Chattahoochee National Forest's hundreds of miles of trails, numerous lakes, mountain streams, and nature preserves. The region is a mecca for outdoors enthusiasts in search of mountain biking, golf, fishing, horseback riding, canoeing, kayaking, white-water rafting, camping, backpacking, and wilderness adventures. An abundance of waterfalls range from dramatic torrents to delicate cascades. Few are visible from the road or parking lots, so hikes—most of which are short—are required to get a glimpse of them. The scenery is spectacular, and local residents are friendly.

The area is also rich in quaint villages, historic country inns, country cooking and fine dining, and shopping for antiques, folk art, pottery, fine crafts, and handmade country pine furniture.

This region has a wealth of Native American history because north Georgia was the capital of the Cherokee Nation during the mid-1700s. Visitors enjoy stories, legends, and lore about that era.

Tallulah Gorge, one of the Seven Wonders of Georgia, is 2 miles long and 1,000 feet deep, making it second in depth only to the Grand Canyon. A testament to how ancient the area is, it is believed to have taken 250 to 500 million years for the river to cut the gorge to its current depth. The gorge has been attracting visitors for more than a century. A series of six waterfalls cascaded through the gorge but have been tamed for power generation. The Tallulah Falls Railway was built in 1882 to bring tourists to the area, making this the first tourist attraction in Georgia. Several large resort hotels were built, which unfortunately no longer survive except for the **York House,** which was built in 1896 and is still in operation. (See *Lodging—Bed & Breakfasts.*) In 1883 a Professor Bachman walked a tightrope across the gorge. Karl Wallenda repeated that spectacular feat in 1970. You may recognize the gorge from scenes in the movies *Grizzly* and *Deliverance.*

GUIDANCE When planning a trip to the Clarkesville area—including Alto, Cornelia, and Demorest—consult the **Habersham County Chamber of Commerce** (706-778-4654 or 1-800-835-2559; www.habershamchamber.com), 668 Clarkesville Street, Cornelia 30531. Open 8:30–5 weekdays.

To learn more about Clayton and the surrounding area—including Dillard, Lakemont, Mountain City, Rabun Gap, Tallulah Falls, and Tiger—contact the **Rabun County Chamber–Rabun Convention and Visitors Bureau and Welcome Center** (706-782-4812; www.gamountains.com), 232 US 441 North, Clayton 30525. Open 9–5 Monday, Tuesday, Thursday, and Friday; April–October open 8:30–5 weekdays.

To find out more about Toccoa, contact the **Toccoa–Stephens County Chamber of Commerce** (706-886-2132 or 1-877-4CURRAHEE; www.toccoagachamber.com), 160 North Alexander Street, Toccoa 30577. Open with staff 8–5 weekdays, with staff 10–4 Saturday, without staff 10–4 Sunday.

GETTING THERE *By air:* The closest airports to this area are in Athens; Atlanta; Greenville-Spartanburg, South Carolina; and Asheville, North Carolina. A traveler coming from any distance would almost certainly have to make a connection in Atlanta, so it might make more sense to fly into there and rent a car rather than taking all the extra time to make a connection into one of the smaller airports. In all cases, see "What's Where in Georgia" for airport, airline, and car rental information.

By bus: The nearest **Greyhound Lines** station is in Gainesville (see the Gainesville chapter).

By car: I-85 and I-985 running north–south near the area make access easy. The primary north–south route within the region is US 441.

By train: **AMTRAK** (1-800-USA-RAIL; www.amtrak.com), 47 North Alexandria Street, Toccoa. The Crescent, which travels from New York City to Atlanta and New Orleans via Washington, D.C., stops in Toccoa.

WHEN TO GO It's not unusual for the mountainous area to get snow or ice in the winter, although it rarely stays on the ground very long, but travelers should be aware of the possibility. Some campgrounds and other establishments that are geared to outdoor activities close for a few months in the winter or cut their hours back significantly, so it's best to call ahead to check.

MEDICAL EMERGENCY Call 911.

VILLAGES Clarkesville, in Habersham County, is a pleasant small town noted for bed & breakfasts and shopping for mountain arts and crafts. **Moccasin Creek State Park** is located nearby (see *Green Space—Nature Preserves and Parks*). A Civil War ironworks in the county produced guns and cannons for the Confederacy, which might have marked it for destruction as Union forces moved south, but it was spared when Confederate troops turned back the Union Cavalry near Currahee Mountain.

Clayton is world-renowned as the home of the Foxfire series, a collection of oral histories gathered by local high school students and published in magazines and books.

✳ To See

CULTURAL SITES ✿ ✐ ♿ **Georgia Heritage Center for the Arts/Tallulah Falls Gallery** (706-754-5989; www.georgiaartists.com), 11785 US 441 North, Tallulah Falls. Open 10–5 Monday–Saturday, 1–5 Sunday. The arts center promotes emerging Georgia artists. Changing exhibits in the Art Heritage Room and the opportunity to watch working artists bring back repeat visitors. The fruits of the labors of these artisans are for sale in the gift shop. Free.

HISTORIC HOMES AND SITES ✿ ✐ ♿ **Big Red Apple Monument,** 102 Grant Place, Cornelia. Open daily. Apples have been such an important part of Cornelia's economy since the early 1900s that town fathers erected a monument to the crisp, sweet fruit in 1926. The concrete apple weighs 5,200 pounds and is 7 feet tall and 22 feet around, making it the largest apple monument in the world. Free.

✿ ✐ **Traveler's Rest Historic Site** (706-886-2256; www.gastateparks.org/TravelersRest), 4339 Riverdale Road, Toccoa. Open 9–5 Saturday. Built in 1815 along the Unicoi Turnpike as the plantation house of James R. Wyly, it was later sold in 1833 to Devereaux Jarrett, the "richest man in the Tugaloo Valley." He doubled the size of the structure, and it continued as the centerpiece of his thriving plantation and was used as a stagecoach inn. Three generations of the Jarrett family lived there until the State of Georgia bought it in 1955. It has been named a National Historic Landmark. The structure features a 90-foot-long porch. Inside are antique furnishings of the period—many of them original to the site, and some made by local craftsman Caleb Shaw. $2.75–4.

MUSEUMS 🐿 🗡 ♿ **Foxfire Museum/Heritage Center** (706-746-5828; www.foxfire .org), 200 Foxfire Lane, Mountain City. Open 8:30–4:30 Monday–Saturday. Dedicated to the heritage and culture of the Appalachian Mountains, the museum displays many examples of the resilience of the area's early settlers. Visitors can experience Southern Appalachia as documented, photographed, and recorded by the students of Rabun County over the past four decades and shared with the world through their student-produced *Foxfire Magazine* and Foxfire book series. The magazine began in 1966 as an attempt to engage high school English students and increase their interest in learning. In 1972, an anthology of magazine articles was published as the first Foxfire book. Twelve more books and counting have been published, with total sales of 9 million copies. Royalties from the books paid for the land and the acquisition or construction of more than 20 log structures that now comprise the Foxfire Museum. The site includes a gristmill, blacksmith shop, church, and several single- and multiroom cabins. A wagon collection is another treat. Self-guided tours for visitors focus on artifacts such as tools and crafts displayed in and around the cabins. Adults $6, seniors $5, children 7–10 $3, children six and younger free.

🐿 🗡 ♿ **Johnny Mize Athletic Center and Museum** (706-778-3000; www.piedmont.edu), 280 Laurel Avenue, Demorest. Open 6 AM–10 PM Monday–Friday when school is in session; also open when there are sporting events. The museum, located on the campus of Piedmont College, is named for native son Johnny Mize (1913–1983), who returned to Demorest after his career and induction into the Baseball Hall of Fame. The former Piedmont College baseball player, nicknamed "The Big Cat," was known for batting left and throwing right. He played for the Cardinals, Giants, and Yankees between 1936 and 1953, and held numerous records, including hitting three homers in a game six times. The small museum features memorabilia from his career. Free.

🐿 🗡 ♿ **Loudermilk Boarding House Museum** (706-778-2001; www.jonimabe.com), 271 Foreacre Street, Cornelia. Open 10–5 Friday and Saturday beginning in early May. Joni Mabe is so enthralled—dare we say obsessed?—with Elvis Presley, she has amassed 30,000 items associated with the King of Rock and Roll. Her collection, dubbed Joni Mabe's Panoramic Encyclopedia of Everything Elvis, toured the world for 14 years before it finally found a permanent home in 2000 on the third floor of Mabe's great-grandparents' circa 1908 boardinghouse in Cornelia. Mabe professes to have been collecting since Elvis died in 1977. Among all the photos, newspaper and magazine articles, souvenirs, and books about the King are some particularly special pieces. She has a vial that purportedly contains Elvis sweat and a toenail she personally picked up from the carpet of the Jungle Room at Graceland. Even Mabe admits that the authenticity of these artifacts is iffy. Her prize possession, however, is a wart removed

What is foxfire? Several species of bioluminescent fungi that grow on rotting wood in damp forests in warmer months emit a dim blue-green glow seen only in dark areas where there is no light from nearby streetlights and other modern illumination. Old-timers also called it "faerie fire" and "will o' the wisp." Today the word *Foxfire* is synonymous with the magazine and books, and is also the name of a method of classroom instruction.

from Elvis by his doctor. The gift shop stocks everything Elvis as well as Mabe's own artwork.
A highly anticipated annual event at the museum is the **Big E Celebration** honoring the
King's death. This is when visitors can see Elvis impersonators and eat his favorite peanut
butter and banana sandwiches or Moon Pies. Adults $5, children six and younger free.

SCENIC DRIVES ❧ ✿ **Scenic Highway GA 197** (www.scenic197.com). From
Clarkesville head north on Georgia Scenic Highway 197, part of the Southern Highroads
Trail, along which you can shop for antiques, herbs, gifts, and crafts; stop for lunch; fish or
wade in a creek; buy boiled peanuts; meander through gardens; have dinner; and spend the
night. Then slide down the famous sliding rock on Wildcat Creek, a headwater stream that
feeds into Lake Burton.

WINERIES ❧ ♿ **Tiger Mountain Vineyards** (706-782-4777 or 706-782-9256; www
.tigerwine.com), 2592 Old US 441, Tiger. Open 1–5 Sunday–Friday, 11–6 Saturday during
summer; 1–5 Friday–Sunday only remainder of the year. The 2,000-foot elevation, mineral-rich
soil, and well-drained slopes on this five-generation family farm combine to produce award-
winning wines—made entirely from Rabun County–grown grapes, including cabernet franc,
malbec, and cabernet sauvignon. Since 1999, the vineyard's six reds and one white have won
many national and international awards. Vineyard parties are scheduled in fall and spring, and
other special events occur throughout the year. Winery free; charges for some special events.

✳ To Do

BICYCLING ❧ ✿ The **U.S. Forest Service** (Chattooga District office: 706-754-6221;
www.fs.usda.gov) maintains several dirt or gravel roads that are suitable for recreational use.
Riding varies from easy to strenuous. Free.

FISHING River North Fly Fishing (404-403-2808; www.rivernorthflyfishing.com),
Clarkesville. Professional guides accompany anglers to some of north Georgia's best fast-
water, deep-hole fly-fishing. Reservations must be made and confirmed in advance. A typical
day might cost $110–180 (gratuity and flies not included), but call for hours and fees.

GOLF Kingwood Country Club and Resort (706-212-4100 or 1-866-KINGWOOD;
www.kingwoodresort.com), 4966 Country Club Drive, Clayton. Open daylight hours in summer (carts must be back by 7:30); 12:30 or 1–dusk in winter (some holes may not be playable
in winter if ground is frozen). Dramatic changes in elevation make this 18-hole, 6,016-yard,
par-71 course very challenging. Three tees for each hole accommodate any level of player.
$42–49, cart rental extra.

HIKING Nearby hiking trails include Currahee Mountain, Broad River, Panther Creek,
Yonah Dam, Minnehaha, Bartram, and Coleman River. See also the **Chattahoochee
National Forest, Moccasin Creek State Park,** and **Tallulah Gorge State Park** under
Green Space—Nature Preserves and Parks.

HORSEBACK RIDING ✿ **Dillard House Stables** (706-746-2038; 706-782-5630 after
hours; www.dillardhousestables.com), Old Dillard Road, Dillard. Open 9–5 daily by reservation;
rides go out 9–4:30. Off season there are no scheduled times for rides, but rides can be arranged
by advance reservation. The stable offers many different kinds of rides: 30-minute and one-hour
farm rides, one-hour river rides, one-and-a-half-hour trail rides, children's ring rides, and all-day
Chattooga wilderness rides. Lessons are also available. $25–60; $10 for ring rides.

✿ **Sunburst Stables** (706-947-7433 or 1-800-806-1953; www.sunburststables.com), 3181 GA
255, Clarkesville. Open 10–4 daily; rides at 10, 1, and 3 (closed Tuesday in February and

March). Take a group trail ride or enjoy a private lesson in the Chattahoochee National Forest. The company also offers overnight rides of up to four days, summer camps, camping facilities, and several cabins—one with a hot tub to soak your weary bones after a day of riding ($119–125 per night). $40–100.

OFF-ROAD RIDING 🐾 ✍ **Locust Stake ORV Area** (U.S. Forest Service: 706-754-6221; www.fs.usda.gov), Locust Stake Road, Toccoa. The Forest Service offers several off-road riding experiences. Locust Stake, located near the north fork of the Broad River west of Toccoa, provides 9.4 miles of trails for two-, three-, and four-wheel vehicles. Designated trails range from easy to extremely difficult. Users must stay on signed trails to prevent damage to the area. $5.

SPAS ⚹ **Spa at Kingwood Country Club and Resort** (spa: 706-212-4125; 1-866-KINGWOOD; www.kingwoodresort.com), 401 Country Club Road, Clayton. Open 7 AM–9 PM daily, May 1–October 31; 7–7 remainder of the year. Services by appointment. The spa offers massages, reflexology, Vichy showers, mud wraps, facials, therapeutic treatments, manicures, and pedicures. There's a fitness center, pool, sauna, steam room, and whirlpools. $10 for use of the facilities; treatments $25–250.

WATERFALLS Several websites provide information about Georgia's waterfalls: www.n-georgia.com/waterfal.htm and www.georgiatrails.com/gt/Georgia_Waterfalls. *Note:* The rocks are deceptively slippery around these falls. Exercise caution, and don't get too close to the edge.

🐾 ✍ **Becky Branch Falls,** Warwoman Road, Clayton. Accessible daylight hours daily. This small, 20-foot cascade just five minutes from downtown is easily accessible by taking a short walk up a trail to a bridge at the base of the falls. The trail is a portion of the Bartram Trail. Free.

🐾 ✍ **Dick's Creek Falls,** off Sandy Ford Road, Clayton. Accessible daylight hours daily. A viewing area at the top of the falls permits a view of the 60-foot drop over a granite mound into the Chattooga River. Free.

🐾 ✍ **Holcomb Creek Falls and Ammons Creek Falls,** Hale Ridge Road, Clayton. Accessible daylight hours daily. Holcomb Creek Falls drops and flows over shoals for 150 feet, and Ammons Creek Falls has an observation deck. Other waterfalls in the Clayton area include **Angel-Panther Falls, Martin Creek Falls,** and **Mud Creek Falls.** Free.

🐾 ✍ **Minnehaha Falls,** off Bear Gap Road, Tallulah Falls. Accessible daylight hours daily. The waterfall is 60 feet high, and the 0.4-mile Minnehaha Trail leads to the base of the falls. Free.

🐾 ✍ **Panther Creek Falls,** Warwoman Road, Clarkesville. Accessible daylight hours daily. The 5.5-mile hike to the main falls means that it is seen only by those willing to make the 11-mile round-trip trek through hemlock and white pine forests and along steep, rocky bluffs. There are several smaller falls and cascades along the way. The trail is noted for its variety of wildflowers and ferns. Trout fishermen enjoy the stream. Free.

🐾 ✍ ⚹ **Tallulah Falls,** US 441, Tallulah Falls. This is actually a series of six falls that drop a total of 490 feet in 1 mile. They range in height from the smallest, at 16 feet, to Hurricane Falls, the tallest, which plummets 96 feet. You have to time your visit to a scheduled release by Georgia Power Company, however, to appreciate the full volume of the falls. For the great majority of the year, the power company diverts the water through a tunnel, and the various falls are a mere trickle. At full power, the river below Hurricane Falls attracts those who desire a white-water kayak or rafting adventure (permit required). Despite the lack of torrents of water, the view into the gorge from the top is spectacular.

🏕 ✎ ♿ **Toccoa Falls** (706-886-6831; www.tfc.edu), GA 17 Alt., Toccoa Falls. Open 8:30–6 weekdays, 8:30–5 Saturday, noon–5 Sunday, when school is in session. Located on the grounds of Toccoa Falls College, the 186-foot waterfall is 26 feet taller than Niagara Falls. In fact, it is one of the highest free-falling waterfalls east of the Mississippi. Visitors enter the property through Toccoa Falls Books and Gifts, located in Gate Cottage. Therefore, it is open only when college is in session (call ahead). A short, level path leads to the base of the falls. Visitors can enjoy the landscaped grounds as well as the gift shop and the Gate Cottage Restaurant, which offers a Sunday buffet. A monument is dedicated to the 39 students and others who lost their lives when an earthen dam broke in 1977. Adults $2, seniors $1.

WHITE-WATER RAFTING ✎ **Nantahala Outdoor Center** (1-888-905-7238; www .noc.com), Clayton. The center offers exciting guided white-water rafting trips on the Chattooga and Oconee rivers, as well as kayaking instruction, a range of paddling classes, adventure tours, and equipment rentals. The adventure extends beyond the river with mountain biking, hiking, lake kayaking, and more. Each adventure leaves from its own outpost. Prices vary by activity.

✎ **Southeastern Expeditions—Whitewater Adventures** (1-800-868-7238; www.south easternexpeditions.com), 7350 US 76 East, Clayton. The season runs March–October. The adventure company offers white-water rafting, canoe and kayak instruction, and overnight trips. Fees vary by activity.

✎ **Wildwater Rafting** (1-866-319-8870; www.wildwaterrafting.com), Clayton. Hours vary seasonally. The company offers rafting trips on the Oconee, Chattooga, Pigeon, and Nantahala rivers, depending on the season. Kayak clinics also are available, as are zip line canopy tours, Jeep tours, raft and rail trips, a ropes course, and a climbing wall. Meeting places depend on the activity. Fees vary by activity.

✳ Green Space

LAKES Georgia Power Company (706-782-4014 or 1-888-GPCLAKE; www.georgia power.com/gpclake or www.southernco.com/gapower/lakes/home.asp) operates several lakes in this area for power generation and recreation: Burton, Rabun, Seed, Tallulah Falls, Tugaloo, and Yonah. These lakes provide opportunities for swimming, boating, fishing, hiking, and picnicking. Some also have camping facilities. Most are open daylight hours daily, and most activities are free.

🏕 ✎ ♿ **Lake Burton** (706-782-4014 or 1-888-GPCLAKE), 4 Seed Lake Road, Lakemont. The most popular lake in the area, Lake Burton covers 2,775 acres, has 62 miles of shoreline, and offers a recreation area, marinas, a beach, a state park, and boat ramps.

🏕 ✎ ♿ **Lake Rabun,** Lakemont, is the second largest in a string of six lakes in the area and covers 834 acres with 25 miles of shoreline. Nacoochee Park is a popular recreation area, and there are also boat ramps, a beach, and campgrounds.

🏕 ✎ ♿ **Lake Tugaloo,** off US 441 North, Tallulah Falls. This small lake covers 597 acres and has 18 miles of shoreline, along which there is no development other than a

LAKE BURTON

campground. A boat ramp allows visitors to launch their own boats. Boats are restricted to less than 25 horsepower.

🐾 ♪ ♿ **Tallulah Falls Lake,** off US 441 South, Tallulah Falls. The small lake, which covers 63 acres, has a mere 3.6 miles of shoreline. It impounds the water that would have poured over the six falls on the Tallulah River. Along the shores is **Tallulah Gorge State Park,** where there is an interpretive center. The lake also offers a campground. Tallulah Point overlooks Tallulah Gorge.

NATURE PRESERVES AND PARKS 🐾 ♪ ♿ ☘ Black Rock Mountain State Park (706-746-2141; lodging reservations: 1-800-864-7275; www.gastateparks.org/Black RockMountain), 3085 Black Rock Mountain Parkway, Mountain City. Open 7 AM–10 PM daily (closed December–mid-March). With an altitude of 3,640 feet, this is the highest state park in Georgia. The 1,738-acre site, named for its sheer, dark-colored biotite gneiss cliffs, is located on the Eastern Continental Divide. Scenic overlooks provide spectacular 80-mile vistas of the southern Appalachian Mountains and four states: Georgia, Tennessee, and North and South Carolina. The park also offers a summit visitors center and fishing for bass, bream, catfish, perch, and trout on a 17-acre lake. A new fishing pier is handicapped accessible. Eleven miles of hiking trails, ranging in difficulty from easy to difficult, pass lush forests, cascading streams, small waterfalls, and wildflowers. This is a good place for canoeing and kayaking, but there are no rentals. Accommodations are available in cottages and at campgrounds (see *Lodging—Campgrounds* and *Lodging—Cottages and Cabins*). Parking $5.

🐾 ♪ ☘ **Chattahoochee National Forest** (district office: 706-754-6221; www.fs.usda.gov) spans 18 north Georgia counties and covers nearly 750,000 acres with more than 450 miles of trails, 1,600 miles of road, and 2,200 miles of rivers and streams—all of which provide endless opportunities for outdoor pursuits. The pristine, undeveloped forest is laced with wildlife management tracts, recreation areas, and scenic regions. Recreational activities include off-road riding, mountain biking, horseback riding, hiking, fishing, hunting, and camping. Access to forest free; some activities have fees.

🐾 ♪ ♿ ☘ **Moccasin Creek State Park** (706-947-3194; lodging reservations: 1-800-864-7275; www.gastateparks.org/MoccasinCreek), 3655 GA 197 North, Clarkesville. Open 7 AM–10 PM daily (closed December–mid-March). Moccasin Creek, a small park of only 32 acres, is located on the shores of 2,775-acre Lake Burton. Although the park is located in the north Georgia mountains, the terrain is relatively flat, which makes it ideal for children's bicycles and wheelchairs. The park offers a boat ramp, seasonal canoe rentals, a wheelchair-accessible fishing pier—for the exclusive use of the handicapped, seniors, and children—and RV camping (see *Lodging—Campgrounds*). Only children and seniors may fish in the stream. Hiking trails include the 2-mile Hemlock Trail and the 1-mile Non-Game Interpretive Trail, which has an observation tower. A Department of Natural Resources trout-rearing station is located nearby. Parking $5.

🐾 ♪ ♿ **Tallulah Gorge State Park** (706-754-7981; camping reservations: 706-754-7979; www.gastateparks.org/TallulahGorge), 338 Jane Hurt Yarn Drive, Tallulah Falls. Park open 8–dark daily; interpretive center open 8–5 daily. (See the chapter introduction to learn more about the gorge and waterfalls.) Visitors can hike several rim trails to overlooks to get a clear view of the 1,000-feet-deep gorge and the tallest of the falls, sheer cliffs, and rock formations. The more intrepid hikers can obtain a free permit (limit 100 hikers per day) to hike down into the gorge, and the brave can venture out onto the suspension bridge that sways 80 feet above the bottom.

RABUN BALD MOUNTAIN
According to Indian legend, the 4,690-foot mountain is inhabited by fire-breathing demon people. Even in the 21st century, campers and other visitors often report strange sounds in the night.

TALLULAH GORGE

Tallulah Gorge is one of the most spectacular chasms east of the Mississippi. Considered to be one of the Seven Wonders of Georgia, it is reputed to be the oldest gorge in the United States. It was carved over millions of years by the Tallulah River, which flows through Lakes Burton, Seed, and Rabun to join the Tugaloo River, eating its way through quartzite rock along the way. The 2-mile-long, 1,100-foot-deep chasm is second in depth only to the Grand Canyon. When the water is flowing freely (it is regulated by Georgia Power), six falls, the highest of which is 96 feet, plummet into the canyon. The company releases more water on the first two weekends in April and the first three weekends in November, at which time the river is suitable for advanced white-water kayaking.

Exhibits in the Jane Hurt Yarn Interpretive Center focus on the resort era, the rugged terrain, and the fragile ecosystem. An award-winning film takes visitors on a spectacular excursion through the gorge. The 2,799-acre park also contains a 63-acre fishing lake (see Tallulah Falls Lake) with a swimming beach, more than 20 miles of hiking and biking trails, a 1.7-mile paved Rails-to-Trails path, tennis courts, picnicking, and camping facilities (see *Lodging—Campgrounds*). Parking $5.

RECREATION AREAS The **U.S. Forest Service** (706-754-6221; www.fs.usda.gov) operates several recreation areas. Unless otherwise indicated, the recreation areas listed here are open daylight hours daily.

🐾 ✂ ♿ **Rabun Beach Recreation Area,** Lake Rabun Road South/County Road 10, Clayton. Open 7 AM–10 PM daily (until 11 on weekends), mid-April–end of November. In addition to swimming, boating, and fishing, visitors enjoy hiking and picnicking. Campsites also available by reservation (closed in winter). Day use $4; camping $14–24.

RIVERS ✂ **Chattooga Wild and Scenic River** (760-782-3320), US 76 East, Clayton. Accessible daily. With its headwaters at Cashiers, North Carolina, the river flows to the Tugaloo River and into Lake Tugaloo, dropping 0.5 mile in elevation on its route. It is one of the few remaining free-flowing rivers in the Southeast and offers spectacular scenery along its course past dense forests and primitive areas. It was used as the setting for the fictional Cahulawassee River in the movie *Deliverance*. Daredevils can enjoy a heart-pounding, wet-and-wild ride on class II to class V white-water rapids on this river, which extends 56.9 miles through the Chattahoochee National Forest. Of that mileage, 39.8 miles are designated wild, 2.5 miles scenic, and 14.6 miles recreational. From spring through fall, outfitters offer half-day, full-day, and overnight raft trips on Sections III and IV, which boast 30 rapids. No motorized vehicles are allowed within a 0.25-mile corridor on either side of the river. River access free; fees for activities vary.

✳ Lodging

BED & BREAKFASTS

In Alto

♿ **The Lodge on Apple Pie Ridge** (706-776-6012 or 1-888-339-1374; www.lodge onapplepieridge.com), 2154 Apple Pie Ridge Road. Skilled artisans took two years to transform old pine logs, local stone, and reclaimed wood into this handsome lodge on a wooded hillside. Although new, it is reminiscent of national park lodges. All rooms boast a private bath and a private balcony or covered patio. For a particularly romantic stay, choose the Royal Gala or the Braeburn room, both of which have jetted tubs for two. Outdoors, guests enjoy the mountain views and landscaped grounds, fields of wildflowers, herb gardens, grape arbors, and blueberry groves. An arrival snack, evening dessert, turndown service with chocolates, and a full breakfast are included. No smoking. One room wheelchair accessible. $149–259; multiple-night stays may be required during holiday periods.

In Clarkesville

✍ ♿ **Glen Ella Springs Inn and Meeting Place** (706-754-7295 or 1-877-456-7527; www.glenella.com), 1789 Bear Gap Road. Travel down a gravel road and leave the hustle and bustle of daily life behind. This historic inn, which was built as a private home in 1875 and expanded to an inn in 1890, is a member of the prestigious Select Registry, Distinguished Inns of North America (one of only nine in Georgia). Imbued with casual elegance, Glen Ella offers comfortable, handsomely appointed, rustic guest rooms and suites furnished with king- or queen-size beds, antiques, and locally handcrafted items. Each has a private bath, but TV is blessedly absent. Suites boast a whirlpool tub and a gas-log fireplace. All rooms open onto common porches well supplied with rocking chairs. The inn sits on 17 acres with formal gardens, meadows, woods, and an outdoor pool. In addition, the inn is well-known for fine dining (see *Where to Eat—Dining Out*) and a high level of personal service. A full breakfast is included. Beer and wine are served, but not on Sunday. No smoking. Some rooms wheelchair accessible. $150–275; two-night minimum required on weekends during high season; frequent guest discounts and last-minute specials available.

In Clayton

♿ **Beechwood Inn** (706-782-5485; www.beechwoodinn.ws), 220 Beechwood Drive. Recently inducted into the Select Registry, Distinguished Inns of North America, Beechwood Inn joins eight others as the only nine such honored inns in Georgia (four of them are in north Georgia). The 1922 inn offers rustic elegance on a mountainside overlooking Clayton and Black Rock Mountain across the valley. Seven guest rooms, each with private bath, are

GLEN ELLA SPRINGS INN IS CASUALLY ELEGANT.

filled with antiques and locally crafted primitive pieces, and offer queen-size beds with luxury linens. Most rooms boast a working fireplace and/or private balcony. Blueberry Cottage offers a whirlpool tub as well as a living room and a kitchenette. Guests enjoy relaxing on the porches or wandering in the lushly landscaped 100-year-old herb and wildflower gardens. A gourmet breakfast begins each day, and afternoon wine tastings also are offered. The inn, which has won a *Wine Spectator* Award, is known for its wine and food events, many of which include a four-course gourmet dinner (additional cost). No smoking. One room on first floor wheelchair accessible. Two-night minimum on holidays and in leaf season. Rooms $159–219, cottage $219–239.

In Lakemont

🦑 ✍ **Lake Rabun Hotel, Restaurant, Bar, and Marina** (706-782-4946 or 1-800-398-5134; www.lakerabunhotel.com), 35 Andrea Drive. The rustic 1922 hotel sitting across the road from Lake Rabun is surrounded by the Chattahoochee National

Forest. Until very recently the local historic landmark remained almost exactly as it was built, complete with wood-paneled walls and exposed beams, and rooms simply decorated with rustic furniture, most with shared baths. In 2008 the new owners upgraded the furnishings and decor in each of the eight rooms to include a queen-size bed and created a private bath for each room. The rustic charm has been retained, however. Televisions are located in the great room and in the bar, and plenty of board games keep guests entertained. An adjacent Innkeepers Cottage can be rented in several different separate configurations, from a single bedroom to a bedroom with living room or the entire cottage. A full breakfast is included, and the restaurant, which is open to the public, serves country cooking at other meals (see *Where to Eat—Eating Out*). The marina is 4 miles from the hotel and has a dock, as well as a bar that serves drinks and simple fare. No smoking. Not wheelchair accessible. Rooms $99–179, cottage $189–435.

In Rabun Gap

🐾 ♿ 🐾 **Sylvan Falls Mill Bed and Breakfast** (706-746-7138; www.sylvan fallsmill.com), 156 Taylor's Chapel Road. The mill was built in 1840 at the base of a 100-foot waterfall that powers it. The B&B's simple rooms—like those you might have found at your grandmother's house—feature private baths, and the Fireplace Room has a gas-burning fireplace. In addition to enjoying the waterfall, guests can wander through flower and herb gardens. A full breakfast is served. Before guests leave, they often stock up on freshly ground yellow or white grits, yellow or white cornmeal, and whole wheat or rye flour. Pets welcome. No smoking. One room wheelchair accessible. $115; two-night minimum preferred on holidays and during leaf season.

🐾 **York House Bed and Breakfast** (706-982-3023 or 1-800-231-9675; www.ga mountains.com/yorkhouse), 416 York House Road. The inn, tucked in a scenic valley and surrounded by hemlocks and pre–Civil War Norwegian spruces, has been

offering hospitality since 1896. Listed on the National Register of Historic Places, it is the oldest inn in Georgia to be in continuous operation. Each of the 13 guest rooms is furnished with its own individual style. Rooms feature private baths and entrances onto communal wraparound rocking-chair porches on both floors. Suites feature either a working fireplace or private porch. Full breakfast included. Kitchen available for guest use. No pets. No smoking inside. Not wheelchair accessible. $115–145.

In Toccoa

Simmons-Bond Inn Bed and Breakfast (706-282-5183 or 1-877-658-0746; www .simmons-bond.com), 130 West Tugaloo Street. The inn occupies a beautiful 1903 Queen Anne–Greek Revival home that is a showcase for original architectural details such as burnished oak paneling and beveled, stained, and curved glass. Graciously and sumptuously furnished rooms feature private baths and modern conveniences—most boast a working fireplace. Guests are cosseted with coffee and tea, and turndown service with a sweet. A large gourmet breakfast is served. No smoking. Not wheelchair accessible. $89–129.

CAMPGROUNDS For contact information and a description of the amenities at the state parks listed in this section, see *Green Space—Nature Preserves and Parks.*

In Clarkesville

🐾 🐾 ♿ 🐾 **Moccasin Creek State Park** (lodging reservations: 1-800-864-7275). The park boasts 54 tent, trailer, and RV sites. The campground is closed December–mid-March. $25–29.

In Clayton

The **U.S. Forest Service** (706-754-6221; www.fs.usda.gov) operates several campgrounds in the Chattahoochee National Forest. Check for information, rates, and reservations. These campgrounds are **Rabun Beach Campground,** Lake Rabun Road South; **Sandy Bottom Campground,** Forest Road 70; **Tallulah River Campground,** Forest Road 70; **Tate Branch Campground,** Forest Road 70;

and **Wills Knob Campground,** Wills Knob Road.

In Lakemont

🦎 ⚓ **Seed Lake Campground** (706-754-7079 or 1-888-GPC-LAKE; www.georgia power.com/lakes/seed-parks.asp), Crow Creek Road. Open seasonally. The Georgia Power campground offers sites for tents, trailers, and RVs; water and electric hookups; showers and restrooms; laundry facilities; and a dump station. There is a beach area, too. Small boats only. Tent sites $14, RV sites $16; reservations required 10 days in advance; two-night minimum.

In Mountain City

🦎 ⚓ ♿ ❀ **Black Rock Mountain State Park** (lodging reservations: 1-800-864-7275). The park offers 48 tent, trailer, and RV sites with cable TV hookups; 12 walk-in sites; 4 backcountry campsites; and the highest pioneer campground in the state. The campground is closed December–mid-March. $25–28; $15 for walk-in sites, $9 for backcountry sites.

In Tallulah Falls

🦎 ⚓ ♿ ❀ **Tallulah Gorge State Park** (camping reservations: 706-754-7979). Georgia Power Company, which operates the campground, offers 50 tent, trailer, and RV sites, and 3 backcountry Adirondack shelters ($13). $20–25.

COTTAGES AND CABINS

In Clarkesville

⚓ **Burton Woods Cabins and Lodges** (706-947-3926), 220 Brookwoods Lane. One- to four-bedroom cottages that accommodate 4 to 12 people are staggered up the mountainside near Lake Burton. All cabins feature fireplaces and fully equipped kitchens. The two- to four-bedroom cabins have dishwashers and a washer and dryer. For a family reunion or group of friends, accommodations are offered in a lodge with seven bedrooms, five bathrooms, and two kitchens. There's also a recreation building on the property, lawn games, and pontoon boat rentals. Ask about pets. No smoking. Not wheelchair accessible. $85–160; entire lodge $450.

⚓ ♿ **Chalet Village** (706-746-5348 or 1-800-541-0671; www.dillardhouse.com), 768 Franklin Street. Twenty-five A-frame chalets, each of which accommodates 2 to 10 people, offer fully equipped kitchens and several bedrooms and baths. Some have a whirlpool tub and/or a fireplace. No smoking. $99–179.

In Mountain City

🦎 ⚓ ♿ ❀ **Black Rock Mountain State Park** (lodging reservations: 1-800-864-7275). The park has 10 fully equipped cottages with fireplaces and screened porches. Two cottages are dog friendly ($40 per dog; maximum two). The entire park is closed December–mid-March. $125–145.

INNS AND RESORTS

In Clayton

⚓ ♿ **Kingwood Golf Club and Resort** (706-212-4100 or 1-866-KINGWOOD; www.kingwoodresort.com), 401 Country Club Road. Accommodations are offered in 48 lodge rooms as well as fully equipped two- and three-bedroom condominiums and rental homes. The condos feature two baths, a full kitchen, gas fireplace, whirlpool tub, a screened porch or deck, and a washer/dryer. The resort features an 18-hole golf course (see *To Do—Golf*); tennis courts; indoor and outdoor swimming pools; a fitness center with a Jacuzzi, steam room, and wet and dry saunas; and a spa (see *To Do—Spas*). Dining is offered in the main dining room, the **Back Porch,** and the **Fireside Lounge.** Guests enjoy a complimentary breakfast, and the inn also offers a Friday-night reception with live music and complimentary wine, beer, and hors d'oeuvres. No smoking. Lodge rooms $79–99, condominiums $225–250, rental homes $375; condos and rental homes may have two-night minimum stay.

In Dillard

⚓ ♿ **Dillard House** (706-746-5348 or 1-800-541-0671; www.dillardhouse.com), 768 Franklin Street. An outstanding place for a family escape, the 100-year-old working farm offers a petting zoo, tennis, swimming, horseback riding, a waterfall ride, an outdoor hot tub, two stocked trout ponds, volleyball, and horseshoes. Accommodations are offered in the Old Inn (the original Dillard House), as well as in chalets, motels, and cottages, some of which are at other sites. The chalets, which are at a 90-acre location 2 miles away, include small A-frames and chalets big enough to accommodate a large family reunion. Each chalet features a living room with a fireplace and a fully equipped kitchen, and some have a Jacuzzi tub. The Chalet Village has a swimming pool, outdoor hot tub, tennis courts, a trout pond, and hiking trails. Cottages, most of which have a fully equipped kitchen, sleep two to eight people. Motel-style accommodations include some whirlpool tub and fireplace suites, and some with a refrigerator and microwave. No smoking. Rooms at the inn and Rock House $59–179, cottages $79–219, chalets $79–239.

✳ Where to Eat

DINING OUT

In Clarkesville

♪ & **Glen Ella Springs Inn** (706-754-7295 or 1-877-456-7527; www.glenella .com), 1789 Bear Gap Road. Open 6–9 PM daily. Lunch buffets on Easter, Mother's Day, and Thanksgiving. The restaurant at this rustic inn (see *Lodging—Bed & Breakfasts*) has won numerous accolades from *Georgia Trend* magazine and *Southern Living*, among others. Exceptional cuisine features regional recipes and local ingredients to create a distinctive American Continental flavor with a touch of the South. Featured entrées might be created around trout, pork, beef, or lamb. All the desserts are homemade. The restaurant has a beer and wine license but cannot serve alcohol on Sunday. Reservations are strongly recommended. No smoking. $19–29.

In Dillard

♥ ♪ & **Dillard House** (706-746-5348 or 1-800-541-0671; www.dillardhouse.com), 768 Franklin Street. Open 7–10:30 AM and 11:30 AM–8 PM daily. Check the diet at the door when dining at this nationally

renowned, down-home, all-you-can-eat restaurant. There are no menus. Instead, generous portions of farm-fresh, mountain-grown home cooking like Grandma used to fix are served family-style. Expect country ham, country-fried steak, fried chicken, pork chops, a dozen vegetables and sides, and yummy desserts. You won't leave the table hungry. No smoking. Breakfast $14–17, lunch $18–23, dinner $20–25, $19.95 all day Sunday.

EATING OUT

In Dillard

♥ ♪ & **The Cupboard Café** (706-746-5700), 7388 US 441. Open 7 AM–8:30 PM daily. The restaurant serves breakfast all day, as well as a wide assortment of country favorites, including steak, barbecue, fried chicken, meat loaf, vegetables, corn bread, pastas, and homemade desserts. The café also has a gift shop that carries candles; wooden toys; homemade fudge, jams, jellies, and preserves; greeting cards; plush toys; recorded dulcimer music; wind chimes; and Christmas collectibles. No smoking. Breakfast $2–10, lunch and dinner $7–20.

In Lakemont

♪ **Lake Rabun Hotel, Restaurant, Bar, and Marina** (706-782-4946; www.lake rabunhotel.com), 35 Andrea Drive. Open in season (April 1–November 30) for brunch on weekends and dinner Wednesday–Saturday; off season dinner only Thursday–Saturday. The restaurant is presided over by a noted garden-to-table chef who describes his cuisine as having eclectic world-wide influences with a strong Southern twist. Dinner entrées run the gamut from fried green tomatoes to scallops to filet. Save room for dessert. No smoking. Not wheelchair accessible. Brunch $12–15, dinner $14–28.

✳ Entertainment

MOVIES ♥ ♪ & **Tiger Drive-In** (706-782-1611; www.tigerdrivein.com), 2956 Old US 441 South, Tiger. Check the website or call for hours. One of only a few nostalgic drive-ins still operating in Georgia, the Tiger Drive-In offers two-for-one showings of first-run movies on the weekends in season. An additional attraction is Hot Rod Night held the first Saturday June–November. Adults $7, children 4–11 $4.

MUSIC **Northeast Georgia Community Concert Association** (706-297-7121; www.negaconcerts.com), Toccoa. Call for a schedule of guest artists. The series offers national and international entertainment from early fall to late spring, including ballet and dance, national tours of Broadway shows, jazz, cabaret, and classical works by chamber orchestras and ensembles. Performances are held at the Tugaloo Center for the Performing Arts on the campus of Stephens County High School. Adults $20, children $10.

Toccoa Symphony Orchestra and Chorus (www.toccoasymphony.org). The symphony, which has been performing since 1976, presents concerts in December, March, and May at the Georgia Baptist Assembly's Garrison Auditorium, 462 Sunrise Way. Adjuncts of the symphony are the Toccoa Brass Ensemble, a string quartet, and the chorus, which perform throughout the year. Adults $7 in advance or online, $10 at the door; children $3 in advance, $5 at the door.

THEATER **Toccoa Stephens County Community Theater** (706-282-9799; www.tscct.org). Call for a schedule of performances. The group offers musical and nonmusical productions including Shakespeare, farce, comedy, and drama throughout the year at various venues, but primarily at the Schaefer Center for the Performing Arts in downtown Toccoa. Adults $10–15, children ages 8–12 $8–10; discounts for seniors.

✷ Selective Shopping
ANTIQUES ✐ **Old Clarkesville Mill** (706-754-1247; www.oldclarkesvillemill.com), 583 Grant Street, Clarkesville. Art and antiques mall open 10–5:30 Monday–Saturday, 1–5 Sunday; shops open 10–5

Tuesday–Saturday; bowling center open 10–10 Monday–Thursday, 10–midnight Friday, and noon–midnight Saturday. The 6.5-acre Old Clarkesville Mill is the perfect destination for shopping and family fun all under one roof, offering everything from art classes to bowling lessons. There are shops filled with art, antiques, discount books, clothing, pottery, furniture, and home decor, as well as a bowling center, billiards, and a video arcade. As if that's not enough, the Clarkesville Greenways Trail originates at the property and offers opportunities for hiking and biking.

Whistlestop Cornerstone Antique Market (706-282-1386), 202 North Sage Street, Toccoa. Open 10–5:30 Monday–Saturday, 1–5 Sunday. Shop here for antiques, collectibles, crafts, furniture, silver, glass, porcelain, and American pottery dating back to the early 1800s.

ART GALLERIES **Burton Gallery and Emporium** (706-947-1351; www.burtongallery.net), 150 Burton Dam Road, Clarkesville. Open 10–5 Wednesday–Monday, spring–fall; winter hours 10–5 Friday, Saturday, and Monday, and noon–5 Sunday. Representing the works of 350 artists, the eclectic gallery carries everything from fine art to folk art, as well as high-quality handcrafted items. Shop here for paintings, pottery, wood items, jewelry, and Amish pieces. Children enjoy the koi pond and waterfall.

Tallulah Gallery (706-754-6020; www.tallulahgallery.biz), 580 Tallulah George Scenic Loop/Old US 441, Tallulah Falls. Open 10–noon and 1–5 daily, April–December and winter weekends. The gallery, located in what was the "Milking Parlor" from when the school had an agriculture program, offers fine Southern art, including folk art, original paintings, pottery, raku, sculpture, fiber art, jewelry, and photography. Books and furniture can be found here, too. All proceeds go to the scholarship fund of Tallulah Falls School.

CRAFTS **Mark of the Potter** (706-947-3440; www.markofthepotter.com), 9982 GA

197 North, Clarkesville. Open 10–6 daily in summer, 10–5 daily in winter. Located inside the 1931 Grandpa Watts' Grist Mill on the picturesque Soque River, the shop purveys quality, handcrafted, contemporary artworks in wood, metal, pottery, and hand-blown glass. The mill has been restored and a deck added so visitors can get a better view of the falls and the huge native trout that come close to be fed.

FOOD Hillside Orchard Farms (706-782-0858 or 1-866-782-4995; www.hillside orchard.com), 18 Sorghum Mill Drive, Lakemont. Open 8:30–5 Monday–Saturday, 11–5 Sunday (check ahead for hours in winter). The roadside country store is filled with 600 products, including seasonal produce, jams, jellies, and other goodies in a jar; gift baskets; and fall decorations. You can pick your own blueberries in late June. The newest attraction is panning for gems at the indoor gem mine. Special events include a corn maze in the fall (it's haunted in October) and **Old Time Farm Day** on the second Saturday in May (see *Special Events*).

Jaemor Farm Market (770-869-3999; www.jamsjellies.com), 5340 Cornelia Highway, Alto. Open 7–6 Monday–Saturday, September–mid-April; 1–6 Sunday, mid-April–May; 7–7 Monday–Saturday, 1–7 Sunday, June–August. Jaemor Farms grows fruits and vegetables on 100 acres. The peach and apple orchards produce 30 varieties of peaches and 15 varieties of apples. The market specializes in fresh seasonal fruits and vegetables, as well as 150 jams, jellies, canned goods, pickles, relishes, barbecue sauce, cider, salad dressing, salsas, marinades, hot sauces, apple and peach products, Vidalia onion products, and more. The Pie Kitchen's homemade fried pies, other bakery products, and ice cream are famous in these parts. In addition, the market features handmade farmhouse furniture and pottery for the yard. From mid-September through early November, Jaemor Farm offers an 8-acre corn maze, a kiddie maze, farm slide, hand-pump duck races, and hayrides.

FURNITURE Amish Red Barn (706-754-8235), 6345 GA 17, Clarkesville. Open noon–3 Friday–Sunday. The store isn't located in a red barn but in an 1899 farmhouse. There is, however, a red barn with a silo on the property. Amish furniture, artwork, quilts, and crafts from Pennsylvania and Ohio are offered.

SPECIAL STORES Barker's Creek Grist Mill (706-746-6921), Betty Creek Road, Rabun Gap. Open noon–4 first Saturday of each month. The historic mill has been providing milling services since the 1880s. The current mill, which was built in 1944 on the site of an older mill, still produces and sells numerous products ground from wheat and corn. Miller Woody Malot, a physics instructor at the Rabun Gap–Nacoochee School, is from a line of millers stretching back to the 1750s. Students from the school work the mill on a regular basis to produce whole-wheat flour from hard winter wheat, buckwheat flour from Pennsylvania-grown buckwheat, and grits and meal from locally grown hybrid yellow and nonhybrid white corn. Speckled grits and cornmeal are produced from white "keener" corn. A 12-foot overshot wheel powers the mill and the two 16-inch flint/granite stones that do the grinding. If you bring your own grain to be ground, the miller charges one-quarter of what he grinds. The store also carries wool yarn produced by the Rabun Gap–Nacoochee School.

Goats on the Roof (706-782-2784; www.goats-on-the-roof.com), 3026 US 441 South, Tiger. Open 10–6 Friday–Sunday in winter, 10–6 daily in summer. We can just about guarantee that you've never seen a shop like this before. The roof of this rustic structure is covered with grass, and a herd of friendly goats climbs up on the roof to graze. Or at least that's the story. Other theories are that they have Santa Claus Reindeer Envy or that they're actually aliens trying to get as close to the sky as possible so they can be picked up by their mother ship. Kids get a kick out of feeding the goats by an ingenious contraption: They pedal a stationary bike that operates a conveyor belt that takes the Goat Chow food pellets to the roof. Oh, and by the way, inside there are Amish wines and cheeses, jams and jellies, fudge and candies, homemade dog treats, T-shirts and gag gifts, primitive furniture, outdoor furniture, other quality handmade furniture, and other gifts. Big Billy's Old Goats Deli serves sandwiches with names such as the Nanny and the Goatatarian. There's also an ice cream shop. Adults enjoy sitting on the porch with their ice cream while the human kids feed the goats. Also on the property is the Old Goat Mining Company, where you can pan for gems. Small fee for Goat Chow and gem panning. There's another location in Helen (see the Dahlonega chapter).

✳ Special Events

April: **Living History Days at the Foxfire Museum/Heritage Center** (706-746-5828; www.foxfire.org) features period costumes; activities of life in the 1800s, such as cooking, schoolwork, blacksmithing, church services, woodworking, and music; as well as a quilting bee and old-time children's games. Included in regular admission: adults $6, seniors $5, children 7–10 $3, children six and younger free.

May: **Old Time Farm Day at Hillside Orchard Farms** (see *Selective Shopping*). Young visitors enjoy the playground and can feed the goats and see a hog, ducks, turkeys, a cow, a donkey, and chickens in Grandpa's Barnyard. Grown-ups will be interested in the blacksmith shop and sawmill, as well as a moonshine still and old tractors. There's live music and hayrides. Free.

October: **Foxfire Mountaineer Festival** (706-746-5828; www.foxfiremountaineer .org). This festival, which honors the old-timers and the old ways of the region, features pioneer music, crafts and trades, contests, and games. Rides and animals to pet are on-site. A popular event is the scarecrow contest. $5.

November–December: **Toccoa Christmasfest** (706-282-3269). Held in late November and early December, the holiday extravaganza features the lighting of the tree, a festival of trees, a parade, and the arrival of Santa. Free.

DAHLONEGA TO HELEN

Although everyone has heard of the 1849 California gold rush, Dahlonega was actually the site of the nation's first gold rush 20 years earlier in what was then the Cherokee Nation in north Georgia. The rush caused the towns of Auraria and Dahlonega to grow and prosper, and a U.S. Mint was established in Dahlonega, where more than $6 million in gold was coined between 1838 and 1861. Even the domes of North Georgia College and State University in Dahlonega and the Georgia Capitol in Atlanta are covered with gold leaf mined in Dahlonega.

Although active mining stopped more than 150 years ago, it's believed that enough gold remains in the ground to pave the square around the Dahlonega courthouse 1 foot deep. These days, however, panning for gold is purely a pastime for tourists.

Dahlonega also serves as the gateway to the northeast Georgia mountains area, which contains many charming small towns with numerous attractions (see *Villages*) but which may be better known as an outdoors lover's paradise. Rivers, a national forest, recreation areas, wildlife management areas, and numerous state parks provide innumerable opportunities for trout fishing, horseback riding, tubing, white-water rafting, mountain biking, and hiking. The region has more waterfalls and wineries than any other area of the state, as well as a large selection of bed & breakfasts.

GUIDANCE When planning a trip to the Dahlonega area, contact the **Dahlonega–Lumpkin County Chamber of Commerce and Visitors Center** (706-864-3711 or 1-800-231-5543; www.dahlonega.org), 13 South Park Street, Dahlonega 30533. Open 9–5:30 Monday–Saturday, 10–5 Sunday. Pick up a *Dahlonega's Mountain Magic Self-Guided Auto Tour* brochure, which takes you through the Chattahoochee National Forest.

For more information about Dawsonville, consult the **Dawson County Chamber of Commerce** (706-265-6278 or 1-877-302-9271; www.dawson.org), 54 GA 53 West, Dawsonville 30534. Open 9–5 weekdays. The **Welcome Center** is located on GA 400 just north of GA 53.

To learn more about Cleveland, call the **White County Chamber of Commerce** (706-865-5356; www.whitecountychamber.org), 122 North Main Street, Cleveland 30528, also located in an old jail. Open 8–4:30 weekdays.

For information about Helen, contact the **Alpine Helen–White County Convention Center and Visitors Bureau/Welcome Center** (706-878-2181 or 1-800-858-8027; www.helenga.org), 726 Brucken Strasse, Helen 30545. Open 9–5 Monday–Saturday, 10–5 Sunday. Also, contact the **Greater Helen Area Chamber of Commerce** (706-878-1908; www.helenchamber.com), 1074 Edelweiss Strasse, Helen 30545. Open 10–5 weekdays.

GETTING THERE *By air:* Most visitors who plan to arrive by air for a visit to the north Georgia mountains will fly into Atlanta (see "What's Where in Georgia"). It would then be necessary to rent a car to reach and tour the area covered in this chapter. Visitors could also fly into Greenville-Spartanburg, South Carolina, or Asheville, North Carolina, but both those options would probably require a connection that would take more time than driving from Atlanta, and it would still be necessary to rent a car to drive to the area. To learn more about all three options, see "What's Where in Georgia" for airport, airline, and car rental information

By bus: The closest stop on **Greyhound Line**'s Georgia route is in Gainesville (see the Gainesville chapter). It would then be necessary to rent a car to reach and tour the destinations in this chapter.

By car: Access to this area is easy from Atlanta from I-85, I-985, and US 19/GA 400.

By train: The nearest **AMTRAK** station is in Gainesville (see the Gainesville chapter).

GETTING AROUND US 129 is another north–south route. GA 53 is the major east–west route. There is no public transit in the area and few taxis.

WHEN TO GO During the winter temperatures can be somewhat unpredictable. For example, in the course of a week, it's not unusual to experience a fairly warm sunny day, a miserably dreary rainy day, or a snowy winter wonderland. Be forewarned: The narrow country lanes can be severely clogged during the fall leaf season. Some campgrounds and companies that deal with outdoor activities close in the winter or severely curtail their hours.

MEDICAL EMERGENCY Call 911.

VILLAGES **Dawsonville** is considered to be the birthplace of auto racing in Georgia and is also the home of NASCAR legend and hometown hero "Awesome Bill from Dawsonville" Bill Elliott. The history behind auto racing actually begins in the mountains of north Georgia as local moonshiners transporting their illegal "likker" raced to outrun the federal revenuers who were chasing them to destroy their products and arrest them. The moonshiners tinkered with their cars' engines to maximize their speed and created better and better cars. One thing led to another, and soon legitimate races were being run by perfectly law-abiding citizens.

Helen, a replica of a Bavarian village nestled in the midst of the north Georgia mountains, is a curiosity. It's the place to go in north Georgia to shop 'til you drop. There are dozens of stores selling a wide assortment of merchandise—German products, of course, but also homemade quilts, candles, Christmas decorations, apparel, Georgia foods and nuts, antiques, bath and body products, gourd crafts, wines, pottery, silver jewelry, *Gone with the Wind* memorabilia, and so on. The list is endless. Start at one end of Main Street and see if you have the stamina to shop all the way down and all the way back. Don't forget to stop for snacks or meals in the numerous eateries along the way.

The **Sautee and Nacoochee valleys** have been established as an official historic district and named one of "the 100 Best Small Art Towns in America" in a book of the same name.

✳ To See

COVERED BRIDGES ☃ ♂ ♿ **Stovall Mill Covered Bridge** (www.georgiahistory.com), GA 255, Sautee. Accessible daily. A pull-over observation area allows a good view of the state's shortest clear-span covered bridge. Built in 1895 in the Kingpost design, it is only 33 feet long and one span wide. The original Queen post bridge had washed away in the early

1890s. The bridge was featured in the 1951 *I'd Climb the Highest Mountain,* starring Susan Hayward. Free.

CLEVELAND'S BABYLAND GENERAL HOSPITAL IS THE BIRTHPLACE OF THE CABBAGE PATCH KIDS.

FOR FAMILIES 🏛 ✎ ♿ **BabyLand General Hospital** (706-865-2171; www .cabbagepatchkids.com), 300 N.O.K. Drive, Cleveland. Open 9–5 Monday–Saturday, 10–5 Sunday. Fun is born at this museum–attraction–retail store dedicated to the Cabbage Patch Kids, the brainchildren of native son Xavier Roberts, which now number 100 million worldwide. The Travel Channel named it one of the Top Ten Toy-lands. Once located in a turn-of-the-20th-century medical clinic, the hospital has moved to an impressive new facility in the style of a grand antebellum plantation home located on 650 acres outside town. Those who visit the clinic can watch Kids being "born" from Mother Cabbages in the Cabbage Patch and placed in incubators. When the Kids are ready to be placed for adoption, LPNs (Licensed Patch Nurses) are available for consultations. Vignettes throughout the clinic show Kids in every aspect of play. Dolls are available

HELEN REBORN

The tiny hamlet of Helen was once a logging town. When the industry moved on, the village began to die. Residents refused to let that happen, however, and set about to find a way to revive the economy. What they came up with was quite innovative. Bavarian facades were put on the buildings, vendors of Bavarian-type merchandise were recruited to fill the empty stores, and German restaurants attracted diners from miles around. The concept has been so wildly successful that Helen is booming. The result may be a little hokey, with a theme-park or Disneyesque ambience, but everyone should visit Helen at least once. Many return again and again.

BAVARIAN ARCHITECTURE IN HELEN

for "adoption," and outfits and accessories are for sale (see *Selective Shopping*). Several special events occur throughout the year; just one is the **Easter Eggstravaganza** mega Easter egg hunt (see *Special Events*). Free.

🐾 ♂ ♿ **Black Forest Bear Park and Reptile Exhibit** (706-878-7043; www.blackforest bearpark.com), 8160 South Main Street, Helen. Open 10–7 weekdays, 10–8 Saturday, 10–6 Sunday. The park has a collection of live bears used to educate people about different species and their habitats. Visitors see several examples each of grizzly, Syrian grizzly, American black, and cinnamon black bears. The reptile exhibit features many large snakes, including all the poisonous snakes found in North America as well as lizards and spiders. Bear exhibit $5, reptile exhibit $1.

🐾 ♂ ♿ **Charlemagne's Kingdom** (706-878-2200; www.georgiamodelrailroad.com), 8808 North Main Street, Helen. Open 10–5 daily, except Wednesday. A small-scale version of Germany from the North Sea to the Alps has been created, with HO-scale railroads running on 400 feet of track through the 20-by-50-foot layout. Accurate topography, 300 buildings in alpine architecture, seaports, bridges, autobahns, towns, villages, lakes, rivers, and 800 figures along with sound effects lend authenticity. Marvel at the 4-foot-tall carved glockenspiel figures in colorful traditional dress as they dance to German music three times a day. Adults $5, children $2.50.

HISTORIC HOMES AND SITES 🐾 ♂ ♿ **Nora Mill Granary and Country Store** (706-878-1280 or 1-800-927-2375; www.noramill.com), 7107 South Main Street/GA 75, Helen. Open 9–5 Monday–Saturday, 10–5 Sunday. Nora Mill, an authentic working gristmill, was constructed in 1876 on the banks of the Chattahoochee River. The Fain family still grinds grain daily using the original French burr stones or the modern Meal Master stone grinding system and sells grits and meal as well as jams and home-baked pies. Free.

🐾 **Sautee-Nacoochee Indian Mound** (706-878-2181 or 1-800-858-8027; www.helenga .org), GA 75 and GA 17, Helen. Although this mound, believed to have been built by Native Americans between 10,000 and 2500 B.C., is located on the private property of the Hardman-Nichols Estate, it is clearly visible from both highways, and you can pull off the highway to photograph it. The mound is reputed to be the final resting place of two tragic lovers from warring Cherokee and Chickasaw tribes—Sautee, the son of a Chickasaw chief, and Nacoochee, the daughter of a Cherokee chief. They were reputed to have committed suicide when they couldn't marry. The Victorian gazebo, which sits atop the mound, was a much more recent addition.

MUSEUMS 🐾 ♂ ♿ **Dahlonega Gold Museum Historic Site** (706-864-2257; www.ga stateparks.org/DahlonegaGoldMuseum), One Public Square, Dahlonega. Open 9–5 Monday–Saturday, 10–5 Sunday. Literally located in the center of the historic town square, the structure in which the museum is housed was the original Lumpkin County Courthouse. Built in 1836 on the site of a log cabin, the courthouse is the oldest public building in north Georgia. The museum tells the story of the local gold rush and mining in Georgia through a film and exhibits, which include mining tools and equipment, gold nuggets (one weighing more than 5 ounces), and gold coins—all very well protected, of course. Second floor not wheelchair accessible. $3.50–6.

🐾 ♿ **Folk Pottery Museum of Northeast Georgia** (706-878-3300; www.folkpottery museum.com), 283 GA 255 North, Sautee-Nacoochee. Open 10–5 Monday–Saturday, 1–5 Sunday. Located at the **Sautee-Nacoochee Art Center** (see *Entertainment—Theater*), this museum contains an extensive collection of more than 150 rare pieces of folk pottery dating from the 1840s to the present. It is the only such collection in the Southeast. Activities at the museum include audiovisual presentations, programs, demonstrations by local potters, seminars, and special tours. Adults $5, seniors $4, children $2.

🐟 ✐ ♿ **Georgia Racing Hall of Fame Museum** (706-216-7223; www.thunderroadusa .com), 415 GA 53 East, Dawsonville. Open 10–4 Monday–Saturday, noon–4 Sunday. Racing cars and Bill Elliott memorabilia are sure to enthrall, while the Georgia Racing Hall of Fame recognizes the contributions of motor sports in the state. The hall of fame features items such as the first NASCAR trophy ever awarded, historic racing vehicles, and videos of memorable moments in racing history played in a replica of a drive-in theater. Adults $4, seniors $3, children 7–13 $2.

🐟 ✐ **Old Sautee Store** (706-878-2281 or 1-888-463-9853; www.oldsauteestore.com), 2315 GA 17 at GA 255, Sautee. Open 10–5:30 Monday–Saturday, noon–5:30 Sunday. Established in 1872, the original store served the community with general merchandise and was even the post office for the entire valley until the 1940s. In continuous operation since its opening, the original front portion of the store is reminiscent of an old-time country store, complete with old fixtures and merchandise from yesteryear in museum-like displays, but now visitors also can shop for special gifts, gourmet foods, fine jewelry, books, and Norwegian and other Scandinavian sweaters. Shoppers can also enjoy coffee and a bagel. Free.

NATURAL BEAUTY SPOTS 🐟 ✐ **Neel's Gap Lookout Point and Mountain Crossings Outfitters at Walasi-Yi Information Center** (706-745-6095; www.mountain crossings.com), 12471 Gainesville Highway/US 19/129, Dahlonega. Open 8:30–7 daily. The Appalachian Trail passes directly through this rustic center, which was built during the New Deal in 1937, the same year the trail was completed. This is the only covered section on the entire 2,100-mile trail. Outside, the overlook offers stunning views. You can buy hiking gear, maps, guidebooks, and picnic supplies, as well as homemade crafts. Employees make appointments to advise anyone who wants to make any length trip on the Appalachian Trail.

SCENIC DRIVES 🐟 ✐ **Russell-Brasstown Scenic Byway** (www.helenga.net/russell -brasstown-scenic-byway). This 41-mile windy scenic loop with hairpin turns stretches between Helen and Hiawassee, and reveals some of the most dramatic scenery in the state. It was awarded National Scenic Byway designation on June 15, 2000. Included in the route is Brasstown Bald (Georgia's highest mountain), the Bavarian-themed town of Helen, several wildlife management areas, the headwaters of the Chattahoochee River, and a section of the Appalachian Trail. Along the way several state parks offer an array of recreational opportunities such as hiking, camping, and fishing. Several highlights include **Anna Ruby Falls, Dukes Creek Falls, Raven Cliffs Falls** (see *To Do—Waterfalls*), and High Falls.

🐟 ✐ **Sautee-Nacoochee Valleys–Scenic 197–Southern Highroads Trail** (706-878-2181; www.southernhighroads.org). The Sautee-Nacoochee Valleys Association and the Scenic 197 Business Association have joined with the Southern Highroads Trail Association to create a special gateway loop route. Along the route visitors will pass pastures filled with cows and horses; beautiful mountain and valley scenery; special shops, some of them purveying fine arts and crafts; restaurants; and unique lodgings.

✳ To Do

BALLOONING **Balloons Over Georgia** (678-947-9866), Helen. Soar high above the north Georgia mountains for a bird's-eye view of the region. Call for schedules, prices, and reservations. A ballpark figure is $325 per person, with a minimum of two.

BICYCLING 🐟 ✐ **Woody's Mountain Bikes** (706-878-3715; www.woodysmtb.net), 457 GA 356, Helen. Open 10–5 Tuesday–Saturday, mid-March–November. Woody, a former Florida state mountain bike champion, operates a full-service mountain bicycle shop that provides sales, repairs, bike rentals, and escorted tours suitable for all skill levels over some of the 60 bike trails in the north Georgia mountains. Rentals include a bicycle, helmet, and, in some cases, return shuttle service. The $50 Gap Ride is the most popular for families. Reservations recommended. Call for prices.

BOAT EXCURSIONS ℘ **Appalachian Outfitters River Trips** (706-864-7117; www .canoegeorgia.com), 2084 South Chestatee/GA 60 South, Dahlonega. Open daily, June– August; Call for hours the rest of the year. Reservations are strongly suggested. Thrills and chills are guaranteed on half-hour to overnight guided canoe, kayak, and tube trips on the Chestatee and Etowah rivers. Canoes, kayaks, and rafts can be rented for self-guided excursions. Call for prices.

℘ **Wildwood Outfitters** (706-865-4451 or 1-800-553-2715; www.wildwoodoutfitters.com), 6865 Helen Highway, Helen. Hours vary seasonally, so call ahead. Guided and unguided canoe, kayak, and raft trips (class I and II) on four sections of the river are available, as well as rock-climbing instruction and camping. Equipment is also available for sale. Call for prices.

FARM TOURS ❧ ℘ ♿ **Bradley's Pumpkin Patch and Christmas Trees** (770-380- 3636; www.bradleyspumpkinpatch.com), 25 Lawrence Drive, Dawsonville. Open in the fall only; call for hours. Visitors can pick their own pumpkins to take home to create jack-o'- lanterns. They also can pick out fresh apples, gourds, and Indian corn, or even a Christmas tree in season. In spring the farm is noted for its daylilies. The gift shop carries jams and jellies, honey, apple cider, and other goodies such as local homemade quilts, handmade soaps, gardening books, and wooden toys. Free.

❧ ℘ ♿ **Burt's Farm** (706-265-3701 or 1-800-600-BURT; www.burtsfarm.com), 5 Burt's Farm Road off GA 53 East, Dawsonville. Open 9–6 daily, September–November 5. In the autumn, Burt's is a sea of colorful pumpkins, gourds, and Indian corn. Visitors also can watch corn being processed for popcorn, take a tractor-pulled hayride on weekends, and see talking pumpkin heads. The gift shop carries honey, cider, popcorn, and an array of autumn decorations. Farm visit free; hayride: adults $5, children younger than 12 $4.

❧ ℘ ♿ **Goofy Rooster Corn Maze** (706-878-1777 or 1-877-498-6294; www.goofy rooster.com), 7264 Highway 75A, Cleveland. Open Tuesday–Sunday, after Labor Day– Thanksgiving. Call for specific hours. The corn maze is haunted on evenings in October. Other fun activities include a swinging bridge, hayrides, a barrel train, and a fire pit for roasting marshmallows for s'mores. Combo ticket: adults $12, seniors $10, children $9; tickets for activities can be purchased separately: $3–8.

❧ ℘ ♿ **Uncle Shuck's Corn Maze and Pumpkin Patch** (770-772-6223 or 1-888- OSHUCKS; www.uncleshucks.com), 4520 GA 53 East, Dawsonville. Open Labor Day– Thanksgiving. Call for hours and prices. The challenging, intricate maze with 3 miles of trails and fun for all ages is created from a cornfield each autumn. In addition, the farm sells pumpkins, gourds, and Indian corn. On weekends prior to Halloween, ghosts, goblins, and witches take over the maze dusk–10 PM. Hayrides are also offered. Several ticket combinations include the maze, the haunted maze, and hayrides.

FISHING **Smithgall Woods State Park** (706-878-3087; www.gastateparks.org/Smithgall Woods), 61 Tsalaki Trail, Helen. North Georgia's premier trout stream, Dukes Creek, runs through this property and offers superb fishing opportunities. At this angler's paradise, catch- and-release trout fishing is offered on Wednesday, Saturday, and Sunday to a limited number of the public and daily for overnight guests. For those who do not want to fish, 5 miles of trails and 18 miles of roads wind through the property. Reservations required. Call for schedules and prices.

Unicoi Outfitters (706-878-3083; www.unicoioutfitters.com), 7280 South Main Street/GA 75, Helen. Open 9–5 daily in winter, 8–5:30 daily in summer. Located right on the Chattahoochee River at Nacoochee Bend, this establishment—the oldest full-service fly shop in north Georgia—is a must-stop place for fly fishermen or wannabes. The company offers fly-fishing and tying classes, as well as guided fly-fishing excursions. The fly shop, of course, stocks fly-fishing equipment as well as Orvis-endorsed clothing, gifts, and luggage. Call for class and excursion fees.

FOR FAMILIES ⚲ ✑ ♿ **Chestatee Wildlife Preserve** (678-864-9411; www.chestatee wildlifepreserve.org), 469 Old Dahlonega Highway, Dahlonega. Open 10–4 daily. The star of the show is Pippi the Zedonk. Her mom is a donkey, and her dad is a zebra. You'll see the resemblance to Pippi Longstocking as soon as you see her striped legs. Located on 20 acres, the preserve is the home of 100 animals, including white Siberian tigers, Bengal tigers, lions, Canadian lynx, servals, chimps, ring-tailed lemurs, capuchin monkeys, wolves, grizzly bears, and others. The sanctuary promotes preservation of exotic and domestic wildlife through education. Adults $10, children younger than 12 $5.

⚲ ✑ ♿ **Nacoochee Village** (www.nacoocheevillage.com). Phone numbers and addresses listed with individual entries. Located just a half mile south of Helen, the village boasts a variety of activities for the entire family, including **Nora Mill Granary,** a historic gristmill (see *To See—Historic Homes and Sites*); **antiques shops** (see *Selective Shopping— Antiques*); the **Nacoochee Grill** (see *Where to Eat—Dining Out*); a **paint-your-own pottery studio** (see *Selective Shopping—Crafts*); and a **day spa** (see *Spas*). Free.

GEM AND GOLD PANNING ⚲ ✑ ♿ **Dukes Creek Gold and Ruby Mine** (706-878-2625), 6145 Helen Highway/GA 75, Sautee-Nacoochee. Open 10–5 daily. Pan for gold and screen for gems or fossils. With so many choices, everyone from your future geologist to your future princess will be hooked. If you don't find the gem of your dreams, the mine carries gifts, 10–14 carat gold, gems and birthstones, Southwest Indian jewelry, sterling silver, and Navajo horsehair pottery. No charge for admission or parking. Individual buckets $8–18; family buckets $40.

⚲ ✑ ♿ **Gold 'n Gem Grubbin' Mine** (706-865-5454; www.goldngem.com), 75 Gold Nugget Lane, Cleveland. Open 9–6 daily. Visitors can try their luck panning for gold and gemstones. Between spring and fall you can tour the mine, too. Fishing and camping are also available (see *Lodging—Campgrounds*). Adults $15–25, children $7.50–12.50.

GOLF ⚲ **Innsbruck Golf Club** (1-800-642-2709; www.innsbruckgolfclub.com), 664 Bahn Innsbruck, Helen. Voted one of the best golf courses in the country by *Golf Digest,* Innsbruck was designed to challenge both the avid golfer and the enthusiastic novice. Amenities include a swimming pool, tennis court, and clubhouse. $30–40.

HIKING ⚲ ✑ **Appalachian Trail** (www.appalachiantrail.org). Always accessible. The southern terminus of the 2,174-mile footpath is at Springer Mountain. Access to the 78-mile Georgia section of the trail, the most hiked trail in Georgia, is via an 8-mile approach trail from Amicalola Falls State Park and from seven other spots between there and Bly Gap at the North Carolina border. The easiest access is at the Walasi-Yi Center, where the trail crosses US 19 north of Dahlonega. Free.

HORSEBACK RIDING ✑ **Chattahoochee Stables** (706-878-7000; www.chattahoochee stables.com), 2180 GA 17, Sautee-Nacoochee. Open 10–5 daily year-round, until 7 in the summer. Reservations suggested but not required. All ages can ride, and there are no weight limits. At this 143-acre ranch in the Sautee-Nacoochee Valley, you can have a *City Slicker* experience on one of these 3.5-mile guided trail rides, of which 1.5 miles parallel the Chattahoochee River. Riders enjoy lush scenery and perhaps see some wildlife. $30; $40 if a small child rides double with an adult.

🐎 **Gold City Corral and Carriage Company** (706-867-9395; www.goldcitycorral.com), 49 Forrest Hills Road, Dahlonega. Open daily. First rides leave at 10 AM, and rides operate every two hours until 6. Call for reservations. The company offers guided one- and two-hour rides down forest trails and scenic mountain back roads. Half-day trail rides with lunch included are also offered, as are chuck-wagon dinner rides and carriage rides. For the more experienced rider, try an overnight camping trip. One- and two-hour trail rides $35 per person per hour, children $32; half-day ride $150. Call for prices for dinner, carriage, and overnight rides.

🐎 **Sunny Farms North** (706-867-9167; www.sunnyfarmsnorth.com), 1332 Longbranch Road, Dahlonega. Call for hours. Riders see pastures and mountain trails on these one- or two-hour trail rides catering to all riding levels. Reservations required. $35 per hour.

MINE TOURS 🐎 **Consolidated Gold Mine** (706-864-8473; www.consolidatedgold mine.com), 185 Consolidated Gold Mine Road, Dahlonega. Open 10–4 weekdays, 10–5 weekends. Although the mine closed 100 years ago, it was the largest gold mine east of the Mississippi when it was operating. Guides take you 250 feet below ground on a tour of a massive underground network of tunnels where they explain the techniques used by early miners. Once back on the surface, you can learn how to pan for gold or gemstones. (Mine tour not wheelchair accessible, and participants are advised that open shoes or sandals are not permitted.) Adults $15, children 4–14 $9, including tour and gold panning; panning without the tour $6–15.

🐎 ♿ **Crisson Gold Mine** (706-864-6363; www.crissongoldmine.com), 2736 Morrison Moore Parkway East, Dahlonega. Open 10–5 daily, until 6 in summer. This mine, which began operation in 1847, opened as a gold-panning destination in 1970 and is operated by the fourth generation of a mining family. Georgia's only stamp mill, its century-old machine was used to crush rock so the gold could be removed. Visitors see other working mine machinery and can pan for gold or gemstones. Indoor panning is offered in the winter. Call for prices.

MINIATURE GOLF 👹 🐎 ♿ **Alpine Miniature Golf** (706-878-3328), 7914 South Main Street, Helen. Open 10–10 daily, March–November; weekends December–February (but call ahead). This quaint 18-hole course was designed to resemble a tiny Bavarian village. Children of all ages will be charmed by its miniature chalets and lodges. All the open areas are filled with gardens and flowers. Adults $8, children younger than 12 $7.

SPAS ♿ **Forrest Hills Mountain Hideaway Resort** (770-534-3244, 706-864-6458, or 1-800-654-6313; www.foresths .com), 135 Forrest Hills Road, Dahlonega. The menu of spa services offered here is comprehensive and unique. The facility offers everything from paraffin facials to reflexology to stone massage to full-body

A GOLD-PANNING DEMONSTRATION AT CONSOLIDATED GOLD MINE

massage. Couples also can enjoy private couples massage training. $95–250, depending on services. See also *Lodging—Resorts*.

&. **Nacoochee Crossing Wellness Center and Day Spa** (706-878-0036; www.nacoochee wellness.com), 35 Nacoochee Way/GA 255 and 17, Sautee-Nacoochee. Open 9–6 daily. The center offers acupuncture, reflexology, massage, yoga, and a wide variety of spa treatments and services. $35–135.

TUBING 🐾 ✂ **Cool River Tubing** (706-878-2665 or 1-800-896-4595; www.coolriver tubing.com), 590 Edelweiss Strasse, Helen. Open 9–6 daily, Memorial Day–Labor Day; weekends in September. Enjoy scenic one- or two-hour floats down the Chattahoochee River or try the water slide. $5.

🐾 ✂ **Helen Tubing and Waterpark** (706-878-1082; www.helentubing.com), 9917 GA 75 North, Helen. Open daily, Memorial Day–Labor Day. Float down the Hooch on one-and-a-half- or three-hour trips, or enjoy the water park's 14 slides, tubes, and lazy river. The facility also has a game room and gift shop. Tubing all day $8; water park: adults $15, anyone under 42 inches tall $10, children two and under free.

WATERFALLS 🐾 ✂ &. **Amicalola Falls,** 418 Amicalola Falls State Park Road, Dawsonville. See *Green Space—Nature Preserves and Parks*. Accessible 7 AM–10 PM daily. The star of this 829-acre park is, of course, the spectacular waterfall. In fact, *Amicalola* is the Cherokee word for "tumbling waters." With a drop of 729 feet, Amicalola is one of the highest waterfalls in the Southeast and is included in the Seven Wonders of Georgia. Visitors can drive almost to the base of the falls or to an overlook at the top to admire it without any strenuous exercise, but there is one trail that leads about halfway up from the bottom and another trail that leads partway down from the top. Exercise caution, because the rocky paths can be slippery due to spray from the falls. Parking $5.

🐾 ✂ &. **Anna Ruby Falls** (706-878-3455), Anna Ruby Falls Road off GA 356, Helen. Accessible 9–8 daily in summer, 9–7 daily in spring and fall, 9–6 daily in winter. Anna Ruby Falls is actually two falls: Curtis Creek and York Creek flow parallel to each other, then drop as side-by-side cascades. Curtis Falls plummets 153 feet; York Falls plunges 50 feet. A paved path leads to the base. In addition to the double falls, the area on Tray Mountain features hiking, picnicking, a visitors center, and a craft shop. The Lion's Eye interpretive trail, 0.5 mile round-trip, is accessible to people with visual and physical disabilities, and includes Braille signs. A trail from here leads to Unicoi State Park. $2.

🐾 ✂ **DeSoto Falls and DeSoto Falls Recreation Area** (Forest Service District Office: 706-745-6221; www.fs.usda.gov), US 19/129 North, Dahlonega. Accessible 7 AM–10 PM daily. Explorer Hernando de Soto scouted in this area in the 1500s, and a plate of armor reputedly was found near here in the 1880s; hence the name DeSoto was chosen for the falls. Because the elevation changes from 2,000 feet to 3,400 feet within a very small area, the streams that flow through the area plummet from the higher level to the lower in three separate falls dropping 35 feet, 90 feet, and 200 feet. Two can be reached by easy hiking trails; the third requires a strenuous trek. In addition to viewing the falls, visitors can enjoy camping, fishing, hiking, picnicking, and wildlife viewing at the recreation area. Free.

🐾 ✂ **Dukes Creek Falls and Recreation Area** (Forest Service District Office: 706-754-6221; www.fs.usda.gov), GA 348, Helen. Accessible 8 AM–10 PM daily. Dukes Creek Falls plummets 400 feet into a scenic gorge, which can be reached by a steep 0.5-mile trail. The path has a series of switchbacks, however, so it's not too strenuous. Despite its name, the falls are actually on Davis Creek at its confluence with Dukes Creek. An observation deck at the foot of the falls allows a beautiful view. The upper portion of the trail from the parking lot to an observation deck permits a glimpse of the falls from above and is wheelchair accessible. Free.

❦ ♂ **Raven Cliffs Falls** (Forest Service District Office: 706-754-6221; www.fs.usda.gov), Russell-Brasstown Scenic Byway, Helen. Open daylight hours daily. Considered to be the most unusual waterfall in the area, Raven Cliffs Falls results from water flowing through a split in the face of a solid rock outcropping. The falls drop 100 feet total: 60 feet behind the rock, 20 feet from the split to the pool, and 20 more feet to Dodd Creek. The 2-mile trail fords streams, climbs steep grades, and crosses a rocky bluff. $3 access fee.

WHITE-WATER RAFTING See **Appalachian Outfitters River Trips** and **Wildwood Outfitters** under *Boat Excursions.*

WILDERNESS SCHOOL ♂ **Medicine Bow** (706-864-5928; www.medicinebow.net), 104 Medicine Bow, Dahlonega. Call for a schedule of classes and fees. Classes for all ages in ancient skills and Native American lore teach students about man's unique relationship with the forest. Just a few classes include Wonders of Water, Plains Indian Sign Language, and Animal Tracking. There are parent-child weekends and summer camp, too.

WINERY TOURS ❦ ♿ **Dahlonega Tasting Room** (706-864-8275; www.dahlonega tastingroom.com or www.habershamwinery.com), 16 North Park Street, Dahlonega. Call for hours and fees. This establishment features reserve wines and a tasting facility, along with a shop that sells wine accessories, home decor, and gift items, and also has a wedding registry. Another tasting room is in Helen at 7025 South Main Street/GA 75.

❦ ♿ **Frogtown Cellars** (706-865-0687; www.frogtownwine.com), 700 Ridge Point Drive, Dahlonega. Tasting room open 10–6 Monday–Saturday, 12:30–6 Sunday; later hours in sum-mer. Tours and tastings available; group tours for 10 or more by appointment. This 28-acre vineyard produces 15 varieties of wine made with 100 percent Frogtown grapes. Many visi-tors prefer to skip the tour and get right to the wine. The facility also serves lunch Friday–Sunday and brunch some Sundays (see *Where to Eat—Eating Out*). Tours and tastings $15 for nine whites and rosés, $15 for nine reds; combo tasting $24.

❦ ♿ **Habersham Winery** (706-878-9463; www.habershamwinery.com), 7025 South Main Street/GA 75, Helen. Open 10–6 Monday–Saturday, 12:30–6 Sunday. One of Georgia's old-est and largest wineries, Habersham operates an outlet in Nacoochee Village just south of Helen, where visitors can sample wines and view the tank room, oak barrel room, and bot-tling line. A large gift shop features wine-related merchandise and gourmet food products.

❦ ♿ ✿ **Three Sisters Vineyards and Winery** (706-865-9463; www.threesistersvineyard .com), 439 Vineyard Way, Dahlonega. Tasting room open 11–5 Thursday–Saturday, 1–5 Sun-day, other weekdays by appointment; closed in January. The 184-acre vineyard boasts a rus-tic, laid-back, casual atmosphere. Children are welcome, and pets are permitted on the property, though not in the winery. Free; tastings $5–30.

❦ ♿ **Wolf Mountain Vineyards and Winery** (706-867-9862; www.wolfmountainvineyards .com), 180 Wolf Mountain Trail, Dahlonega. Open noon–5 Thursday–Saturday, 12:30–5 Sun-day. This boutique winery produces wines from 100 percent Georgia-grown grapes hand-picked at the 1,800-foot elevation north of Dahlonega. Enjoy the beautiful views, winery tour, a delicious lunch or sumptuous brunch buffet in the **Vineyard Café** (see *Where to Eat—Dining Out*), and delicious wines. A light lunch menu is also available weekends. Tour and tasting $30; tastings $10–20.

❋ Green Space

NATURE PRESERVES AND PARKS ❦ ♂ ♿ **Amicalola Falls State Park and Lodge** (park: 706-265-4703; lodge reservations: 1-800-575-9656; camping and cottage reser-vations: 1-800-864-7275; www.gastateparks.org/AmicalolaFalls), 418 Amicalola Falls State

Park Road, Dawsonville. Open 7 AM–10 PM daily. In addition to Amicalola Falls (see *To Do— Waterfalls*), there are other hiking trails, including an 8-mile access trail to the southern end of the Appalachian Trail and access to the 20-room **Len Foote Hike Inn** (see *Lodging— Other Lodging*), which can only be reached on foot. The popular park also features an interpretive center, weekend programs, a 57-room lodge with a restaurant, 14 cottages, and camping (see *Lodging—Inns and Hotels*, *Lodging—Campgrounds*, and *Lodging—Cottages and Cabins*). Parking $5.

🦌 ♂ **Chattahoochee National Forest** (770-297-3000; www.fs.usda.gov) spans 18 north Georgia counties and covers nearly 750,000 acres with more than 450 miles of trails, more than 1,600 miles of "road," and 2,200 miles of rivers and streams—all of which provide endless opportunities for outdoor pursuits. The pristine, undeveloped forest is laced with wildlife management tracts, recreation areas, and scenic regions. Recreational activities include off-road riding, mountain biking, horseback riding, hiking, fishing, hunting, and camping. Access free; some activities have fees.

♂ ♿ **Smithgall Woods State Park** (706-878-3087; lodging reservations: 1-800-864-7275; www.gastateparks.org/SmithgallWoods), 61 Tsalaki Trail, Helen. Open 7–6 daily. Once a private estate, this beautiful property offers trout fishing (see *To Do—Fishing*), hiking, biking, picnicking, and wildlife observation. Four miles of trails and 18 miles of roads allow hikers and cyclists to explore far afield. Several cottages of various sizes provide upscale accommodations (see *Lodging—Cottages and Cabins*).

🦌 ♂ ♿ **Unicoi State Park and Lodge** (programs: 706-878-2201; lodge reservations: 706-573-9659; camping or cottage reservations: 1-800-864-7275; www.gastateparks.org/Unicoi), 1788 GA 356, Helen. Open 7 AM–10 PM daily. Beautiful mountain scenery and a 53-acre lake bring families to this 1,050-acre park for outdoor pursuits. The park has a swimming beach, seasonal canoe and pedal-boat rentals, handicapped-accessible fishing docks, a ropes course, four lighted tennis courts, a softball and volleyball area, and various ranger programs that focus on natural, cultural, historical, and recreational resources. Hikers and cyclists enjoy 7 miles of scenic mountain hiking trails and 8 miles of biking trails. Especially popular are those leading to **Anna Ruby Falls** (see *To Do—Waterfalls*) and the town of Helen. Overnight guests can stay in the lodge (see *Lodging—Inns and Hotels*), which has a restaurant; in the cottages (see *Lodging—Cottages and Cabins*); or at the campground (see *Lodging—Campgrounds*). Craft lovers shouldn't miss the gift shop, which carries handmade quilts, pottery, and other local mountain crafts. Parking $5.

✳ Lodging

BED & BREAKFASTS

In Cleveland

🦌 ♿ **Lodge at Windy Acres** (706-865-6635 or 1-800-435-5032; www.thelodgeat windyacres.com), 16 Windy Acres Road. This comfortable retreat, located halfway between Helen and Cleveland, was built in 1988 specifically to be a B&B. There are five queen rooms with private baths and a porch or deck access. Other amenities include a library and game room, laundry facilities, a fireplace in the common area, and kitchen privileges. A full breakfast is included. Not for children or pets. Smoking outdoors only. Wheelchair accessible, but bathrooms not handicapped equipped. $75–85.

In Dahlonega

♿ **Cedar House Inn and Yurts** (706-867-9446; www.georgiamountaininn.com), 6463 US 19 North. This ecofriendly B&B offers two types of accommodations. The three charming white-pine-paneled rooms have queen beds, private baths, and private entrances. Guests are also free to enjoy the common living and dining rooms, as well as the patios and other outdoor spaces. From June through September, the facility also offers accommodations in two unique yurts (a domed canvas structure on a wooden base) in the woods. They are surprisingly luxuriously furnished. A bathhouse is nearby. No smoking. Rooms in main house wheelchair accessible. Not for children or pets. Rooms $115–135, yurts $135. Two-night minimum during festivals and leaf season. Reservations required Sunday–Thursday, recommended Friday and Saturday.

Historic Worley House Bed and Breakfast (706-864-7002 or 1-800-348-8094; www.bbonline.com/ga/worley), 168 West Main Street. Once a stagecoach stop, this 1845 home just off the square in Dahlonega now operates as an upscale B&B within easy walking distance of North Georgia College and State University. In mint condition and furnished with graceful antiques, it features cozy, romantic rooms, some with fireplaces, all with private baths. Full country breakfast included. Not for children or pets. Smoking outdoors only. Not wheelchair accessible. $129–149; all-inclusive packages available.

Lily Creek Lodge (706-864-6848; www.lilycreeklodge.com), 2608 Auraria Road. Experience a European-style getaway at this cozy and romantic lodge nestled on 9 acres in the woods. This three-diamond facility offers 13 guest rooms furnished with European antiques and art from around the world. The Tango Suite boasts a whirlpool tub and a separate shower. Amenities include arrival refreshments, large decks with rocking chairs, gardens and walking paths, a secluded swimming pool with a waterfall, an outdoor hot tub, a comfortable and relaxing tree house, a boccie court, and the lodge's great room, the perfect place for guests to meet new friends. A full breakfast is included. No smoking. Not wheelchair accessible. $104–199.

Mountain Laurel Creek Inn and Spa (706-867-8134; www.mountainlaurelcreek.com), 202 Talmer Grizzle Road. This special mountain getaway has six deluxe guest suites, all with two-person whirlpools, separate showers, private balconies, and sitting areas with a fireplace. Great mountain views and sumptuous breakfasts are just some of the inn's other highlights. If that's not enough, visit the **Oasis Day Spa** and enjoy a massage or skin treatment. No smoking. Not wheelchair accessible. $115–195 weekends; special weekday rates.

&. **Mountain Top Lodge at Dahlonega** (706-864-5257; www.mountaintoplodge.net), 447 Mountain Top Lodge Road. Relax in the beautiful 5-acre setting and enjoy the scenery from this private mountaintop location. Some of the 12 guest rooms in this facility boast whirlpool tubs and fireplaces. Additional accommodations are offered in the adjacent Hillside Lodge. Another unique amenity is a back porch with a sweeping view of the north Georgia mountains and valley below. A crow's nest with a telescope further enhances viewing opportunities. Full gourmet breakfast included and served on brightly colored antique Fiestaware. No smoking. $100–155.

In Helen

&. **Black Forest B&B and Luxury Cabins** (706-878-3995; www.blackforest-bb.com), 8902 North Main Street. This charming and quaint facility offers several lodging solutions, from charming individual rooms and suites to private cabins. Some feature a private entrance, gas-log fireplace, a heart-shaped whirlpool tub, and a refrigerator. Rooms have queen-size beds; suites feature king-size beds. The property boasts a waterfall and a koi pond. The full gourmet breakfast features European and specialty cuisine. Best of all, the B&B is located within easy walking distance of all the area's best attractions. No smoking. Rooms and suites $135–250, cabins $150–225.

&. **Lucille's Mountain Top Inn and Spa—A Luxury B&B Inn** (706-878-5055 or 1-866-245-4777; www.lucillesmountaintopinn.com), 964 Rabun Road. Experience mountain luxury at this deluxe facility. Rates include rooms with private baths (some with whirlpool tubs and see-through fireplaces), mountain or valley views, robes, and towel warmers. Located on 5 acres, the property offers badminton and croquet. A full range of services and treatments—including massages, facials, body polish, destress cocoon, and hand and foot treatments—are offered at the spa ($45–130). Children younger than 14 not permitted. No pets. No smoking. $129–194.

In Sautee

 ♿ 🐾 **Nacoochee Valley Guest House** (706-878-3830; www.letsgotobernies.com), 2220 GA 17. Besides three cozy, intimate rooms (one with a whirlpool tub and one with a fireplace), guests are treated to a full breakfast and use of the pleasant library, fireplaces, decks, and gardens. Outdoors, guests enjoy magnificent views of the Sautee-Nacoochee Valley and surrounding mountains. Pets welcome ($20 for a small dog, $30 for a large dog). No smoking. Limited wheelchair accessibility from patio porch. Two-night minimum on weekends and holidays. $161–184.

 🦪 **Sautee Inn** (706-878-8287; www.sautee inn.com), 2178 GA 17. Open April–Oktoberfest. This historic 1892 home features a wraparound porch on both floors with views of the Smoky Mountains, terraced gardens, and cozy and comfortable guest rooms with full-, queen-, or king-size beds. Baths are shared. The antiques throughout the inn are available for purchase, and a continental breakfast is included with each stay. The inn is within walking distance of several attractions, and on the property guests can enjoy a stroll through the pasture to a creek. Children welcome; pets not permitted. No smoking. Not wheelchair accessible. $95–175.

 🦪 🔍 **Stovall House Bed and Breakfast** (706-878-3355; www.stovallhouse.com), 1526 GA 255 North. This intimate 1837 farmhouse is located on 26 acres. The five guest rooms have mountain views in all directions. Each is furnished with antiques and has its own bath. A continental breakfast is included. Children welcome, but no pets. No smoking. Not wheelchair accessible. $100.

CAMPGROUNDS

In Cleveland

 🦪 🔍 ♿ **Gold 'n Gem Grubbin' Mine** (706-865-5454; www.goldngem.com), 75 Gold Nugget Road. After you've panned for gold and gems, found your treasure, and had it mounted (see *To Do—Gem and Gold Mining*), camp in this beautiful tent and RV campground. Tent sites are primitive, but RV sites have full hookups. Campground amenities include a clean log-cabin bathhouse. Fish for trout in the stream. There is also a studio apartment adjacent to the bathhouse that sleeps two (call for price and availability). Tent sites $18, $20 on river; RV sites with full hookups $28.

 🦪 🔍 ♿ **Leisure Acres Campground** (706-865-6466 or 1-888-748-6344; www .leisureacrescampground.com), 3840 Westmoreland Road. Open year-round. This campground offers both full-hookup pull-through RV sites and tent sites. Amenities include a camp store, swimming pool, playground, coin-operated laundry, modern bathrooms with hot showers, a game room, pavilion, fishing pond, and cool mountain stream. $32–36. Three-night minimum on holiday weekends.

In Dawsonville

 🦪 🔍 ♿ 🐾 **Amicalola Falls State Park** (camping reservations: 1-800-864-7275). The campground features 24 tent, trailer, and RV sites. $25–28. See also *Green Space—Nature Preserves and Parks.*

In Helen

 🦪 🔍 🐾 **Unicoi State Park** (camping reservations: 1-800-864-7275). The park offers 82 tent, trailer, and RV sites, as well as 33 walk-in sites. $29–35; walk-in sites $25. See also *Green Space—Nature Preserves and Parks.*

COTTAGES AND CABINS

In Dahlonega

 🔍 ♿ 🐾 **Bend of the River Cabins and Chalets** (706-219-2040; www.bendof theriver.net), 319 Horseshoe Lane. Located between Dahlonega and Helen, the cabins, chalets, and private homes are available year-round. Most have two to three bedrooms and can accommodate from 1 to 14 guests. Some of the units are even wheelchair accessible. Others are pet friendly. Priced for every budget; call for details.

In Dawsonville

🦌 🐾 ♿ 🐾 **Amicalola Falls State Park and Lodge** (cottage reservations: 1-800-864-7275). The park features 14 fully equipped cottages. Two are dog friendly ($40 per dog; maximum two). No smoking. Wheelchair accessible. $85–166. See also *Green Space—Nature Preserves and Parks.*

🦌 **Amicalola View** (706-265-8154; www .amicalolaview.com), 200 Sign Broad Gap Road. This lovely two-bedroom log cabin has a full kitchen, dining room, covered front porch, and private deck. Located next to the state park; the view of the falls is spectacular here. Smoking outdoors only. No pets. Not wheelchair accessible. $100; two-night minimum.

In Helen

🐾 ♿ **Smithgall Woods State Park** (1-800-864-7275). Scattered around the 5,555-acre property are five cottages ranging in size from one to five bedrooms and from fairly simple to grandly luxurious. Their isolation makes them particularly ideal for a romantic getaway, although the cottages with multiple bedrooms are suitable for family reunions or friends traveling together. Some whirlpool tubs. One-bedroom Laurel and Garden cottages $154–204; three-bedroom Creekside Cottage $304–404; four-bedroom Smithgall and five-bedroom Dover cottages $404–504. Two-night minimum on weekends. No pets. No smoking. Some wheelchair accessible. See also *Green Space—Nature Preserves and Parks.*

🐾 ♿ 🐾 **Tanglewood Resort Cabins** (706-878-3286 or 1-866-6343-1686; www .tanglewoodcabinrentals.com), 3387 Sautee-Nacoochee/GA 356. The rustic log cabins range in size from one to six bedrooms, all nestled on 75 wooded acres near Unicoi State Park and not far from Helen. In order to offer something for everyone, some cabins are geared toward families, and others are romantic (with hot tubs); some are rustic log cabins, but others are luxurious; some are very private, while others are pet friendly (under 25 pounds; $25 nonrefundable). No smoking. $109–259. One-time cleaning fee $35–125 in cash.

🦌 🐾 ♿ 🐾 **Unicoi State Park** (cottage reservations: 1-800-864-7275). The park features 30 fully equipped cottages. Three are dog friendly ($40 per dog; maximum two). No smoking. $90–139. See also *Green Space—Nature Preserves and Parks.*

INNS AND HOTELS

In Dahlonega

🐾 **Smith House** (706-867-7000 or 1-800-852-9577; www.smithhouse.com), 84 South Chestatee Street. Located in a house that was built as a family home in 1899, the Smith House has served as an inn and restaurant (see *Where to Eat—Eating Out*) since the 1920s. Some of the simple rooms are located in the historic house, while others are in an addition of more recent construction. The inn also features a swimming pool, and guests can pan for gold. The inn is within easy walking distance of the historic Dahlonega town square, attractions, theaters, and restaurants. No smoking. Not wheelchair accessible. $99–249.

In Dawsonville

🐾 ♿ **Amicalola Falls State Park and Lodge** (lodge reservations: 1-800-573-9656). The 57-room, four-story lodge features guest rooms and suites with private porches and breathtaking views through huge windows, as well as a restaurant that serves a buffet for breakfast, lunch, and dinner. Reservations essential during leaf season. No smoking. $55–180. See also *Green Space—Nature Preserves and Parks.*

In Helen

🐾 ♿ **Unicoi State Park and Lodge** (lodge reservations: 1-800-573-9659). The modern 100-room lodge features an all-buffet restaurant, conference center, and craft shop. Reservations essential during leaf season. No smoking. $75–135. See also *Green Space—Nature Preserves and Parks.*

RESORTS

In Dahlonega

♿ **Forrest Hills Mountain Hideaway Resort** (770-534-3244 or 1-800-654-6313; www.forresthillsresort.com), 135 Forrest Hills Road. Located on 140 acres adjacent to the Chattahoochee National Forest, this resort provides private cabins with an accent on romance. Whether styled as rustic, contemporary, or Victorian, each cabin is in a private wooded area. Luxury cabins feature a whirlpool tub for two, fireplace, and private deck. Accommodations are also offered in bilevel luxury suites and group lodges ranging in size from 4 to 16 bedrooms. Some include breakfast; others feature a kitchenette. Resort amenities consist of several dining rooms to cater to individual needs (including candlelit dinners in the Secret Garden dining room for couples only), massages, a day spa (see *To Do—Spas*), an outdoor pool, tennis courts, an outdoor hot tub, fitness center, nature trails, and riding stables. Excursions offered at Forrest Hills by Gold City Corral (see *To Do—Horseback Riding*) include guided trail rides, carriage rides, horseback riding, horse-drawn wagon rides, and half-day adventures. The property also boasts a wedding pavilion, a wedding chapel, and wedding gardens. No smoking. Rooms $149, cabins $149–199, group lodges $99 per room; packages available.

In Helen

✍ & **IGLS** (pronounced "eagles") **Villas at Innsbruck** (706-878-2400 or 1-800-204-3536; www.innsbruckresort.com), 98 Schwarzwald Strasse. Three-bedroom villas contain modern comforts such as kitchen and a fireplace or a whirlpool tub. Recreational facilities include an 18-hole golf course, tennis courts, pool, hot tub, and bar and grill. Smoking permitted. $500–900 per week; call for daily rates.

In Sautee

✍ & **Black Bear Lodge and Cabins** (706-219-3303; www. blackbearlodge.com), 310 Black Bear Ridge. The resort provides a serene base from which guests can explore the area. The 11-suite lodge is furnished with antiques; 13 luxury one-, two-, and three-bedroom log cabins contain full kitchens, fireplaces, hot tubs, and decks. Bear Cub Suites boast a gas-log fireplace, a whirlpool tub in the bath, and a hot tub on the deck. No smoking. Two cabins wheelchair accessible. $149–310.

In Dahlonega

🐾 ✍ 🏕 **Hiker Hostel** (770-312-7342; www .hikerhostel.com), 7693 US 19 North. This unique facility is located just north of Dahlonega near the Appalachian Trail and the Benton MacKaye Trail. The staff will cheerfully supply shuttle service for people who are hiking during the day or even overnight. For those coming off the Appalachian or other trails, they will even provide transportation to local restaurants. Breakfast included. No smoking. Not wheelchair accessible. Well-mannered, housebroken, "relatively" clean pets are welcome. Be prepared to leash them if necessary. Pets are not allowed on the furniture or in an area where food is being prepared. $17 for shared bunk room, $40 for private room, $3 for laundry; no additional charge for pets.

In Dawsonville

🐾 ✍ **Len Foote Hike Inn** (706-867-6203 or 1-800-581-8032; www.hike-inn.com), 240 Amicalola Falls Lodge Road. This special eco-lodge retreat just for hikers, located at **Amicalola Falls State Park** (see *Green Space—Nature Preserves and Parks*), is reached by a 5-mile moderate trail through the Blue Ridge Mountains. Four buildings provide a total of 20 rooms. A bathhouse with hot showers is centrally located. A hearty breakfast and family-style dinner are included, and trail lunches can be ordered for an additional fee. No smoking. Not wheelchair accessible. Advance reservations are encouraged. From $97 for single occupancy, $70 per person for double; discounts available for children younger than 12.

✳ Where to Eat
DINING OUT

In Dahlonega

& **Corkscrew Café** (706-867-8551; www .thecorkscrewcafe.com), 51 West Main Street. Open 11:30–9 Tuesday–Thursday, 11:30–10 Friday and Saturday, noon–9 Sunday (brunch noon–3). Lunch favorites include quiche, paninis, seafood, and a variety of sandwiches. Dinner entrées include filet mignon, lamb, pork, duck, beef tips, local fish, and seafood. The restaurant, located next to the Holly Theater (see *Entertainment—Theater*), is the perfect place to eat before the show. It was voted Best in Fine Dining and Best Dinner for 2011 by members of the community in a survey given by the *Dahlonega Nugget*, the local paper. Reservations recommended. No smoking. Lunch $9–11, dinner $16–30, brunch $9–15.

The McGuire House (706-864-6829), 135 North Chestatee Street. Open 4–9 Monday–Thursday, 4–10 Friday and Saturday. The restaurant specializes in steak and seafood. No smoking. Not wheelchair accessible. $16–21.

& **The Oar House** (706-864-9938), 3072 East GA 52. Open 11–9 Monday–Thursday, 11–10 Friday and Saturday. This contemporary bistro located in a charming old house overlooking the Chestatee River offers casual fine dining. Menu items include seafood, lamb, beef, and pasta. No smoking in eating area. $18–26.

& **Vineyard Café at Wolf Mountain Vineyards** (706-867-9862; www.wolf mountainvineyards.com), 180 Wolf Mountain Road. Open noon–3 Thursday–Saturday, seatings at 12:30 and 2 Sunday (brunch), March–mid-December. Experience gourmet dining in a casual setting with beautiful mountain views. Accompany your meal with the handcrafted wines (see *To Do—Winery Tours*). Live entertainment is offered with brunch. Reservations required. No smoking. Lunch $11–20, brunch $30. Wine extra. Occasional special dinners such as Valentine's Day, $80.

In Helen

🍴 & **Nacoochee Grill** (706-878-8020; www.nacoocheegrill.com), 7277 South Main Street. Open 11:30–9 Monday–Thursday, 11:30–10 Friday and Saturday, 11–3:30 and 4:30–9 Sunday; winter hours 4–9 Tuesday–Thursday, 11–9 Friday and Saturday. A renovated 1900s farmhouse is the location of this ultra-successful "live-fire" grill. Hand-carved Angus steaks, fresh Gulf seafood, ribs, and chops are cooked to perfection over applewood, oak, and hickory. No

smoking. Wheelchair accessible from side entrance. Lunch averages $10, dinner $15–21, brunch $8–14.

In Sautee-Nacoochee

& **Bernie's Restaurant** (706-878-3830; www.letsgotobernies.com), 2220 GA 17. Open 11:30–2 Wednesday–Saturday, 6–8:30 Thursday–Saturday. Located in a charming 1920s cottage with beautiful views of the Sautee-Nacoochee Valley, the restaurant offers gourmet fine dining overseen by mother-daughter team Bernie and Monda, who have more than 60 years of hospitality and culinary experience between them. Daughter Monda was trained at the Culinary Institute of America in Hyde Park, New York. Lunch features sophisticated choices such as a Maryland crabcake sandwich, French dip, a stuffed portobello mushroom sandwich, or the crêpe du jour. Dinner choices include beef, duck, seafood, and lamb. Accommodations are also offered in the associated **Nacoochee Valley Guest House** (see *Lodging—Bed & Breakfasts*). No smoking. Wheelchair accessibility from patio porch. Lunch $8–18, dinner $21–28.

EATING OUT

In Dahlonega

🍴 🐟 & **Back Porch Oyster Bar** (706-864-8623; www.backporchoysterbar.net), 19 Chestatee Street. Open for lunch and dinner Tuesday–Saturday. The focus at this popular restaurant, as the name suggests, is on fresh seafood. Described by the chef as North Carolina cuisine, dishes range from simple fried catfish to the more ambitious pan-seared Chilean sea bass in lemon beurre blanc. Live entertainment is offered, too. No smoking. Lunch $16–17, dinner $17–27.

🍴 🐟 & **Caruso's Italian Restaurant,** home of **Dahlonega Brewing Company** (706-864-4664), 19 East Main Street. Open 11–11 Monday–Thursday, 11 AM–1 AM Friday, 11 AM–midnight Saturday, 11–10 Sunday, but kitchen closes at 9 PM. Menu favorites include an array of pasta dishes and pizzas. The restaurant is also the home of the northernmost brewpub in Georgia.

Several of the beers produced are on tap. No smoking. $8–19.

🍷 ♿ **Frogtown Cellars** (706-865-0687; www.frogtownwine.com), 700 Ridge Point Drive. Open noon–3:30 Saturday, 12:30–3 Sunday. Panini sandwiches (served with a side salad), soups, and pastas are favorites at this unique restaurant connected with the winery (see *To Do—Winery Tours*). Brunch items are served on select Sundays. No smoking. $9–12.

🍷 🍴 ♿ **Smith House** (706-867-7000 or 1-800-852-9577; www.smithhouse.com), 84 South Chestatee Street. Open for lunch daily, dinner Friday–Sunday. The menu, served family-style, includes heaping helpings of fried chicken, honey-cured ham, and a dozen or so vegetables and side dishes, all culminating in traditional Southern desserts like peach cobbler. No smoking. Adults $15–18, children $8–10.

In Dawsonville

🍷 🍴 ♿ **Dawsonville Pool Room** (706-265-2792; www.dawsonvillepoolroom.com), 78 East First Street. Usually open 7 AM–10 PM Monday–Thursday, 7 AM–11 PM Friday and Saturday. Call ahead before you visit. Part hamburger joint, part pool room, part museum, this popular eatery displays a collection of memorabilia from early moonshine runners as well as racing memorabilia from the NASCAR career of native son "Awesome Bill from Dawsonville" Bill Elliott. Popular choices are the Bully Burgers, handcut fries, and sweet tea. No smoking. About $7; pool $1 per game.

In Helen

🍷 🍴 ♿ **Café International** (706-878-3102), 8546 Main Street/GA 75. Open 11–8 Monday–Saturday, 11–7 Sunday; open only for lunch November–March. As is implied by the name, the cuisine at this casual restaurant mixes American, Continental, and international influences. In addition to Reubens, for which the eatery is noted, other menu items include salads, sandwiches, lemon-pepper trout, veal and chicken parmigianas, and German specialties such as knockwurst, schnitzels, and strudels. Sit out on the covered deck over-

looking the river, where you can enjoy gentle breezes and watch folks wading in the stream or floating by on inner tubes. Smoking permitted on deck. Lunch about $9, more for dinner.

🍷 🍴 ♿ **Hofer's Bakery and Café** (706-878-8200 or 1-800-525-4964), 8758 North Main Street. Open 8–5 daily; closed Tuesday and Wednesday February–early March. This authentic Bavarian bakery and café offers an amazing collection of cakes, pies, pastries, and European breads. In addition, the restaurant also serves a relaxed breakfast and lunch in the dining area until 3 daily. Menu favorites include schnitzel, bratwursts, spaetzle, Reubens, and po'boys. On holidays and during Oktoberfest, a dinner menu is added as well. In summer the outdoor Biergarten is open Friday–Sunday. No smoking. $7–15.

🍷 🍴 ♿ **Old Bavaria Inn Restaurant** (706-878-3729; www.theoldbavarianinn rest.com), 8619 North Main Street. Open 11–8 Sunday–Thursday, 11–9 Friday and Saturday. The restaurant serves authentic German and American cuisine, specializing in favorites such as schnitzels, sauerbraten, sausages, Reubens, German potato pancakes, beer-battered mushrooms, smoked salmon, spaetzle, fresh local trout, and homemade apple strudel. No smoking. Lunch averages $10, dinner $10–20.

🍷 🍴 ♿ **Safari Steakhouse & Grill, Inc.** (706-878-2083), 8717 North Main Street. Open 5–9 Friday, 11–9 weekends. One wonders why there's an African safari–themed restaurant in Bavarian Helen, but ours is not to reason why—obviously it's working. The menu includes great sandwiches, burgers, and appetizers, as well as delicious steak, seafood, and chicken dinners. Children enjoy choosing from the Pigmy Meals and virgin cocktails. Smoking and nonsmoking areas. $9–25.

COFFEEHOUSES

In Dahlonega

🍷 🍴 ♿ **Crimson Moon Café** (706-864-3982; www.thecrimsonmoon.com), 24

North Park Street. Open 10–9:30 Wednesday and Thursday, 8 AM–11 PM Friday and Saturday, 8 AM–9:30 PM Sunday. What this establishment is known for is its live entertainment, offered every weekend and other times (call or check the website for a schedule). In fact, Crimson Moon is known as the South's Most Intimate Music Venue. In addition to all your coffee favorites, menu selections include sandwiches, desserts, baked potatoes, soups, quiches, and salads. No smoking. Breakfast $4–9, other meals $8–16.

✳ Entertainment

THEATER ♪ **Historic Holly Theater** (706-864-3759; www.hollytheater.com), 69 West Main Street, Dahlonega. Box office hours 9–5 weekdays. A small restored movie theater, the Holly offers movies, theatrical performances, dinner theater, children's theater, and other special performances. Past shows have included such favorites as *Willy Wonka and the Chocolate Factory.* Call for a schedule of performances and prices.

🎭 ♪ ♿ **Sautee-Nacoochee Art Center** (706-878-3300; www.snca.org; purchase tickets online at www.snca.tix.com), 283 GA 255 North, Sautee. This thriving community arts center contains not only a theater in the old cafeteria but also an on-site regional history museum and an art gallery. Housed in an old 1928 schoolhouse situated on 8 acres, the center offers community theater productions, dinner and a show, concerts, playwright readings, lectures, environmental workshops, summer youth camps, and visual and performing-arts classes. The history museum features Native American artifacts, pioneer tools, gold-mining relics, old photographs, and school memorabilia. Monthly community folk dances are held in the old gymnasium. The newest addition is a wing showcasing the best of north Georgia folk potters (see *To See—Museums*). The only known surviving slave cabin in northeast Georgia has been relocated to the campus as well. Museum and gallery free. Call for a schedule of performances and ticket prices.

✳ Selective Shopping

ANTIQUES **Nacoochee Village Antiques Mall** (706-878-4069), 7091 South Main Street, Helen. Open 10–6 daily. Discover treasures and bargains at Helen's largest antiques gallery. The emporium specializes in antique furniture, kitchen and dining ware, books, and paintings. Don't miss the attic Christmas store.

CRAFTS ♿ **The Glassblowing Shop** (www.glassblowingshop.com). 10 South Chestatee Street, Dahlonega (706-864-9022) and 8600 Main Street, Helen (706-878-3156). Open 10–6 daily. Call for specific demonstration times. Enjoy these clear and brightly colored works of art. Favorites include frogs, hummingbirds, feeders, and garden orbs, but there is tons more to choose from.

The Gourd Place (706-865-4048; www .gourdplace.com), 2319 Duncan Bridge Road, Sautee. Open 10–5 Monday–Saturday, 1–5 Sunday; closed January–March except by appointment. The retail shop sells interesting items made from gourds, while the museum features more than 200 gourds from 23 countries.

The Willows (706-878-1344; www.the willowspottery.com), 7275 South Main Street, Nacoochee Village. Open 10–6 Monday–Saturday, 12:30–6 Sunday. This unique shop allows budding artists to paint their own pottery. Most days visitors can observe the resident potters at their wheels making decorative and functional pieces.

OUTLET MALLS **North Georgia Premium Outlets** (706-216-3609; www .premiumoutlets.com/northgeorgia), 800 US 19/GA 400 South, Dawsonville. Open 10–9 Monday–Saturday, noon–7 Sunday. The upscale center features 140 designer apparel and brand-name stores such as Off 5th (a Saks Fifth Avenue outlet), Banana Republic, Escada, Hugo Bass, Liz Claiborne, Gap, Polo Ralph Lauren, Timberland, Tommy Hilfiger, and many more. Services include a large food pavilion, stroller rentals, wheelchairs, and a children's play area.

SPECIAL STORES BabyLand General Hospital (706-865-2171; www .cabbagepatchkids.com), 300 N.O.K. Drive, Cleveland. Open 9–5 Monday–Saturday, 10–5 Sunday. After visiting the museum (see *To See—For Families*), proceed to the gift shop, where visitors can "adopt" a Cabbage Patch Kid, then outfit and accessorize it for every possible occasion.

Goats on the Roof (706-892-1250; www .goats-on-the-roof.com), 1204 Ridge Road, Helen. Open 10–6 Friday–Sunday in winter, 10–6 daily in summer. We can just about guarantee that you've never seen a shop like this before. The roof of this rustic structure is covered with grass, and a herd of friendly goats climbs up on the roof to graze. Or at least that's the theory. Some conjecture that the goats have Santa Claus Reindeer envy, or could it be that they're really aliens waiting to be picked up by their mother ship? Kids get a kick out of feeding the goats by an ingenious contraption: They pedal a stationary bike that operates a conveyor belt taking the Goat Chow food pellets to the roof. Oh, and, by the way, inside there are Amish wines and cheeses, jams and jellies, fudge and candies, homemade dog treats, T-shirts and gag gifts, primitive furniture, outdoor furniture, other quality handmade furniture, and other gifts. Big Billy's Old Goats Deli serves sandwiches with names such as the Nanny and the Goatatarian. There's also an ice cream shop. Adults enjoy sitting on the porch with their ice cream while the human kids feed the goats. There's another location in Tiger (see the Clarkesville chapter).

❧ **Scarlett's Secret** (706-878-1028; www .scarlettsecret.com), 1902 GA 17, Sautee. Open 11–4 Monday–Saturday, 1–4 Sunday. Appropriately located in a plantation-style home furnished to resemble the *Gone with the Wind* era, the shop sells vintage and new GWTW merchandise.

✳ Special Events

March or April: **Easter Eggstravaganza** (706-865-5356). Held at BabyLand General Hospital in Cleveland the Friday and Saturday of Easter weekend, the event features a parade, breakfast with the Easter Bunny, a 25,000-plus egg hunt for children, dancing with Cabbage Patch costumed characters, an Easter bonnet contest, a treasure hunt for adults, and an arts and crafts fair. Free, except for $10 breakfast.

April: **Bear on the Square Mountain Festival** (706-348-1370; www.bearonthe square.org). This annual music festival takes place in historic downtown Dahlonega. Events include concerts, workshops, jam sessions, a children's play and teddy-bear picnic, storytelling, mountain dancing such as Flatfoot Buck Dancing, singing and yodeling, a pie contest, and a country auction featuring folk art and gifts. Outdoor events free; concert prices free–$10.

May: **Annual Helen to the Atlantic Hot Air Balloon Race** (706-878-2271). The South's oldest balloon event, it is the only long-distance event in the country. For the actual race, about 30 balloons create an awe-inspiring sight when they lift off at 7 AM. That alone would be worth a visit, but by far that's not all, however. There are three days of events, including several local mass balloon flights. Other activities include tethered balloon rides ($10 per person) and one-hour champagne flights ($300 per person); reservations required.

Mountain Flower Fine Arts Festival (706-864-3711). This juried event draws artists from all over the country and attracts thousands of people to the picturesque mountain village of Dahlonega. Free.

June: **Georgia Wine Country Festival** (706-865-WINE). Held at Three Sisters Winery in Dahlonega the first three weekends in June, this event highlights Georgia's many wine resources. Activities include live music, gourmet food, folk art, farm exhibits and live demonstrations, and, of course, wine. Free; fees for food and wine.

Mountain Top Rodeo (706-864-6444; www.rranchga.com). Selected as one of the Southeast Tourism Society's Top 20 Events of 2004, this Professional Rodeo Cowboys Association rodeo features world-class competition in Dahlonega's beautiful mountain setting. Adults $10 in advance, $12 at the gate; children $6. Parking $2.

July: **4th of July Family Celebration** (706-864-3711). This Dahlonega event, a perennial winner of the Southeast Tourism Society's Top July Events designation, is the largest celebration of its kind in north Georgia. Events include patriotic speeches, a flag-raising ceremony, clogging, music, arts and crafts demonstrations, gold panning, food, Firecracker 5K and 10K runs, pet show, watermelon cutting, and antique auto show culminating with fireworks. Free.

Mid-September–early November: **Oktoberfest** (706-878-1908; www.helenchamber .com). What started more than 70 years ago as a small-town festival has grown into one of the most talked-about events in the state. Although the name suggests October only, this festival actually goes on for two entire months. It begins with a parade and the Tapping of the Keg, and goes on to favorite activities such as browsing Helen's many unique shops, a visit (or two) to a beer garden, and at night a trip to the famous Festhalle, where entertainment includes German bands, dancing, food, beer, and much more. Book your reservations early, because lodging during this event sells out fast. Free; admission charges for some events.

October: **Gold Rush Days** (706-864-7247). An annual tradition since 1956, this festival takes place on the third weekend in October in Dahlonega. Celebrate the 1828 discovery of "gold in them thar hills." History is re-created with buck dancing, gospel, greased-pig chasing, a beard contest, fashion show, gold-panning contest, king and queen coronation, wrist-wrestling contest, hog-calling contest, pioneer parade, and more than 300 arts and crafts exhibitors. Free.

DALTON AND
NORTHWEST GEORGIA

Nestled in the foothills of the Appalachian Mountains, this area of extreme northwest Georgia features serene, fertile valleys and plateaus. Wind and water have sculpted the limestone and sandstone for millions of years, creating awe-inspiring cliffs, dramatic waterfalls, incredible rock formations, and panoramic valleys with hundreds of varieties of ferns, flowers, plants, shrubs, and trees. In addition to scenic beauty, the area offers an abundance of recreational opportunities, from cave exploration to hang gliding.

The area is also rich in Native American and Civil War history, and many sites are on the **Blue and Gray Trail,** which traces battles and events from Chattanooga to Atlanta. Whitfield County has 32 historical markers, more than any other Georgia county. For more information, consult the website at www.ngeorgia.com/travel/bgtrail.html. Several sites are on the **Georgia Civil War Heritage Trails,** which interpret the events that took place in the state. For more information, consult the website at www.gcwht.org or call 1-800-331-3258. A valuable website for Civil War buffs is www.civilwartravelers.com.

Visitors to this area enjoy carpet factories and sales showrooms, an outlet mall, the famous Rock City Gardens, museums, a winery, state parks, wilderness areas, lakes, and even ghost tours. Among the many quaint towns to explore, Dalton is the primary city.

GUIDANCE If you're arriving from Tennessee, stop at the **Georgia Visitor Information Center–Ringgold** (706-937-4211; www.exploregeorgia.org), 2726 I-75 South, Ringgold 30736. Open 8:30–5:30 daily; restrooms open 7 AM–11 PM.

For information about Chatsworth, contact the **Chatsworth Local Welcome Center, Chatsworth–Murray County Chamber of Commerce and Welcome Center** (706-695-6060; www.murraycountychamber.com), 126 North Third Avenue, Chatsworth 30705. Open 9–5 weekdays.

To learn more about Dalton, Tunnel Hill, and Varnell, contact the **Dalton-Whitfield Convention and Visitors Bureau** (706-270-9960 or 1-800-331-3258; www.daltoncvb.com), 2211 Dug Gap Battle Road, Dalton 30720. Open 9–5 Monday–Saturday. When you arrive in the area, visit the **Dalton Welcome Center** (706-272-7676 or 1-800-824-7469; www.nwgtcc .com), located inside the **Northwest Georgia Trade and Convention Center,** at the same address as the CVB. Open 8:30–5 weekdays.

To learn more about Chickamauga, LaFayette, Lookout Mountain, and Rossville, contact the **Walker County Chamber of Commerce** (706-375-7702; www.walkercochamber.com), 10052 North US 27, Rock Spring 30739. Open 8:30–5 weekdays.

GETTING THERE *By air:* The nearest airports to this region in Atlanta and Chattanooga, Tennessee. For airport, airline, and car rental information about either, see "What's Where in Georgia."

By bus: Service to this area is provided by **Greyhound Lines** (706-278-3139 or 1-800-231-2222; www.greyhound.com), at the Pilot Travel Center, 142 Carbondale Road, Dalton. Then a rental car would be needed to get around.

By car: Northwest Georgia is bisected by the north–south route I-75, so access to the area is easy. Get off the interstate and explore via the scenic routes US 27 and US 411, and east–west US 76. I-59 and I-24 connect this corner of Georgia to Alabama and Tennessee.

By train: The nearest **AMTRAK** station is in Atlanta (see "What's Where in Georgia"). A rental car would be needed to get to this area.

GETTING AROUND In Dalton, rental cars can be obtained from **Enterprise Rent-A-Car** (706-226-7770), 1503 East Walnut Avenue. In Chatsworth, car rentals are available from **Enterprise** (1-800-257-1136), 301 South Third Avenue.

WHEN TO GO The mountainous areas of Georgia occasionally get snow that sticks to the ground for a couple days and impedes transportation. A few campgrounds and other companies or establishments geared to outdoor activities close for several months in the winter, so be sure to call ahead to avoid disappointment.

MEDICAL EMERGENCY Call 911.

VILLAGES Dalton, located 90 miles north of Atlanta and 25 miles south of Chattanooga, boasts more than 100 carpet outlets, earning the title "Carpet Capital of the World." The town also offers Cherokee and Civil War history as well as discount shopping. After Native Americans were ousted from the region in 1838, the Western and Atlantic Railroad began laying track, and settlers came pouring in. Before the city was incorporated, it was known as Cross Plains. In 1852 the City of Dalton was laid out in a 1-mile radius from a survey post where the Dalton Depot now stands.

During the Civil War, Confederate hospitals and manufacturing facilities in Dalton were important for supporting the South's efforts. In May 1864, after the Union victory at Chattanooga, the war turned south toward Atlanta, and several important battles occurred nearby.

Dalton once had the nickname "Peacock Alley" because of the wide array of chenille bedspreads hung out for sale along the highway. This significant cottage industry—a truly American business—began in the early 1900s when a farm girl named Catherine Evans Whitener used the colonial art of tufting to make a bedspread she sold for $2.50. Soon all the ladies in the area were making them. By the 1950s, advances in technology transformed the bedspread industry into carpet making—now a multimillion-dollar industry.

Today historic downtown Dalton features a theater, shopping, and restaurants. Downtown Dalton is a great place for train viewing, too. The CSX and Norfolk-Southern lines travel side by side, and more than 35 trains pass through each day. Stop at the **Dalton Welcome Center** in the **Northwest Georgia Trade and Convention Center** (see *Guidance*) to pick up a brochure for the **Chieftans Trail** (www.chieftainstrail.com), a 150-mile path that dates back to 1000 B.C. Nine sites open to the public are included on the trail.

Chickamauga, once known as Crawfish Springs, was the site of one of the bloodiest battles of the Civil War. The Battle of Chickamauga, fought nearby on September 19 and 20, 1863, was one of the early battles in the Union's push toward Atlanta from Chattanooga and was a rare victory for the Confederacy, although it resulted in 34,000 casualties total. The small town near the site of one of the first National Battlefield Parks in the nation has several historic sites.

Durham Iron and Coal Company later built long lines of beehive ovens to turn coal into coke for iron and steel foundries in Chattanooga, a practice that continued until the coal ran out during the Depression. A Chickamauga park created around the ovens has wetlands demonstration ponds, a bird sanctuary, and a nature trail. The park is the site of the **Arts and Crafts Festival** held each September in conjunction with **War Between the States Day.** At that event, reenactors erect a camp and living-history demonstration area around the springs. Nearby, the **Holland-Watson Veterans Memorial Park,** which displays a Huey helicopter, honors Chickamauga veterans of all American wars.

Fort Oglethorpe was established in 1902 and served as the home of the 6th, 7th, 10th, 11th, and 12th Cavalries. During World War I, the parade ground served as a detention camp for enemy aliens and prisoners of war. During the 1920s and 1930s, the fort became one of the most elite posts in the country, complete with polo matches and fox hunts. In fact, the Sunday-afternoon polo matches were so famous throughout northwest Georgia and southeast Tennessee, the parade ground became known as the Polo Field. Equally renowned were the fort's horse shows, drill team, mounted band, and mounted guard performances.

During World War II, the post became an induction center and once again served as an internment center for enemy aliens and POWs. In 1943, it became a training center for the Women's Third Army Corps. At the end of the war, the post became a center for processing returning GIs until it was closed in 1947. Across from the fort grounds is the Georgia unit of the **Chickamauga and Chattanooga National Military Park.** Today a museum describes the various phases the fort went through, but it focuses on the Sixth Cavalry.

Lookout Mountain was formed millions of years ago. Native Americans inhabited it, and two missionaries arrived in 1823 to minister to them. They described the area as a citadel of rocks arranged in streets and lanes (hence Rock City). The slopes of the mountain saw much action during the Civil War. A Union officer and a Confederate nurse both contended that seven states could be seen from the summit. Beginning in the 1890s, Lookout Mountain became a major attraction, with grand hotels and three railroads to the top. Generations of Americans and foreign visitors were familiar with SEE ROCK CITY signs painted on barn roofs.

Tunnel Hill came into being when a 1,477-foot tunnel was built through Chetoogeta Mountain to connect the port of Augusta to the Tennessee River Valley. Construction began in 1848, and the first Western and Atlantic train passed through in 1850. The new town of Atlanta became one of the railroad's major hubs. The tunnel was the site of several historic events during the Civil War. Afterward, heavier rail traffic and larger train cars often caused trains to become stuck in the tunnel, so a larger parallel tunnel was built in 1928. The abandoned tunnel was neglected for 70 years but was restored and reopened to the public in 2000 in time for its 150th birthday. Today the tunnel and several historic attractions and festivals bring tourists to Tunnel Hill.

✳ To See

FOR FAMILIES 𝓮 ᕼ 🐾 **Rock City Gardens** (706-820-2531 or 1-800-854-0675; www .seerockcity.com), 1400 Patten Road, Lookout Mountain. Open year-round from 8:30 AM, closes at different times depending on season. Gigantic and often bizarre rock formations created over millions of years by changing temperatures, wind, and water create the basis for this 14-acre park. During the 1920s, Garnet and Frieda Carter created their own private garden here, eventually opening it to the public in 1932. Today 4,100 feet of paths wind through rock formations where visitors can get spectacular views and enjoy 400 different species of native wildflowers, plants, shrubs, and trees. The brave-hearted will want to test their courage on the 180-foot Swing-Along Bridge. The more faint-of-heart will enjoy Fat Man's Squeeze, Fairyland Caverns, Mother Goose Village, the 90-foot waterfall, and the view of seven states from Lover's Leap. Rock City sponsors many special events throughout the year: **Rock City Raptors Birds of Prey Take Flight** (Memorial Day weekend through Labor Day weekend), **Summer Blooms at Rock City** (late June through September), the **Enchanted Maize** (see *To Do—For Families*), and **Enchanted Garden of Lights and Winter Wonderland** (mid-November through December; see *Special Events*). Partially handicapped accessible. Pets allowed on a leash. $11–19.

GUIDED TOURS ❧ Carpet Mill

Tours (706-270-9960 or 1-800-331-3258; www.daltoncvb.com). Weekdays, subject to availability. Carpet mill tours lasting about one and a half hours can be arranged through the Dalton Convention and Visitors Bureau (see *Guidance*). No one under 16 allowed in the mill. Free.

HISTORIC HOMES AND SITES

🐾 ☙ ♿ **Chickamauga and Chattanooga National Military Park** (706-866-9241; www.nps.gov/chch), 3370 Lafayette Road, Fort Oglethorpe. Visitors center open 8–5 daily; park open daylight hours. The scene of a bloody battle that resulted in a rare Confederate victory, the Chickamauga bat-

SPECTACULAR VIEWS AWAIT VISITORS TO ROCK CITY GARDENS.

tlefield in Georgia is part of the country's oldest and largest military park. Preserved by veterans from the North and South, the 8,000-acre park—which also includes several sites in Chattanooga, Tennessee—was the first of its kind in the country and endures as a symbol of unity. Nearly a million visitors tour the battlefield annually, making it the most visited military park in the country. Begin at the Chickamauga visitors center to see an audiovisual presentation describing the battle, view the Fuller Gun Collection and other exhibits, and pick up a brochure for a self-guided tour. The Georgia area of the park features driving roads, hiking paths, horse trails (BYOH—bring your own horse), monuments, cannons, and historical markers. The best place from which to get a bird's-eye view of the battlefield is from the top of the 85-foot Wilder Tower, a memorial to Col. John T. Wilder, who commanded the Lightning Brigade. In addition to the Georgia attractions in the park described here, there

ROCK CITY BARNS

When Garnet and Frieda Carter opened Rock City Gardens to the public in 1932, Garnet realized that the attraction was so far off the beaten path he needed to get people's attention in a big way. He hired a sign painter named Chuck Byers to travel the nation's highways and offer to paint farmers' barns for free if they would agree to let him paint SEE ROCK CITY in huge letters on the roof. At one time there were 900 of these barns, and they could be seen as far north as Michigan and as far west as Texas. Sadly, only a few of these treasured national landmarks remain.

are several attractions in Tennessee, including the Cravens House and Point Park. Partially handicapped accessible. Free.

🦌 🎣 ♿ **Chief Vann House Historic Site** (706-695-2598; www.gastateparks.org/ChiefVann House), 82 GA 225 North, Chatsworth. Open 9–5 Thursday–Saturday; last tour 45 minutes prior to closing. Called the "Showplace of the Cherokee Nation," this beautiful two-story Federal-style residence was the home of Cherokee chief James Vann, a political leader and wealthy plantation owner. He amassed 1,000 acres, making his property the largest and most prosperous Cherokee plantation. Constructed in 1804, this was the first brick home within the Cherokee Nation and the only mansion built by an early Native American. The interior features a "floating" or cantilevered staircase, hand carvings of the Cherokee rose, and period furniture. Vann brought Moravian missionaries to the Cherokee Nation to build schools and teach the children, and they established the Springplace Moravian Mission School. Vann was murdered in 1809. His son, Joseph, inherited the home and became a Cherokee statesman and businessman. "Rich Joe," as he was known, was forced off the property when the Cherokee were removed from Georgia and sent along the Trail of Tears. Also located on the grounds are a small log cabin and the **Robert E. Chambers Interpretive Center,** which has several exhibits and a short video interpreting Native American life and the clash of cultures with settlers. The most special event of the year is the **Moravian Christmas at the Chief Vann House,** held the second weekend in December. Located just 300 yards from the house is the **Springplace Mission Cemetery,** where such notables as Chief Charles R. Hicks, Margaret "Peggy" Vann Crutchfield (James Vann's widow), and missionary Anna Rosina Gambold are buried. Visitors center and first floor of house wheelchair accessible. $3.50–6.

🦌 🎣 ♿ **Dalton Depot** (706-226-3160), 110 Depot Street, Dalton. Built in 1847 and used by the railroad until 1978, the facility is one of only a few surviving antebellum depots. During the Civil War, it served as a Confederate Army ordnance depot. During the Great Locomotive Chase in 1862 (see the Northern Suburbs chapter in part 1: "Atlanta Metro"), it was here that 17-year-old Southerner Edward Henderson was dropped off to telegraph a message to Chattanooga to stop the stolen General. Today the depot houses a restaurant and Trackside Tavern lounge (see *Where to Eat—Eating Out*). The original survey post around which Dalton was laid out is still embedded in the wooden floor of the depot.

🦌 🎣 **Dug Gap Battle Park** (historical society: 706-278-0217; CVB: 1-800-331-3258), 2211 West Dug Gap Battle Road, Dalton. Open daylight hours daily. Although outnumbered 10 to 1 on May 8, 1864, Confederate soldiers successfully repelled a Union attack by using a stone wall, 1,000 feet of which survives, and by constructing 1,200-foot breastwork entrenchments that are still evident. Visitors also can take the Dug Gap Mountain hiking trail to the summit and enjoy scenic views of Dalton and the surrounding area. The park is maintained by the Civil War Roundtable of Dalton. Free.

CHIEF VANN HOUSE HISTORIC SITE

🕯 **Gordon-Lee Mansion** (706-375-4728 or 1-800-487-4728; www.gordon-leemansion.com), 217 Cove Road, Chickamauga. House open 11–4 Saturday, Memorial Day–Labor Day; log cabin open 11–4 Tuesday–Saturday, April–October. The imposing historic home was built between 1840 and 1847 with bricks made on the grounds. It is the last surviving structure used during the Battle of Chickamauga, making it an official site on the Civil War Discovery Trail and the Blue-Gray Trail. Union general William S. Rosecrans used the home for his headquarters during the battle, and the home's graceful library served as a grisly operating room. It was reported that there was so much blood on the floors that they had to be covered with mats. The graciously furnished mansion is open for tours, and the 1835 log cabin on the property serves as the **Gordon-Lee Mansion History Theater** museum, where a continuous-feed DVD describes the history of the area and the house. House: adults $4, children $1; log cabin: free.

🕯 ⚲ ♿ **Lee and Gordon's Mills** (706-375-6801; www.leeandgordonsmills.com), 71 Red Belt Road, Chickamauga. Park open 1–5 Wednesday–Saturday during winter, longer in summer; mill open only during special events. Located on the east bank of Chickamauga Creek, the original mill, which was built by James Gordon, was constructed in 1836. During the 1863 Civil War Battle of Chickamauga, the mill served as the headquarters of the Confederate Army of Tennessee under the command of Gen. Braxton Bragg. On the second day of the battle, Bragg withdrew to LaFayette, and Union troops occupied the mill. The original mill burned in 1867 and was replaced by one built by James Lee. That mill has been restored to operating condition, and cornmeal ground there can be purchased during special events. Free; donations appreciated. The **Veterans of All Wars Museum** (423-304-1722) is located in the upper building. Open 10–4 Tuesday–Friday, 10–3 Saturday, 2–4 Sunday. Adults $2, children $1.

🕯 ⚲ ♿ **Prater's Mill** (706-694-6455; www.pratersmill.org), 500 Prater's Mill Road/GA 2, Varnell. Park open daylight hours daily; mill building open only during festivals. The historic gristmill was built by slaves in 1855, but the Civil War intruded on the area not long after that. The grounds were used by 600 Union soldiers under Col. Eli Long in February 1864 and then by 2,500 Confederate soldiers under Gen. Joseph Wheeler two months later. Today the site offers fishing on Cohulla Creek, hiking on a nature trail, and a popular fall country fair (see *Special Events*).

🕯 ⚲ ♿ **Tunnel Hill Heritage Center–Western and Atlantic Railroad Tunnel** (706-876-1571; www.tunnelhillheritagecenter.com), 215 Clisby Austin Road, Dalton. Open 10–5 Monday–Saturday. The 1,477-foot tunnel built by the Western and Atlantic Railroad through Chetoogeta Mountain is the oldest tunnel south of the Mason-Dixon Line and was the first link between the Atlantic and the Ohio Valley. Completed in 1850, it was the engineering marvel of its time. It also was the site of several skirmishes during the Civil War and figured in the Great Locomotive Chase. When the tunnel was restored, the railbed was surfaced to provide easy visitor access.

Near the tunnel is the historic 1850 **Clisby Austin House,** which was built to be a summer getaway in the cool mountains but was used as a hospital during the Battle of Chickamauga. Confederate general John Bell Hood was sent there to recuperate. General Sherman used the house as a headquarters during the Battle of Dalton on May 7, 1864, as he planned the final legs of the Atlanta Campaign. Plans are to open it for tours soon.

Located in another building, the heritage center houses historical displays about the Tunnel Hill area, local families, the Clisby Austin House, Foster Cemetery, the Great Locomotive Chase, and the chenille bedspread industry of Peacock Alley. Exhibits about Civil War and railroad history and Native American artifacts also are displayed. The CSX Railroad tracks adjacent to the heritage center are perfect for train viewing and photography because they are part of a busy rail corridor between Dalton and Chattanooga. The **Battle of Tunnel Hill Reenactment** takes place here each September the weekend after Labor Day (see *Special*

GENERAL HOOD'S LEG

Confederate general John Bell Hood had been seriously wounded at Gettysburg, resulting in the loss of use of one of his arms. Then he was so grievously wounded in the leg at Chickamauga that it had to be amputated. Amputated limbs were normally discarded, but the doctors were so certain that Hood would die, they sent his leg along with him when he was moved to the Clisby Austin House in nearby Tunnel Hill so it could be buried with him. As he so often did, however, Hood rallied and went on to fight in many more battles. Therefore, his leg was buried in the family cemetery at the Clisby Austin House.

Events), and April's **Celtic and Heritage Festival** highlights Scottish and Cherokee influences on the area. Adults $5, children 12 and younger $3; reenactment also $5/$3.

MUSEUMS ✿ ♦ ⚅ **Sixth Cavalry Museum** (706-861-2860; www.6thcavalrymuseum .com), 6 Barnhardt Circle, Fort Oglethorpe. Open 9–4 Tuesday–Saturday. The Sixth Cavalry was formed in 1861 and was stationed here from 1919 to 1942 (see *Villages—Fort Oglethorpe*). Today it serves in Germany and Korea, but this museum, which is located on the old parade ground/polo field, relives the days when it was stationed here. Exhibits include artifacts, uniforms, and weapons. Visitors enjoy seeing a Patten tank and a Cobra Gunship Helicopter up close. Adults $3, students $2, family $10.

✿ ♦ ⚅ **Walker County Regional Heritage and Train Museum** (706-375-4488), 200 Gordon Street, Chickamauga. Open 10–4 Thursday–Saturday. The first railroad with a stop at Chickamauga (then Crawfish Springs) made two daily round-trips between Chattanooga, Tennessee, and Cedartown (see the Rome chapter). Trains pulled by steam locomotives still make excursions from Chattanooga during the summer with stops at the Chickamauga Depot. The stone depot built by Central of Georgia Railroad has been restored and now houses exhibits of Native American artifacts and displays about the Civil War, World War I, and antique guns and furniture. Guests also can see a complete working display of Lionel O-gauge model trains that date back to the 1940s. $2.

SCENIC DRIVES **Backroads and Battlefields** (CVB: 1-800-331-3258; www.nw georgiabackroads.com). Stop at the Dalton Visitors Center (2211 Dug Gap Battle Road) to pick up a brochure for this historic and scenic tour of northwest Georgia, which is packed with Native American and Civil War history.

Cohutta-Chattahoochee Scenic Byway (CVB: 1-800-331-3258; www.nwgeorgiabackroads .com). Stop at the Dalton Visitors Center (2211 Dug Gap Battle Road) to learn about this 54-mile corridor, which highlights the scenic, cultural, and historic rural back roads from Dalton east to the top of Fort Mountain, including Chatsworth, historic Prater's Mill, and Fort Mountain State Park.

✳ To Do

FOR FAMILIES ✿ ♦ ⚅ **Enchanted Maize by Rock City** (706-820-2531 or 1-800-854-0675; www.seerockcity.com), 271 Chattanooga Valley Road, Flintstone. Open noon–8 or 10 Thursday–Sunday, September and October. The twists and turns of the intricately designed 10-acre cornfield maze at Blowing Springs Farm at the base of Lookout Mountain are sure to create excitement. As if that's not enough, there are hayrides, a playground, a kiddie hay maze, hay pyramid, pumpkin patch, scarecrow and pumpkin design contests, refreshments, and more. On Halloween weekend experience flashlight tours of the maze. Adults $8, children 4–12 $6. Evenings in October, the farm morphs into **Blowing Screams Farm.** The Forest of Fear features a haunted house in a century-old farmhouse, Ghost Ride is a hayride like no other, and 3-D special effects offer plenty of thrills and chills. $15 for each attraction or $25 for both. Visitors can purchase a combo ticket for $30 to enjoy both the day and evening experiences.

✑ ♿ **Lake Winnepesaukah** (706-866-5681 or 1-877-525-3946; www.lakewinnie.com), 1730 Lakeview Drive, Rossville. Open Thursday–Sunday, April–September; hours vary (longest hours are 10–10), so call ahead. Affectionately known as Lake Winnie, this family-oriented amusement park has been open since 1925. In addition to popular rides such as the Cannonball Coasters, Matterhorn, Genie, Tilt-A-Whirl, and an antique carousel, the park offers 30 other thrill, family, and kiddie rides, as well as an arcade, miniature golf, paddleboats, a gift shop, and a picnic area. $25 allows unlimited rides; limited tickets for less.

HANG GLIDING ✑ **Lookout Mountain Flight Park and Training Center** (706-398-3541 or 1-800-688-5637; www.hanglide.com), 7201 Scenic Highway, Rising Fawn. Office and pro shop open 9–6 Thursday–Monday. Call for flight hours. Enjoy a special view of Lookout Mountain while quietly soaring 2,000 feet over the area. Lessons are available as well as tandem flights with instructors, but if you don't want to participate, spectators are welcome, too. The 44-acre mountain retreat also offers camping and lodging. Fees vary by activity; tandem flight $149.

HIKING 🐾 ✑ **Disney Trail** (www.georgiatrails.com/gt/Disney_Trail). It's hard to imagine in this forbidding terrain, but this was the site of the fierce Civil War Battle of Rocky Face on May 8–10, 1864. Named for Confederate soldier George Disney, who fell during that battle and whose crude grave site lies at the end of the trail, this steep 2.4-mile path that ascends Rocky Face Mountain is the most challenging short trail in the state. Located west of Dalton, it is also one of the oldest trails in the state—predating the Appalachian Trail by 20 years. From here, there is access to 6 miles of other trails.

🐾 ✑ **Pinhoti Trail, National Forest Service** (www.georgiapinhoti.org), accessible across from Dug Gap Battle Park (see *To See—Historic Homes and Sites*) and several other points. Consult the website for a complete trail guide. Open daylight hours daily. *Pinhoti* is the Cherokee word for "turkey," so the trail is blazed with representations of turkey feet. When complete, the multiuse trail will be the state's longest. Plans call for it to be 245 miles long, connecting the Appalachian Trail in northeast Georgia to the Talladega National Forest in Alabama. Free.

THE AREA'S LAKES ARE PERFECT FOR CANOEING AND KAYAKING.

HORSEBACK RIDING ✑ **Fort Mountain Stables** (706-517-4906; www.fortmountainstables.com), 548 Cliff Mines Road, Chatsworth. Open 9–2 daily. Horseback riding adventures from one hour to overnight are offered on 37 miles of scenic trails at Fort Mountain State Park (see *Green Space—Nature Preserves and Parks*). Reservations required. $30 per hour up to $100 for four hours; overnight $200.

MINIATURE GOLF 🐾 ✑ **Dalton Falls Miniature Golf and Laser Tag** (706-272-3574; www.daltonfallsgolf.com), 2817 Airport Road, Dalton. Call for hours; they vary widely depending on the season. The facility features a naturalistic 18-hole course with waterfalls, ponds, streams, and hills; an arcade room; and a concession stand. A 16,000-square-foot facility with 27 barriers is devoted to laser tag. Play Capture the Flag, VIP, and Last Man Standing. Laser tag: $7 for 30 minutes, $12 for an hour. Mini golf: adults $6, children $5; check for many specials.

WINERY TOURS 🏪 ⚐ ♿ **Georgia Winery Taste Center** (706-937-WINE; www.georgia wines.com), 6469 Battlefield Parkway, Ringgold. Open 10–6 Monday–Saturday; tours at 2 and 4 Saturday. The 52-acre site has been producing wines since 1983. Reds, whites, rosés, and blushes are produced primarily from muscadine grapes. The gift shop offers wines, gourmet foods, gifts with a wine or grape theme, and winemaking supplies. Tour and tasting $20 including a wine glass, or just visit the gift shop.

✳ Green Space

LAKES 🏪 ⚐ ♿ **Carters Lake** (706-334-2248; www.sam.usace.army.mil). Office at 1850 Carter's Dam Road, Chatsworth. Located at the southern end of the Blue Ridge Mountains, this is one of the most scenic lakes in the Southeast as well as one of the best recreational reservoirs. Impounding the Coosawattee River, the 3,220-acre lake and its surrounding area boast eight public-use parks. The area is perfect for boating (launching ramps and rentals available), camping, fishing, hiking, hunting, mountain biking, and picnicking. Camping and cottages are available (see *Lodging—Inns and Resorts*).

NATURE PRESERVES AND PARKS 🏪 ⚐ ♿ 🐾 **Cloudland Canyon State Park** (706-657-4050; lodging reservations: 1-800-864-7275; www.gastateparks.org/Cloudland Canyon), 122 Cloudland Canyon Park Road, Rising Fawn. Open 7 AM–10 PM daily. Spectacular scenery is one of the main reasons visitors come to Cloudland Canyon State Park, at the western edge of Lookout Mountain. The 3,485-acre park encompasses a deep gorge cut by Sitton's Gulch Creek, which results in elevation ranging from 800 to 1,980 feet. Beautiful vistas can be seen from the picnic area parking lot as well as from along the rim trail. Hardy travelers can hike down into the canyon to view two waterfalls not visible from the summit. (Just remember: While it's easy going down, it's all uphill on the way back.) Hikers like the 4.8-mile West Rim Trail and the 2-mile Backcountry Trail. More challenging are the 9-mile Cloudland Connector Trail and the 6.5 Sitton's Gulch Trail. The park also features fishing, bike rentals, tennis courts, and disc golf ($3). There are also a campground and cottages (see *Lodging—Campgrounds* and *Lodging—Cottages and Cabins*). Parking $5.

🏪 ⚐ ♿ 🐾 **Fort Mountain State Park** (706-482-1932; lodging reservations: 1-800-864-7275; www.gastateparks.org/Fort Mountain), 181 Fort Mountain Park Road, Chatsworth. Open 7 AM–10 PM daily. Named for the ruins of an ancient 855-foot-long rock wall that tops the 2,800-foot-high

CLOUDLAND CANYON STATE PARK

mountain, the park offers numerous recreational activities. The wall may have been built by Native Americans as a fortification against other tribes, but the most widely held theory is that it was built for ceremonial purposes. Believed to have been constructed around A.D. 500, the wall is situated so that the sun rises and sets perfectly over each end. A hike to the wall takes about 15 minutes. The 3,712-acre

> ### WETLAND, MARSH, OR SWAMP?
> A wetland is an area where shallow water covers the land at least several weeks out of the year. If it is dominated by trees, it's called a swamp. If it's dominated by herbaceous plants, it's called a marsh.

park—located in the Chattahoochee National Forest near the Cohutta Wilderness—boasts 14 miles of hiking, 27 miles of mountain biking trails, and 37 miles of horseback riding trails (you can BYOH—bring your own horse); a 17-acre lake with a sandy beach; swimming; canoe, fishing boat, and pedal-boat rentals in season; miniature golf seasonally (additional fee); and horseback riding (see *To Do—Horseback Riding*). The park offers a campground and cottages (see *Lodging—Campgrounds* and *Lodging—Cottages and Cabins*). Parking $5; fee for use of mountain biking trails.

🐾 ♿ **Spring Creek Wetlands Preserve** (Dalton Utilities: 706-278-1313), Boyles Mill Road, Dalton. Open 9–6 weekends; reservations required for weekday visits. Well-marked trails provide opportunities for visitors to see a wide variety of flora and fauna in this 200-acre water and wildlife habitat. The preserve supports a secondary trout stream and is the breeding ground for several endangered species. Visitors see frogs, toads, salamanders, wood ducks, reptiles, turtles, snails, great blue herons, and green-backed herons. The 1-mile trail is one easy flat terrain. Free.

✳ Lodging

BED & BREAKFASTS

In Chatsworth

Hearthstone Lodge Bed and Breakfast (706-695-0920; www.thehearthstonelodge.com), 2755 US 76/GA 282. The beautiful cedar-log home features three guest suites named for apples. Each room offers a private bath, queen-size bed, sitting area, and entertainment center. The B&B also features five fireplaces, decks and porches, a hot tub, steam room, pool table, and darts. A gourmet breakfast, afternoon refreshments, evening desserts, and bedtime sweets are provided. A short hike takes visitors through forest to creeks and waterfalls. Ages 21 and older only. No smoking. No pets. Not wheelchair accessible. $179 per night; two-night minimum.

♿ **Overlook Inn Bed and Breakfast** (706-517-8810; www.theoverlookinn.com), 864 Wilderness View. Located atop Fort Mountain in the Cohutta Wilderness, with spectacular views of the Blue Ridge Mountains, this rustic inn features tree-trunk support beams, a stone fireplace, hardwood floors, and an antler chandelier. The five surprisingly elegant guest rooms are uniquely decorated in natural hues. Although there are blessedly no telephones or televisions, amenities include private entrances and porches, in-room or porch hot tubs, and fireplaces. A three-course Southern gourmet breakfast, afternoon wine and cheese, and candlelight desserts are pleasant extras. For a truly romantic evening, guests can purchase dinner served in your room ($49). A woodland trail is accessible from the inn. No children. No pets. Smoking outdoors only. Limited wheelchair accessibility. $149–239.

In Lookout Mountain

♿ **Chanticleer Inn** (706-820-2002 or 1-866-424-2684; www.stayatchanticleer.com), 1300 Mockingbird Lane. A member of Select Registry, Distinguished Inns of North America, this hostelry is located on 5 landscaped acres in the historic Fairyland neighborhood atop Lookout Mountain. The inn, built in the late 1920s, has a mountain-stone exterior similar to that of nearby Rock City Gardens (see *To See—For Families*). Seventeen rooms and five cottages were completely renovated in 2002 using a country theme with English antiques much more upscale than the simple exterior would imply. Each boasts a private bath, cable TV, and feather-top beds. Some rooms have private patios, gas or electric fireplaces, whirlpool tubs, and stocked refrigerators. The inn's swimming pool is open seasonally. A Southern breakfast buffet is served each morning, and afternoon refreshments are also included. No smoking. $135–245; two-night minimum May 1—November 1. Several special packages available.

& **Garden Walk Bed and Breakfast Inn** (706-820-4127 or 1-800-617-0502; www.gardenwalkinn.com), 1206 Lula Lake Road. A series of cottages are nostalgically, romantically, or whimsically decorated in themes. Rooms are available with queen-, king-, or twin-size beds. Each offers a private bath, mini fridge, coffeemaker, and cable TV. Some feature a fireplace and/or Jacuzzi. Other amenities include an outdoor pool and hot tub along with beautifully landscaped gardens. A full hot breakfast is provided. Adults and youth 16 and older only. Smoking outside only. No pets. Limited wheelchair accessibility (one cabin has no steps, but its bathroom will not accommodate a wheelchair). $90–195.

CAMPGROUNDS

In Chatsworth

🦌 ✐ & 🐾 **Fort Mountain State Park** (camping reservations: 1-800-864-7275). The park offers 70 tent, trailer, and RV sites ($25–28), as well as four walk-in sites ($15), six platform sites ($15), four backcountry sites ($9 per person), and primitive equestrian campsites ($50). See also *Green Space—Nature Preserves and Parks*.

In Rising Fawn

🦌 ✐ & 🐾 **Cloudland Canyon State Park** (camping reservations: 1-800-864-7275). The park's campground offers 72 tent,

trailer, and RV sites ($25–28), as well as 30 walk-in sites ($16) and 11 backcountry sites ($6 per person). See also *Green Space—Nature Preserves and Parks*.

In Trenton

🦌 ✐ **Lookout Mountain KOA** (706-657-6815 or 1-800-562-1239; www.lookoutmountainkoa.com), 930 Mountain Shadows Drive. The 37-acre forested site offers beautiful mountain views. Activities and amenities include hiking, a lookout point, and a large pool. In addition to camping sites, accommodations are offered in basic cabins. Some are basically four solid walls and a roof over your head. Others have a bathroom. In either case, you must bring your own linens. No pets allowed. RV sites $34–35, cabins with bathroom $52, cabins without bathroom $46.

COTTAGES AND CABINS

In Chatsworth

✐ 🐾 **Fort Mountain State Park** (cottage reservations: 1-800-864-7275). The park offers 15 fully equipped cottages. Two are dog friendly ($40 per dog; maximum two). $125–145. See also *Green Space—Nature Preserves and Parks*.

🦌 ✐ & 🐾 **Wilderness View Cabin Rentals** (706-517-8810 or 1-866-517-8810; www.wildernessviewcabins.com), 9420 Highway 52. Because these cabins are located on a 100-acre private preserve and each sits on 5 to 7 acres, guests are ensured the ultimate in privacy. Each one- to four-bedroom, one- to three-bath cabin features a full kitchen, wood-burning fireplace, and outdoor hot tub. A few are pet friendly. Smoking outdoors only. Limited wheelchair accessibility. $199–239; two-night minimum; three-night minimum during fall leaf season and some holidays.

In Rising Fawn

✐ 🐾 **Cloudland Canyon State Park** (cottage reservations: 1-800-864-7275). Sixteen fully equipped cottages are offered. Two are dog friendly ($40 per dog; maximum two). $135–160. See also *Green Space—Nature Preserves and Parks*.

THE MOUNTAINS

In Chatsworth

✶ ✦ ❀ **Carters Lake Marina and Resort** (706-276-4891; www.carterslake .com), 575 Marina Road. Accommodations, which range from basic rooms to cabins to houseboats, fit every budget. Luxury cabins with spectacular views of the lake feature two bedrooms, a sleeping loft, bathroom, gas-log fireplace, fully equipped kitchen, covered porch, deck, and barbecue grill. Family log cabins feature two bedrooms, one bath, a sofa bed, and a fully equipped kitchen. Basic rooms feature one bed and one bath. All basic rooms have a coffeemaker; some also have a refrigerator and microwave. Some cabins are dog friendly. Houseboats feature sleeping room for eight, as well as a full kitchen, one bathroom, front and back decks, and an upper deck. They can be rented for three, four, or seven nights. Guests are welcome to bring one personal boat and use the resort's docks at no extra charge; additional boats or Jet Skis are $10 per night. Pontoon boats are available to rent ($255–295), and a snack bar operates during the summer. For boat customers, service, repairs, fuel, and supplies are available. No smoking. Some wheelchair accessible. Lakeside rooms $39.95–49.95, cabins $100–190, houseboats $1,000–3,000.

In Chickamauga

❁ ✶ ✦ **Hidden Hollow Resort** (706-539-2372; www.hiddenhollowresort.com), 463 Hidden Hollow Lane. The small, secluded, rustic resort provides a perfect getaway from modern-day life's hectic pace. The 135 wooded acres lie at the foot and along the side of Lookout Mountain. Guests take long walks, play lawn games, relax on the porches, sit around the fireplace, or participate in sing-alongs or marshmallow roasts. There is a small lake and a creek on the property, too. Accommodations are provided in a quaint country inn or in cozy log cabins, most with fireplaces and all with a kitchen or kitchenette. There is only one central phone, and rooms do not have televisions (although you can bring your own). Paddleboats and canoes are available. No

smoking. No pets. Limited wheelchair accessibility (one cabin has no steps). $48–198.

✶ Where to Eat

DINING OUT

In Rising Fawn

✶ ✦ **The Canyon Grill** (706-398-9510; www.canyongrill.com), 189 28 Scenic Highway. Open 5–9 Wednesday–Sunday; call ahead for priority seating. *Georgia Trend* magazine has named this eatery one of Georgia's Top Ten Dining Destinations. Located at the southern end of Lookout Mountain, the popular restaurant's signature dish is Slash and Burn Catfish, which is crispy fried catfish accompanied by black bean sauce. Other entrées include fish and seafood, duck, pork, pastas, and lamb—many of which are cooked on the eatery's Tuff Grill, which they invented and now sell. The restaurant does not have a liquor license, but diners can BYOB. No smoking. $14–38.

EATING OUT

In Chickamauga

❁ ✶ ✦ **Crystal Spring Smokehouse** (706-375-9269), 505 West Ninth Street. Open 7 AM–8 PM Tuesday–Friday, 7–2 Saturday. This restaurant specializes in smoked barbecue plates and sandwiches. No smoking. Breakfast $5–8, lunch $4–6, dinner $7–15.

❁ ✶ ✦ **Greg's Restaurant** (706-375-4788), 12560 North Highway 27. Open 6:30 AM–8 PM Monday–Friday, 6:30–2 Saturday. A local favorite for its Friday night catfish, the casual eatery offers home cooking. Breakfast is served all day. No smoking. Breakfast less than $7, lunch and dinner $9.

In Dalton

❁ ✶ ✦ **Dalton Depot Restaurant and Trackside Tavern** (706-226-3160; www .thedaltondepot.net), 110 Depot Street. Open 11–10 Monday–Saturday. The historic depot (see *To See—Historic Homes and Sites*) is occupied by two restaurants. For a quieter, more personal dining experience in the atmosphere of a bygone era, try the Dalton Depot Restaurant. For a faster pace in a more contemporary setting, the Trackside Tavern has big-screen televisions, video games, interactive trivia games, pool tables and tournaments, live music, and karaoke. Both eateries feature house specialties such as double-cut pork chops, baby-back ribs, chicken or veal Parmesan, and shrimp and grits. Their menus also contain a full array of appetizers, seafood, steaks, and lighter fare. Murals and railroad relics are reminders of the building's history. No smoking. Lunch about $9, dinner $14–18.

✳ Entertainment

THEATER **Dalton Little Theater** (706-226-6618; www.daltonlittletheatre.com), 210 North Pentz Street, Dalton. With its first production in 1869, the group claims to be the oldest community theater in Georgia. Today operating out of the converted Historic Old Firehouse, the organization produces a wide range of live shows as well as the Firehouse Film Festival throughout the year. Call for a schedule of performances and ticket prices.

& **Historic Wink Theatre** (706-226-WINK; www.winktheatre.com), 114 West Crawford Street, Dalton. The opulent 1941 theater, designed to be a small-town version of the extravagant Fox Theatre in Atlanta, is the only example of art moderne architecture in north Georgia. The theater had a long career as a movie house until it closed in the 1970s. Now fully restored, it offers a variety of concerts, theatrical productions, classic movies, and other entertainment that keep it filled almost every weekend. Call for a schedule of performances and prices.

✳ Selective Shopping

ANTIQUES **Gateway Antiques and Collectibles Mall** (706-858-9685; www .gatewayantiques.com), 4103 Cloud Springs Road, Ringgold. Open 9–8 daily. More than 300 dealers purvey everything imaginable in the way of antiques and collectibles.

Le Frou Frou (706-375-7701), 112 Gordon Street, Chickamauga. Open 11–5 Tuesday–Friday, 11–4:30 Saturday. The shop carries a blend of vintage and classic antiques, as well as the Rachel Ashwell Shabby Chic line of bedding, accessories, and baby items.

BOOKS **The Book Nook and Cubby Hole Café** (706-226-8886), 229 North Hamilton Street, Dalton. Bookstore open 10–6 weekdays, 10–10 Saturday; café open 11–2:30 weekdays. Peruse the used hardbacks, paperbacks, and audiobooks, then enjoy soups, salads, coffees, and desserts. $4–12.

CARPETS **Carpets of Dalton** (706-277-3132 or 1-800-262-3132; www.carpetsof dalton.com), 3010 Old Dug Gap Road, Dalton. Open 8–6 Monday–Saturday. The emporium not only is a complete floor-covering store, but also houses the American Home Showplace, where shoppers can buy quality furniture; Buy the Room, where shoppers can buy furniture at discount prices; and World of Outdoor Living, a place to buy outdoor furniture and accessories.

Myers Carpet Company (706-277-4053 or 1-800-450-5551; www.myerscarpet.com), 3096 North Dug Gap Road, Dalton. Open 8:30–5 weekdays, 10–5:30 Saturday. The company, Dalton's oldest floor-covering

THE U.S. CARPET INDUSTRY

- The United States supplies 45 percent of the world's carpet.
- 80 percent of the U.S. carpet market is supplied by mills within a 65-mile radius of Dalton, Georgia.
- 90 percent of the carpet produced is tufted, a process that grew out of the chenille bedspread industry.
- The Georgia manufacturer with the largest number of employees (30,000) is a carpet manufacturer.
- The world's four largest carpet manufacturers are located in Georgia.

retailer, is the largest independent wool carpet dealer in the Southeast. It also produces custom-designed area rugs.

OTHER GOODS The Galleries on Gordon (706-375-9849), 111 Gordon Street, Chickamauga. Open 11–4 Monday, 10–5:30 Tuesday–Friday, 11–4 Saturday. Eighteen shops in one building purvey everything from antiques and art to home and garden decor, pottery, stationery, handbags, gourmet foods, and baby gifts.

OUTLET STORES Market Street Shops (706-277-2688), 1001 Market Street, Dalton. Open 9–9 Monday–Saturday, noon–6 Sunday. The outlet center features more than 24 designer and specialty shops—including Bass, Bon Worth, OshKosh B'gosh, and others—offering a wide variety of merchandise.

SPECIAL SHOPS Mountain City Mercantile (706-375-3800), 126 Gordon Street, Chickamauga. Open 10–6 Thursday–Saturday. Whether you want to purchase authentic Civil War reproductions or just browse, this 19th-century clothier and sutlery serves the reenactment and living-history community with quality merchandise that meets historical requirements. The offerings include Confederate and Union uniforms, footwear, accessories, cookware, haversack stuffers, and other items. The shop also offers cowboy merchandise from the period 1830–1899, as well as Victorian-era ladies' clothing and accessories.

✳ Special Events

September: **Battle of Tunnel Hill Civil War Reenactment** (706-871-1571; www .tunnelhillheritagecenter.com). Weekend after Labor Day. An exciting battle with 1,000 reenactors, cannon fire, and thundering horses showcases life during the Civil War. Visitors can walk through Union and Confederate camps, shop at sutlers' tents, see the tunnel, and enjoy food and entertainment. Held on the grounds of the historic Clisby Austin House in Tunnel Hill (see *To See—Historic Homes and Sites*). Adults $5, children $3.

War Between the States Day and Arts and Crafts Festival (Walker Chamber: 706-375-3177). This festival in Chickamauga features living-history programs with reenactors demonstrating camp life, artillery firing, period cooking, and life for area farm families affected by the battle. Another popular event is the Blue-Gray Barbecue Cookoff. Free.

October: **North Georgia Agricultural Fair** (706-278-1217). This popular 10-day agricultural and cultural event in Dalton features livestock, agricultural exhibits, a petting zoo, pony rides, a pageant, wrestling, midway rides and games, food, and live entertainment. Adults $5, children 4–12 $2; special discounts available.

Prater's Mill Country Fair (706-694-6455; www.pratersmill.org), 500 Prater's Mill Road off GA 2, Varnell. Columbus Day weekend. The old-fashioned country-fair-type festival features 200 quality artists and craftspeople, music, food, and other amusements. The mill, which was built by slaves in 1855 (see *To See—Historic Homes and Sites*), grinds corn during the fair. Visitors can take a self-guided tour of the mill, the Shugart Cotton Gin, the 1898 Prater's Store, and Westbrook Barn, and also examine the Gardner-Smith Farm Collection. Old-time demonstrations include blacksmithing, rug hooking, spinning, wood carving, quilting, and flint knapping. Adults $5, children under 12 free.

Mid-November–after New Year's: **Enchanted Garden of Lights at Rock City Gardens** (706-820-2531 or 1-800-854-0675; www.seerockcity.com), 1400 Patten Road, Lookout Mountain. Open 6–9 PM. This dazzling lights extravaganza features millions of lights and 30 holiday scenes that transform the garden (see *To See—For Families*) into a fantasyland. Other activities include entertainment, "snow," a visit with Santa, and refreshments. Adults $19–22, children $11–12; dinner with Santa extra.

GAINESVILLE AND LAKE LANIER

A s the county slogan proclaims, "From shorelines to finish lines to fabulous finds," Gainesville–Hall County offers some of the finest recreation in the South, from water sports to motor sports to major-league football.

Gainesville, once known as Mule Camp Springs, boasts a beautiful art deco–inspired downtown, unlike those of so many Georgia towns with historic town centers from the late 19th century. Although Gainesville's significance as a business and trading center goes back 200 years, a 1936 tornado demolished the downtown and killed many residents. President Franklin D. Roosevelt's New Deal programs made construction of a new downtown possible, thus reflecting the art deco style of the time. A monument to the president is in Roosevelt Square.

In recent years the city has earned the titles "Queen City of the Mountains," "Poultry Capital," and "Hospitality Capital of the World." The revitalized downtown features boutiques, cafés, antiques and collectible shops, and shops featuring the works of local artisans. In May and October, locals and visitors can enjoy Blue Sky Concerts (770-297-1141) during the noon hour. Bring a lunch or pick one up at a nearby eatery and settle back on one of the square's Victorian benches to enjoy the concert.

Lake Sidney Lanier, named after the beloved Georgia poet, is a 38,000-acre U.S. Army Corps of Engineers lake with 540 miles of shoreline, 60 recreational areas, and 7 commercial marinas. The lake, which was formed by the damming of the Chattahoochee River, is a major source of power in Georgia as well as a recreational playground. One of the lake's most popular attractions is Lake Lanier Islands, a resort area with hotels, a water park, golf, horseback riding, and other recreational activities.

GUIDANCE To find out more about Braselton, Buford, or Duluth, contact the **Gwinnett Convention and Visitors Bureau** (770-813-6054 or 1-888-494-6638; www.gcvb.org), 6500 Sugarloaf Parkway, Suite 200, Duluth 30097. Open 8–5 weekdays.

To learn more about Gainesville, contact the **Gainesville–Hall County Convention and Visitors Bureau** (770-536-5209 or 1-888-536-0005; www.gainesvillehallcvb.org), 117 Jesse Jewell Parkway, Gainesville 30503. Open 9–5 weekdays. Visitors also can stop by the **Greater Hall Chamber and Gainesville Welcome Center** (770-532-6206; www.greater hallchamber.com), 230 East Butler Parkway, Gainesville 30501. Open 8:30–5 Monday–Thursday, 8:30–4 Friday.

Some other helpful websites with information about the entire area include www.visitnorth eastgeorgia.com and www.georgiatouristguide.com.

GETTING THERE *By air:* The nearest full-service airport is in Atlanta (see "What's Where in Georgia"). Car rentals are available on-site and off-site. Several shuttle companies offer service to outlying locations.

By bus: In this area, **Greyhound Lines** (770-532-2641; www.greyhound.com) stops only in Gainesville (1780 Martin Luther King Jr. Boulevard). A visitor would then need a rental car to get around.

By car: The cities and towns described in this chapter are easily accessible from either I-85 or I-985, which run north–south, as do US 23, US 129, and US 441. GA 53 runs east–west.

By train: **AMTRAK**'s (1-800-USA-RAIL; www.amtrak.com) daily Crescent makes one of its three Georgia stops in Gainesville (116 Industrial Boulevard).

MEDICAL EMERGENCY Call 911.

VILLAGES AND NEIGHBORHOODS In Gainesville, visit the **Green Street Historic District.** Walk or drive along this half-mile, tree-lined historic street to enjoy turn-of-the-20th-century Queen Anne and neoclassical residences and businesses. A walking-tour brochure is available from the Gainesville–Hall County Convention and Visitors Bureau (117 Jesse Jewell Parkway).

Historic Downtown Gainesville's revitalized commercial district, centered on the Downtown Square, features an art center, art galleries, museums, restaurants, and specialty shops.

✴ To See

CULTURAL SITES 🐾 ⌖ **Historic Buford–Tannery Row Artist Colony** (770-904-0572; www.TanneryRowArtistColony.com), 554 West Main Street, Building C, Buford. Hours vary; see end of listing. Historic Buford stretches along Main Street from South Lee Street to Hill Street. The revitalized area boasts antiques shops, art galleries, and monthly arts events. The Tannery Row Artist Colony–Tannery Row Cultural Arts Center has a 13-acre facility in the former Bona Allen Shoe and Horse Collar Factory. Today, 17 artists—including glassblowers, jewelers, painters, photographers, sculptors, and wood-carvers—open their studios to allow the public to view works in progress (call or check the website for a schedule). Each month there is a festive opening reception 6–9 PM on the third Saturday for a show of an outstanding artist's work; studios are open that evening as well. Each month's show can be viewed noon–5 Tuesday–Saturday in the Tannery Row Gallery.

🐾 ⌖ **Quinlan Visual Arts Center** (770-536-2575; www.quinlanartscenter.org), 514 Green Street NE, Gainesville. Open 9–5 weekdays, 10–4 Saturday. Located in the Green Street Historic District, this regional arts organization, housed in an imposing Italian Renaissance building, sponsors classes, workshops, and world-class exhibitions. The center owns more than 100 pieces in its permanent collection but also shows the work of emerging, midcareer, and master artists as well as traveling exhibits in its two galleries. Free.

🐾 ⌖ **Smithgall Arts Center** (770-534-2787; www.theartscouncil.net), 331 Spring Street SW, Gainesville. Open 8:30–5 weekdays. Call for a schedule of events. The arts center is housed in a restored 1914 passenger train depot located next to the downtown square. The depot itself is unusual in that it is the only two-story depot in northeast Georgia. Activities include art exhibitions, the Pearce Series of guest performers, evenings of jazz and theater, outdoor summer concerts, the

NO FORKS ALLOWED

There is a city ordinance on the books in Gainesville, the Poultry Capital of the World, forbidding the use of utensils when eating fried chicken.

filmmakers series, movies on the green, and more (see the **Arts Council** under *Entertainment*). Free; some events have a fee.

FOR FAMILIES 🐾 ⚲ ♿ **Elachee Nature Science Center** (770-535-1976; www.elachee .org), 2125 Elachee Drive, Gainesville. Museum open 10–5 Monday–Saturday (shorter hours late November–March); trails open 8–dusk daily (except in extreme weather). The natural history museum and nature complex located in the 1,500-acre Chicopee Woods Nature Preserve features exhibits and live animals. The newest exhibit, *Waters of Time: the Chicopee Woods Story,* features two authentic fossilized mosasaur skeletons. Highlights include a Dino Dig box with real fossils to find, a 1-ton petrified log to climb on, a fossil collection to make rubbings from, and goop with which to create forest animal tracks. Astronomy Hall acquaints visitors with the solar system, while a live-animal room features fish, reptiles, and amphibians. Red-tailed hawks live in the aviary. The nature center sponsors many special activities, including **First Quarter Moon Fridays, First Saturday Hikes, Elachee's Spring Bird Festival, Elachee's Annual Snake Day,** and **Elachee's NightFall Halloween Festival.** See *Green Space—Nature Preserves and Parks.* Museum admission: adults $5, children 2–12 $3; trails free; admission charged for most special events and festivals.

🐾 ⚲ **Interactive Neighborhood for Kids (INK)** (770-536-1900; www.inkfun.org), 999 Chestnut Street, Gainesville. Open 10–5 Monday–Saturday, 1–5 Sunday. The children's museum contains hands-on interactive activities, including a dentist's office, Inkie's Market, Soda Pop's (a '50s diner), a bank, INK Clinic, a train depot, WINK radio station, and more. Guests up to four years old can enjoy Preschool Paradise, an area based on *Jack and the Beanstalk.* Not wheelchair accessible. Adults and children two and older $8.

HISTORIC HOMES AND SITES 🐾 ♿ **Banks County Historic Courthouse** (706-677-2108 or 1-800-638-5004; www.bankscountyga.org), 106 Yonah Homer Road, Homer. Open 9–1 weekdays. One of the four oldest courthouses in Georgia, this one houses the chamber of commerce and the local **Historical Society Museum,** which features art, World War II memorabilia, collector items, and historical records. Free.

🐾 ⚲ ♿ **Shields-Ethridge Heritage Farm** (706-367-2949; www.shieldsethridgefarminc .org), 2355 Ethridge Road, Jefferson. Open daylight hours daily April–October for self-guided tours of the grounds using an iPhone/iTouch app. This outdoor historical agricultural museum allows visitors to see a blacksmith shop, cotton gin, gristmill, fully stocked commissary, 1900 schoolhouse, mule barn, and a wheat house—some still in use—as well as historic farm equipment. The farm was established by James Shields in 1799 and lived in by generations of the same family for 200 years. Many special events occur at the farm, including the annual **Mule Day,** which includes demonstrations of traditional farm equipment by the Georgia Old Time Plow Club. Free except for special events.

MUSEUMS 🐾 ⚲ ♿ **Barrow County Museum** (770-307-1183), 74 West Athens Street, Winder. Open 1–4 weekdays. The museum, maintained by the Barrow County Historical Society, is housed in the old Barrow County Jail—a Gothic Revival castlelike structure that was built in 1915. A State Historic Site and listed on the National Register of Historic Places, the building features the original "hanging tower" (which was never used) and three original jail cells. Hundreds of artifacts have been donated by local citizens and placed into exhibits relating to native son Senator Richard B. Russell, county history, and nearby Fort Yargo, which was created as a defense against hostile Indians. Free.

🐾 ⚲ ♿ **Crawford W. Long Museum** (706-367-5307; www.crawfordlong.org), 28 College Street, Jefferson. Open 10–5 Tuesday–Friday, 10–4 Saturday. Known as "the Birthplace of Anesthesia," the museum honors the doctor who performed the first painless surgery, on March 30, 1842, using ether for surgical anesthesia. In the days when many doctors were self-trained or learned through an apprenticeship, Dr. Long was highly educated. He noticed that friends who were using ether for recreational purposes felt no pain from injuries sustained during their "frolics." He deduced ether could be used to lessen the effects of surgery, and he was correct—earning him the title "father of painless surgery." The Medical Museum houses Long's personal artifacts, documents highlighting his life and work in pharmacology, and early anesthesia equipment. The antebellum Pendergrass Store Building houses a re-created 1840s doctor's office and apothecary shop, and a replica of a 19th-century general store. Some household items trace the development of textiles from home spinning to "store bought" and the advancement of canned goods. There's also performance space for story-telling, live musical performances, and demonstrations. Outside, the Knot Garden features culinary and medicinal herbs. The Mulberry Tree museum shop carries works by local artisans, books, apparel, keepsakes, children's items, old-fashioned toys, herbal products, and regional souvenirs. The museum offers several history camps during the summer. Adults $5, seniors $4, students and military $3.

♀ ✂ ♿ **Flowery Branch Historic Train Depot Museum and Historic Caboose** (770-967-6371; www.flowerybranchga.org), Railroad Avenue and Main Street, Flowery Branch. Open 11–2 Saturday. The 100-plus-year-old depot is typical of the Craftsman style. The museum houses exhibits, pictures, and documents relating to the city's history. The 1914 wooden caboose is open to visitors as well, and a simulated railroad track walkway lies along the Railroad Avenue side of the building. Free.

♀ ✂ ♿ **Northeast Georgia History Center at Brenau University** (770-297-5900; www.negahc.org), 322 Academy Street, Gainesville. Open 10–4 Tuesday–Saturday. In addition to a display chronicling the history of the area, the museum includes a gallery dedicated to Ed Dodd, who created the *Mark Trail* environmental preservation comic strip; exhibits on black history, industrial history, and folk pottery; arts and crafts by north Georgians; the Northeast Georgia Sports Hall of Fame; an exhibit about Confederate general James Longstreet; and a separate railroad museum. Also on the grounds is **Chief White Path's Cabin,** circa 1780, a typical Cherokee home. The cabin—originally a one-room dwelling with a loft—was built by White Path's parents in what is now Ellijay. When land and property were taken away from the Cherokee in 1832, the cabin was acquired by a settler family who added a dogtrot central hallway and another downstairs room, as well as continuing the loft into a full second story. The cabin was relocated here in 1995 with the help of Counte Cooley, a descendant of Chief White Path. Artifacts and authentic period furnishings in the cabin permit visitors to get a glimpse into what life was like for Native Americans and early white settlers in northeast Georgia. The site also features vegetable and herb gardens typical of a Cherokee home. Before leaving the museum, visitors can get information for a self-guided **Longstreet Tour.** General James Longstreet, who was considered Robert E. Lee's right-hand man, retired to Gainesville for the last 29 years of his life and served in various local and federal governmental capacities and engaged in several business pursuits. He is buried in Gainesville at Alta Vista Cemetery. Adults $5, seniors $4, children $3.

CHIEF WHITE PATH

Born in 1761, his Cherokee name, Nunna-tsune-ga, translates to "I dwell on the peaceful (or white) path." In 1814, White Path and a small band of Cherokee joined Andrew Jackson to fight the Creeks at the Battle of Horseshoe Bend in Alabama, where they were instrumental in ensuring victory by stealing the Creeks' canoes and cutting off their escape. Unfortunately, the Cherokee were repaid with Andrew Jackson's removal policies. In 1838, when White Path was 77, he helped organize the removal to the West that was later known as the Trail of Tears. White Path didn't make it to Oklahoma but died in Hopkinsville, Kentucky, where he is buried.

ONE OF THE TRAINS ON DISPLAY AT THE
SOUTHEASTERN RAILWAY MUSEUM

🐾 ✍ ♿ **Southeastern Railway Museum**
(770-476-2013; www.southeasternrailway
museum.org), 3595 Peachtree Road,
Duluth. Open 10–5 Thursday–Saturday
year-round, also Monday and Wednesday in
summer and selected Sundays. The 30-acre
museum site, which is operated by volunteers of the Atlanta Chapter of the National
Railway Historical Society and designated as
Georgia's Official Transportation History
Museum, is dedicated to preserving, restoring, and operating historically significant
railway equipment. The chapter owns and
displays 90 pieces of retired rolling stock,
including wooden freight cars, vintage
steam locomotives, Pullman cars, and
maintenance-of-way equipment. Among the
vintage cars are a 1910 steam locomotive; the 1911 private car Superb, which was used by
President Warren G. Harding in 1923; and the Washington Club, a 1930 first-class lounge
car. Also on display are a 1940s railway post office, a rare World War II troop kitchen, and a
1922 Pullman coach. Vintage diesels pull the caboose train each Saturday as well as some
other heavily attended days, such spring break. The museum sponsors several special events
throughout the year. Wheelchair accessibility to the building but not the rail cars. Adults $8,
seniors $6, children 2–12 $5; Caboose Train Ride $3.

✳ To Do

AUTO RACING ✍ ♿ **Atlanta Dragway** (706-335-2301 or 770-682-3782; www.atlanta
dragway.com), 500 East Ridgeway Road, Commerce. The National Hot Rod Association
Power Aid drag-racing facility is the home of the Southern Nationals each May. Call for a
schedule of events and ticket prices.

✍ ♿ **Gresham Motorsports Park** (706-367-9461; www.greshammotorsportspark.com), 388
Lyle Field Road, Jefferson. Among the events held here are the Hooters Pro Cup and Georgia Asphalt Series. Check the website or call for a schedule of events and ticket prices.

✍ ♿ **Lanier National Speedway** (770-967-8600; www.lanierspeedway.com), One Raceway
Drive, Braselton. Races every Saturday evening, March–October. Georgia's only NASCAR
asphalt short track features stock-car races. The speedway hosts 2,500 spectators and 100
competitors every week, with racers coming from all over the Southeast to compete for
NASCAR points. Major events include the
Southern All Star Stock Car Racing Series,
USCS Outlaw Thunder Sprint Cars, ASA
Racing Series, and NASCAR All Pro 200.
The track offers spectators grandstand seat-
ing, track-side parking, and VIP suites.
Check the website or call for a schedule of
events and ticket prices.

✍ ♿ **Road Atlanta** (770-967-6143 or
1-800-849-RACE; www.roadatlanta
.com), 5300 Winder Highway, Braselton.
The area's premier road-racing facility,
Road Atlanta features one of the most

**FIRST FEMALE MAYOR IN
GEORGIA**
Alice H. Strickland (1861–1947) promised to
clean up the city of Duluth and rid it of
"demon rum." She allowed her home to be
used as a hospital where children could
have their tonsils removed and led conservation movements to protect forestlands. Her
donation of an acre of land for a community
forest was the first in the area.

challenging and exciting racetracks in the country. It is recognized as one of the world's best road courses. The 2.54-mile, 12-turn Grand Prix road course, which is home to the American LeMans Series and Panoz Motorsports, hosts internationally acclaimed events such as the Suzuki American Motorcycle Association Superbikes Showdown, Sports Car Club of America Trans Am Southern Dash, and Petit LeMans. Other attractions include professional and amateur auto and motorcycle races, Panoz Racing School, Audi Driving Experience, Audi Teen Driving Experience, Kevin Schwartz Suzuki School, and testing for professional and amateur racing teams. Limited camping is available in the infield for all races; reservations are required. Prebooked hot laps are available to the public. Check the website or call for a schedule of events and ticket prices. Parking free for most events; fee for infield parking.

BICYCLING ♂ **Chateau Elan Winery and Resort** (678-425-0900, ext. 49; www.chateau elan.com/energize/bike-trails), 100 Rue Charlemagne, Braselton. Seven miles of trails meander through the 3,500-acre property, through wooded areas, quiet nature paths, around the equestrian center, past the vineyards, along the championship golf courses, and through the exclusive residential area. Bikes, many of them Mountain Comfort models, can be rented through and picked up at the front desk. Bike rental $20 per day.

BOATING ♂ ♿ **Aqualand Marina** (770-967-6811; www.flagshipmarinas.com/marinas /aqualand, click on "Aqualand"), 6800 Lights Ferry Road, Flowery Branch. Open 9–5 daily. The full-service marina offers a fuel dock, pump-out facilities, boat docks, repairs, in-and-out services, shower and bath facilities, and a fully stocked store. The Windsong Sailing Academy (770-931-9151) is based here, and visitors can enjoy a meal at the Dockside Grill. Jet Ski and boat rentals are available. Call for hours and rates.

♂ ♿ **Gainesville Marina** (770-536-2171; www.gainesvillemarina.com), 2145 Dawsonville Highway, Gainesville. Open 8–5 daily. The full-service marina sells new and used boats, provides wet and dry storage and Jet Ski storage, supplies parts and gas, and has a pump-out station, bathhouse, and Skogie's Restaurant (678-450-1310; open 11–9 Wednesday–Friday, 8 AM–9 PM Saturday, 8–8 Sunday seasonally; breakfast $5–9, lunch and dinner $8–15).

♂ ♿ **Harbor Landing Marina** (770-932-7255 or 1-800-677-5304; www.lakelanierislands .com/harbor), 7000 Lake Lanier Islands Parkway, Lake Lanier Islands. Open 9–5 daily in summer; reduced hours the remainder of the year. With more than 90 rental boats, Harbor Landing offers the largest fleet on the lake. Choose from ski or pontoon boats or a houseboat. Fishing, tubing, and ski equipment are also available for rent. Call for rates, as they vary widely by season, type of boat, and length of rental; cheapest two-hour rental for an eight-passenger pontoon boat with a 25 horsepower motor: $100.

FAMILIES CAN RENT BOATS AT LAKE LANIER ISLANDS AND VARIOUS MARINAS ON THE LAKE.

♂ ♿ **Holiday Marina on Lake Lanier** (770-945-7201; www.holidaylakelanier.com), 6900 Lake Lanier Islands Parkway, Buford. Open 8–5 daily. The full-service marina offers boat and Jet Ski rentals, and also offers bathhouses and laundry facilities. The surrounding property features rental cabins and restaurants. Call for rates.

FISHING Lake Lanier is noted for its black, spotted, and largemouth bass. The

FISHING IS A POPULAR PASTIME AT LAKE LANIER.

striped bass, which is normally found in salt water, is stocked by the Georgia Department of Natural Resources and has adapted well.

Harold Nash Lake Lanier Striper and Bass Fishing Guide Service (770-967-6582; www.lanierfishingguide.com). The guide service specializes in trophy angling for giant stripers and bass. Call for schedules, fees, and meeting places.

Larry's Lanier Guide Services (770-842-0976 or 770-844-0976; www.lanierguide.com). Services are offered to novice anglers and pros. Call for a schedule, fees, and meeting places.

FLYING ✈ **Lanier Flight Center** (678-989-2395; www.lanierflightcenter.com), 1660 Palmour Drive at Lee Gilmer Memorial Airport, Gainesville. Office open 8–6 daily. Sight-seeing tours by air over Lake Lanier and the north Georgia mountains are available, as are flying lessons. Call for options and fees.

FOR FAMILIES ✿ ✈ ♿ **Lake Lanier Islands** (770-932-7200 or 1-800-677-5304; www.lakelanierislands.com), 7000 Lake Lanier Islands Parkway, Lake Lanier Islands. This 1,500-acre area on the southernmost shores of Lake Sidney Lanier is a not only a year-round vacation destination but also the most heavily visited water recreation area in the country. Facilities include a luxury hotel, numerous dining options, a spa, lake house rentals, and lakeside camping, as well as a par-72 golf course, tennis, horseback riding, boat rentals, a beach and water park (see next entry), and a zip line. One of the premier seasonal activities is the **Magical Nights of Lights** in December (see *Special Events*). Entrance fee $10 per car.

✈ ♿ **Lanierworld** (formerly Lake Lanier Islands Beach and Waterpark) (770-932-7218 or 1-800-840-LAKE; www.lanierworld.com), 6950 Lake Lanier Islands Parkway, Buford. Open weekends in May; 10–8 Sunday–Friday, 10 AM–11 PM Saturday, late May–early August; weekends only through late September. Located right on the lake, this exciting water park has 12 thrilling water attractions, including Wild Waves, the state's largest wave pool. Youngsters enjoy Kiddie Lagoon and Wiggle Waves. The park also boasts a 0.5-mile-long sandy white beach, beach volleyball, three dining options, and concessions. Sometimes there are concerts by popular groups and Saturday "dive-in" movies. Tube, locker, cabana, and umbrella rentals. Adults $34.99; children, seniors, and active military $19.99; reduced after 3 and again after 6.

GOLF Chateau Elan Golf Courses (tee times: 678-425-0900, ext. 44; 1-800-233-9463; www.chateauelan.com/golf), 6060 Golf Club Drive, Braselton. Open 7:30–dusk. So passionate about golf is Chateau Elan Resort that it has four golf courses: two public 18-hole courses—both of which are rated as among the top four courses in Georgia by the ESPN Zagat Survey; a nine-hole, par-3 executive walking course; and a private course. The public **Chateau Course** is 7,030 yards, par 71, with contoured fairways, three lakes, and two streams. Water comes into play on 10 holes. The public **Woodlands Course** is considered to be the most picturesque of the resort's courses. The 6,735-yard, par-72 course has numerous elevations, lakes, and tree-lined holes. The executive walking course behind the inn is the perfect venue for the golfer without a lot of time, for beginners, or for children. Holes vary in length from less than 100 yards to more than 200 yards. Amenities within the golf complex include clubhouses with restaurants and pro shops at the Chateau and Woodlands courses. Accommodations are available in two- or three-bedroom golf villas in addition to the inn or the spa (see *Lodging—Cottages and Cabins*). The practice facility, which has one of the highest ratings in the state, is the home of the **Dave Pelz Scoring Game School.** The program includes comprehensive practice facilities, highly skilled instructors, and video and computer analysis. There is a driving range, short game area, and putting green. $60–70. A real bargain is 9–5 Friday–Sunday: It costs only $18 to play the nine-hole course.

Legacy on Lanier Golf Club (770-945-8789; www.lakelanierislandsgolf.com), 7000 Lake Lanier Islands Parkway, Lake Lanier Islands. Open 7:10–5:30 daily. This award-winning, Billy Fuller–designed 18-hole, par-72 course boasts 12 holes with dazzling water views of Lake Lanier. The course features instruction, a pro shop, and the Golf Club Grille. $84–94.

HORSEBACK RIDING ✔ **Lake Lanier Islands Equestrian Center** (770-932-7233; www.lakelanierislands.com/equestrian.php), 7000 Lake Lanier Islands Parkway, Lake Lanier Islands. Open 10–5 daily, April–October; 11–4 daily, November–March; reservations recommended. Saddle up on one of the island's gentle horses for a scenic guided trail ride through the woods and along the lakeshore. Pony rides are available for children six and younger. Individual and group Western or English lessons are also available. $35 for 45-minute scenic trail ride, $15 for 30-minute pony ride, $45 for hour lesson. This is also the place to rent standard and multispeed bikes. The gently rolling roads throughout the resort make for easy to moderate rides.

MINIATURE GOLF ✸ ✔ ♿ **The Oaks Miniature Golf** (770-534-9547; www .oaksminigolf.com), 3709 Whiting Road, Gainesville. Open 11–9 daily, Memorial Day weekend–Labor Day weekend; call the rest of the year. The Oaks is the only mini golf course in the world that immerses visitors in the native environment—the oak-hickory forest of the Georgia Piedmont. The course is also the only one ever to win a design award from the American Society of Landscape Architects for environmental responsibility. There are no windmills or elephants, only a subtle nature theme with native Georgia plants. Adults $5–6.25, children $4–5.25.

SAILING ✔ **Lanier Sailing Academy** (770-945-8810 or 1-800-684-9463; www .laniersail.com), 6900 Lake Lanier Islands Parkway, Buford. Open 9–6 daily. One of the top American Sailing Association schools, the academy offers sailing classes from practical sailing to offshore passage and also provides the largest sailboat rental fleet on Lake Lanier. To rent a boat, sailors

SAILING ON LAKE LANIER

must be certified. Sunset sails are very popular. Half day $180–220. Call for other lesson and rental prices.

SPAS ☐ **The Healing Arts Spa on Green Street** (678-450-1570; www.spaongreen street.com), 635 Green Street, Gainesville. Open 10–7 Monday–Saturday (last appointment at 5:30). Located in the beautiful and historic Dunlap House, a Colonial Revival home that until recently was an upscale bed & breakfast, the spa does BioEnergetic assessment, acupuncture, massage, body treatments, and skin care. Treatments and services $40–150, packages $135–259, bioenergy and wellness $90–150.

☐ **The Spa at Chateau Elan Winery and Resort** (appointments: 678-425-0900, ext. 41; www.chateauelan.com/spa), 100 Rue Charlemagne, Braselton. Open 8–8 daily. Indulgences at the serene and romantic spa are guaranteed to make you feel renewed. Located beside a sparkling lake surrounded by trees, manicured green lawns, and flowering shrubs, the spa is contained within a French country–style Spa Mansion (678-425-6064), which also offers exquisite accommodations (see *Lodging*) and healthful gourmet dining for breakfast, lunch, and dinner at the sunny Fleur-de-Lis restaurant. Spa treatments are available à la carte or may be purchased as an overnight package with accommodations at the inn. All-day or overnight spa packages include use of the steam room, sauna, whirlpool, indoor resistance pool, and fitness area, plus classes, a spa lunch, afternoon tea, and a tour of the winery; some overnight packages include other meals as well. The fitness room, which is open 24/7, features a variety of health and fitness equipment. The spa also offers the **LOTUSEA Wellness Program,** which includes a personal health assessment, comprehensive lab testing, classes, and spa amenities. Use of the facilities $25–35 for guests, $50 for nonguests. Spa services $50–230 for individuals, $200–345 for couples; packages $190–685; wellness program $200–300.

☐ **Tranquility, The Spa** (678-318-7887 or 1-800-677-5304; www.lakelanierislands.com /activities/spa), 7000 Lake Lanier Islands Parkway, Lake Lanier Islands. Open 10–5 Tuesday–Thursday and Sunday, 10–6 Friday, 9–6 Saturday. Located at the **Legacy at Lanier Resort** (see *Lodging—Inns and Resorts*), the spa offers numerous ways to relax and fortify the mind, body, and spirit, including six types of massage and a wide array of body treatments, facials, manicures, pedicures, and hair services. Treatments and services $25–190, packages $145–265.

SPORTING EVENTS ☐ ☐ **Chicopee Woods Agricultural Center** (770-531-6855; www.hallcounty.org/parks), 1855 Calvary Church Road, Gainesville. Office open 8–5 weekdays. All kinds of events occur here, including equestrian competitions, rodeos, animal expositions, mountain bike races, archery competitions, and festivals. Call for a schedule of events and ticket prices.

☐ ☐ **Clarks Bridge Park/Lake Lanier Olympic Center** (parks department: 770-535-8280; Lanier Canoe and Kayak Club: 770-287-7888; www.lckc.org), 3105 Clarks Bridge Road, Gainesville. Call for a schedule of events and ticket prices. Once the site of the 1996 Centennial Olympic Summer Games' rowing, sprint canoe, and kayak events, and the Lanier Canoe 2003 World Championships, the facility has amphitheater seating, a state-of-the-art finish tower, and a unique race course that shelters paddlers from wind and provides clean water year-round. The center provides a permanent facility for two sports and still sponsors national and international canoe, kayak, and rowing events throughout the year. Canoe and kayak rentals are available, and there is also a beach and boat ramp.

☐ ☐ **The Equestrian Center at Chateau Elan** (678-425-0900, ext. 6207; www.chateau elan.com/events/equestrian), 100 Rue Charlemagne, Braselton. With a covered and lighted arena, four large and lighted all-weather rings, two smaller warm-up areas, 196 permanent stalls, and room for 200 temporary stalls, the center is the site of many equestrian and canine shows throughout the year. Concerts, arts and crafts shows, and car shows also are held here. Call for a schedule of events and ticket prices.

❡ & **Georgia Force** (770-609-1300; www.georgiaforce.com). The Force plays arena football at the Arena at Gwinnett Center, Sugarloaf Parkway. Check the website or call for a schedule of games and ticket prices. Single ticket price $14.15–109.20.

WALKING TOURS ❡ ❡ & **Solar System Tour: Gainesville Scale-Model Walking Tour of Our Solar System** (contact North Georgia Astronomers: www.northgeorgiaastronomers.org/scale model/index.html). The 1.8-mile tour takes visitors from the sun, on the square, down to Pluto, on Lake Lanier. Ask for a brochure.

WINERY TOURS ❡ & **Chateau Elan Winery and Resort** (678-425-0900, ext. 6354; www.chateauelan.com/epicurean /winery), 100 Rue Charlemagne, Braselton. Open 10–8 Sunday–Thursday, 10–9 Friday, 10–10 Saturday. Two tours weekdays ($5), five tours weekends ($10). Housed in a replica of a 16th-century-style French

CHATEAU ELAN WINERY AND RESORT

château that rises out of a northeast Georgia field filled with grapevines, this full-production winery is the largest producer of premium wines in Georgia. Approximately 75 acres are planted with *vinifera* French and French-American hybrid grapes, from which 11 wines are produced. Wine tours of the operation are offered and culminate with a tasting of several varieties.

Naturally, after touring the winery and tasting some of its vintages, visitors may wish to take some home. The **Wine Market** (ext. 6354), located just adjacent to the tasting room, sells Chateau Elan wines and a wide variety of wine-related gifts, as well as Irish crystal, quality golf shirts with the Chateau logo, custom-made gift baskets, and other unique gift items. **Le Clos** (see *Where to Eat—Dining Out*) is the winery's fine-dining restaurant. The informal, bistro-style **Café Elan** (ext. 6317) has the cozy ambience of a provincial European restaurant, where chefs create Mediterranean dishes. Open 11–4 and 5–10 daily; reservations recommended.

✳ Green Space

LAKES Lake Lanier is a water-lover's paradise. The huge lake is 26 miles long, covers 38,000 acres, has 540 miles of shoreline, and touches five counties. It offers many water sports and other outdoor recreation. (Under *To Do*, see *Boating, Fishing, Flying, For Families, Golf, Horseback Riding,* and *Sailing,* and under *Lodging,* see *Campgrounds, Cottages and Cabins,* and *Inns and Resorts.*)

NATURE PRESERVES AND PARKS ✿ ✸ ♿ **Chattahoochee-Oconee National**

Forest (district office: 770-297-3000; www.fs.usda.gov), 1755 Cleveland Highway, Gainesville. Office open 9–4 Tuesday–Friday; park open daylight hours daily. The vast forest offers opportunities for bird-watching and wildlife observation, camping, fishing, hiking, horseback riding (BYOH—bring your own horse), photography, and riding off-road vehicles. Call or check the website for specifics, including fees.

✿ ✸ ♿ **Elachee Nature Preserve** (770-535-1976; www.elachee.org), 2125 Elachee Drive, Gainesville. Open 8–dusk daily. *Elachee* is the Cherokee word for "new green earth." The 1,500-acre nature preserve is among the largest land trusts in north Georgia and one of the biggest within city limits east of the Mississippi River. It features the **Elachee Nature Science Center** (see *To See—For Families*). Outside are native plant and rain demonstration gardens, a wheelchair-accessible path, a 1-mile loop trail along a gently flowing creek, and 12 miles of trails throughout pine forests, hardwood ridges, streams, and wetlands. A new addition is the **Chicopee Woods Aquatic Studies Center and Chicopee Lake,** which was created to study pond life and wetland inhabitants. Located some distance from the nature center building, it can be reached by a 2.5-mile trail or by car. Use of the trails free; admission fee for museum.

✿ ✸ ♿ 🐾 **Fort Yargo State Park** (770-867-3489; lodging reservations: 1-800-864-7275; www.gastateparks.org/FortYargo), GA 81, Winder. Open 7 AM–10 PM daily. Named for a 1792 log fort built by early settlers as protection against Creek and Cherokee Indians, the 1,814-acre park offers camping and cottages (see *Lodging—Campgrounds* and *Lodging—Cottages and Cabins*); the 260-acre Marbury Creek Reservoir, with a swimming beach and canoe, fishing, and pedal-boat boat rentals in season; 8 miles of hiking and biking trails along the lakeshore; picnicking; and miniature and disc golf (additional fees). Other recreational amenities include boat ramps and tennis courts. Private boats are allowed but restricted to 10 horsepower. Numerous special events occur throughout the year. Parking $5.

✿ ✸ ♿ **Hurricane Shoals Park** (706-652-2370; www.hurricaneshoalspark.org), 416 Hurricane Shoals Road, Maysville. Open 9–9 daily, April–October; 9–6 weekends, March and November; closed December–February. The wooded park is named for the shoals that are popular for swimming, wading, and tubing. Alongside the stream is an old gristmill, and a heritage village is being developed around it. Historic buildings moved here from other places include a chapel, courthouse, log cabins, blacksmith shed, tool shed, smokehouse/wagon shelter, privy, barn, and covered bridge. Other features of the park include a playground and an amphitheater. The mill operates during the **Art in the Park** arts festival, held here in September. Free.

✴ Lodging

BED & BREAKFASTS

In Flowery Branch

✿ ✸ ♿ **Whitworth Inn** (770-967-2386; www.whitworthinn.com), 6593 McEver Road. With its columns and verandas on both floors, the inn looks like a gracious Southern mansion of old, but it was actually built to serve as a bed & breakfast. Ten rooms with private baths are individually decorated to create distinct personalities. Some feature four-poster beds; one has two double beds. A full breakfast is included.

No smoking. One room wheelchair accessible. $85.

CAMPGROUNDS

In Gainesville

✿ ✸ ♿ **River Forks Park** (770-531-3952; www.hallcounty.org/parks), 3500 Keith Bridge Road. Open March 1–December 31. The park offers 63 campsites with water and electric hookups, a bathhouse with showers, restrooms, and a pump-out station, as well as all the facilities of the park, which include horseshoes, volleyball, playgrounds, a boat ramp, and a swimming beach on the lake. Campsites $20, tent sites $15.

At Lake Lanier Islands

🐾 🍃 ♿ **Lake Lanier Islands Campground** (770-932-7270 or 678-482-0332; www.lakelanierislands.com/accommodations /campground.asp), 7000 Lake Lanier Islands Parkway. The campground offers 300 year-round sites, a fishing pier, boat ramp, pavilion, and camp store. The resort also operates the **Shoal Creek Campground** (6300 Shadburn Ferry Road). It features 100 sites on a peninsula where many sites are waterfront or have a water view. The campground features a bathhouse, laundry facilities, a boat ramp, playground, swimming area, and dump station. $21–39.

In Winder

🐾 🍃 ♿ 🐾 **Fort Yargo State Park** (lodging reservations: 1-800-864-7275). The park offers 40 tent, trailer, and RV sites, and 9 walk-in sites. $25–29, walk-in sites $23. See also *Green Space—Nature Preserves and Parks.*

COTTAGES AND CABINS

In Braselton

🍃 ♿ 🐾 **The Golf Villas at Chateau Elan Winery and Resort** (678-425-0900, ext. 41; www.chateauelan.com/golf/villas.html), 100 Rue Charlemagne. The villas are located on the 15th fairway of the Chateau Course and within walking distance of the pro shop and Clubhouse Grille (see *To Do—Golf*). Each villa has two or three bedrooms and baths, a large open plan, a fully equipped kitchen, and a living room with a fireplace. Golf packages include accommodations, breakfast, and one round of golf on the Chateau or Woodlands course. Pets allowed. $295–445.

At Lake Lanier Islands

🍃 **The Lake Houses at Legacy on Lanier** (1-800-677-5304; www.lakelanier islands.com/accommodations/lakehouses .asp), 7000 Holiday Road. The waterfront New England–style cottages are nestled among towering pines. Each cottage offers

two bedrooms (one with a king-size bed, the other with two doubles) and baths, a great room with a fireplace, high-speed Internet access, a washer and dryer, and modern kitchen. Outside on the deck are a gas grill and a heated spa. $329–409.

In Winder

🐾 🍃 ♿ 🐾 **Fort Yargo State Park** (lodging reservations: 1-800-864-7275). The park features three fully equipped cottages and six yurts. One cottage is dog friendly ($40 per dog; maximum two). $120, yurts $70. See also *Green Space—Nature Preserves and Parks.*

INNS AND RESORTS

In Braselton

🍃 ♿ **The Inn at Chateau Elan Winery and Resort** (678-425-0900; www.chateau elan.com), 100 Rue Charlemagne. The four-star, four-diamond property is truly a resort in every sense of the word, with multitudinous offerings in addition to exquisite guest accommodations. The property, located on the site of a winery, is the flagship of Chateau Elan Hotels and Resorts, a group of luxury properties in the United States and overseas. The French country château–style inn features 275 deluxe guest rooms, including 20 suites, a Presidential Suite, a Governor's Suite, and 17 fully wheelchair-accessible rooms. Each guest accommodation boasts all the modern amenities along with a luxurious bath with an oversized tub and separate shower. There are also a swimming pool and a conference center. Also within the inn building are the following dining venues: **Versailles** restaurant, which serves breakfast and lunch buffets and à la carte dinners daily, and **L'Auberge** lounge, with large-screen televisions, championship-size pool tables, light foods, and live entertainment on Friday and Saturday evenings. Other restaurants at the resort include **Le Clos** (see *Where to Eat—Dining Out*) and **Café Elan in the Winery, Fleur-de-Lis** in the Spa Mansion, the **Clubhouse Grille** on the Chateau Golf Course, and **Paddy's Irish Pub** (see *Where to Eat—Eating Out*). The centerpiece of the resort is the winery (see *To Do—Winery Tours*). The resort also boasts accommodations at the spa (see next entry) and in golf villas (see *Cottages and Cabins*); several golf courses and a golf academy (see *To Do—Golf*); a spa (see *To Do—Spas*); walking/biking trails and bike rentals (see *To Do—Bicycling*); and an equestrian center (see *To Do—Sporting Events*). No smoking. No pets. $164–259.

⑁ **Spa Mansion at Chateau Elan Winery and Resort** (678-425-0900; www.chateauelan.com), 100 Rue Charlemagne. Located in a separate building from the main inn, the 14 luxurious spa suites exude style and comfort. Each features a two-person air-jet tub and/or a Raindance shower. The spa facilities (see *To Do—Spas*) are located in this building, as is the **Fleur-de-Lis** restaurant. All the other amenities of the resort are located nearby. No smoking. Some wheelchair accessible. $400–450.

At Lake Lanier Islands

🐾 ⑁ **Legacy Lodge and Conference Center** (1-800-677-5304; www.lakelanierislands.com), 7000 Lake Lanier Islands Parkway. The centerpiece of Lake Lanier Islands is the resort hotel, which features 287 guest rooms and suites—many with lake views. Rooms and suites, which can be rented in different configurations, are also offered in the Legacy Villas. Spa services are available (see **Tranquility, The Spa** under *To Do—Spas*). The resort has two restaurants: **Windows Restaurant,** open for a breakfast buffet daily as well as special events such as monthly wine-tasting dinners and a summertime seafood buffet; and **Bullfrog's Bar and Grille,** a publike eatery serving lunch and dinner daily. Diners can eat inside or poolside. The resort also offers a championship 18-hole golf course (see *To Do—Golf*), horseback riding (see *To Do—Horseback Riding*), a summertime beach and water park (see *To Do—For Families*), a fleet of rental boats (see *To Do—Boating*), tennis courts, a swimming pool, fitness center, gift shop, business center, and jogging trails. $139 in season, $119 off-season.

✴ Where to Eat

DINING OUT

In Braselton

⑁ **Le Clos at Chateau Elan Winery and Resort** (678-425-0900, ext. 6317; www.chateauelan.com), 100 Rue Charlemagne. Open 6–9 PM Friday and Saturday; reservations and upscale casual attire required. The intimate fine-dining room resembles a Mediterranean courtyard. In this setting, seasonal French classic cuisine with American influence is served. Plan to make an evening of it, because the five-course prix-fixe dinner typically takes up to two and a half hours to complete. The staff will recommend two, three, or five wine pairings to accompany the meal for an additional charge, or diners may purchase wine by the bottle. No children or cell phones. No smoking. Prix-fixe three-course $58, five-course $78, plus wine pairings with Chateau Elan wines $35.

In Gainesville

⑁ **Luna's Restaurant and Piano Lounge** (770-531-0848; www.lunas.com), 200 Main Street. Open 11:30–2:30 and 5–10 weekdays, 5–11 Saturday. Located on the ground level of the Hunt Tower, Luna's offers American-Continental fine dining. An intimate romantic ambience is created by wall murals, crisp white table linens, candlelight, and soothing music. Luncheon items include salads, sandwiches, and pastas. Dinner items include steaks, seafood, lamb, chicken, and pork selections. Friday and Saturday nights, the lounge, with its grand piano and fireplace, offers music, dancing, and drinks. No smoking. Lunch $10–11, dinner about $21.

EATING OUT

In Braselton

🐾 ⑁ **Paddy's Irish Pub at Chateau Elan Winery and Resort** (678-425-0900, ext. 6074; www.chateauelan.com), 100 Rue Charlemagne. Open 2–midnight daily. All the fixtures and furnishings at Paddy's are completely authentic, created in Ireland, shipped to the resort, and then reassembled. The pub serves traditional Irish food and beverages, and provides Irish music and song on Friday and Saturday evenings beginning at 8:30. No smoking. Single menu for lunch and dinner $15–30.

In Duluth

⚓ **Park Café** (770-476-2989; www.park cafeduluth.com), 3579 West Lawrenceville Street. Open 11–3 and 5–9 Tuesday–Thursday, until 10 Friday and Saturday. Reservations suggested but not required. In this quaint, relaxing restaurant, located in the century-old Knox House overlooking the town green, diners can enjoy casual American dining with a Southern flair. There are chef's specials almost every evening, special menus to accommodate theatergoers on their way to a production at the **Red Clay Theatre,** and wine tastings at 6:30 every Wednesday. Dinner entrées include seafood, steaks, salads, and Southern favorites. Some diners prefer the patio, which is enclosed and heated in winter. The café's market sells wine, cheese, gourmet food items, and gift baskets. No smoking. Lunch $9–10, dinner $17–25.

At Lake Lanier Islands

These three eateries are located at the **Legacy on Lanier Resort** and can all be reached at 1-800-677-5304.

🎣 ⚓ **Bullfrog's Bar and Grille.** Open 11–10:30 daily. Diners can eat inside or poolside in season, enjoying such light fare as salads and sandwiches to more substantial entrées. While this eatery can please any palate, Bullfrog's isn't just a place to eat—it's a place to play. There's Ping-Pong, Foosball, ice hockey, bumper pool, chess, Scrabble, and backgammon. Lunch $11–15, dinner $11–25.

🎣 ⚓ **Sunset Cove Beach Café and Club.** Open 11–11 daily in summer, weekends May and September. The casual eatery is open-air, so it's open only seasonally depending on the weather. Tiki torches and giant fire pits create the ambience for this party place. There's often live music or other entertainment. Wake Board Wednesdays feature a stunt show. Full Moon Parties (monthly at the full moon) feature music, dance, a juggler, fire eater, stilt

walker, and fireworks. Inside there's a big-screen TV for watching sporting events. Oh yes, the food: burgers, brats, hot dogs, barbecue, and seafood. $10–14.

🎣 ⚓ **Windows Restaurant at Legacy on Lanier Resort.** Open 8:30–10:30 AM Monday–Saturday for breakfast buffet, 10:30–1 Sunday for brunch buffet, and 6–9 PM Friday and Saturday for dinner buffet. The restaurant is known for its buffets—especially the lavish brunch buffet; the Friday-night seafood buffet laden with lobster, shrimp, crab, and oysters on the half shell; and the Saturday-night lowcountry boil buffet. Breakfast buffet $15, brunch and dinner buffets $29.99.

✳ Entertainment

The Arts Council (770-534-2787; www.theartscouncil.net), 331 Spring Street SW, Gainesville. The council represents various art forms and sponsors the Pearce Series, Evenings of Intimate Jazz, the outdoor Summer MusicFest, Theatre at the Depot, and numerous other events (see **Smithgall Arts Center** under *To See—Cultural Sites*). Check the website or call for a schedule of events and prices.

🎣 ⚓ **Georgia Mountains Center** (770-534-8420; www.georgiamountainscenter.com), 301 Main Street SW, Gainesville. Box office open 8–5 weekdays. The event and concert venue presents theatrical performances, musical groups, and other events. Check the website or call for a schedule of events and prices.

⚓ **John S. Burd Center for the Performing Arts at Brenau University** (770-535-6246), 429 Academy Street, Gainesville. The **Hosch Theatre** is the venue for musical concerts, dance and theatrical productions, and other performing arts. The center also houses the **Banks Recital Hall** and an art gallery. Call for a schedule and ticket prices.

DANCE **Gainesville Ballet Company** (770-532-4241; www.gainesvilleballet.org), mailing address: P.O. Box 1663, Gainesville 30501. The company, made up of students and professionals, has been performing classics such as *The Nutcracker* and *Alice in Wonderland* for more than 30 years. Performances at Pearce Auditorium at Brenau University. Call for a schedule of performances and ticket prices.

MUSIC **Gainesville Symphony** (770-532-5727; www.gainesvillesymphony.com). The orchestra, which performs at Brenau University, performs a classical masterworks series as well as pops. Two much-anticipated events are the July Patriotic Pops and the Holiday Pops. Adults $27, seniors $20, children $12.

THEATER **Gainesville Theatre Alliance** (box office: 678-717-3624; www.gainesvilletheatrealliance.org), mailing address: P.O. Box 1358, Gainesville 30503. The Gainesville Theatre Alliance (GTA), a collaboration by Gainesville College, Brenau University, and the community through the Theatre Wings organization, is a training ground for theater professionals and educators. GTA is the first college- and community-based theater in the state to be funded by the Georgia Council for the Arts, and it is consistently rated among the top 10 theaters in the state. GTA has performance spaces at Brenau University's **Hosch Theatre,** Pearce Auditorium, and Little Theatre, and Gainesville College's Ed Cabell Theatre. GTA produces three drama, comedy, musical, or classic productions annually in November, February, and April. The Discovery Series, often the thesis projects of graduating seniors, can be edgy and more off the beaten path than main-stage productions. Check the website or call for a schedule of performances and ticket prices.

✳ Selective Shopping

Several areas are particularly noted for shopping. The **Flowery Branch Main Street Square** features unique shops and restaurants. **Gainesville's Main Street Marketplace,** built in 1886, is an open-air market with an array of distinctive shops and restaurants. Many people died here during a 1936 tornado, and legend has it that many of their spirits still inhabit the space, but modern-day visitors are more interested in the shops. **Banks Crossing,** in Commerce, is one of the most popular outlet centers in the South.

CRAFTS **Raven's Nest Artisans Marketplace** (770-242-3901), 3109 South Main Street, Duluth. Open 10–6 Tuesday–Friday, 10–5 Saturday. Shop here for handcrafted potpourri, teas, herbs, spices, fragrance oils, herbal bath products, stained glass, jewelry, photography, antiques, folk art, crocheted and knitted items, woodwork, and more. Classes and live musical entertainment are often scheduled.

FLEA MARKETS **Pendergrass Flea Market** (706-693-4466 or 1-866-234-3532; www.pendflea.com), 5641 US 129 North, Jefferson. Open 9–6 weekends. At the 250,000-square-foot flea market, 500 dealers sell just about anything you can think of, including but not limited to antiques, collectibles, furniture, produce, and even livestock. Stay all day; there's a food court. Free admission and parking.

OUTLET STORES **Commerce Factory Stores** (706-335-6352), 199 Pottery Factory Drive, Commerce. Open 9–9 Monday–Saturday, noon–6 Sunday. A pipsqueak compared to its much larger cousin, Tanger Outlets, this center has 20 stores, including Lenox and Dress Barn.

Tanger Outlets of Commerce (706-335-3354 or 1-800-405-9828; www.tangeroutlet.com/commerce), Tanger I: 111 Tanger Drive; Tanger II: 800 Steven B. Tanger Boulevard, Commerce. Open 9–9 Monday–Saturday, 11–7 Sunday. Located for easy access at US 441 and I-85, the centers offer 125 manufacturer and designer stores ranging from A (Adidas) to Z (Zales). For the serious shopper, several hotels and restaurants are nearby.

POTTERY 🐾 ♿ **Crocker Folk Pottery** (770-869-3160), 6345 West Country Line Road, Lula. Open 9–5 weekdays. Michael

Crocker, a nationally acclaimed north Georgian folk potter, has work on display at the Smithsonian. He is known for face jugs and jugs encircled by representations of north Georgia snakes. Other folk potters also have their work for sale here.

Hewell's Pottery (770-869-3469; www .hewellspottery.com), 6305 Highway 52, Gillsville. Open 7:30–5 Monday–Thursday, 7:30–4 Friday and Saturday. Generations of the Hewell family have been making pottery since 1860—everything from flowerpots to glazed collector pieces. Three generations are currently working there. Hewell's is the largest producer of unglazed horticultural ware in the East and Midwest, and it's all created by hand in a 10-wheel shop. The shopping area is open year-round to sell folk pottery fired in a wood-burning groundhog kiln, garden pottery, churns, pocket berry planters, nostalgic signs, bent hickory furniture, home accessories, and gift items.

Turpin Pottery (706-677-1528; www .turpinpottery.com), 2500 US 441, Homer. Open 8–2 Monday–Thursday, by appointment Friday–Sunday. Steve Turpin has been creating pottery for more than 30 years, and his pieces are highly sought after. Also for sale are pieces made by Steve's daughter, Abby. She started with face jugs but has moved on to include small chickens and snake jugs.

✳ Special Events

June: **City Lights Festival** (706-335-3164). Held the third weekend in June, this event could be called "Nashville Comes to Commerce." Native son and country music legend "Whispering" Bill Anderson brings stars from Nashville—performers such as Charley Pride, Jimmy Dean, Jan Howard, Mel Tillis, and Vince Gill—to perform at the City Lights Concert. In addition, the festival features eight events over three days, including a golf tournament, Dinner with the Stars, Stars 'N' Cars, Bark in the Park, live music, arts, crafts, and food. Some activities free; others have a small fee.

North Georgia Folk Potters Festival (call Steve Turpin: 706-677-1528; www .northgafolkpotteryfestival). Held in Homer at Banks County Middle School, 712 Thompson Street, this giant pottery sale is an opportunity to purchase directly from a wide variety of potters gathered in one spot. Older collectible pieces are offered for sale as well. Free.

August: **Chateau Elan Vineyard Fest** (www.chateauelan.com/exclusives/vineyard -fest). Activities include the tasting of 100 wines from around the world, wine seminars, cooking demonstrations, a food pavilion, a tour of the winery in Braselton, live musical entertainment, dancing, and grape stomping. $75 advance ticket sales only.

September: **Duluth Fall Festival** (770-476-0240 or 1-855-385-8841; www.duluth fallfestival.com). The weekend festival in Duluth kicks off with a parade, and then the action moves to the Festival Center and Amphitheater, where there's a carnival, 250 arts and crafts and food vendors, continuous entertainment, a children's area, an auction, and more. Free; some activities have a fee.

Mid-November–December 30: **Magical Nights of Lights** (770-932-7200; www .lakelanierislands.com/tickets). Village open 5–10 nightly. The annual extravaganza at Lake Lanier Islands claims to be the largest animated light display in the world. More than 1 million lights create gigantic animated characters and scenes along a 7-mile drive. Visitors can tune their car radios to a special station to listen to holiday favorites while making the drive. At the end there is a holiday village, where there's a zip line, petting zoo, pony rides, carnival rides, shopping, refreshments, an opportunity to visit with Santa, and a bonfire for roasting marshmallows. $40 per car Monday–Thursday, $60 Friday–Sunday. The zip line, petting zoo, pony rides, and carnival rides are all priced separately, $4–20, or you can get an all-inclusive ticket for $99 for two people.

HARTWELL AND ELBERTON

T his area of northeast Georgia is defined by significant lakes and the granite industry. It also has one of the largest concentrations of state parks in Georgia, making it a magnet for outdoor-recreation enthusiasts. Here, the waters from the Broad and Savannah rivers are impounded in the largest man-made lake east of the Mississippi. The lake, which straddles the Georgia–South Carolina border, has a split personality. In Georgia it's called Clarks Hill Lake; in South Carolina, Strom Thurmond Lake. Whatever you call it, this lake offers innumerable opportunities for water sports and other outdoor pursuits.

The area is also rich in historic sites, Native American lore, bed & breakfasts, casual eateries, antiques and other shopping, and a variety of special events.

Some of the most unusual attractions in the state are found here.

GUIDANCE When planning a trip to Elberton, consult the **Elbert County Chamber and Welcome Center** (706-283-5651; www.elbertga.com), 104 Heard Street, Elberton 30635. Open 9–5 weekdays.

To learn more about Hartwell, contact the **Hart County Chamber of Commerce** (706-376-8590; www.hart-chamber.org), 31 East Howell Street, Hartwell 30643. Open 8:30–5 weekdays.

To find out more about Lavonia, consult the **Lavonia Chamber of Commerce** (706-356-8202; www.lavonia-ga.com), 12221 Augusta Road, Lavonia 30553. Open 9–noon and 1–5 weekdays. Or stop by the **Georgia Visitor Information Center–Lavonia** (706-356-4019; www.exploregeorgia.org), 938 County 84, Lavonia 30553. Open 8:30–5:30 daily, restrooms 7 AM–11 PM. In addition to obtaining brochures and other information here, travelers can enjoy the use of picnic tables and grills. There is also a pet walking area.

GETTING THERE *By air:* Most visitors fly into Atlanta, Athens, or Greenville-Spartanburg, South Carolina. For airport, airline, and car rental information at each, see "What's Where in Georgia."

By bus: **Greyhound Lines** (706-549-2255 or 1-800-231-2222; www.greyhound.com) offers service to nearby Athens (see the Athens chapter in part 3: Historical South), but then a visitor would have to rent a car to get to and around this area.

By car: The towns described in this chapter are located near the Georgia–South Carolina border and are easily accessed via I-85 from Atlanta to the southwest or from Greenville-Spartanburg, South Carolina, and other points from the northeast. US 29 also runs north–south; GA 72 runs east–west.

By train: **AMTRAK** (see "What's Where in Georgia") operates service to Atlanta and Augusta (see the Augusta chapter in part 3: Historical South), but then a visitor would need a car to get to and around this area.

MEDICAL EMERGENCY Call 911.

VILLAGES AND NEIGHBORHOODS **Hart County** and its county seat, **Hartwell,** were named for Nancy Morgan Hart, a Revolutionary War hero. But even before settlers had moved in, the Cherokee met here to trade with tribes from more southerly regions. Their meeting place was known to them as the Center of the World. After the Revolutionary War, veterans settled here; their gravestones can be found in local cemeteries.

The **Hartwell Historic District** has several commercial buildings and residences of historic and architectural interest. Hartwell also is revitalizing its downtown, which is the site of many festivals throughout the year. New, trendy shops and exciting restaurants are popping up near the art center and the historic post office. **Historic Depot Street,** named for the old train station, offers gift shops, antiques stores, art galleries, a candle factory, Bluegrass Music Hall, and the **Hart County Community Theatre** (see *Entertainment*).

The hard-rock town of **Elberton,** the top producer of granite in America, calls itself "the Granite Capital of the World" because of the amount of granite extracted from nearby quarries. Most of the stone is produced for gravestones, but some is used for building material and some for sculpture. It's reported that the remaining granite deposit is 35 miles long, 6 miles wide, and 2 to 3 miles deep. That's enough to fill the Rose Bowl 2 million times! When in town, be sure to drive by the Elbert County Courthouse, a granite and marble landmark on the square in downtown. Also located on the town square is the Bicentennial Memorial and Fountain, which was donated by the granite industry in 1976. It lists significant periods of local history on 13 panels symbolic of the 13 original colonies. A sculptured American eagle sits atop the central shaft. Before leaving the area, don't miss the **Elberton Granite Museum** (see *To See—Museums*) and the mysterious **Georgia Guidestones** (see *To See— Special Places*).

✳ To See

COVERED BRIDGES ✤ ✍ ♿ **Cromer's Mill Covered Bridge** (chamber of commerce: 706-384-4659; www.franklin-county.com), GA 106 East at Nails Creek (access via Baker Road), Carnesville. One of Georgia's precious few remaining covered bridges, this one was built in 1907, so it has surpassed its centennial birthday. The bridge, constructed in the Town Lattice design, is one lane wide and 132 feet long. Just admire and photograph it—it's not open to traffic.

At **Watson Mill Bridge State Outdoor Recreation Area** (see *Green Space—Nature Preserves and Parks*), you'll find Georgia's longest covered bridge.

HISTORIC HOMES AND SITES ✤ ✍ ♿ **Nancy Hart Cabin** (contact the Elbert County Chamber: 706-283-5651; www.elbertga.com), Elberton. Nancy Hart, after whom the county was named, was a skilled doctor and a staunch patriot as well as reputedly being a crack shot. She is most famous, however, for being a spy for the colonials during the Revolutionary War and is credited with capturing several British Tories. While the cabin is a replica, the stones in the chimney are original, and it is surrounded by 5 acres of park. Free.

MUSEUMS ✤ ✍ ♿ **Elberton Granite Museum and Exhibit** (706-283-2551; www.ega online.com), One Granite Plaza, Elberton. Open 2–5 Monday–Saturday. Three levels of self-guided exhibits include antique granite-working tools and historical exhibits, artifacts, educa-

NANCY MORGAN HART—WAR WOMAN

Myth and truth often intermingle, but by any account Nancy was a firebrand and an exceptional woman. She is reputed to have been a flaming redhead and more than 6 feet tall.

Around 1760, Nancy married Benjamin Hart, who was related to Thomas Hart Benton and the wife of Henry Clay. They had eight children and settled in the Broad River area of northeast Georgia, where they owned 400 acres on the banks of a creek that the Indians named Wahatchee ("War Woman") Creek in her honor. There, Nancy grew a medicinal garden and doctored her family and neighbors. She was reputedly such a crack shot, one side of her cabin was allegedly covered with antlers from deer she had killed.

During the Revolutionary War, Nancy kept her farm going while her husband hid from the Tories. She also contributed to the war effort, by disguising herself to gain information. But the story that cemented her legendary reputation concerned a group of Tories who had shot and killed her neighbor, patriot Col. John Dooley. These redcoats allegedly came to her cabin and forced her to cook dinner for them. According to the story, she regaled them with stories and plied them with drink as she cooked. When they began to nod off, she sent her daughter Sukey to alert neighbors that she needed help. Meanwhile, she began gathering up their rifles and slipping them out through chinks in the wall.

As the story goes, the soldiers eventually became aware of what she was doing, so she was forced to hold them at gunpoint. When they tried to disarm her, she reportedly killed one and wounded another. When her husband and neighbors arrived, they wanted to shoot the rest of the Tories for killing Dooley, but Nancy said shooting was too good for them, so they were hanged while she sang "Yankee Doodle." Although some historians didn't believe the account, six bodies were found in one grave on that very spot in the early 1900s.

Nancy has a highway, a town, a state park, and a county named for her (in fact, this is the only county in Georgia named for a woman).

tional displays, and materials relating to the past and current granite industry in Elberton. One of the most fascinating items in the museum is the statue called *Dutchy*. The first granite statue created in Elberton, it was meant to be a Civil War memorial. Unfortunately, *Dutchy* was unpopular with local citizens, who thought he looked like a cross between a Pennsylvania Dutchman (hence his name) and a hippopotamus. They also felt that his uniform looked suspiciously Northern. As a result, the statue was pulled down and buried facedown—a sign of military disgrace. After 82 years, *Dutchy* was dug up and run through a car wash to remove the Georgia red clay, and he now resides in the museum. While at the museum, watch the film about the **Georgia Guidestones** (see *To See—Special Places*). The film explains how the monument came to be built, why the site was chosen, a little about the mysterious benefactors without identifying them, and what the various sayings mean. Free.

🐾 🍴 ♿ **Ty Cobb Museum** (706-245-1825; www.tycobbmuseum.org), 461 Cook Street, Royston. Open 9–4 weekdays, 10–4 Saturday. Native son and baseball great Tyrus Raymond "Ty" Cobb, known as "the Georgia Peach," was born in Royston in 1886. Many years after his death, Cobb, who threw left and batted right, is still considered by many to be the best player in baseball history. He set or equaled more records than any other player, including having the highest lifetime major league batting average, and in 1936 he was the first player to be inducted into the Baseball Hall of Fame. His life and career are memorialized at this museum, which features personal belongings, memorabilia including his 1907 American League Batting Champion Award, rare films, and photographs. He was the first pro athlete to appear in a movie—the film *Somewhere in Georgia*, in 1917. The museum also provides information about baseball history during Cobb's era and his impact on the game. In the

Cobb Theater, which boasts a beautiful mural and stadium seating, a video features interviews with players and analysts. Adults $5, seniors $4, and children $3.

SPECIAL PLACES ☀ ♂ ⚕ Georgia Guidestones, GA 77 North, Elberton.

Accessible daily. This mysterious granite monument consists of three 19-foot-high blue granite stones—reputedly the largest granite blocks ever quarried—connected by a capstone. Called America's Stonehenge, the 119-ton monolith was erected in a field near Elberton in 1980. Only a few people know the identity of the group of sponsors who provided the specifications and the funds for the monument, and they're not talking. The stones are engraved with a 10-part philosophical message in 12 languages providing counsel for the preservation of mankind—a total of 4,000 letters sand-blasted into the polished surface. The

GEORGIA GUIDESTONES IS CALLED AMERICA'S STONEHENGE.

Guidestones also serve as an astrological observatory with a sundial: a diagonal hole aligned to Polaris, the North Star, and a slit that marks the sunrise and sunset at the winter and summer solstices. Before or after seeing the Guidestones, watch the explanatory film at the **Elberton Granite Museum** in downtown Elberton (see *Museums*). Free.

✳ To Do

BALLOONING For ballooning information in northeast Georgia, call 1-877-BALLOON.

GOLF ⛳ **Arrowhead Pointe at Richard B. Russell State Park** (706-283-6000; www.gastateparks.org/RichardBRussell or www.golfgeorgia.org), 2650 Russell State Park Road, Elberton. Open 8–7 daily. The park's 18-hole, 6,800-yard golf course is called Arrowhead Pointe after the Native American sites that were discovered nearby. Located on a peninsula, the course offers stunning water views, with 10 of the 18 holes skirting the lake. There are no visible houses from any vantage point on the course, which is consistent with the state-park golf-course theme of "no crowds, no houses, no noise." (See *Green Space—Nature Preserves and Parks.*) Greens fees $44–49 with cart.

TAKING IN THE GEORGIA SCENERY FROM HOT-AIR BALLOONS

⛳ **Highland Walk Golf Course at Victoria Bryant State Park** (pro shop: 706-245-6770; 1-866-317-7789; tee times: 1-800-434-0982; www.gastateparks.org/VictoriaBryant or www.golfgeorgia.com), 1415 Bryant Park Road, Royston. Open 7:30–7 daily, mid-March–October, 8–5 daily,

November–mid-March. The park's 18-hole course features challenging steep rolling hills. Amenities include a clubhouse, pro shop, and junior and senior discounts. Reservations required weekends and holidays. (See *Green Space—Nature Preserves and Parks*.) $30–36.

✳ Green Space

LAKES 🦆 𝒮 ⟁ **Clarks Hill Lake** (1-800-533-3478; www.sas.usace.army.mil/lakes /thurmond), 2959 McCormick Highway/US 378 East, Lincolnton (see the Madison chapter in part 3: Historical South). Open daily. A mecca for water sports enthusiasts, Clarks Hill Lake straddles the Georgia–South Carolina border. (It's known as Strom Thurmond Lake on the South Carolina side.) This lake, which is the largest reservoir in the Southeast, boasts 71,000 acres and 1,200 miles of shoreline, of which 400 are in Lincoln County. Its 6 million annual visitors enjoy 11 Corps of Engineers recreation areas and 13 Corps campgrounds, 5 commercial marinas, 6 state parks, and 4 county parks. Free.

🦆 𝒮 ⟁ **Lake Hartwell** (office: 706-856-0300; 1-888-893-0678; www.sas.usace.army.mil /lakes/hartwell), office: 5625 Anderson Highway, Hartwell. Visitors center open 8–4:30 daily. Visitors can drive across this beautiful lake as they travel between Georgia and South Carolina on I-85. The 55,590-acre lake, which boasts 962 miles of shoreline, dotted with public parks, marinas, and campgrounds, provides many opportunities for water sports and outdoor recreation. It is one of the top five most-visited Corps lakes in the country. From the Lake Hartwell Dam, visitors can get a panoramic view of the lake and the Savannah River. Parking is at the Big Oaks Recreation Park on US 29. Free.

🦆 𝒮 ⟁ **Lake Richard B. Russell** (706-213-3400 or 1-800-944-7207; www.sas.usace.army .mil/lakes/Russell), 4144 Russell Dam Road, Elberton. Visitors center open 8–4:30 daily. With 540 miles of shoreline and 26,650 surface acres of water surrounded by an additional 26,500 acres of land, the lake provides multitudinous opportunities for outdoor recreation and water sports. There is a visitors center at the dam and a fishing pier below it. Free.

NATURE PRESERVES AND PARKS 🦆 𝒮 ⟁ 🌳 **Bobby Brown Outdoor Recreation Area** (Not staffed. For information contact Elijah Clark State Park: 706-359-3458; www.gastateparks.org/BobbyBrown), 2509 Bobby Brown, Elberton. Open 7 AM–10 PM daily. The land on which this pretty park sits has an interesting history. In the 1790s an old town called Petersburg, which was surrounded by plantations, was located here, where the Broad and Savannah rivers meet. When the water is low, visitors can still see some of the town's old foundations. The 665-acre park, named in honor of U.S. Navy lieutenant Robert T. Brown, who lost his life in World War II, uses its location on the shores of 70,000-acre Clarks Hill Lake to offer visitors boating, fishing, and waterskiing. Park facilities include 2 miles of hiking trails, a self-guided compass course, and a boat ramp and dock. Campsites are offered on a self-registration basis (see *Lodging—Campgrounds*). Parking $5.

🦆 𝒮 ⟁ 🌳 **Hart State Outdoor Recreation Area** (Not staffed. For information contact Richard B. Russell State Park: 706-213-2045; www.gastateparks.org/Hart), 330 Hart Road, Hartwell. Open 7 AM–10 PM daily. Boating, fishing, swimming, and waterskiing are the primary reasons to visit this park on 55,590-acre Lake Hartwell (see *Lakes*). A swimming beach, two boat ramps, and docks offer easy access to all water sports. An angler's heaven, the lake yields largemouth bass, hybrid bass, striper, black crappie, bream, rainbow trout, and walleyed pike. A 1.5-mile multiuse trail attracts hikers and cyclists. Lakeshore accommodations are offered at seasonal self-registration campsites (see *Lodging—Campgrounds*). Parking $5.

🦆 𝒮 ⟁ 🌳 **Richard B. Russell State Park** (706-213-2045; lodging reservations: 1-800-864-7275; www.gastateparks.org/RichardBRussell), 2650 Russell State Park Road, Elberton. Open 7 AM–10 PM daily. Paleo-Indians lived in the area more than 10,000 years ago at a site now called Rucker's Bottom, which was completely covered over when 26,500-acre Lake

Richard B. Russell was filled in 1980 (see *Lakes*). Perched on the shores of the lake, this park offers some of Georgia's best fishing and boating. Facilities for water sports include a swimming beach, rowing area, boat ramps, and canoe and pedal boat rentals in season. Other outdoor pursuits include 6 miles of nature trails also used by hikers and cyclists, disc golf (additional fee), beach volleyball, and an 18-hole golf course (see *To Do—Golf*). A campground and cottages provide overnight accommodations (see *Lodging—Campgrounds* and *Lodging—Cottages and Cabins*). Parking $5.

🦆 𝒹 ⚁ 🌴 **Tugaloo State Park** (706-356-4362; lodging reservations: 1-800-864-7275; www .gastateparks.org/Tugaloo), 1763 Tugaloo State Park Road, Lavonia. Open 7 AM–10 PM daily. The park is named for the Native American word for the river that flowed freely before the Hartwell Dam built to impound Lake Hartwell (see *Lakes*). The small 393-acre park's location on the lake makes it a popular destination for devotees of water sports. Because so many boaters want to launch their boats here, the park has not only two smaller boat ramps, but also a six-lane megaramp that is perfect for launching many boats at a time during fishing tournaments. Fishing is excellent year-round, particularly for largemouth bass. During the summer, boating, sailing, swimming, and waterskiing are favored pursuits, as are tennis, volleyball, horseshoes, and miniature golf (additional fee). Canoes are rented seasonally. Hikers can enjoy 4 miles of trails, including the wooded Crow Tree and Muscadine nature trails. Accommodations are offered at campsites and in cottages (see *Lodging—Campgrounds* and *Lodging—Cottages and Cabins*). Parking $5.

🦆 𝒹 ⚁ 🌴 **Victoria Bryant State Park** (706-245-6270; lodging reservations: 1-800-864-7275; www.gastateparks.org/VictoriaBryant), 1105 Bryant Park Road, Royston. Open 7 AM–dark daily. Visitors come to this 502-acre park to enjoy the rolling hills of Georgia's upper Piedmont region, hike the 8 miles of trails along the beautiful stream or around the perimeter, get a glimpse of wildlife, cycle, swim in the park's pool (seasonally, additional fee), and play golf (see *To Do—Golf*). Campers can overnight at the park (see *Lodging—Campgrounds*). Two fishing ponds are open only to campers and disabled visitors. Parking $5.

🦆 𝒹 ⚁ 🌴 **Watson Mill Bridge State Outdoor Recreation Area** (Not staffed. For information contact Victoria Bryant State Park: 706-245-6270; www.gastateparks.org/WatsonMill), 650 Watson Mill Road, Comer. Open 7 AM–10 PM daily. The centerpiece of the 1,018-acre park is Georgia's longest covered bridge still in its original position. The 229-foot Town Lattice Truss design bridge was built in 1885 by W. W. King, son of freed slave and famous covered bridge builder Horace King, to span the South Fork River and is one of only 16 of the state's original 200 covered bridges still in existence. The scenic park, a mecca for outdoors enthusiasts, offers 5 miles of biking trails and 7 miles of hiking trails; 14 miles of equestrian trails (BYOH—bring your own horse); fishing for bass, bream, and catfish in the 5-acre millpond; picnicking; and seasonal canoe and pedal-boat rentals. In summertime visitors like to romp in the cool river shoals below the bridge. Seasonal self-registration camping in developed and primitive campsites, self-registration equestrian campsites available year-round, and even accommodations for the horses (see *Lodging—Campgrounds*). Reservations required for horse stalls. Parking $5.

✳ Lodging
BED & BREAKFASTS
In Elberton
Rainbow Manor Bed and Breakfast
(706-213-0314; www.rainbowmanor.com), 217 Heard Street. Stay in this beautiful antebellum home (circa 1882), which has been lovingly restored and decorated with antiques. Of the five guest rooms, one has a private bath. The others are in pairs with shared baths, making them perfect for families or friends traveling together. A full country breakfast is included. No smoking. No pets. Not wheelchair accessible. $95–125.

In Lavonia

🔱 ♿ **RenStone Bed and Breakfast and Spa** (706-356-1198 or 1-866-862-4517; www.renstone.com), 560 Chandler Place Drive. From beautifully appointed rooms to a full range of professional spa services, RenStone is the place to go and be pampered. It is located in a quiet deep-water cove on Lake Hartwell (see *Green Space—Lakes*). The two-bedroom Wits End guest suite has a full kitchen, satellite television, a VCR, whirlpool, washer and dryer, a large bath with his-and-hers vanities, and its own lakeside entrance. Full Southern breakfast included. Spa services include facials, body wraps, waxing, and massages. Smoking on porches and decks only. Rooms $69–89, suite $139–169. Spa services extra.

CAMPGROUNDS To learn more about the amenities at all the following parks, see *Green Space—Nature Preserves and Parks.*

In Comer

🔱 🚿 ♿ 🐾 **Watson Mill Bridge State Outdoor Recreation Area** (see *Green Space—Nature Preserves and Parks*). The park features 21 tent, trailer, and RV sites, as well as 11 equestrian campsites and horse stalls ($11 each). General campsites are available mid-March—mid-September on a first-come, first-served self-registration basis; equestrian sites (also self-registration) available year-round. $25–28.

In Elberton

🔱 🚿 ♿ 🐾 **Bobby Brown State Outdoor Recreation Area** (see *Green Space—Nature Preserves and Parks*). The park features 61 tent, trailer, and RV sites. Sites are available mid-March–mid-September on a first-come, first-served self-registration basis. $24–26.

🔱 🚿 ♿ 🐾 **Richard B. Russell State Park** (lodging reservations: 1-800-864-7275). The campground, which is near the shoreline of Lake Richard B. Russell, offers 28 tent, trailer, and RV sites with cable TV hookups. $25–28.

In Hartwell

🔱 🚿 ♿ 🐾 **Hart State Outdoor Recreation Area** (see *Green Space—Nature Preserves*

and Parks). The park offers 62 tent, trailer, and RV sites, and 16 walk-in sites. Sites are available mid-March–mid-September on a first-come, first-served self-registration basis. $19–26; walk-in sites $19.

In Lavonia

🔱 🚿 ♿ 🐾 **Tugaloo State Park** (lodging reservations: 1-800-864-7275). Most of the park's 108 tent, trailer, and RV sites are situated on a wooded peninsula with spectacular views of Lake Hartwell in every direction. There are also five primitive campsites. $23–30; primitive sites $15.

In Royston

🔱 🚿 ♿ 🐾 **Victoria Bryant State Park** (lodging reservations: 1-800-864-7275). The park features 27 tent, trailer, and RV sites, as well as eight platform tent sites. $25–28; walk-in sites $27.

COTTAGES AND CABINS

In Elberton

🔱 🚿 ♿ 🐾 **Richard B. Russell State Park** (lodging reservations: 1-800-864-7275). The park features 20 cottages on the shores of Lake Richard B. Russell. Two are dog friendly ($40 per dog; maximum two). $13–140. See Green *Space—Nature Preserves and Parks.*

In Lavonia

🔱 🚿 ♿ 🐾 **Tugaloo State Park** (lodging reservations: 1-800-864-7275). All of the park's 20 cottages are located on a wooded peninsula, and many have excellent views of Lake Hartwell. Three are dog friendly ($40 per dog; maximum two). $135. See *Green Space—Nature Preserves and Parks.*

✳ Where to Eat
DINING OUT

In Hartwell

♿ **Waterfall Grille** (706-856-GOLF; www.cateechee.com), Cateechee Golf Club, 140 Cateechee Trail. Open 11:30–2 Tuesday–Sunday, 5:30–9 Tuesday–Saturday. The menu features delicious Southern regional cuisine. Favorites include Georgia white shrimp, prime rib, cold-water lobster tails, sandwiches, chef's specials, unique and creative salads, appetizers, and desserts. No smoking. Single menu for lunch and dinner $9–23.

EATING OUT

In Elberton

🦐 🍴 ♿ **Clifford's Restaurant at Beaverdam Marina** (706-213-0079 or 706-213-6462; www.BeaverdamMarina.com), 1155 Marina Drive. Open 11:30–10 Friday and Saturday, 11–7 Sunday, March–November. This fun, casual family restaurant specializes in seafood, steaks, and chicken. Nightly specials include prime rib on Friday, chef's specials such as Cajun catfish on Saturday, and snow crab legs on Sunday. No smoking. $7.50–13.

🦐 🍴 ♿ **Granite City Restaurant** (706-283-6928), 225 College Avenue. Open 7 AM–9 PM Monday–Saturday. This is the place to go for value and all your hometown favorites. Choices change each day. No smoking. Breakfast $4, lunch $7, dinner $9.

🦐 🍴 **Time Square Sandwich Cafe** (706-283-1235), 103 Heard Street. Open 10:30–1:30. This restaurant serves a wide variety of lunch favorites, including sandwiches, chicken fingers, and salads. No smoking. Not wheelchair accessible. $4–9.

In Hartwell

🦐 🍴 ♿ **Downtown Café and Pizzeria** (706-377-3055), 63 Depot Street. Open 11–9 daily, until 10 Friday and Saturday. In addition to great pizza, the Greek/Mediterranean/Italian menu items include authentic pasta dishes as well as seafood. No smoking. $6–17.

🦐 🍴 ♿ **Jim's Family-Style Restaurant** (706-376-9287), 50 South Forest Avenue. Open 6 AM–1:45 PM Monday–Friday. The menu can be characterized as old-time soul food. Great value. Favorites include meat loaf, fried chicken, liver and onions, chicken fried steak, turnip greens, and more, but hamburgers, sandwiches, and the like are also offered. No smoking. $2–7.

In Lavonia

🦐 🍴 ♿ **Downtown Café and Pizzeria** (706-356-2535), 203 West Main Street. Open 11–9 Sunday–Thursday, until 10 Friday and Saturday. Fare includes pizza, a full range of Italian/Mediterranean/Greek pasta dishes, stromboli, chicken fingers, and salads. No smoking. $6–15.

🦐 🍴 ♿ **Gumlog Bar-B-Que and Fish Lodge** (706-356-4061), 106 Whitworth School Farmer Road, Gumlog. Open 11–9:45 Friday and Saturday, 11–7:45 Sunday. Besides fish dishes such as catfish, perch, and flounder, menu items include barbecue, steaks, smoked pork, ham, ribs, burgers, and sandwiches. Every table gets two pitchers of iced tea, "one sweet, the other ain't." No smoking. $8–16. Cash only.

🦐 🍴 **211 Main Street Restaurant** (706-356-2877), 211 West Main Street. Open 10:30–3 weekdays, 5–8:30 Friday. Enjoy homemade soups and salads, sandwiches, and daily meat specials served with two vegetables. Save room for dessert—there are always eight pies, two cheesecakes, and four cakes to choose from. No smoking. Not wheelchair accessible. Around $7–9.

TAKE-OUT

In Lavonia

🦐 🍴 **Finley's Café** (706-356-8281), 12800 Jones Street. Open 11–8 Monday–Saturday. Menu items include hot dogs, hamburgers, Polish sausages, and the like. Although this is primarily a take-out restaurant, there are two outdoor tables. Smoking outdoors only. Not wheelchair accessible. $8–10.

✴ Entertainment

THEATER Elberton Theatre Foundation (706-283-1049; www.elberttheatre .org), 100 South Oliver Street, Elberton. This volunteer theater company stages five events per season, plus two children's performances as well as concerts and films. Additional income is earned by renting the theater out to churches, schools, and various bands. Check the website or call for a schedule of events and prices.

Hart County Community Theatre (706-376-5599; www.hartcountycommunity theatre.com), 83 Depot Street, Hartwell. Box office open 10–2 Tuesday–Friday. The group produces plays quarterly in the renovated Weatherly Furniture Building. Check the website or call for a schedule of performances and ticket prices.

✳ Selective Shopping

ART GALLERIES **Bendzunas Glass Studio and Glass Gallery** (706-783-5869), 89 West South Street, Comer. No regular hours, but visitors encouraged to come by anytime until 10 PM. World-renowned glass artists Paul and Barbara Bendzunas create their imaginative works here, where two generations work side by side crafting one-of-a-kind hand-blown functional and decorative glass art.

✳ Special Events

April: **Antique Boat Show** (706-376-8590; www.acbs.org). Lake Hartwell provides the backdrop for exhibitors from across the United States to display their classic 1920–1960 wooden boats at this national Antique and Classic Boat Society event held at Hartwell Marina. Spectators free; parking $1.

Spring Fever Regatta on Lake Hartwell (www.twinhulls.com). The exciting three-day racing event is the largest catamaran regatta in the United States. It's advertised as "The World's Finest Regatta by a Dam Site" because it's held from the Milltown Campground near Hartwell Dam. There's nothing much more beautiful than seeing brightly colored sails packed together as they fly across the lake maneuvering the course. Check the website for details. Free for spectators.

September: **ARTS in hARTwell Festival of Heritage and Fine Arts** (706-376-0188). This event on Hartwell Square includes an assortment of activities, including a juried fine arts show, live heritage music, craft demonstrations, storytelling, and children's activities. Free.

November: **Annual Granite City Fall Festival** (706-283-5651), on downtown square, Elberton. This fun-filled day for the whole family includes visits to a quarry and skilled craftspeople etching images onto granite. Events include a 4-H animal corner, children's activities, food, music, dancing, and arts and crafts. Free; some activities have a fee.

HIAWASSEE, BLAIRSVILLE, AND YOUNG HARRIS

Most visitors to Hiawassee, Blairsville, and Young Harris come for water sports on Lake Chatuge and Lake Nottely or for hiking and other outdoor pursuits in the Chattahoochee National Forest. Georgia's highest point, Brasstown Bald, is in this area, and the Benton MacKaye and Appalachian trails begin their northward trek along the ridges of the Blue Ridge and Cohutta mountains. The Benton MacKaye Trail follows the western ridge for 250 miles to Virginia, and the Appalachian Trail follows the eastern ridge 2,000 miles to Maine. In July, folks come from near and far for the **Georgia Mountain Fair** (see *Special Events*).

GUIDANCE For more information about Blairsville, contact the **Blairsville–Union County Chamber of Commerce** (706-745-5789 or 1-877-745-5789; www.blairsville chamber.com or www.visitblairsville.com), 129 Union County Recreation Road, Blairsville 30512. Open 9–5 weekdays, 10–1 Saturday, May–October.

To learn more about Hiawassee and Young Harris, consult the **Towns County Chamber of Commerce and Local Welcome Center–Towns County Tourism Association** (706-896-4966 or 1-800-984-1543; www.mountaintopga.com), 1411 Jack Dayton Circle, Young Harris 30582. Open 9–5 weekdays; also 9–4 Saturday, April–December.

GETTING THERE *By air:* Most air travelers fly into Atlanta, but another option is Chattanooga, Tennessee. For airport, airline, or car rental information at either, see "What's Where in Georgia."

By bus: The closest bus service is provided by **Greyhound Lines** to Gainesville (see the Gainesville chapter). A visitor would need to rent a car to get to and around this area.

By car: Blairsville, Young Harris, and Hiawassee are strung out along US 76 from west to east along the north-central edge of Georgia. There are no interstates in this part of the state except for the extension of I-575 out of Atlanta that becomes GA 5. GA 400 is a multilane limited-access highway out of Atlanta that becomes US 19.

By train: The closest **AMTRAK** train service is in Gainesville (see the Gainesville chapter).

WHEN TO GO Brasstown Bald, the highest point in the southern United States, has weather comparable to Vermont's. Even down in the valleys, the temperature seldom breaks into the 80s and can easily drop below freezing late into the spring and early in the fall. There can be snow or ice storms in winter. This weather, which is unusual for Georgia, dictates that most visitors prefer visiting from late spring through late fall. Many, however, enjoy visiting around the Christmas season. Some campgrounds and organizations that provide outdoor activities close in the winter or cut their hours significantly.

MEDICAL EMERGENCY Call 911.

VILLAGES **Blairsville** is not only the county seat but also the only incorporated town in Union County (which, by the way, was not named for the Federal side during the Civil War, but for the Union Party, which was formed 28 years before that war). **Brasstown Bald,** the highest point in the state, is nearby (see *To See—Natural Beauty Spots*). The surrounding area is popular for outdoor pursuits, including those offered at **Vogel State Park** (see *Green Space—Nature Preserves and Parks*) and on the Appalachian Trail.

Hiawassee is a Cherokee word meaning "meadow." Although the beautiful town with this name is in the mountains of north Georgia, it is surrounded by many open areas. The town and the Hiawassee River attracted tourists from the 1800s to the 1930s, when wealthy families from the lowlands of Georgia and neighboring states summered in the mountains to escape the heat and disease prevalent in their home areas. Fortunately, the mountains, lakes, and recreational activities have since become affordable for everyone. Another attraction is the **Fred Hamilton Rhododendron Garden** (see *Green Space—Gardens*), which features 2,000 rhododendrons, azaleas, and wildflowers.

Colleges often are named after the towns in which they are located, but in the case of **Young Harris,** the town was named for the college. Young Harris College, named for Judge Young Loftin Gerdine Harris, existed before the town came into being. Its planetarium is open to the public (see *To See—Planetariums*). One of the state's fine resorts, **Brasstown Valley Resort** (see *Lodging—Inns and Resorts*), is nearby, as is **Crane Creek Vineyards** (see *To Do—Winery Tours*).

✳ To See

FOR FAMILIES ✆ ✎ ♿ **Misty Mountain Train Museum** (706-745-4786; www.misty mountaininn.com), 55 Misty Mountain Lane, off Town Creek School Road, Blairsville. Open for tours at 2 Monday, Wednesday, Friday, and Saturday, May–December; Monday, Wednesday, and Saturday, January–April. Located at **Misty Mountain Inn and Cottages** (see *Lodging—Bed & Breakfasts*), the 3,400-square-foot model train layout, which has 14 O-gauge Lionel trains operating on nearly a mile of track with 12 bridges, 4 trestles, and 15 tunnels, is the largest privately owned O-gauge train collection in the nation. The backdrop represents the southern Appalachian Mountains in Georgia and Tennessee, and includes representations of Gainesville, Helen, Kennesaw, and Tallulah Gorge in Georgia as well as Copperhill, Tennessee, and the Biltmore Estate in North Carolina. The tableau is populated with miniature figures and enhanced with 300 Department 56 buildings and accessories. $3 donation requested; proceeds given to charity.

HISTORIC HOMES AND SITES ✆ ✎ ♿ **Pioneer Village at the Georgia Mountain Fairgrounds** (706-896-4191; www.georgiamountainfairgrounds.com), 1311 Music Hall Drive, off US 76, Hiawassee. Open during special events, of which there are many throughout the year. During these events, craftsmen demonstrate old-time mountain activities such as soapmaking, moonshining, hominy making, and blacksmithing. Several authentic historical structures have been moved to the site from around north Georgia, including a one-room schoolhouse, a general store, blacksmith shop, repair shop, house, and smokehouse. The exhibit hall features memorabilia from more than 50 years of events as well as antique machinery. Purchase homemade jams and jellies here. Free with admission to the events.

THE MOUNTAINS

MUSEUMS 🐾 ✎ **Union County Historical Society Museum** (706-745-5493; www
.unioncountyhistory.org), Old Union County Courthouse on the Square, Blairsville. Open
10–4 Monday–Saturday; closed Saturdays January–April. Housed in the opulent old courthouse with its impressive bell and clock tower, the museum contains county memorabilia
from Civil War artifacts to 19th-century farm equipment. The star of the show is the Mar-
garita Morgan Miniature House Collection of tiny meticulously furnished structures.
Another favorite is an exhibit created by moving the original bell and clock works from the
tower down to the grounds, where visitors can actually see them up close. Other exhibits
include Native American pottery and arrowheads, spinning wheels, quilts, early medical
equipment, and vintage clothing. Military displays include uniforms, medals, and weapons.
Adults $2, children 6–12 $1.

NATURAL BEAUTY SPOTS 🐾 ✎ ♿ **Brasstown Bald** (forestry service: 706-745-
6928; visitor information center: 706-896-2556; www.fs.usda.gov), GA 180 Spur, Blairsville.
Visitors center open 10–5 daily, Memorial Day–October; weekends only March–May and
November; closed December–February. Road open year-round. At 4,784 feet above sea
level, Brasstown Bald is Georgia's highest mountain and one of the highest in the Southeast.
From the summit, visitors can see a 360-degree view of four states: Georgia, North Carolina,
South Carolina, and Tennessee. Below the peak to the north and east is the only "cloud forest" in Georgia, an area that's usually dripping wet from the moisture in the clouds that hang
low over it. The environmentally sensitive slope features lichen-covered yellow birch and
spectacular wildflower displays. Cars can drive most of the way up the mountain. Access to
the summit from the parking lot is by way of a steep half-mile paved trail or by shuttle in
season. Tourists are rewarded at the top with a visitor information center that offers exhibits
of flora and fauna not usually found this far south; in fact, they're more typical of Maine.
Films, interpretive programs, and an audio-animatronic Ranger Woody—the Barefoot
Ranger—are sure to fascinate. The park also features picnicking and four hiking trails ranging from 0.5 to 6 miles. Because of the elevation, the weather can be quite cool, and the area
gets snow and ice in the winter. Check the website at www.ngeorgia.com/travel/brasstown
.html for a weather cam's look at conditions before you go. A trail from the parking lot connects with the Appalachian Trail. Day use and visitors center $2 per person; shuttle $3
round-trip per adult, $2 children 3–10.

PLANETARIUMS 🐾 ✎ ♿ **Rollins Planetarium** (706-379-4312 or 1-800-241-3754;
www.yhc.edu/external/planet), One College Street, Young Harris. Open for 30 shows per
year (check the website or call for dates and times). Located on the campus of Young Harris
College, this planetarium is one of the largest in the state. It has a 40-foot dome, and guests
can relax in reclining seats during the show. Special shows include *Fright Light* in October
and *Season of Light*—the Christmas show. The college also has an observatory, which is open
immediately after planetarium shows, at Twiggs Overlook, on state property near Brasstown
Valley Resort. The observatory features a Schmidt-Cassegrain telescope. Adults $3, children
$2.

SCENIC DRIVES **Georgia Mountain Parkway** (www.ngeorgia.com/gmp). The parkway, which runs 65 miles from Hiawassee to Jasper, is full of stops along the way in nostalgic
towns and recreation areas for sight-seeing, shopping, festivals, and outdoor pursuits.

Russell-Brasstown Scenic Byway. The 41-mile loop trail anchored by Blairsville and
Helen runs through the Chattahoochee National Forest and provides some of the most spectacular scenery and views in the state. Off this windy road filled with hairpin turns there are
numerous overlooks along the way, as well as access to Brasstown Bald, waterfalls, and the
Appalachian Trail. Be warned, traffic is heavy during leaf season. For more information, see
the Dahlonega to Helen chapter.

BOAT EXCURSIONS ⚓ ♿ **Romantic Lake Cruises** (828-389-2255; www.romantic lakecruises.com), Dock D, the Ridges Resort Marina, 3499 US 76 West, Hiawassee. Open daily, April 15 through leaf season in late October. Cruises on the Lake Chatuge Love Boat include a variety of offerings, from a bare-bones one-hour cruise to a sumptuous dinner cruise with live music and complimentary drinks. Family-oriented cruises are available as well, and there are packages with various add-ons. $30–52.

BOATING ⚓ ♿ **Boundary Waters Resort and Marina** (706-896-2530 or 1-800-323-3562; www.boundarywatersresort.com), 528 Sunnyside Road/Highway 288, Hiawassee. Open 8:30–5:30 daily. Located on Lake Chatuge, the full-service marina rents ski, deck, or wakeboard boats; Jet Skis; runabouts; pontoon boats; canoes; kayaks; and paddleboats. Boat rental prices vary $10–225.

⚓ ♿ **The Ridges Resort Marina** (706-896-2112 or 1-888-834-4408; www.theridgesresort .com), 3499 US 76 West, Hiawassee. Hours vary seasonally, so call first. The full-service marina rents pontoon boats, fishing boats, canoes, kayaks, and aqua cycles. Rental prices vary $10–140.

FISHING ⚓ ♿ **Upper Hi Fly Fishing Outfitters** (1-866-899-5259; www.reelangling adventures.com), 3375 US 76 West, Hiawassee. Open 9–5 Monday–Saturday, 9–2 Sunday; reservations required. Expert guides know the best places and the best techniques for successful fly-fishing on Lake Chatuge and other places. Options include wild trout treks, wade trips, private waters trophy trout, and drift boat trips. The store carries fishing tackle, clothing, accessories, gifts, and fine art. Call for prices and meeting places.

FOR FAMILIES 🎏 ⚓ ♿ **Fun World** (706-896-7777), 1150 Jack Dayton Circle, Young Harris. Open 4–8 Thursday, 4–10 Friday, noon–11 Saturday, 1–7 Sunday; longer hours in summer. Heaven forbid that there should be a rainy or snowy day when your family is visiting the mountains, but if there is, the kids won't go stir crazy in your hotel room if you take them to Fun World, where they can enjoy the roller rink, Xbox gaming center, Air Zone inflatables, Adrenaline Rush Extreme Obstacle Course, Corkscrew the Mechanical Bull, Lagoon of Doom log roll game, and arcade games. Tiny tots aren't left out. They have their own Toddler Town area with a castle, bouncy house, foam factory, and little surf slide. Adults aren't left out, either. On the first Monday there's an adult skate night. Activities priced individually.

🎏 ⚓ ♿ **Southern Tree Plantation** (706-745-0601; www.southerntreeplantation.com), 2531 Owltown Road, Blairsville. Open 10–6 Saturday, noon–6 Sunday, early–late October; 10–6 Monday–Saturday, 10–6 Sunday, day after Thanksgiving–December 23 for Christmas trees. Families can choose their own pumpkins in October or their own Christmas tree during the holiday season at this 60-acre farm. The fun doesn't stop there, however. Other family-oriented activities include a barnyard playground and wooden maze, an inflatable slide, horseshoes, volleyball, hayrides, fishing, marshmallow roasting around a roaring fire, and train rides aboard the Southern Tree Express, a miniature train. On selected days there are pony rides. The petting zoo allows children to get up close and personal with lovable farm critters such as Buckwheat the potbellied pig, Bo and Peep the sheep, or Poncho the donkey. Wildlife is represented by Donner the deer. Local crafts also are sold here, and on selected weekends in the fall the farm sponsors a hoedown with bluegrass music and an all-you-can-eat buffet. Southern Tree Plantation is the largest Christmas tree farm in north Georgia, growing more than 25,000 trees at any one time. Days with pony rides: adults $10, children $12. Other days no entrance fee, $5 per activity or there are unlimited packages.

GOLF Brasstown Valley Resort (706-379-4613 or 1-800-201-3205; www.brasstown valley.com), 6321 US 76, Young Harris. Open daylight hours daily. North Georgia's premier mountain golf resort, Brasstown Valley offers an abundance of outdoor activities beyond the award-winning Scottish links–style course designed by Denis Griffiths. The championship par-72 course is consistently ranked by *Golf Digest* as one of the best places to play golf in Georgia and is a member of the prestigious Leading Golf Courses of America. The environmentally sensitive course design uses the natural landscape to create a challenging, well-bunkered course with water on 10 holes. The course also features PGA professional instruction, a driving range, and a pro shop. During the summer season, golfers can get back into the swing of things by attending the Brasstown Valley Resort's K.I.S.S. Golf School, which is tailored to women and couples. Led by LPGA pro Lori McCabe and professional instructors, the school features instruction for both novices and experienced players. Call for rates, which vary seasonally.

HIKING For the **Appalachian Trail** (www.appalachiantrail.org), see the Dahlonega chapter.

For the **Benton MacKaye Trail** (www.bmta.org), see the Cartersville chapter.

HORSEBACK RIDING ✍ **A Step Above Stables** (706-745-9051; www.astepabove stables.net), 696 Mauney Circle off Highway 19/129 North, Blairsville. Open 9–sunset Wednesday–Sunday; reservations required. The 90-acre facility offers guided rides along wooded trails through hardwood forests, along trout streams, through open meadows, and to a Lake Nottely overlook. Children welcome. Those under six can do a pony ride in the riding ring. Instruction is offered. Trail rides $30 per hour, pony rides $10.

✍ **Brasstown Valley Resort** (706-379-4613 or 1-800-201-3205; www.brasstownvalley.com), 6321 US 76, Young Harris. Open at 9:15 Wednesday–Sunday; first ride goes out at 9:15 AM, and the last ride at 2:15 PM; reservations required. This family-oriented resort has added stables and offers 5-mile trail rides for all levels of riding skill. $45 for one hour, $77 for two hours.

✍ **Trackrock Stables** (706-745-5252 or 1-800-826-0073; www.trackrock.com), 202 Trackrock Camp Road, Blairsville. Open year-round. Reservations suggested but not required. Guided one-hour trail rides meander through Trackrock Campground, mountain meadows, and along tree-shaded paths beside gurgling streams. They have horses for riders of all skill levels as well as some particularly trained for younger children. Nonriders in your group can enjoy hayrides or spend time fishing, swimming, or hiking. $30 per hour.

RIDERS OF ALL SKILL LEVELS CAN TAKE TO THE TRAILS AT TRACKROCK STABLES.

SPAS ⅃ **Equani Spa at Brasstown Valley Resort** (706-379-2336 or 1-800-201-3205; www.brasstownvalley.com), 6321 US 76, Young Harris. Closed Monday and Wednesday. Pamper yourself with body treatments, facials, massages, or take advantage of the sauna, steam rooms, outdoor hot tub, and relaxation areas. What sets this spa apart, however, are the unique rituals indigenous to the Cherokee. Use of the facilities is complimentary for overnight guests; day passes can be purchased for outsiders. Treatments and services $20–225, Cherokee rituals $225–280.

WATERFALLS *Note:* The rocks are deceptively slippery around these falls. Exercise caution.

🦞 ♂ **Helton Creek Falls** (706-745-5789 or 1-877-745-5789; www.georgiatrails.com), US 129 South, Blairsville. Accessible daylight hours daily. The falls is near Vogel State Park. The 0.3-mile Helton Creek Falls Trail follows the creek to two waterfalls. The trail accesses the lower falls at both the bottom and top, and it ends at the bottom of the upper falls. The total vertical drop is more than 100 feet. An observation deck provides a good view and lots of photo ops. Free.

🦞 ♂ **High Shoals Falls and High Shoals Scenic Area** (Forest Service: 706-745-6928; www.fs.usda.gov), Forest Service Road 283 off GA 75 just past GA 180, Hiawassee. Accessible daylight hours daily. An observation deck provides views of five falls. Several trails traverse the area. Free.

WINERY TOURS 🦞 ♿ **Crane Creek Vineyards** (tasting room: 706-379-1236; www.cranecreekvineyards.com), 916 Crane Creek Road, Young Harris. Open 11–5 Tuesday–Saturday, 1–5 Sunday in winter, until 6 April–December. The family-owned and family-operated vineyard produces a full spectrum of traditional wines. Numerous wine dinners are scheduled throughout the year, as well as the **Spring Art and Wine Fest** and the **Fall Harvest Festival.** The Vintner's Tasting in the 1800s farmhouse on Saturday includes a tasting of all of the vineyard's wines and a souvenir glass. The store sells gourmet food items, gifts, and wine-related items. Check out the Friday Evening Tapas and the Soup Kitchen Saturdays. The winery and store are wheelchair accessible, but not the tasting room. Tour free, standard tasting $5, Vintner's Tasting $7.

✳ Green Space

GARDENS 🦞 ♂ ♿ **Fred Hamilton Rhododendron Garden** (706-896-4191; www.georgia-mountain-fair.com), 1311 Music Hall Drive, Hiawassee. Open daily year-round, in bloom April–May. In the spring and early summer, more than 3,000 rhododendrons and azaleas bloom alongside wildflowers sloping steeply down to the shores of Lake Chatuge. The pine-bark trail has numerous switchbacks, but the walk is not strenuous. Limited wheelchair accessibility. $3.

LAKES 🦞 ♂ ♿ **Lake Chatuge.** The 7,500-acre, 13-mile-long TVA reservoir, which is shared by Towns County, Georgia, and Clay County, North Carolina, has 132 miles of shoreline and offers numerous water sports and activities. Resorts, rentals, and restaurants overlook the lake.

🦞 ♂ ♿ **Lake Nottely,** US 19 and US 129 North, Blairsville. Open daylight hours daily. The picturesque 20-mile-long, 4,180-acre TVA lake with 106 miles of shoreline offers all sorts of water sports and outdoor recreation, including boating, camping, fishing, picnicking, and swimming.

NATURE PRESERVES AND PARKS 🦞 ♂ ♿ **Cooper's Creek Wildlife Management Area** (706-745-6928; www.fs.usda.gov), GA 60 at GA 180, Blairsville. Open daylight hours daily. Outdoors fans enjoy the 30,000-acre area for bird-watching, camping, fishing, horseback riding (BYOH—bring your own horse), hunting, and picnicking. The challenging Duncan Ridge Trail, which stretches from north of Dahlonega to the Benton MacKaye Trail in Fannin County, offers stunning scenery and waterfalls. Be careful hiking during hunting season. Free.

🐾 🦯 ♿ **Sosebee Cove Scenic Area** (706-745-0601; www.fs.usda.gov), GA 180, Blairsville. Open daylight hours daily. The 175-acre area is a large, north-facing cove with many high-elevation flora and fauna. Of particular note are the huge buckeye and tulip trees. The area has an easy loop trail from which visitors can view the natural beauty of the area and bird-watch. This area was a favorite of Ranger Woody, the Barefoot Ranger, who negotiated the purchase of the acreage for the Forest Service. Today it's a particular favorite of photographers because of the 20 to 30 species of wildflowers and ferns—some of them rare. Free.

🐾 🦯 ♿ **Vogel State Park** (706-745-2628; lodging reservations: 1-800-864-7275; www.ga stateparks.org/Vogel), 405 Vogel State Park Road, Blairsville. Open 7 AM–10 PM daily; museum open daily in summer, weekends in spring and fall, closed in winter. One of the oldest preserves in the state park system, Vogel State Park is located at the foot of Blood Mountain in the Chattahoochee National Forest. The 233-acre park is particularly popular in the autumn, when the area is a sea of brilliant colors. A small 20-acre lake with a beach allows for swimming and fishing. Boats without motors are allowed. Hikers and backpackers enjoy 17 miles of trails. Among them are the 4-mile Bear Hair Gap loop, the easy lake loop to Trahlyta Falls, and the challenging 13-mile Backcountry Trail. In addition, the park features a Civilian Conservation Corps museum, a general store, seasonal miniature golf (additional fee), and seasonal pedal-boat rentals. Accommodations are offered in campsites and cottages (see *Lodging—Campgrounds* and *Lodging—Cottages and Cabins*). Parking $5.

✳ Lodging

BED & BREAKFASTS

In Blairsville

♿ **Davis-Reid-Sampson Inn B&B** (706-835-2469 or 770-921-8187), 147 Rogers Street. Open only on weekends between June 1 and October 1; reservations required. This 1865 home, on the National Register of Historic Places, is decorated with Victorian-era antiques. No smoking. One wheelchair-accessible room on first floor. Prefers two-night minimum. $150.

🐾 **Misty Mountain Inn and Cottages** (706-745-4786; www.mistymountaininn .com), 55 Misty Mountain Lane. This comfortable Victorian-era farmhouse is decorated with period antiques. Four rooms feature a private bath and a fireplace; three feature a balcony. Continental breakfast included. (Also see **Misty Mountain Train Museum** under *To See—For Families.*) No smoking. Not wheelchair accessible. $110.

CAMPGROUNDS

In Blairsville

🐾 🦯 ♿**Trackrock Campground and Cabins** (706-745-2420; www.trackrock

.com), 141 Trackrock Camp Road. This year-round facility offers 95 tree-shaded campsites with full or partial hookups on 300 acres. Amenities include bathhouses, a recreation building, laundry facilities, and sales of ice, firewood, and liquefied petroleum gas. One- and two-bedroom lakeside and rustic wooded cabins are offered as well. These cabins feature a stone fireplace, covered porch, and fully equipped kitchen. Activities include fishing, swimming, horseback riding (separate fee; see *To Do— Horseback Riding*), and hayrides. No smoking in cabins. Camping. $27–39.

🐾 🦯 🐾 **Vogel State Park** (lodging reservations: 1-800-864-7275). This park offers 103 tent, trailer, and RV sites as well as 18 walk-in sites and backcountry sites. Campers can enjoy all the facilities of the state park (see *Green Space—Nature Preserves and Parks*). Some sections close in the winter. $25–28, backcountry sites $19.

In Hiawassee

🐾 🦯 ♿ **Georgia Mountain Fairgrounds** (706-896-4191; www.georgiamountain fairgrounds.com/campgrounds.php), 1311 Music Hall Drive. Campers can enjoy all the facilities, amenities, activities, and entertainment of the Georgia Mountain Fair facility. Many of the 189 campsites are lakefront on Lake Chatuge. Many others enjoy a lake view. Amenities include two playgrounds, a boat ramp, and two tennis courts. $20–33.

CONDOS

In Hiawassee

✔ ⛵ & **The Ridges Resort Lake Villas** (706-896-2262 or 1-888-834-4409), 3379 US 76 West. Located on the grounds of the resort overlooking Lake Chatuge, the two-, three-, and four-bedroom condos are individually decorated. Each features a fully equipped kitchen, a balcony or patio, a whirlpool tub, a fireplace, and a washer/dryer. There's a pool for the exclusive use of condo guests, and many of the resort amenities are available as well. No pets. No smoking. $334–660 high season (May–October), $275–475 off-season.

COTTAGES AND CABINS

In Blairsville

🐾 ✔ & **Misty Mountain Inn and Cottages** (706-745-4786). In addition to B&B rooms in the main house (see *Lodging— Bed & Breakfasts*), Misty Mountain offers six cozy two- and three-bedroom cabins. Each features a kitchenette, a fireplace, and a rocking chair porch. Pets are welcome ($20 per pet). Meals are not included. Limited wheelchair accessibility. $140.

✔ & **Trackrock Campground and Cabins** (see *Campgrounds* as well as *To Do— Horseback Riding*). Lakeside and Rustic Wooded one- and two-bedroom cabins are available. Each features a full kitchen and a stacked-stone fireplace. Bedding and kitchen linens are provided, but not towels. Cabins are not wheelchair-accessible. Two-night minimum, three nights on holidays. $109–139.

🐾 ✔ & ✿ **Vogel State Park** (lodging reservations: 1-800-864-7275; www.ga stateparks.org/Vogel). The park features 35 fully equipped cottages, many of them lakeside. Three are dog friendly ($40 per dog;

maximum two). Campers enjoy all the amenities of the park (see *Green Space— Nature Preserves and Parks*). $95–160.

INNS AND RESORTS

In Hiawassee

✔ & **Boundary Waters Resort** (706-896-2530 or 1-800-323-3562; www.boundary watersresort.com), 528 Sunnyside Road. Closed January and February. Lakeside suites that sleep two to six are offered, along with the fully equipped three-bedroom Mallard Point Lake House. Guests receive complimentary dockage for their boats and use of canoes, kayaks, and paddleboats. No pets. No smoking. Limited wheelchair accessibility. Suites $115–135, cabin $135–150.

✔ & **The Ridges Resort** (706-896-2262 or 1-888-834-4409; www.theridgesresort.com), 3499 US 76 West. Cradled along the shores of Lake Chatuge, the getaway features 66 upscale rooms with private balconies, complimentary continental breakfast in the Moosehead Lounge, the four-star **Oaks** (see *Where to Eat—Dining Out*), **Yacht Club Boat House** (see *Where to Eat— Eating Out*), swimming pool, tennis courts, exercise room, volleyball, horseshoes, badminton, playground, and walking paths. The property is an Audubon-listed wildlife sanctuary. The on-site marina provides all kinds of rentals and activities (see *To Do— Boating*). No smoking. $199–255 in high season (May–October), $169–230 off-season.

In Young Harris

✔ & ✿ **Brasstown Valley Resort and Spa** (706-379-9900 or 1-800-201-3205; www.brasstownvalley.com), 6321 US 76. This luxurious resort offers accommodations in a 1,074-room lodge, five one-bedroom suites, and eight four-bedroom cottages. Some have a balcony and/or a gas-log fireplace. The cottages can be rented in configurations from one to four bedrooms with or without the common room with wood-burning fireplace and full kitchen. Each has a deck and a gas grill. The over-the-top Spa Suite has a private rooftop deck, two-person whirlpool tub, fireplace, and kitchenette. Its Experience Shower boasts double drench showerheads, steam aromatherapy, LED lights, marine speakers, and 12-head Swiss shower bars. Renowned for its high-country cuisine, the restaurant serves authentic north Georgia dishes paired with wines from local vintners. Dining options include a dining room and a casual eatery. (See *Where to Eat— Dining Out* and *Where to Eat— Eating Out.*) Activities on the 503-acre resort include an 18-hole golf course (see *To Do—Golf*), four lighted tennis courts, a swimming pool, state-of-the-art fitness center and spa and wellness center (see *To Do—Spas*), stables (see *To Do—Horseback Riding*), 9.2 miles of interpretive hiking and horseback riding trails, Brasstown Creek trout fishing, and more. Pet-friendly cottages. No smoking. $154–$184. $10 nightly fee covers the use of the fitness center, steam room, sauna, bass fishing pond, tennis courts, and the business center.

OTHER LODGINGS

In Hiawassee
🦐 🍃 ♿ **Enota Mountain Retreat** (706-896-9966 or 1-800-990-8864; www.enota .com), 1000 GA 180. Enota Mountain offers accommodations in cabins, RV and tent sites, and motel-type units. The non-profit spiritual retreat and animal rescue facility, surrounded by 1 million acres of national forest featuring five streams and four waterfalls, provides accommodations for visitors in order to help finance its conservation work. Cabins are on or across from a stream. Each features a full kitchen, deck, grill, and fire ring. Two boast a whirlpool tub. They are pet friendly ($15 per night). Most of the shaded 33 camping sites are on a stream. They are also pet friendly ($5 per night). There are family-only and adult-only tent areas. All the camping areas have bathhouses. The facility features a spa and wellness center that offers massages and full body aromatherapy. Other amenities include trout fishing, pony rides ($10), daily farm tour and animal feeding, three inground trampolines, horseshoes, volleyball, playground, tand Saturday hayrides ($3). From Labor Day through

ACTIVITIES AT BRASSTOWN VALLEY RESORT RANGE FROM HORSEBACK RIDING TO RELAXING ON THE PORCH.

November 30, dinner is served on Friday and Saturday night ($12) and breakfast is served weekends ($10). No smoking. One cabin wheelchair accessible. Tent sites $25–34, RV camping $34–39, cabins $110–175. $10 per stay conservation fee.

✳ Where to Eat
DINING OUT

In Hiawassee
🍃 ♿ **The Oaks at the Ridges Resort** (706-896-4141 or 1-888-834-4409), 3499 US 76 West. Open 5–10 daily. Happy hour and early bird specials. This very upscale dining establishment serves steaks, prime rib, freshwater fish, lobster, and pastas for dinner. No smoking. $13–24.

In Young Harris
🍃 ♿ **Dining Room at the Brasstown Valley Resort** (706-379-4613 or 1-800-201-3205; www.brasstownvalley.com), 6321 US 76. Open 7 AM–9 PM daily, Sunday brunch. The resort's seafood and prime rib buffets are particularly popular. The à la carte menu is always available. No smoking. Breakfast and lunch $8–14, dinner $20–40, buffets $18–37, brunch $21.

In Hiawassee

🍴 🗑 ⛐ **Boat House at the Marina, the Ridges Resort** (706-896-1919), 3499 US 76 West. Open for lunch and dinner daily. This "boater's casual" eatery serves burgers, meat and two sides, soup of the day, and freshly baked desserts. Other dining options at the resort include the Moosehead Lounge for continental breakfast, snacks, and cocktails; the seasonal Tiki Bar, where live music is offered evenings on the patio, and the Oaks (see *Dining Out*). No smoking. $6–24.

In Young Harris

🍴 🗑 ⛐ **Brassies at the 19th Hole/ Brasstown Valley Resort** (706-379-4613 or 1-800-201-3205; www.brasstown valley.com), 6321 US 76. Open 11–11 Sunday–Thursday, until midnight Friday and Saturday. The casual eatery serves burgers, salads, and snacks. No smoking. $8–15.

✳ Entertainment

MUSIC Anderson Music Hall (706-896-4191; www.georgiamountainfairgrounds .com), Georgia Mountain Fairgrounds, 1131 Music Hall Road off US 76, Hiawassee. The 2,900-seat music hall is the site of many concerts throughout the year, including the **Superstar Concert Series** and **Georgia's Official State Fiddler's Convention.** In just five months there were appearances by Willie Nelson, Jeremy Camp, Travis Tritt, Randy Travis, Colt Ford, Mercy Me, George Jones, Happy Together Tour, and Vince Gill, so that's the caliber of entertainment offered. Check the website or call for schedule and prices, which are priced dependent on the show but generally range $30–45.

✳ Selective Shopping

ANTIQUES Hiawassee Antique Mall (706-896-0587), 460 North Main Street, Hiawassee. Open 10–5 Monday–Saturday, noon–5 Sunday. Sixty dealers sell a large selection of antiques, with an emphasis on mountain country items.

✳ Special Events

May: **Rhododendron Festival** (706-896-4191; www.georgia-mountain-fair.com). Held at the Fred Hamilton Rhododendron Gardens at the Georgia Mountain Fair, the festival celebrates the beautiful rhododendron gardens, which bloom from early April to late May. The festival also features craft vendors and food, plus plants for sale. $3.

July: **Georgia Mountain Fair** (706-896-4191; www.georgiamountainfairgrounds .com/georgiamountainfair.php), US 76, Hiawassee. Fair hours: 10–9 Monday–Thursday, 10–10 Friday, 9 AM–10 PM Saturday, 9–6 Sunday. Towns County's oldest tourist attraction, the 10-day celebration features music, demonstrations of old-time skills, food, arts and crafts, exhibitions, flower show, midway rides, access to the **Pioneer Village** (see *To See—Historic Homes and Sites*), and entertainment. Gate $5, music shows $10 each, parking $2.

October: **Georgia Mountain Fall Festival** (706-896-4191; www.georgia-mountain -fair.com). Similar to the Georgia Mountain Fair in the summer, the 10-day fall festival is also the official **State Fiddlers Convention,** with performances by numerous artists and groups included in the admission price. Gate $5, music shows $10 each, parking $2.

MOUNTAIN MIDNIGHT COON DOG HOWL

Celebrate New Year's Eve at a unique event where you can come in bibbed overalls or a tux, jeans or a sequined ball gown, and sit on hay bales at tables covered with white linen cloths. Held at the Hiawassee River Trout Lodge (706-896-7400), the shabby-chic celebration includes an ugly coon dog contest, coon dog howling contest, hog calling contest, favors, entertainment, and champagne for toasting at midnight. Food and beverages available for purchase. $15.

ROME AND CALHOUN

Located in the heart of northwest Georgia, this area is rich with history. Long the home of Native Americans, it served as the last capital of the Cherokee Nation, the largest of the five civilized tribes of the Southeast, before the Indians were removed and sent west along the Trail of Tears. The Civil War played a significant part in the region's history, and the Battle of Resaca was one of the bloodiest battles in the Atlanta Campaign. For history buffs, numerous museums and historic homes tell the stories of the Native Americans, white settlers, and military campaigns.

Three large rivers flow through the area—the Conasauga, the Oostanaula, and the Coosawattee—as well as numerous smaller rivers and streams. The Chattahoochee National Forest provides splendid views of nature's beauty and a gorgeous setting for outdoor activities, as do several state parks, city and county parks, lakes, and recreation areas.

GUIDANCE When planning a trip to the Rome area, including Cave Spring, contact the **Greater Rome Convention and Visitors Center Bureau and Welcome Center** (706-295-5576 or 1-800-444-1834; www.romegeorgia.org), 402 Civic Center Drive, Rome 30161. Open 9:30–5 weekdays, 9:30–3 Saturday. For specific Cave Spring information, check out www.cavespringgeorgia.com.

For more information about Adairsville and Resaca, contact the **Cartersville–Bartow County Convention and Visitors Bureau** (770-387-1357 or 1-800-733-2280; www.not atlanta.org), located in the Clarence Brown Conference Center, 5450 GA 20, Cartersville 30120. Open 8:30–5 weekdays, 11–4 Saturday.

For information about Calhoun or Resaca, contact the **Calhoun–Gordon County Convention and Visitors Bureau, Calhoun Local Welcome Center, Gordon County Chamber of Commerce** (706-625-3200 or 1-800-887-3811; www.gordonchamber.org), 350 South Wall Street, Calhoun 30701. Open 8:30–5 weekdays.

GETTING THERE *By air:* The nearest airports are in Atlanta and Chattanooga in nearby Tennessee (see "What's Where in Georgia").

By bus: **Greyhound Lines** (706-291-4775; www.greyhound.com) provides service to Rome (868 Spider Web Drive).

By car: North–south I-75 in Georgia and I-59 in Alabama provide easy access to this area, but why not get off the interstates and use the more scenic US 27? East–west routes include US 278, US 411, and GA 20.

By train: The nearest **AMTRAK** (see "What's Where in Georgia") station is in Atlanta.

GETTING AROUND **Rome Transit** (706-236-4523) offers mass transit service on several routes within the city limits from 5:45 AM to 6:30 PM. Service includes paratransit services for the disabled. One-way ticket price: adults $1, seniors and students $0.50. In Rome, car rentals are available from **Budget** (706-290-0244) and **Enterprise** (706-290-1093). In Calhoun, car rentals are available from **Enterprise** (706-602-1841) and **Nugent Auto Rental** (706-625-3765).

PARKING Downtown parking on Broad Street in Rome is free and allowed in two-hour increments. Visitors may receive passes for longer parking by contacting the **Greater Rome Convention and Visitors Bureau** (1-800-444-1834). Parking passes are issued on a case-by-case basis and are not allowed for special-event parking.

WHEN TO GO The mountainous areas in the northern part of the state experience longer periods of colder temperatures as well as occasional snow or ice. Some campgrounds and other establishments focusing on outdoor activities close for a few months in the winter, so call ahead if traveling in the winter to avoid disappointment.

MEDICAL EMERGENCY Call 911.

VILLAGES AND NEIGHBORHOODS **Rome,** the only city in the region described in this chapter, has a population of 91,000 and 800 acres of parkland. Rome boasts Shorter College, one of the finest music schools in the Southeast; Berry College, which has the largest campus in the world; Floyd College; and Coosa Valley Technical College. The official symbol for Rome is its clock tower, which sits atop one of the city's seven hills and is actually a cleverly disguised water tower.

Rome's **Between the Rivers Historic District** is aptly named in that it encompasses the old downtown area of Rome where the town was first founded in 1834. Defined by the Etowah, Oostanaula, and Coosa rivers, this area contains most of Rome's oldest (mostly turn-of-the-20th-century, Victorian-style) homes, churches, and commercial buildings. Broad Street, the second widest in Georgia, offers many trendy shops and restaurants. Get a walking tour brochure from the visitors center.

Adairsville is noted for the part it played in the Great Locomotive Chase during the Civil War (see the Northern Suburbs chapter in part 1: Atlanta Metro). In this century, it is also known for the world-class **Barnsley Gardens Resort,** which offers superior accommodations, dining, and sporting options (see listings throughout this chapter). Once a private, 10,000-acre estate called Woodlands, the property has seen its share of tragedies. Julia, wife of original owner Geoffrey Barnsley, died during construction. The Civil War ruined Barnsley's fortunes, and soldiers from both sides ravaged the estate. Later, a 1906 tornado tore the roof off the villa and forced the family into the kitchen annex. The estate was rescued in 1988 by Prince Hubertus Fugger and Princess Alexandra of a small principality in southern Germany. They restored the gardens and stabilized the ruins, then added cottages, dining establishments, a spa, a golf course, and other amenities.

A Norman Rockwell kind of town, Adairsville was the first town in Georgia to be listed in its entirety on the National Register of Historic Places. Antebellum and Victorian homes and churches fill the 170-acre historic district. Today it attracts tourists, history buffs, and antiques lovers. Adairsville also hosts the three-day **Great Locomotive Chase Festival** the first weekend in October (see *Special Events*).

Calhoun's past is largely influenced by the Cherokee Indians who lived here. The area eventually became the capital of the Cherokee Nation and was the birthplace of the Cherokee alphabet, written language, and newspaper, the *Cherokee Phoenix* (see **New Echota Cherokee Capital Historic Site** under *To See—Historic Homes and Sites*).

Cave Spring, a classic small Southern town south of Rome, was named for the pure spring found in a limestone cave located in what is now known as **Rolater Park** (see *Green Space—Nature Preserves and Parks*). The town's natural wonders were known to several cultures of Native Americans, and legend has it that tribal meetings and games occurred at the site. The park site also was the campus of the Cave Spring Manual Labor School, later renamed Hearn Academy. One of the historic school buildings now operates as the **Hearn Inn** (see *Lodging—Bed & Breakfasts*), and the old Baptist church is used for weddings, meetings, and special events. Including the school buildings, the picturesque village has 90 structures on the National Register of Historic Places. Homes exhibit Gothic, Queen Anne, and Plantation styles. The 1867 Presbyterian church has been restored and is open to the public as an art gallery on weekends. Still central to the village is the 29-acre park where the spring flows into a pond and then into a 1.5–acre swimming pool shaped like the state of Georgia. Cave Spring is widely known for the quality and quantity of its antiques shops, and several antiques, gift, and home decor shops and popular eateries surround the park. A renowned arts and crafts festival also is held each June in the park (see *Special Events*).

Cedartown's claim to fame is that it was the hometown of Sterling Holloway, whose raspy voice portrayed Winnie-the-Pooh in numerous animated movies. He began performing here in early childhood by putting on neighborhood variety shows. A marker at College Street and Sterling Holloway Place memorializes the native son. Today Cedartown has a history museum and is the home of a skydiving company.

Kingston claims to have more historical markers per capita than any other town in Georgia. Kingston grew during the heyday of the railroads because there was a major rail facility downtown. During the Great Locomotive Chase in April 1862, Andrews's Raiders lost a precious hour in the rail yard until freight trains cleared the tracks. Rescuers missed them by only four minutes but took a locomotive from there to continue the chase. Union general William Tecumseh Sherman headquartered here, consolidating his position early in the Atlanta Campaign. While in Kingston during the Civil War, General Sherman made plans for and awaited approval from Gen. Ulysses Grant for his March to the Sea. He destroyed the town when he left. The last contingent of Confederate troops east of the Mississippi was surrendered by Gen. William Wofford and pardoned in Kingston on May 12, 1865. That same year, ladies of the town observed Confederate Memorial Day by decorating the graves of 250 Confederate soldiers and two Union unknowns in the town cemetery on the last Sunday in April. That ceremony became known as Decoration Day and eventually evolved into the Memorial Day we celebrate today, although a separate Confederate Memorial Day is still observed. After the Civil War, Kingston became known for its ministers, whose renown spread through the reports of rail passengers who visited local churches while waiting for their trains. Today Kingston is well-known as the home of the **Atlanta Steeplechase** (see *Special Events*).

✳ To See

CULTURAL SITES 🐾 🌢 ♿ *Capitoline Wolf* (CVB: 607-295-5576; 1-800-444-1834; www.romegeorgia.org), 601 Broad Street, Rome. Open daily. This 1,500-pound statue of a suckling wolf in front of City Hall was a gift from the government of Rome, Italy, to the people of Rome, Georgia, in 1929. The statue is an exact replica of the *Capitoline Wolf* suckling the twins Romulus and Remus (orphaned offspring of Mars, the god of war, and Rhea Silvia, the daughter of King Numitor), an Etruscan statue that stands in the Palazzo dei Conservatori on the Capitoline Hill in Rome. Some folks found the statue so shocking that when important events were scheduled the twins were diapered and the wolf draped. In 1933 one of the twins was stolen and a replacement had to be created. Because of anti-Italy sentiment during World War II and threats to dynamite the statue, it was put into storage until 1952. Free.

❦ ⚲ **Berry College Campus** (706-238-7966;
www.berry.edu/oakhill), 2277 Martha Berry Highway NW, Mount Berry. In the early 20th
century, Martha Berry began teaching poor children in her playhouse. Eventually her
efforts created a college. She called on Henry Ford and other philanthropists for help, and
many of the beautiful buildings on campus were constructed with financial contributions
from Ford. Today, with 26,000 acres, Berry has the largest campus in the world. Among its
interesting sites are Oak Hill and Martha Berry Museum (see *Museums*); the Old Mill,
where corn is sometimes ground with the second-largest working overshot waterwheel in
the world; and an All-American Selections Display Garden. Self-guided tours free, guided
campus tours $20.

❦ ✎ ⚲ **New Echota Cherokee Capital Historic Site** (706-624-1321; www.gastateparks
.org/NewEchota), 1211 Chatsworth Highway NE/GA 225, Calhoun. Open 9–5 Thursday–
Saturday. Contrary to popular opinion, all Native Americans did not live in tepees or grass
huts. Many lived just as the white settlers did. In 1825 the Cherokee national legislature
established a capital called New Echota at the headwaters of the Oostanaula River, marking
one of the earliest experiments in national self-government by an Indian tribe. The Cherokee built log cabins, frame homes, outbuildings, and public structures. They published a
bilingual newspaper at an on-site print shop—the first Indian-language newspaper in the
country. They instigated a court case that went all the way to the U.S. Supreme Court.
Unfortunately, when gold was discovered in north Georgia, the white men decided to take
the land of the Native Americans. A treaty was signed that relinquished all Cherokee land
east of the Mississippi River. The infamous Trail of Tears began here with Native Americans
assembled for removal to the west in 1838. Today the site contains original and reconstructed buildings, including the council house, courthouse, print shop, missionary Samuel
Worcester's home and tavern, an 1805 store, and farm outbuildings such as barns, corncribs,
and smokehouses. The modern visitors center provides space for an introductory movie,
interpretive exhibits, and a gift shop where visitors can purchase authentic Native American
arts, crafts, and music. The site also features a 1-mile nature trail and Coosawattee River
fishing. $4.50–6.50.

❦ ✎ ⚲ **Oakleigh** (706-629-1515), 335 South Wall Street, Calhoun. Open 1–4 Monday,
Wednesday, and Friday or by appointment. General Sherman used this stately home as his
headquarters when his Union troops were advancing from Chattanooga to Atlanta. Today the
1850 house serves as the headquarters of the Gordon County Historical Society. In addition
to admiring the home and its antique furniture, female visitors are fascinated by the fantastic
collection of nearly 2,000 dolls from the 1930s to the early Barbies, all of which were collected by one woman. The historical society also has many genealogy resources. Free.

❦ ✎ ⚲ **Paradise Gardens** (678-641-8700; www.finsterparadisegardens.org), 84 Knox Street,
Summerville. Closed in winter. Howard Finster, 1915–2001, known as the "Grandfather of
Modern American Visionary Art," was one of the most celebrated and prolific artists of the
last century, with 46,000 pieces of original art. His works have appeared at the Library of
Congress, the Smithsonian, and the High Museum, among others. He began creating primitive outsider art laced with prophetic religious statements in 1961 after he received a vision
telling him to create sacred art. His philosophy on this type of art was that "It preaches for
them after they're gone." The entire 4-acre complex of structures and sculpture is created
with found objects covered with text and includes the Paradise Gardens Art Gallery and the
World's Folk Art Chapel. The annual **Finster Fest,** held the first weekend in May in downtown's Dowdy Park, includes shuttles to tour Paradise Gardens.

MUSEUMS ❦ ✎ ⚲ **Adairsville Rail Depot Age of Steam Museum** (770-773-1775),
101 Public Square, Adairsville. Open 10–5 Tuesday–Friday. This 1847 Western and Atlantic
Railroad Depot was a silent witness to the Great Locomotive Chase. Today it contains

displays describing the town's role in the Civil War, railroad memorabilia, tributes to early life in Adairsville, and the role of peaches and chenille in the town's economy. Free.

🌸 ✍ ⚅ **Chieftains Museum–Major Ridge Home** (706-291-9494; www.chieftainsmuseum .org), 501 Riverside Parkway, Rome. Open 9–5 Wednesday–Saturday. Located on the banks of the Oostanaula River, the original home of Major Ridge, an early-19th-century leader of the Cherokee Nation, was given the National Park Service National Trail of Tears designation. Ridge, who tried to conform to white men's culture while preserving his own, served as a mediator during many disputes. He fought with Andrew Jackson at the Battle of Horseshoe Bend in 1814, which is where he earned the rank of major. Ridge and his family were ferryboat operators, storekeepers, tavern owners, and slaveholders. The core house was built in 1794 and enlarged and remodeled many times until it attained its current white clapboard plantation house appearance. Exhibits focus on the Ridge family, artifacts found on the property, the Cherokee, the clash of cultures with white settlers, and the Trail of Tears. Displays include Native American artifacts, photographs, furniture, and artwork. Adults $5, seniors $3, children $2.

🌸 ✍ ⚅ **Eubanks Museum and Gallery** (706-291-2121 or 1-800-868-6980; www.shorter .edu), 315 Shorter Avenue, Rome. Open 8:30–5 weekdays. This museum, in the welcome center on the campus of Shorter College, contains the collection of J. Robert Eubanks, a life trustee and benefactor of the college. Natural-history exhibits display family artifacts from safaris to Africa and India. Other exhibits include antique telephones, early American hardware, and Native American pottery, tools, and hunting items. Free.

🌸 ⚅ **Kingston Woman's History Museums** (770-336-5540 or 770-387-1357; www.not atlanta.org), 13 East Main Street, Kingston. Open 1–4 Saturday and Sunday or by appointment. Although it started as a women's museum concentrating on candlelit tours, today the Kingston Woman's History Club displays artifacts, scrapbooks, and photographs in two museums. The Civil War Museum portrays the town's role in the Civil War and the Kingston Memorial Day observances, which are the oldest in the nation. The Martha Mulinix Annex displays memorabilia relating to life in Kingston after the Civil War, housing displays of old farm equipment and exhibits related to Kingston schools, stores, and churches. Free; donations accepted.

🌸 ✍ ⚅ **Oak Hill, Martha Berry Museum** (706-238-7966; www.berry.edu/oakhill), 2277 Martha Berry Highway NW, Mount Berry. Open 10–5 Monday–Saturday. A magnificent example of Colonial Revival architecture, Oak Hill was the home of Martha Berry, founder of the Martha Berry School, which is now Berry College (see *Historic Homes and Sites*). The house, which was built in 1847, remains as it was lived in from 1860 to 1942. The museum, in a separate building and location, chronicles Martha Berry's life and work as related to her founding the school for less fortunate children. The museum also contains an extensive art collection amassed by Miss Berry's sister, Eugenia, wife of Prince Enrico of Italy. The collection includes Italian and American artists and spans 1,000 years. The crowning glory of the estate is the gardens, which were designed between 1927 and 1933. In keeping with early-20th-century landscaping trends, the gardens also display classical statuary and fountains. Trails include the Fernery Nature Trail and Martha Berry's Walkway of Life. Just a small piece of trivia: Oak Hill appeared as the Carmichael mansion in the film *Sweet Home Alabama*. Also on the estate is the Carriage House, which features vintage vehicles; the original log cabin, also known as the "Birthplace of Berry," where Berry began teaching mountain children; and Aunt Martha's Cottage, the restored home of Berry's beloved cook and house servant, "Aunt Martha" Freeman. Limited wheelchair accessibility. Special events include the **Berry College Ford Festival** and **Candles and Carols.** Adults $4, children 6–12 $3.

🌸 ✍ ⚅ **Polk County Historical Society Museum** (770-749-0747; www.polkhist.org), 205 College Street, Cedartown. Open 2–4 Wednesday and 1:30–5 the last Sunday of each month. Once a children's library, the building now houses a local museum where exhibits chronicle the history of the county. Displays include town and farm memorabilia from the 19th through the early 20th century, vintage clothing, and furniture. Free.

❦ ⅃ **Roland Hayes Museum** (706-629-2599; www.harrisartscenter.com/roland-hayes -history-museum), 212 South Wall Street, Calhoun. Open 10–6 Monday, 10–4 Tuesday– Thursday, 10–2 Friday, Saturday by appointment. Housed within the **Harris Arts Center** (see *Entertainment*), the museum honors Roland Hayes (1887–1977), a native of Calhoun, the son of a slave, and one of the first African Americans to have a concert and operatic career. He performed at Carnegie Hall and with the Boston Symphony and all over Europe—in fact, performing for King George V and Queen Mary at Buckingham Palace. He was one of the highest paid singers of his time—of any color. The museum displays memorabilia related to Hayes's career and includes his grand piano. Visitors can listen to his music and see a film about his life. Free; donations appreciated.

❦ ⅃ **Rome Area History Museum** (706-235-8051; www.romehistorymuseum.com), 305 Broad Street, Rome. Open 10–4 Wednesday–Friday, 10–6 Saturday. Exhibits cover subjects such as Native American history, explorer Hernando de Soto's visit to the area, early settlers, and wars from the Civil War to the present. Learn about quilting, weaving, the importance of steamboats and cotton, and the devastation caused when Union troops burned the city to the ground. These stories are told through documents, maps, blueprints, photographs, personal letters, business records, and much more, including temporary exhibits. It's somewhat light on actual artifacts. Adults $4, seniors $3, children 6–12 $2.

SPECIAL PLACES ❦ ⅃ ❀ **Silver Comet Trail and Riverwalk** (770-684-8760 or 1-800-226-2517; www.silvercometga.com), Rockmart. Open daily. This paved Rails-to-Trails route stretching from Atlanta to the Georgia-Alabama state line is popular with walkers, joggers, skaters, and cyclists. It is suitable for wheelchairs and strollers. It is accessible from downtown Rockmart at mile marker 37.6 and also in Cedartown at the depot. The trail is named for the Seaboard Airline Railroad's silver passenger train, which traveled through here on a route between New York and Birmingham from May 1947 to April 1969. Free.

✳ To Do

BICYCLING ⌁ **Barnsley Gardens Resort** (770-773-7480; resort: 1-877-773-2447; www.barnsleyresort.com), 597 Barnsley Gardens Road, Adairsville. Reservations required. The rolling landscape is ideal for novice riders, although there are more thrilling options. Rentals include a mountain bike or cruiser, helmet, water bottle, and trail map. Minimum age 6; adults must accompany riders age 6–11. $10 per hour, $35 for full day; trail use fee $10 for riders with their own bikes.

BOATING ❦ ⌁ **Barnsley Gardens Resort** (see *Bicycling*). Reservations required. Canoes and kayaks are available on a first-come, first-served basis for use on the resort's 10-acre lake. Boaters must be at least 11 years old unless accompanied by an adult. Complimentary for overnight guests; included in the $15 admission price for day visitors.

Canoe Trails. Rome has 50 miles of canoe trails on the **Oostanaula River.** The gradient drops only 1 foot along the entire length—guaranteeing smooth water and a leisurely paddle. Put-in points are along GA 225.

FARM TOURS ❦ ⌁ ⅃ **Pumpkin Patch Farm** (770-773-2617; www.pumpkinpatch farm.net), 230 Old Dixie Highway NW, Adairsville. Open 10–5 weekends in October. Activities include a petting zoo, hay maze, hayrides, pumpkin and autumn crafts, scarecrow making, and more. There's a huge selection of gourds, Indian corn, straw, and cornstalks to purchase for your home decorations. Admission $6; activity prices vary.

FISHING ✍ **Barnsley Gardens Resort** (see *Bicycling*). Reservations required. Anglers enjoy fly- and spin-fishing on Lower Pond or the 10-acre lake. Instruction is offered, and guides can take anglers on daylong fishing excursions to local rivers such as the Noontoola, a private trophy-trout stream. Minimum age of 14 unless accompanied by an adult. $90–150 for instruction and equipment; if fishing on your own, $25 for fishing permit, $15–30 for equipment, $4 for lures; $375 for guided fishing trips.

FRISBEE GOLF 🐾 ✍ **Barnsley Gardens Resort** (see *Bicycling*). The nine-hole course meanders through gardens and meadows. Complimentary for overnight guests, $15 for day visitors.

GOLF Barnsley Gardens Resort (see *Bicycling*). Pro shop open 8–6; course opening depends on weather (in winter, frost must be off the course before it can open, then play is until dark), so call for hours. The resort's course, called "the General" for the famous train hijacked during the Great Locomotive Chase, is a Jim Fazio–designed championship course ranked 13th in the state by *Golf Digest*. The 18-hole, 7,350-yard, par-72 course covering 378 acres features an outstanding collection of par-3 holes. The course winds through hardwood forest, tall reeds, cattails, and thick brush past a creek and pond, with abrupt changes in elevation. $85–100; rental clubs $55.

HORSEBACK RIDING ✍ **Barnsley Gardens Resort** (see *Bicycling*). Open 7 AM–10 PM daily. Reservations required. Guests can enjoy a guided Western horseback ride. One-hour trail rides, two-hour scenic wilderness rides, and children's rides are offered. Picnic meals can be added to any ride at an additional cost. $75 per hour, two-hour Wilderness Ride $115, corral ride $45 for 30 minutes, Saturday lessons $65 per hour.

PAINTBALL ✍ **Barnsley Gardens Resort** (see *Bicycling*). Families and groups may enjoy the exciting challenges of a Paint Ball Adventure in the Wolf Care Mountain Field. Admission $20, gun and safety equipment $15, paintballs $50.

SHOOTING SPORTS Barnsley Gardens Resort (see *Bicycling*). By appointment 9–4:30 Monday–Saturday; reservations required. The resort offers sporting clays, lessons, and clinics overseen by the prestigious British School of Shooting at the Spring Bank Plantation, as well as quail and pheasant hunts (call for prices). $90 for 100 clays with Barnsley equipment, $60 for 100 clays with your own equipment, $50 per hour for lessons.

SKYDIVING Atlanta Skydiving Center (770-684-3483 or 1-800-607-5867; www.asc skydiving.com), 493 Airport Road, Cedartown. Open 8 AM–9 PM daily year-round. The largest skydiving center in the Southeast offers tandem skydiving with qualified instructors. Participants can receive a video or photo of their accomplishment (additional cost). Call for prices.

SkyDive The Farm (1-888-494-6964; www.proskydiving.com), Rockmart. Open 7:30–sunset Wednesday–Sunday. The company offers a full range of skydiving opportunities for the more adventurous among us. The site offers breathtaking panoramas for those who are too faint of heart to try skydiving. There are also bunkhouses and camping. $179 tandem, $269 solo, $269 accelerated free fall, $90 audiovisual package.

SPAS ♿ **Barnsley Gardens Resort** (see *Bicycling*). Check the website or call for hours. At the Spa at Barnsley Gardens, guests can be pampered with a wide array of massages, skin treatments, body wraps, and aromatherapy. Overnight guests have complimentary use of the large coed whirlpool; ladies' and gentlemen's saunas, steam rooms, and whirlpools; fitness center; and the Grecian-style swimming pool. Must be 18 years old to use spa facilities. Spa rates vary by treatment $20–185; packages available.

TENNIS ✺ ✑ **Rome–Floyd County Tennis Center** (706-290-0072), 301 West Third Street SW, Rome. Open 9 AM–10 PM Monday–Thursday, 9–9 Friday, noon–8 Saturday. The design of the award-winning center has earned an "Outstanding Tennis Facility Design" award from the U.S. Tennis Association, and *Tennis Magazine* calls Rome one of the top tennis cities in America. The 16-court lighted facility offers instruction and league play, and hosts state and regional tournaments. $3 per hour.

✳ Green Space

GARDENS ✺ ✑ ✿ **Barnsley Gardens Resort** (see *To Do—Bicycling*). Open sunrise–sunset daily. The 160-year-old gardens with 100 varieties of heirloom roses were rescued from oblivion in 1988 and have been restored to the showcase of the South they once were. One of the most spectacular displays is the sea of thousands of cheery yellow daffodils in the spring. Enjoy guided or self-guided tours of the gardens, the manor house ruins, and the small museum. Complimentary for overnight guests. Day visitors: adults $10, seniors $8, children $5.

THE LOVE OF HIS LIFE

Geoffrey Barnsley set out to build an estate worthy of his wife, Julia. In 1842 he began construction of a grand 24-room Italianate villa with modern conveniences such as hot and cold running water. He surrounded the villa with formal gardens designed in the style of Andrew Jackson Downing, the architect who designed the grounds of the U.S. Capitol and the White House. Unfortunately, Julia died before the home and gardens were completed. Brokenhearted, Barnsley abandoned construction until Julia allegedly appeared to him in the formal gardens one night and told him she wanted the house finished. You'll find a likeness of Julia on the fountain in the knot garden. Various visitors and employees report ghostly occurrences, including sightings of Julia and Geoffrey.

LAKES ✺ ✑ ✿ **Carters Lake** (706-334-2248; www.sam.usace.army.mil/carters), 1850 Carters Dam, Chatsworth. Open 8–4:30 weekdays, 9–5 weekends. The 3,200-acre, 450-feet deep U.S. Army Corps of Engineers lake with 62 miles of shoreline is impounded by the tallest earthen dam east of the Mississippi. The lake and surrounding 6,000 acres of public land offer opportunities for boating, developed and primitive camping, fishing, hunting, and picnicking. One of the appealing facets of this lake is that there are no private docks or development. Corps-operated marinas and cabin and boat rentals are available. Mountain biking and hiking are popular land-based activities. Free access to lake; some activities have fees.

NATURE PRESERVES AND PARKS ✺ ✑ ✿ **Chattahoochee National Forest** (district office: 706-695-6736; www.fs.usda.gov). Open daylight hours daily except for campers. The pristine, undeveloped forest boasts 750,000 acres, 10 wilderness areas, 2,200 miles of rivers and streams (of which 1,367 miles are trout streams), and 430 miles of hiking trails—many of these located in northwest Georgia. (See also the Cartersville, Clarkesville, Dahlonega, Dalton, and Hiawassee chapters.) All of them provide endless opportunities for outdoor pursuits in wildlife management tracts, recreation areas, and scenic regions. Recreational activities include off-road riding, mountain biking, horseback riding, hiking, fishing, hunting, and camping. Free.

✺ ✑ ✿ ❀ **James H. (Sloppy) Floyd State Park** (706-857-0826; lodging reservations: 1-800-864-7275; www.gastateparks.org/JamesHFloyd), 280 Sloppy Floyd Lake Road, off US

27, Summerville. Open 7 AM–10 PM daily. Isolated from the hustle and bustle of city life, this tranquil 561-acre park is surrounded by rural countryside and the Chattahoochee National Forest (see previous entry). Fishing is offered on two stocked lakes, and hikers can use the 3 miles of lake loop trails or access the Pinhoti Trail. Two boat ramps are available (electric motors only are allowed). There are two fishing piers, one of which is wheelchair accessible. Children enjoy the playgrounds, feeding the fish from the boardwalk, and renting pedal boats in season. The park also offers camping and cottages (see *Lodging—Campgrounds and Cottages*). Parking $5.

Lock and Dam Regional Park (706-234-5001; www.rfpra.com), 181 Lock and Dam Road, off Blacks Bluff Road, Rome. Park open dawn–dusk daily; store open 8–5 daily in winter, 7–5 in summer. The 73-acre regional park was created around the Mayo Lock and Dam, which was completed and opened for navigation in 1913. Enjoy the best in river fishing for crappie and striper as well as canoeing on the Coosa River from the park, which also includes picnic shelters, a playground, an exhibition center, horseshoe pits, canoe rentals, a boat ramp, and restrooms. The Coosa River Trading Post sells snacks and beverages, fishing licenses, bait, and supplies, while the Coosa River Nature Center has live reptile exhibits and natural history displays. Camping at 31 fully equipped RV campsites and primitive sites are available. The campground features a bathhouse, laundry facilities, and a nature preserve. Two-night minimum on weekends, three-night minimum on holidays. Parking $2, boat ramp $3, RV sites $22–24, tent sites $14.

Rolater Park, Cave Spring (706-777-8904 or 706-777-9944; www.cavespringgeorgia.com), 13 Cedartown Street/US 411/GA 53, Cave Spring. Park open daylight hours daily; cave open 10–6 daily in summer. The 300,000-year-old cave, where the spring originates, has impressive stalagmites and the legendary "Devil's Stool" formation. The spring pumps 3 to 4 million gallons of water a day, and the award-winning springwater is noted for its purity and taste. Although it can be purchased commercially, many visitors bring jugs to fill and take home. Park free; cave $1.

Salacoa Creek Park (706-629-3490), GA 156, Calhoun. Open 7 AM–8 PM daily the first Saturday in March–October 1. The 343-acre Gordon County park features a 126-acre lake and offers a quality swimming beach, a boat ramp, picnic areas, and fishing. Bass, bream, catfish, and crappie are stocked in the lake. Private boats are permitted on the lake (motorboats are limited to 10 mph), and canoeing is popular. The waters are open for legal fishing when the park is open. Anglers age 16 and older must have a valid state or nonresident fishing license. No night fishing is allowed except during special events. In addition, the park offers nature trails and tent and RV campsites (see *Lodging—Campgrounds and Cottages*). Free.

RECREATION AREAS **Rocky Mountain Recreation and Fishing Area** (706-802-5087; www.georgiawildlife.com), 4054 Big Texas Valley Road NW, Rome. Open daily; fishing permitted sunrise–sunset. Enjoy nature at its finest, as well as outdoor pursuits such as fishing, hunting, picnicking, hiking, camping, and swimming. The 5,000-acre area offers two recreation lakes—Antioch and Heath. Restrictions on Heath Lake limit its use to only the 1st through the 10th of each month. There are also limits on size and number of fish caught. Largemouth bass and sunfish are the most common fish caught, but the lakes are also filled with channel catfish, black crappie, bluegill, redear sunfish, and hybrid white-striped bass. White-tailed deer, turkey, and waterfowl are present for wildlife observation. There are two boat ramps, fishing jetties, scenic overlooks, and hiking trails. Only fishing boats are allowed, and they must run at idle speed regardless of boat or motor size. Anglers age 14–65 must have a valid fishing license unless disabled. RV campsites and walk-in sites are available. $3 per car, primitive campsites $12, RV sites $25–50.

✳ Lodging

BED & BREAKFASTS

In Cave Spring

🦐 🍴 ♿ **Hearn Inn** (706-777-8502 or 706-676-4579; www.cavespringhistoricalsociety .com), 13 Cedartown Street SW. The 1839 building, once the dormitory for the Cave Spring Manual Labor School or Hearn Academy, now houses a bed & breakfast. Located in Rolater Park, where it has easy access to downtown as well as the cave and the pool, the simply furnished inn offers seven rooms, one with a private bath. Other rooms share baths, making them suitable for a family or friends traveling together. A continental breakfast is included in the nightly rate. A communal hot tub is a hit with guests. No smoking. Limited wheelchair accessibility. $65–75.

🦐 **Tumlin House Bed and Breakfast** (706-777-0066 or 1-800-939-3880), 38 Alabama Street. The sprawling 1842 home, purchased by ancestors of the present family in 1886, offers four beautifully decorated guest rooms—two with private baths and two with a shared bath, making them ideal for families or friends traveling together. In addition, the B&B boasts a 1,400-square-foot wraparound porch, a screened porch, and a swimming pool. A full gourmet breakfast is included in your stay. A six-course fixed price dinner is served on Saturday nights by reservation for $40 per person (BYOW—bring your own wine). The B&B is within easy walking distance of **Rolater Park** (see *Green Space—Nature Preserves and Parks*), antiques shops, and restaurants. No pets. Children 12 and older welcome. Smoking outdoors only. Not wheelchair accessible. $75–85.

In Rome

♿ **Claremont House Bed and Breakfast** (706-291-0900 or 1-800-254-4797; www .theclaremonthouse.net), 906 East Second Avenue. One of the most striking Victorian-era mansions in Rome, the Claremont House (circa 1882) offers elegant guest rooms furnished in Victorian opulence. Spacious guest accommodations feature 14-foot ceilings, heart-pine floors, elaborately carved woodwork, a fireplace, a private bath, gorgeous furnishings, and luxury linens. Accommodations are also offered in the 1879 cottage where the family lived while their dream house was being built. It features a bedroom, bath, living room, and fully stocked kitchen. Included in the nightly rates is a gourmet candlelit breakfast. Ask about pets. No smoking. Some rooms wheelchair accessible. $95–175.

In Summerville

🦐 **Dillard's Bed and Breakfast** (706-822-9948), 625 East Washington Street. A more-than-100-year-old farmhouse provides three beautifully appointed guest rooms, each with a private bath, television, VCR, and small refrigerator. Two rooms feature a sitting area and a claw-foot tub. A screened porch overlooks the stone patio and affords an opportunity to observe birds and wildlife. In fact, the property is certified as a National Wildlife Federation Backyard Wildlife Habitat. A continental breakfast is included weekdays, and weekends feature a full Taste of the South breakfast. No smoking. Not wheelchair accessible. $85.

CAMPGROUNDS AND COTTAGES

In Calhoun

See **Salacoa Creek Park** under *Green Space—Nature Preserves and Parks.*

In Rome

See **Lock and Dam Regional Park** under *Green Space—Nature Preserves and Parks* and **Rocky Mountain Recreation and Fishing Area** under *Green Space— Recreation Areas.*

In Summerville

🦐 🍴 ♿ 🐾 **James H. Floyd State Park** (lodging reservations: 1-800-864-7275). The park offers four fully equipped cottages. One is dog friendly ($40 per dog; maximum two). In addition, the park offers 25 tent, trailer, and RV sites. Guests can use all the park's facilities (see *Green Space—Nature Preserves and Parks*). Campsites $25–28, cottages $135–145.

THE MOUNTAINS

In Adairsville

♂ & ❀ **Barnsley Gardens Resort** (770-773-7480 or 1-877-773-2447; www.barnsley resort.com), 597 Barnsley Gardens Road. Barnsley Gardens is the premier resort in north Georgia and one of the most outstanding in the entire state—or the Southeast, for that matter. Thirty-three exceptional cottages containing 70 suites feature English-cottage architecture. The cottages sport 12-foot ceilings, heart-pine floors, private porches, and period-inspired private baths with ball-and-claw iron soaking tubs and a separate shower. Each suite is appointed with antiques and fine period reproductions, a king-size bed, a wood-burning fireplace, and the latest electronics. Many also offer a sofa bed to accommodate additional guests. Other cottages are available with multiple bedrooms from two to seven, making them ideal for families or friends traveling together or for groups. In addition to superior lodging, fine and casual dining, and a spa, the resort features a golf course, hunting and sporting clays, horseback riding, fly-fishing, Frisbee golf, paintball, bicycle and boat rentals, two clay tennis courts, and a swimming pool open seasonally, as well as several dining options (see separate entries throughout chapter). World-class dining options abound at the **Rice House Restaurant** and the **Woodlands Grill** (see *Where to Eat—Dining Out*). Barnsley Gardens doesn't merely have a concierge, but has a Fairy Godmother who can arrange to make almost any dream come true. Pets are welcome and are pampered with beds, bowls, bottled water, and treats for an additional $75 fee for cleaning. No smoking. Four cottages wheelchair accessible. $259–2,303; many packages and specials available.

✳ Where to Eat
DINING OUT

In Adairsville
& **Rice House, Barnsley Gardens Resort** (770-877-9497; see *Lodging—Resorts*). Open 5:30–10 PM Wednesday–

Saturday; closed January–March. The Rice House, Barnsley's formal dining restaurant, serves classic Southern cuisine. Located in an 1854 farmhouse that was the home of Fleming Rice, the house's exterior is still marred by bullet holes from a Civil War battle. Dining options include the formal dining room, with its original stone fireplace, or the glass-enclosed dining porch overlooking the gardens and ruins. The elegant meals feature beef, wild game, and seafood. Reservations strongly recommended. $24–36.

♂ & **Woodlands Grill, Barnsley Gardens Resort** (770-877-9497; see *Lodging—Resorts*). Open 7 AM–10 PM daily. The Woodlands Grill, a steakhouse that serves prime meats and fish, is a little more casual than the Rice House and has both indoor and outdoor seating from which guests enjoy a panoramic view of the golf course. The restaurant also has Dugan's Tavern, an English pub with a fireplace and billiards table. No smoking. Breakfast $3–12, lunch $3–20, dinner $10–30.

In Cave Spring
Tumlin House Bed and Breakfast (see *Lodging—Bed & Breakfasts*). Open Saturday 7 PM. Reservations required at least 24 hours in advance. A six-course gourmet dinner is served at a single seating. Guests may bring their own wine. No smoking. Not wheelchair accessible. $40.

In Rome
& **LaScala Italian Restaurant** (706-238-9000), 413 Broad Street. Open 5:30–10 Monday–Saturday. This upscale restaurant offers Italian cuisine, traditional dishes, and candlelight dining, as well as a cozy lounge. Menu choices include seafood, pastas, gourmet salads, and desserts, and the restaurant also has a fully stocked bar and an extensive wine list. No smoking. $16–30.

EATING OUT

In Adairsville
🍺 ♂ & **The Beer Garden at Barnsley Gardens Resort** (see *Lodging—Resorts*). Open seasonally, 4–9 Friday, noon–9 Saturday, noon–6 Sunday; may be closed in

inclement weather. The authentic Bavarian-style outdoor Beer Garden serves imported German beers, including the house specialty, Munich's Spaten, as well as cuisine that ranges from sausages and pretzels to ribs and panini. An open-fire pit warms diners at night and provides a place to roast marshmallows. Smoking allowed since this is outdoors. $6–12.50.

🍴 🍷 ♿ **Maggie Mae's Tea Room at the 1902 Stock Exchange** (770-773-1902), 124 Public Square. Open 10:30–3 Tuesday–Saturday. Tearoom fare includes imported teas and coffees, chicken salad, three kinds of quiches, a daily hot special, and a choice of scrumptious desserts, such as hummingbird cake, turtle cheesecake, or pie. When the weather is pleasant, eat in the charming brick courtyard. No smoking. $4.95–6.95.

In Rome

🍴 🍷 ♿ **Harvest Moon Café** (706-292-0099; www.harvestmooncafe.com), 234 Broad Street. Open 11–3:30 Monday, 11–9 Tuesday–Thursday, 11–10 Friday and Saturday, 11–2:30 Sunday. "Food that makes your tongue smile"—that's the slogan of this popular café known for specialty sandwiches on home-baked breads, homemade soups, burgers, salads, and delicious desserts at lunchtime. The dinner menu features an extensive array of appetizers, rib-eye steaks, shrimp, pork chops, pastas, and veggie platters. Music, fun, and games are on tap on the Moon Roof from 2:30 to late night Tuesday–Saturday. A gargantuan brunch buffet is served on Sunday. There is also an on-site wine market. The café's Wicked Pimina Cheese (aka Pimp Cheese) and Wicked Bacon Gorgonzola Dip are now sold in supermarkets in northwest Georgia. No smoking. Lunch $5–11, dinner $9–22, brunch $11.

🍴 🍷 ♿ **Jefferson's** (706-378-0222), 340 Broad Street. Open 11–10 Monday–Wednesday, 11–11 Thursday–Saturday, 11:30–10 Sunday. This casual eatery and sports bar serves up hot dogs, nachos, and platters and baskets of oysters and seafood, and it's known for its wings—which come in mild, medium hot, or turbo varieties. Beer

is the most popular beverage, and there are many choices, bottled or on tap. No smoking. $6–9.

✴ Entertainment

Harris Arts Center (706-629-2599; www.harrisartscenter.com), 212 South Wall Street, Calhoun. Open 10–9 Monday, 10–4 Tuesday–Thursday, 10–2 Friday and Saturday. The center, which occupies the restored 1930-era Rooker Hotel, contains an art gallery, the **Roland Hayes Museum** (see *To See—Museums*), and the Milton Ratner Performing Arts Theater, where the Calhoun Little Theater produces plays and where the Calhoun Community Adult Chorus performs. The Music Guild brings in performers from all over the country. The art gallery hosts a fine arts show and numerous exhibitions throughout the year. Free to tour building, museum, and art gallery; event prices vary.

MUSIC Cedartown Performing Arts Center (770-748-4168 or 1-877-263-9372; www.cedartownshows.com), 205 East Avenue, Cedartown. Performances of all kinds—bluegrass, Broadway, classical, and other genres—are held throughout the year here. Check the website or call for a schedule of performances and ticket prices.

Rome Symphony Orchestra (706-291-7967; www.romesymphony.org), office mailing address: P.O. Box 533, Rome 30162. One of the oldest orchestras in the South, the symphony was created in 1921. The orchestra presents a series of four classics concerts and another of three pops concerts at the Rome City Auditorium in addition to outdoor performances during Pops in the Park and the First Friday series. Check the website or call for a schedule of performances. In advance: adults $15, seniors $10, students $3; at the door: $20, $15, and $6.

PROFESSIONAL SPORTS
🍴 🍷 ♿ **Rome Braves** (tickets: 706-378-5144; 1-800-326-4000; www.romebraves .com), office: 755 Braves Boulevard, Rome. Call or visit the website for a schedule of games. Between April and September, the

2003 South Atlantic League baseball champions play 70 home games at State Mutual Stadium. The Three Rivers Club, for club level ticket holders only, at the stadium is open 11–2 weekdays for lunch. Wheelchair-accessible seating. No smoking. Tickets $4–10, parking $4.

🐾 🐕 ♿ **Rome Gladiators** (706-512-5656 or 1-800-868-6980; www.wbagladiators.com), Rome. Call or visit the website for a schedule of events. Between March and June, the World Basketball Association team plays home games in the Berry College Ford Gym. $8.

THEATER Public Square Opera House at the 1902 Stock Exchange (770-773-1902), 124 Public Square, Adairsville. The facility offers dinner-theater productions highlighting historical themes, such as *A Circuit Rider's Wife* by local author Corra Harris, which inspired the film *I'd Climb the Highest Mountain;* Mark Twain's *The Diaries of Adam and Eve;* and Louisa May Alcott's *Little Women.* Special performances are often geared to holidays such as Valentine's Day, Mother's Day, and Christmas. Call for a schedule of productions and prices. The 1902 Stock Exchange also houses **Maggie Mae's Tea Room** (see *Where to Eat—Eating Out*), as well as numerous shops purveying antiques and collectibles (see *Selective Shopping*).

Rome Little Theatre (706-295-7171; www.romelittletheatre.com), 530 Broad Street, Rome. Check the website or call for a schedule of performances. The organization offers quality entertainment for the whole family at the historic 1929 DeSoto Theater in downtown Rome. Named for explorer Hernando de Soto, who passed through the area, and beautifully restored, the theater was originally built for "talkies," but it closed as a movie theater in 1982. Visitors admire the art deco marquee, the French mirrored entrance hall, and the Georgian interior as much as they enjoy the live performances and the Rome International Film Festival. Each season usually includes a children's show, Christmas show, comedy, drama, and musical. Generally adults $12–14, students and seniors $10–12.

✳ Selective Shopping

ANTIQUES 1902 Stock Exchange (770-773-1902), 124 Public Square, Adairsville. Open 10–5 Tuesday–Saturday, 1–5 Sunday. Individual gallery shops sell Victorian and Civil War collectibles, fine linens and lace, baby gifts, china, crystal, silver, antique wedding dresses, military weapons, antique furniture, Coke collectibles, Christmas decorations, antique toys, paintings, and prints. The **Corra Harris Bookstore,** named for the novelist from nearby Pine Log and author of *A Circuit Rider's Wife,* carries out-of-print-books and works by Georgia authors. The complex also houses **Maggie Mae's Tea Room** (see *Where to Eat—Eating Out*) and the **Public Square Opera House** (see *Entertainment—Theater*).

OUTLET STORES Calhoun Premium Outlets (706-602-1305 or 1-877-GO-OUT-LETS; www.premiumoutlets.com), 455 Belwood Road, Calhoun. Open 10–9 Monday–Saturday, 11–7 Sunday. More than 50 designers, manufacturers, and other retailers, including Ann Taylor, Tommy Hilfiger, Jones New York, Coach, Polo Ralph Lauren, and Nike, offer discount prices.

✳ Special Events

April: **Atlanta Steeplechase** (404-237-7436; www.atlantasteeplechase.org). Known as the "best lawn party in the state" as well as Georgia's biggest single horse-racing event, the steeplechase is part of the Triple Crown Circuit and is the region's premier spring social event. The series of races is held at 435-acre Kingston Downs along the Etowah River. Other activities include the Disc Dog Southern Nationals, terrier races; pony rides; hayrides; hat, tailgating, and tent-party-decor contests; and a parade of hounds. $30 per person, plus $20 vehicle pass. Packages available for $250–2,500, which include a varying number of tickets, parking pass, and pre- and/or post-race cocktail party. Call Ticketmaster.

May: **Battle of Resaca Reenactment** (Gordon Chamber of Commerce: 706-625-3200; 1-800-887-3811; www.georgiadivision

.org/bor_reenactment.html). The reenactment, held the third weekend in May each year, occurs on 650 acres of Chitwood Farm, the 1864 battle's original site. In addition to battles at 2 PM both days, spectators see reconstructed breastworks and a redoubt, demonstrations of spinning and other skills, a re-created field hospital, civilian and refugee camps, entertainment from a regimental band, and sutlers' and vendors' wares. There is a memorial service at the Resaca Cemetery on Saturday and a church service on Sunday. Except for handicap parking, other parking is at a distance, and shuttle buses bring spectators to the site. It is recommended to bring lawn chairs. Adults $5, children $2; portion of proceeds goes to battlefield preservation.

Georgia String Band Festival (706-629-2599; www.harrisartscenter.com), held at the Northwest Georgia Fairgrounds, Calhoun. Sponsored by the Harris Arts Center, the festival features competitions for cash prizes in string band, fiddle, banjo, buck dancing, and junior players. Impromptu jam sessions throughout. $10.

June: **Cave Spring Fine Arts and Crafts Festival** (city hall: 706-777-3382). Held the second weekend in June at **Rolater Park** (see *Green Space—Nature Preserves and Parks*), the homespun fair features juried artists and an antique car show. $5.

October: **Chiaha Harvest Fair** (706-235-4542; www.chiaha.org). Call for dates. Held Saturday and Sunday on the banks of the Oostanaula River in Rome's Ridge Ferry Park, the festival, sponsored by the Chiaha Guild of Arts and Crafts, includes 120 artists, demonstrating craftspeople, continuous live entertainment, Southern cooking, and children's art activities. Adults $5, students and seniors $4, children younger than 12 $1, free parking; fees for some activities.

Great Locomotive Chase Festival (770-773-3451, ext. 26). Held the first weekend (Friday–Sunday) in the Public Square in Adairsville, the festival features arts and crafts, parades, pageants, fireworks, and street dancing, as well as demonstrations of old-time skills such as chair caning, basket weaving, quilting, beadwork, quilting, and making corn husk dolls, nut dolls, and chenille. $3.

Southern Rivers 5

INTRODUCTION

PEACHES, PECANS, PEANUTS, PLANTATIONS, AND PRESIDENTS

Located in the southwestern corner of the state, the Southern Rivers region, which is further subdivided into the Plantation Trace and Presidential Pathways, is one of the most tranquil areas of Georgia and the least touristy. The absence of large cities also blessedly means the absence of heavy traffic, so travelers can cruise down miles and miles of almost deserted country roads at their own pace. Just remember to watch for the occasional slow-moving tractor or cotton-picking machinery. This is truly an area where you can get off the beaten track to find one-of-a-kind attractions.

People stereotypically believe that plantations were literally gone with the wind after the Civil War, and so they are quite amazed to learn that not only do vast plantations still exist, but that the region between Thomasville and Tallahassee, Florida, has the largest concentration of working plantations in the country—thus the area being designated as the Plantation Trace.

Two presidents called southwestern Georgia home. Franklin D. Roosevelt came to Warm Springs for polio treatment and ended up building a small house nearby, which came to be known as the Little White House. He died there in 1945, and the house is now a state historic site. Jimmy Carter grew up in Plains and returned there after his presidency, and several sites in and around town are designated as National Historic Sites. The presidential connection resulted in part of the region being dubbed Presidential Pathways.

Seemingly endless rural areas are filled with farms and orchards that produce peaches, pecans, and peanuts. Purchase the region's bounty in season and take home numerous products made from them. Visitors also can learn about the importance of agriculture to the area at such sites as the Georgia Museum of Agriculture in Tifton, the Old South Farm Museum in Woodland, and Westville in Lumpkin.

One of the most important gardens in the Southeast, Callaway Gardens, is located in this region. Callaway Gardens is also a resort with a variety of lodging options, restaurants, and recreational activities. Flowers are also the main attraction at Ferrell Gardens in LaGrange and in Thomasville, which is known as the Rose City.

Abundant rivers such as the Chattahoochee, Flint, and Ochlocknee; lakes such as Blackshear, George T. Bagby, Seminole, Walter F. George, and West Point; several state parks; and thousands of acres of undeveloped and protected forestlands and preserves provide innumerable opportunities for outdoor recreation.

Only a few small cities dot this area: Albany, Americus, Bainbridge, Columbus, LaGrange, Pine Mountain, Thomasville, Tifton, and Valdosta. Each offers numerous histori-

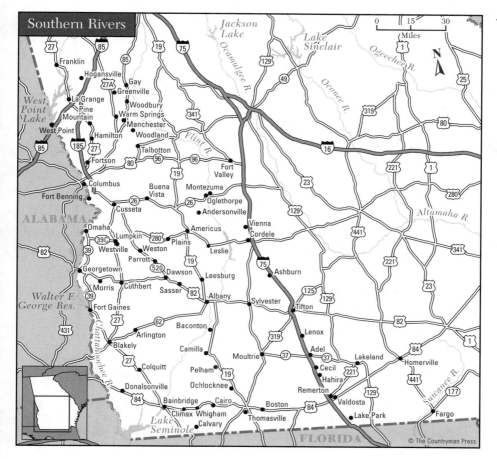

cal attractions and museums, as well as a wide range of cultural activities and distinctive accommodations, restaurants, and shopping.

The remainder of the region is made up of dozens of distinctive small towns, each with a special attraction, such as the Kolomoki Mounds Historic Park in Blakely or the Georgia Rural Telephone Museum in Leslie. Eleven state parks and historic sites can be found in this region.

History is always on display in this area. Various aspects of the Civil War can be examined at the Andersonville National Historic Site and National Prisoner of War Museum near Andersonville and the Port Columbus National Civil War Naval Museum in Columbus.

ALBANY

The first residents of what became the Albany area were the Creek Indians, who called it Thronateeska, which meant "the place where flint is picked up." It's no surprise, then, that the Flint River flows through Albany.

The town was founded in 1836 and grew to incorporate several prosperous plantations. There were no battles fought in the area during the Civil War to interrupt production at these plantations, so they were able to supply critical food and cotton for the Confederacy. Albany became a rail center at the turn of the 20th century. Union Station, the convergence point for seven railroads, saw as many as 55 trains a day.

Like most Southern cities, Albany experienced upheaval during the civil rights movement of the 1960s and was the site of marches and protests. But the success of black voter registration led to a runoff election for a city commission seat in 1962. The following spring, all segregation statutes were removed from the books.

Albany, the eighth-biggest city in the state, with a population of 76,000, is currently experiencing an exciting renaissance with significant downtown renewal. The city suffered two devastating floods in the 1990s. In July 1994, Hurricane Hugo dumped 17 inches of rain on the area in a short time, and the water rose as much as 8 feet, exceeding the levels of a 500-year flood. A flood of the proportions of a 100-year flood occurred in 1998. Reconstruction from both disasters has given Albany a new lease on life and provided a vibrant backdrop for the city's symphony orchestra, theater, a ballet company, and an excellent art museum.

One of the Seven Wonders of Georgia is found just outside Albany. Radium Springs, the largest natural spring in Georgia, produces 70,000 gallons per minute. The water, which eventually flows into the Flint River, maintains a temperature of 68 degrees year-round.

The plantations of yesteryear are now hunting preserves, and Albany, which is known as the Quail Hunting Capital of the World, annually hosts the Quail Unlimited Celebrity Hunt and the United Kennel Club Coon Dog Hunt. The Flint River and Lake Chehaw provide innumerable opportunities for water sports.

The surrounding small towns and countryside are noted for peanut production, hunting, tennis, and antiques shopping.

GUIDANCE When planning a trip to the Albany area, contact the **Albany Convention and Visitors Bureau and Welcome Center** (229-317-3760 or 1-866-750-0840; www .visitalbanyga.com), 112 North Front Street, Albany 31701. Open 9–5 weekdays, 10–4 Saturday, and noon–4 Sunday.

GETTING THERE *By air:* Visitors to Albany can fly into **Southeast Georgia Regional Airport.** (For airport, airline, and car rental information, see "What's Where in Georgia.")

By bus: **Greyhound Lines** (1-800-231-2222; www.greyhound.com), 300 West Oglethorpe Boulevard, Albany, offers bus service.

By car: US 19 and US 82 intersect in Albany. The easiest route to take there is US 82 west from I-75. The smaller towns described here are located along east–west US 82 or north–south US 19.

By train: Rail travel to the Albany area is not convenient. The closest **AMTRAK** station (1-800-USA-RAIL; www.amtrak.com) is in Atlanta (see "What's Where in Georgia").

GETTING AROUND In Albany, in addition to car rentals at the airport, rental cars are available from **Economy Rent-A-Car** (229-883-7141), 524 West Oglethorpe; **Enterprise Rent-A-Car** (229-889-8020), 407 Sands Drive; and **Thrifty Car Rental** (229-434-7368), 712 West Oglethorpe.

MEDICAL EMERGENCY For life-threatening emergency, call 911.

✳ To See

FOR FAMILIES 🐾 ✿ ♿ **Flint RiverQuarium** (229-639-2650 or 1-877-GOFLINT; www.flintriverquarium.com), 117 Pine Avenue, Albany. Open 10–5 Monday–Saturday, 1–5 Sunday. Descend to the depths of an underwater spring without even getting wet at this aquarium. The facility tells the story of the Apalachicola, Chattahoochee, and Flint river basins and the mysterious blue-hole springs that help create the Flint River, which begins as a tiny trickle south of Atlanta and flows 350 miles to the Gulf of Mexico. The facility also showcases southwest Georgia's unique underwater inhabitants. An open-air, 175,000-gallon freshwater tank is filled with scores of fish, turtles, and alligators native to the area. Also displayed are reptiles, amphibians, and regional plants. The World of Water gives visitors an insider's view of rivers around the world. Adults $9, seniors $8, children 4–12 $6.50.

🐾 ✿ ♿ **Parks at Chehaw** (229-430-5275; www.chehaw.org), 105 Chehaw Road, Albany. Open 9–5 daily. This 800-acre park has a little something for everyone—the Wiregrass Express miniature train ride; water sports at **Lake Chehaw** (see *Green Space—Lakes*); a **BMX Bike Park** (229-894-5822); a Play Park, one of the state's largest play parks for children; a Wild Animal Park; nature trails along Muckalee Creek; picnicking; and camping. An exciting annual event is the **Chehaw Native American Cultural Festival** (see *Special Events*). The centerpiece of the complex is the **Chehaw Wild Animal Park,** open 9:30–5 daily, a 100-acre park-within-a-park that is southwest Georgia's only American Zoo Association–accredited wild animal park. Its trails and elevated walkways allow visitors to see 212 specimens representing 55 species, including native Georgia wildlife as well as more exotic fauna such as buffalo, rhinos, elks, llamas, ostriches, lemurs, and zebras roaming in natural habitats. The new Land Down Under habitat showcases emus and red kangaroos. The alligator feeding at the Muckalee Swampland Station is a big hit. The park was originally designed by Albany native Jim Fowler of *Wild Kingdom.* Admission to park only: adults $2; seniors, military, and children 4–12 $1. Admission to both park and zoo: adults $8.75, seniors $7.75, military and children

BALD EAGLES AT THE PARKS AT CHEHAW'S WILD ANIMAL PARK

4–12 $5.75. A 20-minute train ride on the Wiregrass Express: $3 per person, children under two ride free. Special events may require additional charge.

HISTORIC HOMES AND SITES 🌸 ⑤ **The Albany Civil Rights Movement Museum at Old Mount Zion Church** (229-432-1698; www.albanycivilrightsinstitute.org), 326 Whitney Avenue, Albany. Open 10–4 Tuesday–Saturday. Located in the historic Freedom District, the Mount Zion Missionary Baptist Church was the site of many mass meetings during the Albany Movement in the early 1960s. Dr. Martin Luther King Jr. and many other civil rights leaders spoke there. Now a museum, the old church, which is set up to reflect its appearance during that period, celebrates the courage of ordinary people who struggled for equality during extraordinary times. The Freedom Singers, a group organized during the civil rights movement, perform at 1 PM on the second Saturday of each month. Adults $6; seniors, military, and students $5; 1st–4th grade $3; preschool children $2; children under four accompanied by an adult free.

MUSEUMS 🌸 🌿 ⑤ **Albany Museum of Art** (229-439-8400; www.albanymuseum.com), 311 Meadowlark Drive, Albany. Open 10–5 Tuesday–Saturday. Southwest Georgia's only nationally accredited art museum, the Albany Museum of Art offers six galleries. The museum's permanent collection features 19th- and 20th-century American and European art, but it is its sub-Saharan African art that shines. The stunning collection, the largest in the Southeast, features masks, musical instruments, religious and ceremonial devices, sculpture, pottery, baskets, jewelry, gold weights, and textiles. The interactive children's wing is called AMAzing Space. (*Note:* The museum is planning to move to a bigger and better space, so check the website or call ahead to make sure of the current address.) Free.

THE ALBANY CIVIL RIGHTS MOVEMENT MUSEUM AT OLD MOUNT ZION CHURCH

🌸 🌿 ⑤ **Thronateeska Heritage Center** (229-432-6955; www.heritagecenter.org), Heritage Plaza, 100 West Roosevelt Avenue, Albany. Open 10–4 Thursday–Saturday. Planetarium shows are regularly scheduled for 10:30, 11:30, 1, 2, and 3 Thursday–Saturday (shows are rotated, so it is recommended that visitors call ahead to see which shows will be shown when). Model railroad exhibit open noon–4 Saturday. Actually a complex of historic buildings and three attractions in one, the center consists of the old railroad depot and an adjacent railway express office, as well as some restored vintage railcars. The History Museum, which occupies the historic 1912 Union Depot, uses changing exhibits of artifacts to trace the history of Albany and southwest Georgia, including the riverboat days and the great floods of 1925 and 1994. In the adjacent Railway Express building, it's always a starry night as the Wetherbee Planetarium presents information about the solar system, stars, and galaxies. Programs change monthly. Also housed in that building is the Science Discovery Center, where visitors can participate in hands-on activities relating to light, electricity, magnetism, sound, weather, and other scientific topics. A model train exhibit, operated by the Flint River Model Railroad Club, occupies an old baggage and mail car. Museum and model railroad exhibit free. Planetarium shows: age three and up $3.50 plus tax.

THE THRONATEESKA HERITAGE CENTER CONSISTS OF AN OLD RAILROAD DEPOT, RAILWAY EXPRESS OFFICE, AND RAILCARS.

✳ To Do

CANOEING AND KAYAKING
𝒮 Flint River Outpost (229-787-3004; www.flintriveroutpost.com), 11151 Old GA 3, Baconton. Open 8–5:30 Tuesday–Sunday. The outfitter provides canoe and kayak rentals, return shuttle service for Flint River trips, and primitive campsites. Prices vary by activity.

FARM TOURS **The Farmyard** (229-883-3308), 3810 Gillionville Road, Albany. Open 9–6 Monday–Saturday. In addition to pumpkin and gourd painting, visitors can pick their own sunflowers or go fishing. Free admission; products for sale.

Mark's Melon Patch (229-698-4750; www.marksmelonpatch.com), 8580 Albany Highway, Sasser. Shop open year-round: 8–7 daily, spring–fall; 9–6 daily in winter. The big attraction is fall and Halloween. Be sure to bring a flashlight to experience the haunted maze. The effect of the maze and the jack-o'-lanterns is most dramatic at night, and it's less crowded then, too. Many school groups visit during the day. Other attractions include carved pumpkins, hayrides, and a bouncy house. Choose your own pumpkin or pick sunflowers. Free admission; products for sale.

FOR FAMILIES **𝒮 All-American Fun Park** (229-436-8362; www.allamericanfunpark .com), 2608 North Slappey Boulevard, Albany. Open 10–10 Monday–Thursday, 10–midnight Friday and Saturday, 1–10 Sunday, 363 days per year (closed Christmas and Easter). The family-oriented fun center features 36 holes of miniature golf, the largest game room in the Southeast, bumper boats, go-carts, batting cages, laser tag, and a rock-climbing wall. $6 for 1 activity, $20 for 4, $40 for 10. Several specials are offered during the season; check the website or call for details.

🐾 𝒮 ♿ **Turtle Grove Play Park** (contact Albany Tomorrow: 229-430-3910), along Front Street, Albany. A magnet for youngsters, the fun park is filled with giant representations of turtles painted with various scenes, as well as six interest areas: a Dino Dig, Tot Lot, Critters Area, Big-Kids Area, a mosaic tile area, and a music area. The park is located next to the Flint RiverQuarium and is also a popular spot from which to watch the Fourth of July fireworks. Free.

✳ Green Space

LAKES 🐾 𝒮 **Lake Chehaw.** On the 1,400-acre lake in Albany, opportunities abound for canoeing, boating, fishing, waterskiing, and picnicking. A canoe trail winds through the lake. A large portion of the lake is within the city limits of Albany. See also **Parks at Chehaw** under *To See—For Families.*

NATURE PRESERVES AND PARKS 🐾 🛶 ♿ **Veterans Riverfront Park** (229-434-8799 or 1-800-475-8700; www.albanyga.com or www.albanytomorrow.com), Oglethorpe Boulevard, Albany. Open dawn–dusk daily. This pleasant park is an appealing place to walk, jog, cycle, or relax with a book. An amphitheater and various monuments honor veterans and victims of several wars. The **Flood of 1994 Memorial** honors those who died and the many volunteers who contributed time and labor to rebuild the city after the catastrophic inundation. The downtown park also features gardens, a fountain that's animated with music and lights, the **Turtle Grove Play Park** (see *To Do—For Families*), the trailhead to **Flint River Greenways Trail System,** and the **Riverwalk.** The park features an interactive water fountain, which is particularly popular on hot summer days, so wear your bathing suit. Connected to the park is **Ray Charles Plaza,** dedicated to the Albany native. It is a life-size representation of the legendary musician seated at a baby grand piano. Water flows down the pedestal, and Charles's music emanates from loudspeakers. The surrounding walkways resemble piano keyboards. Free.

RIVERS 🐾 🛶 The **Flint River** is central to much of the area's outdoor activities, including boating, fishing, tubing, and other water sports. (See **Flint River Outpost** under *To Do—Canoeing and Kayaking.*) The river flows from Atlanta 212 miles south to Lake Blackshear, but because of its meandering nature it actually covers 350 miles. The Flint is one of only 40 rivers in the country that flows more than 200 miles unimpeded by a dam. It also offers the only class II to class IV rapids in south Georgia. Access free; fees for some activities.

✳ Lodging

CAMPGROUNDS

In Albany

🐾 🛶 **Parks at Chehaw** (229-430-5295; www.parksatchehaw.org), 105 Chehaw Park Road. RV sites offer full hookups; tent sites have water hookups. The campground also features a bathhouse, laundry facilities, vending machines, and a dump station. Tent sites $15; RV sites $28 for full hookup, $20 for just power and water.

INNS AND HOTELS

In Albany

🐾 🛶 ♿ **Merry Acres of Albany, Georgia** (229-435-7721; www.merryacres.com), 1500 Dawson Road. Merry Acres is an institution in Albany. The gracious manor house, which serves as the registration and office center, was built in 1934 as a country home, and Albany has since grown up around it. The company retained 10 acres around the house and has built a lodging, dining, shopping, and conference complex connected by gardens and pathways. Merry Acres is the only all-suite boutique hotel in Albany. Recreational amenities include a secluded swimming pool, shuttle service to the airport and some of the local restaurants, and a state-of-the-art fitness center. There's also the **Merry Acres Restaurant** (see *Where to Eat—Eating Out*) and **Merry Acres Galleria,** a collection of specialty shops. No smoking. Wheelchair accessible, including some fully adapted bathrooms. The entire property was refurbished in 2011–2012. $77–222.

✳ Where to Eat

DINING OUT

In Albany

♿ **Henry Campbell's Steak House** (229-594-9288; www.stewbos.com), 629 North Westover Boulevard. Open 4–10 Monday–Saturday. Fine dining occurs in this meat lovers' paradise with prime cuts of steak, quality fresh seafood from their sister property (the Catch), and an extensive wine list. No smoking. Wheelchair accessible, including handicapped bathrooms. $22–50.

♿ **The Sunset Grill** (229-878-6738), 2601 Dawson Road. Open 11–9 weekdays, 11–10 Saturday, 11–8 Sunday. The menu includes American and Caribbean dishes, chops, steaks, and pastas. Smoking in bar only. Lunch $4–8, dinner $12–24.

In Albany

🦐 🍷 ♿ **Harvest Moon Pizza** (229-439-7077; www.stewbos.com), 2347 Dawson Road. Open 11 AM–3 AM Monday–Saturday. Pizza, calzones, and wraps; an ever-changing variety of more than 50 craft and imported beers; and live music keep "the Moon" a place to meet, eat, and drink. No smoking. $4.50–20.

🦐 🍷 ♿ **Merry Acres Restaurant** (229-439-2261; www.merryacres.com), 1504 Dawson Road. Open 11–3 daily. The restaurant serves soups and sandwiches, as well as a buffet with two to three meats and a choice of vegetables. No smoking. $5–7.

✴ Entertainment

ARTS Albany Area Arts Council (229-439-ARTS; www.albanyartscouncil.org), 215 North Jackson Street, Albany. Open 10–4 weekdays. Housed in a beautiful historic 1906 Carnegie library, the council presents exhibits showcasing regional artwork, as well as seminars, workshops, festivals, tours, and children's programs. Free.

Albany Darton College (229-317-6554 or 229-317-6875), 2400 Gillianville Road, Albany. The college's theater program presents three major productions a year. Various music ensembles also perform throughout the year, and there are numerous art exhibits. Call for a schedule of events and ticket prices.

Albany Municipal Auditorium (229-430-3990), 200 Pine Avenue, Albany. The historic auditorium hosts many of Albany's performing arts companies. Call for a schedule of performances and ticket prices.

Albany State University Department of Fine Arts (229-430-4849), 504 College Drive, Albany. The university offers numerous performances and exhibitions of student and faculty work. Under the umbrella of the Department of Fine Arts are the ASU Theater Ensemble, the popular Marching Rams Show Band, the Jazz Band, the Concert Band, and the ASU Concert Chorale. Call for a schedule of events and ticket prices.

DANCE Albany Ballet Theater (229-439-7141), 200 Pine Avenue, Albany. Annual performances held in the **Albany Municipal Auditorium** (see *Arts*) include classical and modern ballets as well as jazz. Call for a schedule of performances and ticket prices.

MUSIC Albany Chorale (229-439-2787), mailing address: P.O. Box 70942, Albany 30708. Performing for more than 75 years, the chorale presents everything from Bach to rock, including classical, jazz, madrigal, and American folk music. The chorale also has a Chamber Ensemble that performs with the Albany Symphony Orchestra at Christmas and other times. The season, which runs from late August to June, features three major concerts, a dinner show, and outreach programs. Call for a schedule of performances and ticket prices.

Albany Concert Association (229-439-2787), mailing address: P.O. Box 1607, Albany 31702. Founded in 1935, the organization sponsors quality entertainment by professional artists. The four- or five-concert series features dance; musical theater; solo instrumentalists; vocal, string, or bass ensembles; and other genres. Concerts are held at the **Albany Municipal Auditorium.** Call for a schedule of performances and ticket prices. Admission is by membership or single ticket.

Albany Symphony Orchestra (229-430-8933; www.albanysymphony.org), mailing address: P.O. Box 70065, Albany 30707. One of southwest Georgia's professional orchestras, the Albany Symphony is under the direction of a full-time resident conductor and performs at **Albany Darton College** and the **Albany Municipal Auditorium.** The orchestra, which is often heard on Peach State Public Radio, performs American music, orchestral repertory, new music, and lesser-known classics. Regional soloists and national and international artists perform with the orchestra. The season includes five subscription concerts, children's concerts, a holiday pops program, and "Pops in the Park at Chehaw." Check the website or call for a schedule of performances and ticket prices.

THEATER **Theatre Albany** (box office: 229-439-7141; www.theatrealbany.com), 514 Pine Avenue, Albany. Box office open noon–4 Tuesday–Friday. Formed in 1932, Theatre Albany is the oldest cultural organization in Albany as well as one of its most respected. Productions take place in the John A. Davis House, one of Albany's elegant restored antebellum landmarks. The five-production main-stage season features an eclectic mix of drama, comedy, and musicals. In addition, the theatrical organization offers productions in its intimate Studio Theater, as well as children's theater, reader's theater, and workshops. Check the website or call for a schedule of performances. Adults $40, seniors $15, children and active military $10.

✳ Selective Shopping

ANTIQUES **Maridean's Marketplace** (229-623-4123; www.parrottga.com /Marideans-antiques.html), 110 East Main Street, Parrott. Open 10–5 Tuesday–Saturday. The emporium sells European and American antiques, porcelains, and other merchandise.

FOOD **Mark's Melon Patch** (229-698-4750; www.marksmelonpatch.com), 8580 Albany Highway/US 82, Sasser. Open 8–7 daily, 9–6 in winter. Shop here for cantaloupes and watermelons, but also for gourds, Vidalia onions, butter beans, and other fresh produce. Hayrides and a maze are offered at Halloween (see *To Do— Farm Tours*).

SPECIAL STORES **Sound Play** (229-623-5545; www.soundplay.com), 108 Railroad Street, Parrott. Open 10–6 daily. Guided tours are available. Unusual outdoor musical instruments made from recycled materials are fashioned into fanciful shapes.

✳ Special Events

April: **Chehaw Native American Cultural Festival** (229-430-5275; www.chehaw .org). A major cultural event in the entire Southeast, the three-day festival in Albany features traditional Native American crafts, dances, skills demonstrations, and storytelling. Included with admission to the Parks at Chehaw: adults $8.75, children younger than 13 $5.75.

July: **Local Palooza at the Parks at Chehaw** (229-430-5275; www.parksat chehaw.org). The popular Albany event features 12 bands. Adults $8.75, children younger than 13 $5.75.

October: **Boo at the Zoo at the Parks at Chehaw** (229-430-5275; www.parksat chehaw.org). Have a hauntingly ghoulish time with games, prizes, food, and costume contests at this Halloween event in Albany. Adults $8.75, children younger than 13 $5.75.

Georgia Peanut Festival (229-776-6657; www.gapeanutfestival.org). Held in Sylvester on the fourth Saturday in October. This annual event, which has been celebrated since 1963, features arts and crafts, the Peter Pan Peanut Parade, a barbecue, cuisine utilizing peanuts, a 5K run, bike tour, pageants for several age groups, and other activities. The Peanut Festival holds the world's record for the largest peanut butter sandwich at 12 feet by 12 feet. Free; some activities have a fee.

December: **Festival of Lights at Parks at Chehaw** (229-430-5275; www.chehaw.org). During December the park in Albany is festooned with thousands of lights. Visitors can tour in their own vehicle or aboard the Wiregrass Express train. $12 per vehicle.

AMERICUS

T his area of southwest Georgia, while still relatively undiscovered by most travelers, is rich in history, culture, scenic beauty, state parks, and outdoor recreational activities.

The area in and around the sleepy town of Plains is designated as the Jimmy Carter National Historic Site (see *To See—Historic Homes and Sites*). The former president and Nobel Prize winner grew up here and still makes Plains his home, and you may even see him when you're in town. You also can attend Maranantha Baptist Church, where he often teaches Sunday-school classes. President and Mrs. Carter are always on hand for the annual Plains Peanut Festival (see *Special Events*), held each September. The Carters award prizes, watch the parade, and sign their books.

Georgia may be known as the peach state, but peanuts and pecans are major parts of the economy in southwest Georgia. In fact, the area is known as "the Pecan Capital of the World" and is renowned for the nut itself as well as for pies, cakes, cookies, candies, and other treats made from pecans. Watermelon is king in Cordele, known as the "Watermelon Capital of the World." This area is also home of the largest barbecue cook-off in the state (see *Special Events*).

The Civil War intruded here as it did almost everywhere in Georgia, but rather than being the site of many battles, this area was home to the notorious prison camp at Andersonville. The prison camp, national cemetery, and National Prisoner of War Museum attract many visitors every year, as does the small village of Andersonville (see *To See—Historic Homes and Sites*).

Some surprises in this region include an 1850s living-history village at Westville, a deep canyon known as Georgia's Little Grand Canyon, and a telephone museum with an outstanding collection. Numerous festivals celebrate or memorialize the watermelon, dogwood, peanuts, and a flood (see *Special Events*).

GUIDANCE For information about Americus, contact the **Americus Welcome Center** (229-928-6059 or 1-888-278-6837; www.therealgeorgia.com), 123 West Lamar Street, Americus 31709. Open 9–5 weekdays. Pick up an *Americus Driving Tour* brochure here.

CORDELE IS KNOWN AS THE "WATERMELON CAPITAL OF THE WORLD."

To learn more about Andersonville, contact the **Andersonville Welcome Center** (229-924-2558; www.andersonvillega.freeservers.com), 114 Church Street, Andersonville 31711. Open 9–5 daily. Information about the town, the prison, and the cemetery are available here.

For information on Cordele, contact the **Cordele-Crisp Chamber of Commerce** (229-273-1668 or 1-866-426-3566; www.cordele-crisp-chamber.com), 502 South Second Street, Cordele 31015. Open 8:30–5 Monday–Thursday, 8:30–4 Friday.

To learn more about Plains, contact the **Plains Visitor Information Center** (229-824-7477), 1763 US 280 East, Plains 31780. Open 9–5 Tuesday–Saturday, noon–5 Sunday.

For information about Vienna, contact the **Dooly County Chamber of Commerce** (229-268-8275; www.doolychamber.com), 117 East Union Street, Vienna 31092. Open 9–5 weekdays. Also consult the website www.cityofvienna.org.

GETTING THERE *By air:* The two closest airports to Americus and the towns described in this chapter are in Columbus and Macon (see "What's Where in Georgia").

By bus: The closest **Greyhound Lines** stations are also in Columbus and Macon (see those chapters).

By car: The towns and attractions described in this chapter are accessible from I-75 southwest of Atlanta. East–west US 280 and GA 26 connect to I-75 as well as US 19, US 27, and GA 520.

By train: The closest **AMTRAK** (1-800-AMTRAK; www.amtrak.com) station is in Atlanta (see "What's Where in Georgia").

MEDICAL EMERGENCY In life-threatening situations, call 911.

VILLAGES Americus, established in 1832, is the county seat of Sumter County. The name Americus is the masculine version of *America,* which was named for Amerigo Vespucci. Americus is the only city in the nation that uses that name. Some wags claim, however, that the town got its name from "A-Merry-Cuss," a person with a high-spirited zest for life. Four years before his solo flight across the Atlantic in 1927, Charles Lindbergh bought his first plane in Americus. He came to Souther Field, a U.S. Army aviation training camp, to obtain a single-engine World War I–surplus "Jenny." Although he had flown with other barnstormers, when Lindbergh took the plane on a test flight, it was his first solo. The momentous occasion is marked by a plaque at the Americus airport. Famous people from Americus include Dan Reeves, the longtime former head coach of the Atlanta Falcons, and Chan Gailey, the former coach of the Dallas Cowboys. Today Americus is the international headquarters for Habitat for Humanity, the nonprofit organization dedicated to eliminating substandard housing around the world. Habitat is one of the top 10 home builders in the nation.

Andersonville, tiny as it is, became infamous during the Civil War. In 1864, with the war going badly for the Confederacy, it was decided to move Union prisoners of war from near Richmond to an area out of reach of Federal troops. Andersonville was chosen, and Camp Sumter was established as a prison. The unfortunate soldiers are remembered in many ways in a national park, a national cemetery, and several museums.

The area around what is now **Cordele** served as the temporary capital of Georgia during the waning days of the Civil War, when Governor Joseph E. Brown used his rural farmhouse here to escape the Union March to the Sea. Cordele, the county seat, was founded in 1888 at a junction of the Savannah, Americus and Montgomery Railroad. It was named for Cordelia Hawkins, the daughter of the president of the railroad. Today Cordele is so well-known nationwide for its big, luscious watermelons it has earned the title "Watermelon Capital of the World."

Montezuma is in Mennonite farm country, where you can pick your own fruit or buy it fresh, and where folk arts and crafts are readily available. Montezuma, which was named for the Aztec warrior by local soldiers returning from the Mexican War, was a railroad and steamboat town on the Flint River. The bustling economic center had hotels, livery stables, cottonseed processing plants, and agricultural industries. Now it is the home of Southern Frozen Foods for the McKenzie Brand of frozen fruits and vegetables, which are sold all over the country. Today, instead of providing an avenue for steamboat transportation, the Flint River supplies the area with natural resources and recreational opportunities. The river, however, has occasionally caused terrible devastation. Major floods hit the area in 1902, 1929, 1948, and 1994, when 20 inches of rain fell in 24 hours, causing the Flint to crest at 35 feet. Montezuma calls itself "the Town That Refused to Drown" and has restored its historic downtown buildings and created new parks and streetscapes. After a devastating downtown fire, volunteers created Charlie Jackson Park by clearing the debris and replacing it with a stage, arbors, a wall of fame, and a fountain representing a phoenix rising from the ashes.

Plains (population 776 at the 2010 census) revolves around farming, church, and school. The small rural town produced James Earl "Jimmy" Carter, naval officer, peanut farmer, governor of Georgia, president of the United States, and Nobel Peace Prize winner, who still lives there and often can be seen around town.

While in town, visit the **Jimmy Carter National Historic Site** (see *To See—Historic Homes and Sites*).

✳ To See

FOR FAMILIES 🐾 ✐ ♿ **Habitat for Humanity Global Village and Discovery Center and International Headquarters** (229-924-6935 or 1-800-HABITAT; www.habitat .org/gvdc), headquarters at 322 West Lamar Street, Americus; Global Village at 721 West Church Street, Americus. Self guided tours 9–5 Monday–Friday, 10–2 Saturday. Watch an orientation film at headquarters, then drive a couple blocks to tour the Global Village and Discovery Center. This 6-acre attraction features different types of Habitat residences built in 15 countries. Visitors begin in the Living in Poverty Area, where conditions mirror those experienced by millions of people worldwide—in fact, one in five people live in poverty. In the Village Area, the examples of Habitat houses show how simple local materials can be used to provide adequate housing and an increased standard of living. In the Experience Area, you can actually make bricks. The Marketplace contains a photo gallery, exhibits, a theater with short films about Habitat, an exploration center, and a store. Contributions are welcome.

🐾 ✐ ♿ **Smiling Peanut.** What better icon should greet visitors to Plains than the Smiling Peanut on GA 45 (south of US 280)? This giant grinning goober, spokesman for this region

GEORGIA PEANUTS

- The peanut is Georgia's official state crop, producing $390 million in revenue yearly.
- Georgia is the nation's largest producer of peanuts, producing nearly 42 percent of the U.S. crop.
- More than 70 Georgia counties produce 1.5 billion pounds of peanuts annually.
- Georgia has between 5,000 and 15,000 peanut farms, and 37,000 people work on the farms, in shelling plants, in factories that roast peanuts or make candy or peanut butter from them, or in peanut-related agribusiness.
- Favorite ways to eat peanuts in Georgia are boiling them in salt water while still in the shells or dropping shelled peanuts in your Coca-Cola.

of Georgia, isn't just any peanut. The 13-foot-tall goober has a very recognizable toothy smile—that of the 39th president, Jimmy Carter. It was constructed by Democratic friends Loretta Townsend, Doyle Kifer, and James Kiley of Evansville, Indiana. Recognizable worldwide, the happy peanut has even appeared on *Jeopardy*. The must-stop photo op is located at the edge of town about a half mile from Carter's campaign headquarters, which was in the old Seaboard Railroad depot.

CIVIL WAR HISTORY COMES TO LIFE AT THE ANDERSONVILLE NATIONAL HISTORIC SITE.

HISTORIC HOMES AND SITES

🐾 ✎ ♿ **Andersonville Civil War Village** (229-924-2558; www.andersonvillega.free servers.com), 109 Church Street, Andersonville (in the front of the Drummer Boy Civil War Museum). The entire center of the tiny town is a restored Civil War–era village where visitors can see the **Drummer Boy Civil War Museum** (see *Museums*). The remainder of the commercial establishments are occupied by shops and restaurants. During the Civil War, Andersonville was where Federal prisoners arrived by rail before being marched to nearby Camp Sumter–Andersonville Civil War Prison. The village became a supply center for the prison. Visitors can explore an old-time farm complete with a log cabin and barn, as well as live animals, a sugarcane mill, and a syrup kettle. Andersonville's log-and-fieldstone church, **Pennington St. James,** is open daily. Built in 1927, it was designed by Cramm and Ferguson, the architectural firm that designed St. John the Divine in New York City.

🐾 ✎ ♿ **Andersonville National Historic Site** (229-924-0343; www.nps.gov/ande), 496 Cemetery Road, Andersonville. Park grounds, historic prison site, and cemetery open 8–5 daily (until 6 the Sunday before Memorial Day); museum open 8:30–5 daily except Thanksgiving, Christmas, and New Year's Day. A brochure and audiotape are available for a free self-guided tour. During the Civil War, Camp Sumter was a notorious Confederate prison where more than 40,000 Union troops were incarcerated in a space that was created to hold 10,000. About 13,000 men died from disease, malnutrition, poor sanitation, overcrowding, and exposure—the highest percentage of deaths at any prison camp, North or South.

After the war, famed nurse Clara Barton came to Andersonville to find out the fate of many missing Union soldiers. She and her helpers located and marked the graves of most of the dead, but 500 remain unknown. The 500-acre site preserves the **Andersonville National Cemetery** and the location of the stockade. On Memorial Day, the cemetery is a sea of small, fluttering American flags placed on every grave.

The historic site is also the home of the **National Prisoner of War Museum,** which traces America's wars from the Revolution to the present and honors more than 800,000 Americans

---

MIRACLE AT THE ANDERSONVILLE PRISON CAMP

The small granite Providence Spring House at the Andersonville National Historic Site marks the site of a miracle at the prison camp. The only source of drinking water within the stockade was a small spring, which was constantly polluted by human waste and by men washing in the water. The prisoners prayed for rain so they could collect clean water and get some relief from the summer heat. During a downpour that cleaned out the creek, lightning struck the ground, and a spring began to flow from that spot. Not only did it provide a balm for the POWs, it is also still flowing to this day. The springhouse was built over it in 1901 by the Women's Relief Corps.

who have been captured during wartime. This is the only unit in the national park system that serves as a memorial to prisoners of war. Begin with the 27-minute film *Echoes of Captivity*, then see touching exhibits that trace the lives of POWs from capture to release or escape. Interactive displays and short video clips heighten the experience. Then walk or drive around the cemetery and prison site. A free audio driving tour is available at the museum's front desk. Interpretive programs are presented at the national park at 11 and 2 daily. During periodic living-history presentations at the site, reenactors describe the inhumane conditions POWs endured. With so much suffering and death here, it's not surprising that ghost stories persist. Sometimes visitors claim to feel hands reaching out to them, while others experience hovering shadows. Others feel cold spots by the Providence Spring and Stockade Creek. Some claim to have seen the ghost of a one-legged Confederate soldier on crutches in the cemetery. (See also *To Do—Hiking* to learn about the **Andersonville Prison Historical Hike.**) Free.

Jimmy Carter National Historic Site (229-824-4104; www.nps.gov/jica), 300 North Bond Street, Plains. Visitors center open 9–5 daily except Thanksgiving, Christmas, and New Year's Day; depot open 9–4:30; boyhood farm open 10–4. Begin at **Plains High School,** the official State School of Georgia and the visitors center. President Carter, his wife, Rosalynn, and their three sons were all educated here. A film and exhibits of photographs, documents, and other memorabilia in the former classrooms chronicle the life of the former president from tiny Plains to Washington, D.C., and beyond. The visitors center also keeps a schedule of times President Carter teaches Sunday school at Maranantha Baptist Church, which visitors are welcome to attend. Then visit the old **Plains Depot,** Main and M. L. Hudson streets, which was Carter's 1976 campaign headquarters and is the oldest structure in town. The highlight of a visit to the historic site is the **Carter Boyhood Home,** located in nearby Archery. The 360-acre farm is restored to its 1930s pre-electricity appearance and features the house, barn, blacksmith shop, and pump house. In several rooms, visitors can hear recorded reminiscences of the former president. You can get to the farm by car or aboard the SAM Shortline Railroad (see *To Do—Train Excursions*). Free.

Westville (229-838-6310 or 1-888-733-1850; www.westville.org), One Martin Luther King Drive, Lumpkin. Open 10–5 Thursday–Saturday. Westville never actually existed as a town and no one ever lived here, but by moving more than 30 antebellum homes, stores, workshops, churches, a courthouse, a school, and other buildings from various places in Georgia, a preindustrial town representing the 1850s has been created. Homes run the gamut from log cabins to elegant Greek Revival town houses. Nearly every artifact has been donated. Costumed living-history reenactors demonstrate old-time skills such as quilting, potting, blacksmithing, woodworking, and open-hearth cooking. Gardens are planted as they would have been in the 1850s. The **Kiser Restaurant** (229-838-4655; open 10–4:30; $2.50–5) serves burgers, hot dogs, sandwiches, and barbecue (not exactly the menu of 1850, but welcome nonetheless). There are monthly special events to keep visitors coming back, too. Some of the bigger events are the **Spring Days Festival, Independence Day Celebration, Fall Harvest Festival, Deck the Halls,** and **Christmas at Westville** (see *Special Events*). Adults $10; seniors, military, and college students $8; children K–12 $5; pre-K and younger free.

YOUNG JIMMY CARTER'S BEDROOM AT THE JIMMY CARTER NATIONAL HISTORIC SITE

♂ & **Windsor Hotel** (229-924-1555 or 1-888-297-9567; www.windsor-americus.com), 125 West Lamar Street, Americus. Whether you stay at the Windsor or not, you should stop in to admire it, perhaps have a meal at **Amelia's** (see *Where to Eat—Dining Out*), or visit the gift, clothing, art, and antiques shop. A whimsical confection of various architectural styles, the massive hotel, which occupies an entire city block, was fashioned after the finest hotels in 19th-century Europe and built in 1892 to attract winter visitors from the North. It is Italianate in style but also features a Flemish-style stepped roof, a Romanesque tower, and a Moorish atrium. Some famous former guests include heavyweight boxing champion John L. Sullivan, congressman William Jennings Bryan, American labor leader Eugene V. Debs, and soon-to-be president Franklin D. Roosevelt. It's even rumored that Al Capone and John Dillinger spent the night in what is now the Bridal Suite while their armed bodyguards were posted at the foot of the stairs. The depressions of 1893 and the 1930s seriously impacted tourism and the hotel, and it began a long decline. The hotel finally closed in the 1970s and sat empty for almost 20 years. It was donated to the city by the family of the last owner, and city government had to make a major decision: tear it down for a parking lot or restore it. Fortunately, they chose the latter. The Windsor was beautifully restored and reopened in 1991. Former president Jimmy Carter and Mrs. Carter cut the ribbon. Many of its original architectural features and fixtures survive.

MUSEUMS 🐾 ♂ **Bedingfield Inn Museum** (229-838-6419; www.bedingfieldinn.com), 100 Cotton Street, on the square, Lumpkin. Open 1–5 Friday and Saturday. The circa 1836 Greek Revival–style building, a former stagecoach inn that also serves as the visitors center for Stewart County, has been restored and furnished to represent the period 1836–1850. The inn and original period furnishings show visitors what overnight stops were like in the early days. If travelers could pay a high price, they would get a private room, but more often several strangers would sleep in the same bed or on the floor. Also located on the property is a dependency kitchen building and an 1845 dogtrot house. Before leaving the museum, pick up a *Stagecoach Trail Tour* brochure, for a driving tour past 23 pre-1850 homes. Adults $5, children $2.

🐾 ♂ & **Drummer Boy Civil War Museum** (229-924-2558; www.andersonvillegeorgia .com), 109 Church Street, Andersonville. Open 9–5 daily. The idea for the museum was based on two drummer boys—one a Yank, one a Reb. Exhibits feature 15 mannequins wearing authentic Civil War uniforms, including a colorful red and blue New York Fire Zouave uniform and, of course, Union and Confederate drummer boy uniforms complete with original drums. Other exhibits display weapons, documents, and photographs taken by famed Civil War photographer Matthew Brady. Flags on exhibit include a 35-star U.S. flag and the last national flag of the Confederacy. An extensive collection of artifacts belonged to Gen. Thomas T. Eckert, president of Western Union and chief of the U.S. Military Telegraph Department under President Lincoln. One of the interesting pieces on display is the bonnet of Mary Surratt, which was removed from her head and given to Eckert just before her hanging with others convicted in the conspiracy to assassinate Lincoln. A large diorama

FLOYD'S PUB

The quaint watering hole on the second floor of the Windsor Hotel overlooking downtown Americus was named for Floyd Lowery, an employee who worked at the hotel for 40 years. During the restoration, workers found an old safe and were eager to open it and see what was inside. Instead of money, jewels, or stock certificates, it contained one of Floyd's worn-out uniforms. The pub was named in honor of Floyd, but what's ironic about the choice is that Floyd was a complete teetotaler who had never taken a drink.

depicts the Andersonville Confederate Prison and the village of Andersonville as they were in 1864. Adults (over 17) $5, children 13–17 $1, children under 13 free.

🔌 🗐 ⚲ **Georgia Rural Telephone Museum** (229-874-4786; www.grtm.org), 135 Bailey Avenue, Leslie. Open 9:30–3:30 weekdays. It's astonishing that in a town of fewer than 500 there is one of the world's largest telephone museums. Housed in a circa 1920s cotton warehouse, the astounding personal collection of Tommy C. Smith, owner of Citizens Telephone Company, contains more than 2,000 artifacts. Visitors can trace the evolution of communications in this country from the smoke signals in a re-created Creek Indian village to the modern cell phone. Showcased are some of the oldest, rarest, and largest examples of telecommunications from 1876 to the present. One of the prize artifacts is Alexander Graham Bell's 1876 liquid transmitter, the first transmitter through which a voice was relayed. A re-creation of Bell's workshop includes many of the telephones envisioned by the inventor. Among other exhibits are wooden voice boxes; early pay telephone booths; rare 1882 50-line switchboards; turn-of-the-20th-century headsets; a model of Tel-Star, the first communications satellite; antique clocks; a late-1800s pipe organ; and antique service vehicles. Several vignettes portray early telephone workers at their jobs. Nominal charge.

🔌 🗐 ⚲ **Georgia State Cotton Museum** (229-268-2045), 1321 East Union Street, Vienna. Open 9–4 weekdays. Farm tools, cotton bolls, periodicals, a cotton bale, and other agricultural implements tell the story of cotton in this rustic museum. A small patch of cotton is growing outside. Before leaving, be sure to pick up a *Driving Tour of Vienna* brochure, which guides visitors past 60 historic buildings, the imposing 1892 Romanesque-style courthouse, and the **Walter F. George Law Museum** (open only by appointment). Free.

🔌 🗐 ⚲ **Georgia Veterans State Park** (park: 229-276-2371; www.gastateparks.org /GeorgiaVets), 2456 US 280 West, Cordele. Open 7 AM–10 PM daily. Developed to honor U.S. veterans, the 1,308-acre state park features a museum with uniforms, medals, weapons, and other memorabilia from the Revolutionary War through the Gulf War. Outdoors, visitors can get up-close looks at several vintage military airplanes, including a Boeing B-29A; tanks; and other vehicles. Parking $5.

NATURAL BEAUTY SPOTS

🔌 🗐 ⚲ **Providence Canyon State Conservation Park** (229-838-6870; www.ga stateparks.org/ProvidenceCanyon), 8930 Canyon Road, Lumpkin. Open 7–6 daily, September 15–April 14; 7 AM–9 PM daily, April 15–September 14. Known as Georgia's "Little Grand Canyon," this gorge, which is 150 feet deep at its greatest depth, presents a vision of breathtaking pink, orange, red, and purple hues and undulating patterns. Formations resembling above-ground stalagmites punctuate the chasm. What's totally amazing is that the canyon

AN UNUSUAL ROCK FORMATION AT PROVIDENCE CANYON STATE CONSERVATION PARK

isn't millions of years old but was caused by erosion due to poor farming practices in the 1800s. Visitors can view the ravines from the rim trail or make the 3-mile trek into the canyon. Backpackers can overnight along the 7 miles of backcountry trails. The interpretive center at the 1,109-acre park has exhibits about the formation of the canyon. The rare orange plumleaf azalea grows only in a small 50-mile-radius area that stretches from the canyon to Callaway Gardens (see the Pine Mountain chapter), and the park is often dotted with colorful wildflowers. In fact, the park is noted for having the largest concentration of wildflowers in Georgia. Special events include **Wildflower Day, Kudzu Takeover Day, and Photography Day.** Parking $5.

SCENIC DRIVES Andersonville Trail (229-924-0343). The looping trail stretches 75 miles from Byron (see the Macon chapter in part 3: Historical South) to Cordele. Visitors enjoy quaint towns, historic homes, museums, cotton and canola fields, peach and pecan orchards, and two National Historic Sites. Highlights of the trail include **Massee Lane Gardens,** national headquarters of the American Camellia Society (see the Macon chapter); **Habitat for Humanity Global Village and Discovery Center and International Headquarters** (see *For Families*); **Georgia Veterans State Park** (see *Museums*); and the **Museum of Aviation–Georgia Aviation Hall of Fame** (see the Macon chapter). Along the way there are numerous opportunities for antiquing and other shopping, camping, fishing, and hunting. Stop at roadside stands for watermelons, peaches, peanuts, and pecans.

✹ To Do
AUTO RACING Watermelon Capital Speedway (229-271-9301; www.watermelon capitalspeedway.com), 385 Farmers Market Road, Cordele. The ⅜-mile, medium-banked, high-speed asphalt track is the scene of Bandolero, Legends, Mini Stock, Enduro, Pure Stock, Superstreet, and Pro Late Model races. Check the website or call for a schedule of events and ticket prices.

FRUIT AND BERRY PICKING 🍓 ✐ ♿ **Kauffman's Strawberry and Farm Market** (478-472-8833; www.kauffmansfarmmarket.com), 1305 Mennonite Church Road, Montezuma. Open 8–6 Monday–Saturday; strawberries April–June, sweet corn May–June, peaches June–July. Pick your own strawberries, sweet corn, and peaches in season. When you've worked up an appetite or a sweat, cool off with ice cream or lemonade. Take home cakes, pies, tarts, and produce. Fees vary.

GOLF ⛳ **Georgia Veterans Memorial Golf Course** (golf course: 229-276-2377 or 1-877-736-8897; tee times: 1-800-434-0982) at **Georgia Veterans State Park** (see *Green Space— Nature Preserves and Parks*). Open 8–dusk. This 18-hole, 7,059-yard, par-72, four-star championship course was designed by Dennis Griffith. The course's clubhouse features light snacks and drinks, as well as a full-service pro shop. $41–45.

HIKING 🥾 ✐ **Andersonville Prison Historical Hike.** The 3-mile walking history lesson explores the **Andersonville National Historic Site** (see *To See—Historic Homes and Sites*) and the town of Andersonville. The route is directed by a questionnaire available at the information desk at the National Prisoner of War Museum, goes through the prison site and into the town of Andersonville, and ends up at the Andersonville National Cemetery.

TRAIN EXCURSIONS ✐ **SAM Shortline–Southwest Georgia Excursion Train** (229-276-2715, 1-800-864-7275, or 1-877-GA-RAILS; www.samshortline.com), mailing address: P.O. Box 845, Cordele 31010. Generally operates Friday and Saturday, but not every week. Operates some Sundays. Call or check the website for dates and times. Restored vintage rail cars provide a nostalgic way to see this area of southwest Georgia along a 42-mile route through pecan country. Called the SAM Shortline because the route was once part of the Savannah, Americus and Montgomery line, the railroad now operates the Americus Adventurer, the Archery Explorer, the Southwest Georgia Arrow, and the Presidential Flyer. Stations are at Georgia Veterans State Park, Leslie, Americus, Plains, and Archery, but every route doesn't stop at every station, so make sure the one you choose stops where you want it to. Special runs to additional cities are offered throughout the year. Reservations are strongly recommended. Coach: adults $27.99, seniors and active military $25.99, children $17.99; Premium Car: adults $35.99, children $25.99; Hawkins Car: $35.99.

✳ Green Space

LAKES ✺ ⚲ ⚶ **Lake Blackshear** was created in 1930 by damming the Flint River to provide power to Crisp County. The 8,600-acre lake provides water and shore recreation including boating and fishing for bass, crappie, catfish, and bream.

✺ ⚲ ⚶ **Lake Walter F. George** on the Chattahoochee River contains 45,000 acres of water surface and innumerable opportunities for water sports and other outdoor recreation. The lake actually has two names. It is called Lake Walter F. George on the Georgia side but is known as Lake Eufaula on the Alabama side.

NATURE PRESERVES AND PARKS ✺ ⚲ ⚶ **Florence Marina State Park** (229-838-6870; www.gastateparks.org/FlorenceMarina), 218 Florence Road, Omaha. Open 7 AM–10 PM daily. The 173-acre park is located at the northern end of 45,000-acre Lake Walter F. George. Recreational amenities at the park include a natural deep-water marina with 66 slips, a boat ramp and dock, boat rentals in season, a lighted fishing pier, two playgrounds, a 0.75-mile nature trail, and miniature golf (additional fee). The park's **Kirbo Interpretive Center** teaches visitors about Native Americans, local history, and nature. Displays include artifacts from prehistoric Paleo-Indians to the present. Accommodations are available (see *Lodging—Campgrounds and Lodging—Cottages and Cabins*). Parking $5.

✺ ⚲ ⚶ **Georgia Veterans State Park** (park: 229-276-2371). Open 7 AM–10 PM daily. The park is located on the shores of 8,600-acre Lake Blackshear. Water sports include swimming at the beach, fishing, waterskiing, and boating. Private boats are permitted on the lake, and rentals are available at the park's marina. The 1,308-acre park offers even more. It boasts privately owned and operated **Lake Blackshear Resort and Golf Club** (see *To Do—Golf, Lodging—Cottages and Cabins,* and *Lodging—Resorts*) as well as camping, a 1-mile nature trail, a fitness course, a radio-controlled model airplane flying field, disc golf (additional fee), bike rentals, a hummingbird-wildflower meadow, and an indoor-outdoor military museum (see *To See—Museums*). In addition, the **SAM Shortline/Southwest Georgia Excursion Train** stops at the park, giving visitors an opportunity to travel to Plains and back (see *To Do—Train Excursions*). Special events throughout the year include the **Georgia Veterans Memorial Triathlon and Duathlon** in August, the **Fall School Day Fair** in September, and **Tribute to Veterans** in November. Parking $5.

RIVERS The **Flint River** makes a transition north of this area from the Piedmont region to the Coastal Plain. Unlike areas of shoals and rapids where white-water rafting is possible, this section of the river is characterized by deeply cut, sandy banks and broad, forested floodplains. The river here is deep, wide, and slow. When rainfall is heavy upstream, the river overflows, sometimes with devastating results. Periodic flooding has resulted in a vast floodplain known as the Great Swamp. It actually consists of two swamps—north of GA 96 (which runs east from Columbus to Fort Valley) is the Magnolia Swamp, south of the highway is Beechwood Swamp. During floods they cover thousands of acres. The stream channel is continuously migrating and creating new sandbars, which make good places to camp or fish for flathead and channel catfish. Bends in the river often cause oxbow lakes, which are fishermen's closely guarded secrets. Boating can be impeded by tree snags, but these same snags provide homes for turtles, water snakes, bluegill, and bass. North of Montezuma is an escarped area referred to as the Montezuma Bluffs, where weathering has resulted in a 150-foot escarpment overlooking the Beechwood Swamp and the river. Not only can visitors see fossilized limestone that was part of a marine ecosystem 50 million years ago, but the steep, moist slopes contain one of the state's largest concentrations of the rare and endangered relic trillium. The area remains relatively pristine because access is only by boat.

✴ Lodging

BED & BREAKFASTS

In Americus

& **Americus Garden Inn Bed and Breakfast** (229-931-0122 or 1-888-758-4749; www.americusgardeninn.com), 504 Rees Park. This 1848 mansion surrounded by 1.3 acres has a wraparound porch and gingerbread accents. The inn offers eight guest accommodations: two rooms on the first floor, five on the second, and the Executive Suite in the Olde Schoolhouse. Some rooms boast a Jacuzzi. Outdoors, enjoy the garden, gazebo, koi pond, and waterfall. A full gourmet breakfast is included. Smoking outdoors only. $129–189; on special event weekends, two-night minimum required.

✺ **1906 Pathway Inn** (229-928-2078 or 1-800-889-1466), 501 South Lee Street. The stunning neoclassical home provides the most elegant accommodations in town. Public rooms and guest rooms are beautifully and luxuriously decorated with antiques. The guest rooms are named for famous people connected with the region: Carter, Rosalynn, Lindbergh, Roosevelt, Presidential, and Bell. Make time to enjoy the superb architectural elements, the pleasant veranda, and the gardens. A full gourmet breakfast is included in the nightly rate. Small pets allowed with prior approval and additional fee. Smoking outdoors only. Not wheelchair accessible. $89–135.

In Montezuma

✾ **The White House Farm** (478-472-7942; www.whitehousefarmbnb.com), 1679 Mennonite Church Road. The Nisly's home is located on a 250-acre dairy farm. Their two-story home was built in the 1950s with help from members of the Mennonite community—similar to an old-fashioned barn raising. Guest accommodations include cannonball and four-poster beds

and soft floral fabrics. A full breakfast gets your day off to a good start. The Nisly family also bakes typical Mennonite favorites. No smoking. Not wheelchair accessible. $70–90.

CAMPGROUNDS

In Cordele

✺ ✔ ✾ **Georgia Veterans State Park** (camping reservations: 1-800-864-7275). The park offers 77 tent, trailer, and RV sites with hookups. $25–28. See *Green Space—Nature Preserves and Parks*.

In Lumpkin

✺ ✔ ✾ **Providence Canyon State Conservation Park** (229-838-6870; camping reservations: 1-800-864-7275). The park has six hike-in backcountry campsites. $9 per person per night. See *Green Space—Nature Preserves and Parks*.

In Omaha

✺ ✔ ✾ **Florence Marina State Park** (lodging reservations: 1-800-864-7275). The park offers 43 tent, trailer, and RV sites with cable TV hookups and all the amenities of the park. $25–28. See *Green Space—Nature Preserves and Parks*.

COTTAGES AND CABINS

In Cordele

✔ & ✾ **Lake Blackshear Resort and Golf Club** (1-800-459-1230; www.lakeblackshearresort.org) at **Georgia Veterans State Park** (229-276-2371 or 1-800-864-7275; www.gastateparks.org/GeorgiaVets), 2459-H US 280 West. The resort has 10 private, fully equipped cottages, each with two bedrooms, one bath, complete kitchen, living room with a fireplace, and a large screened porch, as well as a grill and picnic table. Pet friendly (one free, two or more

$25). Some wheelchair accessibility. $115–199.

In Omaha
🦆 🐾 ♨ **Florence Marina State Park** (lodging reservations: 1-800-864-7275). The park has six fully equipped cottages, two of which are dog friendly ($40 per dog; maximum two), and eight efficiency units. $90–115. See *Green Space—Nature Preserves and Parks.*

INNS AND HOTELS

In Americus
🐾 ♿ **Windsor Hotel** (229-924-1555 or 1-888-297-9567; www.windsor-americus .com), 125 West Lamar Street. (See *To See—Historic Homes and Sites* for a complete description of the structure.) Choose from 53 period-style guest rooms and suites, each different and each with all the modern amenities. There are several two-room executive suites, too. The one on the third floor is named for Jessica Tandy and its connecting room for Hume Cronin. The famous couple stayed at the hotel during the making of the Hallmark Hall of Fame film *To Dance with the White Dog.* In addition, there are two suites: the James Earl Carter Presidential Suite and the bridal suite, which has its own private stairway. **Amelia's** is open for breakfast daily and dinner every night except Sunday (see *Where to Eat—Dining Out*). Cocktails and musical entertainment can be enjoyed in Floyd's Pub and its adjacent veranda. Floyd's is open from 5 PM Monday–Saturday and offers Trivia Night on Wednesday and live music on Friday. Continental breakfast is included in the nightly rate. Smoking and nonsmoking rooms. $100–225; numerous special packages available.

In Plains
🐾 ♿ **Plains Historic Inn and Antiques Mall** (229-824-4517; www.plainsgeorgia .com/accommodations.html), 106 Main Street. In this historic commercial establishment, the ground floor is devoted to an antiques mall (see *Selective Shopping— Antiques*), but charming accommodations can be found upstairs. "Every room is a history lesson," the website proclaims. In fact,

each guest room is dedicated to a decade in President Jimmy Carter's life, from 1920 to 1980, and the decor reflects the style of that era. President and Mrs. Carter actually had input into the choices of decor. Guests have access to a huge common room and a balcony overlooking the historic square. Complimentary continental breakfast is included. No smoking. $74.50–110.

RESORTS

In Cordele
🐾 ♿ ♨ **Lake Blackshear Resort and Golf Club** (229-276-1004 or 1-800-459-1230; www.lakeblackshearresort.org) at **Georgia Veterans State Park** (229-276-2371 or 1-800-864-7275; www.gastate parks.org/GeorgiaVets), 2459-H US 280 West. The resort offers 14 rooms in the contemporary lodge as well as in 64 villas, each of which has a private screened porch or balcony overlooking the lake. These rooms contain a small refrigerator. Accommodations also are offered in 10 cottages (see *Cottages and Cabins*). The lodge features fine dining in **Cordelia's** restaurant (see *Where to Eat—Dining Out*), casual dining seasonally in the Cypress Grill, and 88's Lakeside Bar. Guests have access to all the amenities of the state park (see *Green Space—Nature Preserves and Parks*) and Lake Blackshear, including an 18-hole golf course (see *To Do—Golf*), beach and swimming area, fitness center, indoor-outdoor pool with whirlpool, lake activities, nature trail, gift shop, and business center. Pet friendly (first dog free, two or more $25). Smoking and nonsmoking rooms available. Some rooms and villas wheelchair accessible. $139–159 for rooms and villas; $159–199 for cottages (two-night minimum on weekends).

✳ Where to Eat
DINING OUT

In Americus
🦆 🐾 ♿ **Amelia's at the Windsor Hotel** (229-924-1555; www.windsor-americus .com), 125 West Lamar Street. Open for breakfast 6:30–9:30 AM daily, for dinner 6–9 PM Monday–Saturday. Dinner reservations recommended. Savor a sophisticated

dining experience in the epitome of Victorian elegance. Dinner choices include regional and national favorites made with beef, seafood, chicken, and pork. No smoking. Continental breakfast $6, à la carte entrées $9–11; dinner $12–26.

In Cordele

🦪 🍷 ♿ **Cordelia's** (229-276-1004 or 1-800-459-1230; www.lakeblackshearresort .com), at the Lake Blackshear Resort and Golf Club, 2459-H US 280 West. Open 7–10:30 for breakfast, 11–2 for lunch, and 7–9 for dinner, Sunday–Friday; 7–10:30 for breakfast, 11–2 for lunch, and 6–10 for dinner Saturday. The city of Cordele was named for Cordelia Hawkins in 1888, and she was also the inspiration for this upscale restaurant. The cuisine is a blend of Italian and local cuisines, with the dinner menu being primarily classic Italian. Get the day off to a good start with traditional breakfast choices ranging from egg dishes and pancakes to French toast. If you can tear yourself away from outdoor activities, lunches include soups, salads, sandwiches, wraps, and burgers. À la carte dinner choices include classic Italian fare and steaks, chicken, and seafood. Diners enjoy lake views while savoring their meal, and some folks even come by boat. Adjacent to the restaurant, 88's Lakeside Bar, named because the state of Georgia was officially created in 1788 and the city was founded in 1888, serves cocktails and light fare in a casual, eclectic setting overlooking the lake. No smoking. Breakfast $4.50–9.95, lunch $5.95–8.95, dinner $9.95–35.95.

🦪 🍷 ♿ **Daphne Lodge** (229-273-2596; www.daphnelodge.com), 12 US 280 West. Open 5:30–9:30 Tuesday–Saturday; reservations recommended on weekends. Located in a vintage red cottage with a long rocker-filled front porch nestled among the pines near Georgia Veterans State Park, Daphne Lodge is a great casual place to go for "Georgia lake country eatin.'" It's particularly known for its catfish, but also for seafood and steaks. Lots of small dining rooms are decorated with country charm. No smoking. $11–34.

EATING OUT

In Americus

🦪 ♿ **Monroe's Hot Dogs and Billiards** (229-924-4106), 318-A West Lamar Street. Open 10:30–8 Monday–Friday, open until 5 on Saturday. Monroe's bills their famous hot dogs as "the best dog ever bitten by a man." Drop in to try one out for yourself, and stay to enjoy the billiards and game room. Smoking allowed. Hot dogs $1–1.50; pool $1.25 per person for 30 minutes.

In Montezuma

🦪 🍷 ♿ **Yoder's Deitsch Haus Restaurant, Bakery, and Gift Shop** (478-472-2024), 5252 GA 26 East. The bakery is open at 7, restaurant is open 11:30–2 and 5–8:30 Tuesday, Thursday, Friday, and Saturday; 11:30–2 only on Wednesday. Menu items at the nationally renowned restaurant include roast beef, chicken, fish, chops, casseroles, Southern-style vegetables, and homemade desserts. Pies are a specialty. No smoking. Restaurant wheelchair accessible, restrooms are not. $7–9.

In Plains

🦪 🍷 ♿ **Mom's Kitchen** (229-824-5458), 203 Church Street. Open 6 AM–3 PM Tuesday–Thursday for breakfast and lunch, 6–8 PM Friday and Saturday for dinner, 11–3 Sunday. Southern specialties such as corn fritters, sweet potato pie, and collard greens are served buffet-style. No smoking. Wheelchair accessible. Buffet $6.99–8.99.

✳ Entertainment

THEATER 🍷 ♿ **Rylander Theatre** (229-931-0001; www.rylander.org), 310 West Lamar Street, Americus. Box office open 11–4 Tuesday–Friday. Americus businessman Walter Rylander constructed this premier performance theater and movie palace in 1921. At that time it was called "the Finest Playhouse South of Atlanta." The theater's interior is a visual feast, featuring ornate plasterwork, beautiful stencil patterns, and painted murals. Despite having closed in 1951 and sitting empty for many years, its architectural details are intact. The beautifully restored theater is now a venue for live performances, including productions of the Sumter Players (see next); organ concerts on the 1928 Moller pipe organ; classic movies; and other special events. Guided tours available. Check the website or call for a schedule of performances and ticket prices.

Sumter Players (229-924-2645; Rylander box office: 229-931-0001; www.sumter player.org). Box office open 11–4 Tuesday–Friday, 11–8 Thursday–Saturday on days of performances, 1–2:30 Sunday on days of performances. Check the website or call for a schedule of performances. The all-volunteer theater troupe has been entertaining the community since the 1960s. Adults $15; seniors, students, and Habitat volunteers $10.

✳ Selective Shopping

ANTIQUES **Plains Historic Inn and Antiques Mall** (229-824-4517; www.plains georgia.com), 106 Main Street, Plains. Open 10–6 Monday–Saturday, 1–5 Sunday. Twenty-five booths offer a wide variety of antiques and other merchandise. Accommodations, which include a continental breakfast, are offered upstairs (see *Lodging—Inns and Hotels*).

CRAFTS ♿ **Yoder's Deitsch Haus Restaurant, Bakery, and Gift Shop** (478-472-2024), 5252 GA 26 East, Montezuma. The bakery and gift shop opens each day at 7; the restaurant is open 11:30–2 and 5–8:30 Tuesday and Thursday–Saturday, 11:30–2 only on Wednesday. Shop here for quality crafts and traditional Pennsylvania Dutch and Southern foods.

FOOD **Yoder's Country Market** (478-472-2070), 7402 GA 26 East, Montezuma. Open 7 AM–9 PM Monday–Saturday, 8–7 Sunday. Shop here for cheeses, jams, and spices.

✳ Special Events

March: **Andersonville Revisited Living-History Weekend** (229-924-0343; www .nps.gov/ande). During the event at the Andersonville National Historic Site (see *To See—Historic Homes and Sites*), living his-

tory begins with the arrival of the prisoners, and various scenarios continue throughout the weekend, including issuing rations, shelter building, inspection, escape and punishment, guard drills, and artillery demonstrations. At 3 each day, visitors will want to see *Every Stone Has a Story*—tales of some of the men buried here. Interpretive programs 10–4 Saturday, 10–3 Sunday. Free.

April: **Antique Dogwood Festival** (229-874-1259). The festival, held in Leslie, features antiques dealers from all over Georgia with a variety of merchandise from coin collections to Civil War memorabilia to furniture. $5.

Spring Days Festival (229-838-6310 or 1-888-733-1850). See plowing, planting, and garden preparation using mules. Participate in crafts and games, and listen to musicians playing traditional instruments. Included in regular admission to Westville (see *To See—Historic Homes and Sites*).

May and October: **Andersonville Historic Fair** (229-924-2558; www.andersonville georgia.com). The festival features living history, mock battles, a parade, arts and crafts, and old-time craftspeople—as well as entertainment. A flea market offers bargains. Adults $4, children $1.50.

July: **Independence Day Celebration** (229-838-6310 or 1-888-733-1850). The event in Westville includes a barbecue, watermelon, bluegrass musical entertainment, mid-19th-century games and races, and a special treat—blowing the anvil every hour. Included in regular admission (see *To See—Historic Homes and Sites*).

Watermelon Days Festival (229-273-1668 or 1-800-621-3456; www.cordelecrisp ga.com). The Cordele festival has been held annually since 1955. For two weeks in late June and early July, a multitude of events take place at various locations: a pageant, 5K and fun run, car race, entertainment, arts and crafts, parade, photo contest, 4-H dog show, fishing rodeo, horseshoe tournament, waterskiing show, puppet show, Mr. Melon contest, gospel sing, and, of course, watermelon-decorating, seed-spitting, watermelon-chucking, and watermelon-eating contests. A special event is Fireworks on the Flint, seen from aboard the SAM Shortline train (see *To Do—Train Excursions*). Festival free; small charge for some activities.

September: **Plains Peanut Festival** (229-824-5373; www.plainsgeorgia.com/peanut _festival.html). The festival celebrates peanut production with a 1-mile fun run and a 5K road race. Former president Jimmy Carter awards the prizes for these events. Then there's a downtown parade with VIPs, beauty queens, bands, and floats. President and Mrs. Carter view the parade from the balcony of the Plains Historic Inn. The festival continues at Maxine Reese Park on Main Street with arts and crafts, food, and continuous entertainment. The annual folk play *If These Sidewalks Could Talk . . . Comin' Home,* performed on Friday and Saturday evenings, is an amusing look at life in a small town. Festival free; small charge for some activities.

Late September or early October: **Big Pig Jig** (229-268-8278 or 229-268-8275; www .bigpigjig.com), Big Pig Jig Boulevard, Vienna. This is the oldest and largest of Georgia's barbecue cooking championships. In addition to the contest, there's something for everyone at this event: crafts, collectibles, a midway with games, golf tournament, specialty food vendors, hog-calling contests, and barbecue tastings. Evening concerts, a parade, a pageant, children's activities, and the 5K Hog Jog round out the fun. On Saturday after the judging, samples of the barbecue can be purchased for $5 a carton until they run out. Admission: $8 Friday, $5 on Saturday during the day; $8 after 3 when there is entertainment.

October: **Montezuma's Beaver Creek Festival** (478-472-4777; www.montezuma -ga.org). The annual event, which began after a devastating flood in July 1994 decimated the downtown area, was originally called the Flood Festival. Held at Charlie Jackson Unity Park, which was created after a disastrous fire, the renamed festival celebrates the accomplishments that continue to be made in reviving the town of Mon-

BARBECUE IS KING AT THE BIG PIG JIG, HELD EVERY FALL IN VIENNA.

tezuma. The festival features arts and crafts, live entertainment, and good food, and culminates in the Great Beaver Creek Duck Race fund-raiser. Free.

November: **Fall Harvest Festival** (229-838-6310 or 1-888-733-1850; www .westville.org). Traditional activities at this Westville event include bluegrass music, crafts, harvest chores, and skills demonstrations such as ginning cotton, cooking sugarcane syrup, and candle and soap making. Included in regular admission to Westville (see *To See—Historic Homes and Sites*).

December: **Deck the Halls** and **Christmas at Westville** (229-838-6310 or 1-888-733-1850; www.westville.org). Held on two separate Saturdays in Westville. **Deck the Halls,** held on the first Saturday, is a decorating workshop where participants learn how to make authentic period decorations that are then placed throughout the village. Since you'll be working, the event is free. The second Saturday is **Christmas at Westville.** Visitors can make and take period crafts and decorations, visit Father Christmas, and participate in the Lighting of the Lanterns procession, which ends with candlelight carols at the courthouse. Included in regular admission (see *To See— Historic Homes and Sites*).

BAINBRIDGE AND
SOUTHWEST GEORGIA

T his area of extreme southwest Georgia is, in fact, much closer to Alabama and the Florida Panhandle than it is to most of Georgia, and it's probably more familiar to travelers from those states than it is to citizens of Georgia. There are no large towns, but there are several large lakes, several state parks, the Chattahoochee and Flint rivers, and lots of opportunities for outdoor recreation.

The area is characterized by small towns and red-clay fields of peanuts, corn, and cotton. Visitors are rewarded with sights such as a covered bridge, murals painted on downtown buildings, a monument to the peanut, a variety of museums, a winery, and the official Georgia folklife play, *Swamp Gravy.* Some of the state's most unusual festivals—among them those celebrating mules, swine, and even rattlesnakes—draw lots of guests to the region.

GUIDANCE If you are planning a trip to Bainbridge and Climax, contact the **Bainbridge–Decatur County Chamber of Commerce** (229-246-4774; www.bainbridgegachamber .com), 100 Boat Basin Circle, Bainbridge 39817. Open 8–5 weekdays. When you are in the area, stop by the office, which is located in the **McKenzie-Reynolds House,** a 1921 neo–Classical Revival home. For more information about the entire area of southwest Georgia, call or stop in at the **Southwest Georgia Visitor Information Center** (229-243-8555; www.bainbridgega.com), 101 Airport Road, Bainbridge 39817. Open 8–5 Monday–Friday. The visitors center provides information on statewide as well as local attractions.

Visitors planning a trip to the Blakely area, including Arlington, should consult the **Blakely–Early County Chamber of Commerce** (229-723-3641; www.blakelyearlycountychamber .com), 214 Court Square, Blakely 39823. Open 8:30–5 weekdays.

For more information about Colquitt, contact the **Colquitt–Miller County Chamber of Commerce** (229-758-2400; www.colquitt-georgia.com), 302 East College Street, Colquitt 39837. Open 9–5 weekdays.

To learn more about Donalsonville, contact the **Donalsonville–Seminole County Chamber of Commerce** (229-524-2588; www.donalsonvillega.com), 122 East Second Street, Donalsonville 31806. Open 9–5 weekdays. In addition to general information, the **Southern Rivers Birding Trail** (see *To Do—Birding*) guide and map are available here.

To learn more about Fort Gaines, contact the **Clay County Library/Visitors Bureau and Information Center** (229-768-2248; www.fortgaines.com), Clay County Library, 208 Hancock Street, Fort Gaines 39851. Open 9–6 Monday–Wednesday, 9–5 Friday and Saturday. Both the library and **George T. Bagby State Park and Lodge** (see *Green Space—Nature*

Preserves and Parks) provide audio guides and brochures for the **Fort Gaines Walking Tour** (see *To See—Walking Tours*) of the area.

GETTING THERE *By air:* Getting to this area by air requires flying into a nearby airport and renting a car. The closest airport to Cuthbert and Fort Gaines is in Columbus. The closest airport to Blakely, Arlington, and Colquitt is in Dothan, Alabama. The closest airports to Donalsonville, Bainbridge, Calvary, Whigham, and Climax are in Dothan, Alabama, or Tallahassee, Florida. For airport, airline, and car rental information about any of these, see "What's Where in Georgia."

By bus: The **Greyhound Lines** (229-248-8774) station in Bainbridge (2331 Dothan Highway) is the only one in the area covered by this chapter. Other options are in Albany, Columbus, or Thomasville (see those chapters), or Dothan, Alabama (285 South Foster Street).

By car: The two major towns are Bainbridge, at US 84 and US 27, and Blakely, at US 27 and GA 62. Cuthbert is at US 27 and US 82.

MEDICAL EMERGENCY In life-threatening situations, call 911.

VILLAGES Bainbridge, located near Lake Seminole, is the county seat of Decatur County. The town was incorporated in 1829 and is named for Commo. William Bainbridge, commander of the USS *Constitution,* "Old Ironsides." Historic downtown Bainbridge surrounds Willis Park and contains an intact group of architecturally significant commercial buildings that date from 1860 to 1920. Numerous outdoor recreational activities are available in the area, including **Seminole State Park** (see *Green Space—Nature Preserves and Parks*).

Fort Gaines, established in 1814 around a fort on the Chattahoochee River, is one of the oldest towns in Georgia. The fort was established to protect settlers during the Creek Indian Wars. Fort Gaines's position on the Chattahoochee River led to the town becoming a shipping point for cotton planters on both the Georgia and Alabama sides of the river. Fort Gaines remained a key market until railroads replaced river freight. The tiny town and the surrounding area have numerous attractions, including a museum, two lakes, and several state parks. The area around Fort Gaines is also the last refuge of the *Trillium reliquum,* an endangered plant species, and is the home of the largest magnolia tree in Georgia. Wildlife is plentiful. In fact, Clay County is reputed to have three times more deer than people.

Blakely is known as "the Peanut Capital of the World" because so many peanut products are made here, although you'll have seen in other chapters that several other areas also claim the title. A peanut monument on Courthouse Square salutes the industry. Blakely is also known for the Indian mounds nearby, a covered bridge, a 140-plus-year-old Confederate flagpole, a restored 1930s theater, and several festivals.

With a population of fewer than 2,000 people, **Colquitt** belies its size in the number of things going on there. Located in the southwest corner of Georgia, Colquitt is 50 miles east of Dothan, Alabama, southwest of Albany, and north of Tallahassee, Florida. The town is known as "the Mayhaw Capital of the World." Mayhaws are a tart fruit from the rose family that grow in swampy areas; boats and nets are often required to harvest them. Colquitt is also the home of a 23-foot carved face of an Indian brave as well as *Swamp Gravy,* the official Georgia folklife play. Many events occur throughout the year here, including the **National Mayhaw Festival** (see *Special Events*).

✳ To See

COVERED BRIDGES 🐾 ✎ ♿ **Coheelee Creek Covered Bridge** (229-273-3741; www.blakelyearlycountychamber.com), GA 62 and Old River Road, Blakely. Accessible daylight hours daily. Built in 1891, the 96-foot-long, two-span bridge, which crosses narrow, rambling Coheelee Creek in Fannie Askew Williams Park, is one of only 16 covered bridges left in Georgia. The bridge has an even more significant designation: It is the southernmost historic, authentic covered bridge in the United States. Even more rare in the flat plains of south Georgia is that the swiftly flowing creek drops over some rocks to create a small waterfall just past the bridge. Free.

CULTURAL SITES 🐾 ✒ ♿ **Donalsonville Murals** (chamber of commerce: 229-524-2588; www.donalsonvillega.com), Donalsonville. Local artist Earl Burke painted two murals on local businesses depicting Donalsonville history: *The Local Depot* on Lions Hall, 105 South Tennille, and *Farming of Yesterday* on the north end of Seminole Auto Parts, 301 South Wiley Avenue.

🐾 ✒ ♿ **Millennium Murals** (Colquitt–Miller County Arts Council: 229-758-5450; www .swampgravy.com/mural_project.php), Town Square and throughout town, Colquitt. Fifteen murals (so far) painted by artists from all over the United States constitute the project, which was started in 1999. The murals help promote the importance of storytelling and oral histories, with many of the scenes depicted coming from *Swamp Gravy,* Georgia's official folklife play. *We've Got a Story to Tell* depicts the three dominant cultures of the South—Native American, African American, and European. This mural features not only life-size figures but native plants, crops, and even insects. *Saturday on the Square* depicts the town in the early 1900s, the 1920s, the 1930s and 1940s, and the 1950s. The *Ghost Story Alley* mural depicts several eerie tales of mystery, death, and heartache, including the "Red-Haired Woman," "White's Bridge Ghost," and "Big Black Beautiful Stallion." When the 10th mural was completed, the project became eligible to belong to the International Mural Society, which promotes public art. In 2010, Colquitt hosted representatives from all over the world for the Global Mural and Arts Conference.

🐾 ✒ ♿ **Tribute to the American Indian** (229-758-2400; www.colquitt-georgia.com), 166 South First Street/US 27, Colquitt. Hungarian-born sculptor Peter Toth has devoted his life to carving memorial monuments, which he calls "Whispering Giants," in each state in honor of the spirit of the Native Americans who inhabited our land before European settlers arrived. His Georgia contribution is a 23-foot red-oak head of an Indian brave. Toth said he chose Colquitt for the site of Georgia's tribute statue because of the spirit of hospitality, friendship, and cooperation he received when he first visited in the 1980s.

FOR FAMILIES 🐾 ✒ ♿ **Peanut Monument** (229-273-3741; www.blakelyearlycounty chamber.com), North Main Street, on the square, Blakely. Accessible daily. Early County produces more peanuts than any other county in America. Although the county has more acres planted in cotton, it still has more acres planted in peanuts than any other county in Georgia and produces millions more dollars in income. This monument, which is an 8-foot-tall stone plinth with a carved peanut on top, pays tribute to the crop on which the city and county's economy is based and extols its health benefits to the world.

HISTORIC HOMES AND SITES 🐾 ✒ ♿ **Frontier Village** (Clay County Library: 229-768-2248; www.fortgaines.com/frontier_village.html), Bluff Street, Fort Gaines. Open daylight hours daily. Its strategic position on a bluff overlooking the Chattahoochee River was the reason for situating a frontier fort here in 1814. It served as an Indian fort in 1836. Bluff Park, where the village is located, has existed since the turn of the 20th century. Many structures have been relocated here to form the village: the 1928 Woman's Club House, a 1928 Boy Scout cabin, an 1820s tollhouse, a gristmill and smokehouse, several log cabins and simple settler houses, and the watchtower of a Confederate fort. Visitors to the park also can see a Civil War cannon, which has rested in the same spot since the war, and the Otis Micco statue. Micco was a Native American overwhelmed by American forces in the early days of the town. The artist, Phillip Andrews, retired in Fort Gaines. Free.

🐾 ✿ ♿ **Kolomoki Mounds Historic Park** (229-724-2150; www.gastateparks.org/Kolomoki Mounds), 205 Indian Mounds Road, off US 27, Blakely. Park open 7 AM–10 PM daily; museum open 8–5 daily. Kolomoki is both an important archaeological site—the oldest and largest Woodland Indian site in the Southeast—and a recreational area. Central to this 1,293-acre park are seven Native American earthen mounds built between A.D. 250 and 950 by Swift Creek and Weeden Island Indians. Although the site, which was one of the most populous settlements north of Mexico, is believed to have been inhabited from 1000 B.C., the highest level of development was between A.D. 350 and 600. The seven mounds include the state's oldest temple mound as well as two burial mounds and four ceremonial mounds. An interpretive museum, partially situated inside an excavated mound, explains the significance of the mounds, and it offers a film as well as displays of artifacts discovered on the site. To learn about the recreational attractions and lodging opportunities at the park, see *Green Space—Nature Preserves and Parks* and *Lodging—Campgrounds*. Parking $5; museum admission $4–5.

🐾 ✿ ♿ **Outpost Replica** (Clay County Library: 229-768-2248; www.fortgaines.com), Commerce Street, Fort Gaines. Open daily. The replica re-creates a smaller version of the old blockhouse at the original fort. The village that was used to protect early settlers from Creek and Seminole Indian attacks between 1814 and 1830 consists of original log houses from around the city that have been moved to the site. Free.

MUSEUMS 🐾 ✿ ♿ **Cotton Hall–Storytelling Museum–Museum of Southern Culture** (229-758-5450; www.swampgravy.com/storytelling_museum.php), 116 East Main Street, Colquitt. Open only during performances, which are given frequently throughout the year. Cotton Hall was built in the 1930s as part of the New Deal, but it was used as a cotton warehouse for only four years before the boll weevil decimated the cotton industry. Now it has a new life. The community-based museum has 10,000 exhibits relating to Southern culture, rural Southerners, storytelling, and folklife. Familiar and frequented places around town are re-created: the doctor's office, barber–beauty shop, railroad depot, post office, newspaper, dry goods store, picture show, and farm. The characters who operated these businesses invite visitors to explore the museum through the stories of their ancestors. Visitors also can use the storytelling room to share their own life stories. Free.

SCENIC DRIVES 🐾 **Bainbridge Heritage Tour** (229-246-4774). Brochures can be picked up from several locations: the Bainbridge–Decatur County Chamber of Commerce (see *Guidance*); **Main Street–Tourism Office** (229-248-2000; www.bainbridgecity.com), 107 South Broad Street; or the Southwest Georgia Visitor Information Center (see *Guidance*). Several magnificent mansions from the turn of the 20th century are described.

WALKING TOURS 🐾 **Fort Gaines Walking Tour** (Clay County Visitors Bureau and Information Center: 229-768-2248; www.fortgaines.com), Clay County Library, 208 Hancock Street, Fort Gaines. The tour includes 34 historic sites. Brochures can be picked up at the library or at George T. Bagby State Park and Lodge, off GA 39 in Fort Gaines.

✴ To Do

BIRDING 🐾 ✿ ♿ **Southern Rivers Birding Trail** (478-994-1438). More than 263 species of birds, 20 of them rare and endangered, inhabit the area. This 30-site Georgia Department of Natural Resources trail winds its way from the rolling hills of the Georgia Piedmont to the Coastal Plain and eventually to the Okefenokee Swamp. Many of the prime observation sites are located along the Chattahoochee and Flint rivers. Maps and bird lists are available at local visitors centers, on the River Way South website (www.riverwaysouth .org), or by calling the number at the beginning of this listing.

BOATING Numerous opportunities are available for sailing, motorboating, waterskiing, canoeing, kayaking, and the use of personal watercraft on **Lake Walter F. George** (see *Green Space—Lakes*) and **Lake George W. Andrews.** Boaters are urged to be cautious of commercial barge traffic, possible underwater hazards, and low-hanging power lines.

FISHING Although Georgia and Alabama have a reciprocal agreement honoring each other's fishing licenses, the two states differ in daily limits and size restrictions for some species, so check ahead. Bank fishing is excellent at public fishing docks, by bridges, and at the mouths of creeks. The Georgia Department of Natural Resources maintains a series of fish attractors for better fishing. Cedar trees have been placed in the lakes to create new fish concentration areas, and these are marked with buoys.

GOLF 🏌 **Meadow Links Golf Course at George T. Bagby State Park and Lodge** (pro shop: 229-768-3714 or 1-877-591-5574; tee times: 1-800-434-0982; www.gastate parks.org/GeorgeTBagby or www.golfgeorgia.com), GA 39, Fort Gaines. Open 8–dusk except Christmas Day; tee times can be scheduled by reservation, which is particularly recommended on weekends and holidays. The state park features Meadow Links, an 18-hole, 7,007-yard, par-72, Willard Byrd–designed golf course that challenges any golfer. This newest state park course was named the sixth-best new affordable public course in America when it opened in 1998. Amenities include a pro shop, snack bar, and instruction. Golf packages are available combined with accommodations in the park's lodge or cottages (see *Lodging—Cottages and Cabins* and *Lodging—Inns and Resorts*). $30–37.

WINERY TOURS 🍷 ♿ **Still Pond Vineyard and Winery** (229-792-6382 or 1-800-475-1193; www.stillpond.com), 1575 Still Pond Road, Arlington. Open 10–5 Monday–Saturday. Still Pond is the largest winery in the state as well as the only winery in south Georgia. At Still Pond, you'll find acres and acres of muscadine (also known as scuppernong or swamp grapes) vines. Visitors can tour the vineyards and winery, and then enjoy complimentary tastings of the 11 Still Pond premium wines from the comfort of a custom-made rocking chair. Tastings of other Georgia wines are available for a small fee. In addition to producing its own wines, Still Pond Winery also supplies muscadine juice to other wineries and retailers. The gift shop sells Still Pond wines, wine-related gifts, and cheeses. Several special events occur throughout the year, including spring, summer, and fall wine festivals, and a Christmas open house. Free.

✳ Green Space

LAKES 🏊 ⛵ ♿ **Lake Seminole** (229-662-2001; www.sam.usace.army.mil/op/rec /seminole), Donalsonville. When completed in 1957, Jim Woodruff Lock and Dam created the 37,500-acre lake at the confluence of the Chattahoochee and Flint rivers. The lake was named for the last Native American tribe that was pushed out of Georgia into central Florida. Interpretive displays can be found at the Lake Seminole Visitor Center at the Resource Management Office in nearby Chattahoochee, Florida. The lake's 376 miles of shoreline extend 30 miles up the Chattahoochee and 35 miles up the Flint. The lock and dam improve navigation, generate electricity, and provide recreation. Before construction, the

THE LEGEND OF STILL POND

Although we pictured this isolated pond at the vineyard and winery as being tranquil and serene, therefore "still," that's not how the pond got its name. During the Civil War, the landowner had a still on the banks of the pond, where he turned out peach brandy for exhausted Confederate soldiers to give them some comfort, relaxation, and escape.

Chattahoochee was only 3 feet deep. Today, a channel 9 feet deep and 100 feet wide allows commercial river traffic to reach Columbus on the Chattahoochee and Bainbridge on the Flint. The area's moderate climate and sandy, acid soils produce a diversity of distinctive Coastal Plain flora, which in turn supports a vast abundance of mammalian, reptilian, amphibian, bird, and fish species. In fact, Lake Seminole is one of the most highly regarded fishing lakes in North America for largemouth bass, striped and hybrid bass, bream, crappie, and catfish. In addition to fishing, the lake is popular for swimming, boating, and waterskiing. Numerous boat ramps make access to the lake easy. Fishing supplies, licenses, and other supplies are readily available at marinas and bait and tackle shops. Boat rentals are also available at marinas. You can cruise all the way from Columbus, Georgia, to Panama City Beach, Florida, by going through the locks (call the superintendent for schedules). Shore-based activities include hiking, hunting, camping, bird-watching, and nature photography.

🐾 ✿ ♿ **Lake Walter F. George, U.S. Army Corps of Engineers Visitors Center** (229-768-2516 or 1-866-772-9542; www.sam.usace.army.mil/op/rec/wfg), 427 Eufaula Road, off GA 39, Fort Gaines. Lake open daily dawn–dusk; visitors center open 8–4:30 weekdays year-round, plus 9:30–6 Saturday and Sunday in summer. The 48,000-acre lake occupies 85 miles of the Chattahoochee River separating Georgia and Alabama (on the Alabama side, it's called Lake Eufaula). The lake boasts 640 miles of shoreline, 13 Corps of Engineers day-use parks, 8 county and local day-use parks, and 4 campgrounds. The day-use parks on the Georgia side of the lake are Cool Branch and East Bank. Some of the day-use parks offer beaches, boat ramps, fishing docks and piers, picnic tables, horseshoe pits, and volleyball areas. Most of them have restrooms. Fishing is a major attraction, with the principal species being largemouth bass, white bass, crappie, channel catfish, and bream. Fishing is good from boats, banks, and piers at the mouth of tributary creeks and along several bridges. The two states have reciprocal acceptance of state-issued fishing licenses. The lake also offers boating, camping, swimming, and waterskiing. Access to lake free; day-use areas with beaches have a $4 daily fee; those with boat ramps have a $3 use fee.

NATURE PRESERVES AND PARKS 🐾 ✿ ♿ **Earl May Boat Basin and Cheney Griffin Park** (229-248-2012), Boat Basin Circle, Bainbridge. Open daily. This 500-acre park on the banks of the Flint River features a visitors center, swimming area in a spring-fed lake, boat-launching ramps, fishing pier, 3.4 miles of hiking and nature trails, a boardwalk along the river, camping, playground, historic steam locomotive, lighted tennis courts, and a performance amphitheater where monthly concerts are held from May to October. Free.

🐾 ✿ ♿ ❀ **George T. Bagby State Park and Lodge** (229-768-2571; lodging reservations: 1-800-864-7275; www.gastateparks.org/GeorgeTBagby), 330 Bagby Parkway, off GA 39, Fort Gaines. Open 7 AM–10 PM daily. Located on 48,000-acre **Lake Walter F. George** (see *Lakes*), the 700-acre resort park offers endless water sports. The state record for a blue catfish was caught here in 2010. Water enthusiasts are drawn to its swimming beach, pool (lodge and cottage guests only), full-service marina, docks and boat ramps, and canoe and fishing boat rentals. Other recreational amenities include an award-winning golf course with a pro shop (see *To Do—Golf*), tennis courts, bike rentals, 3 miles of hiking trails through hardwoods and pines, beach volleyball, and picnicking. Bird-watching and wildlife observation are popular activities, too. Accommodations are available in a lodge, in cottages, and in campsites (see *Lodging*), and a restaurant is also on-site (see *Where to Eat—Eating Out*). Pets are permitted in the campground and selected cottages, but not the lodge. Special events throughout the year include a summer nature photography contest, Labor Day celebration and luau, Halloween celebration, and holiday open house. Parking $5.

Kolomoki Mounds Historic Park (229-724-2150; www.gastaeparks.org/KolomokiMounds). The centerpiece of the park is the Native American archaeological site (see *To See—Historic*

Homes and Sites). However, the 1,294-acre park offers recreational facilities including a 50-
acre and an 80-acre lake for both fishing and boating. There is a dock and a boat ramp. Private boats are allowed with a 10 horsepower limit. Pedal boats and canoes are rented in season. Other amenities include picnicking, miniature golf (additional fee), and 5 miles of trails. Camping is available as well (see *Lodging—Campgrounds*). Parking $5.

❦ ☙ ⚅ **Mayhaw Wildlife Management Area** (229-430-4254; www.georgiawildlife.com), north of Colquitt; call for directions. Open 24/7. The 4,700-acre preserve is perfect for birdwatching, hiking, camping, and hunting, and there is also a firing range (open sunrise–sunset Tuesday–Sunday). Mostly dirt roads take visitors through hardwood bottoms, cypress-gum wetlands, and young and mature pines. Birdwatchers enjoy the ibis and wood storks that congregate here during the summer. Georgia Outdoor Recreation Pass (GORP) required for anyone 16–64 who does not already have a hunting or fishing license: $3.50 for three days.

❦ ☙ ⚅ ☀ **Seminole State Park** (229-861-3137; lodging reservations: 1-800-864-7275; www.gastateparks.org/Seminole), 7870 State Park Drive, off GA 253, Donalsonville. Open 7 AM–10 PM daily. Lake Seminole, with 37,500 surface acres, is rated the fifth-best bass-fishing lake in the nation (see *Lakes*). Naturally it is immensely popular for fishing but also for all other water sports, including boating, swimming, and waterskiing, as well as for bird-watching. Although the lake is shallow, natural lime sinkholes create areas of cool, clear water that attract a variety of fish. The 604-acre park, which boasts one of the largest longleaf pine forest in the state park system, features a swimming beach, five boat ramps, three docks, picnic area, 2.2-mile nature trail, and miniature golf (additional fee). Georgia's state reptile, the endangered gopher tortoise, resides along the nature trail, which interprets the wire-grass habitat. Visitors may also see alligators, osprey, and eagles. Canoe and boat rentals are available. Accommodations are available in campsites and cottages (see *Lodging—Campgrounds* and *Lodging—Cottages and Cabins*). The park is located near a wildlife management area, which attracts duck and deer hunters—many of whom stay at the park. Parking $5.

RIVERS ❦ ☙ **Chattahoochee River.** Open dawn–dusk daily. The Chattahoochee River begins as a mere trickle in north Georgia; wends its way through metro Atlanta, where it is designated as the Chattahoochee River National Recreation Area; and then creates the border between Georgia and Alabama before emptying into Lake Seminole at the Georgia-Florida border. The river has rapids in its upper reaches, but the river in this region flows placidly through the Coastal Plain. Although the Chattahoochee is navigable up to Columbus and was once a major transportation artery, today its main uses are for power generation, drinking water, and recreation, and it remains one of the most important ecological and economic assets to the region. Public boat ramps and day-use areas afford opportunities for fishing, boating, waterskiing, bird-watching, picnicking, and hiking. Free.

❦ ☙ **Flint River,** which begins in metro Atlanta and flows all the way to the Florida border into Lake Seminole, has three distinct sections. The Lower Flint River Basin, in the Bainbridge area, flows through Coastal Plain and Dougherty Plain. Many natural springs create blue holes, where swimmers cool off on hot summer days because the water temperature is 68 degrees year-round. These cool temperatures are critical to the survival of the Gulf strain of striped bass. Meanwhile, shoals in the river provide habitats for several rare and threatened fish and freshwater shellfish. When the river reaches Bainbridge, it is discharging 3 million to 11 million gallons of water daily, which is essential to the ecosystems of Lake Seminole, the Apalachicola River, Apalachicola Bay, and the Gulf of Mexico. The river provides innumerable opportunities for swimming, fishing, camping, waterskiing, boating, bird-watching, wildlife observation, and plant identification.

✷ Lodging
BED & BREAKFASTS
In Bainbridge
The Commodore Bed and Breakfast (229-248-0081; www.commodorebedand breakfast.com), 320 Washington Street. The magnificent white-columned antebellum home is the epitome of a Southern mansion. Built in 1840, the virgin longleaf-pine structure is supported by 40-foot-high cypress columns. Guest rooms and public spaces are filled with antiques, fine furniture, and collectibles. The second-floor sitting area features an art gallery. All four accommodations feature a sitting area; two have private baths and two share, making them ideal for families or friends traveling together. Beautifully landscaped grounds boast fountains, a gazebo, and a swimming pool. All this within walking distance of the downtown square and the Flint River. A full breakfast is included. No pets. Smoking outdoors only. Not wheelchair accessible. $95–115.

In Colquitt
♂ & **Tarrer Inn** (229-758-2888 or 1-888-282-7737; www.tarrerinn.com), 155 South Cuthbert Street. The inn, built in 1905 and restored in 1994, is listed on the National Register of Historic Places and is the recipient of the prestigious Georgia Trust for Historic Preservation award. Its 12 elegant accommodations are furnished with fine period antiques and boast hand-painted fireplaces and luxurious baths. From embroidered bed linens to wireless Internet access, the inn provides a combination of elegance and convenience. Continental breakfast is included. For other meals, authentic Southern cuisine is featured at sumptuous lunch and dinner buffets in the dining rooms (see *Where to Eat—Dining Out*). Outstanding personal service proves the truth of Southern hospitality. No smoking. $99–125.

In Fort Gaines
♀ & **Sutlive House Bed and Breakfast** (229-768-3546), 204 South Washington Street. Two suites, each with a bedroom, sitting room, and private bath with a Jacuzzi tub, are offered in the 1820 plantation-style home. No smoking. $90–125.

CAMPGROUNDS
In Bainbridge
♀ ♂ **Wingate's Marina** (229-246-0658; www.wingateslodge.com), 139 Wingate Road. Wingate's offers a variety of lodging options and a full-service marina with two in-and-out ramps. The campground features a dump station, 30- to 50-amp hookups, a bathhouse, picnic tables, and fire rings. Wingate's also offers a variety of brick cottages, two-bedroom log cabins, motel rooms, and mobile homes. Campsites $20 with full hookups, rooms and cottages $50, cabins $75.

In Blakely
Kolomoki Mounds Historic Park (reservations: 1-800-864-7275). The park offers 24 tent, trailer, and RV sites. $25–27. See *To See—Historic Homes and Sites*.

In Donalsonville
Seminole State Park (lodging reservations: 1-800-864-7275) offers 50 tent, trailer, and RV sites. $25–28. See *Green Space—Nature Preserves and Parks*.

In Fort Gaines
♀ ♂ & **Cotton Hill Park Campground** (229-768-3061; www.reserveusa.com), GA 39 North. The Corps of Engineers campground, which is open year-round, offers 91 campsites, all with full water, electric, and sewage hookups, and 10 tent, electric-only sites. Many of the sites are lakefront. Amenities include a fish-cleaning station, coin laundry, three bathhouses with showers, a boat ramp and courtesy dock, playgrounds, a dump station, and wheelchair-accessible restrooms and fishing. The campground also features a hiking trail with interpretive markers for nature lovers. Tent sites $20, other sites $24; reservations must be made at least four days in advance; two-night minimum on weekends, three-night minimum on holiday weekends.

♀ ♂ & ✿ **George T. Bagby State Park and Lodge** (229-768-2571 or 1-800-864-7275; www.gastateparks.org/GeorgeTBagby), off GA 39, Fort Gaines. The park offers five tent, trailer, and RV sites, as well as a pioneer campground. $23–28. See *Green Space—Nature Preserves and Parks*.

COTTAGES AND CABINS

In Bainbridge
See **Wingate's Marina** under *Campgrounds*.

In Donalsonville
🍴 ♿ & 🐾 **Seminole State Park** (lodging reservations: 1-800-864-7275) offers 14 fully equipped cottages, many of which are located at the water's edge and have excellent lake views. Two are dog friendly ($40 per dog; maximum two). $125–135. See *Green Space—Nature Preserves and Parks*.

In Fort Gaines
🍴 ♿ & 🐾 **George T. Bagby State Park and Lodge** (229-768-2571 or 1-800-864-7275; www.gastateparks.org/GeorgeTBagby), off GA 39, Fort Gaines. Guests can stay in one of five two-bedroom cottages, each with digital satellite TV, fireplace, a kitchen with stove and refrigerator, living and dining areas, and all utensils and linens. One is dog friendly ($40 per dog; maximum two). $125–150. See *Green Space—Nature Preserves and Parks*.

INNS AND RESORTS

In Fort Gaines
🍴 ♿ & **George T. Bagby State Park and Lodge** (229-768-2571 or 1-800-864-7275; www.gastateparks.org/GeorgeTBagby), off GA 39, Fort Gaines. The park's lodge features 60 rooms, including two junior suites, as well as a restaurant (see *Where to Eat—Eating Out*). Many of the traditional hotel rooms offer a view of the lake. Each accommodation has all the modern conveniences. In addition, there is a group lodge that sleeps 10. No smoking. Rooms $65–125; group lodge $125–150. See *Green Space—Nature Preserves and Parks*.

✳ Where to Eat
DINING OUT
In Colquitt
& **Tarrer Inn** (229-758-2888; www.tarrerinn.com), 155 South Cuthbert Street. Open 11:30–2 Tuesday–Friday and Sunday, 6–9 Friday. Also open for dinner Thursday and Saturday evenings during *Swamp Gravy* performances (see *Entertainment—*

Theater). Several dining rooms ensure intimate dining. Rich in the tradition of Southern cooking, the restaurant serves buffet-style meals with regional dishes such as fried chicken, glazed pork roast, and catfish, along with a vast array of vegetables, salads, breads, and desserts like peach cobbler, pecan pie, strawberry trifle, and banana pudding. No smoking. $9.50–12.

EATING OUT
In Bainbridge
🍴 ♿ & **Boyd's Pit Bar-B-Que and Grill** (229-246-0797), 721 East Calhoun Street. Open 11–3 Monday–Wednesday, 11–9 Thursday–Saturday. The specialty here is rubbed and hickory-smoked ribs cooked "Southern, smoky, and slow." Diners can get a half slab, whole slab, basket, or plate of ribs. Check for the night of the all-you-can-eat ribs special. If ribs aren't your thing, there are a wide variety of sandwiches, salads, plates, and burgers, as well as a Kids Korner menu. The eatery advertises its fried tenderloin sandwich as the largest sandwich on a bun. No smoking. $3.75 for a sandwich to $17.49 for a whole slab.

In Fort Gaines
🍴 ♿ & **Pilot House Grille at George T. Bagby State Park and Lodge** (229-768-2571). Open 7–10 AM and 11 AM–2 PM daily, 5–8 PM Monday–Saturday. The lakeside restaurant offers sumptuous buffets, as well as an à la carte menu. No smoking. Breakfast $3.25–7, lunch $5.50–8, dinner $11–18.

TEAROOMS
In Cuthbert
🍴 & **Julianna's Antiques, Gifts, and Tea Parlor** (229-732-5523), 80 South Peachtree Street. Open 10–5 Tuesday–Saturday. Afternoon and high tea served Friday and Saturday by reservation only. Located in the original Bank of Randolph, which was built in the 1800s, the Victorian-style tearoom serves English tea with a Southern twist, in the parlor or in the Savannah-style garden. Afternoon tea features tea sandwiches and sweets; high tea also features an entrée. The ambience, service, and food are flawless. Even if you don't have tea, peruse the

gift shop for wonderful finds including irresistible gifts for the tea lover, as well as other gift items, antiques, and collectibles. No smoking. Afternoon tea $14.95, high tea $18.95, lunch items less than $7.

✳ Entertainment

MUSIC 🎵 🎷 ⚬ **River Music Concert Series** (229-248-2010), performing arts amphitheater at **Earl May Boat Basin and Cheney Griffin Park** (see *Green Space—Nature Preserves and Parks*), Boat Basin Circle, Bainbridge. Call for a schedule of events or check the city website. Concerts occur throughout the summer and feature a variety of musical genres, from gospel to barbershop to Army band selections to '50s music. The July concert also includes fireworks. Bring a blanket or lawn chair and a picnic. Most concerts free.

THEATER **Bainbridge Little Theatre** (229-246-8345; www.bainbridgelittle theatre.com), 220 East Troupe Street, Bainbridge (mailing address: P.O. Box 1245, Bainbridge 39818). Check the website or call for a schedule of performances. Entertaining Bainbridge residents and those from the surrounding area since the 1970s, this award-winning theater presents four productions each year, including dramas, comedies, and musicals. Plays: adults $12, students $7; musicals: adults $15, students $10.

Cotton Hall Theater, *Swamp Gravy* (229-758-6686; tickets: 1-800-514-3849; www.swampgravy.com), 164 East Main Street, Colquitt. The play is performed weekends in March and October and during the annual Mayhaw Festival in April (see *Special Events*). Check the website or call for a schedule of performances. The Museum of Southern Culture is open only during performances. The restored 70-year-old cotton warehouse is the home of the **Museum of Southern Culture** (see *To See—Museums*) and the performance venue of Georgia's official folklife play, *Swamp Gravy*, which depicts the ordinary, comic, and tragic life and culture of rural southwest Georgia families and communi-

ties through original and traditional song and dance. The play, which has a cast of more than 100, was first performed in 1992. With a new play created each year, however, it's still attracting scores of playgoers. All the plays are based on real-life stories obtained from taped interviews and adapted for the stage by a local playwright. *Swamp Gravy* attracted national attention through a Cultural Olympiad appearance at the 1996 Centennial Olympic Summer Games and another at the Kennedy Center. Cotton Hall, which features four stages, arena-style seating, and a state-of-the-art lighting system, hosts other performances throughout the year. Performed in January and April, *May-Haw* is a hilarious musical. A show featuring children and youth is often performed in the summer. Tickets about $27.

⚬ **Olive Theater** (229-524-8209), 203 South Woolfork Avenue, Donalsonville. Once a 1930s-era movie palace, the theater has been restored and upgraded to a state-of-the-art performance venue for the productions of the Seminole County Arts Council. Call for a schedule of performances and ticket prices.

✳ Selective Shopping

Market on the Square (229-758-8480), 164 South First Street, Colquitt. Open 10–5:30 weekdays, 10–2 Saturday; special hours during holidays and productions of *Swamp Gravy*. Market on the Square is a mini mall with 20 shops featuring antiques, arts and crafts, jewelry, gifts, home accents, Christmas items, children's clothing, and food items such as mayhaw jelly and peanut products.

WHAT IS SWAMP GRAVY?

Indigenous to the area, the stewlike dish is made by pouring the drippings from frying fish over tomatoes, potatoes, onions, and whatever else is at hand. It can be a side dish or even the whole meal if there isn't enough fish for everyone.

T&W Auction Company (229-400-8170), 3017 Thomasville Highway, US 84 East, Bainbridge. Auctions at 6 PM on second and last Saturday of each month; previews 9–4 weekdays. The company specializes in antiques auctions and also does estate and business liquidation auctions. Shoppers may find flow blue, various china, pottery, oil paintings, collectibles such as Hummels, art glass, advertising items, jewelry, old coins, Persian rugs, tools, and much more. Although much of the excitement is the auction itself, you don't have to be present; left bids, online bids, and phone bids are accepted.

✳ Special Events

January: **Rattlesnake Roundup** (229-377-3663). This event, a popular attraction since the 1960s, is held on the last Saturday in January at the Rattlesnake Grounds in Whigham. In addition to snake-handling demonstrations, the festival features arts and crafts, concessions, entertainment, and children's rides. Free.

April: **National Mayhaw Festival** (229-758-2400; www.colquitt-georgia.com). Held the third weekend in April at the Spring Creek Recreational Park in Colquitt, the festival celebrates the mayhaw, small red berries often used in jams and jellies. The event includes a parade, arts and crafts, entertainment, children's activities, and lots of good food. The musical comedy *May-Haw* is performed Friday and Saturday nights. Festival free; some events have a charge; *May-Haw* performances $26.56.

July: **Tama Intertribal Pow-Wow** (229-762-3165). Held over the July Fourth weekend in Whigham's Tama Tribal Town, the event is sponsored by the Lower Muscogee Creek Tribe. The festival includes Native American crafts and exhibits, as well as dancing, drumming, and storytelling. Bluegrass and gospel are also featured. $3 per car. Pets must be kept leashed.

November: **Christmas at the Fort** (229-768-2249). The annual arts and crafts fair, held at Fort Gaines's **Frontier Village** (see *To See—Historic Homes and Sites*), features arts and crafts vendors, Christmas items, food, continuous entertainment, and demonstrations of old-time skills. Festival free; some events have a charge.

Mule Day (229-377-3663; www.calvary lionsmuleday.com). Held in Calvary the first Saturday in November, the festival, which attracts 75,000 visitors, features a parade of mule-drawn wagons; mule judging; a mule show; contests in skills such as plowing; demonstrations of cane grinding, meal grinding, and syrup making; all-day entertainment; arts and crafts booths; a flea market; a slingshot turkey shoot; and food. The Mule Museum takes visitors back to the days of shade tobacco farms. Events prior to Mule Day include a golf tournament, trail ride, chicken dinner, and auction. Festival free; some events have a charge.

Swine Time Festival (229-246-3300; www.swinetimefestival.com). Held the Saturday of Thanksgiving weekend in Climax, the festival features a parade, food, arts and crafts, a homemade quilt auction, entertainment, and demonstrations of old-time skills. Contests include the best-dressed pig, hog and turkey calling, pig racing, a greased pig chase, corn shucking, chitterlings eating, syrup making, and baby crawling. Antique engines and vehicles are displayed. There is a historic log cabin to visit, and there are camper sites available at a very reasonable price. Festival free; some activities have a small charge.

COLUMBUS

Although Columbus is far inland from the Gulf of Mexico, the Chattahoochee River is navigable to Columbus, making it a real river city. Therefore, in the 1800s it was a shipbuilding center, and, in fact, the Confederate ironclad CSS *Jackson* was built there. Unfortunately, before it could be put into service, it was destroyed by Union troops, with only its below-water hull surviving. It rested on the bottom of the Chattahoochee until it was recovered in the 1960s. Today it is the centerpiece of the Port Columbus Civil War Naval Museum (see *To See—Museums*).

Throughout the years, three things have played major roles in Columbus's history: cotton, clay, and Coca-Cola.

Columbus also has a rich African American heritage. In addition to Mother of the Blues "Ma" Rainey, Columbus was the home of Eugene Bullard, the world's first black combat aviator, and Horace King, a former slave who became a master bridge builder.

Novelist Carson McCullers, author of *The Heart is a Lonely Hunter* and *The Member of the Wedding*, was also a Columbus native. Visitors can walk or drive by her house at 1519 Stark Avenue, now privately owned, and read the historical marker.

Today bustling Columbus is the state's third-largest city, with a population of 189,885. Among the oddities in Columbus is the Scramble Dog, a strange concoction served at the Dinglewood Pharmacy (see *Where to Eat—Eating Out*). The city also claims to have the highest concentration of barbecue restaurants anywhere.

Nearby is Fort Benning, the world's largest infantry training center and home of the National Infantry Museum (see *To See—Museums*). Tiny Buena Vista is the home of Pasaquan, the colorful compound of an audacious artist (see *To See—Historic Homes and Sites*).

GUIDANCE For information about Columbus and the greater Columbus area, contact the **Columbus Convention and Visitors Bureau** (706-322-1613 or 1-800-999-1613; www .visitcolumbusga.com), 900 Front Avenue, Columbus 31901. Open 8:30–5:30 weekdays, 10–2 Saturday. Stop by to see a video orientation to the city and pick up brochures.

There's also a **Georgia Visitor Information Center** (706-649-7455), 1751 Williams Road, Columbus 31904, that is open daily 8:30–5:30.

GETTING THERE *By air:* **Columbus Metropolitan Airport** (706-324-2449; www.fly columbusga.com) is served by **American** and **Delta Airlines.** Car rentals are available, and several hotels provide shuttle service.

By bus: **Greyhound Lines** (1-800-231-2222; www.greyhound.com), 818 Veterans Parkway, provides bus service to and from Columbus.

By car: Columbus is on the Georgia-Alabama line. From the north it is reached by I-85, then I-185. From the south it is reached by US 280. The major east–west route is US 80, plus GA 26 and GA 96.

By train: There is no **AMTRAK** service to Columbus. Train riders have to transfer by bus or car from Atlanta, which is three hours to the north.

MEDICAL EMERGENCY For a medical emergency, call 911.

NEIGHBORHOODS Columbus has several designated historic neighborhoods: **Uptown,** which includes the Springer Opera House; **High Uptown,** which includes opulent residences such as the **Rankin House** (see *To See—Historic Homes and Sites*), known for its ornamental ironwork; and the **Historic District,** which includes the Chattahoochee promenade and the **Port Columbus Civil War Naval Museum** (see *To See—Museums*).

✳ To See

HISTORIC HOMES AND SITES ✿ ✐ **Pasaquan** (Pasaquan Preservation Society: 912-649-9444; www.pasaquan.com), Eddie Martin Road, off County 78, Buena Vista. Open the first Saturday of the month May–November or by appointment (but it's worth the effort). This bizarre 4-acre fantasy compound created by artist Eddie Owens Martin (1908–1988), son of a local sharecropper, is one of the most unusual sights anyone will ever see and one of the premier outsider-art sites in the country. Martin, who freely admitted to dabbling in drugs, mystic religions, and the occult, dubbed himself St. EOM (his initials), the Wizard of Pasaquan. Martin claimed that God spoke to him and told him to create Pasaquan, which he translated to mean "bringing the past and future together." Drawing from African, Asian, and Native American mythology, he created flamboyantly painted outdoor sculptures, pagodas, temples, totem poles, and walls. If these figures were envisioned when Martin was in a drug-induced state, it must have been a happy place considering the many representations of smiling humans and grinning snakes. Inside the main house, floors, walls, ceilings, and furniture are also painted within an inch of their lives. Upon his death, Martin willed the compound to the Marion County Historical Society, which struggles to preserve it. Admission $5, children under six free (but the society would be ever so grateful for any additional amount you might feel like donating).

✿ **Rankin House** (706-322-0756; www .nscdaga.org/nscdaga-museums/the-rankin -house/), 1440 Second Avenue, Columbus. Open 9–5 weekdays. Located in the High Uptown Historic District and serving as the headquarters of the Historic Columbus Foundation, the grand 1860s mansion features exquisite iron grillwork, cast-iron windowsills and doorframes, and a flying balcony outside. Heart-pine floors and a solid-walnut double stairway grace the interior, as well as lovely Victorian-era antiques representing the era 1850–1870. The National Society of Colonial Dames of America–Georgia assisted with the restoration and maintains two rooms. Free.

THE QUIRKY COMPOUND KNOWN AS PASAQUAN OVERFLOWS WITH COLORFUL ART.

MUSEUMS 🍴 🎨 ♿ **Columbus Museum** (706-748-2562; www.columbusmuseum.com), 1251 Wynnton Road, Columbus. Open 10–5 Tuesday–Saturday (until 8 on Thursday), 1–5 Sunday. The second-largest museum in the state, the Columbus Museum contains collections of Native American, American impressionist, and contemporary mixed-media art, as well as American furniture and many changing exhibits. The Chattahoochee Legacy is a regional history gallery where a film and life-size period settings tell the story of the Chattahoochee River Valley. Here visitors see dwellings, an old schoolroom, exhibitions on Rood Creek Indians, and old photos. Hands-on activities in the children's discovery gallery encourage curiosity and imagination. Free.

🍴 🎨 ♿ **National Infantry Museum and Soldier Center** (706-685-5800; www.national infantrymuseum.com), 1775 Legacy Way, Fort Benning. Open 9–9 Tuesday–Saturday, 11–5 Sunday. Fort Benning is the world's largest infantry training center, so it's no surprise that a museum connected with the foot soldier would be located here or that it houses one of the most complete collections of military memorabilia from U.S. infantrymen. The striking new building is located just outside the gates to the fort. The evolution of the dogface is chronicled from the 1607 wilderness of Virginia to the French and Indian War to the 1991 Persian Gulf War. This museum has an example of every gun ever used by the U.S. Army, and other artifacts from each of America's military engagements are displayed, including uniforms, footwear, mess equipment, helmets, vehicles, military band instruments, captured enemy paraphernalia, military documents signed by each of America's presidents, silver presentation pieces, and much more. Some of the more interesting artifacts include a document signed by John Hancock, a bust of Adolph Hitler, a gas mask for a horse, and a prisoner of war uniform. The collection is so immense it cannot all be exhibited at the same time, so displays change often, giving even frequent visitors something new to see. Films are shown daily in the Infantry Theater and in 3-D IMAX theater (fee). Combat simulators allow participants to experience a Humvee, Black Hawk, and/or rifle range (fee). The museum's gift shop sells military-related bears, books, toys, and many other items. Meals from light snacks to more substantial meals are available in the Fife and Drum Restaurant (open 11–5 Tuesday– Saturday, noon–5 Sunday). Outside, visitors can tour Heritage Walk, Founders Circle, and the Memorial Walk of Honor, as well as the World War II Street, the only fully preserved set of series 700 buildings in existence. These seven buildings include a barracks, mess hall, orderly room, supply room, headquarters, chapel, and Gen. George S. Patton's sleeping quarters, as well as a Sherman tank. Free, but $5 donation appreciated. IMAX films: adults $8–10; seniors, military, and youth $7–9; children 4–12 $6–8. Infantry Adventures Combat Simulators $10–20. Rifle range $7–10.

🍴 🎨 ♿ **Port Columbus Civil War Naval Museum** (706-327-9798; www.portcolumbus .org), 1002 Victory Drive, Columbus. Open 10–4:30 Tuesday–Saturday, 12:30–4:30 Sunday and Monday. This museum, dedicated to the naval battles of the Civil War, was created to display the remains of two Confederate Navy ships. The museum's star attraction is what remains of the CSS *Jackson,* the largest surviving scratch-made ironclad ship in the world. Since so little of it is left, a steel ghost skeleton was constructed over the hull to give an idea of the ship's size. The hull can be viewed from above and below. The museum's hundreds of exhibits also feature remnants of the CSS *Chattahoochee,* a warship built in Columbus and scuttled by Union troops; a partial replica of the USS *Hartford,* Union admiral David Farragut's flagship; a full-size sectional reconstruction of the USS *Monitor;* as well as the country's only full-size ironclad Civil War combat simulator. Both Confederate and Union weapons and uniforms are shown, as well as rare Confederate naval flags. To fully understand the story, begin with the audiovisual presentations about the Union attack. Adults $7.50, seniors and active military $6.50, students $6.

NATURAL BEAUTY SPOTS A **waterfall** in downtown Columbus marks the north-ernmost navigable point on the Chattahoochee River. It can be seen from the **RiverWalk** (see *Special Places*).

SCENIC DRIVES Purchase an area map and enjoy the 68-mile drive from **Columbus to Providence Canyon.** There are good secondary roads that meander south of Columbus, through the forested part of Fort Benning Military Reservation, through various small towns, past the scenic Chattahoochee River and the Walter F. George Lake and Dam, and continuing through Florence Marina State Park to beautiful Providence Canyon State Park. Other points of interest along the way include American Indian mounds and Westville Historic Village (c. 1800s). For more information about these sites, see the Americus chapter.

SELF-GUIDED TOURS **Black Heritage Trail Tour.** Pick up a brochure for this driving tour from the **Columbus Convention and Visitors Bureau** (see *Guidance*). Twenty-nine sites on this drive-by tour include historic black churches, cemeteries, the Liberty Theater, and the last home of Gertrude "Ma" Rainey. Born to minstrel-show parents in Columbus in 1886, Gertrude Pridgett began performing early. She married Will Rainey, but it didn't last long. She took on the name "Ma" and went on to a career as one of the first female recording stars, earning the titles "Queen of the Blues" and "Mother of the Blues." Someday the house may be a museum, but for now visitors can only drive by her home at 805 Fifth Avenue. Visitors also can drive by the home of Eugene Ballard, the first African American combat pilot.

SPECIAL PLACES ❀ ✿ ♿ **Columbus RiverWalk,** located along the scenic bluffs and banks of the Chattahoochee River. The 15-mile linear park is a favorite spot for walking, cycling, skating, and fishing. The brick-paved promenade is punctuated with decorative ironwork, gazebos, fountains, historical markers, sculptures, and benches. Free.

✴ To Do

FOR FAMILIES ❀ ✿ ♿ **Coca-Cola Space Science Center** (706-649-1470; www.ccssc .org), 701 Front Avenue, Columbus. Open 10–4 Monday–Friday, 10:30–8 Saturday. Science center open only to groups of at least 20, but observatory and theater open to all. *Hands-on* is the byword at this space and astronomy facility, one of 31 Challenger centers in America, where visitors can experience landing on the moon or probing a comet's tail. See a full-size replica of the nose cone of a NASA space shuttle orbiter, the first Coca-Cola drink dispenser taken into space, a space suit, and an interactive view of 88 constellations. The Mead Observatory is open once a month for astronomical viewing. At the state-of-the-art Omnisphere Planetarium Theater, spectacular laser concerts, star shows, and children's shows take place. Adults $6, military and students $5, children $4.

❀ ✿ ♿ **Hollywood Connection** (706-321-8286), 1683 Whittlesey Road, Columbus. Open 11:30–9 Sunday–Thursday, 11:30–midnight Friday and Saturday. There's something for everyone in the family here. In addition to megaplex movie theaters with stadium seating, the complex offers Caddyshack miniature golf, Fun Zone amusements and rides, Mind Games arcade, Krazy Kars bumper cars, Ultrazone Laser Tag Arena, Xanadu Skate Center, and a teen club. Animal House is a two-story soft play area for younger kids. Lieutenant's, a '50s-style restaurant, is open for lunch daily. Prices vary by activity.

HORSEBACK RIDING ✿ **Snyder Farms Stables** (706-324-4806), 936 McCrary Road, Fortson. Snyder Farms offers one-hour guided trail rides through 100 acres of wooded countryside. Western riding lessons and camps are also offered. Rides are open to age six and older. Call for rates and hours.

OUTDOOR ADVENTURES ✔ **Chattahoochee Riverwalk Outfitters** (706-660-2999), 1000 Bay Avenue, Columbus. Open 8–8 daily. The company rents bikes, canoes, kayaks, and skates—everything needed for outdoor fun. Call for rates.

TENNIS ✿ ✔ **Cooper Creek Tennis Center** (706-317-4186), 4816 Milgen Road, Columbus. Open 8 AM–10 PM Monday–Thursday, 8–8 Friday and Sunday, 8–6 Saturday. This is the South's largest clay-court tennis facility, with a total of 30 lighted courts. $2.50 an hour for Muscogee County residents, $3.50 an hour during peak hours for nonresidents.

✳ Green Space

LAKES ✿ ✔ ♿ **Lake Walter F. George** (229-768-2516; www.sam.usace.army.mil/op/rec /wfg) boasts 45,000 acres and includes many opportunities for deep-water fishing as well as other water sports. Birdwatchers will want to stay alert as herons, egrets, and the occasional bald eagle inhabit these shores. The lake is ringed with marinas, parks, and recreation areas, as well as a state park.

NATURE PRESERVES AND PARKS ✿ ✔ ♿ **Oxbow Meadows Environmental Learning Center** (706-687-4090; http://oxbow.columbusstate.edu), 3535 South Lumpkin Road, Columbus. Open 9–4 Tuesday–Friday, 10–3 Saturday, noon–5 Sunday. More than 1,600 acres provide homes for native wildlife such as alligators, birds, butterflies, dragonflies, hawks, opossums, owls, and turtles. The center provides opportunities for outdoor education, wildlife observation, and recreation. Two walking trails wind between ponds to allow visitors to see the flora and fauna. The hands-on nature discovery center interprets the natural history of the area with mounted specimens of birds, mammals, and reptiles, along with a small live-animal collection of amphibians, fish, insects, and reptiles. Free.

✳ Lodging

BED & BREAKFASTS

In Buena Vista

✿ **Sign of the Dove Bed and Breakfast** (229-649-3663 or 1-888-690-3663; www .sign-of-the-dove.com), 108 North Church Street. This 1905 historic home is on the National Register of Historic Places. Neoclassical architecture blends Greek and Roman influences with Southern details like the large wraparound porch. Besides the sleeping area, each guest room features a sitting area and a private bath with a clawfoot tub. A restaurant also is on-site. No pets. $75 single or double occupancy includes full breakfast; $100 single occupancy includes a full breakfast and a four-course dinner; $125 double occupancy and up includes a full breakfast and a four-course dinner for two.

In Columbus

♿ **Rothschild-Pound House Inn and Cottages–Cafe 222** (706-322-4075; www

.thepoundhouseinn.com), 201 Seventh Street. A gorgeous Second Empire Italianate painted lady filled with antiques, the mansion offers elegant AAA four-diamond bed & breakfast accommodations—some with whirlpool tubs, balconies, and fireplaces. In addition to starting the day with a full gourmet breakfast, cocktails and hors d'oeuvres are served in the afternoon. In addition to those in the main house, accommodations are offered in four cottages. No smoking. $125–365, special $85 military rate (two-night minimum).

CAMPGROUNDS

In Buena Vista

✿ ✔ **Country Vista Campground** (229-649-2267), 1634 GA 41 South. Amenities include laundry facilities and separate men's and women's bathhouses. Full hookups with water, sewer, and electric are available. Tent sites $14; hookups $18 per day.

ROTHSCHILD-POUND HOUSE INN IN
COLUMBUS

In Columbus

🦐 🐾 **Lake Pines Campground and RV
Park** (706-561-9675; www.lakepines.net),
6404 Garrett Road. Amenities include a
bathhouse, laundry, and swimming pool.
Full hookups with water, sewer, and electric
are available. Tent sites $22 per day for two
people, RV full hookups $35 per day.

INNS AND HOTELS

In Columbus

🐾 ♿ **Marriott Hotel** (706-324-1800), 800
Front Avenue. A section of the riverfront
hotel uses the historic century-old Empire
Mills. A sporting motif sets a relaxing backdrop at Houlihan's. The Grist Mill Coffee
Shop is a kiosk purveying beverages and
pastries. No smoking. $164–195 for stan-
dard room.

✳ Where to Eat

DINING OUT

In Columbus

♿ **Buckhead Grill** (706-571-9995; www
.buckheadbarandgrill.com), 5010 Armour
Road. Open 5–10 daily; opens at noon
Sunday. Menu highlights include USDA-
certified prime Angus beef, fish, pasta, and
ribs, as well as a full array of burgers, salads, and sandwiches. No smoking. $10–25.

In Columbus

🦐 🐾 ♿ **Dinglewood Pharmacy** (706-322-
0616), 1939 Wynnton Road. Open 9–6
weekdays, 10–4 Saturday. Since the 1940s,
the Scramble Dog has been served at the
lunch counter and booths of this 1918-era
pharmacy. Two hot dogs and a bun are split
open; then piled with cheese, chili, dill
pickles, and mustard; then topped with oyster crackers. Why a visitor would want to
order anything else, we can't possibly imagine, but hamburgers, chicken sandwiches,
and deli sandwiches are also on the menu.
No smoking. Wheelchair accessible through
back entrance. Scramble Dog $4.25.

🦐 ♿ **Minnie's Uptown** (706-322-2766),
104 Eighth Street. Open 11–2:30 Sunday–
Friday. This eatery in the historic district
offers award-winning Southern cooking. No
smoking. About $10 per person, including
drinks and dessert.

🦐 🐾 ♿ **Miriam's Café and Gallery** (706-
327-0707), 1330 13th Street. Open 11–3
Monday–Saturday. Miriam's, an upscale
deli with European flair, serves lunch
only. There are creative specials every day

SOFT DRINK CAPITAL

One of Columbus's claims to fame is that it
was the birthplace of the world-famous soft
drink Coca-Cola. A local pharmacist, Dr.
John Stith Pemberton, concocted the original formula for French Wine of Coca, a fore-
runner of Coca-Cola, in his apothecary shop
in 1850 and later dispensed it at a soda
fountain. It wasn't until after the Civil War,
when he moved to Atlanta, that he per-
fected the formula and sold it to Asa Candler for a mere $1,750. When Candler sold it
in 1917, he made $25 million. What Coca-
Cola is worth today is beyond comprehen-
sion. Most folks are amazed to learn that
not only Coca-Cola but Royal Crown Cola
and Nehi were concocted by Columbus citizens as well.

and exciting menu choices. No smoking. About $7.

🍴 ✎ ♿ **The Rankin Quarter** (706-322-8151), 21 East 10th Street. Open 11–3:30 Sunday–Friday. Menu features deli sandwiches, burgers, salads, and grilled items. No smoking. Restaurant wheelchair accessible, but restrooms are not. Less than $8.

✳ Entertainment

MUSIC Columbus Symphony Orchestra (706-323-5059; www.csoga.org), 935 First Avenue, Columbus. Founded in 1855, the CSO was the third symphony in America. It performs concerts October through May at the RiverCenter for the Performing Arts (see next entry). There is also a children's series of concerts. Check the website or call for a schedule of performances and ticket prices.

RiverCenter for the Performing Arts (706-256-3620 or 1-888-332-5200; event hotline: 706-256-3600; www.rivercenter .org), 900 Broadway, Columbus. Box office open noon–5 weekdays. This enormous showplace, the centerpiece of a new arts and entertainment district, contains multiple recital halls and a theater. The facility is the home of the nationally touring Broadway Series, Columbus Symphony Orchestra (see previous entry), Columbus State University Schwob School of Music, and other local music and dance companies. Check the website or call for schedules of events and prices.

NIGHTLIFE ♿ **Oxygen** (706-596-8397), 1040 Broadway, Columbus. Open 9 PM–3 AM Friday and Saturday. Located in the historic district, Oxygen is a high-energy, Top 40 nightclub. Dress is upscale. No smoking. Cover charge $10; ladies admitted free until 11.

PROFESSIONAL SPORTS

✎ **Columbus Cottonmouths Hockey** (706-571-0086; www.cottonmouths.com), 400 Fourth Street, Columbus. The season runs late October–mid-March. Competing for a decade, the Cottonmouths, a Southern Professional Hockey League team, play at the Columbus Civic Center. During the 2004–2005 season, the Cottonmouths won the SPHL President's Cup Championship. Check the website or call for a schedule. $12–28.

THEATER Human Experience Theater (706-323-3689), 1047 Broadway, Columbus. Season runs September–May. Box office open 10–2 Tuesday and Thursday, 2–6 Wednesday, Friday, and Saturday. Unique to this theater is its "bring-your-own-dinner" concept. Call for a schedule and prices.

Liberty Theater Cultural Center (706-653-7566; www.columbusjazzsociety.com /liberty.htm), 823 Eighth Avenue, Columbus. Office open 10–5 weekdays. This historic, 300-seat theater, which opened in 1925, once drew performers such as Marian Anderson, Cab Calloway, Duke Ellington, Ella Fitzgerald, Lena Horne, Ma Rainey, Bessie Smith, and Ethel Waters. When it was built as an African American movie house/performing arts theater, it was actually the biggest theater in town—bigger than any of the whites-only theaters. Now restored and placed on the National Register of Historic Places, the theater once again hosts performances of dramas and musicals. Check the website or call for tours, schedules, and prices.

✎ **Springer Opera House** (706-327-3688; www.springeroperahouse.org), 103 10th Street, Columbus. Tours at 3:30 Monday and Wednesday. A jewel in Columbus's crown, the magnificent plush-and-gilt theater was built in 1871 and saw performances by Irving Berlin, Edwin Booth, John Philip Sousa, Will Rogers, Oscar Wilde, and many other luminaries from the late 1800s through the Great Depression. Like many theaters of the day, it was converted to a movie house and began a long decline. Designated as the State Theater of Georgia, the Springer Opera House has been restored to its 1901 Edwardian splendor. Museum areas on the first and second floors display artifacts and furnishings such as 19th-century theater seats, vintage photographs, portraits, programs, posters, and other memorabilia. The theater's main-stage season September through May hosts Broadway musicals, comedies, and dramas. In addition, there is a colorful Children's Series. The No Shame Theater on Friday nights at 10:30 is a forum for improv, music, comedy, poetry, and dance with "no censors, no discrimination, and no shame!" Check the website or call for a schedule of events and ticket prices. Tours $5.

✷ Selective Shopping

ART GALLERIES Galleria Riverside (706-653-1950), 1658 Rollins Way, Suite 300, Columbus. Open 10–5:30 weekdays, 10–4 Saturday. In addition to artwork, the gallery offers antiques, handcrafted furniture, and gifts.

Joseph House Gallery Cooperative (706-321-8948), 828 Broadway, Columbus. Open 11–5 Tuesday–Friday, 1–5 Saturday. The historic structure houses the work of 65 regional artists and more than 1,000 original paintings, drawings, pottery, photography, woodwork, and china.

✷ Special Events

April: **Riverfest Weekend–Salisbury Fair** (706-323-7979). Held the last full weekend in April along the Columbus RiverWalk, this event consists of several parts. The **Salisbury Fair** features artists at work, arts and crafts, a 5K road race, fireworks, and a food court. The **Folklife Village** consists of a folk-art show, crafters, youth art show, fine art exhibition, children's activities, and Native American demonstrations. The **Greater Columbus Pig Jig Barbecue Cook-Off** is a Memphis in May–sanctioned barbecue cook-off. Entertainment features local, regional, and national talent performing jazz, blues, country, and rock on three stages. Other activities include a carnival, collectibles, and even pig racing. General admission $5, concerts $15.

October: **Help the Hooch Watershed Festival.** For more information, contact **Keep Columbus Beautiful** (706-653-4008). The clean-up program and festival began in 1994 with 500 volunteers. During the 2011 cleanup, more than 12,000 volunteers turned out to help. Attendance at the Watershed Festival afterward, a reward for all the hard work, was also record-breaking. The festival includes games, exhibitors, refreshments, inflatables, prizes, and T-shirts.

LAGRANGE

This area calls itself "Georgia's West Coast" because of its location on the Chattahoochee River and West Point Lake at the Georgia-Alabama border. Together the river and lake provide an immense area of water and endless recreational opportunities.

Historically, the Creek Indians, who occupied west Georgia before the Indian Springs Treaty of 1825, used a warpath that ran through what is now downtown LaGrange. All but a few of the Creeks were gone by 1827, when the area was opened for settlement. The area is primarily rural, with most of the population living in LaGrange and a few small towns.

Visitors primarily come to LaGrange to see its two art museums and two magnificent historic homes. While there, many decide to take the walking tour or watch some drag racing. Outdoor recreation enthusiasts can find a million things to do at West Point Lake, the West Point Wildlife Management Area, and other parks. Campers are particularly pleased with the wide selection of campgrounds.

Visitors to LaGrange's downtown park won't find the statue of a founding father of the state or city, nor a monument to Confederate soldiers, nor a memorial to some politician. Instead they'll see a statue honoring the Marquis de Lafayette, the French hero of the Revolutionary War. In fact, the town itself is named after Lafayette's estate in France. It seems that when Lafayette was traveling through this then undeveloped area in 1825, he remarked that the surroundings reminded him of his home, which he called LaGrange. In 1828, when a seat for Troup County was created, the name LaGrange was chosen for the town. In 1976 city fathers named the downtown park Lafayette Square and commissioned a fountain centered with a bronze statue of Lafayette.

The nearby towns of Franklin, Hogansville, and West Point offer one or more sightseeing attractions, bed & breakfasts, campgrounds, restaurants, and interesting shops.

GUIDANCE For visitors planning a trip to LaGrange, contact the **LaGrange–Troup County Chamber of Commerce** (706-884-8671; www.lagrangechamber.com), 111 Bull Street, LaGrange 30240. Open 8:30–5:30 weekdays. The chamber of commerce has brochures on the Chattahoochee Trace, the Chattahoochee-Flint Heritage Highway, the *Historic Courthouse Corridor Travel Guide,* and the *Presidential Pathways Travel Guide.*

While in the area, stop at the **Georgia Visitor Information Center** (706-645-3353), I-85 North at the Georgia-Alabama line. Open 8:30–5:30 daily; restaurant open until 11:30.

GETTING THERE *By air:* The nearest airport is in Atlanta. For airport, airline, and car rental information, see "What's Where in Georgia."

By bus: **Greyhound Lines** (706-882-1897 or 1-800-231-2222; www.greyhound.com) has a terminal (1328 Greenville Street) in LaGrange.

"HERE YOU GO, LAFAYETTE"

When Lafayette was in LaGrange, he reportedly told Col. Julius C. Alford about a French custom of tossing a coin into a well to wish for good luck. When Alford left for the Creek Indian War of 1836, he tossed a coin into one of LaGrange's two wells and said, "Here you go, Lafayette." All the men who were going off to war did the same, as did their sweethearts, and a custom was born.

Eventually, townsfolk began throwing two coins into the well to double their wish. According to tradition, the first coin is tossed over one's shoulder, standing back-to-back with the statue; the second is tossed while facing the statue.

After the courthouse burned in 1936 and a fountain was placed in the square, people transferred the two-coin custom to the fountain. In 1976, when the statue of Lafayette was placed in the fountain, the phrase "Here you go, Lafayette" took on added meaning.

By car: LaGrange is 65 miles southwest of Atlanta on I-85. US 27 is the other north–south route.

By train: The closest **AMTRAK** (1-800-USA-Rail; www.amtrak.com) station is in Atlanta (see "What's Where in Georgia").

GETTING AROUND Rental cars can be obtained in LaGrange from **Advantage Rent-a-Car** (706-812-8797), 1237 Lafayette Parkway, and **Enterprise Rent-a-Car** (706-883-8800), 1504 Lafayette Parkway.

MEDICAL EMERGENCY For life-threatening emergencies, call 911.

✷ To See

CULTURAL SITES ✿ ♿ **Lamar Dodd Art Center** (706-880-8211; www.lagrange.edu), 302 Forrest Avenue, LaGrange. Open 8:30–4:30 weekdays, September–June. Located in a modern edifice on the campus of LaGrange College, the center houses a permanent collection of the works of 20th-century painter and native son Lamar Dodd. The art center also hosts rotating exhibits of the works of numerous other contemporary painters and graduating seniors. Some interesting Indian artifacts are also part of the permanent display. Free.

HISTORIC HOMES AND SITES ✿ **Bellevue Historical Home** (706-884-1832), 204 Ben Hill Street, LaGrange. Open 10–noon and 2–5 Tuesday–Saturday. This opulent antebellum home, the former residence of U.S. senator Benjamin Harvey Hill, is considered one of the finest examples of Greek Revival architecture in Georgia. Designed and built over two years in the early 1850s, the exterior features Ionic columns supporting wide porticos. Other outstanding architectural features include unique woodwork, such as massive carved cornices over the doors and windows. The interior is further embellished with black Italian marble mantels and ornate plaster ceiling medallions. In the 1930s, the Fuller E. Callaway Foundation purchased the house and later presented it to the LaGrange Woman's Club. The house was restored in 1974 and 1975. Bellevue is furnished with period pieces to reflect the 1850s as well as with family mementos, such as portraits of Senator Hill and his wife, Caroline Holt Hill, and framed rubbings from Hill family tombstones. In fact, the rosewood piano in the formal parlor has been there since the home's earliest days. Adults $5, students $3.

✿ ✎ ♿ **Fort Tyler** (334-642-1503; www.forttyler.com), Sixth Avenue and West 10th Street, West Point. Open daylight hours daily. A paved path leads to a small earthen fort built in 1863 and named in honor of Gen. R. C. Tyler, quartermaster of the Confederate army. It was the last Confederate fort to fall at the end of the Civil War. Three cannon replicas are located at the fort, which is an official Civil War Discovery Trail site, and interpretive signs describe the site. Free.

🔌 ♿ **Hills and Dales** (706-882-3242; www.hillsanddalesestate.org), 1916 Hills and Dales Drive, LaGrange. Open 10–6 Tuesday–Saturday, 1–6 Sunday, March–June; 10–5 Tuesday–Saturday, July–February. The centerpiece of this 35-acre estate is the opulent 1916 Italian-style villa. Designed by Neel Reid, one of the founders of the Georgia School of Classicism, the historic estate was the home of textile magnate Fuller E. Callaway Sr. and his wife, Ida Cason Callaway. Upon their deaths, it passed to their son, Fuller E. Callaway Jr., and his wife, Alice Hand Callaway. After the younger Callaway and his wife passed away, the estate was given to the Fuller E. Callaway Foundation to be opened for the enjoyment and enrichment of the public. The mansion tour includes the majestic rooms and family furnishings on all three floors.

Of equal interest at the same site are the **Ferrell Gardens,** which date to 1841 and are named for Sarah Ferrell, whose family lived on the property in a much smaller house before the Callaways bought the estate and built the mansion. Sarah opened the grounds to the public after church on Sundays, and the Callaways continued the tradition. These gardens feature extensive boxwood plantings in Italian Renaissance and Baroque designs, as well as fountains, descending terraces, a greenhouse, and many religious elements introduced by Sarah. The site also includes an herb garden, a sunken garden, and many planted walks, terraces, and lanes. The Callaways acquired outdoor statuary on their world travels, and many of these pieces continue to grace the gardens as well.

Begin at the opulent **visitors center,** a newer but classically inspired building that blends beautifully with the existing Neel Reid architecture. There you can see educational exhibits and watch a film about Sarah Ferrell and two generations of the Callaway family. Then take a tram up the steep hill to the house for the guided tour and finish by strolling through the gardens on your own. Plan on at least two hours to experience everything. Children younger than six are not admitted to the house. House and garden admission: adults $15, students age seven–college $7. Admission to gardens only: adults $8, students age seven–college $4; audio tour of the gardens $3.

MUSEUMS 🔌 ✏ **Heard County Historical Center and Museum** (706-675-6507; www.heardgeorgia.org), 161 Shady Street, Franklin. Open 9–noon and 1–5:30 Tuesday and Thursday. Located in the county's "Old Jail," the beautiful Romanesque Revival structure served as the county jail and sheriff's office as well as his residence from 1912 to 1964. Visitors can still see the cells and gallows, along with other exhibits relating to county history. Movie buffs delight in learning about local legends such as Miss Mayhaley Lancaster, a pivotal character from the best-selling novel and movie *Murder in Coweta County.* She was a lawyer, a schoolteacher, and a political activist, but she claimed to be a psychic and "oracle of the ages." Free.

🔌 ♿ **LaGrange Art Museum** (706-882-3267; www.lagrangeartmuseum.org), 112 Lafayette Parkway, LaGrange. Open 9–5

THE ITALIAN-STYLE VILLA IS THE CENTERPIECE OF HILLS AND DALES ESTATE.

Tuesday–Friday, 11–5 Saturday. Focusing on contemporary art and encompassing more than 500 pieces, the museum annually features 10 to 13 exhibitions showcasing the works of well-known and emerging Southeastern artists. Workshops and gallery talks spotlight artists whose work is currently on display. Every other year, the museum hosts the paintings, prints, and drawings portion of the LaGrange National Biennial, which brings the most current trends in contemporary art to LaGrange. Located just off Lafayette Square in historic downtown LaGrange, the 1892 building itself is interesting because it served as the Troup County Jail until 1946. The building was completely renovated in 1978 to create contemporary galleries, allowing paintings to hang where criminals were once hanged. Free, but donations are gratefully accepted.

✳ To Do

BICYCLING Contact the LaGrange–Troup County Chamber of Commerce (see *Guidance*) to request the *Backroads Bicycling on Georgia's Chattahoochee–Flint Heritage Way* bicycling brochure.

FISHING Fishing is the most popular activity on **West Point Lake.** A dozen creeks and 40 square miles of lake provide prime fishing spots for several species of monster-size bass, bream, channel catfish, and crappie. Bank and pier fishing is excellent, and all piers are wheelchair accessible. Interestingly, West Point Lake has more annual fishing tournaments than any other lake in Georgia.

SWIMMING 🐾 ✐ ⛓ **Water Wiz** (706-845-7655; http://3creeksentertainment.net/), 305 Old Roanoke Road, LaGrange. Open 10–7 Monday–Saturday (until 6 on Wednesday), 2–5 Sunday, May–September. The popular water park boasts 275- and 300-foot water slides in addition to a 30-by-60-foot swimming pool. The complex also features a batting cage where future big-leaguers can swing at six balls for $0.25. The batting area stays lit until 10 PM. $11.95 for anyone taller than 4 feet tall, $8.95 for children shorter than 4 feet tall, free for children two and younger.

WALKING TOURS 🐾 **Historic Downtown LaGrange Walking Tour** (706-884-1828 or 706-884-8671; www.trouparchives.org). Pick up a free brochure in LaGrange from the Troup County Historical Society and Archives, 136 Main Street, or the LaGrange–Troup County Chamber of Commerce (see *Guidance*).

✳ Green Space

LAKES 🐾 ✐ ⛓ **West Point Lake** (706-645-2937 or 1-877-444-6777; www.sam.usace.army .mil/westpt), 500 Resource Management Drive, West Point. Most facilities open 8–4:30 weekdays, October–March; 8–5 daily, April–September. The U.S. Army Corps of Engineers lake extends 35 miles along the Chattahoochee River. The 26,000-acre reservoir has 500 miles of shoreline and is surrounded by forests. Although the lake's purpose is to control flooding, generate electricity, and maintain depths downstream that permit navigation by tugboats, barges, and other riverboats, it is a mecca for recreation even in the winter, with day-use parks, campgrounds, marinas, beach areas, boat launching areas, and fishing piers surrounding the lake. If water sports are your main interest, there are hundreds of coves and two secluded slalom courses for waterskiing enthusiasts. Without all the heavy traffic of other lakes, West Point is also perfect for tubing, kneeboarding, swimming, and cruising. There is also a white sand beach and a play area for children. For fishermen, this resort is heaven, famous for monster-size largemouth bass, hybrid bass, spotted bass, white bass, stripers, and crappie. It also offers more fishing tournaments than any other lake in the state. Two privately owned marinas provide fuel, repairs, rentals, supplies, and other necessities. Because of West Point Lake's many recreation possibilities and its proximity to three major metropolitan areas, the lake is identified by the Corps of Engineers as a Recreational Demonstration Project, and therefore additional recreational facilities not commonly found at other lakes are provided here. Some of the day-use areas have tennis courts, ball fields, basketball courts, and fishing piers with fish attractors placed under them for the disabled. The **visitors center at the Project Management Office** has displays concerning the management of the lake and its lands.

NATURE PRESERVES AND PARKS **West Point Wildlife Management Area** (478-825-6354; www.georgiawildlife.com). Nearly 10,000 acres provide habitat for ospreys, bald eagles, deer, bobcats, and dozens of species of songbirds. The area also offers excellent hunting for deer, turkey, dove, quail, wood duck, and other waterfowl. Hunters need a Georgia Wildlife Management Area stamp to hunt seasonally and participate in special quota hunts.

✴ Lodging

BED & BREAKFASTS

In LaGrange

🌿 **Thyme Away Bed and Breakfast** (706-885-9625; www.lagrangechamber.com /clientsites/thymeaway.html), 508 Greenville Street. This attractive Greek Revival B&B (circa 1840) boasts five deluxe guest rooms. Each individually decorated room features a private bath with whirlpool tub, gas-log fireplace, TV, VCR, refrigerator, and wireless Internet access. Be sure to enjoy the beautiful gardens surrounding the house, too. Full breakfast is included. No smoking. Ask about children. No pets. Not wheelchair accessible. $75 single, $85 double.

CAMPGROUNDS

In Franklin

🌿 ✍ **Brush Creek Park** (706-675-2267 or 706-645-3778; www.franklingeorgia.com /BrushCreekPark.html), 1328 Brush Creek Park Road. Campgrounds open April–November. This countymaintained recreation area on West Point Lake offers both primitive and RV campsites, bathhouses, picnic pavilions, a baseball field, basketball court, playground, and direct boat access. Of further interest, this campground is located on the site of the old Indian community of Chattahoochee. It is from this early settlement that the Chattahoochee River got its name. $12–16.

In LaGrange

🌿 ✍ **Highland Marina and Resort** (706-882-3437 or 1-800-378-7001; www .highlandmarina.com), 1000 Seminole Road. If camping is your thing, the marina has many RV sites (sorry, no tent camping) on West Point Lake. Get there early, because reservations are not accepted and sites rent on a first-come, first-served basis. $25–35.

🌿 ✍ **Three Creeks Campground** (706-885-7655; www.3creeksentertainment .net/3_creeks_camp_ground), 305 Old Roanoke Road. With both pop-up and RV sites, a bathhouse, laundry facilities, playground, and catfish lake, this campground has a lot, but it's on the same property at the Water Wiz water park and Red's 2 skating rink, so there's more than enough to do even on a rainy day. If that's not enough, it's located only 0.25 mile from the closest boat launch at West Point Lake. $28–32.

RESORTS

In LaGrange

✍ **Highland Marina and Resort** (706-882-3437 or 1-800-378-7001; www .highlandmarina.com), 100 Seminole Road. Georgia's most affordable and beautiful marina is actually a complete resort that sits on 200 acres of peace and quiet. During your stay, enjoy a seemingly endless list of activities or just take time to relax and refresh. Anglers can fish for largemouth, hybrid, spotted, and white bass, as well as stripers and crappie. The resort also has a store that sells fishing tackle, bait, food, and beer, and has on-the-water gas pumps to fill up your boat. A restaurant is open for lunch and dinner daily year-round; breakfast March through November. The most expensive entrée is $6. In addition to camp-sites (see *Campgrounds*), the resort offers 33 fully equipped, one- to three-bedroom waterfront cabins and chalets with full kitchens, central heat and air, cable televi-sion, and decks with grills. For complete privacy, rent a private dock for your cabin as well. $70–320 per night.

✳ Where to Eat
DINING OUT
In LaGrange
🍴 ♿ **Banzai Japanese Steakhouse** (706-882-0750), 1510 Lafayette Parkway. Open 4:30–10 Monday–Thursday, 4:30–11 Friday and Saturday. Enjoy Japanese-style cuisine from grilled chicken to a steak-and-seafood combination platter. Entrées are served with rice and a vegetable. No smoking. $15–25.

EATING OUT
In Hogansville
🍴 🍴 ♿ **Roger's Bar-B-Q Hogansville** (706-637-4100; www.rogersbbq.com), 1863 East Main Street. Open 11–9 Monday–Thursday, 11–11 Friday and Saturday. The menu at this barbecue restaurant, which was originally established in West Point in 1945, includes ribs, chicken, steak, stew, and catfish, as well as salads, vegetables, and homemade lunches. All the barbecue items are pit cooked on-site. No smoking. $8–17.

In LaGrange
🍴 🍴 ♿ **Charlie Joseph's** (706-884-5416), 128 Bull Street and (706-884-0469), 2238 West Point Road. Open 9–5:30 Monday–Saturday (Wednesday they close at 2). The menu includes hot dogs, ham-burgers, sandwiches, and stews. No smok-ing. $2–5.

🍴 🍴 ♿ **Hog Heaven** (706-882-7227), 2240 West Point Road. Open 11–9:30 Monday–Thursday, 11–10 Friday and Saturday. Proclaimed the "Best Barbecue in Troup County" two years in a row by the *LaGrange Daily News*, this restaurant definitely lives up to its name. Menu favorites include baby-back ribs, steaks, burgers, salads, and smoked pork, chicken, and turkey. Fresh-cooked pork skins can be delivered to your table still crackling. There's also a free bucket of peanuts on every table (just throw the shells on the floor). No smoking. $3–19.

🍴 🍴 ♿ **Jim Bob's** (706-882-9917), 108 Cor-porate Plaza Drive. Open 10–9 Monday–Saturday. Chicken fingers, wings, and cat-fish fillets are among the specialties of this restaurant. No smoking. Under $10.

🍴 ♿ **Venucci** (706-884-9393; www.the downtownrestaurantgroup.com), 129 Main Street. Open 11–2 for lunch and 5:30–9:30 for dinner Monday–Saturday. Meals are served family-style at this traditional Italian restaurant. The eatery caters to a business crowd at lunch, and therefore the lunch menu is much more extensive (and also expensive) than the more limited din-ner menu. No smoking. Lunch $7–23, din-ner $7–9.

In West Point
🍴 🍴 ♿ **Heart of the South Tea Room** (706-643-0544; www.heartofthesouth.biz/), 1111 Second Avenue. Open 11–3 Sunday–Friday. Menu favorites include salads, sandwiches, muffalettas, po'boys, veggie plates, daily specials, and the tearoom's unique corn bread salad. No smoking. $5–8.

TAKE-OUT
In LaGrange
🍴 🍴 ♿ **Big Chic** (706-882-5615), 503 Vernon Street. Open 11–8:30 Tuesday–Saturday, 11–7 Sunday. This take-out-only restaurant has a variety of favorites, includ-ing chicken dishes, seafood items, and great desserts. No smoking. $3–6.

✳ Entertainment

MUSIC LaGrange Symphony (706-882-0662; www.lagrangesymphony.org), office: 301 Church Street, LaGrange. The orchestra enriches the community through music, cultural experience, educational programs, and performance opportunities usually performed at the Callaway Auditorium. Check the website or call for performance schedules. Tickets $5–25.

THEATER Lafayette Theatre Company/Lafayette Society for the Performing Arts (706-882-9909; www.lspa arts.com/lspaltc.html), 214 Bull Street, LaGrange. This community theater delivers a wide variety of high-quality presentations. Check the website or call for a schedule of events and ticket prices.

✳ Selective Shopping

ART GALLERIES Artists in Residence (706-885-9900), 300 South Greenwood Street, LaGrange. Open by chance or appointment. This facility houses a retail store, artists' studios, and a teaching section for arts and pottery.

✳ Special Events

Early May: **An Affair on the Square** (706-882-3267; www.lagrangega.info/fairs .htm), 112 Lafayette Parkway, LaGrange. Held on the square on the second weekend in May, this fine-arts fair, sponsored by the **LaGrange Art Museum** (see *To See— Museums*), has lots of food and entertainment for the whole family. Free; fee for some activities.

Early July: **Fourth of July Festivities** (706-883-1670; www.lagrangega.info/fairs .htm), 1220 Lafayette Parkway, LaGrange. This Independence Day celebration includes the Sweet Land of Liberty children's parade, activities and entertainment all afternoon at **Pyne Road Park** on West Point Lake, and a fireworks display over the lake that night. Free; fee for some activities.

October: **Hogansville Hummingbird Festival** (706-637-9497; www.lagrangega .info/fairs.htm). This charming annual festival is held the third week in October in downtown Hogansville. In addition to a food court and various entertainment, there are sales and demonstrations of unique arts and crafts, as well as special children's activities. Free; fee for some activities.

PINE MOUNTAIN, CALLAWAY GARDENS, AND WARM SPRINGS

T his region is the home of one of the best-known resorts in the Southeast: Callaway Gardens. In fact, this entire chapter could have been written about the gardens alone, but we've added some nearby places as well. The vast 14,000-acre garden, resort, and preserve complex was the brainchild of Cason Jewell Callaway and his wife, Virginia Hand Callaway. He longed for a place where man and nature could commingle to the advantage of both. The resort features various types of accommodations and eateries, as well as numerous activities and pursuits. Whether you desire a quiet place for leisurely strolls and observation of nature or prefer an action-packed sports experience and other adventures, you can find what you want at Callaway Gardens.

The area described in this chapter is included in the region known as Presidential Pathways because of its association with Franklin D. Roosevelt and Jimmy Carter. (For more information about the part of the Presidential Pathways region that relates to Jimmy Carter, see the Americus chapter.) FDR came to Warm Springs to try the curative waters for relief from his polio. After several visits, he built the only house he ever bought on his own. That home, which became known as the Little White House, draws many visitors annually (see *To See—Historic Homes and Sites*).

Many other outdoor activities, such as fishing, hiking, and horseback riding, attract visitors year-round, as do a wild animal park, a covered bridge, an aquarium, museums, and shopping.

GUIDANCE To learn more about Pine Mountain, contact the **Pine Mountain Tourism Association and Welcome Center** (706-663-4000 or 1-800-441-3502; www.pinemountain .org), 101 East Broad Street, Pine Mountain 31822. Open 9–5 weekdays, 10–4 Saturday.

For information about Warm Springs, contact the **Warm Springs Area Tourism Association–FDR Warm Springs Welcome Center** (706-655-3322 or 1-800-337-1927; www.city ofwarmsprings.com), One Broad Street, Warm Springs 31830. Open 10–5 Monday–Saturday, 1–4 Sunday.

GETTING THERE *By air:* Visitors could fly into Atlanta or Columbus (see "What's Where in Georgia").

By bus: **Greyhound Lines** does not stop in any of the towns described in this chapter. The nearest stations are in LaGrange, Columbus, and Fort Benning (see the LaGrange and Columbus chapters). A visitor arriving into one of those cities by bus would then need a rental car to get to and around this area.

By car: The towns described in this chapter lie between I-75, I-85, and I-185. The primary north–south routes through the area are US 27 Alt. and GA 85.

By train: There is no train service to this area. The closest **AMTRAK** station is in Atlanta (see "What's Where in Georgia").

GETTING AROUND There are no taxis, buses, or shuttles in the area, so visitors must have a car, either their own or a rental.

MEDICAL EMERGENCY In life-threatening situations, call 911.

VILLAGES Pine Mountain is the nearest town to Callaway Gardens. Founded in 1882 as the railroad town of Chipley, it's now known as "the Gateway to Callaway," but Pine Mountain has attractions of its own, including a bed & breakfast, a museum, restaurants, and interesting shops.

Warm Springs is deeply rooted in the historical era of four-term President Franklin D. Roosevelt. Downtown's Warm Springs Village has been restored and now features a bed & breakfast, several restaurants, and numerous shops.

✳ To See

Callaway Gardens is a world unto itself, with gardens, accommodations, restaurants, shops, and recreational activities. The resort features 13 man-made lakes for boating, fishing, and swimming; Robin Lake Beach; several swimming pools; a 10-mile biking trail, hiking trails, and a fitness trail; boat and bike rentals; a fly-casting center; 36 holes of golf; tennis; lodging; and restaurants. Among the many special events are the Summer Family Adventures, Harvest Festival, Steeplechase at Callaway, and Fantasy in Lights. The resort is mentioned so many times in this chapter, in order to avoid repetition, contact and other general information is listed only once here: Callaway Gardens (706-663-2281 or 1-800-225-5292; www .callawaygardens.com), 17800 US 27, Pine Mountain. Open 9–8 mid-March–Sunday of Labor Day weekend, 9–5 the remainder of the year (except longer during some special events). Adults $18, seniors $15, children 6–12 $9; additional admission price for some special events. Unless otherwise indicated in the separate entries that follow, activities at Callaway Gardens are included in the daily admission price and for overnight guests.

COVERED BRIDGES ♣ ✐ **Red Oak Covered Bridge,** GA 85 Alt./Covered Bridge Road, Imlac near Woodbury. Open daylight hours daily. This is the last existing covered bridge built by Horace King, the famous freed slave who became a master bridge builder all across the South. This bridge was built in the 1840s in the Town Lattice Truss design using wooden pegs. It is the oldest covered bridge in Georgia and also the longest, at 391 feet. That's actually a technicality. The covered portion is 253 feet, which is slightly shorter than the Watson Mill Covered Bridge, but with the long wooden open approach, Red Oak claims the title. There's no dispute about the fact that its 115 feet that's totally unsupported is the longest such span in the state. What's even more amazing is that the bridge is still used by cars and small trucks—one of only a few in the state still in use. Free.

FOR FAMILIES ✐ ♿ **Butts Mill Farm** (706-663-7400; www.buttsmillfarm.com), 2280 Butts Mill Road, Pine Mountain. Open 10–6 daily; last ticket sold one hour prior to closing. Spend a fun day at this operational farm, complete with a gristmill and a covered bridge. Other features include a fishing pond, Mega Discovery Zone, go-cart track, hayrides, miniature golf course, petting farm, pony and horseback rides, Super Down Hill Slide, train rides, and much more. Adults $15.95, children 3–9 $13.95; some activities, such as horseback riding, go-carts, and paintball, have a separate fee in addition to the admission fee.

♂ ᕫ **Cecil B. Day Butterfly Center** at **Callaway Gardens,** named for the founder of the Days Inn motel chain and given in his honor by his widow, is a butterfly-filled rain forest in west-central Georgia. In fact, upward of 1,000 butterflies of 50 lepidopteron species call the glass-enclosed space home. One of the oldest and largest butterfly conservatories in North America, it was the first to incorporate butterflies with horticulture and the first in the world to showcase butterflies from Africa. These "flying flowers" nibble on bananas and oranges, and, if you're quiet, light on you for colorful photo ops. A video called *On Wings of Wonder* plays continuously. Take time to admire the artwork in the lobby, which was also donated by Deen Day Sanders, the original donor. Free with gardens admission.

♀ ♂ ᕫ **Old South Farm Museum and Agricultural Learning Center** (706-975-9136; www.oldsouthfarm.com), Pleasant Valley Road and GA 41, Woodland. Open 9–5 Monday–Saturday, but call first. This interactive farm museum features live animals and examples of authentic farm machinery, such as balers, combines, cultivators, hay presses, seed cleaners, and Allis Chalmers half-size tractors—the forerunners of riding lawnmowers. There is a canning plant, a moonshine still, and a peach-packing shed. The Old South Drive-Through section features such Southern farm scenes as a blacksmith shop, cotton gin, dairy farm, gristmill, poultry house, sawmill, milking shed, and syrup mill. Inside the museum are exhibits that include a complete barber shop and an immense collection of different types of barbed wire. Adults $3, children 3–12 $1.

♂ ᕫ **Virginia Hand Callaway Discovery Center** at **Callaway Gardens,** situated at the end of Mountain Creek Lake, features informational films, permanent and traveling exhibits, and educational programs. The ***Birds of Prey Show,*** presented at the Discovery Center either outdoors at the amphitheater or indoors, depending on rainy or excessively hot weather, features such free-flying raptors as the bald eagle, falcon, hawk, owl, or vulture. There are a dozen birds in the program, and three to five appear in each show, so visitors can see the show many times and see something different. There are one to three shows daily depending on the season, so check the website or call for a schedule. Discovery Center and raptor shows free with gardens admission.

STATUE OF VIRGINIA HAND CALLAWAY AT HER NAMESAKE, THE VIRGINIA HAND CALLAWAY DISCOVERY CENTER AT CALLAWAY GARDENS

♂ ᕫ **Wild Animal Safari** (706-663-8744 or 1-800-367-2751; www.animalsafari.com), 1300 Oak Grove Road, Pine Mountain. Open at 10–5:30 daily, fall–winter; longer hours spring–summer. Check the website or call for a schedule. This park contains 500 acres, which provide habitats for 200 animal species from six continents. Take a guided Zebra Bus tour in season or drive your own car along the 3.5-mile road through the park. You can also rent a Zebra Van for $12–16. Many of the kinder, gentler animals are wandering freely and may come right up to your car to be petted or fed (special food is sold at the park entrance). Some of the more unusual animals are ligers, zedonks, zonies, yakatusi, and guar. An aviary, monkey house, and the Snake Pit (a serpentarium open seasonally) offer views of other exotic species. At Old McDonald's Farm and the Petting Zoo, visitors can cuddle up with more docile critters, bottle-feed a calf, or milk a cow. The park also features the Georgia Wildlife Museum, the Barrel of Fun Arcade, Serengeti Gift Shop, and the Safari Cafe. Don't forget your camera. Adults $19.95, seniors and children $16.95.

HISTORIC HOMES AND SITES 🐾 ✈ ♿ Roosevelt's Little White House Historic Site

(706-655-5870; www.gastateparks.org/LittleWhiteHouse), 401 Little White House Road, Warm Springs. Open 9–4:45 daily; last tour at 4. Because Franklin D. Roosevelt inherited his mother's magnificent home at Hyde Park, New York, and then lived in the White House, this small cottage is the only one he ever built on his own. In fact, he personally drew the original plans. After being stricken with polio in 1921, Roosevelt came in 1924 to swim in the waters of what is now known as the Roosevelt–Warm Springs Institute for Rehabilitation, hoping for a cure. Although the cure didn't happen, the waters gave him some relief, and, while running for president in 1932, he built a simple vacation cottage on the side of Pine Mountain that later became known as the Little White House. It was during his many trips here that he talked to the county residents and learned of their difficulties. These conversations led to the inspiration for New Deal programs like the Rural Electrification Administration, the Civilian Conservation Corps, and the Tennessee Valley Authority. FDR suffered a stroke here on April 12, 1945, while sitting for a portrait being painted by Elizabeth Shoumatoff, and he died a few hours later.

The house and furnishings have been preserved almost as he left them that day. In fact, the leash of FDR's little Scottie, Fala, is still hanging in the closet. Visitors also can see the guesthouse and servants' quarters. A new $5 million museum on the property features a film narrated by Walter Cronkite, while "Fireside Chats" play on the radio in a typical 1930s kitchen. Exhibits contain memorabilia about FDR's life and presidency, including his struggle with polio, his role in the country's recovery from the Great Depression, and his leadership in World War II. Two of the most popular exhibits are the unfinished portrait and the president's 1938 Ford convertible, which had been adapted with hand controls. A stagecoach that was owned by FDR and used in local parades is also on display. More than 100,000 visitors come to the Little White House each year. A commemorative ceremony is held each year on April 12, the date of FDR's death. Also on the grounds, see the Memorial Fountain and the Walk of Flags and Stones, which displays a flag and a boulder from each state. Adults $10, children and seniors $6; parking free.

ROOSEVELT'S LITTLE WHITE HOUSE HISTORIC SITE

NATURAL BEAUTY SPOTS

🐾 ✈ ♿ Dowdell's Knob at F. D. Roosevelt State Park (706-663-4858; www.ga stateparks.org/FDRoosevelt), 2970 GA 190, Pine Mountain. Open 8–8 daily, April–September; 8–5 daily, October–March. A rocky spur of the Pine Mountain ridge, Dowdell's Knob sits at 1,395 feet above sea level, where it offers a panoramic view of Pine Mountain Valley. It was one of President Franklin D. Roosevelt's favorite spots. When Roosevelt drove up here in his 1938 Ford convertible, sometimes alone, sometimes with friends for a picnic, the route was a barely cleared dirt track. Of course, when a president of the United States has a picnic, it may not be the casual affair we

THE WARM SPRINGS

Long before Franklin D. Roosevelt founded the Roosevelt Warms Springs Institute for Rehabilitation in 1927, Native Americans had recognized the powers of the springs. Following battle or other injuries, they came to the springs to seek healing. After white settlers discovered the springs, a spa was created there. Water emerging at 900 gallons per minute and maintaining a temperature of 88 degrees year-round made the springs a popular stagecoach stop. Statesmen John C. Calhoun and Henry Clay are known to have visited the springs.

At the turn of the 20th century, well-to-do families began erecting summer homes nearby. A hotel was built as well as a swimming pool so that people could get better access to the warm, buoyant waters. FDR came to the pools and built his own home nearby. Today his institute treats all kinds of disabilities, and the springs are still part of the therapy.

mere mortals are accustomed to. It's reported that tables and chairs, linen tablecloths and napkins, china, and silver were part of the setup. Roosevelt made his last trip to Dowdell's Knob on April 10, 1945, just two days before his death. It is reported that he had Secret Service agents drive him there, walk back down the road, and not return until he honked the car's horn. He sat alone in his car for two hours. We can only imagine what he was contemplating. Today the road to Dowdell's Knob is paved, and picnic tables and grills have been added so that visitors can eat and enjoy the view as FDR did. A historical marker titled THIS WAS HIS GEORGIA tells about FDR's fondness for the spot. Sometimes when FDR came here, aides simply took the seat out of his car for him to sit on. A life-size bronze statue of FDR sitting on a car seat enables visitors to sit beside him for a unique photo op. Atlanta sculptor Martin Daw created the statue, which is the only one of FDR that shows his leg braces. (The statue in Washington, D.C., is the only one that shows him in a wheelchair.) The memorial also features an interpretive panel detailing some of FDR's important programs. Parking $5.

SCENIC DRIVES **Chattahoochee Flint River Heritage Highway Tour** (US 27), from Roscoe to St. Marks (northwest of Greenville). Part of the 150-mile scenic highway is included in this chapter. The area, once occupied by the Creek Indians, features historic sites, unique architecture, and beautiful vistas.

SPECIAL PLACES ✔ ♿ **Ida Cason Callaway Memorial Chapel** at **Callaway Gardens** is a memorial to Cason Callaway's mother. Situated at the end of a lake, the Gothic-style stone chapel is surrounded by forests and streams. Six striking stained-glass windows depict local forests and the changing seasons. The Moller pipe organ fills the chapel and woodlands with heavenly music. A peaceful place for contemplation, the chapel is also very popular for weddings.

✳ To Do

BICYCLING ♿ ✔ **Callaway Gardens** offers a 10-mile paved **Discovery Bicycle Trail** over gently rolling terrain, which is an invigorating way to see the property. The trail is situated so that it provides access to all the major gardens. Bring your own bike or rent one at the Callaway Discovery Center.

CIRCUS ✔ ♿ **Flying High Circus** at **Callaway Gardens.** Performances at 3:30 Monday, Thursday, and weekends; also at 8 Friday and Saturday. Since 1961, the Florida State University Flying High Circus has been in residence during the Summer Family Adventure Program at the resort. The college students train and perform, and serve as camp counselors teaching rudimentary circus skills to the campers. Whether your family is participating in the summer camp program or not, you'll want to catch a performance of the circus to see juggling and acrobatic skills such as trapeze, balance, and tightwire.

FISHING 🐟 ✐ ♿ **Callaway Gardens** offers a variety of angling opportunities. **Mountain Creek Lake** offers some of the finest fishing in the region, and both spin- and fly-fishing enthusiasts extol the resort. Guides can lead fly-fishing excursions to private lakes. Two-day fishing schools and private lessons also are offered by Certified FFF instructors and a Master Certified Casting Instructor. A Georgia fishing license is not required. There are additional fees for boat rentals, fishing equipment, instruction, and guided fishing trips.

GOLF Callaway Gardens Golf. Open 8–5 daily. Opportunities for golfers are almost limitless at this Pine Mountain resort, where superbly designed and meticulously maintained courses feature woodland borders and lakeland settings. The original course, which has been renovated, is the 18-hole, par-70 **Lake View** course, designed by world-famous golf architects Dick Wilson and J. B. McGovern. Beautiful landscaping with azaleas, dogwoods, and seasonal flowers belies the challenges of the nine water holes. Innovations include new bunkers, TifEagle greens, and new cart paths. The **Mountain View** course, also designed by Wilson, is a 7,057-yard, par-72 championship course, which served for 10 years as the home of the PGA Tour's Buick Challenge. The course is ranked among the nation's top courses by *Golf Digest* and *Golf* magazines. The Twin Oaks Practice facility features multiple target greens, two large sand bunkers, multiple chipping and pitching areas, and a large practice putting green. $50–80 for Lake View course, $65–100 for Mountain View course.

HIKING 🐟 ✐ **Callaway Gardens** features **nature trails** varying in length from 0.5 mile to 1.6 miles. These trails showcase plants and wildlife, and provide changing scenery throughout the year. Some of the trails are dedicated to azaleas, wildflowers, holly, and rhododendrons. Other trails include the **Mountain Creek Lake Trail, Laurel Springs Trail,** and the **Whippoorwill Lake Trail.**

🐟 ✐ **Pine Mountain Trail** (www.pinemountaintrail.org) in **F. D. Roosevelt State Park** (see *Green Space—Nature Preserves and Parks*). Get a trail map from the state park office (706-663-4858). Twenty-three miles of blazed trail run from the Callaway Country Store on US 27 in Pine Mountain to the WJSP-TV tower on GA 85 in Warm Springs on land that once belonged to FDR. The trail, which runs along the ridge, sometimes provides views of the valley, while at other times it winds through forests and past streams, waterfalls, and rocky outcroppings. Blazes, cairns, and mile markers guide hikers through the trail system. Various trailheads make it possible to hike small portions of the trail. The 4.3-mile **Dowdell's Knob Loop,** near the center of the trail and the highest point on it, is popular for its stunning views and historical backdrop (see *To See—Natural Beauty Spots*). Many claim that the **Wolfden Loop** is the most beautiful trail in the Southeast. The 6.5-mile trail passes beaver dams, goes over Hogback Mountain, and continues along the **Mountain Creek Nature Trail.** There are very

GOLFERS HAVE TWO COURSES TO CHOOSE FROM AT CALLAWAY GARDENS.

few steep grades along the entire Pine Mountain Trail, so hiking is not difficult. Those who want to hike the complete length of the trail can camp out at nine different sites. More than 60,000 visitors, from every state and many foreign countries, hike all or part of the trail each year.

HORSEBACK RIDING ✧ **Roosevelt Riding Stables** (706-628-7463; www.Roosevelt Stables.com), 1063 Group Camp Road, Pine Mountain. Open daily; call for hours. Saddle up for a horseback-riding adventure on 28 miles of trails that wind through the mountains and valleys of **F. D. Roosevelt State Park** (see *Green Space—Nature Preserves and Parks*). Trail rides of various lengths last from one to four hours and accommodate riders of all skill levels. Some rides are coupled with lunch or an overnight experience. Lessons and wagon rides are also available, and moonlight rides and overnight excursions are offered seasonally. Riders must be at least six years old. Pony rides are available for younger children. The trails are also open to riders who bring their own horses ($7 trail use fee). Stalls are available for those who want to keep a personal horse there overnight ($22). Reservations are strongly recommended. Trail rides $30–135, depending on length; overnight rides $200.

SUMMER YOUTH PROGRAMS ✧ ♿ **Callaway Summer Family Adventure Program** at **Callaway Gardens.** Camp activities offered 9–3 daily. Who hasn't wanted to run off and join the circus at one time or another? From early June to early August, kids age three and older can fly high at weeklong sessions of this glorified summer camp. Members of the Florida State University Flying High Circus not only provide entertainment in regular circus performances but also serve as camp counselors. There's a wide range of structured activities for three- to six-year-olds at the child care center. When children reach the age of seven, they can join the circus, where they'll learn simple magic tricks and circus acts such as juggling, tightrope walking, tumbling, and even flying on a trapeze. Youngsters who have attended year after year progress in the difficulty of acts they can perform. While the kids are busy, Mom and Dad can enjoy the resort's many sports options and amenities. The program also includes parent-child time in the evening for campfires and marshmallow roasting, games, movies, scavenger hunts, sports, stage shows, theme dinners, and more. Families are normally housed in the resort's cottages, which have full kitchens (see *Lodging—Cottages and Cabins*). Rates for packages including accommodations vary widely, so call for details. If the circus doesn't strike your child's fancy, there are many additional age-appropriate activities for them, including TreeTop Adventures, laser tag, geocaching, tennis and golf clinics, astronomy, teen activities, and more mundane activities such as biking, hiking, and swimming.

SWIMMING ✧ ♿ **Robin Lake Beach** at **Callaway Gardens** is the longest man-made inland white-sand beach in the world. It travels 1 mile around 65-acre Robin Lake and is the hub of water activities at the resort from Memorial Day to Labor Day. It's also the place from which to watch the annual Masters Water Ski and Wakeboard Tournament. In addition to sunning and swimming, other activities around the beach include shuffleboard, miniature golf, table tennis, and the performances of the Flying High Circus. Available at an additional fee are the Aqua Island Floating Playground, Blaster Boats, Light Laser Tag, and waterskiing. Rounding out the amenities are beach chair and umbrella rental, food concessions at the Beach Pavilion and Rockin' Robin's Malt Shop and Pizzeria, and the Sand Bucket Gift Shop.

TENNIS ✧ **Mountain Creek Tennis Center** at **Callaway Gardens** (706-663-5032) is consistently recognized as one of the Top 50 Tennis Resorts in America by *Tennis* magazine with a five-star rating. Ten outdoor lighted tennis courts (eight hard surface, two soft surface) and two indoor racquetball courts combine to form an excellent venue. Private and group lessons available, as are racquet and ball machine rental. Check the website or call for rates.

ZIP-LINE ADVENTURES ✔ **TreeTop Adventures** at **Callaway Gardens.** Open daily. Check the website or call for times. Located behind the Virginia Hand Callaway Discovery Center, the system, which traverses nearly 1,500 feet horizontally and soars up to 30 feet above the forest floor, features five zip lines ranging from 44 to 210 feet long. The course also includes 19 more sections comprised of ladders, wires, logs, discs, netting, and other suspended surfaces, each requiring a high-level balancing act that must be carefully executed in order to reach the next challenge or zip line. The entire high-flying challenge takes about 60 to 90 minutes to complete. $30 per person in addition to garden admission (participants must be at least 54 inches tall and under 260 pounds).

✳ Green Space

GARDENS All the following gardens are within Callaway Gardens.

✔ ♿ **Callaway Brothers Azalea Bowl** at **Callaway Gardens,** the world's largest azalea garden at 40 acres, is named for Ely Reeves Callaway and his brother, Fuller Earle Callaway, the father of the garden's founder, Cason Callaway. More than 3,400 hybrid azaleas erupt in pink, red, and white each spring. The rare orange plumleaf azalea, which blooms in profusion at Callaway Gardens, is found only within a 50-mile radius in west Georgia. Additionally, 2,000 trees and shrubs as well as seasonal flowers provide an array of color and blooms throughout the year. Bubbling streams, walking paths, an arched bridge, and a reflection pool make this an excellent place to relax.

✔ ♿ **John A. Sibley Horticultural Center** at **Callaway Gardens,** an indoor/outdoor conservatory, contains everything from exotic to native plants, unique sub-Mediterranean plantings, and seasonal displays such as chrysanthemums in the autumn and poinsettias during the holidays. Visitors are assured something different almost every time they come because the indoor displays are changed eight times a year and the outdoor plantings are changed five times a year. An impressive 350 gallons of water per minute plummet over the 22-foot waterfall into a pool below. Gigantic folding doors allow the conservatory to be closed off in rare cold weather. Outdoors, winding paths through 5 acres and strategically placed old-fashioned swings invite visitors to linger to enjoy the grounds and the sculpture garden.

✔ **Lady Bird Johnson Wildflower Trail** (near Callaway's Pioneer Log Cabin) displays plants native to Georgia as well as rare, threatened, and endangered species. Meadow, bog, Coastal Plain, Piedmont forest, and southern Appalachian forest habitats are represented. Along the trail are a gazebo, a waterfall, and a picturesque bridge overlooking Mountain Creek Lake.

✔ ♿ **Mr. Cason's Vegetable Garden** at **Callaway Gardens** is a 7.5-acre demonstration garden originally planted by founder Cason Callaway to demonstrate proper growing techniques. Today flowers, vegetables, fruits, and herbs grow in the garden, where Southern segments of the

MR. CASON'S VEGETABLE GARDEN AT CALLAWAY GARDENS

long-running PBS television series *The Victory Garden* are filmed. The garden also incorporates an All America Trials Garden.

✔ ⟡ **Overlook Garden and Azalea Trail** at **Callaway Gardens** contains an impressive collection of more than 700 varieties of azaleas.

NATURE PRESERVES AND PARKS ❀ ✔ ⟡ **F. D. Roosevelt State Park** (706-663-4858 or 1-800-864-7275; www.gastateparks.org/FDRoosevelt), 2970 GA 190, Pine Mountain. Open 7 AM–10 PM daily. Stretching from Pine Mountain to Warm Springs and encompassing more than 9,000 acres, Georgia's largest state park is named for the four-term president who loved the area so much. In fact, his favorite picnic spot, at **Dowdell's Knob** above Kings Gap (see *To See—Natural Beauty Spots*), is within the park. The 23-mile **Pine Mountain Trail** winds through forests of hardwoods and pines, but there are 14 miles of other trails (see *To Do—Hiking*). Two lakes provide opportunities for water sports. Many of the park's buildings and the Liberty Bell–shaped swimming pool (closed) were constructed during the Great Depression by the Civilian Conservation Corps. Activities available in the park include backpacking, boating, camping (see *Lodging—Campgrounds*), fishing, horseback riding (see *To Do—Horseback Riding*), and picnicking. In season, fishing boats, canoes, and kayaks are available for rental. Parking $5.

✳ Lodging

BED & BREAKFASTS

In Greenville

⟡ **Georgian Inn Bed and Breakfast** (706-672-1600), 566 South Talbotton Street/US 27 Alt. Five sumptuous, lavishly decorated rooms with all the modern conveniences are offered in this stately, white-columned historic house built in 1914. Outdoors, guests can enjoy the summer house; perennial, herb, hummingbird, and butterfly gardens; and typical Southern flowering shrubs such as gardenias, azaleas, camellias, sasanquas, and others. An abundant Southern country breakfast is offered each morning. No smoking. One downstairs room wheelchair accessible. From $120 per night weeknights.

In Pine Mountain

❀ ✔ ⟡ **Chipley Murrah House Bed and Breakfast** (706-663-9801 or 1-888-782-0797; www.chipleymurrah.com), 207 West Harris Street. Truly a "wedding cake" type of painted lady, this gorgeous Queen Anne Victorian home was built in 1895. Today the antiques-filled home offers spacious rooms with private baths (one is in the hall), king- or queen-size beds, and Southern hospitality. Two- and three-bedroom cottages with full kitchens are perfect for families. All guests enjoy the wraparound porch, swimming pool, and putting green. A hearty breakfast is served to guests in the main house; breakfast is not included for those staying in the cottages. Children younger than 12 in cottages only. No pets. No smoking. One room on first floor of main house, and cottages, wheelchair accessible, but bathrooms not fully equipped. Rooms $85–140, cottages $140–225; two-night minimum on weekends in main house; closed in January.

In Warm Springs

✔ ⟡ ❦ **Hotel Warm Springs Bed and Breakfast Inn** (706-655-2114 or 1-800-366-7616; www.hotelwarmspringsbb.org), 47 Broad Street. It's appropriate that the town's historic 1907-era hotel is once again serving up hospitality, this time as a bed & breakfast. When President Franklin D. Roosevelt was in residence at his nearby Little White House, national and international heads of state and other dignitaries as well as journalists and Secret Service agents stayed at the hotel. Restored to its 1941 appearance, the venerable old hotel offers accommodations in spacious, high-ceilinged individually themed rooms filled with antiques and Roosevelt memorabilia. Unexpectedly, the Honeymoon Suite features an oversized, red, heart-shaped hot tub. The nightly rate includes a late-afternoon social hour and a full Southern breakfast with cheese grits. Pet friendly. No smoking. Rooms $65–110, suites $120–190. For those who want only a room and no amenities, room rates start at $50.

CAMPGROUNDS

In Pine Mountain

🦐 ⌀ ♿ ☸ **F. D. Roosevelt State Park** (reservations: 1-800-864-7275). The park offers 140 tent, trailer, and RV sites; 13 backcountry sites; and a bathhouse. Some sites overlook the lake; others are nestled in the woods. $25–28; backcountry sites $9 per person. See *Green Space—Nature Preserves and Parks.*

COTTAGES AND CABINS

In Pine Mountain

⌀ ♿ **Callaway Gardens.** The resort features spacious one- or two-bedroom cottages at the **Southern Pine Cottages** and luxurious one- to four-bedroom homes at the **Mountain Creek Villas.** All feature a fully equipped kitchen, a living-dining area with a fireplace, a deck, and a screened-in porch. The cottage area has its own swimming pool, laundry, and Rockin' Robin's Malt Shop and Pizzeria restaurant. The villas feature a bathroom for every bedroom and a washer and dryer. The nightly rate includes admission to the gardens, use of the fitness center, and admission to Robin Lake Beach in season (see *To Do— Swimming*). No smoking. Cottages $159–259, villas $189–508.

⌀ ♿ ☸ **F. D. Roosevelt State Park** (reservations: 1-800-864-7275). The park has 22 historic stone cottages built by the Civilian Conservation Corps. Each is equipped with a fireplace and grill, as well as linens and kitchen utensils. Some of the cottages sit on the mountaintop and have fabulous views; others hug the lakeshore. No smoking. Two cottages wheelchair accessible. Two are dog friendly ($40 per dog; maximum two). $90–135. See *Green Space—Nature Preserves and Parks.*

♿ ☸ **Homestead Log Cabins** (706-663-4951 or 1-866-652-2246; www.homestead cabins.com), mailing address: P.O. Box 311, Warm Springs 31830. Secluded in the mountains in four different locations, but close to attractions, these log cabins, which sleep from 2 to 18, vary from very rustic to sleek contemporary. Some offer a fireplace, whirlpool tub, and a full kitchen. Many are pet friendly ($10 additional charge). No smoking. Wheelchair accessible, but bathrooms not totally equipped. Call for rates and special discounts.

♿ ☸ **Mountain Top Inn and Resort** (706-663-4719 or 1-800-533-6376; www .hide-away.com), GA 190 and Hines Gap Road. At this unique resort, accommodations are available in one- to five-bedroom log cabins with world-theme guest rooms, fireplaces, and double Jacuzzis. Each is located on 1 to 5 acres, which ensures privacy. The resort also has hiking trails, tennis, and a pool with a waterfall. For the hopelessly romantic, the resort has a charming **log wedding chapel** (1-800-ITAKETHEE), so couples can have their wedding and honeymoon on-site. Some cabins pet friendly ($20 additional). No smoking. Some wheelchair accessibility. Call for rates and special discounts.

⌀ ♿ **Pine Mountain Club Chalets Family Resort** (706-663-2211 or 1-800-535-7622; www.pinemountainclubchalets.com), 14475 GA 18 West. Quaint one- to eight-bedroom alpine chalets surround a fishing lake or are nestled in the woods. Each chalet features a fully equipped kitchen, living and dining room, and a private deck. Linens are provided. The resort also features a fishing lake, tennis courts, a swimming pool, a nine-hole miniature golf course, basketball and shuffleboard courts, and a playground. The Family Center features Ping-Pong and pool tables for the occasional rainy day. No pets. No smoking. Wheelchair-accessible cabins available. $125–395; holidays require three-night minimum.

INNS AND RESORTS

In Pine Mountain

✏ ♿ **Callaway Gardens** offers motel-room accommodations in the **Mountain Creek Inn,** which also features restaurants, a cocktail lounge, and a swimming pool. The nightly rate includes admission to the gardens, use of the fitness center, and admission to Robin Lake Beach (see *To Do—Swimming*) in season. No smoking. $119–139.

✱ Where to Eat

DINING OUT

In Pine Mountain

✏ ♿ There are several options for fine dining at **Callaway Gardens,** including the **Gardens Restaurant** (open 5:30–9 Tuesday–Saturday, 11:30–2 Sunday; $8–25) within the gardens, which has a lovely porch overlooking Mountain Creek Lake and the Lake View Golf Course; the **Plant Room** in the Mountain Creek Inn (open 6:30–10:30 AM daily for breakfast [$12], 5–9 PM Friday for a Surf and Turf buffet [adults $25.95, children 6–12 $12.95], and 5–9 PM Saturday for a Southern buffet [adults $25.95, children 6–12 $12.95]); and **Vineyards Green** at the inn (open 11:30–9 Sunday–Thursday [until 10 Friday and Saturday]; $6–20). At all Callaway restaurants, children five and younger eat free.

♿ **Cricket's Restaurant** (706-663-8136; www.cricketsrestaurant.com), 14661 GA 18. Open 5–9 nightly. Located in a quaint chalet in a wooded setting, the restaurant offers steak, seafood, and New Orleans cuisine. No smoking. $10–29.

EATING OUT

In Pine Mountain

🍴 ♿ **The Bakery and Café at Rose Cottage** (706-663-7877; www.rosecottage ga.com), 111 East Broad Street. Open 9–3 Sunday–Friday, 9–4 Saturday. This bakery–café–tearoom–antiques shop serves gourmet sandwiches, soups, salads, quiche, desserts, English teas, and fine wines. In addition, diners can purchase English

antiques and gifts, gourmet foods, and baby's and children's gifts. No smoking. $3–12.50.

🍴 ✏ ♿ There are several options for inexpensive meals at **Callaway Gardens,** including the **Discovery Café** (open 11–3 daily; $3–7) in the Virginia Hand Callaway Discovery Center, which features salads and sandwiches; **Rockin' Robin's Malt Shop and Pizzeria** (open Memorial Day–Labor Day; $10–15) at the cottages for sandwiches and pizza; the **Country Kitchen** (open 8–8 daily; $7–25) in the Callaway Country Store on US 27, which serves down-home cooking, including blue plate specials and pit-cooked barbecue; and **Champion's Grille at the Mountain View Golf Course** (open 11–6 daily; $5–10), which serves light fare including box lunches, sandwiches, and bar food. Seasonally at Robin Lake Beach, light fare is available at the **Veranda** walk-up windows at Robin Lake Pavilion and at the **Beach Bar.** Always check times and prices before finalizing your plans, because what's open and what they are serving will change seasonally. At all Callaway restaurants, children five and younger eat free.

In Warm Springs

🍴 ✏ ♿ **Bulloch House** (706-655-2736; www.bullochhouse.com), 47 Bulloch Avenue/US 27A/US 41. Open 11–2:30 daily for lunch, 5–8:30 Friday and Saturday for dinner. "Country with class" is the motto at this popular all-you-can-eat restaurant, located in a charming circa 1892 Victorian-style cottage. No smoking. Lunch $8.95, dinner $10.95.

✱ Selective Shopping

Callaway Gardens has numerous shopping outlets. The **Callaway Gardens Country Store** stocks Callaway specialty food items such as their famous muscadine sauce and jelly, as well as home decor, apparel, and more. The **Inn Store** carries sundries. Gift shops in the **Virginia Hand Callaway Discovery Center, Day Butterfly Center,** and **Sibley Horticultural Center** purvey nature and garden items.

The **pro shops** at the golf and tennis facilities make sure visitors are properly outfitted for their respective sports, while **Kingfisher Outfitters** has all the equipment anglers need for fishing. Beach items can be purchased at the **Sand Bucket** at Robin Lake Beach in season. All these items also can be purchased online at www.callawaygardens.com.

Warm Springs Village (welcome center: 706-655-3322 or 1-800-337-1927; www.cityofwarmsprings.com), 69 Broad Street, Warm Springs. Historic buildings grouped around the Bullochville and Magnolia courtyards contain a variety of specialty shops that purvey everything from furniture and accessories to antiques, fine collectibles, and crafts.

ANTIQUES **Antiques and Crafts Unlimited Mall** (706-655-2468; www.acum.org), 7679 Roosevelt Highway, Warm Springs. Open 10–6 daily. In addition to antiques, this emporium of 114 shops offers art, collectibles, crafts, furniture, glassware, pottery, and more. The **Visions Art Gallery** (www.visionsartgallery.net) features the work of regional artist Arthur Riggs.

Pine Mountain Antique Mall (706-663-8165; www.pinemountainantiquemall.com), 230 Main Street, Pine Mountain. Open 10–6 daily. Thousands of antiques range from the ordinary to the sublime and include books, coins, dolls, jewelry, period glass, primitives, sterling silver, and wind chimes.

OTHER GOODS **Country Gardens** (706-663-7779), 155 Main Street, Pine Mountain. Open 10–6 daily. In addition to everything you could want for your garden, including herbs and native plants, the emporium offers antiques and accessories for the home.

❋ Special Events

May: **Masters Water-Ski and Wakeboard Tournament** (Callaway Gardens: 706-663-2281 or 1-800-225-5292; www.masterswaterski.com). Held Memorial Day weekend on Callaway Gardens' Robin Lake, the extravaganza has been going strong since 1959. Pavilion seating is available. General admission only; included in Callaway Gardens admission.

May and October: **Cotton Pickin' Fair** (706-538-6814; www.cpfair.org), 18830 Highway 85. A peach-packing shed, cotton gin, and an 1891 farmhouse in Gay are some of the attractions. Skilled artisans present their wares, and there are also antiques, great Southern food, and live entertainment presented on six stages. Adults $7, children age 4–12 $3.

September: **Sky High Hot Air Balloon Festival** (706-663-2281 or 1-800-225-5292; www.callawaygardens.com/specials/specials.sky-high-hot-air-ballon.specials.aspx). The premier activity at this festive event at Callaway Gardens is the balloon glow on Friday night. There are balloon flights and tethered morning and afternoon flights throughout the weekend, entertainment, family activities, a barbecue, classic car show, sand-castle construction, exhibits, and disc dog demonstrations. Adults $25, seniors $20, children 6–12 $12.50

October: **Ossahatchee Indian Festival and Pow-Wow** (www.ossahatchee.org). Held at the Harris County Soccer Fields on GA 116E in Hamilton, the festival features Native Americans from all over the country participating in dance and drum competitions, including hoop dances. Also popular with spectators are primitive skills demonstrations, authentic arts and crafts, and traditional Native American food. Adults $8, children $5.

Railroad Days (706-846-5341). The Saturday railroadiana show at the Manchester Mill (110 Callaway Street, Warm Springs) features HO and Atlantic Coast S-gauge model layout displays, personal collections, and vendor sales. Rides are available on train cars pulled by live steamers—handmade 7.5-inch scale engines A few blocks away, the Manchester railroad yard features a covered platform where you can watch the passing trains. Adults and children older than 12 $2.

November: **Fala Day** (706-655-3322 or 1-800-337-1927; wwwwarmspringsga.com).

STEEPLECHASE AT CALLAWAY

The annual tribute to FDR's little Scottie is presented in Warm Springs by the Scottie Club of Greater Atlanta. Everyone brings their Scotties, and there's a parade and dog show at the park, as well as other festivities. Free admission; some events may have a fee.

Steeplechase at Callaway (706-324-6252; www.steeplechaseatcallaway.org). Held at Callaway Gardens, the event is the third and final leg of the "Sport of Kings" Challenge in the United States. One of the premier social events in all of southwest Georgia, the steeplechase provides numerous horse races over timber and brush hurdles, including junior races and five sanctioned races. Other just-for-fun races include a Stick Pony Race and Jack Russell terrier races. Additional activities include bagpipers, pony rides, a Kids Corral, and a parade of Midland foxhounds. Then there are the contests: Southern Views Hat Contest, Sunny 100 Tailgating Competition, and the Ledge-Enquirer Terrace Box Competition. Seating is in tents, box seats, and the infield. Needless to say, there's lots of food. $25–85 per person, additional $20–50 per car for parking.

November–December: **Fantasy in Lights** (706-663-2281 or 1-800-225-5292; www.callawaygardens.com), GA 18 and GA 354, Pine Mountain. Open evenings from Friday before Thanksgiving through late December at Callaway Gardens. A true winter wonderland, this 5-mile drive-through extravaganza of a dozen Christmas scenes—illuminated with 8 million white and colored lights and enhanced with sound and music—is the largest in the Southeast. Just a few of the scenes include Toy Soldiers, Snowflake Valley, 'Twas the Night Before Christmas, the Nativity, and the Enchanted Rainbow Forest. Drive your own car or ride the Jolly Trolley. At the end of the ride, there are refreshments at eight venues; 10 Christmas shops; entertainment, including raptor shows; and a visit with Father Christmas. Adults $16–25, children $8–12.50. It's far more economical to buy tickets in advance for a weeknight. Several packages available for overnight stays.

FANTASY IN LIGHTS FUN FACTS

- Two million visitors attend each year.
- 3,500 extension cords are used.
- 12 million cables ties are used.
- If all the strings of lights were connected, they would stretch 731 miles—that's the circumference of South Carolina or the distance from Callaway Gardens to Baltimore.
- It takes 3,900 man hours over six weeks to install the display.
- To turn on the display each night, 1,000 switches must be flipped.
- After the season, the lights are stored in a 6,500-square-foot warehouse.

THOMASVILLE

Make time to smell the roses in Thomasville, a city in the Red Hills region of southwest Georgia. The land, with its extremely fertile soil, is home to tall stands of longleaf pines, graceful live oaks, and a profusion of azaleas, dogwood, wisteria, and roses (more about them later).

The town was established in the 1820s with the introduction of cotton plantations. Still prosperous to this day, the region between Thomasville and Tallahassee boasts more working plantations than anywhere in the country—71 plantations encompass more than 300,000 acres. They are private and hidden away behind gates, but one is open for tours and offers accommodations.

Although most of the South suffered during and after the Civil War, Thomasville prospered. Not only was it far removed from Union forces, but it also benefited from its timber industry and an agricultural economy not entirely dependent on cotton. Later, the extension of northern railroads into the area brought commerce, visitors, and new residents.

One of the first cities in Georgia to recognize the importance of historic preservation, Thomasville formed Thomasville Landmarks in 1964. Concentrating on residential restoration, the program has documented seven historic districts in the city. Even though the gargantuan turn-of-the-20th-century hotels of the Winter Resort Era are "gone with the wind," many of the mansions built during that period survive as private homes and businesses, so the town retains much of the charm of that bygone age. Thomasville was named one of the Top Five Main Street Cities in America, and its Main Street Program has restored more than 100 buildings so far.

Thomasville claims to have more roses than people (population 20,000), and if you're riding around the fragrant, colorful streets in the late spring and early summertime, you can easily believe it. The city plants and maintains more than 7,000 rosebushes—each of which blossoms with hundreds of flowers—and many residents nurture their own impressive rose gardens.

The small towns in this region boast one or more attractions, outdoor recreation, lodgings, restaurants, and special events.

GUIDANCE To learn more about Thomasville and Ochlocknee, contact the **Thomasville–Thomas County Visitors Center** (229-228-7977 or 1-866-577-3600; www.thomasvillega .com), 401 South Broad Street, Thomasville 31792. Open 8–5 weekdays, 10–3 Saturday. This is the place to pick up brochures for the **Historic Walking and Driving Tour** and the **Thomasville Black History Heritage Trail Tour Guide** (see *To Do—Walking Tours*).

GETTING THERE *By air:* The nearest airport is in Tallahassee, Florida. For airport, airline, and car rental information, see "What's Where in Georgia."

THOMASVILLE REPORTEDLY HAS MORE
ROSES THAN PEOPLE.

By bus: The closest **Greyhound** bus service is in Albany. (See the Albany chapter.)

By car: Thomasville is at the intersection of US 84/221, US 319, and US 19/GA 300.

By train: There is no train service to Thomasville or the surrounding area.

GETTING AROUND In addition to car rentals at Tallahassee Regional Airport, off-site car rentals are available from **Budget** (1-800-527-7000) and **Thrifty** (850-576-7368).

MEDICAL EMERGENCY Call 911.

NEIGHBORHOODS AND VILLAGES Thomasville boasts several historic districts with a wide range of turn-of-the-20th-century homes and buildings, and a vast array of architectural styles. The **Dawson Street Historic District** stretches from Jackson to Walcott streets. The **Downtown Historic District** extends from Walcott and Dawson streets to Broad Street. The **Stevens Street Historic District,** which includes West Calhoun, Oak, Monroe, Stevens, Pine, West Clay, West Washington, Jefferson, Webster, Walcott, Jerger, and Forsyth streets, was a neighborhood for affluent African Americans. Some other historic districts include the **Paradise Park Historic District** and the **Tockwotton–Love Street Historic District.** Numerous historic buildings line **Hansell Street.**

✳ To See

CULTURAL SITES 🐾 ✎ ♿ **Thomasville Cultural Center** (229-226-0588; www.thomasvillearts.org), 600 East Washington Street, Thomasville. Galleries open 9–5 weekdays, 1–5 Saturday during exhibitions. The center hosts art exhibits as well as performances and conducts visual and performing arts classes. In the Orientation Room, artifacts, memorabilia, and photographs offer an in-depth look at the cultural history of the city and county. Multiple galleries on several levels of the center feature the works of local, regional, and national artists on a rotating basis. There is also an impressive permanent gallery, and a period classroom is filled with children's artwork. The three-story building is interesting in itself. It was originally constructed in 1915 for the Eastside Elementary School, the city's first public school built with tax revenue. Free.

HISTORIC HOMES AND SITES 🐾 ✎ **Lapham-Patterson House Historic Site** (229-225-4004; www.gastateparks.org/LaphamPatterson), 626 North Dawson Street, Thomasville. Open 1–5 Friday, 10–5 Saturday, and 2–5:30 Sunday. Guided tours start on the hour and last about 45 minutes; last tour at 4. This whimsical Queen Anne house is a testimonial to ingenuity, engineering, and craftsmanship. Some of its interesting architectural features are its fish-scale shingles in several different patterns, Oriental-style molding on the porch, longleaf pine inlaid floors, a double-flue chimney with a walk-through staircase, and a cantilevered balcony, but two things are especially interesting: None of the rooms are square or rectangular, and all 19 rooms have an outside exit. C. W. Lapham, an affluent Chicago shoe manufacturer, had suffered lung damage in the infamous 1871 Chicago fire. When he built this house as a winter "cottage" in 1885, he made sure he could get out easily no matter where he was in his home. In addition to satisfying his safety concerns, he made sure the house featured all the modern conveniences of the time: a gas-lighting system, hot and cold running water, and built-in closets. All this was created for the then astronomical price of $4,500. Admission $1–5.

🦌 ♿ **Old Magnolia Cemetery, Lieutenant Henry O. Flipper's Grave,** 700 North Madison Street, Thomasville. Of all the notable African American citizens buried in this graveyard, one is of particular interest. Lieut. Henry Ossian Flipper, a Thomasville native, was born into slavery in 1856. He went on, however, to become the first African American graduate of the U.S. Military Academy at West Point and subsequently had a career with the U.S. Cavalry's buffalo soldiers, where he achieved many firsts for African American soldiers: cavalry officer, surveyor, cartographer, civil and mining engineer, translator, editor, author, and special agent for the Justice Department. Unfortunately, Flipper was erro-

THE LAPHAM-PATTERSON HOUSE HISTORIC SITE OVERFLOWS WITH UNIQUE ARCHITECTURAL FEATURES, AS SEEN FROM THIS VIEW FROM THE REAR.

neously accused of embezzling government funds. Although he was found not guilty, his clumsy attempt to replace the money to make the problem go away resulted in a dishonorable discharge from the Army. Through the prodigious efforts of family members, the Army finally granted him a posthumous honorable discharge in 1976, and President Clinton granted him a pardon in 1999, 59 years after his death. To honor his memory, the city of Thomasville named the park across the street from the cemetery Henry O. Flipper Park, and a bust of Flipper resides in the Thomas County Library's Flipper Room.

🦌 ✏ ♿ **Pebble Hill Plantation** (229-226-2344; www.pebblehill.com), 1251 US 319, Thomasville. Open 10–5 Tuesday–Saturday, 1–5 Sunday (final tour at 4); closed in September. Pebble Hill is currently the only one of the Thomasville area's many plantations that is open for tours. With more than 3,000 acres, the plantation is a prime example of the opulent late-19th- and early-20th-century shooting plantations developed by wealthy Northerners. Although the plantation had existed as a working farm since 1820, when it had been established by Thomas Jefferson Johnson, the founder of Thomas County, when it was acquired by Cleveland entrepreneur Howard Melville Hanna in 1896, it became a place of leisure pursuits. The original house was destroyed by fire in the 1930s with the exception of the loggia. The current 40-room mansion was designed by Abram Garfield, son of the nation's 20th president. Hanna's granddaughter and last of the Hanna heirs, Elisabeth Ireland Poe, known as "Miss Pansy," filled the house with antique furnishings, period wall murals, decorative arts, silver, an astounding collection of sporting art and wildlife scenes, and an extensive collection of 33 Audubon prints, Native American artifacts, shells, sporting trophies, and other personal mementos. On her death in 1978, Miss Pansy left the estate to be used as a museum. Visitors would see the house much as if the family had just stepped out for a while. So engrossed would visitors be in looking at the furniture and collections that much of the magnificent art was not shown to advantage. Recently the upstairs bedrooms have been converted to galleries with museum-quality lighting to better showcase the English and American sporting art. Outside, visitors can tour the stables, kennels, dog hospital, log-cabin schoolhouse, infirmary, fire engine house, garage filled with vintage carriages and autos, swimming pool, graveyards (both human and canine), and a child-size Noah's Ark that serves as a playhouse–jungle gym. Plan on several hours here. Children younger than six are not permitted in main house, but there are plenty of other things for them to see outdoors, including the horses, mules, and dogs. Accommodations are available in the Overflow Cottage ($350–450 per night) or the Firehouse Apartment ($250). Admission to property: adults $5, children younger than 12 $2; mansion tour: adults $15, children 6–12 $6.

MUSEUMS 🐾 **Grady County Museum and History Center** (229-377-9728), 101 North Broad Street, Cairo. Open 10–4 Tuesday, Thursday, and Friday; 1–6 Wednesday. The Grady County Historical Society operates this museum, where visitors can see antiques, collectibles, memorabilia, and photographs that depict the rich heritage of the county. Among the displays are household and agricultural items, but the focal point of the museum is a historic mural on permanent loan from the post office. Free.

🐾 ✎ ♿ **Thomas County Museum of History** (229-226-7664; www.thomascountyhistory .org), 725 North Dawson Street, Thomasville. Open 10–11:30 and 2–3:30 Monday–Saturday; closed last two weeks in August. Step into this 1923 Jeffersonian Revival house and discover the stories of early Thomasville residents. The story of the Winter Resort Era and its wealthy visitors is told through photographs and artifacts from the hotels and plantations, but African American, Civil War, antebellum, World War II, and pioneer Thomasville history are not neglected. A particularly interesting exhibit details the lives of African American families who lived and worked on plantations. Also located on the grounds are several historic buildings either original to the property or moved from other locations. The circa 1860 **Rufus Smith House** is a pioneer log cabin, while the circa 1877 **Emily Joyner House** is a modest Victorian cottage. Something most visitors have never seen anywhere else is the self-contained **Ewart Bowling Alley,** a turn-of-the-20th-century bowling alley built of heart pine. It is the oldest in Georgia and perhaps the oldest in the South. The newest addition to the complex is the circa 1892 **Metcalf Courthouse,** a simple country courthouse. Adults $5, children 6–18 $1.

SPECIAL PLACES 🐾 ✎ ♿ **The Big Oak,** East Monroe and North Crawford streets, Thomasville. The pride and joy of Thomasville, as well as its oldest natural landmark, is this mighty live oak, which grew from a tiny acorn in about 1685, making it about 327 years old in 2012. Think about it: That means this oak predates the founding of this nation by many years. The venerable tree is more than 66 feet tall, has a limb span over 165 feet wide, and is 26 feet in circumference, making it the largest live oak east of the Mississippi. The Big Oak is one of the original members (#49) of the Live Oak Society, enrolled in 1936. The sprawling branches are often covered with resurrection fern. Non-Southerners may not be familiar with resurrection fern, which is found in abundance on this and other trees. It may look as if it's dried up and dead, but any moisture—even morning dew—brings it miraculously back to life. In order to protect the Big Oak, there are restrictions about what can be driven under it. For example, don't try to drive an RV under it. Free.

WINTER RESORT ERA

Thomasville's pleasant climate, lack of mosquito-laden marshes, abundance of wild game, and easy access by railroad caused Northerners to flock to the area in the late 1880s, creating the Winter Resort Era and turning cotton plantations into quail-hunting estates. The Northerners even believed that the area's pine-scented air had beneficial qualities for pulmonary ailments. Large resort hotels sprang up and attracted presidents, potentates, tycoons, and entertainers. Many of these visitors decided to stay at least part of the year and built grand homes they modestly called "cottages." Eventually the railroads pushed into Florida and the fickle idle rich moved on to trendier locales, but Thomasville still retains the charm of that area with many surviving homes.

✳ To Do

BIRDING ✿ ✎ **Birdsong Nature Center** (229-377-4408 or 1-800-953-BIRD; www.birdsongnaturecenter.org), 2106 Meridian Road, Thomasville. Open 9–5 Wednesday, Friday, and Saturday; 1–5 Sunday. This pristine sanctuary for birds and wildlife, located on what was originally Birdsong Plantation, boasts 565 acres of fields, pine and hardwood forests, ponds, swamps, and wildflower meadows. The most unusual feature of the center is the Bird Window. Within the historic house, which now serves as the visitors center, a large picture window allows visitors to observe birds up close. Providing food for the birds in the intimate enclosed garden outside the window has attracted more than 160 species. Visitors can easily see 25 different species in one sitting. At the Listening Place, a screened pavilion overlooking Big Bay Swamp, visitors can hear a symphony of bird calls and the songs of frogs, alligators, and other wildlife. The Butterfly Garden is vibrant with multicolored butterflies from April through November, while the best time to see purple martins is from January to July. Ten miles of nature trails include the Bluebird Trail, along which 40 nest boxes are placed in ideal bluebird habitat. More than 100 bluebird fledglings are born here each year during the nesting season from mid-March to August. Adults $5, children 4–12 $2.50.

SAY "CHEESE"
For a one-of-a-kind souvenir, stand in front of the Big Oak behind the white sign and dial 229-236-0053 on your cell phone. Look at the camera on the telephone pole across the street, follow the instructions you hear on your cell phone, and strike a pose. Find your picture online at http://BigOak.Rose.net.

WALKING TOURS ✿ **Historic Walking and Driving Tour** (www.thomasvillega.com /scenic_tour.htm). Available for purchase from the Thomasville–Thomas County Visitors Center, 401 South Broad Street, the self-guided 4.5-mile tour includes more than 70 homes and buildings. Every historic building downtown contains a marker listing the year of construction and the original business that occupied the space, though many of the residences are private homes not open to the public. You can get a sample of what you'll see on the tour by consulting the website.

✿ **Thomasville Black History Heritage Trail Tour** (www.thomasvillega.com/black _history.htm). Free booklets available at the visitors center and the Thomas County Historical Society, 725 North Dawson Street, have pictures and an easy-to-follow map. The self-guided tour points out 68 significant African American historical sites, including the grave site of Lieut. Henry Ossian Flipper (see **Old Magnolia Cemetery** under *To See—Historic Homes and Sites*), a post office named in Flipper's honor, the only remaining African American one-room country school, the historic Stevens Street Historic District, and the Douglas High School Memorial Monument.

THE BIG OAK IN THOMASVILLE IS MORE THAN 300 YEARS OLD.

✳ Green Space

GARDENS ✿ ✎ ⚹ **Thomasville Rose Garden,** Smith Avenue and Covington Drive near Cherokee Lake, Thomasville. Open daylight hours daily. Although quite small, this colorful garden showcases more than 250 species and more than 500 prize rose-bushes. Free.

495

THOMASVILLE

NATURE PRESERVES AND PARKS 🦆 ✎ ♿ **Paradise Park,** bounded by Broad, Hansell, and Metcalf streets, was originally nicknamed Yankee Paradise because the Northerners who stayed at the resort hotels used the park. John Philip Sousa's band entertained in the bandstand. Today the 26-acre park remains in its natural state for all to enjoy.

RIVERS 🦆 ✎ The **Ochlocknee River** in Cairo has several boat landings and many opportunities for canoeing and fishing.

✳ Lodging
BED & BREAKFASTS

In Camilla
🦆 **Eagle Eyrie and the Smokehouse Antiques** (229-336-8811), 135 East Broad Street. This circa 1906 house boasts 22 rooms, four of which are reserved for guests at this charming B&B. A wraparound porch with swings and rockers graces the entrance, and guests are invited to shop for antiques in the converted smokehouse. A full breakfast is included in the nightly rate. Smoking not permitted indoors. Not wheelchair accessible. $95.

In Thomasville
1884 Paxton House Inn (229-226-5197; www.1884paxtonhouseinn.com), 445 Remington Avenue. Located in an opulent Victorian Gothic mansion recognized for its outstanding renovation by the Georgia Trust for Historic Preservation, this AAA four-diamond B&B offers luxurious accommodations in the historic main house and several recently constructed cottages. The house was originally built by Col. J. W. Paxton of Wheeling, West Virginia, as a vacation residence during the Winter Resort Era. Owner Susie Sherrod has many fascinating collections from her world travels—Lalique, Waterford, Hummel, and Russian dolls among them. She's just as fascinating herself. Among the surprises are a communal indoor lap pool and a hot tub in one of the cottages. The pool is available for use by all guests 9–9; earlier or later than that, it is available only to guests in that cottage. A gourmet breakfast is served in the Garden Room of the main house with fine china, silver, and crystal. No smoking. Not wheelchair accessible. $175–375.

CAMPGROUNDS

In Ochlocknee
🦆 ✎ **Sugar Mill Plantation RV Park** (229-227-1451), 4857 McMillan Road. In addition to the 48 level, shady RV sites, the facility offers cabins, three clubhouses, an exercise room, shuffleboard, horseshoes, a basketball court, fish ponds (no license required), a fishing pier, hiking trails, restrooms and showers, laundry, a lending library, and even a woodworking shop. $28 per night, $175 per week.

✳ Where to Eat
DINING OUT

In Thomasville
♿ **Liam's Restaurant** (229-226-9944; www.liamsthomasville.com), 113 East Jackson Street. Open 11–2 Tuesday–Friday for lunch, 5:30–10 Thursday–Friday for dinner,

STUMPING BOYS
In 1868 a simple lane that was the precursor to the present-day Broad Street in Camilla was created by cutting down virgin pines, leaving their stumps behind. The town's first mayor, T. J. Butler, inaugurated a "stumping contest" in which he contributed dimes to the boys who uprooted the most stumps to clear the lane. He gave dimes from his own pocket because the town treasury had no money in it.

Saturday 9–1 for brunch and 5:30–whenever for dinner. A *Georgia Trend* Silver Spoon Award winner, the restaurant features eclectic seasonal fare with a rotating menu. In addition to the food, diners enjoy the warm atmosphere, open kitchen, artwork by local artists, Sweet Grass Dairy cheeses, and garden dining when the weather permits. No smoking. Brunch $6–8, lunch $6–11, dinner $26–32.

EATING OUT

In Thomasville

🦐 ✂ ♿ **George and Louie's Fresh Seafood Restaurant** (229-226-1218), 216 Remington Avenue. Open 11–8 Monday–Saturday. Located in what was once a 1950s burger joint, this eatery serves up catfish, oyster, scallop, shrimp, and snapper plates accompanied by fries or grits, hush puppies, and salad. Deviled crab, chicken or seafood kebabs, sandwiches, salads, and burgers are also on the menu, but they're really famous for their fried green tomatoes, Greek salads, and Greek wines. If you're in a big hurry, call in your order and pick it up at the drive-through window. No smoking. $9–17.

🦐 ✂ ♿ **Market Diner** (229-225-1777), 502 Smith Avenue. Open 10:15–9 Monday–Thursday, 10:15–10 Friday and Saturday, 10:15–8:30 Sunday. A bustling place, this restaurant is located in the **State Farmer's Market** (see *Selective Shopping—Food*). Plain and simple, the eatery's staple is its buffet, but its specialty is chicken gizzards. You also can order seafood platters, quail, a variety of vegetables, and homemade desserts. There's an all-you-can-eat seafood buffet on Friday and Saturday nights. No smoking. Wheelchair accessible. Lunch $6–7, dinner $9–11.

SNACKS AND TAKE-OUT

In Thomasville

🦐 ✂ ♿ **The Billiard Academy** (229-226-9981), 121 South Broad Street. Open 9–7 Monday–Saturday. Is it the hot dogs or the billiards or both that bring folks here from far and near? The franks, slathered in a special chili sauce, can be purchased at the sidewalk window or enjoyed at the lunch counter inside. Between 200 and 300 dogs are sold on any normal day, but during festivals and special events the number may soar to 1,000. Billiards is enjoyed in the back room. No smoking. Wheelchair accessible.

🦐 ✂ ♿ **The Scoop Ice Cream and Deli** (229-551-0012), 118-A South Broad Street. Open 9:30–5:30 Monday–Saturday. When in the mood for dessert, stop at the Scoop for fresh ice cream, milk shakes, and sundaes. The eatery also serves salads, sandwiches, and soups. Primarily meant to be a take-out place, it has one table inside and several outside. No smoking. Wheelchair accessible. Entrées under $10.

✳ Entertainment

The best way to find out what is happening in the area, as well as where, when, and admission prices, is to check this website: www.thomasvillega.com/Calendar/Show/6/Month/events-and-festivals.html.

🦐 **Thomasville Cultural Center** (229-226-0588; www.thomasvillearts.org), 600 East Washington Street, Thomasville. Galleries open 9–5 weekdays, 1–5 Saturday and Sunday. Theatrical and musical productions are staged in the renovated auditorium. In collaboration with the Thomasville Entertainment Foundation, a nine-month-long season brings national performers to the stage. Classic films are shown during the Summer Music Series, and annual events include the **Plantation Wildlife Arts Festival** (see *Special Events*). Admission to galleries free. Times and prices vary for productions; check the website or call for a schedule of events and ticket prices.

MUSIC Thomasville Entertainment Foundation (229-226-7404; www.tefconcerts.com). Performances held at Thomasville Cultural Arts Center auditorium, 600 East Jackson Street, Thomasville. Founded in 1937, the foundation is one of America's oldest all-volunteer concert series presenters. Patrons are treated to internationally renowned dancers, instrumentalists, pianists, and singers in six concerts between October and April. Check the website or call for a schedule of performances. Adults $35, students $15.

THEATER ❧ Thomasville On Stage & Company (229-226-0863; www.tosac.com), 117 South Broad Street, Thomasville. Performances Friday and Saturday nights and Sunday afternoons. A local theater group, the company stages three shows a year, one of which is usually a musical. Check the website or call for a schedule of performances. Adults $12, students $10.

✳ Selective Shopping

ANTIQUES Toscoga Marketplace Antiques (229-227-6777; www.toscoga .com), 209 South Broad Street, Thomasville. Open 10–6 Monday–Saturday, noon–5 Sunday. Ninety dealers offer antiques, collectibles, and gifts.

BOOKS The Bookshelf and Gallery (229-228-7767), 126 South Broad Street, Thomasville. Open 9–5:30 weekdays, 10–5:30 Saturday. Those who appreciate the ever-decreasing independent bookstores will want to stop here for a wide selection of new and used books, audiobooks, cards, and gifts. The store will help you locate out-of-print books, too.

FOOD State Farmer's Market (229-225-4072), 502 Smith Avenue, Thomasville. Open 8–6 Monday–Saturday; auctions held 2–6 Monday–Saturday, May–November. Second in size only to Atlanta's farmer's market in the Southeast, the Thomasville market sells the best and freshest regional produce, everything from mayhaw berries to the world-famous sweet Vidalia onions. Among the homemade jams, jellies, relishes, and pickles is mayhaw jelly, created from berries that grow on trees in swamps. **Market Diner,** the on-site restaurant, is open 10–9:30 daily (see *Where to Eat—Eating Out*). Local cookbooks, white oak baskets, and souvenirs are also available.

✳ Special Events

April: **Thomasville Rose Show, Parade, and Festival** (229-227-3310). Visitors have a blooming good time at this festival, held annually since 1921, which celebrates the 7,000 rosebushes planted throughout the city. Among the activities are special rose displays; historic home, garden, and museum tours; street dances; arts and crafts shows; walking and running races; a golf classic; Jump for the Roses horse show; the Pebble Hill Plantation Ball; a juried rose show; lectures; nursery vendor displays; and, of course, the parade. During the festival, the Lapham-Patterson House is the "House of a Hundred Roses," with hundreds of roses on display. Free; some activities have a small fee.

Late April or early May and October: **Picker's Paradise Park Festival** (229-221-5467), 2217 Maddox Road, Ochlocknee. The twice-yearly bluegrass festival is held on a scenic 10-acre lake. Music starts informally on Thursday night but officially starts at 7 on Friday. People are usually playing informally all day in "picking circles." Home-cooked food is also an integral part of the festival. $5 Thursday evening only; $10 per day Friday and Saturday; $25 Festival Pass for all three days, in and out privileges throughout, and primitive camping.

Mid-September: **Friends and Family Days at Pebble Hill Plantation** (229-226-2344; www.pebblehill.com) features entertainment and storytelling. Free with admission.

Early October: **Pelham Wildlife Festival** (229-294-4924). Held on the first Saturday of October, the biggest wildlife event in southwest Georgia features wildlife education shows, arts and crafts, and all-day entertainment. Free.

Mid-October: **Thomasville Fly-In** (229-226-4753; www.thomasvilleflyin.com). Held the second weekend of the month at Thomasville Municipal Airport. The fastest-growing area of the fly-in is the Vendors and Fly Market. The Aircraft Engine

Museum is another draw, and peanut boiling is a long-standing Saturday-morning tradition. The Rose City Soaring Club offers sailplane and glider rides, and many folks get their first plane ride at the fly-in. Children's activities include a parade and the Candy Drop—50 pounds of candy dropped from a helicopter. Free for spectators; small charge for some activities.

Mid-November: **Plantation Wildlife Arts Festival** (229-226-0588; www.pwaf.org). Held in Thomasville 10–5 Saturday and Sunday preceding Thanksgiving. The **Thomasville Cultural Center** (see *To See—Cultural Sites*) presents a juried wildlife arts show featuring painting, sculpture, and photography by renowned artists. Prices for items for sale range from $10 to $50,000. An annual highlight is a visit from *Wild Kingdom* host Jim Fowler, who entertains visitors with furred and feathered wildlife. Also featured are children's activities, demonstrations, lectures, and wildlife and sporting films. Check the website or call for annual details and prices.

Early December: **Victorian Christmas** (229-227-7020; www.downtownthomasville .com/victorian.html). The 1890s are recreated in Thomasville during two evenings with jingle-bell horse-drawn carriage rides, citizens in period costumes, stores and restaurants decorated for the holidays, and food and holiday delicacies. Most anticipated, however, are the street performances by actors, storytellers, carolers, choirs, dancers, bands, mimes, jugglers, and an organ grinder. Other activities include a Victorian Museum, a live Nativity, and a visit from St. Nicholas. In addition, during Victorian Christmas there is an open house at the **Lapham-Patterson House** (see *To See—Historic Homes and Sites*), a holiday show from the Thomasville Music and Drama Troupe, and the Thomas County Museum of History's Candlelight Tour of Homes. Some events free; others, fees vary by activity. Call for details.

Mid-December: **Pebble Hill Plantation Family Christmas** (229-226-2344; www .pebblehill.com). Held on Saturday of second weekend in December near Thomasville (see *To See—Historic Homes and Sites*). During the evening open house, guests tour the downstairs of the main house, decked out in all its holiday finery. Other activities include a visit with Santa, coach rides, and games, $20 per car.

TIFTON AND MOULTRIE

I n the heart of rural south Georgia, prime agricultural land with scenic, sprawling farmsteads is the norm. The region, however, is a growing leisure destination. The only big towns are Tifton and Moultrie, but there are numerous hamlets with enough attractions and activities to draw visitors. Travelers find plentiful outdoor recreational activities, art museums and galleries, outdoor murals and other public art, historic and quirky museums, gardens, state parks, wildlife refuges, cultural events, unusual festivals, antiques and outlet shopping, and bed & breakfasts in historic homes.

In Georgia, towns and counties with the same name are not usually paired up (Clayton is not in Clayton County, Lumpkin is not in Lumpkin County, and so on), so Tifton and Tift County are unusual in that they were both named for the same family—although not for the same person. Tift County was named for Nelson Tift, and the town of Tifton was named for his nephew Henry Tift.

GUIDANCE When planning a trip to the Tifton area, contact the **Tifton–Tift County Tourism Association** (229-382-8700; www.tiftontourism.com), 115 West Second Street, Tifton 31793. Another source of information is the **Tifton–Tift County Chamber of Commerce** (229-382-6200; www.tiftonchamber.org), 100 North Central Avenue, Tifton 31794. Open 8:30–5 weekdays.

If planning travel to the Moultrie area, contact the **Moultrie–Colquitt County Chamber of Commerce** (229-985-2131 or 1-888-40-VISIT; www.moultriechamber.com), 116 First Avenue SE, Moultrie 31768. Open 8–5 weekdays.

GETTING THERE *By air:* Tifton is located within one hour's drive of the Valdosta and Albany airports (see the Valdosta chapter and "What's Where in Georgia").

By bus: Bus service is provided by **Greyhound Lines** (229-382-1868 or 1-800-231-2222), 4431 Union Road, Tifton.

By car: Tifton is conveniently located at I-75, US 319, US 82, and US 41.

By train: The nearest **AMTRAK** (1-800-USA-RAIL) stations are in Atlanta (see "What's Where in Georgia") and Madison, Florida.

GETTING AROUND In Tifton, car rentals are available from **Enterprise** (229-382-6614 or 1-800-736-8222), 1401 Tift Avenue.

MEDICAL EMERGENCY In life-threatening situations, call 911.

VILLAGES Tifton, the largest municipality in this area, was founded in 1890 by sawmill supervisor Henry Harding Tift. Today 70 percent of the downtown buildings are on the National Register of Historic Places. Because Tifton, listed in the book *100 Best Small Towns in America* by Michael Crampton, participates in the nationwide Main Street improvement program, downtown buildings have been spruced up to house trendy shops, boutiques, and restaurants. The city offers museums, art galleries, shopping, historic sites, and outdoor recreational activities.

Moultrie, the county seat of Colquitt County, was incorporated in 1859 and named for Gen. William Moultrie, a Revolutionary War hero. The city's opulent 1902 courthouse has been voted the prettiest in the state. Moultrie, which rivals Tifton in population, boasts a rejuvenated downtown with more than 50 specialty shops and restaurants. Called "the Antique Capital of South Georgia," it boasts more than 36 downtown antiques dealers. Moultrie is also the home of the **Sunbelt Agricultural Exposition,** the largest farm show in the country (see *Special Events*), and hosts several other festivals. Moultrie is in the midst of prime quail hunting plantations, too.

✳ To See

CULTURAL SITES 🐾 ♿ **Atlantic Coastline Artists Station** (229-382-5589), 119 Love Avenue, Tifton. Open 2–4 Wednesday or by appointment. The town's restored railroad freight depot houses a permanent collection and changing exhibitions. Outside, *Our Town Tifton* is a 30-foot bas-relief folk-art wall that was created by combining the whimsical minisculptures made by hundreds of area residents. Free.

🐾 ♿ **Citizen's Art Collection** (229-382-6231), 130 East First Street, Tifton. Open 8:30–5 weekdays. Several dozen works of art depicting Tifton and south Georgia as seen through the eyes of local and regional artists are displayed at the historic Myon Hotel, which now serves as Tifton City Hall. Free.

🐾 ♦ ♿ **Landscape Murals.** Always accessible. Outdoor murals of regional scenes, lakes, and flowers adorn a building at Main and Second streets and another at Commerce Way and Third Street, both in Tifton. Free.

🐾 ♦ ♿ **Milltown Murals** (229-482-9755), at Main, Center, and Murrell streets, as well as Valdosta Highway, Lakeland. Always accessible. Twenty-three life-size murals painted on downtown buildings depict the citizens, landscape, and important events of Milltown, which was Lakeland's name until 1925. The murals depict life in the 1920s. Maps to help visitors locate all the murals can be obtained from the **Lakeland–Lanier County Chamber of Commerce** (www.lakelandlanier chamber.com).

🐾 ♦ ♿ **World's Largest Peanut Monument,** along I-75, Ashburn. Accessible 24/7. Ashburn is the home of the world's largest peanut processing plant, so it's only natural that a tribute to the important crop would be raised here. Erected in 1975, the 10-foot-tall peanut emerges from a large yellow crown proclaiming GEORGIA FIRST IN PEANUTS, which is mounted on a 15-foot column. Each point on the crown is festooned with a colored glass globe resembling a jewel, so the entire monument really sparkles when lit at night. Although

LITTLE ELEPHANT

Anyone who has ever wanted to run off and join the circus will smile at this touching little gravestone in the old Pleasant Grove Primitive Baptist Church cemetery on GA 37 in Moultrie. As a boy at the turn of the 20th century, William F. Duggan wanted to do just that. When he grew up, his dream came true and then some—he bought a circus. Duggan died in 1950, and, as a tribute to his father's dream, his son commissioned a gravestone that is topped with the likeness of a baby elephant.

the 13-foot Smiling Peanut representing former president Jimmy Carter in Plains (see the Americus chapter) may have a taller nut, with the crown and pedestal, this representation of the goober wins the "largest" title hands down.

HISTORIC HOMES AND SITES 🦐 ♦ ♿ **Fulwood Garden Center** (229-386-8347; www.fulwoodgardencenter.com), 802 West 12th Street, Tifton. Open for self-guided tours 9–noon weekdays; guided tours by reservation. A beautiful home from the early 1900s has been restored by the Tifton Garden Club and surrounded by a garden filled with native and exotic plants. Free.

🦐 ♦ ♿ **Georgia Museum of Agriculture and History Village** (229-386-3344 or 1-800-767-1875; www.abac.edu/museum), 1392 Whiddon Mill Road, Tifton. Open 9–4:30 Tuesday–Saturday; train operates Saturday only. By moving 35 historical homes and commercial buildings from various locations in south Georgia to the 95-acre site, a town and surrounding farmsteads have been assembled to depict the wire-grass region during the period 1870 to 1910. The site is divided into five sections: a traditional farm community of the 1870s, a progressive farmstead of the 1890s, an industrial site, a rural town, and a national peanut complex and Museum of Agriculture Center. Costumed docents describe life in a simpler time and demonstrate old-time skills. In addition to several historic homes—from a preacher's cabin to the opulent Tift House and two farmsteads—the town contains an apothecary, church, cotton gin, country store, feed and seed store, water-powered gristmill, Masonic lodge, newspaper office and print shop, railroad depot, sawmill, one-room school, woodworker's shop, cooper's works, blacksmith shop, and turpentine still. A steam locomotive pulls a train of open-air wooden cars around the site on Saturdays. Visitors can buy small, interesting, old-timey gifts at the country store. Cotton ginning, cane grinding, and turpentine stilling are demonstrated at various times throughout the year. The Wiregrass Opry performs some Saturday nights. Among the special events that occur throughout the year are the **Historical Halloween Carnival** and the **1890s Victorian Christmas Celebration.** Adults $7, seniors $6, children $4; on Saturday the train ride is included: adults $10, seniors $8, children $5; children four and younger free all days.

🦐 ♦ ♿ **Old Colquitt County Jail** (229-985-2131 or 1-888-40-VISIT; www.moultriechamber.com), 116 First Avenue SE, Moultrie. Open 8–5 weekdays. Now the location of the chamber of commerce, the 1915 building served as a jail, and the original gallows are still in place. The structure is notable for its Oriental brick, terrazzo floors, and Georgia granite. Free.

MUSEUMS 🦐 ♦ ♿ **Crime and Punishment Museum and Last Meal Café** (229-567-9696; www.jailmuseum.com), 241 East College Street, Ashburn. Open 10–4:15 Tuesday–Saturday. Built in 1906, the Turner County Jail was nicknamed "Castle Turner" by inmates because of its Romanesque style. Among things to see here are the original cells, death cell,

OLD MEETS NEW AT THE GEORGIA MUSEUM OF AGRICULTURE AND HISTORY VILLAGE.

hanging hook, and trapdoor where two men were hanged for murder. The facility also features the **Last Meal Café** (see *Where to Eat—Eating Out*). Call ahead to verify current admission fees and that the Last Meal Café will be open.

🐾 ✒ ⚹ **Museum of Colquitt County History** (229-890-1626; www.colquittmusem.org), 500 Fourth Avenue SE, Moultrie. Open for self-guided tours 10–5 Friday and Saturday, 2–5 Sunday, or by appointment; guided tours by reservation. Changing exhibits chronicle the diverse history of the area. Displays range from Native American history to more recent events, such as wars in which Colquitt County citizens have participated. Artifacts date back to pre-Columbian times. Free; donations appreciated.

🐾 ⚹ **Tifton Museum of Arts and Heritage** (229-382-3600), 255 Love Avenue, Tifton. Open based on exhibit schedule, so call for hours; tours by reservation. The museum is housed in a restored 1901 Romanesque church, which was Tifton's first brick church. The building retains its exquisite stained-glass windows and other significant architectural elements including heart-pine floors, vaulted ceilings and buttresses, a bell tower, and fanlight doorways. The museum features quarterly traveling exhibits of paintings, works in wood, porcelain, and other media. Free; donations appreciated.

SPECIAL PLACES **Magnolia Tree Park** (229-386-0216), Magnolia Industrial Park Drive, Tifton. Accessible 24/7. More than 400 years old and 61 feet tall, with a crown spread of 105 feet, the second-largest magnolia in the country is the star of this park. If this is the second largest, we'd love to see the largest. The best time to see the tree is in the late spring or early summer, when it is covered with thousands of waxy white blooms. Free.

✳ To Do

AUTO RACING ✒ ⚹ **South Georgia Motorsports Park** (229-896-7000; www.sgmp racing.com), 2521 US 41 North, Cecil. Located near Valdosta, the facility features a full weekly schedule of "dragway" and speedway racing, including monster truck shows, swap meets, and motorcycle days. Tiered seats accommodate 6,000. The 4,100-foot dragway is on one side of the stands; a 0.5-mile oval track for stock car racing is on the other side. Call or check the website for a schedule of events and ticket prices.

BICYCLING 🐾 ✒ ⚹ **The Bike Trail** (229-985-1056). Open daily. This Rails-to-Trails project beside South Main Street in downtown Moultrie offers easily accessible opportunities for biking, walking, jogging, and in-line skating. Free.

BIRDING See **Reed Bingham State Park** under *Green Space—Nature Preserves and Parks*. The best locations are near the bridge and dam, and along the nature trails at dusk. Buzzard viewing (actually black and turkey vultures) is best in the morning and late afternoon. Visitors may be rewarded with sightings of nesting bald eagles.

FISHING 🐾 ✒ ⚹ **Paradise Public Fishing Area** (229-533-4792; www.georgiawildlife .org/PFA/Paradise), Brookfield-Nashville Road off US 82 East, Tifton. Open sunrise–sunset Wednesday–Sunday. Sixty-eight lakes and ponds totaling 525 acres of water provide plenty of fishing opportunities, but you must have a valid fishing license. In addition, there are 568 acres of forest and 123 acres of open fields. The entire Georgia Department of Natural Resources–operated area is excellent for wildlife observation. Many areas can be seen from a vehicle or a small boat, except for some longleaf pine–wire-grass areas, which can be reached only on foot. A variety of wading birds and waterfowl, bald eagles, hawks, many mammals, nine-banded armadillos, snakes, and the endangered gopher tortoise can be seen. (*Note:* When venturing off roads and trails, snake leggings are recommended.) The facility offers restrooms, a boat ramp, fishing pier, dock, and primitive camping. Some of the facilities are handicapped accessible. Several tournaments occur throughout the year, some specifically for children. A Georgia Outdoor Recreation Pass (GORP) is required for anyone 16–64 who does not already have a hunting or fishing license. $3.50 for three days, $19 for an annual pass.

HIKING ❦ ♂ **Robert Simpson Nature Trail** (229-482-9755), North Temple Street, Lakeland. Open dawn–dusk daily. The trail, on a 75-acre tract alongside Lake Irma, meanders through pristine forested areas where visitors can see abundant plant life, natural bogs, and native wildlife. The exceptional scenery attracts both seasoned and novice hikers. Fishing opportunities are excellent as well. Free.

HUNTING **Live Oak Plantation** (229-896-2112 or 1-800-682-4868; www.huntliveoak .com), 675 Plantation Road, Adel. Open daily October 1–March 31. A sportsman's paradise, the facility offers not only quail and pheasant hunting, but also golf and fishing. Bobwhite quail abound on the 3,000-acre private reserve. Professional hunting guides and champion bird dogs lead the way to the action. A handsomely decorated rustic lodge provides accommodations and meals. Prices vary.

WALKING TOURS ❦ **Walking Tour of Moultrie** (www.gpb.org/georgiastories/videos /walking_tour_of_moultrie). Go to the website and print out the walking tour information, which leads visitors past the courthouse, war memorials, and other downtown historic buildings constructed in the Beaux Arts, neoclassical, Colonial Revival, Craftsman–Mediterranean Revival, and art deco styles. In addition, brochures for walking and driving tours of the county are available at the **Moultrie–Colquitt County Chamber of Commerce** (see *Guidance*).

✳ Green Space

NATURE PRESERVES AND PARKS ❦ ♂ **Banks Lake National Wildlife Refuge** (229-482-9755; www.fws.gov/bankslake/), US 221, Lakeland. Open dawn–dusk daily. The refuge provides opportunities for wildlife observation, and its boat ramps are popular with boaters who launch from there. Free.

❦ ♂ ♿ **Bert Harsh Park** (229-985-2131 or 1-888-40-VISIT; www.moultriechamber.com), Fifth Street SE, Moultrie. Open daylight hours daily. This is the first historic grove of trees to be planted in a USA Certified Tree City. Trees in the park were planted and named in honor of Moultrie people and famous Americans, most of them Southern: for example, the Jimmy Carter slash pine, the Juliette Gordon Lowe magnolia, or the Robert E. Lee sweet gum. Free.

❦ ♂ ♿ **Coastal Plain Research Arboretum** (229-391-6868), Rainwater Road and South Entomology Drive, Tifton. Open daylight hours daily for self-guided tours; guided tours by

---

WHAT'S IN A NAME?

Unusually named Adel, originally called Puddleville, has interesting stories about the origin of its name. One story is that the founders of the city and Cook County wanted just a piece of city life for their small town, so they took the middle four letters from the thriving city of PhilADELphia as the name of the town. An alternative legend is that the first postmaster, Joel "Uncle Jack" Parrish, wanted to change the town's name from Puddleville, and when he saw the name "Philadelphia" on a crocus sack, he struck out the first four and the last four letters to create the town's name.

reservation. Thirty-eight acres of forest and wetlands provide opportunities for plant identification and wildlife observation. The arboretum is planted with 280 different species of trees, shrubs, and herbaceous plants native to the Coastal Plain of Georgia. Free.

🦅 🐾 ♿ **Reed Bingham State Park** (office: 229-896-3551; lodging reservations: 1-800-864-7275; www.gastateparks.org/ReedBingham), 542 Reed Bingham Road, Adel. Open 7 AM–10 PM daily. Central to the 1,613-acre park is a 375-acre lake, which has become a major boating, fishing, and waterskiing mecca in south Georgia. Fishing for bass, catfish, and crappie is excellent. Recreational amenities include a swimming beach, three boat ramps, a wheelchair-accessible fishing dock, a playground, miniature golf, and 4 miles of hiking trails. Boat rentals are available, too. The park's Coastal Plain Nature Trail and Gopher Tortoise Nature Trail wind through a cypress swamp, sand hills, a pitcher plant bog, and other habitats where visitors may see waterfowl, the endangered gopher tortoise, harmless indigo snakes, and other wildlife; however, the most famous residents are thousands of black vultures and turkey vultures that arrive in November and stay through April. Camping is offered at 46 campsites (see *Lodging—Campgrounds*). Parking $5.

RIVERS 🦅 🐾 ♿ **Alapaha River,** US 221 and GA 37, Lakeland. Open dawn–dusk daily. The river offers numerous opportunities for fishing, canoeing, bird-watching, and wildlife observation, not to mention simple relaxation. Free.

✳ Lodging
BED & BREAKFASTS
In Moultrie
Pecan Hill Inn Bed and Breakfast (229-985-7869), 2458 Sylvester Highway. The stately century-old Queen Anne Victorian home, also known as the Coleman House, sits on 5 acres with 22 pecan trees. The home has an interesting past, including use as a boardinghouse for teachers and home of the Georgia State Patrol. It is listed on both the Georgia and National Registers of Historic Places. Also on the property is a livestock and cattle barn listed on the National Register and a carriage house. Four well-appointed guest rooms with private baths, fireplaces, and bay windows are offered. A bountiful gourmet breakfast is served. No smoking. Not wheelchair accessible. $125–135.

In Tifton
Mockingbird Ridge (229-382-8454), 4935 GA 125 North. Many lodgings claim to offer guests a home away from home, but this bed & breakfast really delivers. Accommodations are offered in a private brick home with a bedroom and bath, living room, fully stocked kitchen, front porch, swimming pool, and gardens on 10 acres

with a fishing pond. Smoking outdoors only. Not wheelchair accessible. $75–125.

CAMPGROUNDS
In Adel
🦅 🐾 ♿ 🏕 **Reed Bingham State Park** (camping reservations: 1-800-864-7275). The park offers 46 tent, trailer, and RV sites. $25–28. See *Green Space—Nature Preserves and Parks*.

In Tifton
🦅 🐾 **Tifton KOA** (229-386-8441; reservations: 1-800-813-3274; www.tiftonkoa.com), 4632 Union Road. The park's 55 pull-through sites offer 30- or 50-amp hookups. Amenities include a swimming pool, playground, and catch-and-release fishing pond. Accommodations also are offered in one cozy cabin. Rates vary with season.

✳ Where to Eat
DINING OUT
In Tifton
🦅 🐾 ♿ **Charles Seafood** (229-382-9696), 701 Seventh Street West. Open 11–2 and 5–9 Monday–Saturday. Although the restaurant is casual, it offers the most upscale din-

ing in town. No smoking. Lunch $2.50–4.25, dinner $7.50–14.99.

EATING OUT

In Ashburn

🐾 🍴 ♿ **Last Meal Café** (229-567-9696 or 1-800-471-9696; www.jailmuseum.com), 241 East College Street. Open 11 AM–1 PM Tuesday–Saturday. There is a long-standing tradition of allowing death-row inmates to request a lavish last meal. The café, located at the **Crime and Punishment Museum** (see *To See—Museums*), serves desserts to die for (just be glad you don't have to) as well as other favorite Southern dishes. No smoking. Call for current menu and prices.

In Tifton

🐾 🍴 ♿ **Giggles Café** (229-382-7997), 219 Main Street South. Open 8–5 Monday–Friday, 11–3 Saturday. This casual eatery serves an array of homemade soups, salads, sandwiches, wraps, and desserts. No smoking. $1.45–7.25.

🐾 🍴 ♿ **La Cabana Mexican Restaurant** (229-382-1011), 211 Main Street South. Open 11–10 Monday–Saturday, 11–9 Sunday. This casual eatery serves authentic Mexican cuisine. No smoking. Lunch $4.50–5.50, dinner $7.50–17.95.

✳ Entertainment

ARTS Colquitt County Arts Center (229-985-1922; www.colquittcountyarts .com), 401 Seventh Avenue SW, Moultrie. Open 10–5:30 Monday–Friday, 10–2 Saturday. The 1929 Moultrie High School was restored to create this entertainment center. Throughout the year the center stages art exhibits, theatrical performances, and other arts programs. Free admission to building; check the website or call for a schedule of events and ticket prices.

MUSIC Arts and Entertainment Series, First Tuesday Series, Stafford Steinway Series (AE: series 229-291-4820; First Tuesday Series: 229-391-4943; www .abac.edu/arts). In collaboration with several arts groups, the Tifton–Tift County

Arts Council presents an annual series of dance, music, and stage plays performed by artists from all over the world. Performances are held at the Chapel of All Faiths, Howard Auditorium on the campus of Abraham Baldwin Agricultural College, the Tift County High School Performing Arts Center, and other venues. Check the website or call for a schedule of events. $5–15.

THEATER Tift Theater for the Performing Arts (229-386-5150 or 229-391-3903; http://downtowntifton.com/?page _id=9), 318 Main Street, Tifton. The art deco–style theater in the heart of downtown Tifton was built in 1937 with a Carerra glass facade embellished with neon lights. Fully restored, the theater now hosts local and traveling musical and theatrical performances, pageants, and big-screen movies. Check the website or call for a schedule of events and ticket prices.

✳ Selective Shopping

ANTIQUES Moultrie's Antiques Trail (229-890-5455 or 1-888-40-VISIT; www

THE 1937 TIFT THEATER FOR PERFORMING ARTS HAS BEEN COMPLETELY RESTORED.

.moultriega.com), downtown Moultrie. Open Monday–Saturday; hours vary. Moultrie bills itself as "the Antique Capital of South Georgia" and boasts more than 36 antiques dealers purveying middle- to upper-end merchandise.

FOOD Calhoun Produce (229-273-1887; www.calhounproduce.com), 5075 Hawpond Road, Ashburn. Open 8–6 daily, March–December. Shoppers can choose from fresh fruits, vegetables, and gift baskets. Take a break from shopping for a treat of ice cream or lemonade.

State Farmer's Market (229-891-7240; www.moultriechamber.com), First Avenue SE, Moultrie. Open 7–6 Monday–Saturday, year-round. Locals and visitors can purchase fresh seasonal produce directly from local farmers. It's also a popular place to purchase a Christmas tree in December.

✴ Special Events

March: **Arts in Black Festival** (Abraham Baldwin Arts Connection: 229-391-4820). In Tifton, African and African American heritage is showcased, including music, poetry, storytelling, dance, drums, foods, and crafts. Activities take place in Fulwood Park, except for an evening talent show at the Tift Theater ($5). Free.

Fire Ant Festival (229-386-0216 or 229-567-9696; www.fireantfestival.com). Held on the fourth Saturday of March in Ashburn, this hilarious tribute to south Georgia's nemesis features a fire ant calling contest, a giant fire ant maze, and more typical festival activities including a car and bike show, pet parade, art show, barbecue cook-off, strawberry cook-off, beauty pageant, photography contest, and entertainment. $12 in advance, $15 at the gate.

March and November: **Calico Arts and Crafts Shows** (229-985-1968). Artists at more than 300 booths at this Moultrie event display and sell handmade arts and crafts. Adults $5, younger than 12 free.

May: **Love Affair Fine Arts Festival** (Abraham Baldwin Arts Connection: 229-391-4820; www.abac.edu/arts/LoveAffair).

The renowned three-day cultural arts extravaganza, which is presented in Fulwood Park and other historic downtown Tifton venues, features quality visual and performing arts. Other events include hands-on activities for children, heritage crafts demonstrations, and strolling performers. Free.

October: **Sunbelt Agricultural Exposition** (229-985-1968; www.sunbeltexpo.com). Like an old-fashioned county fair on steroids, this Moultrie festival, the largest agricultural expo in North America, features livestock exhibits; stock dog, sheep, and cattle trials; alpaca and equine demonstrations; an antique tractor parade; hot-air balloon flights; entertainment; and hunting and fishing demonstrations. Visitors can see the wares of more than 1,000 exhibitors. Adults $10, children under 12 free with an adult; $20 multiday pass.

December: **Hometown Holiday Celebration** (contact Tifton–Tift County Tourism Association: 229-386-0216; www.tifttourism.com). A parade, musical performances, live Nativity scene, breakfast with Santa, the Candy Cane Express to Fulwood Park's Wonderland Tour of Lights, a tree lighting, arts and crafts, a tour of homes, and the Hall of Trees and Gingerbread Houses at the Museum of Arts and Heritage set the mood for the holiday season in Tifton. Some events free; fees for some activities.

THE LOVE AFFAIR FINE ARTS FESTIVAL FEATURES PLENTY OF HANDS-ON ACTIVITIES FOR PARTICIPANTS.

VALDOSTA AND
THE OKEFENOKEE SWAMP

Valdosta, which is only 18 miles north of the Georgia-Florida border, is named after an estate owned by former Georgia governor George Troup. The name is believed to have been derived from Val de Aosta, a district in the Alpine Mountains of Italy. The English translation is "Vale of Beauty." The city certainly lives up to its name with an abundance of flowering azaleas—which have earned Valdosta the nickname "the Azalea City"—as well as gardens blooming throughout the spring and summer.

Valdosta is also known as "Winnersville" because it is the home of the winningest high school football team in the nation. The city, the 10th largest in Georgia, is recognized as the business, cultural, leisure, medical, and retail hub for an 11-county area of south Georgia and north Florida. Another claim to fame is that Valdosta was the boyhood home of notorious outlaw John Henry (Doc) Holliday. His home still exists, but it is a private residence.

Valdosta State University is an integral part of cultural life in Valdosta, presenting theatrical and musical productions and opening its art gallery to the public.

The small towns in this chapter offer attractions, outdoor recreation, special lodgings and restaurants, and fairs and festivals.

GUIDANCE If you are planning a trip to the Valdosta area, contact the **Valdosta–Lowndes County Conference Center and Tourism Authority** (229-245-0513 or 1-800-569-TOUR; www.valdostatourism.com), 1 Meeting Place, Valdosta 31601. Open 8–5 weekdays. While there, get a brochure for the **Valdosta Historic Driving Tour** (see *To See—Scenic Drives*). When you arrive in the area, visit the **Georgia Visitor Information Center–Valdosta** (229-559-5828), 5584 Mill Store Road, Lake Park 31636. Open 8:30–5 daily.

GETTING THERE *By air:* **Valdosta Regional Airport** (229-333-1833), 1750 Airport Road, Valdosta, is served by **ExpressJet.** Car rentals are available on-site from **Avis** (229-242-4242) and **Hertz** (229-242-7070).

The nearest large commercial airport served by several airlines is **Tallahassee Regional Airport.** See "What's Where in Georgia" for airport, airline, and car rental information.

By bus: Service is provided by **Greyhound Lines** (229-242-8575 or 1-800-231-2222; www.greyhound.com), 200 North Oak Street, Valdosta.

By car: These cities and towns are easily accessible from I-75. Other north–south routes are US 129 and US 441; east–west access is via US 84.

By train: The nearest **AMTRAK** (1-800-USA-RAIL; www.amtrak.com) station is 27 miles away at 1000 South Range Street in Madison, Florida, which is on the *Sunset Limited* coast-to-coast route with three trains per week.

GETTING AROUND In addition to the car rental companies at the airport (see "What's Where in Georgia"), car rentals are also available in Valdosta from **Enterprise** (229-241-8560), 803 North Ashley Street, and **Thrifty** (229-241-7368), 2704 Bemiss Road.

ALL SORTS OF GREENERY GROWS IN THE OKEFENOKEE SWAMP.

MEDICAL EMERGENCY In life-threatening situations, call 911.

NEIGHBORHOODS AND VILLAGES Valdosta has several districts on the National Register of Historic Places: Brookwood North Historic District, Valdosta Commercial Historic District, East End Historic District, Fairview Historic District, and midtown's North Patterson Street Historic District. Of particular interest is the **Fairview Historic District,** which concentrates on River, Varnedoe, and Wells streets and Central Place downtown. The village of Fairview predates the incorporation of the city of Valdosta. The neighborhood underwent three primary periods of development: 1840–1860; the late-1890s Victorian era, when opulent homes were built; and the 1910–1920s period of Prairie and Craftsman influence.

The **Okefenokee Swamp,** one of the most intriguing areas in Georgia (or in the country, for that matter), features moss-laden cypress trees reflecting off black swamp waters. Visitors to the **Okefenokee National Wildlife Refuge** can view alligators, turtles, raccoons, black bears, deer, and other creatures from elevated boardwalks, on guided boat trips, or by renting motorboats or canoes.

✳ To See

CULTURAL SITES ✿ ✍ ⅙ **Annette Howell Turner Center for the Arts** (229-247-2787; www.turnercenter.org or www.lvac.org), 527 North Patterson Street, Valdosta. Open 10–6 Tuesday–Thursday, 10–4 Friday and Saturday. Operated by the Lowndes-Valdosta Arts Commission, the center has art galleries and is the home of the Little Actor's Theater, where children put on several productions each year. In addition to four rotating galleries that feature new exhibits each month, the permanent gallery has a collection of East African art. The center also sponsors a spring festival and summer art camps. Free; donations accepted.

HISTORIC HOME AND SITES ✿ ⅙ **Barber-Pittman House** (229-247-8100; www.valdostachamber.com), 416 North Ashley Street, Valdosta. Open 9–5 weekdays. This imposing, white-columned neoclassical home, considered to be one of the most outstanding examples of architectural design in the Southeast, was built in 1915 for E. R. Barber, an inventor and the first bottler of Coca-Cola outside Atlanta. When the house was threatened with demolition, Ola Barber Pittman, the original builder's daughter, bequeathed it to the citizens of Valdosta with a provision that it not be sold. Mrs. Pittman died in 1977, the mansion was restored by local architects and the Valdosta Junior Women's Club in 1979, and it now serves as the home of the **Valdosta–Lowndes County Chamber of Commerce**. Visitors are welcome to see the beautiful interior architectural features as well as the original light fixtures, admire the original family furnishings, and stroll through the formal gardens. Free.

❧ **The Crescent** (229-244-6747), 904 North Patterson Street, Valdosta. Open 2–5 weekdays or by appointment. Neoclassical in design, the Crescent, built in 1898 by U.S. senator William Stanley West, acquired its name from the distinctive semicircular portico supported by 13 Doric columns representing the 13 original colonies. The Crescent is Valdosta's most recognized landmark. Rescued from demolition in 1951, it is now the home of the Garden Club of Valdosta and is the scene of many weddings and other special events. At the 23-room mansion, the grand staircase, ballroom, original pieces, and period antiques give a glimpse into turn-of-the-20th-century sophistication. The grounds boast beautiful test gardens, an octagonal schoolhouse, and a quaint chapel. Free; donations accepted.

MUSEUMS ❧ ♿ **Lowndes County Historical Society and Museum** (229-247-4780; www.valdostamuseum.org), 305 West Central Avenue, Valdosta. Open 10–5 weekdays, 10–2 Saturday. Housed in a historic Carnegie library built in 1913, the museum's exhibits display an extensive collection of artifacts from early Lowndes County families, including historical photographs, documents, costumes, and more. Special displays tell about the local hospital, Moody Air Force Base, and prominent local families. There is also an extensive genealogical library available for research. Free.

SCENIC DRIVES **The Azalea Trail,** available from the Valdosta–Lowndes County Conference Center and Tourism Authority (229-245-0513 or 1-800-569-TOUR; www .valdostatourism.com), 1 Meeting Place, Valdosta. The map leads visitors past the most cultivated azalea areas in the city.

Valdosta Historic Driving Tour, also available from the Valdosta–Lowndes County Conference Center and Tourism Authority (see previous listing). The tour leads visitors past 56 historic sites, including the early-1900s courthouse, stately homes, churches, and a cemetery.

✳ To Do

FOR FAMILIES ✍ ♿ **Wild Adventures Theme Park** (229-219-7080; www.wild adventures.net), 3766 Old Clyattsville Road, Valdosta. Open year-round; hours vary by season—generally open daily March–Labor Day, Friday–Monday rest of the year, but call ahead to be sure. Splash Island Water Park open during regular park hours March–September, weekends in October. Although this is a family-owned regional park, rides, roller coasters, and water rides in the Splash Island Water Park vie with national theme parks. Splash Island features the five-story Rain Fortress, an interactive wet play area with

THE AZALEA CITY

R. J. Drexel came to Valdosta as its parks superintendent in 1925. He planted azaleas along city streets, in the cemetery, on church grounds, and around government buildings, and each spring he would give five azalea plants to citizens who wanted them. Later the Garden Club sold azaleas for 10 cents each to raise money for the purchase and renovation of the Crescent, a historic home that serves as its headquarters (see *To See—Historic Homes and Sites*). Drexel Park, at Brookwood Drive and Patterson Street, is named in R. J. Drexel's honor, and the Azalea Trail is a scenic driving route through the most beautiful azalea areas (see *To See—Scenic Drives*). One of the biggest events in the community is the Valdosta–Lowndes County Azalea Festival (see *Special Events*).

21 platforms and various slides. The Safari Train Ride permits views of many of the 500 wild animals scattered in natural habitats throughout the park. Adventure Quest, for which there is an additional fee, is a park-within-a-park with an 18-hole adventure golf course, climbing wall, game arcade, and go-cart raceway. Up to a dozen entertainment shows each day may include acrobats, musical revues, and Western melodramas. National headliners—from Christian to country, pop to R&B—take the stage at the All-Star Amphitheater. General seating is included in park admission, and visitors are encouraged to bring their own lawn chairs so they can watch the concerts in comfort. Reserved seating under the pavilion is an additional $15–20 depending on the show. No one will starve to death while spending a day here. There's a Lone Star Bar-B-Que restaurant and snack concessions. Of course, several gift shops are on-site. Adults $45.99, seniors and children 3–9 $40.99. Parking $10, RV $12.

WALKING TOURS **The Camellia Trail** (229-333-5800), Georgia Avenue, Valdosta. Open daily. Take a leisurely stroll along the 3,000-foot trail on the campus of Valdosta State University, which was begun in 1944. During the fall through spring camellia season, more than 430 varieties of camellias are showcased within a longleaf pine grove. A memorial gateway honors the collection's founder, Jewell Whitehead, who was known as "the Camellia Lady." Free.

✷ Green Space

NATURE PRESERVES AND PARKS ✤ ✐ **Grand Bay Wildlife Management Area** (229-245-8160; www.georgiawildlife.com), Bemiss Road, Valdosta. Open Saturday and Sunday year-round. The site is composed of 1,350 acres within a 13,000-acre wetlands system, the second-largest natural blackwater cypress-blackgum wetland in the Coastal Plain of Georgia after the Okefenokee Swamp. The preserve is open year-round for fishing, canoeing, hiking, bird and wildlife observation, camping, and deer and small-game hunting. In the areas east of the Flint River, a Georgia Outdoor Recreation Pass (GORP) is required for anyone 16–64 who does not already have a hunting or fishing license: $3.50 for three days.

✤ ✐ ❧ **Okefenokee National Wildlife Refuge** (912-496-7836; www.fws.gov/okefenokee), Folkston. The 680-square-mile wetland wilderness provides crucial habitat for wildlife. For humans, the refuge offers boating, canoeing and kayaking, fishing, camping, wildlife observation, bicycling, hiking, and guided tours. (For much more information about the swamp, see the Brunswick and the Waycross chapters in part 2: The Coast.) In this area, access to the swamp is through **Stephen C. Foster State Park** (see next).

✤ ✐ ❧ ❧ **Stephen C. Foster State Park** (park: 912-637-5274; lodging reservations: 1-800-864-7275; www.gastateparks.org/StephenCFoster), 17515 GA 177, Fargo. Open 7–7 in fall and winter, 6:30 AM–8:30 PM in spring and summer. (Because the park is located within the Okefenokee National Wildlife Refuge, the gates are locked at closing.) One of the primary entrances to the primordial Okefenokee Swamp, this remote 80-acre park is named for songwriter Stephen Foster. There is a 1.5-mile Trembling Earth Nature Trail as well as 25 miles of day-use waterways. Canoe and fishing boat rentals are available, and private boats are permitted, though there is a 10-horsepower limit. There is a boat ramp for launching, too. Fishing is popular, but don't trail your catch behind the boat; you'll attract alligators. Accommodations are available in cottages and at the campgrounds (see *Lodging—Campgrounds* and *Lodging—Cottages and Cabins*). Stop at the park's **Suwannee River Interpretive Center** on US 441 to watch a short film about the swamp and to see exhibits and live animals. The building itself has won an award for its environmentally responsible construction. Parking $5; guided boat tours $8–12.

✳ Lodging

BED & BREAKFASTS

In Valdosta

Fairview Inn Bed and Breakfast (229-244-6456; www.fairviewinn.info), 416 River Street. Located in the historic Fairview neighborhood, one of Valdosta's oldest, the commodious inn takes visitors back to the opulence of the late 1800s. Five uniquely decorated guest rooms feature modern amenities such as cable television, Bose CD radios, high-speed Internet access, and hair dryers. A full breakfast is served 7–9 AM. Guests can choose to enjoy their repast in the old-world dining room or the cozy kitchen. The inn is within walking distance of the **Lowndes County Historical Society and Museum** (see *To See—Museums*), the historic courthouse, and downtown shops. Smoking outside only. Not wheelchair accessible. $85–125.

CAMPGROUNDS

In Fargo

Stephen C. Foster State Park (camping reservations: 1-800-864-7275). The park offers 66 tent, trailer, and RV sites. $25–30. See *Green Space—Nature Preserves and Parks.*

COTTAGES AND CABINS

In Fargo

🐾 **Stephen C. Foster State Park** (cottage reservations: 1-800-864-7275). The park features nine fully equipped cottages, of which one is dog friendly ($40 per dog; maximum two). $115–125. See *Green Space—Nature Preserves and Parks.*

✳ Where to Eat

DINING OUT

In Valdosta

👍 **The Bistro Restaurant and Piano Bar** (229-253-1253), 130 North Ashley Street. Open 5–10 Monday–Saturday. The Bistro features fine dining. Its French/American-inspired cuisine includes Angus beef, seafood, chicken, lamb, sashimi tuna, and pasta. No smoking. $14.95–24.95.

👍 **Charlie Tripper's Fine Food and Fruits of the Vine** (229-247-0366), 4479 North Valdosta Road. Open 6–10 Tuesday–Saturday; bar opens at 5. In this four-star, casual-but-fashionable restaurant, intimate dining is assured in small rooms with white table linens and low lighting. The eclectic decor features exposed brick accented with artwork and memorabilia. Entrées include Angus beef, filets, rib eye, New Zealand lamb, pork, and seafood. Vegetarian plates can be requested. Save room for decadent desserts such as bananas Foster, bread pudding, crème brûlée, cobblers, and tarts. No smoking. $16.95–25.95.

🍴 👍 **Gulio's Greek-Italian Restaurant** (229-333-0929; www.giuliosrestaurant.com), 105 East Ann Street. Open 5–10 Tuesday–Saturday. A beautiful setting in a turn-of-the-20th-century home sets the scene for European-inspired cuisine specializing in seafood and charbroiled steaks. Gulio's is not too formal, however. You're just as likely to see jeans as tuxedos. No smoking. $10–20.

👍 **306 North** (229-249-5333; www.306north.com), 306 North Patterson Street. Open 11–9 Monday–Thursday, 10–10 Friday, 5–10 Saturday. This upscale eatery features white tablecloths even for their patio dining. Lunch features choices ranging from eggplant fries to a shrimp and mushroom crêpe. Dinner features many beef and seafood choices. Lunch $6–12, dinner $19–26.

EATING OUT

In Valdosta

🍴 👍 **Covington's** (229-242-2261; www.covingtonscatering.com), 310 North Patterson Street. Open 11–2 Monday–Saturday. Covington's serves soups, such as creamy crab, as well as appetizers, salads, sandwiches, pasta, lasagna, quesadillas, fish, quiche, and desserts. No smoking. $6.50–9.

🍴 🐾 👍 **Two Friends Café and Market** (229-242-3282; www.twofriendscafe.net), 3338-B Country Club Road. Open 7:30–2 Tuesday–Friday, 9–2 Saturday; market open 10–4 Tuesday–Saturday. The café offers light breakfast items such as a sweet-potato biscuit with baked ham, homemade granola, muffins, and fruit. Lunch includes the specialty hot baked chicken salad as well as soups, salads, sandwiches, appetizers, and desserts. Take-out items include breads, desserts, casseroles, salads, pastas, quiches, lasagna, jambalaya, potpie, meat loaf, and appetizers. No smoking. Breakfast $4.50–5.25, lunch $5–10.

✴ Entertainment

MUSIC Valdosta Symphony Orchestra (229-333-5804; www.valdosta.edu/music). Four concerts presented annually November–May. The group consists of Valdosta State University faculty as well as students and professional musicians from the community. Guest artists are often featured, and a youth orchestra also performs. Concerts are held in the Fine Arts Building on the Valdosta State University campus. Check the website or call for a schedule of performances and ticket prices.

NIGHTLIFE ♿ Bayou Bill's North Cajun Grill (229-241-8825), 1811 Jerry Jones Drive, Valdosta. Open 4 PM–2 AM Monday–Saturday. This casual eatery serves mainly wings, appetizers, and raw oysters. Bayou Bill's North is known for daily drink specials and nightly entertainment. Smoking allowed. Cover charge $5 when there is live entertainment.

♿ **Mikki's** (229-242-3248), 402 Northside Drive, Valdosta. Open 4 PM–2 AM weeknights, 3 PM–2 AM Saturday, 4 PM–midnight Sunday. In addition to live bands, Mikki's offers a big-screen television, pool tables, karaoke on Friday nights, and darts. Smoking allowed. Cover charge $5.

THEATER The Dosta Playhouse (229-247-8243; www.theatreguildvaldosta.com), 122 North Ashley Street, Valdosta. The art moderne structure, built in 1941, reflects the era just after the Great Depression. Free of much ornamentation, the theater still features glass bricks, porthole windows, and curved corners created to celebrate cruise ships and the automobile. The theater is home to **Theatre Guild-Valdosta,**

which presents four main shows and two children's productions each year. Check the website or call for a schedule of performances and ticket prices.

Peach State Summer Theater (229-259-7770; www.valdosta.edu/psst). The nine-week summer season features three musicals in rotating repertory. Check the website or call for a schedule. Performances take place at the Sawyer Theater in the Valdosta State University Fine Arts Building. The professional summer-stock theater company is composed of 60 actors-singers and backup personnel. Previous visitors to Georgia may have experienced the works of this group in its former incarnation as the Jekyll Island Musical Theatre Festival. Tickets: adults $25, seniors and students $20.

Valdosta State University Theatre (229-333-5973; www.valdosta.edu/comarts /theatre.shtml). The theater arts program at the university presents a seven-production season. Check the website or call for a schedule of performances. Plays with a small number of actors are presented in the intimate Lab Theatre; larger-scale works are presented in the Sawyer Theatre. Adults $12, seniors $10, children $8; VSU students free.

✴ Selective Shopping

Remerton Village (Plum Street and Baytree Place) in Valdosta features quaint restored mill houses now occupied by specialty shops that offer antiques, collectibles, crafts, a pottery, a coffeehouse, and several restaurants.

ANTIQUES Just off Main (229-794-1118), 103 North Lowndes Street, Hahira. Open 10–5 Tuesday–Saturday. Located in a restored home in the heart of Hahira, the shop sells antiques, furniture, lamps, accessories for the home, and vintage collectibles.

BOOKS Hildegard's (229-247-6802), 101 East Central Avenue, Valdosta. Open 8 AM–11 PM (kitchen open 8 AM–9 PM). The nonprofit bookstore/café features a coffee and tea lounge, deli, wireless Internet access, an art gallery, and performance space.

CLOTHING Country Cobbler (229-242-1430), 1737 Gornto Road, Valdosta. Open 10–9 Monday–Saturday, 1–6 Sunday. Every shoe lover's dream, this store carries a fine and large selection of women's and men's shoes from Steve Madden to Brighton at affordable prices.

FOOD South Georgia Pecan Gift Shop (229-244-0686 or 1-800-627-6630), 403 East Hill Avenue, Valdosta. Open 9–5 weekdays. The shop offers a wide variety of fresh nuts, syrups, gift baskets, and much more.

OUTLET STORES Lake Park Outlets (229-559-6822 or 1-888-SHOP-333; www .factoryoutletstores/georgia/lake-park -outlets.html), 5327 Mill Store Road, Lake Park. Open 9–8 Monday–Saturday, 10–6 Sunday. Whether you're interested in fashion, gifts, or home accessories, choose from more than 48 famous designer names and national brands at this outlet center. Nestled within the larger factory center, **Farm House Plaza** features 14 shops selling china, books, diamonds and gold, carpets, and linens. The facility also offers an antiques and crafters mall with 125 dealers and a country restaurant.

✳ Special Events

March: **Valdosta–Lowndes County Azalea Festival** (229-269-9381; www .azaleafestival.com). Held in Valdosta's Drexel Park, the event features a parade, sporting events, circus, arts and crafts, musical entertainment, home tours, food,

children's activities, and more. An international village displays costumes and exhibits while offering food and entertainment. There are also events in the weeks preceding the festival, including the Azalea Asian Cultural Experience Festival and an international extravaganza with bands, a parade of nations, entertainment, fireworks, and food. Parking is allowed in all Valdosta State University lots. Most events free; small participation fees for some activities and events.

October: **Hahira Honey Bee Festival** (229-794-3097 or 229-794-2813; www .hahirahoneybeefestivalinc.com). Sponsored by the Hahira Honey Bee Committee, the weeklong festival features live bee demonstrations, arts and crafts, gospel singing and other live entertainment, a 5K run, beauty pageant, dog show, climbing wall, and parade. Free; fee for some activities and events.

November: **Lowndes County–South Georgia Fair** (229-242-9316; www .valdostatourism.com). Held at the Lowndes County Civic Center in Valdosta, the fair features livestock shows, exhibits, booths, and carnival rides. Free.

Mid-November–December 30: **Wild Adventures Christmas Wonderland** (229-219-7080; www.wildadventures.net). For this, one of the South's largest holiday celebrations, the Wild Adventures Theme Park in Valdosta (see *To Do—For Families*) is transformed into a magical land filled with millions of dazzling lights, holiday displays, sounds of the season, a living Nativity, and holiday shows. The Wonderland Express is a merry train ride, and, of course, no visit would be complete without a visit with St. Nicholas. Included in regular park admission.

INDEX